# EVIDENCE IN FAMILY PROCEEDINGS

# EVIDENCE IN FAMILY PROCEEDINGS

David Burrows, Solicitor Advocate

*with contributions by*

David Bedingfield, Barrister
Glenn Brasse, Barrister, District Judge at the Principal Registry
Jane Keir, Partner, Kingsley Napley, Solicitors
Caroline Reid, Barrister

**Family Law**

1999

Published by
Family Law, a publishing imprint of
Jordan Publishing Limited
21 St Thomas Street, Bristol BS1 6JS

**British Library Cataloguing-in-Publication Data**
A catalogue record for this book is available from the British Library.

ISBN 0 85308 224 3

Typeset by Mendip Communications Ltd, Frome, Somerset
Printed by MPG Books Ltd, Bodmin, Cornwall

# Preface

This book has had a long gestation period. Suggested first by the publishers in the summer of 1992, it appears, finally, seven years later. The plan was for it to be written jointly by a member of the Bar and a solicitor. I prepared a synopsis and started writing. The remaining seven years were spent finding a member of the Bar, or maybe two or more, to write the balance. I am fortunate indeed to have District Judge Glenn Brasse, David Bedingfield, Caroline Reid and, most recently, Jane Keir to provide the counter-balance to my own contribution.

My first intended collaborator was Judith Parker QC; and to her I owe a substantial debt of gratitude. Her enthusiasm saw the project off to an excellent start, which – sadly – we could not sustain; but the form which the book takes now owes much to her ideas and to the plans we prepared together in October 1992.

At that stage, the Children Act 1989 had been in operation for only a year. Since then, family law has seen such developments as two Child Support Acts, the Family Law Act 1996 (Parts I, II and IV in operation), the Ancillary Relief Pilot Scheme, and all the time, the Woolf reforms have been in the background. The Civil Procedure Rules 1998 are now a looming presence which no family lawyer can entirely ignore.

In the field of evidence, the Civil Evidence Act 1995 has reached the statute book; and the Civil Procedure Act 1997 has had an impact on the rules of evidence. However, most of the important developments – as is so often of significance for the family lawyer – have mostly been in case-law. Res judicata has been shown to be relevant to family proceedings and has been judicially explained three times, at least. The role of opinion evidence – especially in children proceedings – has been examined frequently. In 1995–1996, evidence in children proceedings – and, separately, the related question of privilege – was considered on three occasions in the House of Lords. The duty of disclosure – hitherto a doctrine known only to family law – found its way into civil proceedings in late 1997; and Lord Woolf has now adopted the term, and redefined it, for civil proceedings.

Had I been asked earlier this year whether it was the law of England and Wales that a litigant could call such evidence as he or she chooses (subject to relevance and to any other appropriate exclusionary rules), I would have said: Yes, unquestionably. It is now no longer clear that that is right; and, in time, this may radically alter the subject of this book.

My error, if it be an error, arises from the terms of the Civil Procedure Rules 1998, r 32.1, which reads:

**'32.1 Power of court to control evidence**
(1)  The court may control the evidence by giving directions as to –
  (a)  the issues on which it requires evidence;
  (b)  the nature of the evidence which it requires to decide those issues; and
  (c)  the way in which the evidence is to be placed before the court.
(2)  The court may use its power under this rule to exclude evidence that would otherwise be admissible. ....'

This rule, if it is intra vires the rule-making body, presents a fundamental change to the rights of Her Majesty's subjects. Most people, before the introduction of this rule, would have thought – subject to certain exclusionary rules (such as having leave to call opinion evidence) – that the calling of evidence relevant to the issue before the court was a matter of right. Perhaps it still is; but that depends on a reading of the Civil Procedure Act 1997, Sch 1, para 4, which provides:

'Civil Procedure Rules may modify the rules of evidence as they apply to proceedings in any court within the scope of the rules.'

From this provision – set out, be it noted, in the Schedule to the Act; not in the body of the statute – one or two questions arise: is the control of evidence and of what the court is willing to try, a 'rule of evidence', or is it something more fundamental which affects individual rights? If it is the latter, can it be altered by a paragraph in a Schedule to a statute and a procedural rule?

I should like to dedicate this book to the Solicitors Family Law Association (SFLA), many of whose members have, over the past few years, worked hard to change the way family law is practised. Collectively, family lawyers can do so much to help their clients. That each party, individually, has a significant point of view and a recognition by each solicitor that this must be taken into account, is perhaps what can distinguish family litigation from any other. The SFLA has done so much to promote a climate in which a respect for – or, at least, an understanding of – the other party's point of view can flourish. To personify the SFLA, I should like, in particular, to dedicate this to John Cornwall, its first chair and a great mentor, and to Philippa Pearson, as a representative of the next generation of the Association.

The law is stated as I understand it to be at 1 June 1999.

DAVID BURROWS
*Bristol*
*August 1999*

# Contents

# Table of Cases

**References are to paragraph numbers and Appendices.**

# Table of Statutes

**References are to paragraph numbers and Appendices.**

# Table of Statutory Instruments

# Table of Conventions

**References are to paragraph numbers.**

# Table of Conventions

# Chapter 1

## INTRODUCTION: EVIDENCE IN A DISCRETIONARY JURISDICTION

### 1 INTRODUCTION

#### Evidence defined

**1.1**   Evidence is the means whereby a fact in issue in proceedings is proved to the satisfaction of the court. Evidence of fact enables the court to pronounce its findings on matters in issue between the parties to an application, while a combination of findings of fact and opinion[1] may assist the court where its decision is a matter of discretion. Thus, on the basis of the evidence in a particular case, the court is able to adjudicate on applications before it whether a decision turns on a matter of proof of a given set of facts, or the decision is a matter for the discretion of the court. The corollary of this is that without evidence the court is unable to make a decision and no individual may pursue an application before the court.

**1.2**   As will be seen,[2] discretion plays a significant part in the adjudication of applications in family proceedings. However, even in a discretionary jurisdiction,[3] the court cannot proceed in the absence of evidence from the parties, even if the terms are agreed between them.[4]

#### From evidence of fact to the exercise of discretion

**1.3**   Thus, there will be instances where the court will move from evaluation of factual evidence to assessment of information before the court, including opinion evidence, for the purposes of exercise of a judicial discretion. For example, in an application for a care order under the Children Act 1989, s 31(2)[5] the court deals with a mixture of issues of fact[6] and questions for the exercise of its discretion. At the first

---

1   For a consideration of this terminology, see **3.5** below.
2   See eg **1.8** below.
3   Eg whether or not to make an order under Children Act 1989, s 8 and, if so, what order; what form of order for financial relief to make upon an application under Matrimonial Causes Act 1973, ss 23 and 24.
4   In the case of matrimonial ancillary relief orders, see Matrimonial Causes Act 1973, s 33A(1); Family Proceedings Rules 1991, SI 1991/1247, r 2.61.
5   Children Act 1989, s 31(2) provides that a court may make a care order:
    'if it is satisfied –
       (a) that the child concerned is suffering, or is likely to suffer, significant harm; and
       (b) that the harm … is attributable to –
          (i) the care given to the child [etc …]'
6   The evidence required for such an application and the rules of evidence which apply were considered extensively in *Re H (Minors) (Sexual Abuse: Standard of Proof)* [1996] AC 563, [1996] 1 FLR 80, HL, considered further at **4.21** and **11.10** below.

stage, the court makes findings on the facts alleged by the applicant local authority: this involves deciding whether or not the applicant has proved certain facts to the satisfaction of the court. Secondly, if the facts are proved, the court considers the following: do the facts proved amount to harm to the child; if they do, is that harm attributable to the treatment of the child 'not being what it would be reasonable to expect a parent to give to him'; and, if it is, is the harm 'significant' in the view of the individual judge or bench of magistrates? If the applicant has satisfied the court that the child has suffered significant harm then, finally, and entirely as a matter of its discretion, the court considers whether to make an order.[1] If an order is to be made, and after a finding under s 31(2), an order will almost invariably follow, the court must then decide what order from those available under the Act it should make.

## Evidence and the issue before the court

**1.4**      In terms of evidence, the issue – whether or not the court should make a care order in respect of the particular child – has gone through three distinct stages: the stage at which facts must be proved to the satisfaction of the court; the stage at which the court must decide objectively whether what has been found amounts to harm and, then subjectively, whether or not that harm should be regarded as significant; and, finally, as a matter of discretion, the form of order which should be made. The first stage is a question of proof or disproof of facts. At the second stage, the court must make decisions based on what it has heard and (perhaps) seen, and on the basis of the facts it has found proved. The third stage will depend largely on an assessment of the future for the child based on the facts found and, to an extent, on the opinions expressed concerning the child and his parents.

## 2    THE NECESSITY FOR RULES OF EVIDENCE

## Evidence, pleading and procedure

**1.5**      While the object of evidence is to prove a fact to the satisfaction of the court, procedure is the means whereby court process is regulated; and this includes the means whereby evidence comes before the court.[2] The object of pleadings, at any rate in general terms, is to enable the court and the parties to set out the facts of the case and to define, from that, the matters at issue between them. The distinction between these aspects of court process is explained by *Phipson*[3] as follows:

> 'The rules of *procedure* regulate the general conduct of litigation; the object of *pleading* is to ascertain for the parties and the court the material facts in issue in each particular case; *proof* is the establishment of such facts by proper legal means to the satisfaction of the court, and this sense includes disproof.'

---

1    Children Act 1989, s 1(5) (presumption of no order).
2    See eg Rules of the Supreme Court 1965, Ord 38 (civil proceedings generally); Family
     Proceedings Rules 1991, rr 4.17, 4.18 and 4.20 (children proceedings in High Court and county
     courts) and rr 2.58–2.60, 2.62 and 2.63 (matrimonial ancillary relief proceedings).
3    *Phipson on Evidence* 14th edn (Sweet & Maxwell, 1990) para 1-01.

## Pleadings and the family jurisdiction

**1.6**    One of the very real difficulties of the family jurisdiction is the fact that pleadings – properly so called – are more or less absent.[1] A variety of forms of application and other means of commencing process are used. Few of these go far to define the issues between the parties. For example, the Form M13 in matrimonial ancillary relief proceedings[2] does no more than recite, in the most general way, the relief sought by the applicant, while the issues are left to be pleaded in the affidavit in support of the application.[3] Even in Children Act 1989 proceedings, the prescribed form requires only that an applicant set out his case in the briefest way;[4] and, although the rules prescribe a form of acknowledgement of the application,[5] this form does nothing to define issues between the parties. Thus, it is frequently the case that a definition of the issues between the parties is best deduced from what are essentially forms of evidence (affidavits, sworn statements or statements) or from documents – quasi-pleadings – prepared by the parties themselves as trial of the issue approaches (statements of the issues, chronologies and skeleton arguments).[6]

**1.7**    One of the main functions of the procedural rules will be to define the means whereby evidence comes before the court. Frequent reference to what are essentially procedural matters will occur in this book;[7] but that is inevitable in a consideration of how evidence works and how it fits into the court process.

## Law or discretion

**1.8**    The distinction between what is a matter of fact and what is a matter of law will largely be unimportant in the field of family law. This is the province of the case tried by jury since, generally speaking, in such trials it is for the judge to determine matters of law, while the jury tries matters of fact. The more important distinction, although it is derived from law, is to determine whether a question is one of fact or law, on the one hand, or a matter of judicial discretion on the other. This question is one which recurs throughout the field of family law, and is particularly important in two fields: the extent to which the judge is bound by precedent in making his decision; and the extent to which an appellate court may review the decision of a lower court. Although a previous case may be persuasive upon the judge in the exercise of his discretion, strictly speaking there is no such thing as precedent where the court's discretion is to be exercised in the making of a decision.[8] Save in the case of an appeal to a judge from a district judge,[9] where the appeal is from a decision which arises from

---

1    See Chapter 2 for consideration of pleadings and defining the issues between the parties.
2    Family Proceedings Rules 1991, r 2.58(1).
3    See further **2.4** below.
4    Family Proceedings Rules 1991, r 4.4(1) and (1A). The forms are set out in Appendix 1 to the Rules.
5    Ibid, r 4.9.
6    See further on 'quasi-pleadings' at **2.11** below.
7    For example, evidence generally: Rules of the Supreme Court 1965, Ord 38; production appointments (Ord 38, r 13; Family Proceedings Rules 1991, r 2.62(7)); interrogatories and enquiries (Ord 26, r 2.63); discovery (Ord 24).
8    See further **1.21** below.
9    Family Proceedings Rules 1991, r 8.1(3) (explained in *Marsh v Marsh* [1993] 1 FLR 467, CA); Rules of the Supreme Court 1965, Ord 58, r 1 and County Court Rules 1981, Ord 37, r 6; and see further **14.12** below.

a judicial discretion, an appeal lies only where the appellate court finds the decision of the court below to be plainly wrong.[1]

**1.9**     To revert again to the Children Act 1989, s 31(2),[2] the question of whether or not a child has suffered harm, and whether that harm is significant, is a matter of fact. If the facts are found in accordance with the subsection then the form of the order to be made – including a care or supervision order – will be a matter for the court's discretion, to be exercised in accordance with the welfare principles set out in s 1, and having regard to the factors set out in the checklist in s 1(3).

## Evidence and family proceedings

**1.10**     It may be objected that there is little by way of rules of evidence in the family jurisdiction. This is not, of course, the case. As will be seen, there is extensive judicial reference to the rules of evidence applicable in this jurisdiction. There can be frequent misunderstandings among lawyers of the extent to which rules of evidence apply at all in the family courts. For example, it is only in proceedings 'in connection with the upbringing, maintenance or welfare of a child'[3] that evidence is not excluded by any rule of hearsay. Thus, the rules against hearsay, such as they are[4] (at least, in theory) are as applicable in family proceedings (other than most children proceedings) as in any other civil proceedings. Many practitioners are aware that leave of the court or the agreement of other parties is required for the calling of expert evidence,[5] for example evidence from accountants or an actuary in financial relief proceedings, or medical evidence in children proceedings. The rules relating to privilege ('without prejudice' correspondence[6] and documents privileged from disclosure[7]) represent an area of the subject which is not only open to misunderstanding, but is also, as matters now stand, open to judicial reinterpretation and explanation.

**1.11**     The fact is that evidence in family proceedings weighs very little with the major textbook writers. For example, specific reference to examples drawn from family cases feature hardly at all in *Phipson* or *Cross and Tapper*.[8] One of the most important cases on evidence for the family lawyer is *Jenkins v Livesey (formerly Jenkins)*,[9] which deals with the crucially important subject of disclosure in ancillary relief proceedings;[10] yet that case does not merit a reference in either of these two major reference works on evidence. However, many of the principles considered by such textbooks are an essential part of the family lawyer's sphere of expertise, as will

---

1     *G v G (Minors: Custody Appeal)* [1985] FLR 894, HL.
2     See **1.3** above.
3     Children (Admissibility of Hearsay Evidence) Order 1993, SI 1993/621, art 2; and see **4.51** below.
4     For a full consideration of the rules of hearsay, see **4.44** below.
5     Rules of the Supreme Court 1965, Ord 38, r 36; and see **5.16** below.
6     See further **7.29** et seq below. With the advent of the mediated 'memorandum of understanding' and 'negotiated agreements' and 'financial arrangements' under the Family Law Act 1996, s 9(2)(a) and (b), existing principles of law (see eg *Edgar v Edgar* [1981] 1 WLR 1410, (1981) FLR 19, CA and **7.36** below) in this area are likely soon to be reconsidered judicially.
7     See, generally, chapter 7. It is most unlikely that *Re L (Police Investigation: Privilege)* [1997] AC 16, [1996] 1 FLR 731, HL (considered further at **7.15** et seq below) will be the last judicial word in the family law field on the subject of confidentiality and litigation privilege.
8     *Cross and Tapper on Evidence* 8th edn (Butterworths, 1995).
9     [1984] FLR 452, sub nom *Livesey (formerly Jenkins) v Jenkins* [1985] FLR 813, HL.
10    See further Chapter 6.

be seen by what follows here and by the many judicial pronouncements on a variety of aspects of the rules of evidence, which are discussed in this book.

**1.12**     The lack of a discernible body of rules of evidence specifically applicable to family law, although its rules on disclosure[1] are more or less unique to the jurisdiction, means that heavy reliance will be placed in what follows on judicial *dicta*; for it is in these, especially in the House of Lords and Court of Appeal, that many of the rules and their explanation are to be found.

## Why rules of evidence?

**1.13**     Rules of evidence are no different from any other rules or, indeed, any other law. They exist to seek to ensure that all parties operate within the same bounds and subject to the same constraints. For the law to operate otherwise would create a system which favoured one party as against another. However, in an area of law so widely characterised by judicial discretion, it is clearly more important than ever that the constraints of rules and their importance in doing justice as between the parties are preserved. As was said by Sir Thomas More, in somewhat intemperate tones (perhaps more appropriate to the early sixteenth century when he was writing):[2]

> 'If you take away laws and leave everything to judges, they will either command or forbid nothing, in which cases judges will be useless, or they will rule as their own nature leads or order whatever pleases them, in which case the people will be in no wise more free but worse off... since they will have to submit, not to settled and certain laws, but to uncertain whims changing from day to day.'

These are harsh words, written in the context of a debate between canon lawyers and common lawyers, at a time when a balance between the two was being developed by lawyers such as More. This balance was based on the concept of conscience, or *epieikeia* – the Aristotelian concept of equity to restrain the harshness of the law. Disposal of a case based on conscience, where the rigours of the law might seem to produce unfairness, could be seen as more reliable when compared to the uncertainties of bases of disposal derived from canon law. These uncertainties, it can be argued,[3] remain with family lawyers, and make the appreciation of such rules as there are all the more important.

## Proof to what standard?

**1.14**     If evidence is the means whereby a fact is proved to the satisfaction of the court, the question then arises as to what extent a party must go to prove the fact for the court to be satisfied. Put another way, to what extent is it necessary to prove the truth of a particular allegation? In absolute terms, there is no such thing as absolute truth, as the facts described are all in the past and their explanation depends on the perception of individuals who witnessed those facts. Further, in many family cases, the court will be concerned less with an assessment of truth, than with less tangible factors[4] which

---

1     See further **1.27** and **6.5** et seq below.
2     Quoted by JH Baker in *The Reports of Sir John Spelman, Volume II* (Selden Society, 1978) from JM Headley (ed) *The Complete Works of St Thomas More* (1969) pp 276–279.
3     See further **1.19** below.
4     See eg the lists of factors for consideration by the court in Children Act 1989, s 1(3) and Matrimonial Causes Act 1973, s 25(2).

go to achieving fairness as between the parties. Thus, where the regulation of rights is in issue (as with residence of children or disposition of matrimonial property) the court will be concerned to achieve fairness, which often comes back to the question of conscience.[1] To achieve fairness, it will be necessary to attempt a correct interpretation of the law (where a point of law is involved); but, to do this, it is not always by any means necessary to arrive at a clear assessment of the truth.

## Attaining justice and fairness: the adversarial system

**1.15**     The common law has developed the adversarial[2] system to arrive at an assessment of truth and thereby to seek to achieve justice. By this means, in its technical form, a proposition – a formal application to the court or a pleaded case – is advanced by one party and contradicted by an opposing party. Each side in this debate before the courts is entitled to call its own evidence and to challenge the evidence of its opponent. The culmination of the debate, as pleaded by the parties, is the trial[3] at which oral evidence is given and challenged before the judge, who performs the role of referee and (in almost all civil proceedings) determines the outcome of the proceedings by giving judgment as between the parties and by making an order which disposes of the issues between them.

**1.16**     Within the adversarial system the rules of evidence assume a crucial importance since they determine what information may and may not be admitted to the debate – from the exclusionary rules relating to hearsay, privilege and evidence, which are not relevant to the issues to the court, through discovery and inquiry by means of interrogatory and questionnaire, to disclosure. Rules of evidence determine what evidence may be presumed or treated as already adjudicated upon by the court.

## Fairness in a discretionary jurisdiction

**1.17**     Procedure in family courts has been adapted primarily from procedure in the existing civil courts jurisdiction. This civil court procedure is designed, essentially, to test truth and establish points of law. By contrast, most of the litigation in the family jurisdiction is concerned to establish rights and responsibility in terms of the welfare of children and entitlement as to the distribution of matrimonial or family property and income. With important exceptions,[4] matters of law (as distinct from points of procedure, evidence or jurisdiction) and of statutory construction are only relatively

---

1     See further **1.13** above.

2     'Adversarial' is a term of art applied to a legal procedure for trial, but it need not apply to the way in which that process is conducted. That is to say, family lawyers, by definition (because operating within the English court system) conduct adversarial processes, but they need not conduct them in a way which is adversarial (ie confrontational), as explained by Lord Nicholls in his minority speech in *Re L (Police Investigation: Privilege)* [1996] 2 WLR 395, [1996] 1 FLR 731, HL.

3     The word 'trial' as applied to the legal situation derives from: 'The determination of a person's guilt or innocence, or the righteousness of his cause, by a combat between the accuser and the accused' (*Shorter Oxford English Dictionary*).

4     Eg Children Act 1989, s 31(2) (the establishment of the threshold conditions to lead to the making of a care or supervision order) and proprietary estoppel and implied trusts in relation to family property.

rarely involved.[1] Much more, the family lawyer, as advocate, is concerned with an argument over the way in which the court should exercise its discretion in relation to a particular set of family circumstances, rather than dealing with statutory construction or establishment of liability from a given set of facts. That the family court process has derived from civil procedures means that its development has largely overlooked the extent to which the court's jurisdiction is based upon exercise of judicial discretion in a number of statutory contexts.[2] The importance of the discretionary aspect of the jurisdiction has fed into it a paternal and inquisitorial element which has a particular significance in the area of evidence – disclosure and the extent to which the court adopts an inquisitorial role – which will be considered below.[3]

## 3   EVIDENCE IN A DISCRETIONARY JURISDICTION

**1.18**      In what follows, it will be argued that the prevalence of judicial discretion in many family proceedings creates particular rules of evidence and duties upon the parties which are unknown in other jurisdictions. To arrive at this conclusion, it is necessary briefly to consider the history of the family jurisdiction of the courts, and the developments in the fields of law and equity in that history.

### Law and equity

**1.19**      Aristotle,[4] in the fourth century before Christ, had already understood the need for a difference between law and equity. Law, or legal justice, was framed by the legislators in general terms. This was inevitable, since the law was universal, but: 'there are some things about which it is not possible to pronounce rightly in general terms'. Thus, equity was necessary as: 'a rectification of law in so far as law is defective on account of its generality'. Both justice and equity are 'good', but where they coincide, equity is superior.[5] However, Aristotle conceived of equity being used by the judge: 'to correct the omission by a ruling such as the legislator himself would have given if he had been present there'. Thus, there is the idea of the judge putting

---

1   The variety of family and child law reports available to the beleaguered practitioner will reveal
      that only rarely are important points of legal principle involved, as distinct from points of
      procedure, evidence or exercise of judicial discretion.
2   See eg Matrimonial Causes Act 1973, s 1(3):
      'On presentation of a petition it shall be the duty of the court to enquire ...';
      Matrimonial Causes Act 1973, s 25(1):
      'It shall be the duty of the court *in deciding whether* ...'
      ie the court has an option, regardless of the representations of the parties; the words in italics are
      also used in the Inheritance (Provision for Family and Dependants) Act 1975, s 3(1);
      Matrimonial Causes Act 1973, s 25(2) and Children Act 1989, s 1(3):
      '... the court shall in particular have regard to ...';
      Matrimonial Causes Act 1973, s 25A(1):
      '... it shall be the duty of the court to consider whether it would be appropriate so to exercise
      [its] powers ...'.
3   See **1.21** below.
4   *The Ethics of Aristotle*; the quotes here are taken from the translation of JAK Thompson (1953).
5   Cf Supreme Court Act 1981, s 49(1):
      'wherever there is any conflict or variance between the rules of equity and the rules of the
      common law with reference to the same matter, the rules of equity shall prevail.'

himself in the position of the hypothetical legislator when he delivers a judgment based on equity.

**1.20**    The dilemma of how to interpret strict law flexibly confronted the sixteenth century jurists at a time when the Chancery courts, led by canon lawyers (or sometimes men like Cardinal Wolsey who were not lawyers at all) were seeking to develop their own jurisdiction alongside, but separate from, the common law.[1] A contemporary view of this dilemma is provided by the writings of Christopher St German.[2] He was familiar with the views of Aristotle, probably through the writings of the French theologian, Jean Gerson (1363–1429). He wrote his treatises partially in defence of the initiatives being developed by Sir Thomas More, Wolsey's successor on the Woolsack (1529–1533). More, unlike Wolsey, was a lawyer; and, also unlike Wolsey, he developed his equitable jurisdiction from a sound understanding of the common law. Like Aristotle, St German: 'held that equity is not outside the law, but resides implicitly in it and should be observed in every human law'.[3] Although this approach could be regarded as radical by common lawyers of the time, it contains the seeds of an essentially conservative approach to equity which, in time, developed its own rules as formulistic as those of the common law.

## Discretion in the family jurisdiction

**1.21**    This brief consideration of the origins of equity does not explain the development of the wide discretion now vested in family judges. For this, it is necessary first to return to the roots of certain aspects of the family jurisdiction in ecclesiastical law and, secondly, to consider the paternalistic jurisdiction of the courts, for example in connection with minors and wardship.

### *Divorce and the ecclesiastical jurisdiction*

**1.22**    From the twelfth century, divorce and matrimonial causes were regarded as exclusively matters within the jurisdiction of the ecclesiastical courts.[4] The ecclesiastical jurisdiction came to an end in 1857, when the divorce jurisdiction was vested in a new court for divorce and matrimonial causes by the Matrimonial Causes Act 1857. Under this Act, the court had very limited powers, developed essentially from ecclesiastical law principles, to award financial provision for a wife,[5] although it was not until the Married Women's Property Act 1882 that women achieved full separate proprietary rights separate from their husbands. Divorce and the law relating to financial relief developed further in successive statutory developments culminating in the Divorce Reform Act 1969 and the Matrimonial Proceedings and Property Act 1970, both substantially consolidated into the Matrimonial Causes Act 1973.

---

1    JH Baker provides an excellent introduction to this subject in *The Reports of John Spelman,
     Volume II* (Selden Society, 1978) pp 37–43 and 74–83.
2    TFT Plucknett and JL Barton (eds) *Doctor and Student* (Selden Society, 1974) and JA Guy (ed)
     *Replication of a Serjeant at Arms* (Selden Society, 1985); and see JA Guy *Christopher St
     German on Chancery and Statute* (Selden Society, 1985).
3    JA Guy *Christopher St German on Chancery and Statute* (above) p 71.
4    For a historical introduction, see eg Rayden and Jackson *Divorce and Family Matters*
     (Butterworths, 1991) para 1.1 et seq.
5    Eg the right of the blameless wife to claim alimony.

## *Parens patriae*

**1.23**     Alongside these developments can be seen the concept of the judge, on behalf of the sovereign, who exercises the Crown's prerogative as *parens patriae*. This role is most obvious in the feudal remedy of wardship;[1] but, as an underlying concept, it is also discernable in the paternalistic role, derived from common law,[2] which Parliament has imposed upon the courts[3] and which the judges have assumed for themselves.[4] The *parens patriae* approach to children has been preserved by successive children legislation, culminating in the Children Act 1989, although that Act can be seen as reducing substantially the possible uses of wardship.[5]

## Historical derivation of the discretionary jurisdiction

**1.24**     The last two centuries, and especially the last 30 years, have seen dramatic changes in children law, divorce law and matrimonial property law. However, through all the reforms it is possible to see the influences, first, of the ecclesiastical jurisdiction[6] both in connection with financial relief and in divorce[7] and, secondly, of the *parens patriae* role of the courts. Views derived from history can only be very tentative in the present context, but it is possible to see from these two strands the way in which the discretionary jurisdiction of the courts has developed. The *parens patriae* jurisdiction was theoretically limitless, while the ecclesiastical jurisdiction developed from the more flexible and less precedent-based system of Roman law and pleading, in which conscience – perhaps synonymous, here, with discretion – played a much greater part in judicial decision-making. Both these systems of law imbue the court with a more directly paternalistic role, and this role is reflected today in the extent to which judicial discretion plays such an important part in the decison-making of the family courts.

## Discretion and the inquisitorial system

**1.25**     It might be thought that its derivation from Roman law and its incorporation of an essentially paternalistic role might imply a greater influence of the inquisitorial system of law in family proceedings, a system prevalent, for example, in many parts of continental Europe. In the inquisitorial system the judge enquires into the case, and the allegations upon which it is based. He controls the evidence to be called and determines what questions a witness must answer. This process by judicial enquiry by

---

1     Cretney and Masson *Principles of Family Law* 6th edn (Sweet & Maxwell, 1996) provides a brief background to and commentary upon the uses of wardship (pp 704–707).

2     *Hyman v Hyman* [1929] AC 601, (1929) FLR Rep 342, HL.

3     Eg that no spouse by his own agreement can oust the jurisdiction of the courts: Matrimonial Causes Act 1973, s 34(1).

4     See eg the comments of Waite J in *Hildebrand v Hildebrand* [1992] 1 FLR 244, considered at **6.5** below.

5     Eg by placing on a statutory footing many of the old wardship remedies and by restricting severely the courts' and local authorities' use of wardship to place a child in care: Children Act 1989, s 100.

6     See the history of this traced in relation to the financial relief jurisdiction of the courts in *Wachtel v Wachtel* [1973] Fam 73, (1973) FLR Rep 715, CA.

7     For example, the 'one-third rule' in award of maintenance derives from practice in the ecclesiastical courts; and adultery remains an essentially biblical 'offence'.

no means exists in family courts in England and Wales, although family judges occasionally describe the children jurisdiction as 'inquisitorial'.[1] More judicial intervention and case management are increasingly becoming the norm in most civil proceedings.[2] The family jurisdiction is no exception. Indeed, family lawyers have already encountered a higher level judicial intervention earlier than other divisions of the High Court. Timetabling in children cases has been required since the introduction of the Children Act 1989[3] in October 1991, and the relatively interventionist Ancillary Relief Pilot Scheme,[4] which has operated in a number of county courts and the Principal Registry since 1 October 1996, is due to be adopted in all courts as the procedure applicable for all matrimonial ancillary relief proceedings.

**1.26**      Thus, whatever the role of judicial discretion in determining the outcome of a family case, and whatever the influence of judicial case management, it remains the fact that it is for the individual party before the court to chose what evidence he calls. This is subject to admissibility of the evidence,[5] any applicable exclusionary rule of evidence,[6] compliance with procedural rules concerning the filing of written evidence in advance of a final hearing (affidavits, statements or sworn statements and reports from expert witnesses and other documents), and procedural requirements concerning court leave being obtained to adduce expert evidence.[7] This is in direct opposition to the inquisitorial process, in which the judge determines the evidence to be called and the way it is adduced before the court at trial.

## Evidence in a discretionary jurisdiction

**1.27**      Accordingly, it can be argued with some force that the existence of judicial discretion places a particular duty on parties to be open in their disclosure of relevant information. At present, this duty is almost unique to the family jurisdiction, but over the foreseeable future it is possible to predict a movement (starting, perhaps, from *Vernon v Bosley (No 2)*[8]) away from the haven of certain aspects of privilege in civil proceedings towards the more open regime familiar to family lawyers. A clear divergence may develop between the secretiveness of litigation privilege, on the one hand, and client confidentiality, on the other. The latter is fundamental to the English system of justice, as Lord Taylor explained in the *Derby Justices* case.[9] The former is part of the tactics of the civil litigator which may, in due course, be seen to impair justice and exploration of the truth, rather than helping the court to achieve justice, as nearly as possible, between the parties.

---

1     See an explanation and refutation of this terminology by Lord Nicholls in *Re L (Police Investigation: Privilege)* [1997] AC 16, [1996] 1 FLR 731, HL.
2     *Practice Direction of 31 January 1995 (Case Management)* [1995] 1 WLR 332, [1995] 1 FLR 456 (in the Family Division), which is in comparable terms to *Practice Direction (Civil Litigation: Case Management)* [1995] 1 WLR 508 and *Practice Direction (Chancery Division: Procedure and Case Management)* [1995] 1 WLR 785.
3     Section 11(1) and (2) – in children proceedings 'the court shall ... draw up a timetable with a view to determining the question without delay' (s 11(1)); and rules of court may be framed to deal with these matters (s 11(2)).
4     Now provided for in Family Proceedings Rules 1991, rr 2.71–2.77.
5     Eg on grounds of relevance to the issues before the court (see **4.4** et seq below).
6     Such as privilege (see Chapter 7 below), the rules against hearsay (see **4.44** et seq below) etc.
7     Rules of the Supreme Court 1965, Ord 38, r 36; and see further **5.16** et seq below.
8     [1998] 1 FLR 304, [1997] 3 WLR 683, CA; and see **6.9** et seq below.
9     *R v Derby Magistrates' Court ex parte B* [1996] AC 487, [1996] 1 FLR 513, HL.

**1.28** Principles derived from the equitable jurisdiction give another important dimension to the role of discretion in the family jurisdiction. Thus, the court has power to exclude evidence, because to insist upon it being discovered or called may be regarded as oppressive of a witness. These principles relate to discovery, interrogatories and subpoenas.[1] They are familiar throughout the civil litigation system, not only in the family jurisdiction.

# 4 'FAMILY PROCEEDINGS'

## Towards a definition

**1.29** The term 'family proceedings' is defined in a variety of ways, and according to the context in which the term occurs. There are a number of definitions in individual statutes, and the term is defined differently in different statutory instruments.[2] In the Matrimonial and Family Proceedings Act 1984, s 32,[3] 'family proceedings' are defined as 'family business', which, in turn, by reference to the Supreme Court Act 1981, is defined as:

> 'Business of any description which in the High Court is for the time being assigned to the Family Division and to no other Division under [Supreme Court Act 1981, s 61 and Sch 1].'

The Supreme Court Act 1981, Sch 1, under the heading 'Family Division', provides a narrow list of family proceedings, including matrimonial causes, various children proceedings[4] and 'non-contentious or common form probate business' – not a subject immediately recognised by most family practitioners as part of their routine work. The Children Act 1989 and the Family Law Act 1996 each define 'family proceedings' in similar terms to one another,[5] the latter being an updated version of the former: that is to say, proceedings under the Matrimonial Causes Act 1973, the Adoption Act 1976, the Matrimonial and Family Proceedings Act 1984, Part III, the Children Act 1989, Parts I, II and IV, the Human Fertilisation and Embryology Act 1990, s 30 and the Family Law Act 1996, Parts II and IV and under the inherent jurisdiction of the High Court in relation to children. The Family Proceedings Rules 1991, r 1.2(1) adopts the definition in the Matrimonial and Family Proceedings Act 1984, s 32 (above).

**1.30** In what follows, we shall adopt a wider version of the term 'family proceedings'. Accordingly, we shall include such proceedings as those under the Inheritance (Provision for Family and Dependants) Act 1975 and the Child Support

---

1   See Chapter 6 below.
2   For example, the regime under which costs are dealt with in family proceedings defines the term by reference to a combination of Children Act 1989 and Matrimonial Causes Act 1973, s 50, which is now long repealed: Family Proceedings (Costs) Rules 1991, SI 1991/1832, r 2; and see discussion of this point in *The Family Court Practice* (Family Law, 1999).
3   Civil Procedure Rules 1998, r 2.1(2) refers to 'family proceedings as defined by Matrimonial and Family Proceedings Act 1984, s 40, by which is probably intended s 32; and see **1.31** et seq below for consideration of the application of the Civil Procedure Rules to family proceedings.
4   The list of children proceedings includes legitimacy, wardship, adoption, applications by a minor to consent to marriage.
5   Children Act 1989, s 8(3) and (4) and Family Law Act 1996, s 63(1) and (2).

Acts, and proceedings for judicial review involving children and other family matters (such as review of family decisions by magistrates' courts). We have not attempted a full analysis of evidence as it relates to cohabitants and trust law, since (although this might be regarded as family law) it falls more naturally to be considered in a book relating to evidence in civil proceedings. Within the definition of family law, we therefore include the following statutes and jurisdiction:

- Adoption Act 1976;
- Child Abduction and Custody Act 1985;
- Child Support Acts 1991 and 1995;
- Children Act 1989, Parts II, IV and V;
- Domestic Proceedings and Magistrates' Courts Act 1978;
- Family Law Act 1986;
- Family Law Act 1996, Parts II and IV;
- Human Fertilisation and Embryology Act 1990, s 30;
- Inheritance (Provision for Family and Dependants) Act 1975;
- injunctions in the inherent jurisdiction of the courts,[1] including:
  - *Mareva* injunctions;
  - *Anton Piller* orders;[2]
- judicial review in family matters,[3] such as Children Act 1989, Part III and child support; Married Women's Property Act 1882 (including proceedings under the Law Reform (Miscellaneous Provisions) Act 1970 (proceedings between engaged couples);
- Matrimonial and Family Proceedings Act 1984, Part III;
- Matrimonial Causes Act 1973;
- property proceedings (limited examples, eg the Trusts of Land and Appointment of Trustees Act 1996, s 14);
- Protection from Harassment Act 1997; and
- wardship and the inherent jurisdiction relating to children.

## 'Family proceedings' and the Civil Procedure Rules 1998

**1.31**     As already mentioned, the Civil Procedure Rules 1998 are not intended formally to apply to family proceedings; although, as set out above, there are forms of process – for example, proceedings under the Inheritance (Provision for Family and Dependants) Act 1975 and free-standing family *Mareva* applications – which will not be family proceedings within the definition in the Matrimonial and Family Proceedings Act 1984, s 32. Further, it seems inevitable that many district judges, who will be extensively trained in Woolf procedures, will be influenced by many aspects of the new Rules; and this influence will exhibit itself in their decision-making in family proceedings. Finally, it is probable that before very long the Lord Chancellor will find himself able to apply the new Rules to family proceedings. Accordingly, a very brief discussion of the new Rules follows.

---

1    Under Supreme Court Act 1981, s 31.
2    Now provided for in respect of non family proceedings under Civil Procedure Act 1997, s 7 (and henceforth to be known as 'freezing injunctions' and 'search orders': Civil Procedure Rules 1998, Part 25, r 25.1).
3    Under Supreme Court Act 1981, s 31 and Rules of the Supreme Court 1965, Ord 53.

## Operation of Civil Procedure Rules 1998 and the old Rules

**1.32**    The Civil Procedure Rules 1998 govern practice and procedure in the civil division of the Court of Appeal, the High Court and county courts.[1] The new provisions[2] are contained in the Rules themselves, a set of practice directions[3] and by amending those of the existing Rules of the Supreme Court 1965 and County Court Rules 1981[4] which survive. In parallel, whilst family proceedings remain formally unaffected by the Civil Procedure Rules 1998, the old Rules of the Supreme Court 1965 and the County Court Rules 1981 will remain in force in their entirety and will apply to family proceedings (as defined by Matrimonial and Family Proceedings Act 1984, s 32) as need be.[5] These arrangements, applied to the forms of process set out in the preceding paragraphs, can tentatively be demonstrated by reference to the following table.

---

1    Civil Procedure Act 1997, s 1. Civil Procedure Rules 1998, r 2.1(2) exempts other minor forms of civil proceedings in addition to family proceedings. For a detailed explanation of evidential aspects of the Rules, see Chapter 15.

2    Appendix 1 contains those Civil Procedure Rules 1998 and those of the new practice directions which appear to be relevant to the subject of evidence in family proceedings.

3    Civil Procedure Act 1997, Sch 1, para 6 enables the Civil Procedure Rules 1998 to provide for 'any matter ... by directions'.

4    Eg Rules of the Supreme Court 1965, Ord 53 (judicial review), Ord 99 (Inheritance (Provision for Family and Dependants) Act 1975) and Ord 112 (blood tests) and County Court Rules 1981, Ord 29 (committal) remain, as modified by Schs 1 and 2 of the Rules.

5    Family Proceedings Rules 1991, r 1.3(1). Where possible, in what follows, reference has been made both to the new rule in addition to the existing rule where Civil Procedure Rules 1998, r 2.2(2) disapplies the Civil Procedure Rules 1998 to family proceedings.

# Family proceedings: which Rules apply?

## *(1) Family proceedings*

| *Form of family process* | *FPR 1991 (or other rules)* | *RSC 1965/CCR 1981* | *RSC/CCR (as amended)* | *CPR 1998* |
|---|---|---|---|---|
| Adoption Act 1976 | AAR | | | |
| Child Abduction and Custody Act 1985 | * | * | | |
| Child Support Acts – appeals | * | * | | |
| Children Act 1989[1] | * | * | | |
| Domestic Proceedings and Magistrates' Courts Act 1978[2] | – | – | – | – |
| Family Law Act 1986 | * | * | | |
| Family Law Act 1996, Part IV | * | * | | |
| Human Fertilisation and Embryology Act 1990, s 30 | * | * | | |
| Inheritance (Provision for Family and Dependants) Act 1975 | | | * | * |
| Injunctions in inherent jurisdiction (free standing) | | | | * |
| Judicial review in family proceedings | | | * | * |
| Married Women's Property Act | * | * | | |
| Matrimonial Causes Act 1973 | * | * | | |
| Matrimonial and Family Proceedings Act 1984, Part III | * | * | | |
| Protection from Harassment Act 1997 | | | * | * |
| Trusts of Land and Appointment of Trustees Act 1996, s 14 | | | * | * |
| Wardship and the inherent jurisdiction | * | * | | |

---

1    Family Proceedings Courts (Children Act 1989) Rules 1991 for proceedings in family proceedings courts.

2    Proceedings in the family proceedings court are not in any event 'civil proceedings': Civil Procedure Act 1997, s 1(1).

## (2) Ancillary processes[1]

| | | | | |
|---|---|---|---|---|
| (1) Blood tests under Family Law Reform Act 1969 | | | * | |
| (2) Enforcement of orders | | * | * | |
| (3) Costs[2] | | | | * |
| (4) Appeals<br>(a) District judge to circuit judge in family proceedings (per s 32) | * | * | | |
| (b) Judge to Court of Appeal | | | * | * |
| (c) Family proceedings court to High Court judge | * | * | | |

## The new Rules: a brief introduction

**1.33**    From the above, it will be appreciated that the new Civil Procedure Rules 1998 apply to certain proceedings with which a family lawyer will be concerned, such as those under:

– Inheritance (Provisions for Family and Dependants) Act 1975;
– Protection from Harassment Act 1997;
– Trusts of Land and Appointment of Trustees Act 1996, s 14.

Much of the emphasis in what follows will be on family proceedings covered by the Family Proceedings Rules 1991 and the old rules as originally drafted. Thus, insofar as practice requires that civil proceedings rules be referred on the subject of evidence then for the most part this will be by reference to the Rules of the Supreme Court 1965, Ord 38;[3] but for the above forms of process the Civil Procedure Rules 1998 will apply. Accordingly, a separate chapter, Chapter 15, gives a summary of the new rules; and, where applicable, reference to both sets of rules has been provided in the remainder of the text.

---

1    It is difficult to be categoric as to the way in which any of these processes will be dealt with procedurally: the question may be whether they stand alone as a process (eg a judgment summons or application for a charging order or appointment of a receiver); or whether they are regarded as part of existing proceedings (eg an application to commit for breach of an order or undertaking).

2    Costs in all proceedings are now covered by the Civil Procedure Rules 1998, Parts 43–48 (as partially modified) (Family Proceedings (Miscellaneous Amendments) Rules 1999, SI 1999/1012, r 4(1)).

3    See eg references to Rules of the Supreme Court 1965 and opinion evidence in **5.16** et seq.

# Chapter 2

## EVIDENCE AND PLEADINGS

### 1  PLEADINGS DEFINED

**2.1**    Pleadings perform the role for the court of describing the cause of action, setting out the facts upon which a party bases his case and defining the issues between the parties. Rules of the Supreme Court 1965, Ord 18, r 7(1)[1] sets out the requirement that:

> 'every pleading must contain, and contain only, a statement in a summary form of the material facts on which the party pleading relies for his claim or defence, as the case may be, but not the evidence by which those facts are to be proved, and the statement must be as brief as the nature of the case admits.'

**2.2**    Although pleadings, as the term is understood in civil proceedings generally, are largely absent in family proceedings,[2] it will be argued here that the family lawyer would do well to think in terms of pleading a case when preparing documentation for the court – affidavits, statements and sworn statements – so as to give form to the case which they support; though, as will be seen,[3] these documents are a component of the evidence in the case and must therefore contain particulars of the pleaded case and the evidence in support of it.

**2.3**    The essence of the form of a pleading, as set out in Ord 18, r 7(1), is that it should contain the facts upon which the case is based, not the evidence by which those facts are to be proved; and that the facts be pleaded briefly. These features will now be considered in turn followed by an assessment of the function of the pleadings in defining the issues between the parties.

### Material facts

**2.4**    In terms of pleading, a party is required to set out the facts upon which he relies, so that facts which are not pleaded cannot be relied upon at the trial of the issue concerned. However, whilst it is important to ensure that facts to be relied upon are pleaded, it is almost as important to ensure that facts which are immaterial or

---

1    The equivalent rule for the county courts is County Court Rules 1981, Ord 6, r 1(1) which requires the plaintiff to file particulars of claim which specify 'his cause of action and the relief or remedy which he seeks and stating briefly the material facts on which he relies'. Civil Procedure Rules 1998, rr 16.2 and 16.3 define the contents of a claim pleaded under those rules; and see **15.3** below.

2    Pleading of the main suit is retained in the matrimonial causes jurisdiction. In drafting the particulars of a petition the petitioner is required to set out 'the ground on which relief is sought, together in any case with brief particulars of the individual facts relied on but not the evidence by which they are to be proved': Family Proceedings Rules 1991, App 2, para 1(m).

3    See **3.13** et seq below.

irrelevant to the issues before the court are excluded from pleadings. The facts, as pleaded, must amount to a cause of action. It is not necessary to plead law, save where a point of law is raised – perhaps one for decision on trial of a preliminary issue[1] – in which case it may be pleaded.[2]

## Brevity

**2.5**      The second point stressed by Ord 18, r 7 is the requirement that the pleading must state the case as briefly as possible.[3] The editors of *The Supreme Court Practice*[4] describe this duty as follows:

> 'It cannot be too often stated that the relevant matters must be stated briefly, succinctly, and in strict chronological order. Pleadings should be as brief as the nature of the case will admit. The Court has an inherent jurisdiction to deal with prolix documents.[[5]] But no document is prolix which merely states facts that are material, however numerous.'

## Defining the issues

**2.6**      Perhaps the most important function of pleadings is that, properly drafted, they define the issues between the parties. A definition of the issues is crucial to the decision of what evidence is admissible; for only evidence which is relevant, or sufficiently relevant, to the issues before the court is admissable by the court.[6]

## 2   PLEADINGS AND ISSUES IN THE FAMILY JURISDICTION

**2.7**      The difficulty of imposing a strict rule of pleading in many family proceedings – which are prospective, rather than retrospective in outlook – is illuminated by the case of *M v M (Property Adjustment: Impaired Life Expectancy)*.[7] The husband left the wife and two children of the family in the matrimonial home, and went to live with another woman. The wife had a brain tumour. Notwithstanding radiotherapy, her life expectancy was severely impaired. Despite her wish to stay in the matrimonial home, the district judge ordered that it be sold in one year's time, and the proceeds divided 75 per cent to her and 25 per cent to the husband. Having obtained the order for sale, the husband then asked, at the hearing, for a charge on the property bought by the wife with her share of the proceeds. As her life expectancy was so poor, the district judge acceded to this request. On appeal, both the circuit judge and Court of Appeal upheld the decision. Because of the everchanging circumstances of

---

1     Rules of the Supreme Court 1965, Ord 33, rr 3 and 4(2) enable the court to order that a question of fact or of law be tried as a preliminary issue. For an example of a preliminary issue of fact in children proceedings, and for the recommended procedure in such circumstances, see *Re S (Care Proceedings: Split Hearing)* [1996] 2 FLR 773, Bracewell J.
2     Rules of the Supreme Court 1965, Ord 18, r 11.
3     And see Civil Procedure Rules 1998, Part 16, especially r 16.4.
4     At n 18/7/7.
5     *Hill v Hart-Davies* (1884) 26 ChD 470.
6     See consideration of relevance and admissibility at **4.4** et seq below.
7     [1993] 2 FLR 723, CA.

family life, the court was obliged to deal with the wife's health as it found it to be on the day of the hearing.[1] It could be argued that this was not a matter which could have been pleaded in advance of the hearing, although the husband, a GP, might have given the question some thought.

## Pleadings defined

**2.8** A pleading is a party's written statement of the facts on which he relies for his claim or defence, as the case may be.[2] The term 'pleading' does not, strictly, include a petition, summons or preliminary act;[3] and it has been held that an originating summons is not a pleading.[4] However, for present purposes 'pleadings' will be deemed to include all written applications for orders of court. This is so because it is only by reference to such documents that it is possible, with any reasonable degree of certainty, to discern the grounds upon which it is alleged that the court has jurisdiction to make the order, or to grant the remedy sought. Further, the pleadings, on this broader definition, identify the issues to be tried.

**2.9** In family cases the nature of the proceedings determines the form of the pleading required. Generally, where the rules require specific facts to be pleaded in each case, a prescribed form[5] represents the model that is used; examples are the form used in applications under the Children Act 1989[6] and the form prescribed for issue of applications under the Family Law Act 1996, Part IV.[7] One distinguishing factor of this category of case is that evidence is presented orally even when, as in the example of Children Act 1989 proceedings, the substance of that evidence has to be served prior to the hearing in the form of a statement.[8] In cases concerning applications for ancillary relief, declarations and orders under the Married Women's Property Act 1882, orders under the Inheritance (Provision for Family and Dependants) Act 1975 and applications for injunctions, whether for the protection of persons or property (other than under the Family Law Act 1996, Part IV), are all begun by variations of the originating summons procedure,[9] and are generally supported by affidavit.

### Retrospective pleadings

**2.10.** As has already been observed, as the past is a fixed and determinable quantity, so rules of pleading in respect of incidents which have occurred in the past may, quite reasonably, be strictly enforced. In the county court: 'a plaintiff shall, at the time of commencing an action, file particulars of his claim specifying his cause of action and the relief or remedy which he seeks and stating briefly the material facts on

---

1   Matrimonial Causes Act 1973, s 25(2)(e).
2   Rules of the Supreme Court 1965, Ord 18, r 7.
3   Ibid, Ord 1, r 4.
4   *Lewis v Packer* [1960] 1 WLR 452, [1960] 1 All ER 720.
5   By contrast, a divorce petition must comply with certain prerequisites as set out in Family Proceedings Rules 1991, Appendix 2; but the precise form of the petition is not defined.
6   Family Proceedings Rules 1991, r 4.4 requires applications made under the Children Act 1989 to be 'in the appropriate form in Appendix 1'.
7   Form FL401: Family Proceedings Rules 1991, r 3.8(3).
8   Ibid, r 4.17.
9   See eg Rules of the Supreme Court 1965, Ords 7 and 28 (outline of originating summons and procedure); Family Proceedings Rules 1991, r 2.58 (ancillary relief).

which he relies'.[1] In the High Court: 'every pleading must contain the necessary particulars of any claim, defence or other matter pleaded'.[2] The object of particulars is to prevent the opposite party from being misled or taken by surprise.[3] Thus, the main purpose of pleadings is to inform one party of the case which the other will seek to make against him. 'That is an essential feature of justice.'[4]

**2.11** Pleadings[5] are required to be specific and should state dates, places, the identity of persons, items, conditions of mind, particulars of misrepresentation, fraud, breach of trust, wilful default, undue influence, facts in relation to damages sought, or mitigation of damage.[6] Insufficient particulars may be remedied by a request for further and better particulars.[7] Failure to provide particulars required by the rules or court order may result in the action being dismissed, the defendant debarred from defending, or particulars contained in pleadings being struck out.[8]

## Pleadings in family cases

### (1) Retrospective pleadings

**2.12** In family proceedings, where the issue is retrospective, those strict rules may be applied. Where, for instance, there is an issue as to the beneficial interests in substantial assets, reliance being placed on discussions between the parties, the discussions should be pleaded in the greatest detail in order to enable the court to define the issues and judge the relevance of the evidence adduced. This is especially important in family property cases which, brought by originating summons or application, and supported by affidavit, are not assisted by the procedure for pleading of particulars which exists in actions brought by writ.[9] A failure to plead in a party's affidavit a particular discussion which is later relied on could, arguably, preclude that party from pursuing that part of his claim.

**2.13** In proceedings brought by petition, where allegations relate to past events or states of affairs, strict rules are applied. Petitions must contain 'brief particulars of the individual facts relied on' to prove the fact alleged under s 1(2) of the Matrimonial Causes Act 1973 in suits for divorce or judicial separation, or ground on which relief is sought in other cases.[10] Where an answer, reply or subsequent pleading contains more than a simple denial of the facts stated in the petition, answer or reply as the cases may be, the pleading 'shall set out with sufficient particularity the facts relied on'.[11] The pleadings must not contain the evidence by which the facts alleged are to be

---

1  County Court Rules 1981, Ord 6, r 1(1).
2  Rules of the Supreme Court 1965, Ord 18, r 12.
3  *Stancliffe v Clarke* (1852) 7 Excr 439; *Campbell v Hewlitt* (1851) 16 QB 258; *Gaskill v Skene* (1850) 19 LJQB 275.
4  *Symphony Group plc v Hodgson* [1993] 3 WLR 830 at 845, per Staughton LJ.
5  As defined by Rules of the Supreme Court 1965, Ord 1, r 4(1).
6  Rules of the Supreme Court 1965, Ord 18, rr 6–11 and r 12(1) and (2).
7  See eg ibid, Ord 18, r 12; County Court Rules 1981, Ord 6, r 7.
8  Rules of the Supreme Court 1965, Ord 18; County Court Rules 1981, Ord 13, r 2(2)(b).
9  *H v M (Property: Beneficial Interest)* [1992] 1 FLR 229, per Waite J.
10  Family Proceedings Rules 1991, r 2.3 and Appendix 2, para 1(m): proceedings begun by petition include divorce, nullity, judicial separation, presumption of death and dissolution of marriage, declaration of marital status, declaration of parentage, declaration of legitimacy or legitimation, and declaration of overseas adoption.
11  Family Proceedings Rules 1991, r 2.15. Further particulars can be requested (r 2.19).

proved.[1] However, they may contain admissions which are capable of proving a fact alleged against the party making them. Failure to comply with the rules of court or directions may result in the petition being dismissed, the respondent being debarred from defending, or (where particulars have been ordered) the pleading being struck out unless the order is obeyed within such time as the court may allow.[2] Other examples in family law cases of retrospective pleadings where the strict rule of providing particulars applies include the application to commit a person for breach of a court order,[3] all applications for declaration and enforcement of existing property interests,[4] and interlocutory applications in ancillary relief proceedings for production of documents.[5] In each instance, the pleading is directed at established events or states of affairs, allowing for full particularity of allegation to be both practicable and, in the interests of justice, essential. Thus, the issues are defined and the relevance of evidence is ascertainable.

## (2) Prospective pleadings

**2.14** It has already been observed that applications which seek orders to provide for the future welfare of children and for future financial provision for family members are inherently prospective; insofar as they refer to the past, it is to help predict the future. Thus, in children cases it is proper for the court to enquire into past harm suffered by a child in order to assess the risks of further harm in the future.[6] In ancillary relief cases, past earnings may be a reliable indicator of future earning capacity.[7] Strict rules of pleading in the application forms are not possible much

---

1   Family Proceedings Rules 1991, App 2, para 1(m).
2   Subject to the provisions of the Family Proceedings Rules 1991, the County Court Rules 1981 and the Rules of the Supreme Court 1965 apply to family proceedings (Family Proceedings Rules 1991, r 1.3). Thus, in the county court, failure to comply with an order to provide particulars of a petition, answer or other pleading, or serve a pleading when required to do so may result in the dismissal of the suit, the debarring of the respondent from defending, or the striking-out of particulars as the case may be (County Court Rules 1981, Ord 13, r 2(2)(b)). For general principles to be applied when dismissing for want of prosecution, see *Birkett v James* [1978] AC 297, [1977] 2 All ER 801.
3   In a county court, the request for the issue of the notice of application must identify the provisions of the injunction or undertaking which it is alleged have been disobeyed or broken; and list the ways in which it is alleged the disobedience or breaches have occurred (County Court Rules 1981, Ord 29, r 1(4A); and see *Chakravorty v Braganza* (1983) *The Times*, 12 October; *Chiltern District Council v Keane* [1985] 1 WLR 619, [1985] All ER 118; *Bowen v Bowen* (1987) 9 CL 273a. In the High Court, see Rules of Supreme Court 1965, Ord 45, rr 5–8).
4   Eg under the Married Women's Property Act 1882 (Family Proceedings Rules 1991, r 3.6).
5   Family Proceedings Rules 1991, r 2.62(7); the document required must be specified in the order. Oppressive enquiry or 'fishing expeditions' are not allowed on analogy with Rules of the Supreme Court 1965, Ord 38. The production of the document must be necessary for fairly disposing of the application for ancillary relief, or saving costs (*Frary v Frary* [1993] 2 FLR 696, CA; and see **4.11** et seq and **6.31** (oppressive enquiry)).
6   See eg *Re H (A Minor); Re K (A Minor) (Child Abuse: Evidence)* [1989] 2 FLR 314; Children Act 1989, s 1(3)(e) (harm in consideration of the welfare test) and s 31(2)(a) (significant harm).
7   See eg *Bromilow v Bromilow* [1976] 7 Fam Law 16 (a former unskilled manual labourer was seen as being able to get a job if he wanted to); but contrast *Bennett v Bennett* [1978] 9 Fam Law 19 (an executive who had resigned from his job after 19 years due to a disagreement with the managing director was not expected to have to accept new employment at a much lower salary).

beyond a general description of the relief sought.[1] The evidence in support of the applications, however, must be served in writing, and is capable of being specific about past matters. In ancillary relief applications, further information is obtainable by questionnaire,[2] interrogatory[3] (as appropriate) and production appointments.[4] In children cases, the substance of the evidence contained in the statements or affidavits (which stand as the evidence in chief of the witness) must be sufficiently detailed[5] to show a party's case and the evidence in support of it.

## Quasi-pleadings – skeleton arguments, chronologies, schedules of issues

**2.15**     Such is the pressure on scarce courtroom time that parties are encouraged, as far as possible, to reduce their arguments into written form. This departure from the traditional oral presentation of a case is a trend which has accelerated in recent times. It has long been regarded as good practice, certainly in the High Court, to prepare skeleton arguments and chronologies of material events to assist the clear and expeditious presentation of a case.[6]

**2.16**     In 1983, guidelines were issued on the use of skeleton arguments in the Court of Appeal.[7] The skeleton arguments was envisaged as: 'an abbreviated note of the argument or submission of a party', 'an aide-memoire for convenience of reference', intended 'to dispense with the need for a lengthy, or in some cases any opening'. The skeleton, it was suggested, should contain: the propositions of law; the citations of authorities; the *dramatis personae* of the case; and, if necessary, a glossary of technical terms. A chronology of salient relevant events should be annexed to it. In 1989, skeleton arguments became compulsory[8] in all appeals to the Civil Division of the Court of Appeal, save in those cases of exceptional urgency where time was not sufficient for the drafting, lodgment or service of such a document. Some of the main features can be summarised as follows:

–    to identify, but not argue points;
–    points of law to be stated succinctly, and the authorities relied upon cited;
–    on issues of fact, to state the basis upon which the Court of Appeal was being invited to interfere with the findings of the court below;
–    if the respondent wished to differ with the judgment at first instance in any respect, to put in a skeleton argument, whereas where the respondent agreed with the judgment appealed against, to signify this by letter.

---

1    See consideration of *M v M (Property Adjustment: Impaired Life Expectancy)* [1993] 2 FLR 723, CA, at **2.3** above.
2    Family Proceedings Rules 1991, r 2.63.
3    Rules of the Supreme Court 1965, Ord 26; County Court Rules 1981, Ord 14, r 11.
4    Family Proceedings Rules 1991, r 2.62(7)–(9).
5    *Practice Direction of 31 January 1995 (Case Management)* [1995] 1 WLR 332, [1995] 1 FLR 456 at para 3; Family Proceedings Rules 1991, r 4.17.
6    Directions under the Ancillary Relief Pilot Scheme generally require this of advocates; and, increasingly, judges in children proceedings are directing the filing of skeleton arguments and chronologies.
7    *Practice Direction* [1983] 1 WLR 1055.
8    *Practice Direction* [1989] 1 All ER 891. The requirements in respect of skeleton arguments in Court of Appeal proceedings are now embodied in the Practice Direction to the Civil Procedure Rules 1998, Sch 1 RSC Ord 59. See Appendix 1.

### *Skeleton argument as 'quasi-pleading'*

**2.17**    The skeleton argument was said not to be a pleading. Consequently, it did not need to be answered point by point in the skeleton argument of the other party to the proceedings. However, as it is signed by counsel for the party on whose behalf it is presented, it may be argued that admissions contained in it would be binding on that party in the same way as if they had been made by letter, or indeed by the advocate, orally, in court.

### *Case management and the skeleton argument*

**2.18**    Since 31 January 1995, in cases in the Family Division, care centres, family hearing centres and divorce county courts, whenever practicable and in any matter estimated to last for five days or more, each party should, not less than two clear days before the hearing, lodge and serve a chronology and skeleton argument concisely summarising that party's submissions in relation to each of the issues, and citing main authorities relied upon.[1] The chronology should be cross-referenced with relevant bundles of documents in the case.[2]

## Case management and pre-trial issues

**2.19**    In children cases, where expert evidence is to be called, the experts may be required to discuss the areas of agreement and disagreement between them. A coordinator may be appointed from among the parties' representatives to collate the expert reports and prepare a schedule of the areas of agreement and disagreement between the experts.[3] In ancillary relief proceedings, similar aides to defining the issues may be called for from the parties.[4] In substantial cases the need for such documents should be explored at pre-trial directions hearings. Under the Ancillary Relief Pilot Scheme, in order to encourage the parties to focus on the real issues in the ancillary relief proceedings and reduce the demand for irrelevant discovery, they are required to file and serve a concise statement of apparent issues between them.[5] Each of these documents should be viewed as quasi-pleadings, in that they should be drafted with care, served in compliance with the timetable set by the court, and with due regard to the effect of any admissions that they might contain.

## Pleadings and evidence in proceedings under the Children Act 1989

**2.20**    In the High Court, county courts and family proceedings courts, children applications are made in the forms prescribed by the rules.[6] The applicant must provide a variety of information, some of which is specifically required to establish the court's jurisdiction,[7] and give a summary of the salient features of the case. In

---

1    *Practice Direction of 31 January 1995 (Case Management)* [1995] 1 WLR 332, [1995] 1 FLR 456. In practice, and most regrettably, this Practice Direction has received little attention from judges and district judges.

2    *B v B (Court Bundles: Video Evidence)* [1994] 2 FLR 323, per Wall J.

3    *Re C (Expert Evidence: Disclosure: Practice)* [1995] 1 FLR 204, per Cazalet J.

4    *Evans v Evans* [1990] 1 FLR 319, per Booth J.

5    Family Proceedings Rules 1991, r 2.73(4)(c) (and see **2.17** above).

6    Family Proceedings Rules 1991, r 4.4(1A) and Sch 1; Family Proceedings Courts (Children Act 1989) Rules 1991, SI 1991/1395, r 4(1A).

7    Eg parenthood, the age of the child, residence within the jurisdiction etc.

addition, the grounds for seeking the order and the orders sought must be clearly stated. The local authority, in proceedings for a care or supervision order, should state its care plan in sufficient detail for the court to assess its viability and the extent to which it will serve to safeguard and promote the welfare of the child.[1] Others who need to be served under the rules, and those currently responsible for the children's care, their addresses and their relationship to the child, must also be stated. With this information the court can ensure that all relevant persons will have an opportunity to be heard.

## Applications in family proceedings

**2.21** The application in many family proceedings, whether concerning children or financial relief, is rudimentary. Nearer to a pleading properly so-called, is the affidavit or statement in support. It seems likely that pleadings in family cases are undergoing revolutionary change. The ancillary relief procedure under the pilot scheme currently in force in specified courts is a welcome departure from the relaxed, laissez-faire attitude of the past, and is very much in line with the ethos of the *Practice Direction: Case Management*. The rules establish a strict timetable and an interventionist mode of court control of proceedings. The principle evidence of the parties, stating their means, need, the special factors relied on by them in relation to health, standard of living, pensions or conduct, must be set out as a sworn statement, in a prescribed form (Form E), which must be simultaneously exchanged by the parties not less than 35 days before the date of the first appointment.[2] The prescription of information required is contained in the rules.[3] This procedure produces a hybrid document that is both evidence and a pleading of the party's case. Its prescribed form imposes a consistent approach to pleading a party's case which is comparable to the statement of claim procedure in civil actions. Subsequently, not later than seven days before the first appointment, the parties are required to file and serve questionnaires and requests for the further information and documents each seeks from the other in support of their respective cases.[4] The court alone controls the extent to which these questionnaires and requests require an answer.[5] The avowed purpose of these rules was 'to reduce delay, facilitate settlements, limit costs . . . and provide the court with much greater control over the conduct of proceedings'.[6] To achieve this purpose the pleadings and directions have a declared 'objective of defining the issues and saving costs'. The development in family law of a system of formal pleadings is analogous to that created by Ord 18 of the Rules of the Supreme Court. Although it remains to be seen, therefore, whether judges and district judges use their powers increasingly to direct the filing of what we have identified as 'quasi-pleadings', the Pilot Scheme will give the evolution of pleadings in family law cases a needed impetus.

---

1  *Manchester City Council v F* [1993] 1 FLR 419; *Re J (Minors) (Care: Care Plan)* [1994] 1 FLR 253.
2  Family Proceedings Rules 1991, r. 2.73(1).
3  Ibid, r 2.73(2).
4  Ibid, r 2.73(4).
5  Ibid, r 2.74(1).
6  *Practice Direction of 16 June 1997 (Ancillary Relief Procedure: Pilot Scheme)* [1997] 2 FLR 304.

# Chapter 3

## FORMS OF EVIDENCE

## 1   INTRODUCTION

**3.1**     The purpose of evidence is to put information before the court to prove facts which are in issue in proceedings. Evidence may be oral (whether first-hand, hearsay or opinion), or by means of documents (whether to be agreed by the parties or proved in court). Evidence may also be what is known as 'real evidence' (for example exhibits) and characteristics or demeanour of a witness. Certain information will be placed before the court – and this is especially so in family proceedings – which is not evidence according to the definition, but which is treated as evidence, for example affidavits, statements and reports from expert witnesses.

**3.2**     The form which the evidence takes will depend on the issue before the court and, perhaps, upon the standard of proof demanded by the particular question under consideration.[1] The general rule is that a witness can give evidence only of facts within his personal knowledge or which he has perceived with one or more of his five senses (referred to here as 'primary evidence'); save in the case of the expert witness who may give evidence of opinion (a form of 'secondary evidence') and evidence which is derived from textbooks, from his experience or which he has learned from third parties ('tertiary evidence').

**3.3**     Generally, it is for the parties to call their own evidence in the order which they choose but subject to:

(a)   any obligation they may have to file with the court, and serve on other parties, statements (whether sworn or otherwise) or affidavits from witnesses upon whose evidence they intend to rely;[2]

(b)   any court directions as to the filing and serving of expert evidence.[3]

It is this choice as to the evidence to be called which is an important distinguishing feature of the adversarial system of procedure which applies in most common law systems of justice. This is in contrast to inquisitorial systems of justice, where, for the most part, the judge decides the evidence to be received by the court.[4]

**3.4**     Generally, it is for the applicant to prove his application to the court by means of evidence and subject to the rules on adducing that evidence, considered in this

---

1   See **4.31** below.
2   See eg Rules of the Supreme Court 1965, Ord 38, r 2A; County Court Rules 1981, Ord 20, r 12A; Family Proceedings Rules 1991, SI 1991/1247, r 2.58 (ancillary relief) and r 4.17 (children proceeding); Family Proceedings Courts (Children Act 1989) Rules 1991, SI 1991/1395, r 17; and, in respect of non family proceedings, see Civil Procedure Rules 1998, r 32.4.
3   Rules of the Supreme Court 1965, Ord 38, r 36; County Court Rules 1981, Ord 20, r 27.
4   It remains to be seen to what extent inquisitorial systems develop within the family jurisdiction; see **1.25** above for a further consideration of this question.

chapter. This statement is subject to the exception that there are facts which do not require proof because: judicial notice has been taken of those facts; an estoppel operates to prevent a party to the proceedings denying the facts; a court has already adjudicated upon a set of facts (*res judicata*); or facts have already been admitted by a party to the proceedings.

## 2   CATEGORIES OF EVIDENCE

**3.5**     The extent to which evidence is of value in proving a case depends on the weight, or cogency, of that evidence in persuading the judge of any fact in issue in the proceedings, or which otherwise needs to be established for the purposes of adjudication.[1] The categorisation which follows will be adopted in assessment of the forms of evidence.

### Primary evidence

**3.6**     Primary evidence consists of evidence perceived by the witness or by the court, or of provable evidence which can be adduced by the oral testimony of a witness. This category includes:

–   evidence within a person's knowledge, perceived by one or more of his five senses;
–   real evidence, for example exhibits (a wage slip produced by a witness's employer, a photograph taken by that witness etc) and the fact (as distinct from the contents) of documents;
–   characteristics of a witness or his demeanour in court;
–   photographs and video recordings, the content of which are proved by the maker, or what is photographed is admitted (for example photographs showing injuries to a child who can be identified to the court).

Thus, if these definitions are applied to a video recording, the video cassette itself is primary evidence (as with a document) which may need to be proved (ie an explanation given as to who took the video and in whose possession it has been since then). The interview or other information recorded upon it is hearsay, or secondary (see below), and its cogency will depend on the clarity of the recording, the reliability of the witnesses or the information recorded, and the relevance of the evidence it provides.

### Secondary evidence

**3.7**     Secondary evidence is evidence which is not provable by first-hand experience. (A separate category, 'tertiary evidence', is referred to below for the sources upon which an expert bases his opinion.) The principal area of secondary evidence is hearsay which may be encountered at various removes.[2] Further, it may be adduced not only from oral testimony, but also, for example, from documents, recordings and film.

---

1     For further consideration of cogency, see **4.42** et seq below.
2     For consideration of hearsay evidence, see **4.44** et seq below.

**3.8** Evidence on film, including photographs and video recordings, is secondary. Formally, it may need to be proved by the photographer, although in the family jurisdiction rules on this point are likely to be less rigorous than in the criminal courts unless a particular issue as to proof of film or its content arises.

## Tertiary evidence

**3.9** Tertiary evidence is evidence given by an opinion witness from secondary and other sources and from which the opinion witness[1] deduces his opinion. Examples are:

– consideration of another person's report of the evidence from such sources as medical notes, social work records, photographs of injuries; or, in financial relief cases, a firm's bank or other accounts, and business accounts prepared by an accountant; or, in the case of pensions, information produced by the trustees of the pension fund etc;
– academic sources – books and other reference materials, and discussions with colleagues;
– personal experience in the particular field of expertise.

## 3   ADDUCING THE EVIDENCE

**3.10** Although the general rule is that proof of a case is 'by the examination of witnesses orally and in open Court',[2] most examination-in-chief in family proceedings is – or should be[3] – by means of affidavit, statement or sworn statement. The question of oral evidence is considered below, followed by the variety of forms which other categories of primary evidence may take in practice.

## Oral evidence

**3.11** Thus, under the general rule, the witness who is to be examined 'orally and in open court'[4] must have personal knowledge, perceived by one or more of his five senses, of the facts which he is describing to the court. Two important exceptions to the first-hand knowledge rule relate to hearay evidence[4] and to the opinion witness who is entitled to give evidence based on his expertise.[5] However, most family proceedings are dealt with in chambers rather than in open court, and different rules on adducing evidence have been devleoped for such a venue. Hearings in open court still occasionally occur, for example the hearing of any divorce, judicial separation or nullity petition which is contested or not covered by the 'special procedure',[6] and

---

1   For a full consideration of opinion evidence, see Chapter 5.
2   Rules of the Supreme Court 1965, Ord 38, r 1; Civil Procedure Rules 1998, r 32.2(1).
3   *Practice Direction of 31 January 1995 (Case Management)* [1995] 1 WLR 332, [1995] 1 FLR 456 at para 3.
4   Indeed, Rules of the Supreme Court 1965, Ord 38, r 1 is made subject to the Civil Evidence Act 1968 which deals with hearsay evidence; see **4.44** et seq below.
5   See **5.5** et seq below.
6   Family Proceedings Rules 1991, r 2.28(1) reproduces the wording of Rules of the Supreme Court 1965, Ord 38, r 1 to refer to proof of facts in connection with a petition where it is necessary for this to be heard in open court; see further **9.9** below.

applications to commit for breach of a court order or undertaking.[1] (Judicial review hearings are held in open court, but hearings are mostly on affidavit, with oral evidence being rare.[2])

**3.12**     The Supreme Court Act 1981, s 87(1) permits the making of rules:

> 'for regulating the means by which particular facts may be proved, and the mode in which evidence thereof may be given in any proceedings in the High Court … or on any application in connection with or at any stage of any such proceedings.'

There is no provision which is directly similar to s 87(1) in the County Courts Act 1984; but s 75 gives general rule-making powers, including the provision[3] that:

> '[This section may] authorise the making of rules providing for orders being made at any stage of any proceedings directing that specified facts may be proved at the trial by affidavit with or without the attendance of the deponent for cross-examination, notwithstanding that a party desires his attendance for cross-examination and that he can be produced for that purpose.'

In consequence of these two provisions and their predecessors, a variety of rules of procedure have extensively altered the general rule concerning the examination of witnesses orally, primarily where proceedings are to be held in chambers. In many forms of process, applications are required to be accompanied by an affidavit setting out the case. Children Act 1989 proceedings and other forms of process are required to be accompanied, at the appropriate stage in the process, by statements, and a hybrid (the 'sworn statement') has been developed in recent rules.[4] These are not evidence, according to the strict definition; but they will generally be treated as such by the court. For example, a recent Practice Direction provided:

> 'Unless otherwise ordered, every witness statement or affidavit shall stand as the *evidence in chief* of the witness concerned. The substance of the evidence which a party intends to adduce at the hearing must be sufficiently detailed, but without prolixity; it must be confined to matters of fact …'[5] (emphasis added)

## Affidavits

**3.13**     Family proceedings which follow the originating summons/application procedure[6] – or a procedure akin to it[7] – are always accompanied by affidavits filed in the course of the proceedings. In some cases, they are required to be filed in support of

---

1     See further **9.9** below.
2     See **4.39** and **14.35** below.
3     County Courts Act 1984, s 75(6).
4     See eg Family Proceedings Rules 1991, r 2.73(1) (Form E under Ancillary Relief Pilot Scheme – see further **10.35** et seq below) and r 3.9(1) (applications for occupation and non-molestation orders under Family Law Act 1996, Part IV – see further **13.22** et seq below); and for consideration of sworn statements generally, see **3.24** below.
5     *Practice Direction of 31 January 1995 (Case Management)* [1995] 1 WLR 332, [1995] 1 FLR 456 at para 3.
6     Rules of the Supreme Court 1965, Ord 28, r 1A; County Court Rules 1981, Ord 3, r 4. This will be the procedure used for applications under eg Inheritance (Provision for Family and Dependants) Act 1975, s 1 (and see Rules of the Supreme Court 1965, Ord 99) and Trusts of Land and Trustees Act 1996, s 14.
7     See eg Family Proceedings Rules 1991, r 3.6 (Married Women's Property Act 1882, s 17) and r 3.9 (occupation and non-molestation orders under Family Law Act 1996, Part IV). Proceedings

the application,[1] in other cases after the filing of the originating process.[2] The rules provide no definition of the term 'affidavit'. In some respects, affidavits are being supplanted by the 'sworn statement' in recent rule-making, although the difference, in terms of the status of evidence presented, between a sworn statement and an affidavit, is not clear. Perhaps, as any definition of each document would imply, the terms are intended to be more or less synonymous.[3] Although affidavits in support of applications perform some of the functions of pleadings,[4] in that they do much to set out the issues between the parties, they are not pleadings. The form of an affidavit and rules as to its content are set out in the Rules of the Supreme Court 1965, Ord 41.[5] Order 41, r 5, in particular, stresses the similarity between affidavit evidence and evidence which may be given orally in court. Thus, 'an affidavit may contain only such facts as the deponent is able of his own knowledge to prove';[6] but if, in an affidavit, 'hearsay evidence is to be adduced, the source of the information must be declared or good reason given for not doing so'.[7]

## Content of an affidavit

**3.14**    Because the opportunities to cross-examine the deponent to an affidavit may be limited,[8] it is important that those who prepare affidavits and statements are careful that they do not contain irrelevant or oppressive material and that they comply with the rules of evidence as to, for example, the adducing of opinion or other second hand evidence. Rules provide that if an affidavit contains 'any matter which is scandalous, irrelevant or otherwise oppressive'[9] the court may order that part of the affidavit to be struck out. Further, the court may strike out of an affidavit parts of it which are inadmissible due to their not being relevant to the issues before the court[10] or which are privileged from disclosure, for example because they are part of negotiations for settlement between the parties.[11] Prolixity in the drafting of affidavits is strongly discouraged;[12] and it has been suggested that the court has an inherent discretion to

---

for matrimonial ancillary relief have hitherto (until the introduction of the Ancillary Relief Pilot Scheme (see **10.35** et seq below)) followed a procedure which is similar to the originating summons procedure (Family Proceedings Rules 1991, r 2.58 et seq).

1    See eg Family Proceedings Rules 1991, r 2.58(2) (application for matrimonial ancillary relief) and r 3.6(1) (application under Married Women's Property Act 1882, s 17).

2    Rules of the Supreme Court 1965, Ord 28, r 1A sets out a clear programme for the filing of affidavit evidence; whereas County Court Rules 1981, Ord 3, r 4 is not explicit as to what is required in terms of the filing of affidavits. At most, filing of affidavit evidence can be implied from Ord 28 or such filing must await court directions.

3    See further **3.24** below for consideration of sworn statements.

4    See Chapter 2 above for the function of pleadings.

5    And, in respect of non family proceedings, see Civil Procedure Rules 1998, rr 32.15 and 32.16.

6    Rules of the Supreme Court 1965 Ord 41, r 5(1). *Practice Direction of 31 January 1995 (Case Management)* [1995] 1 WLR 332, [1995] 1 FLR 456 at para 3 requires that affidavits 'be confined to material matters of fact', which comes to much the same thing as r 5(1).

7    *Practice Direction of 31 January 1995 (Case Management)* (above) at para 3.

8    See **3.17** et seq below.

9    Rules of the Supreme Court 1965, Ord 41, r 6.

10    *Savings & Investment Bank Ltd v Gasco Investments (Netherlands) BV* [1984] 1 WLR 271 at 278; and see **4.5** below on admissibility.

11    *Chocoladefabriken Lindt & Springli AG v Nestle Co Ltd* [1978] RPC 287; and see further **7.30** below on privilege.

12    See eg *Practice Direction of 31 January 1995 (Case Management)* (above) at para 3: affidavits 'must be sufficiently detailed, but without prolixity'.

remove an affidavit from the file for prolixity[1] and to disallow costs occasioned by an affidavit's excessive and unnecessary length.[2] The same rules for restricting affidavits may be assumed to apply to statements and sworn statements.

**3.15**      The extent to which affidavits are treated as evidence depends on the proceedings involved. In most interlocutory proceedings, the affidavits will almost invariably stand alone as the deponent's evidence, and in others they will stand alone subject to direction of the court to a witness to attend. Whatever the status of the affidavit as evidence in chief, the evidence in the affidavit will normally be capable of being challenged in cross-examination, subject to the leave of the court being obtained where the form of the proceedings is interlocutory or may otherwise require speedy disposal,[3] or where the court exercises its discretion to receive evidence even though the deponent is not available for cross-examination.[4]

### Oral evidence not called

**3.16**      On a strict definition of the term 'evidence', an affidavit is not evidence, but in some forms of process its function is plainly to perform the role of evidence. Thus, in most forms of interlocutory proceedings, and especially where speed of resolution of the interlocutory issue is important, only affidavits will be before the court as the parties' evidence.[5] Particular types of process will dictate that affidavit evidence be the norm. For example, applications under the Hague Convention on the Civil Aspects of International Child Abduction as enacted by the Child Abduction and Custody Act 1985, will generally be disposed of on affidavit evidence alone, where the need for a swift disposal dictates the necessity of a summary disposal. At most, only limited oral evidence will be directed[6] even though an application under the Convention can sometimes involve clearly disputed facts.[7] Applications for judicial review will be dealt with on affidavit and documentary evidence, and it is rare for oral evidence to be heard, even on the full hearing of the motion for review.[8]

### Affidavits as evidence subject to direction

**3.17**      Where proceedings are begun by originating summons or motion in the High Court, or where they are to be heard in chambers in the county court, evidence may be given by affidavit unless the court directs otherwise.[9] Where the evidence is by way of affidavit, a deponent need not attend to be cross-examined, unless directed by

---

1    Concern with prolixity of documents seems likely to increase with any reforms consequent on Lord Woolf MR *Access to Justice: Final Report* (HMSO, July 1996), and under such schemes as the Ancillary Relief Pilot Scheme (see **10.35** below).

2    *The Supreme Court Practice 1999* (Sweet & Maxwell) para 41/6/1.

3    Eg proceedings under the Hague Convention (see Chapter 12 below).

4    County Courts Act 1984, s 75(6).

5    See eg proceedings under Matrimonial Causes Act 1973, s 37(2) (see **13.7** et seq below). For procedure on interlocutory applications in the county court, see County Court Rules 1981, Ord 13, r 1.

6    Family Proceedings Rules 1991, r 6.7; and see **12.5** below.

7    See eg *Re F (A Minor) (Child Abduction)* [1992] 1 FLR 548 at 552G–554A where Butler-Sloss LJ in the Court of Appeal considered the question of the hearing of oral evidence in some detail.

8    Rules of the Supreme Court 1965, Ord 53, rr 5, 6 and 9.

9    Ibid, Ord 38, r 2(3); County Court Rules 1981, Ord 20, r 5; Family Proceedings Rules 1991, r 10.12.

the court to attend on application of any party to the proceedings.[1] If a person directed to attend fails to do so, his affidavit can be used as evidence only with leave of the court. The Family Proceedings Rules 1991, r 10.12 is in similar terms to Ord 38, r 2(3) of the Rules of the Supreme Court 1965[2] and applies specifically only to proceedings in the High Court on originating summons or notice, or proceedings in the county court for an originating application or any interlocutory application. Rule 10.12 is silent as to whether witnesses should attend for other forms of process covered by the 1991 Rules,[3] for example on the hearing of an application for matrimonial financial relief. Conventionally, parties to an application always attend for cross-examination; other witnesses would normally be expected to attend if notice of their attendance being required is given by one party to the party who filed the affidavit. However, no requirement to this effect appears in the Rules.

**3.18**    Rules of the Supreme Court 1965, Ord 38, r 2(1),[4] enables the court to receive affidavit evidence[5] at trial if, in the circumstances of the case, the court 'thinks it reasonable so to order'. If an order is made under Ord 38, r 2(1), it may be made on such terms as the court sees fit and, subject to such terms, the witness need not be subject to cross-examination and need not attend trial.[6] The availability of Ord 38, r 2(1) should be born in mind where a witness is abroad, is too ill to come to court, or is otherwise unable, for good reason, to attend a hearing; but it is necessary always to recall that its provisions require the leave of the court for a witness not to attend for the hearing.

## Statements

**3.19**    The general rule is that a party need not give notice to any other party of the evidence he plans to call, although, in practice, it is rare that this rule applies today. Most proceedings require that statements of a party's evidence, and that of his witnesses, be filed and exchanged before the final hearing and in accordance with rules of the court; and in many forms of family process these statements will be in the form of affidavits or sworn statements. Thus, in civil proceedings generally, a party may be directed 'to serve on other parties ... written statements of the oral evidence

---

1    Rules of the Supreme Court 1965, Ord 38, r 2(3); County Court Rules 1981, Ord 20, r 5; Family Proceedings Rules 1991, r 10.12.
2    And, in respect of non family proceedings, see Civil Procedure Rules 1998, r 32.5(1).
3    Family Proceedings Rules 1991, r 4.16(1) specifically requires all parties to children proceedings to attend court appointments, unless otherwise directed by the court.
4    County Court Rules 1981, Ord 20, r 6 is in similar terms to Rules of the Supreme Court 1965, Ord 38, r 2(1) and (2); and, in respect of non family proceedings, see Civil Procedure Rules 1998, r 32.5(1).
5    Rules of the Supreme Court 1965, Ord 38, r 2(1) still provides for the affidavit to be 'read at the trial'. Reading of affidavits at trial must nowadays be rare and, for family proceedings, it is specifically provided that the court may limit the reading aloud from documents (*Practice Direction of 31 January 1995 (Case Management)* (above)).
6    Rules of the Supreme Court 1965, Ord 38, r 2(2); and, in respect of non family proceedings, see Civil Procedure Rules 1998, r 32.5(1).

which the party intends to lead on any issue of fact to be decided at the trial'.[1] In children proceedings, similar rules apply. The requirement[2] is that:

'... a party shall file and serve ...
(a) written statements of the substance of the oral evidence which the party intends to adduce at a hearing of, or a directions appointment in, those proceedings...'

### Statements in children proceedings

**3.20**    In proceedings under the Children Act 1989 and since the introduction of the rules under the Act, a part of the requirement of the filing and exchange of statements is to assist control of the process, and its timetabling, by the court. Thus, statements are filed and exchanged as follows:

(a)    in children proceedings generally (other than those referred to below) statements are to be filed as directed by the court or, failing direction, 'before the hearing or appointment';[3]
(b)    in proceedings under the Children Act 1989, s 8 (applications for residence, contact orders etc) no statement may be filed at all until the court directs;[4]
(c)    in proceedings for financial relief for and on behalf of children (Children Act 1989, s 17 and Sch 1) a prescribed statement is filed with the application;[5] and
(d)    for *ex parte* applications[6] and applications for leave to commence proceedings under the Act[7] the position is unclear. A strict adherence to the rules would leave the court with only the information in the prescribed forms on issue of the applications. More information will be needed to enable issue of the application and its consideration to be dealt with. It is therefore submitted that the appropriate course would be to file a statement with the application and formally to seek leave to file at any subsequent hearing.

**3.21**    Statements perform a different role from that of affidavits in the proceedings where each are respectively prescribed; save that in family proceedings, as with affidavits, statements should form the maker's evidence in chief.[8] Statements are not sworn and therefore can in no respect be treated as akin to oral evidence,[9] in the

---

1    Rules of the Supreme Court 1965, Ord 38, r 2A(2). A similar provision in the county courts is mandatory on parties under Rules of the Supreme Court 1965, County Court Rules 1981, Ord 20, r 12A(2); and, in respect of non family proceedings, see also Civil Procedure Rules 1998, r 32.4.
2    Family Proceedings Rules 1991, r 4.17(1); Family Proceedings Courts (Children Act 1989) Rules 1991, r 17(1).
3    Family Proceedings Rules 1991, r 4.17(1) and Family Proceedings Courts (Children Act 1989) Rules 1991, r 17(1).
4    Family Proceedings Rules 1991, r 4.17(5) and Family Proceedings Courts (Children Act 1989) Rules 1991, r 17(5).
5    Family Proceedings Rules 1991, r 4.17(1) and Family Proceedings Courts (Children Act 1989) Rules 1991, r 17(1).
6    Family Proceedings Rules 1991, r 4.4(4) and Family Proceedings Courts (Children Act 1989) Rules 1991, r 4(4).
7    Such applications are dealt with under Family Proceedings Rules 1991, r 4.3 and Family Proceedings Courts (Children Act 1989) Rules 1991, r 3.
8    *Practice Direction of 31 January 1995 (Case Management)* (above) at para 3; and, in respect of non family proceedings, see Civil Procedure Rules 1998, r 32.5(2).
9    *S v Merton London Borough Council* [1994] 1 FCR 186, per Ward J.

absence of their maker appearing in court or of the appropriate hearsay notice,[1] or unless they are agreed or are not challenged. Statements are designed to summarise evidence to be presented orally at court; and the maker of the statement should appear in court to be cross-examined unless his statement is expressly accepted by all parties or the statement is not otherwise challenged. There are no rules equivalent to Rules of the Supreme Court 1965, Ord 41, r 6 (scandalous, irrelevant etc matter in an affidavit);[2] but it is likely that similar rules may be applicable to statements, subject to the fact that the court will have the maker of the statement present to give evidence in a way which will not always be the case with deponents to affidavits.

**3.22**    As with an affidavit, a statement must comply with *Practice Direction of 31 January 1995 (Case Management)*[3] in that:

> '[it] must be sufficiently detailed, but without prolixity; it must be confined to material matters of fact, not (except in the case of the evidence of professional witnesses) of opinion; and if hearsay evidence is to be adduced, the source of the information must be declared or good reason given for not doing so.'

Thus, it seems likely to be judged by the same criterion as an affidavit containing 'only such facts as the [maker] is able of his own knowledge to prove'.[4] Material which is relevant to the issues before the court based on information which is within the knowledge of the maker should thus be the hallmark of a statement in family proceedings.

### Social workers' statements

**3.23**    Preparation of evidence by social workers in support of an application under the Children Act 1989, s 31(2) (care and supervision orders) creates its own special difficulties. Wall J expressed the position thus in *Re JC (Care Proceedings: Procedure)*:[5]

> 'All parties have a duty in family proceedings not to be tendentious in the presentation of their evidence. That duty is, however, particularly acute in relation to local authority evidence, and never more so than when the local authority is advising the court of its view of the outcome of an assessment of parental capacity or otherwise setting out its recommendations and plans. The duty of local authorities to be objective, fair and balanced cannot be overemphasised.'

Much of the evidence which Wall J described will fall more easily in the domain of opinion evidence;[6] but what he said applies equally to factual as well as opinion evidence. In *Rochdale Borough Council v A*,[7] Douglas Brown J stressed the duty on local authority solicitors to the court in the preparation of affidavits in wardship, especially on *ex parte* applications, to be 'accurate, balanced and fair'. Wall J cited Douglas Brown J in *Re JC*,[8] and there can be no doubt that his comments on affidavits

---

1    Civil Evidence Act 1995, s 2; and see **4.48** below.
2    See further **3.14** above.
3    [1995] 1 FLR 456, [1995] 1 WLR 332, para 3.
4    Cf Rules of the Supreme Court 1965, Ord 41, r 5(1); and see **3.13** above.
5    [1995] 2 FLR 77 at 80D.
6    See further **5.39** below.
7    [1991] 2 FLR 192 at 231H.
8    [1995] 2 FLR 77 at 81C.

can be taken as equally applicable to local authority witness statements in all children proceedings.

## Sworn statements

**3.24**    It is not clear what the difference is in evidential terms between an affidavit and a sworn statement. What is clear is that well-established rules apply to affidavits,[1] and such rules have so far not been formally applied to sworn statements.[2] It may be assumed that rules relating to affidavits will be applied to sworn statements.

## Evidence by deposition

**3.25**    The court has power to order that evidence be taken by deposition before an examiner or judge 'where it appears necessary for the purposes of justice'[3] and where a witness will not be able to attend trial. These provisions are only likely to be relevant where evidence on a contested issue is to be heard orally and the witness is unlikely to be able to attend the trial, for example because he is or will be abroad, is ill or is otherwise unable to attend court. A deposition may not be received in evidence unless it was made in accordance with an order under the Rules of the Supreme Court 1965, Ord 39, r 1 and either the party against whom the evidence is called agrees, or the court is satisfied that the deponent is 'beyond the jurisdiction of the court or unable from sickness or other infirmity to attend the [hearing]'.[4] In proceedings where affidavit evidence is admissible, a party will apply to the court for a witness's evidence to be admitted despite his absence, and circumstances where evidence by deposition is likely to be applicable are difficult to conceive.

## 4   DOCUMENTS

## General rule

**3.26**    A document is something which communicates information and thus can include not only written documents, but also tape-recordings, film (including micro-film), maps and plans, graphs and disks containing computer data.[5] The general rule is that a party wishing to rely on a document as part of his evidence must produce the original, but in practice this rule is rarely insisted upon in family proceedings. It will not be necessary to produce the original where:

---

1    See eg Rules of the Supreme Court 1965, Ord 38, r 2 and Ord 41; County Court Rules 1981, Ord 20, rr 5–10, considered fully at **3.14** above; and, in respect of non family proceedings, see Civil Procedure Rules 1998, rr 32.4, 32.9 and 32.15.

2    The Civil Procedure Rules 1998 refer to affidavits as 'sworn statements'; see Glossary to the Rules.

3    Rules of the Supreme Court 1965, Ord 39, r 1; County Court Rules 1981, Ord 20, r 13(1). Family Proceedings Rules 1991 incorporate these sets of rules into matrimonial causes proceedings. In respect of non family proceedings, see Civil Procedure Rules 1998, r 34.8.

4    Rules of the Supreme Court 1965, Ord 38, r 9 (applied in the county court by County Court Rules 1981, Ord 20, r 13(5)(f)).

5    Civil Evidence Act 1968, s 10(1).

(a) the document is in the possesion of another party to the proceedings and he has failed to produce it in response to a formal notice to produce. The service of a list of documents by one party on another in accordance with the provisions of the Rules of the Supreme Court 1965, Ord 24 (discovery and inspection of documents) deems the party served to be given notice to produce at trial such documents specified in his list as are in his possession, custody or power.[1] That is to say all documents in a person's list must be available at the hearing of the proceedings;

(b) the document is in the possession of a third party who has failed to produce it in response to a subpoena *duces tecum*[2] or to an order on a production appointment.[3] It is possible for third parties to claim privilege in respect of documents, although an accountant (in respect of accounts relevant to the financial issues between the parties) has been held to be unable to claim confidentiality in relation to documents and records held by him;[4]

(c) where a document is lost;

(d) where production of the original is impossible – *Cross*[5] cites tombstones as an example under this heading;

(e) banker's books and building society's accounts, which can be proved by production of copies of the records of dealings with the account, although in appropriate cases letters from the bank, cheque stubs and so on may be required.

## Documents officially certified

**3.27**    Where a statute permits, proof of the contents of a document may be by certified or sealed copy,[6] or, where a record is of a public nature and no statute specifically provides for its proof by means of a copy, such proof is admissable by virtue of its public nature.[7] Thus, 'examined copies' or 'certified copies' will be admissible. For example, the Family Proceedings Rules 1991, r 2.6(2) requires that a certificate of marriage is filed with the divorce petition as evidence of the parties' marriage: since the fact of marriage founds the entire jurisdiction under the Matrimonial Causes Act 1973 this document is highly relevant. Sometimes the petitioner will still have her certificate from the day she was married, but in practice the court will accept a more recent copy certified by the registrar. Special rules[8] exist for evidence of marriage abroad to be proved from both the evidence of one of the parties to the marriage and an appropriate certificate or other document attesting to the marriage.

---

1    Rules of the Supreme Court 1965, Ord 27, r 4(3).
2    Ibid, Ord 38, r 14; and note orders to produce other than at trial (ibid, Ord 38, r 13 and *Khanna v Lovell White Durrant (a firm)* [1995] 1 WLR 121; and see, respectively, Civil Procedure Rules 1998, r 34.2(1)(b) and r 34.2(4)(b)).
3    Family Proceedings Rules 1991, r 2.62(7)–(9).
4    *D v D (Production Appointment)* [1995] 2 FLR 497, per Thorpe J.
5    *Cross and Tapper on Evidence* 8th edn (Butterworths, 1995) p 756.
6    Civil Evidence Act 1845, s 1.
7    Evidence Act 1851, s 14.
8    Family Proceedings Rules 1991, r 10.14.

## Court orders

**3.28**    'Office copies' of court orders or a certified copy of an entry in court records is evidence of the order there referred to unless the contrary is proved. Thus, for example, under the Civil Evidence Act 1968, ss 11 and 12 convictions and findings of adultery or paternity may be used in civil proceedings. By ss 11(4) and 12(4), a certified copy of a document recording the court's finding is 'admissible in evidence and shall be taken to be a true copy of that document or part unless the contrary is shown'. In children cases involving child abuse (and occasionally other forms of criminal activity) proof of convictions may be important. The fact of allegations under ss 11 and 12 are required to be pleaded in divorce petitions.[1] The Child Support Act 1991, s 26(2), which prevents a father disputing paternity where he has already been adjudged a parent in earlier proceedings, will depend for its force upon court records if the decision which founds the Agency's assumption of paternity is challenged by the father.

## 5   REAL EVIDENCE

## Material objects

**3.29**    The term 'real evidence' is not one which has gained great currency. It comprises material objects or other information which is directly perceptible by the court. Thus, the main component of this category of evidence is exhibits which form part of the proof of the issue before the court; however, save in the case of documents, family proceedings will rarely turn on the court's perception of a material object.

## Demeanour and personal appearance

**3.30**    Of more significance to the family lawyer in the field of real evidence may be the question of demeanour and, to a lesser extent, appearance of a witness. Demeanour will include the witness's attitude when giving evidence. If he appears truculent when answering questions it may be because he has something to hide; a witness who grimaces when asked a particular question may not want to have to answer it, whereas a witness who answers confidently may be believed more than a witness who answers hesitantly. In an area of law which depends so much on judicial discretion, and where appeals are so frequently turned down because the judge below – not the judges in the Court of Appeal – saw the witness in court, the question of demeanour and appearance and their effects on the court can be particularly important.

## View

**3.31**    Although a site visit by a judge will rarely be of use in family proceedings, photographs may be of assistance to the court, whether the photographs are of injuries to a child involved in care proceedings, the state of a parent's accommodation, or the former matrimonial home from which the husband is saying the wife should move. Video recordings, for example of an interview with a child, is real evidence of the

---

1      Family Proceedings Rules 1991, r 2.6.

facts of the interview occurring and of what was said. It may also provide valuable evidence of the demeanour of the child.

# 6  FACTS NOT NEEDING PROOF

**3.32**    Certain facts do not need to be proved, because the fact can be assumed to be known by the court (judicial notice), because it has already been proved before another court (issue estoppel), or because a fact has been admitted, or can be presumed to have been admitted, by the party in respect of whom it needs to be proved.

## Judicial notice

**3.33**    Judicial notice involves the acceptance of certain facts without admission or proof. A judge has a wide discretion provided he exercises it 'properly and within reasonable limits'.[1] In *Reynolds v Llanelli Associated Tinplate Co*,[2] a judge was criticised by the Court of Appeal for making too much use of his personal knowledge of the prospects of employment of a particular workman in a particular area. Yet assumptions about the 'earning capacity'[3] – and therefore of their prospects of employment of one or other spouse can be an important factor in disposal of a matrimonial financial relief application. Thus, district judges, in particular, routinely make assumptions about the employment prospects of the parties (especially of wives) which is based only on the most vestigial of knowledge and loosely based assumptions in circumstances which might have been criticised by Lord Greene MR in *Reynolds*. Where the court does intend to rely on local knowledge, it should inform the parties of its intention to do so to enable it to comment.[4]

### (1) Judges and judicial notice

**3.34**    In children cases, it is inevitable that a judge will make assumptions based on medical information derived from his experience on the bench or as legal representative. Indeed, in these days of specialist judges and advocates,[5] the reservations expressed by Lord Green MR in *Reynolds*[6] may need to be reconsidered. The area of permitted judicial notice is likely to be much wider; yet a judge will still need to remind himself of the fact that there are occasions when his expertise is limited. In the context of expert evidence, Ward LJ commented that 'The court has no expertise of its own, other than legal expertise',[7] but the comment may be just as valid in the field of judicial notice.

---

1    *Reynolds v Llanelli Associated Tinplate Co* [1948] 1 All ER 140, CA, per Lord Greene MR.
2    Ibid.
3    Matrimonial Causes Act 1973, s 25(2)(a).
4    *Norbrook Laboratories (GB) Ltd v Health & Safety Executive* [1998] TLR 96, (1998) *The Times*, 23 February, QBD.
5    For example, the Law Society's Children Panel.
6    See **3.33** above.
7    *Re B (Care: Expert Witnesses)* [1996] 1 FLR 667 at 670C, CA; and see **5.2** below.

### Magistrates and judicial notice

**3.35**    Justices should be more wary than judges in the extent to which they draw on personal knowledge[1] since, it is said, they are not as well trained as judges to put extraneous knowledge from their consideration. However, they may reasonably be expected to pool their personal knowledge of general matters and use it within reasonable limits, provided always that if they do intend to use such knowledge they should ensure that the parties are aware of this in order to give them an opportunity to comment.[2] However, no clear definition of the extent of those limits has yet been formulated. Human nature will dictate that certain information will be assumed (taken 'as read'); but plainly judges and magistrates must be wary of assuming too much. Meanwhile, the advocate must ensure that facts which need proof are proved. A party is not entitled to assume that the court has any particular knowledge.

## Estoppel – res judicata

**3.36**    An estoppel[3] is a rule which prevents a person from denying a state of affairs which he has previously asserted. Applied to the orders and certain findings of courts of competent jurisdiction an estoppel operates to prevent a person denying such orders and findings in subsequent court proceedings. The estoppel thus:

> 'operates both positively and negatively. First, it prevents the successful party from bringing a fresh suit on the same cause of action ... Secondly, it debars the unsuccessful party from challenging the correctness of that decision in subsequent proceedings. This is a true estoppel, estoppel *per rem judicatem*.'[4]

Where an estoppel operates a party cannot then adduce evidence which tends to contradict the facts already established or adjudicated upon; and from the point of view of the party in whose favour an estoppel operates he need not call evidence to prove the facts to which the estoppel relates. For example, a number of statutory estoppels operate under the Child Support Act 1991, s 26 such that, if a man has been adjudged the father of a child in certain court proceedings, he cannot then deny parentage of the child for child support maintenance purposes.[5] Where there have been previous care proceedings in which a finding was made against a person in relation to his treatment of a child it may not be possible to deny that finding in subsequent children proceedings, subject to a variety of qualifications considered further below.[6]

---

1    *Wetherall v Harrison* [1976] QB 773, [1976] 1 All ER 241, DC.
2    *Norbrook Laboratories (GB) Ltd v Health & Safety Executive* (above).
3    This branch of the law of evidence has no direct relation to equitable estoppel. Estoppel in evidential terms refers to an existing fact – a finding or judgment. By contrast, equitable estoppel relies on a state of affairs presumed from a party's actions, for example promissory estoppel, which relies on a party's expressed intention or promise which is then relied upon by the claimant to his detriment (for a recent decision on promissory estoppel, see eg *Wayling v Jones* [1995] 2 FLR 1029, CA).
4    *Phipson on Evidence*, 14th edn (Sweet & Maxwell, 1990) para 33–23.
5    Child Support Act 1991, s 26(2) (Case F).
6    See **3.47** et seq below; and see eg *K v P (Children Act Proceedings: Estoppel)* [1995] 1 FLR 248, per Ward J.

## *Estoppel by record*

**3.37**    Judgments are conclusive as to the facts they decide as against the parties to the proceedings and their associates (sometimes called 'privies'). Such judgments cannot then be questioned by those parties, and evidence cannot be called by one party in separate proceedings against the other which has the effect of seeking to refute the judgment.[1] For example, allegations in a divorce petition which formed the basis of a decree of divorce cannot be refuted in subsequent children proceedings between the same parties to the extent that they affect the basis on which the earlier decree was granted.[2] These principles are based on the maxims *interest rei publicae ut sit finis litium*[3] and *nemo debet bis vexari pro eadem causa*.[4] In the children jurisdiction, these principles were explained (and justified) by Ward J (as he then was) thus:[5]

> '... when considering the application of the doctrine [of issue estoppel] to child care cases I should take note of the fact that it is founded on considerations of public policy. They are twofold. There is the important principle of certainty of decision, and it is wrong that the same matter should be litigated twice ...; it is expensive and it is wasteful [of the court's time] ... The second consideration is that it is wrong as a matter of principle for a litigant to be vexed twice with having to defend the same complaint made against him.'

Thus, a judgment will be conclusive as between the parties to the proceedings in which the judgment was given, unless it can be open to question in some way or otherwise set aside by some means, for example on grounds that it was given without jurisdiction or without compliance with rules of court;[6] or that the order can be set aside on grounds such as fraud, misrepresentation or failure to disclose material facts.[7]

---

1    And note the separate, though similar doctrine of the collateral attack on a court order considered at **4.43**.

2    To avoid the necessity of defending a divorce petition containing allegations which might affect subsequent financial relief, or children proceedings between the parties to the divorce, a practice has developed of indicating that a petition will not be defended but that the respondent reserves the right to answer allegations in the petition should they arise again in the financial or children proceedings. In such circumstances, no estoppel would operate against a respondent arising from the divorce decree.

3    'It is to the common good that there be an end to litigation'.

4    'No one should be brought to court twice for the same reason'.

5    *K v P (Children Act Proceedings: Estoppel)* [1995] 1 FLR 248 at 256F–H.

6    Where an order is made without compliance with the rules, application can be made to set it aside (Rules of the Supreme Court 1965, Ord 2, r 1; County Court Rules 1981, Ord 37, r 5). The order is a nullity, although not the proceedings to which the order relates (Rules of the Supreme Court 1965, Ord 2, r 1(1); County Court Rules 1981, Ord 37, r 5(1)).

7    A judgment may be set aside and a rehearing ordered where no error of the court is alleged (*Peek v Peek* [1948] P 46; affirmed [1948] 2 All ER 297, CA): 'Is the allegation ... that the court went wrong because evidence on a vital matter was concealed from the court?' (at p 48 per Lord Merriman P). In consequence, a trial of the real issue or issues between the parties in *Peek* was not possible. Application may be made to set aside an order where a party has failed to provide full relevant disclosure (eg *Livesey (formerly Jenkins) v Jenkins* [1985] AC 424, [1985] FLR 813, HL; *T v T (Consent Order: Procedure to Set Aside)* [1996] 2 FLR 640, Richard Anelay QC as deputy judge) where this is required by the court or by statutory provision (eg Matrimonial Causes Act 1973, s 25(1)), or where fresh evidence comes to light which could not have been before the court when the original judgment was given (*Ladd v Marshall* [1954] 1 WLR 1489, [1954] 3 All ER 745, CA), but not where the order was obtained on the basis of bad legal advice (*Harris v Manahan* [1997] 1 FLR 205, CA).

## Judgments in rem and judgments in personam

**3.38**      The principles of issue estoppel apply whether a judgment is *in rem* or is *in personam*. The distinction between these is that a judgment *in personam* binds the parties to an action, while a judgment *in rem* binds not only the parties but the world in general. Thus, a decree of divorce, which effects status, has a bearing on all who are concerned by whether or not an individual is married. An order that the father of a child who was not married to the mother should have parental responsibility,[1] is binding, for example, on those who require parental consent, for example schools, hospitals, doctors etc. In the case of divorce decrees and parental responsibility orders, these bind the parties, but since they affect status they bind anyone else concerned with their status also. By contrast, a judgment *in personam* is binding only on the parties to the proceedings. For example, it may be of concern to the Inland Revenue or the Child Support Agency that a periodical payments order is made, but that order will bind only the spouses concerned in the proceedings.

## Conclusiveness of estoppel per rem judicatem

**3.39**      An estoppel based on the order of a court of competent jurisdiction (*res judicata*) is conclusive in subsequent court proceedings between the same parties. It is conclusive as proof, first, as to the issues decided by the court and, secondly, as to the grounds of the order (so far as these can be discerned from the judgment itself).[2] Thus, the circumstances in which *res judicata* or issue estoppel may arise were summarised by Lord Brandon in *DSV Silo-und Verwaltungsgesellschaft mbH v Owners of The Sennar*[3] as follows:

> 'to create an [estoppel *per rem judicatem*] three requirements have to be satisfied. The first requirement is that the judgment in the earlier action relied on as creating an estoppel must be (a) of a court of competent jurisdiction, (b) final and conclusive and (c) on the merits. The second requirement is that the parties (or privies) in the earlier action relied on as creating an estoppel and those in the earlier action in which that estoppel is raised as a bar must be the same. The third requirement is that the issue in the later action in which the estoppel is raised as a bar must be the same issue as that decided by the judgment in the earlier action.'

### (1) Existing judgment

#### (a) Court of competent jurisdiction

**3.40**      The first requirement is that the decision is of a court of competent jurisdiction and, further, that, as such a court, it is acting in an adjudicative rather than an administrative capacity. Thus, the decision of a magistrates' court or following arbitration, insofar as it resolves an issue between parties, is capable of founding a *res judicata* which will prevent the parties arguing the same point before another court. This will be so even if the procedure of the court or tribunal is partly inquisitorial.[4] By

---

1      Children Act 1989, s 4(1)(a).
2      *Phipson on Evidence* 14th edn (Sweet & Maxwell, 1990) para 33–22.
3      [1985] 1 WLR 490 at 499, [1985] 2 All ER 104 at 110, HL.
4      Eg in *DSV Silo-und Verwaltungsgesellschaft mbH v Owners of The Sennar* (ibid) where the procedures which lead to the findings which founded the estoppel were partially inquisitorial.

contrast, where courts act in an administrative capacity,[1] they do not adjudicate upon an issue between the parties and no estoppel can arise. For example, where a liability order is made by a magistrates' court for child support purposes,[2] no issue is tried before the magistrates: they are asked for the order to enable the Secretary of State to proceed to take further steps to enforce arrears of child support maintenance against an absent parent.

### (b) Judgment: final and conclusive

**3.41**    The judgment must be 'final and conclusive',[3] ie the decision must normally be capable of appeal, whether or not it was appealed against.[4] An order may be final in this context even though interlocutory to proceedings since it is possible to appeal against most interlocutory orders.[5] An appeal may be made against a refusal to make an order[6] (as distinct from dismissal of an application) and, given that there has been a decision of the court based on clear findings, it seems possible to argue that the refusal to make an order could found an estoppel within the terms of the principles now under discussion. More difficult is the issue resolved by a court from which there is no appeal.[7] In such cases, the decision is final and conclusive (even though not capable of being appealed against) and must therefore be capable of raising an estoppel as between the parties. Where a party cannot appeal because he is not a party to proceedings, then in separate proceedings on the same facts and involving him as a party he could not be bound by any estoppel arising from the previous proceedings.[8]

**3.42**    In *Penn-Texas Corporation v Murat Ansalt and Others (No 2)*,[9] Lord Denning MR considered the question of finality as follows:

> 'In my opinion a previous judgment between the same parties is only conclusive on matters which were essential and necessary to the decision. It is not conclusive on other matters which came incidentally into consideration in the course of reasoning . . . One of the tests in seeing whether a matter was necessary to the decision, or only incidental to it is to ask: Could the party have appealed from it?'

Lord Denning laid more stress, in considering conclusiveness, on the question of the importance of particular findings to a decision, and took the view that the question of

---

1    Whereas, although the High Court's jurisdiction in judicial review is declaratory, its declaration will generally follow issues having been joined between a private individual or body and a public body, so that an estoppel may arise.

2    Child Support Act 1991, s 33: the Secretary of State decides whether or not grounds exist to make the order (s 33(1)) and applies to the magistrates' court, which has no choice but to make the order (s 33(3)).

3    In the county courts 'every judgment and order [save where otherwise expressly prescribed] shall . . . be final and conclusive as between the parties' (County Courts Act 1984, s 70) and thus capable of appeal.

4    Supreme Court Act 1981, s 18 sets out a summary of the decisions which may be appealed against, while Rules of the Supreme Court 1965, Ord 59 sets out the procedure.

5    *Midland Bank Trust Co Ltd v Green* [1980] AC 515. For a summary of interlocutory orders against which appeals can be made, see Rules of the Supreme Court 1965, Ord 59, r 1A.

6    *Rickards v Rickards* [1990] Fam 194, [1990] 1 FLR 125, CA.

7    See eg declarations of parentage made by the magistrates' court under Child Support Act 1991, s 27, from which there appears to be no basis for appeal (*T v Child Support Agency and Another* [1997] 2 FLR 875, per Cazalet J).

8    *Re S, S and A (Care Proceedings: Issue Estoppel)* [1995] 2 FLR 244, per Wilson J.

9    [1964] 2 QB 647 at 660.

whether or not a person could appeal against the decision is only one of the tests in considering whether or not an estoppel has been created by a decision.[1]

### (c) Judgment: on the merits

**3.43**    Finally, the judgment must be 'on the merits'. Thus, the decision must follow a consideration of the issues involved in the case – an adjudication 'on an issue raised in the course of an action to which the particular set of facts give rise'.[2] A judgment or finding based on a consideration of facts which are not 'necessary' to the court's determination of an issue before it and without 'any conventional forensic investigation' is not, therefore, 'on the merits' and cannot create an estoppel in respect of the party against whom the findings are made.[3] A consent order is capable of creating an estoppel as between the parties even though the case will not have been considered fully on its merits. They have agreed to its terms, so that an estoppel arises as a result of the order itself,[4] as well as in respect of the agreement between them.

## (2) Same parties and associates

**3.44**    Judgments *in personam* bind parties to the issue before the court and their associates ('privies'). A child who appears by guardian ad litem or next friend will be a party for this purpose. A judgment involving a corporation, such as a local authority, will bind it and its successors. However, where liability of individuals in contract is joint and several – as with a husband and wife with their covenants under a building society mortgage – a judgment against one only does not bind the other and no estoppel will arise in respect of him or her. Where the High Court makes an order in judicial review proceedings, the parties are the Crown and the body concerned as respondent. Where one local authority has obtained a care order in respect of children partially on the basis of findings against a man, a different authority cannot rely on those findings against him in separate proceedings involving other children and a different mother.[5]

**3.45**    An extension of the principle that an estoppel can bind only parties and their associates may be available in children proceedings where a father or stepfather has been proved to the appropriate standard to have abused children and 'the isssue as to his perpetration of those acts has been directly relevant in earlier proceedings relating to that family [and] to which he was a party'. Wilson J (very much *obiter*) took the view that such a father or stepfather could not challenge the finding in separate

---

1    An approach approved of by Balcombe LJ in *Re State of Norway's Application (No 2)* [1988] 3 WLR 603 at 631.

2    Per Lord Diplock in *DSV Silo-und Verwaltungsgesellschaft mbH v Owners of The Sennar* [1985] 1 WLR 490 at 494, [1985] 2 All ER 104 at 106, HL.

3    *Re S, S and A (Care Proceedings: Issue Estoppel)* [1995] 2 FLR 244 at 249A–C, per Wilson J. Wilson J employed Lord Denning MR's concept of 'necessary' derived from *Penn-Texas Corporation v Murat Ansalt and Others (No 2)* [1964] 2 QB 647.

4    Others, such as a solicitor for one of the parties, will not be bound by any estoppel and may be sued by his client in respect of matters which gave rise to the order (*Hall & Co v Simmons; Barratt v Wolf Seddon; Cockbone v Atkinson Dacre & Slack; Harris v Scholfield Roberts & Hill* [1999] 1 FLR 536). But see also *Kelley v Corston* [1997] 4 All ER 466, CA where it was held that to sue an advocate on a consent order constituted a collateral attack on a court order which, as a matter of public policy, can be regarded as an abuse of the process of the court (*Hunter v Chief Constable of West Midlands Police and Others* [1982] QB 529, HL).

5    *Re S, S and A (Care Proceedings: Issue Estoppel)* [1995] 2 FLR 244.

proceedings.[1] This would be the case even though the later proceedings might involve totally different parties, save (possibly)[2] for the man himself. Although such a course may be eminently sensible, it involves a significant departure from the normal rules of issue estoppel since the second of Lord Brandon's requirements[3] is plainly absent: it is very likely that none of the parties to the two actions will be the same.[4] Such an approach to issue estoppel would need to be based on the discretion of a court, especially in children proceedings, to direct the conduct of a case in the way most appropriate to the evidence involved.[5]

### (3) Same issue decided by the judgment

**3.46**     To consider whether or not an issue has been adjudicated upon by the court, it will be relevant to distinguish two factors: whether or not an issue has been adjudicated upon by the court it will be relevant to distinguish two factors: whether it is an issue on which the court was required to make a decision, on the one hand, as distinct from an issue of fact, on the other hand, which was then to form a basis for the court's adjudication. The decision on the main issue is the one which may be appealed and which can raise an estoppel as between the parties. However, the finding of fact alone will not be capable of appeal. Thus, the extent to which a court allows one party to raise an estoppel upon the finding of fact will be a matter for discretion. The findings of fact in care proceedings against the men mentioned in paras **3.44** and **3.45** are examples of findings of fact upon which the final issue was whether or not the children had suffered 'significant harm'[6] and which, if found, could lead to the making of a care or supervision order. Similarly, a finding that a husband owned particular property, which finding formed the basis for an order against him in proceedings under the Matrimonial Causes Act 1973, s 37(2),[7] and which was not appealed against, might render that husband unable to deny the existence of that property in subsequent financial relief proceedings, even though the original order was interlocutory.[8] In both cases, an appeal against the order – final care order or s 37(2) interlocutory order – could involve a challenge to the findings of fact on which they were based.

### Estoppel and children's cases

**3.47**     Following the implementation of the Children Act 1989 in October 1991 there was increasing doubt as to the applicability of the concept of *res judicata* in children proceedings. This doubt arose as much from a general wish of judges not to be too closely bound by old adversarial attitudes (often seen as deriving from over-adherence to rules of procedure and practice), as from a concern to maintain full

---

1     *Re S, S and A (Care Proceedings: Issue Estoppel)* [1995] 2 FLR 244, at 248D–E.
2     He might not necessarily be a party unless joined by his own or another party's application.
3     *DSV Silo-und Verwaltungsgesellschaft mbH v Owners of The Sennar* (see **3.39** above).
4     A fact of which Wilson J is well aware (*Re S, S and A (Care Proceedings, Issue Estoppel)* (above), at 248F).
5     *Re B (Minors) (Contact)* [1994] 2 FLR 1, especially at 4H and 5G–6D.
6     Children Act 1989, s 31(2).
7     Restraint of disposition.
8     *Midland Bank Trust Co Ltd v Green* [1980] AC 515, ie the decision was capable of being appealed against, even though no appeal was made.

flexibility when dealing with children cases. In considering the extent to which courts would consider *res judicata* in relation to children proceedings, Waite J (as he then was) said:[1]

> 'It is because the jurisdiction requires the court to look, in each case, at the totality of the circumstances as they affect the child on the day of the hearing; and, in the lives of children, events seldom stand still for long enough to make it likely that a tribunal considering the same child at successive hearings will find itself confronted at the second hearing with the same facts, requiring assessment from the same perspective, as at the first. The Latin rubric *res judicatur pro verite habetur* is particularly liable, therefore, to find itself at odds, in child care cases, with the homelier English principle that "circumstances may alter cases".'

The pendulum swung back with Ward J (as he then was) stating firmly:[2]

> 'Estoppel *per rem judicatam* is a valuable rule of evidence to contain disputes within a proper compass. It is a tool which the Family Division should not be slow to use where it is appropriate. . . . The court should be slow to permit the relitigation of these questions, for it is time-consuming and wasteful of costs.'

Since then, both Wilson J[3] and Hale J[4] have revisited this field – a little more tentatively, perhaps, than Ward J; although both concluded that issue estoppel has a role in the children jurisdiction. Hale J too the view[5] that:

> '. . . the weight of Court of Appeal authority is against the existence of any strict rule of issue estoppel which is binding upon any of the parties in children's cases. At the same time, the court undoubtedly has a discretion as to how the inquiry before it is to be conducted. This means that it may on occasions decline to allow a full hearing of the evidence on certain matters even if the strict rules of issue estoppel would not cover them.'

### Estoppel and judicial discretion

**3.48**     Where a decision is based upon judicial discretion, estoppel will operate rarely, since the court, in any reconsideration of a particular question, is entitled to look afresh at any matter it so chooses. In the family jurisdiction, examples of a discretionary jurisdiction are numerous: the court's power to make orders for residence, contact etc concerning children;[6] the court's power to make orders for financial relief as between spouses[7] and to vary or discharge a periodical payments order;[8] the court's power to make a care or supervision order (subject to findings of significant harm to children)[9] and to discharge such an order;[10] or the court's power to

---

1    *B v Derbyshire County Council* [1992] 1 FLR 538 at 546D, Waite J.
2    *K v P (Children Act Proceedings: Estoppel)* [1995] 1 FLR 248 at 257G–H; and see *Re S (Discharge of Care Order)* [1995] 2 FLR 639, especially at 646D, per Waite LJ.
3    *Re S, S and A (Care Proceedings: Issue Estoppel)* [1995] 2 FLR 244.
4    *Re B (Children Act Proceedings) (Issue Estoppel)* [1997] 1 FLR 285.
5    Ibid, at 295D.
6    Children Act 1989, s 10(8).
7    Matrimonial Causes Act 1973, ss 23–24.
8    Ibid, s 31(1). The applicant need not formally show a change of circumstances (s 31(7)), although, in practice, a court is likely to take into account any change there may have been (see eg *Flavell v Flavell* [1997] 1 FLR 353, CA).
9    Children Act 1989, s 31(2).
10   Ibid, s 39(1) and (2).

make an occupation or non-molestation order.[1] To talk of *res judicata* in this context would seem to be a misnomer: thus, for example, by effluxion of time, as a result of a child's development or for some other reason, a party can show that circumstances have altered from those which obtained at the time of the first hearing.[2] That is not to say that a party can necessarily litigate indefinitely, certainly in respect of children, where the court has the power to prevent a party from making further application without leave.[3]

### *Estoppel in the family jurisdiction*

**3.49**    The doctrine of issue estoppel applies, unquestionably, in the family jurisdiction, subject to a number of qualifications – the more significant of which may be summarised as follows.

(1)  Circumstances alter cases, so that where issues relate to the welfare of children themselves, as distinct from factors which bear upon those children (eg sexual abuse), or where the court's decision depends on the exercise of judicial discretion, a court will rarely be bound by any form of issue estoppel.[4]

(2)  *Res judicata* is a rule of evidence which can be used to contain litigation where matters have already been adjudicated upon or findings made, and applies equally in the family jurisdiction as in any other.[5]

(3)  There is a public interest in there being an end to litigation. Where the welfare of children demands a swift resolution of proceedings that determination should, where possible, be final, so that issue estoppel prevents parties litigating matters afresh.[6]

(4)  The importance of previous findings may dictate how strictly the court prevents a party seeking a rehearing of an issue already tried,[7] as will the depth of the previous court's consideration of the issue.[8]

(5)  There may be a narrow band of circumstances in which a court would widen the doctrine of issue estoppel beyond an issue between the parties, especially in children proceedings and if their welfare would thus be served.[9]

## Admissions

**3.50**    Parties may admit facts or documents for the purposes of proceedings. This then avoids the need for other parties formally to prove those facts or documents. Formal admission may be made by a party by 'notice [given] by his pleading or

---

1    Family Law Act 1996, ss 33 and 42.
2    See *dicta* of Waite J (as he then was) in *B v Derbyshire County Council* [1992] 1 FLR 538.
3    Children Act 1989, s 91(14). The power under s 91(14) to prevent further application to the court does not arise from an estoppel. It arises solely from the court taking the view, for example, that the welfare of a child is adversely affected by repeated applications concerning him (see eg *Re R (Residence: Contact: Restricting Applications)* [1998] 1 FLR 749, CA).
4    *B v Derbyshire County Council* [1992] 1 FLR 538.
5    *Re S (Discharge of Care Order)* [1995] 2 FLR 639, CA; *K v P (Children Act Proceedings: Estoppel)* [1995] 1 FLR 257, Ward J.
6    *Re S (Discharge of Care Order)* [1995] 2 FLR 639, especially at 646E–F, per Waite LJ.
7    *Re B (Children Act Proceedings) (Issue Estoppel)* [1997] 1 FLR 285 at 296C–E, per Hale J.
8    *K v P (Children Act Proceedings: Estoppel)* [1995] 1 FLR 257, per Ward J.
9    *Re S, S and A (Care Proceedings: Issue Estoppel)* [1995] 2 FLR 244, per Wilson J.

otherwise in writing'.[1] An allegation in a pleading is deemed admitted unless specifically denied.[2] 'Writing' could include an admission made in correspondence or in an affidavit or statement. Further, a document referred to in a list of documents is deemed admitted 'as an original document . . . and [that it] was printed, written, signed or executed as it purports respectively to have been, and that any document described therein as a true copy is a true copy' subject to any other order of the court.[3]

### Notice to admit

**3.51** A party to proceedings may give to another party notice to admit facts[4] or to admit documents.[5] If facts or documents are not admitted and a party goes to the expense of successfully proving the facts or documents, the cost of such proof will, in any event, fall upon the person to whom notice is given.[6] The use of a notice to admit facts can thus perform the valuable role of saving court time or, where that fails, of ensuring payment of costs for the party who gives notice and proves its contents for the purposes of the proceedings.

### Admission 'without prejudice'

**3.52** A fact which should be disclosed, such as information as to a spouse's financial circumstances, cannot be admitted in the course of negotiations and then remain privileged from disclosure.[7] To this extent, *Practice Direction of 16 June 1997 (Ancillary Relief Procedure: Pilot Scheme)*[8] must be regarded as unsafe insofar as it seeks to accord privileged status to admissions made in the course of financial dispute resolution negotiations.[9] In framing the Practice Directions, the President referred to *Re D (Minors) (Conciliation: Privilege)*[10] in which it was held that evidence of statements made in conciliation meetings concerning children could not be given in subsequent proceedings save with leave of the court, and only then where such statement makes it clear that the maker has, in the past, or is likely in the future, to cause harm to the child. The Practice Direction goes much wider than this and relates *Re D* to the altogether different arena of ancillary relief proceedings. In referring to admissions it seems to overlook the duty of disclosure imposed on parties to financial relief proceedings. This duty must make it doubtful whether an admission which

1 Rules of the Supreme Court 1965, Ord 27, r 1; County Court Rules 1981, Ord 20, r 1. These rules are in similar terms, save that Ord 27, r 1 goes on to provide that, once an admission is made, no costs shall be allowed for costs incurred unnecessarily in proof of the facts admitted.
2 Rules of the Supreme Court 1965, Ord 18, r 13(1).
3 Ibid, Ord 18, r 4(1).
4 Rules of the Supreme Court 1965, Ord 27, r 2; County Court Rules 1981, Ord 20, r 2.
5 Rules of the Supreme Court 1965, Ord 27, r 5; County Court Rules 1981, Ord 20, r 3.
6 Rules of the Supreme Court 1965, Ord 62, r 6(7).
7 For further consideration of privilege, see Chapter 7 below.
8 [1997] 2 FLR 304.
9 Under Family Proceedings Rules 1991, r 2.75; and see further **10.34** et seq below. Paragraph (3) of the Practice Direction directs that 'evidence of anything said or of any admission made in the course of an FDR appointment will not be admissible in evidence' save in connection with committal proceedings or in the circumstances of *Re D*.
10 [1993] Fam 23, [1993] 1 FLR 932, CA.

relates to something which should have been disclosed in any event could ever have been privileged[1] since the court requires full relevant disclosure to be able to exercise its discretion under the Matrimonial Causes Act 1973, s 25(1).

**3.53**     If it is correct that an admission, especially one relating to material disclosure, cannot be privileged and can therefore be treated as admissible evidence at any hearing,[2] then it is for the party alleging the admission to prove it. A letter marked 'without prejudice' does not make it privileged if it contains an admission;[3] and therefore that part of the letter containing the admission would be admissible as evidence of the admission.[4] A mediator between the parties could be compelled to give evidence of a relevant admission made in the course of mediation.[5] Whether a district judge who chaired a financial dispute-resolution appointment is compellable is questionable. As a judge, he is probably not compellable 'in relation to his judicial functions'.[6] Whether a district judge at a financial dispute-resolution appointment can be said to be acting 'in relation to his judicial functions' raises different considerations, such as the fact that after the appointment the district judge will be precluded from exercising any further judicial function in relation to the same case[7] (save to give directions);[8] and the fact that at the appointment he sees privileged documents[9] normally not seen by a judge where an issue remains to be resolved by the court. If these factors are taken into account, it may be held that a district judge is compellable to give evidence of an admission made at a financial dispute-resolution appointment.

# 7   PRESUMPTIONS

**3.54**     Presumptions enable the courts to pronounce on an issue where there is no, or insufficient, evidence to support it. They may be presumptions of law or of fact.[10] Presumptions of law may be conclusive or rebuttable, while presumptions of fact are always rebuttable. A presumption of law derives its force from law, while a presumption of fact derives its force from common sense or from assumptions which the court is entitled to make about certain situations. This may come to much the same thing in many instances, although on occasions the law has to state arbitrary presumptions. The presumption of legitimacy is a presumption of law, although it is also a presumption derived from common sense, while that of death after an absence

---

1     The requirement for full relevant disclosure is enunciated by *Livesey (formerly Jenkins) v Jenkins* [1985] AC 424, [1985] FLR 813, HL, and see further **6.7** below.

2     *Buckinghamshire County Council v Moran* [1989] 2 All ER 225, CA.

3     See further **7.30** below.

4     Rules of the Supreme Court 1965, Ord 27, r 1; County Court Rules 1981, Ord 20, r 1; and see **3.50** above.

5     *Re D (Minors) (Conciliation: Privilege)* [1993] 1 FLR 932, CA.

6     *Warren v Warren* [1996] 2 FLR 777 at 785, per Lord Woolf MR in the Court of Appeal.

7     Family Proceedings Rules 1991, r 2.75(1)(a).

8     Ibid, r 2.75(1)(d).

9     Ibid, r 2.75(1)(b).

10    A 'presumption of fact' should be distinguished from an inference to be drawn from facts. The latter is an inevitable incidence of what a judge does, but is not the same as the former (concerning which, see further *Phipson* at 5-02).

of seven years or more is also a presumption of law which is based upon a purely arbitrary date.

## Legitimacy

**3.55** There is a rebuttable presumption that a child is legitimate when born in wedlock. The presumption can be rebutted on the balance of probabilities.[1] While it has been held that a higher standard than the civil standard will be required for proof,[2] it is unlikely that this consideration will any longer weigh heavily with the courts since the introduction of blood tests, and now DNA tests.[3]

## Presumption of death and dissolution

**3.56** The Matrimonial Causes Act 1973, s 19(1) enables a spouse to apply to the court at any time for a decree of dissolution based on a presumption that the other spouse is dead. Section 19(3) goes on to provide that where a spouse has been absent for seven years or more, there will be a rebuttable presumption that the absent spouse is dead. Thus, the burden of proof shifts from the petitioner once the absence of the respondent has exceeded seven years.

## Presumption of intention

**3.57** A presumption that a person intends the foreseeable consequences of his actions may still exist at civil law,[4] but in family cases, if it is ever alleged, a presumption of intention might be more easily rebuttable – most people would accept that a person is not always at his most rational when undergoing the process of relationship breakdown. The onus will normally be upon the party asserting it to show what the foreseeable consequences of an act are, although there may be cases where the court will infer particular consequences from a course of behaviour.[5] While the inferring of consequences from behaviour is different from a party arguing that the court should proceed on a presumption of intention, the inference may often be an alternative to the presumption, so that to try to draw a distinction between the two sets of consequences may be unrealistic. Certainly, it may be valuable to seek to establish a presumption of intention from certain facts where conduct is in issue, as with petitions based on the respondent's unreasonable behaviour,[6] where 'conduct' is in issue in financial relief proceedings[7] or in contempt proceedings. Presumptions from intention as to disposal of assets might also be made in cases of avoidance of disposition.[8]

---

1   Family Law Reform Act 1969, s 26.
2   *Serio v Serio* (1983) FLR 756, CA; and see **4.31** et seq for consideration of 'higher standard'.
3   Family Law Reform Act 1969, s 20 (as amended).
4   Such a presumption no longer exists in criminal law (Criminal Justice Act 1967, s 8; and see further discussion of this subject in *Phipson* at paras 5–18 to 5–19).
5   For example in *K v K (Conduct)* [1990] 2 FLR 225, Scott Baker J held that a husband's drinking and failure to find employment were 'self-inflicted' and were factors which justified him in taking into account the husband's conduct when considering an award of financial provision (Matrimonial Causes Act 1973, s 25(2), especially s 25(2)(g)).
6   Ibid, s 1(2)(b); and see further **19.40** below.
7   Ibid, s 25(1)(g).
8   Matrimonial Causes Act 1973, s 37; and see further **13.25** below.

## Equitable presumptions

**3.58**    It is beyond the scope of this book to consider the subject of equitable presumptions in any detail. However, an overview will be attempted since equitable presumptions can form an important component in proceedings following the breakdown of an unmarried relationship and, to a lesser extent, in proceedings for matrimonial financial relief. It will be appreciated that they will be of little value where proprietory issues arise following marriage breakdown, and the Matrimonial Causes Act 1973, s 25 applies.

### Implied, resulting or constructive trust[1]

**3.59**    The formal requirements for the holding of land are that to create a legal estate in land a deed is necessary; any other interest may also be created in writing.[2] However, equitable doctrines have developed to mitigate the rigours of the law. These doctrines, for present purposes, are based on the intention of the settlor whether presumed or informally expressed. Thus, where one party provides some or all of the purchase price, a resulting trust will be presumed in his favour in the absence of other evidence or of a presumption of advancement;[3] oral evidence is admissible to support the presumption.[4] The consequence of this will be that that party will be entitled in equity to a share proportionate to his investment.[5] Where evidence is accepted that the parties intended, at the date of purchase, that their home be jointly owned, the court will infer an implied trust, provided also that the claimant can also show that she acted to her detriment in a way referable to the purchase or maintenance of the property,[6] normally by making a financial contribution towards the property.

### Presumption of advancement

**3.60**    Where a relationship of dependence exists between the actual purchaser and the person to whom the property is conveyed, the presumption of advancement will rebut any presumption of a resulting trust. Thus, where a man conveys property to his wife or fiancée, or a parent conveys property to his child, it will be presumed that that man or parent intended the property to belong to the named purchaser even though they provided the purchase price.

---

1    This subject is considered fully in eg *Snell's Equity* 29th edn (Sweet & Maxwell, 1990), ch 4. A useful introduction for family lawyers is provided by Cretney and Masson *Principles of Family Law* 6th edn (Sweet & Maxwell, 1996), pp 238 et seq.

2    Law of Property Act 1925, ss 52 and 53. Law of Property (Miscellaneous Provisions) Act 1989, s 2 requires that contracts for sale or other disposition of land must also be in writing.

3    See below **3.60**.

4    Law of Property Act 1925, s 53(2): 'creation or operation of resulting, implied or constructive trusts' not to be affected by the s 53 requirement of writing.

5    For a recent application of the presumption of resulting trust in slightly unusual circumstances, see *Tinsley v Milligan* [1993] 2 FLR 963, HL.

6    *Grant v Edwards* [1987] 1 FLR 87, CA. For contrasting judicial approaches to the presumption applied to unmarried partners, see *Windeler v Whitehall* [1990] 2 FLR 505, per Millet J and *H v M (Property: Beneficial Interest)* [1992] 1 FLR 229, per Waite J.

## Undue influence[1]

**3.61**    In certain relationships, the potential for undue influence in financial dealings will be presumed. In *Barclays Bank plc v O'Brien*,[2] the House of Lords considered the extent to which a lender could be presumed to be fixed by the undue influence of a husband. It is beyond doubt that there is an equity to set aside a transaction where a person is induced to enter into a transaction by undue influence which might be actual or presumed in certain relationships (eg solicitor/client, doctor/patient) where the presumption arises as a matter of law; while in relationships of confidence (eg husband and wife where the husband is responsible for all business affairs) undue influence will be presumed where the the claimant shows the existence of such a relationship. Whether, for example a bank lending money to the husband, takes subject to a wife's interest depends on whether the creditor is held to have been put on notice of the husband's wrongdoing.[3] Thus, the law allows for the 'tender treatment' of married women because 'even today, many wives repose confidence and trust in their husbands in relation to their financial affairs';[4] and this 'tenderness' of the law can extend to others, such as cohabitants, relatives and so on, where there is an emotional relationship between the parties.[5]

## Equity of exoneration

**3.62**    Where joint property is charged by a husband and wife with a debt which is in reality a debt of one of them, then, as between the two parties, and if there is sufficient equity in the property, the equity of exoneration applies to enable the nominal borrower to exonerate her share from the borrowing of the actual borrower.[6] That is to say, there is a presumption which enables the wife (say) to relieve her share in the house from the husband's borrowing.

## Rebutting the presumptions

**3.63**    The presumption of a resulting trust or of advancement can be rebutted by proof of a contrary intention in the actual purchaser. The court will try to envisage

---

1    The subject of 'undue influence' and its consequences in equity are considered more fully in
     *Snell's Equity* 29th edn (Sweet & Maxwell, 1990) pp 551 et seq.
2    [1994] 1 AC 180, [1994] 1 FLR 1, HL.
3    In considering the subject of notice, Lord Browne-Wilkinson in *Barclays Bank plc v O'Brien*
     [1994] 1 FLR 1 at 12E expressed the opinion: 'where a wife has agreed to stand surety for her
     husband's debts as a result of undue influence or misrepresentation, the creditor will take subject
     to the wife's equity to set aside the transaction if the circumstances are such as to put the creditor
     on inquiry as to the circumstances in which she agreed to stand surety'. At the same time as the
     *O'Brien* case, an analogous but contrasting case was considered by the House of Lords in *CICB
     Mortgages plc v Pitt* [1993] 3 WLR 802, [1994] 1 FLR 17, where the lender was held not to be
     fixed by the husband's undue influence because it had no notice of it, either actual or
     constructive.
4    *Barclays Bank plc v O'Brien* [1994] 1 FLR 1 at 12F.
5    Ibid, at 14G. For an example of the treatment of a relative, see eg *Cheese v Thomas* [1994] 1
     FLR 118, CA (88-year-old plaintiff and defendant great nephew; purchase paid by them jointly
     (43:40); house into defendant's sole name; transaction set aside due to great nephew's undue
     influence).
6    In *Re Pittortou* [1985] 1 WLR 58 at 62, Scott J said: 'the debt [to the bank] was not a debt of
     [the wife]. Prima facie, the equity of exoneration applies to entitle [the wife] to require that
     indebtedness to be met primarily out of [her husband's] share in the net proceeds of sale'.

what was his true intention at or about the time of the purchase. Again, parole evidence will be admissible as to the purchaser's intention, although only where this is prior, or sufficiently close to the purchase to form part of the transaction: statements after completion can assist only the nominal purchaser.[1] Even though the transfer to one party is based on an unlawful agreement, the transfer operates in law and the nominal purchaser cannot rebut the presumption of a resulting trust by relying on the illegality.[2]

### *Children applications*

**3.64**    The Children Act 1989 is based upon the presumption – 'the general principle' – that delay by the courts in determining a question relating to a child is prejudicial to that child's welfare;[3] while the public law aspects of the legislation are based on the assumption that children should, where possible, be brought up in their families[4] with removal to care being a last resort. Where children are in care, there is intended to be a presumption that there be 'reasonable parental contact'.[5] Further, certain informal presumptions may apply in children proceedings: that both parents should have contact with their children; that a residential parent will be primarily responsible for their day-to-day care and (perhaps) for ensuring their education; and that a residential parent who reasonably seeks leave to move from the jurisdiction with children should be granted that leave. On this last question, *MH v GP (Child: Emigration)*[6] provides an example of a judicial approach to this presumption. The mother wanted to emigrate to New Zealand and sought leave to take her four-year-old child with her. Thorpe J stated the questions at issue as follows:[7]

> '. . . I apply the principles[8] . . . that, in considering whether to give leave, the welfare of the child is the first and paramount consideration, but that leave should not be withheld unless the interests of the children and those of the custodial parent were clearly shown to be incompatible.
>
> That statement of principle creates a presumption in favour of the reasonable application of the custodial parent, but in weighing whether the reasonable application is or is not incompatible with the welfare of [the child] I have to assess the importance of the relationship between [the child] and his father, not only as it is but as it should develop.'

---

1    *Shephard v Cartwright* [1955] AC 431; citing, with approval, *Snell's Equity* 29th edn (Sweet & Maxwell, 1990) p 180.
2    *Tinsley v Milligan* [1993] 2 FLR 963, HL.
3    Children Act 1989, s 1(2); but see critique of delay in children proceedings in Dame Margaret Booth DBE *Avoiding Delay in Children Act Cases* (July 1996).
4    Children Act 1989, s 17(1)(b) imposes a duty on local authorities 'to promote the upbringing of [children in need] by their families'.
5    *The Children Act 1989 Guidance and Regulations, Volume 1: Court Orders* (Department of Health, HMSO, 1991) para 3.5. Children Act 1989, s 34(1) requires the local authority to allow the child reasonable contact with, among others, his parents, to be terminated only by order of the court (s 34(4)).
6    [1995] 2 FLR 106, per Thorpe J.
7    [1995] 2 FLR 106 at 110G–H.
8    Following *Poel v Poel* [1970] 1 WLR 1469, CA and *Chamberlain v de la Mare* (1983) FLR 434, CA.

## Presumptions and the ancillary relief jurisdiction

**3.65**     Whether formal presumptions should be applied in the ancillary relief jurisdiction is a matter of some debate at the time of going to press. Certain informal presumptions – as in the children jurisdiction – may already be said to apply: that the former matrimonial home be retained during their dependency for the children of the family; and that an agreement reached between parties upon separation with the benefit of competent legal advice shall be upheld by the courts.[1] To speak of a presumption of a 'clean break', however, is misleading: the court is required only to consider whether a 'clean break' is possible as soon as the 'court considers it just and reasonable' after the divorce.[2]

---

1    *Edgar v Edgar* (1981) FLR 19, [1981] 1 WLR 1410, CA; and see **7.37** below.
2    Matrimonial Causes Act 1973, s 25A(1).

# Chapter 4

## RELEVANCE, ADMISSIBILITY AND STANDARD OF PROOF

### 1  INTRODUCTION

**4.1**    The rule that all evidence which is relevant, or sufficiently relevant, to an issue before the court is admissible (subject to any exclusionary rule) is central to the rules of evidence. Rules relating to the relevance of evidence are significant in a variety of areas: for example discovery[1] and interrogatories[2] will only be ordered if the court considers that the documents or the questions are 'necessary either for disposing fairly of the cause or matter or for saving costs'[3] From relevance and admissibility flow such exclusionary rules as those relating to hearsay[4] and to privilege.[5]

**4.2**    In presenting that evidence the advocate will be aware of the standard to which the case he is presenting must be proved. At the conclusion of the hearing, when the admissible evidence has been heard by the judge, it remains for the judge to assess that evidence for its weight and credibility and to decide whether, on the points at issue, the evidence has been proved to the necessary standard. That is a role only the judge can perform working from the evidence called before him.

**4.3**    These principles are as relevant for the family lawyer as for a practitioner in any other field of law. Especially in times of increasing case management by the judiciary,[6] it becomes more important than ever for a lawyer preparing a case to be fully aware of the issues in the case. From that flows an appreciation of what is relevant to those issues; and from that will follow what evidence is admissible by virtue of its relevance.

---

1    Rules of the Supreme Court 1965, Ord 24, r 8; Civil Procedure Rules 1998, r 31.6; and see **6.26** et seq below.
2    Rules of the Supreme Court 1965, Ord 26, r 1(1); Civil Procedure Rules 1998, r 18.1; and see **6.37** et seq below.
3    See, eg, Rules of the Supreme Court 1965, Ord 24, rr 8 and 13.
4    See **4.44** et seq below.
5    See Chapter 7 below.
6    See eg *Practice Direction of 31 January 1995 (Case Management)* [1995] 1 WLR 332, [1995] 1 FLR 456 and Lord Woolf MR *Access to Justice: Final Report* (HMSO, July 1996). The Ancillary Relief Pilot Scheme gives to district judges extensive powers to manage cases and exclude evidence which they consider, at a preliminary stage, to be irrelevant: see further **10.34** et seq below.

## 2   RELEVANCE AND ADMISSIBILITY

### Relevance of evidence

**4.4**    The primary object of evidence is to establish the truth of facts in issue between the parties to proceedings. A court will generally admit evidence which is relevant to those facts in issue, whereas it may exclude evidence which is regarded as irrelevant, or not sufficiently relevant, to those facts. Thus, relevance[1] is tested by an assessment of the proximity of the evidence to the facts in issue. This was explained by Lord Nicholls in *Re H (Sexual Abuse: Standard of Proof)*:[2]

> 'Evidence is the means whereby relevant facts are proved in court. What the evidence is required to establish depends upon the issue the court has to decide. ... At trials ... the court normally has to resolve disputed issues of relevant fact before it can reach its conclusion on the issue it has to decide. ... To decide that issue the court must identify and, when disputed, decide the relevant facts ... Then, but only then, can the court reach a conclusion on the crucial issue.'

### Admissibility of evidence

**4.5**    All evidence which is relevant to the issues before the court will be admissible, subject to any exclusionary rule and any judicial discretion to exclude. That said, evidence which is not strictly relevant to the issues before the court may yet be admissible. *Phipson*[3] draws the distinction between evidence which is relevant as being 'logically probative', while evidence which is admissible is merely evidence which is 'legally receivable': whatever its relevance to the issues the court is entitled to receive it. Relevance, therefore, depends on a logical assessment of the relation of evidence to an issue before the court, or to a connection between the evidence and the issue which makes a particular fact at least probable from the evidence adduced. Admissibility, on the other hand, will depend, first, on the extent to which the judge will allow the evidence to be adduced before him, and then on the question of whether or not the evidence infringes any of the factors which give the judge a discretion to exclude evidence or the rules which require him to exclude.

### Exclusionary rules and the discretion to exclude evidence

**4.6**    The rule that relevant evidence is admissible by the court is subject to a number of exceptions. Where an exception applies, relevant evidence may be excluded from consideration by the judge. This exclusion may operate as a matter of the judge's discretion, or evidence may be excluded by operation of law or as a matter of public policy. Outside these exceptions, there is no general discretion in the court to exclude evidence, even on grounds that its prejudicial effect outweighs its probative

---

1    It may be of interest to note that in *Livesey (formerly Jenkins) v Jenkins* [1985] AC 424, [1985] FLR 813, HL most of their Lordships referred to 'full and frank disclosure' which has truly entered the family lawyer's lexicon; but Lord Hailsham LC preferred 'full relevant disclosure' as the term to be applied to providing information for the purposes of the Matrimonial Causes Act 1973, s 25.

2    [1996] 2 WLR 8; *sub nom Re H and R (Child Sexual Abuse: Standard of Proof)* [1996] 1 FLR 80 at 99C–F, HL.

3    *Phipson on Evidence* 14th edn (Sweet & Maxwell, 1990) para 7–04.

value. Even though the Court of Appeal has expressed the view that judges should have a discretion so to exclude evidence, it has felt unable, in the present state of the law, to find that such a power yet exists.[1]

**4.7** It is important to distinguish between circumstances where exclusion is a matter of law on the one hand, or of judicial discretion on the other.[2] For example, the rules of privilege exist to exclude discovery of confidential documents, so that if a document is privileged from discovery it will be immune from production as a matter of public policy. By contrast, the judge has a discretion to refuse to allow enquiry (eg pursuant to the Family Proceedings Rules 1991, r 2.63, or by subpoena of a witness) where to do so might be oppressive of a party or a witness. A practical consequence of this distinction will relate to the very limited extent to which an appellate court will review the exercise of a judicial discretion,[3] as distinct from a decision based upon the application of a rule.

### Statutory exclusion

**4.8** The following is a list of categories of evidence which may be excluded on the basis of statute, a rule or public policy.

### (a) Confidentiality, privilege and public interest immunity
Documents which are confidential, immune from discovery on grounds of public interest immunity, or which are otherwise privileged from discovery will be excluded on grounds of public policy[4] unless the person protected by the exclusion waives his privilege.[5]

### (b) Hearsay
Evidence is now no longer to be excluded on grounds that it is hearsay,[6] although in civil proceedings a party must give notice of any proposal to adduce such evidence.[7] In civil and family proceedings relating to 'the upbringing, maintenance or welfare of a child' hearsay is admissible regardless of any law excluding hearsay.[8] Bases upon

---

1    *Re M and R (Child Abuse: Evidence)* [1996] 2 FLR 195 at 212E–213D, per Butler-Sloss LJ. In particular, Butler-Sloss LJ referred to the Civil Evidence Act 1972, s 5(3) ('Nothing in this Act shall prejudice (a) any power of the court, in any civil proceedings, to exclude evidence ... at its discretion ...') as implying that there might be a power to exclude evidence, but then felt unable to express an opinion as to whether this was the case.

2    See eg the distinction between the views of Lord Simon and Lord Hailsham in *D v National Society for the Prevention of Cruelty to Children* [1978] AC 171, [1977] 1 All ER 589, (1977) FLR Rep 181, HL on whether or not privileged information was to be excluded as a matter of law or judicial discretion (*Cross and Tapper on Evidence* 8th edn (Butterworths, 1995) p 216).

3    'We are here concerned with a judicial discretion, and it is of the essence of such a discretion that on the same evidence two different minds might reach widely different decisions without either being appealable. It is only where the decision exceeds the generous ambit within which reasonable disagreement is possible, and is, in fact, plainly wrong, that an appellate body is entitled to interfere.' *(Bellenden (formerly Satterthwaite) v Satterthwaite* [1948] 1 All ER 343 at 345, per Asquith LJ; cited with approval in *G v G (Minors: Custody Appeal)* [1985] FLR 894, HL.

4    These subjects are considered fully in Chapter 6.

5    See **7.2** and **7.31** below.

6    Civil Evidence Act 1995, s 1(1).

7    Ibid, s 2.

8    Children (Admissibility of Hearsay Evidence) Order 1993, SI 1993/621, art 2.

which evidence may be excluded on grounds of hearsay in family proceedings will therefore be rare.[1]

### (c) Opinion

Although a witness's opinion on the evidence is inadmissible, in practice the majority of opinion evidence in family proceedings will be from expert witnesses who provide an opinion on matters within their expertise.[2] Such evidence is then admissible subject to compliance of the party calling the evidence with the relevant rules.[3]

## Discretionary exclusion

**4.9**    The following are examples of categories of evidence where the judge has a discretion to exclude.

### (a) Oppressive enquiry

The extent of an enquiry of a party or of a witness may be regarded as oppressive (the court then has a discretion to refuse to require the witness or party to adduce evidence or provide documents[4]). The court may be able to exclude cross-examination as causing the witness suffering out of proportion to the value of the evidence,[5] but there appears to be no discretion to exclude evidence on grounds that its prejudicial effect on a party outweighs its probative value.[6]

### (b) Unnecessary to the fair disposal of an issue, remoteness

Evidence may be excluded because it is regarded as not necessary for disposing fairly of an application before the court or for the saving of costs;[7] or a fact, although technically relevant to the issues before the court, may be regarded as too remote to be of real probative value.[8]

### (c) Limitation of evidence on grounds of cost

A judge may have a discretion to exclude evidence or reduce the time spent in giving evidence by witnesses on grounds of costs attributable to the time taken by the trial.[9]

## Court's discretion to exclude evidence

**4.10**    An immediate difficulty with exclusion of evidence in a jurisdiction which is largely discretionary and, to a degree, inquisitorial, is that it may sometimes be difficult to say what is and is not relevant to the exercise of discretion in the making of the final order. The net cost by the Matrimonial Causes Act 1973 s 25, the Children

---

1    For hearsay, see **4.4** et seq below.
2    Opinion evidence is considered in Chapter 5 below.
3    Rules of the Supreme Court 1965, Ord 38, r 36 et seq; and see **5.16** et seq below.
4    See further **6.40** et seq below.
5    *Vernon v Boseley* (1995) unreported, Sedley J; although in the Court of Appeal the judge was overruled on this ground.
6    *Bradford Metropolitan District Council v K* [1989] 2 FLR 507, per Otton J. *Phipson on Evidence* 14th edn (Sweet & Maxwell, 1990) doubts this assessment by Otton J (at para 28–21).
7    See Rules of the Supreme Court 1965, Ord 24, r 8 (discovery of documents only if necessary: see **4.14** and **6.35** et seq below) and Ord 26, r 1 (interrogatories: see **6.39** below).
8    See further **4.10** below.
9    *Vernon v Boseley* [1994] PIQR 337, CA.

Act 1989, s 1(3) and the Inheritance (Provision for Family and Dependants) Act 1975, s 3 is spread wide indeed. This can make it difficult to decide what evidence the court may exclude on grounds that it is not relevant to, or unnecessary to a determination of, the issues between the parties. However, the fact that a jurisdiction is discretionary may make it easier for the judge – whose 'duty' it is to 'have regard to all the circumstances of the case' – to exclude evidence which will not weigh with him in the exercise of that discretion. As Hoffmann LJ put it in a very different context:[1]

> 'The judge will sometimes rule inadmissible the exploration of side-issues which, though possibly having some potential relevance, do not appear sufficiently relevant to justify the time and expense which would be required to investigate them.'

## Oppressive enquiry

### Questionnaires and interrogatories

**4.11**     Where the court takes the view that one party's enquiry of another party is oppressive, it has a discretion to refuse to order discovery, response to interrogatories or other requests for information, or production of documents by third parties.[2] For example, in *Hildebrand v Hildebrand*,[3] a husband applied for financial relief from his wealthier wife. He served a questionnaire[4] and interrogatories (without leave),[5] both of 'substantial length and detail'. Waite J held that the wife need not answer the interrogatories. He left open the question of whether or not interrogatories apply in the Family Division at all, but assumed for that case – 'without deciding the point' – that they did.[6] However, he considered that the then new procedures for raising interrogatories without leave[7] had been framed for:[8]

> '... restrained and civilised litigants who would confine their interrogatories to the sort of question for which leave would have been granted [under the old rules]. The wide-ranging and oppressively detailed questions raised in the interrogatories – all 51 of them – ... provide a classic example of the oppressive interrogatory which was excluded under the old procedure.'

Waite J then continued by citing *The Supreme Court Practice*[9] which, under the heading 'Oppressive interrogatories will not be allowed', proceeds to state that they 'will not be allowed if they exceed the legitimate requirements of the particular occasion'.

---

1    *Vernon v Bosley* [1994] PIQR 337.
2    For the obtaining of evidence from third parties, see **6.40** et seq below.
3    [1992] 1 FLR 244, per Waite J.
4    Under Matrimonial Causes Rules 1977, SI 1997/1247, r 77(4), now Family Proceedings Rules 1991, r 2.63.
5    Rules of the Supreme Court 1965, Ord 26, r 1.
6    [1992] 1 FLR 244 at 247E. The procedure under Family Proceedings Rules 1991, r 2.63 may be thought to perform much the same role as interrogatories.
7    Rules of the Supreme Court 1965, Ord 26, r 1 enables a party to raise interrogatories 'relating to any matter in question' and, in its present form, came into operation on 5 February 1990.
8    [1992] 1 FLR 244 at 252G–H.
9    (Sweet & Maxwell, 1997) at note 26/1/5(e).

**4.12**      The same argument as was applied to oppressive interrogatories could also be applied to questionnaires under the Family Proceedings Rules 1991, r 2.63.[1] These are limited to raising questions which seek 'further information concerning any matter contained in any affidavit filed by [another party to the application] or any other relevant matter, or to furnish a list of relevant documents'. If the questions are not answered the questioner may 'apply to the district judge for directions'. At this point the issue of whether a party is required to respond to a questionnaire is a matter for discretion of the district judge who is likely to approach the question on grounds of disposing fairly of the issues between the parties or the saving of costs. In *Hildebrand*, the husband's questionnaire was rejected by the judge on two grounds: that it was raised by the husband otherwise than in good faith (he had stolen documents belonging to the wife[2]) and it represented 'an oppressive attempt to get information as to which the questioner is already informed'.[3]

*Third parties: witnesses and production of documents*

**4.13**      A subpoena, *ad testificandum* or *duces tecum*, issues in the High Court for hearings in chambers only with the authority of the court,[4] whereas in the county courts issue of a witness summons cannot be refused, provided the correct formalities have been complied with,[5] save in the case of a summons for a directions hearing in chambers.[6] Once a subpoena has been issued, the court retains a discretion to set it aside[7] on similar bases to the court's powers to refuse to orders discovery, for example: that the subpoena has not been obtained bona fide for the obtaining of relevant evidence;[8] that it is irrelevant, fishing for evidence or speculative;[9] or that it is oppressive. The question of a potentially oppressive subpoena was examined by Watkins J in *Morgan v Morgan*.[10] In that case, a wife sought financial relief from her husband following a 23-year, childless marriage. She was the only daughter of Mr

---

1      See further at **10.30** below. The Ancillary Relief Pilot Scheme excludes r 2.63 since the district judge is responsible for controlling questionnaires at the first appointment (Family Proceedings Rules 1991, r 2.74(1)(a)(i)).

2      See *T v T (Interception of Documents)* [1994] 2 FLR 1083, per Wilson J, in which it was reasonable for a wife to take photocopies of her husband's documents where she thought he might evade discovery, but to use force to do this, to intercept mail and to keep original documents, was wrong.

3      [1992] 1 FLR 244 at 253C–E and 254C.

4      Rules of the Supreme Court 1965, Ord 32, r 7.

5      County Court Rules 1981, Ord 20, r 12; *Senior v Holdsworth ex parte Independent Television News Ltd* [1976] QB 23.

6      County Court Rules 1981, Ord 20, r 12(8).

7      Although there is no clear authority on the point, it must be assumed that, in this respect, the county court has the same power as the High Court.

8      A ground which is analogous with one of the bases for refusing the orders in *Hildebrand v Hildebrand* [1992] 1 FLR 244.

9      *Senior v Holdsworth ex parte Independent Television News Ltd* (above).

10     [1977] Fam 122; (1976) FLR Rep 473; and see *Frary v Frary and Another* [1993] 2 FLR 696, CA (considered further at **4.15** below).

Evans, a Welsh farmer and widower, who appeared to be relatively well off. Watkins J held that 'the evidence he could give [as to his testamentary intentions and property] would be both relevant and admissible'.[1] But should the father be forced to reveal that evidence? The judge put the issue before him as follows:[2]

> 'What power is there, if any, to enable the court to order Mr Evans to, for example, bring to court documents revealing the extent of his assets, to give oral evidence of them or to swear an affidavit about them? … No judge would be entitled to ignore [Mr Evans' evidence] having regard to s 25 of the Matrimonial Causes Act 1973. But is the respondent entitled to force that evidence out of Mr Evans? Is the privacy of a person to be so invaded? Must he reveal, when he may not desire it, his testamentary dispositions and details of his wealth?'

In exercising his discretion on this question, Watkins J held that the judge or district judge who gives leave to issue the subpoena or who considers an application to set aside a subpoena must balance, on the one hand, the need 'to see that the lump sum he awards is the correct figure so far as he is able to calculate it', against, on the other hand, the 'rights of the citizen … to keep to himself … details of his wealth and what he intends to do with it'.[3] On this basis the judge held in *Morgan* that 'it would be oppressive to cause Mr Evans to come under the duress of a subpoena to give evidence to the court about his assets and what he means to do with them'[4] and he rejected what amounted to the husband's application[5] for leave to issue a subpoena.

## Evidence unnecessary to a fair disposal

**4.14** The court will refuse an order for discovery of documents where 'it is of the opinion that discovery is not necessary either for the disposing fairly of the cause or matter or for saving costs'.[6] Similar words are used to found the basis of the court deciding whether or not to order a production appointment,[7] and interrogatories may be raised only where they are necessary for fair disposal of a case or to save costs.[8] The same principles can be applied by the court in exercise of any discretion to exclude evidence because it is regarded as not necessary to a fair disposal of the case. Cases where courts have criticised practitioners for the cost of excessive expert enquiry will be considered elsewhere,[9] but the ground of that criticism is often based on the judge's

---

1   [1977] Fam 122 at 125B. See also *Michael v Michael* [1986] 2 FLR 389 where the Court of Appeal held that in certain circumstances an expectancy of inheritance could be taken into account within the terms of Matrimonial Causes Act 1973, s 25(2)(a) as a financial resource a party 'is likely to have in the foreseeable future'. However, 'In the normal case uncertainties both as to the fact of inheritance and as to the time at which it will occur will make it impossible to hold that the property is property which is likely to be had in the foreseeable future' (at 396E, per Nourse LJ).
2   [1977] Fam 122 at 125B and G; (1976) FLR Rep 473 at 475D and 476A.
3   [1977] Fam 122, at 125H and 126A; (1976) FLR Rep 473 at 476C.
4   Ibid, at 126E; 476G.
5   In fact, the husband had not correctly applied for leave to issue his subpoena under Rules of the Supreme Court 1965, Ord 32, r 7.
6   Ibid, Ord 24, r 8.
7   Family Proceedings Rules 1991, r 2.62(7).
8   Rules of the Supreme Court 1965, Ord 26, r 1.
9   See further consideration at **5.33** below.

perception that the evidence is not necessary to the resolution of the issues between the parties. For example, where a husband's professional practice is among the parties' assets but which is not to be sold, a 'detailed valuation of the business is almost irrelevant': the proper approach for the court is 'a general consideration of [the husband's] sources of income and capital and, in particular, of his liquidity'.[1]

*Evidence of a third party*

**4.15**     On application for an order that a third party produce documents,[2] the court has a discretion over whether or not to require production. In *Frary v Frary and Another*[3] Mr Frary had moved to live with Mrs R. They had signed an agreement regulating their financial arrangements (which agreement was disclosed by Mr Frary to Mrs Frary). Mrs R felt that beyond this agreement her financial affairs were irrelevant to the issues between the parties. Mrs Frary's solicitors said that they intended to subpoena Mrs R to the final hearing, but then issued an application for production of documents. The application was refused by the district judge but allowed, on appeal, by the judge. He made a limited order against Mrs R, in that he required her to produce certain documents if she did not sooner provide 'a simple statement of financial affairs'. The Court of Appeal allowed Mrs R's appeal against that order holding as follows:[4]

> 'In the circumstances of this case I can see no sufficient relevance in the precise limits of Mrs R's very considerable resources to justify the order. The task of the court in the exercise of its discretion is to balance the interests of the petitioner in the obtaining of the information against the interests and wishes of the third party not to divulge it – see *Morgan*[5] ... I have no doubt that the order made was oppressive and unnecessary.'

**4.16**     Where a third party is a person who has been served, or is entitled to be served, with proceedings, does this make any difference to his standing in terms of discovery? This question was considered by Ward J in *Re T (Divorce: Interim Maintenance: Discovery)*.[6] Here a husband's father was entitled to be served with notice of financial relief proceedings as a result of a dispute between him and the husband as to their title to land,[7] although he had not in fact been served. In this context the court considered first whether the father was a party and, if not, whether he should be joined as a party. The court concluded that he was not a party and therefore

---

1      *Potter v Potter* (1983) 4 FLR 331 at 334E, per Dunn LJ; cited with approval by Anthony Lincoln J in *B v B (Financial Provision)* [1989] 1 FLR 119 at 120H.

2      Rules of the Supreme Court 1965, Ord 38, r 13; Family Proceedings Rules 1991, r 2.62(7)–(9); in respect of non family proceedings, see Civil Procedure Rules 1998, r 34.2(4)(b); and see **6.40** et seq below. Under r 2.62(7) the discretion is exercised on the basis of 'disposing fairly of the application ... or for saving costs'.

3      [1993] 2 FLR 696, CA.

4      [1993] 2 FLR 696 at 704E and H, per Ralph Gibson LJ.

5      *Morgan v Morgan* [1977] Fam 122, per Watkins J; considered further at **4.13** above.

6      [1990] 1 FLR 1. This decision can be contrasted with the opposite conclusion in very different circumstances in *T v T and Others (Joinder of Third Parties)* [1996] 2 FLR 357 where Wilson J (who represented the wife in *Re T*) held that the joinder of trustees of a substantial settlement fund made by the husband should continue. It was necessary for them to remain parties to assist the judge in the exercise of his discretion under Matrimonial Causes Act 1973, s 25 and, perhaps, to assist the court in enforcement of any order it might make.

7      Family Proceedings Rules 1991, r 2.59(3) (then Matrimonial Causes Rules 1977, r 74(4)).

discovery could not be ordered against him directly.[1] On the issue of joinder of the father in the proceedings – a consequence of which would be that discovery could be sought against him – the judge referred to the Rules of the Supreme Court 1965, Ord 15, r 6(2)(b) and adopted the following assessment of the sub-rule:[2]

> '[Ord 15, r 6(2)(b)] permits the addition as a party of any person whose presence before the court is necessary to ensure that all matters in dispute in the cause or matter may be effectually and completely determined and adjudicated upon.'

He found that: the primary purpose of the wife in seeking to join the father was discovery of documents; 'the bringing in [of the father] is a not inconsiderable invasion of privacy';[3] and that the cost of still further enquiry 'must be kept within reasonable limits'.[4] He therefore rejected the application to join the father.

### *'Millionaire's defence'*

**4.17**　　　Where a spouse states that whatever order the court makes he has the means to satisfy it, it may be held that to require a party to set out his financial position in full is unnecessary. In *Thyssen-Bornemisza v Thyssen-Bornemisza (No 2)*[5] the Court of Appeal proceeded on analogy with the Rules of the Supreme Court 1965, Ord 24, r 8 (discovery of documents only where necessary 'for disposing fairly of the cause or matter or for the saving of costs'). The court analysed the issue of how much further discovery was needed in the case by reference to the question: would information as to the exact value of the assets of the husband (estimated in 1985 to be in excess of £400 million) alter the way in which the court would exercise its discretion under the Matrimonial Causes Act 1973, s 25? If the answer to that question is that it would not, then further discovery would not be required; the evidence would not be necessary to dispose fairly of the case. Griffiths LJ stated:[6]

> '... what possible purpose is there in mounting a very costly exercise to probe into the precise dimensions of the fortune and the precise legal rights which the baron may possess over the disposition of his fortune? I can see none whatever, and I think it would be very inimical to the public interest, because the longer this case takes going through our courts ... the longer will [others] have to wait for their cases to be tried. I bear in mind that, when exercising a discretion on a matter of discovery, the judge has the guidance provided by Ord 24, r 8, which is that he should refuse discovery if in his opinion it is not necessary for either disposing fairly of the matter or cause or the saving of costs. Nobody has seriously suggested that it is going to save any costs to open up all these issues. For my part, as it cannot possibly make any difference to the petitioner, I do not think that it is necessary for disposing fairly of the matter.'

---

1　This case was decided before the production appointment procedure (Family Proceedings Rules 1991, r 2.62(7)) was part of the ancillary relief rules; although Rules of the Supreme Court 1965, Ord 38, r 13 was available, this does not appear to have been considered by the wife in this case.
2　[1990] 1 FLR 1 at 13E.
3　See also *dicta* of Watkins J on the subject of a third party's privacy in *Morgan v Morgan* [1977] Fam 122 (discussed at **4.13** above).
4　[1990] 1 FLR 1 at 16D, 16G and 16H.
5　[1985] FLR 1069, CA.
6　Ibid, at 1082H–1083C, per Griffiths LJ.

## Limitation of evidence on grounds of cost

### Limiting parties' time in court

**4.18**      Limitation on grounds of cost has featured extensively in consideration of
the two previous exclusionary heads. The grounds for ordering discovery, interrogatories or a production appointment[1] all make reference to 'saving costs' being a
criterion for giving or refusing leave for an order. Cost has also been a factor in the
court's deprecation of excessive expert evidence.[2] Ward J gave 'additional costs and
delay' as a reason for refusing leave to join the husband's father in *Re T (Divorce:
Interim Maintenance: Discovery)*.[3] Time in court was a factor in the court's refusal to
order further discovery from Baron Thyssen-Bornemisza.[4] In *Vernon v Bosley*,[5] the
judge at first instance had imposed time limits on the parties in respect of the calling of
evidence. On appeal to the Court of Appeal this practice, and the question of relevance
generally, was considered by Hoffmann LJ in the following terms:

> 'How relevant must evidence be in order to be admissible? Ordinarily the threshold is
> very low .... But there are limits to the extent to which the parties can be allowed a free
> rein. A party's right to choose how to present his case may have to be balanced against
> other legitimate public or private interests. For example, both the opposing party and the
> general public have an interest in keeping down the length and cost of litigation .... The
> degree of relevance needed for admissibility is not some fixed point on a scale, but will
> vary according to the nature of the evidence and in particular the inconvenience, expense,
> delay or oppression which would attend its reception.'

There are no reported family cases where time for adducing evidence has been limited
by the court; but *Practice Direction of 31 January 1995 (Case Management)*[6] clearly
anticipates this and assumes that the court already has a 'discretion to limit ... (b) the
length of opening and closing submissions; (c) the time allowed for the examination
and cross-examination of witnesses'.[7]

### Woolf and the Ancillary Relief Pilot Scheme

**4.19**      Other straws are floating in the wind. The Ancillary Relief Pilot Scheme[8]
was set up against a background of judicial concern at escalating costs of litigation. In
his foreword to the guide which introduced the scheme, Thorpe LJ criticised 'the
practices and procedures by which some cases are prepared for trial' and then
continued:

> 'The underlying basis of trust was that litigants and their lawyers could be relied upon to
> prepare their cases sensibly and with due regard to proportionality .... It is abundantly

---

1     See **4.9** above.
2     See further **5.4** below.
3     [1991] 1 FLR 1 at 16G.
4     *Thyssen-Bornemisza v Thyssen-Bornemisza (No 2)* [1985] FLR 1069, CA; see quote from
      Griffiths LJ above.
5     [1997] 1 All ER 577, CA.
6     [1995] 1 WLR 332, [1995] 1 FLR 456.
7     Ibid, at para 2.
8     The scheme started life as a President's Direction contained in a guide, Lord Chancellor's
      Advisory Group on Ancillary Relief, *Ancillary Relief Pilot Scheme: Practitioner's Guide* (SFLA
      and FLBA, August 1996). It was given statutory footing by Family Proceedings Rules 1991,
      rr 2.71–2.77 (incorporated into the rules by Family Proceedings (Amendment) (No 2) Rules

obvious in this field, as in the wider field of civil litigation, that there must be far stricter court control together with court led mediation and a proper emphasis on the escalating costs bills. The new procedures have been designed to meet these objectives.'

In *Practice Direction of 25 July 1996 (Ancillary Relief Procedure: Pilot Scheme)*[1] which prefaced the original scheme, Sir Stephen Brown defined its 'objective' (as then drafted), as follows:

'... to reduce delay, facilitate settlements, limit costs incurred by parties to the proceedings and provide the court with much greater control over the conduct of proceedings than exists at present.'

To save time and expense and thereby to limit the parties' costs, the scheme introduces a much greater degree of court control. In particular, it requires a district judge to limit discovery, the answering of questionnaires as between the parties and the adducing of expert evidence;[2] and to remind parties of the costs of their application at each appointment before the court, their legal representatives are required to produce a written estimate of costs to the date of hearing.[3] As part of 'The new landscape' which Lord Woolf sees in his proposals for procedural reform, costs are intended to be limited in part by means of improved case management, limitation of discovery and, where possible, limitation of expert evidence[4] – factors which already feature prominently in the Ancillary Relief Pilot Scheme.

*Rules of the Supreme Court 1965, Ord 40 – the court expert*
**4.20** Concern over the cost of and delay which can be caused by expert evidence is a feature of a number of the proposals for procedural reform. Under the Rules of the Supreme Court 1965, Ord 40 the court already has power to 'appoint an independent expert',[5] although only on the application of a party to the proceedings,[6] not, apparently, of its own motion. This practice was commended by the Court of Appeal in *Abbey National Mortgagees plc v Key Surveyors Nationwide Ltd and Others*;[7] and, as part of its case management function and to save costs, the court is encouraged to limit expert evidence by Woolf.[8] The delay caused by excessive use of experts has been identified by successive Children Act Advisory Committee annual reports.[9] The Advisory Committee commissioned a research report from Dame Margaret Booth specifically on the subject of delay in children cases,[10] which identified the proliferation of expert evidence as amongst the factors leading to delay in children

---

1997, SI 1997/1056). The scheme – or something very like it – seems certain to be introduced in all courts, perhaps alongside the rules reforms which will accompany the coming into operation of the Family Law Act 1996, Part II (divorce orders).

1  [1996] 2 FLR 368.
2  Family Proceedings Rules 1991, r 2.74(1)(a) and (b); and see further **10.40** et seq below.
3  Family Proceedings Rules 1991, r 2.76.
4  Lord Woolf MR, *Access to Justice: Final Report* (HMSO, July 1996). For a summary of these proposals, see Section I, para 8 (pp 4–6 of the report); and see Civil Procedure Rules, rr 35.7 and 35.8.
5  Under Civil Procedure Rules 1998, the court in non family proceedings has power to direct evidence by 'a single joint expert': rr 35.7 and 35.8.
6  See further **5.27** below.
7  [1996] 1 WLR 1534, CA; and see *Re K (Contact: Psychiatric Report)* [1995] 2 FLR 432, CA.
8  *Access to Justice: Final Report* (HMSO, July 1996) at Chapter 13, paras 16–24 (pp 140–142).
9  See eg *Children Act Advisory Committee Annual Report* 1993/94 (p 12) and 1994/95 (p 19).
10  Dame Margaret Booth DBE *Avoiding Delay in Children Act Cases* (July 1996).

proceedings.[1] The powers available to the court – despite what was said in *Abbey National Mortgages* – seem at present to be restricted where the judge seeks to save court time by limiting expert evidence. The Family Proceedings Rules 1991, r 2.74(1)(b), which requires the district judge to direct the 'obtaining and exchanging [of] experts' evidence (including the holding of meetings of experts)', limited where possible to one jointly instructed expert, seems likely to be the beginning of a procedural movement towards the saving of time and cost by court direction which limits the extent to which expert evidence is adduced.

## 3  THE BURDEN AND STANDARD OF PROOF

### Allocation of the burden

**4.21**    The burden of proof defines the duty on a party to establish his case, or to establish the facts relevant to a particular issue, to the satisfaction of the court; whereas the standard of proof defines the degree to which proof on a particular point must be established. The burden of proving a fact rests upon the party asserting it. In *Re H (Sexual Abuse: Standard of Proof)*,[2] in the context of a decision on whether or not the court could be satisfied as to proof of 'significant harm' to children in care proceedings,[3] Lord Nicholls of Birkenhead explained that for the court to be 'satisfied' involved affirmative proof of the facts which the applicant sought to establish before the court: 'The general principle is that he who asserts must prove.'[4]

### *Identifying the burden: issues and pleadings*

**4.22**    In a case where there are formal pleadings, it should generally be clear at commencement of the trial upon whom the burden lies. Alternatively, a statutory provision may make the burden clear, as with the Children Act 1989, s 31(2) or, for example, the Matrimonial Causes Act 1973, s 1(2) which requires that 'the petitioner satisfies the court of one or more of' the five facts set out in the subsection to prove irretrievable breakdown of marriage.[5] However, in many family cases, where pleadings, in the conventional sense of the term, are often only skeletal[6] or where the outcome depends on the court's discretion, it may be difficult to define upon whom the burden lies. Definition of the issues between the parties thus becomes even more

---

1    Dame Margaret Booth DBE *Avoiding Delay in Children Act Cases* (July 1996), at paras 2.8.1 (p 16) and 3.6.7–12 (pp 40–41).

2    [1996] AC 563; *sub nom Re H and R (Child Sexual Abuse: Standard of Proof)* [1996] 1 FLR 80, HL.

3    Children Act 1989, s 31(2) provides that 'a court may only make a care or supervision order if it is satisfied (a) that the child concerned is suffering, or is likely to suffer, significant harm' which is attributable to the care given to him by his parents or to his being beyond parental control.

4    [1996] 1 FLR 80 at 95G.

5    Matrimonial Causes Act 1973, s 1(2) requires proof of irretrievable breakdown of marriage for presentation of a petition for divorce. Proof of that breakdown depends on establishing one or more of the five facts in s 1(2).

6    Divorce is the exception to this generalisation where it is necessary to plead a case for the divorce (Family Proceedings Rules 1991, rr 2.2–2.4); and see *Butterworth v Butterworth* [1997] 2 FLR 336 at 340C, CA where Butler-Sloss LJ was critical of the court's grant of a decree to a

important since this should generally assist in defining on whom any burden of proof lies.[1] That definition, as has already been suggested,[2] should distinguish between primary and secondary, or evidential issues to be considered by the court.

### The burden of proof in a discretionary jurisdiction

**4.23**    Where the jurisdiction of the court is discretionary (for example under the Children Act 1989, s 1(3) or the Matrimonial Causes Act 1973, s 25) questions of burden and standard of proof are largely illusory. More often it may be a question of rebutting a presumption[3] which raises different considerations – mostly of degree. However, for justice to be done it must remain the case – whether the jurisdiction of the court is mandatory or discretionary – that a party who asserts a fact which is contested must prove that fact affirmatively and to the appropriate standard of proof. The court considers the facts and what weight is to be given to facts found to be proved; and in a discretionary jurisdiction the judge then decides which of the facts he wishes to rely upon for the exercise of his discretion. In *Re S (Discharge of Care Order)*,[4] Waite LJ explained the difference between proof of fact and discretion (in the context of an application for discharge of a care order[5]) as follows:[6]

'The inquiry as to whether the threshold requirements [under the Children Act 1989, s 31(2)] are satisfied has to be treated as a clinical issue of fact, determined in the light of the circumstances prevailing when the process was initiated ... and divorced from the discretionary considerations of the child's paramount welfare enjoined by s 1 of the Act. Once, however, they are found to be satisfied, it becomes a matter of discretion for the court to consider whether a care order should be made or not.

Section 39 of the Act allows the court to discharge a care order on the application of (inter alios) a parent. Here the jurisdiction is discretionary from the outset. ... The issue has to be decided by the court in accordance with s 1 of the Act [the welfare principles].'

## Meanings of 'burden'

**4.24**    Two principal meanings of burden of proof can be identified: the legal or persuasive burden; and the evidential burden. If the legal burden is discharged, it may be necessary to move on to discharge the evidential burden relating to facts in issue, whereas if the legal burden is not discharged the court need not go on to consider evidential issues. Similarly, facts may not be in issue: only the legal burden falls to be discharged by considering whether or not the agreed facts amount to a proof of the issue of law before the court.

---

wife where her case was 'not properly pleaded and which the husband was not equipped to meet'.
1    See eg *Cross and Tapper on Evidence* 8th edn (Butterworths, 1995), at p 119: 'The key to clarity in this whole area [of the burden of proof] lies in the precise definition and discrimination of the issues to be tried, and of the facts upon the determination of which they depend'. See also Parker and Burrows 'Identifying the issues in cases relating to children' [1993] Fam Law 637.
2    See **4.5** above.
3    See **3.63** above.
4    [1995] 2 FLR 639, CA.
5    Children Act 1989, s 39(1): 'A care order may be discharged on the application of – (a) any person who has parental responsibility for the child ...'
6    [1995] 2 FLR 639 at 643B–D.

### *Legal or persuasive burden*

**4.25**     The legal or persuasive burden is based on the necessity for a party to prove affirmatively a fact in issue as a matter of substantive law or other legal principle. This burden will remain constant throughout any hearing. Thus, a statutory provision may make the burden clear, as under the Children Act 1989, s 31(2).[1] The applicant, normally the local authority, must satisfy the court as a matter of clinical fact as to the significant harm to the child concerned. This question was considered in detail by Lord Nicholls in *Re H and R (Child Sexual Abuse: Standard of Proof)*:[2]

> 'The expression "if the court is satisfied" … envisages that the court must be judicially satisfied on proper material. There is also inherent in the expression an indication of the need for the subject matter to be affirmatively proved. If the court is left in a state of indecision the matter has not been established to the level, or standard, needed for the court to be "satisfied". … The legal burden of establishing the existence of these conditions rests on the applicant for a care order.'

### *The burden in divorce proceedings*

**4.26**     Matrimonial causes provide a rare example in family proceedings where strict rules of pleading apply.[3] Thus, the Matrimonial Causes Act 1973, s 1(2) requires that 'the petitioner satisfies the court of one or more of' the five facts set out in the subsection to prove irretrievable breakdown of marriage.[4] This places a legal burden on the petitioner to provide evidence to prove one or more of those facts.[5] In practice, this burden will be discharged on relatively rudimentary evidence in the case of undefended petitions,[6] but where a respondent spouse serves a defence he is 'entitled to have the allegations made in the petition against him properly proved to the satisfaction of the court to the civil standard of the balance of probabilities'.[7]

### *The burden in financial relief proceedings*

**4.27**     Financial relief proceedings are based on clear statutory bases and these can indicate how the burden falls. For example, in *Flavell v Flavell*[8] the Court of Appeal considered an application by a wife for variation of an order for periodical payments which was to be terminable at a period of two years from the making of the order.[9] In considering the question of variation, the court specifically rejected any suggestion

---

1    See **4.23** above.
2    [1996] 1 FLR 80 at 95F–G. This case was decided on a majority, Lord Browne-Wilkinson and Lord Lloyd of Berwick dissenting. There appears to have been no real issue on the question of burden of proof (see Lord Browne-Wilkinson at 82B); but for a difference between Lords Nicholls and Lord Lloyd on the issue of standard of proof, see **4.33** and **4.34** below.
3    See Family Proceedings Rules 1991, rr 2.2–2.19.
4    Matrimonial Causes Act 1973, s 1(2) requires proof of irretrievable breakdown of marriage for presentation of a petition for divorce. Proof of that breakdown depends on establishing one or more of the five facts in s 1(2).
5    Ibid, s 1(4) requires that if 'the court is satisfied on the evidence of any such fact [set out in s 1(2)] then, unless it is satisfied that the marriage has not broken down irretrievably it shall … grant a decree of divorce'.
6    See Family Proceedings Rules 1991, r 2.36 (disposal of causes in the special procedure list).
7    *Butterworth v Butterworth* [1997] 2 FLR 336 at 339G, per Butler-Sloss in the Court of Appeal.
8    [1997] 1 FLR 353.
9    Matrimonial Causes Act 1973, s 25A(2) enables the court in awarding periodical payments to order that they run for a defined term.

that there was a legal burden on the wife to 'show exceptional circumstances, or at least a material change in position' since the original order was made before the court's jurisdiction could be invoked:[1]

'The very words of s 31(1)[2] make it plain that there is unrestricted power to vary. The court's jurisdiction is afforded by s 31(1) and there is nothing in the language of that section which requires that jurisdiction be accepted only if there is some exceptional circumstance or some material change.'

**4.28** *Shipman v Shipman*[3] is an example of a case where the legal burden, although not discharged on statutory grounds, was discharged on grounds of legal principle and the inherent jurisdiction of the court. The facts were not in issue. The husband intended to go to live in the United States where he wanted to buy a house, and clear other debts, with his severance pay. On an application by the wife under the Matrimonial Causes Act 1973, s 37(2)(a),[4] the registrar found that the husband had been open in his disclosure of his assets and his explanation of his intentions, but that the husband would not undertake to freeze any of his assets in the jurisdiction. The registrar therefore froze half the sum representing the husband's severance pay, or $300,000 (whichever was the greater), pending the conclusion of ancillary relief proceedings. Anthony Lincoln J, on appeal from the registrar, found that s 37 applied to the transactions proposed by the husband, but specifically rejected the wife's application under s 37(2): 'I do not consider that the evidence taken as a whole establishes any intention on the part of the husband of defeating the wife's claim'.[5] However, the judge then went on to consider whether the court had an inherent jurisdiction to impose an injunction to preserve the husband's assets in the way ordered by the registrar. He concluded that the court had such a jurisdiction[6] and that he would make the order the wife requested. Thus, the evidence did not support an order on statutory grounds, but the burden of satisfying the court that the wife should have an order according to legal principle – in this case the inherent jurisdiction of the court to impose an injunction – was discharged by the wife.

*The burden in children cases*
**4.29** The legal burden in children cases will generally be rare. Care proceedings provide an exception to this statement, essentially because a finding of significant harm may result in parental responsibility being vested in the local authority and, in most cases, in parents being deprived of actual care of a child.[7] Proceedings under the

---

1   [1997] 1 FLR 353 at 356F, per Ward LJ.
2   Matrimonial Causes Act 1973, s 31(1) gives the court 'power to vary or discharge', inter alia, a periodical payments order.
3   [1991] 1 FLR 250.
4   Section 37(2)(a) provides that the court can make an order restraining disposition of property if a respondent to ancillary relief proceedings can be shown by the applicant to be 'about to make any disposition or to transfer out of the jurisdiction or otherwise deal with property', such disposal being 'with the intention of defeating the claim for financial relief'.
5   [1991] 1 FLR 250 at 252E.
6   Ibid, at 253E.
7   'These conditions [ie what became s 31(2)] are the minimum circumstances which the Government considers should always be found to exist before it can ever be justified for a court even to begin to contemplate whether the State should be enabled to intervene compulsorily in family life': Lord Mackay LC, 'Joseph Jackson Memorial Lecture' (1989) 139 NLJ 505. 'In s 31(2) Parliament has stated the minimum conditions which must be present before the court can

Child Abduction and Custody Act 1985 and the Hague Convention[1] provide another exception. For example, under Art 13 of the Convention it is a defence to a claim for return of a child that 'there is a grave risk that his or her return would expose the child to physical or psychological harm'. Thus, in *Re E (A Minor) (Abduction)*[2] where a father sought to retain a child in England against a background of the mother's alleged drug-taking and promiscuity, the Court of Appeal took the view that to make out a defence to an application under the Convention on the basis of 'grave risk' under Art 13 there was a heavy burden on the respondent:

> 'In my judgment there is a very heavy burden indeed upon a person alleged to have abducted a child in bringing himself or herself within the provisions of Article 13, and the court should hesitate very long before it grants what is in effect an exemption from the urgency which is a characteristic of this Convention and the Act incorporating it.'

## The evidential burden

**4.30**     The evidential burden of proof depends on a party being able to produce admissible evidence – where required to do so – which proves or disproves a particular fact in issue before the court; and that proof must be according to the standard of proof required by the court in respect of the evidence concerned. Thus, while the legal burden will remain stable throughout a hearing, the evidential burden may shift or vary according to the facts of a particular case. For example, on a wife's application for financial relief her husband may assert that she should be realising her earning capacity:[3] in the case of a young childless couple the onus will be on the wife to prove her assertion that she cannot work; whereas in the case of a wife looking after two young dependent children, or an older wife whose work experience is limited, the burden will lie on the husband to prove that the wife could indeed be earning. In the case of the older wife, or the wife looking after dependent children, the burden may shift if the husband produces evidence of jobs for which the wife could apply.

## Standard of proof

**4.31**     The standard of proof required by the court in family proceedings will normally be what has come to be described as the 'civil standard' (as distinct from the 'criminal standard', which is 'beyond reasonable doubt'). This standard is defined variously as the 'balance of probabilities', the 'preponderance of the evidence' or the 'preponderance of probability'. Much of what follows will seek to address the question of whether or not, built into the civil standard, there is a degree of flexibility which can enable the court to vary the level of proof according to the seriousness of the evidence before it.

**4.32**     At a basic level the balance of probability can be summarised as follows:[4]

---

look more widely at all the circumstances and decide whether a child's welfare requires that a local authority shall receive the child into their care and have parental responsibility for him' (*Re H and R (Child Sexual Abuse: Standard of Proof)* [1996] 1 FLR 80, per Lord Nicholls).

1    The Convention on the Civil Aspects of International Child Abduction signed in the Hague on 25 October 1980 and incorporated into UK law by the Child Abduction and Custody Act 1985, s 1 and Sch 1 (which sets out the Convention as it applies in UK law).

2    [1989] 1 FLR 135, CA.

3    Matrimonial Causes Act 1973, s 25(2)(a).

4    *Miller v Minister of Pensions* [1947] 2 All ER 372 at 374, per Denning J.

'If the evidence is such that the tribunal can say: "we think it more probable than not", the burden is discharged, but if the probabilities are equal it is not'.

In considering the test the first question must be: what is 'probability'? The term was explained, in the context of care proceedings, by Lord Nicholls in *Re H and R (Child Sexual Abuse: Standard of Proof)*[1] as follows:[2]

'The law looks for probability, not certainty. Certainty is seldom attainable. But probability is an unsatisfactorily vague criterion because there are degrees of probability. In establishing principles regarding the standard of proof, therefore, the law seeks to define the degree of probability appropriate for different types of proceedings.'

### *Preponderance of probability*

**4.33**    For a standard to be applied in family proceedings, Lord Nicholls preferred what he regarded as the more flexible 'preponderance of probability' compared with the concept of 'balance of probability'. Thus, he defined the standard of proof in family proceedings, as he saw it, in the following terms:[3]

'Where the matters in issue are facts the standard of proof required in non-criminal proceedings is the preponderance of probability, usually referred to as the balance of probability. This is the established general principle. There are exceptions such as contempt[4] of court applications, but I can see no reason for thinking that family proceedings are, or should be, an exception. ... Family proceedings often raise very serious issues, but so do other forms of civil proceedings.'

Lord Nicholls then went on to define what he meant by 'preponderance of probability':[5]

'The balance of probability standard means that a court is satisfied an event occurred if the court considers that, on the evidence, the event was more likely than not. When assessing the probabilities the court will have in mind as a factor, to whatever extent is appropriate in the particular case, that the more serious the allegation the less likely it is that the event occurred and, hence, the stronger should be the evidence before the court concludes that the allegation is established on the balance of probability. ... Built into the preponderance of probability standard is a serious degree of flexibility in respect of the seriousness of the allegation.'

(In a minority of one on this issue, Lord Lloyd took the view that the standard of proof 'ought to be the simple balance of probability however serious the allegations'.[6])

### *Flexibility*

**4.34**    Any difference between 'balance of probability' and 'preponderance of probability' may be more in the imagination of lawyers than real. In an earlier decision (concerned with a decision of immigration officers) the House of Lords took the view that the 'flexibility of the civil standard of proof suffices to ensure that the court will require the high degree of probability which is appropriate to what is at

---

1    [1996] 1 FLR 80, HL.
2    Ibid, at 96H.
3    Ibid, at 95H.
4    For a consideration of the standard of proof in contempt proceedings, see **4.39** below.
5    [1996] 1 FLR 80 at 96B–C.
6    Ibid, at 87C.

stake'.[1] Of proof in divorce proceedings, Denning LJ held that the court 'should require a degree of probability which is proportionate to the subject-matter'.[2] In that part of his speech in *Re H and R*, in which he dealt with his view of the flexibility of the preponderance of probability test of proof, Lord Lloyd continued:[3]

> '[A serious degree of flexibility] does not mean that where a serious allegation is in issue the standard of proof required is higher. It means only that the inherent probability or improbability of an event is itself a matter to be taken into account when weighing the probabilities and deciding whether, on balance, the event occurred. The more improbable the event, the stronger must be the evidence that it did occur before, on the balance of probability, its occurrence will be established.'

Whatever it may be termed – 'preponderance of probability' or 'balance of probability' – flexibility may be regarded as the essence of a civil standard of proof: that it should be able to adjust to the seriousness of the allegation before the court and to assess the inherent probability, or not, of the fact sought to be proved.

### The wider evidence – assessment of risk

**4.35**      Of the wider evidence in *Re H and R*, Lord Browne-Wilkinson and Lord Nicholls proposed a supplementary test, especially in relation to assessment of risk. Lord Browne-Wilkinson was particularly concerned at the level of proof required:[4]

> 'If legal proof of actual abuse is a prerequisite to a finding that a child is at risk of abuse, the court will be powerless to intervene to protect children in relation to whom there are the gravest suspicions of actual abuse but the necessary evidence legally to prove such abuse is lacking.'

Both Lord Browne-Wilkinson and Lord Nicholls proposed that proof in relation to assessment of risk that a child 'is likely to suffer significant harm' should be of a yet different standard:[5]

> '... in order to be satisfied that there is a *risk* of such an occurrence, the ambit of the relevant facts is in my view wider. The combined effect of a number of factors which suggest that a state of affairs, though not proved to exist, may well exist is the normal basis for the assessment of future risk.'

Lord Lloyd developed this point as follows:[6]

> 'Evidence which is insufficient to establish the truth of an allegation to a required standard of proof nevertheless remains evidence in the case. It need not be disregarded. ... If the evidence in support of the disputed allegations is such as to give rise to a real or substantial risk of significant harm in the future, then the truth of the disputed allegation need not be proved. ... Even if the evidence falls short of proof of the fact in issue, the court must go on to evaluate the evidence on that issue, together with all the other evidence in the case, and ask itself the critical question as to future risk.'

---

1    *Khawaja v Secretary of State for the Home Department* [1984] AC 74 at 113–114, per Lord
     Scarman.
2    *Bater v Bater* [1951] P 35 at 37.
3    [1996] 1 FLR 80 at 96D–E.
4    Ibid, at 83E.
5    Ibid, at 82–E, per Lord Browne-Wilkinson.
6    Ibid, at 89G, 90G and 91G.

**4.36**     This leads to a yet more flexible approach to evidence in relation to an assessment of the future. In the family jurisdiction, this is an important component of the court's jurisdiction. In children proceedings assessment of risk will be critical to proceedings under the Children Act 1989, s 31(2) (care and supervision orders) not only in considering future risk (whether 'the child concerned is ... likely to suffer significant harm'). An attempt to consider future progress of the child and the respective residential arrangements of the parties to the application is part of an assessment of the welfare of a child when the court considers an application for a residence order.[1] In particular, the court 'shall have regard to' such prospective factors as:[2]

> '(b) [the child's] physical, emotional and educational needs;
> (c) the likely effect on him of any change in his circumstances;
> ...
> (e) any harm which he ... is at risk of suffering;[3]
> (f) how capable each of his parents ... is of meeting his needs ...'

In assessment of a claim for financial relief, the court is again required to take into account matters which refer specifically to the future, such as the 'financial needs' of the parties to the marriage, their 'earning capacity' and 'contributions [they are] likely in the foreseeable future to make to the welfare of the family'.[4] Indeed, the last is but one of three references to the 'foreseeable future' of the parties under the Matrimonial Causes Act 1973, s 25(2).

## *A wider test for assessment of the future – micro facts and macro facts*

**4.37**     In *Re H and R* (above) the House of Lords was able to set out some helpful principles concerning the standard of proof for family proceedings; but one of the difficulties with the case itself was the unusual way in which the local authority chose to present it. The court was required to adjudicate on one issue[5] – whether or not children who lived with a man, who had been acquitted of rape of their older sister, could be said to be likely to suffer significant harm on the basis of a probability of sexual abuse which could be proved against the man as a result of the lower standard of proof said by the local authority to apply in family proceedings. On this narrow issue the House of Lords divided 3:2 in rejecting the local authority's appeal.

**4.38**     In the course of his speech in *Re H and R* (above), Lord Browne-Wilkinson[6] spoke in terms of the major issue (the macro facts) and a number of other facts (the

---

1    Children Act 1989, s 8(1) gives the court power to settle the arrangements as to the person with whom a child shall live. Section 1(1) requires the court to have regard to the principle that, when deciding such issues, 'the child's welfare shall be the court's paramount consideration'.
2    Children Act 1989, s 1(3).
3    In assessing the risk of likelihood of harm under s 1(3)(e), the test is the same as under s 31(2) (*Re M and R (Child Abuse: Evidence)* [1996] 2 FLR 195 at 203F, per Butler-Sloss LJ).
4    Matrimonial Causes Act 1973, s 25(2)(a), (b) and (f).
5    A similar difficulty confronted the Court of Appeal in *Re M and R (Child Abuse: Evidence)* [1996] 2 FLR 195 where, at 203D, Butler-Sloss LJ held: 'If, as in the present case, the court concludes that the evidence is insufficient to prove sexual abuse in the past, and if the fact of sexual abuse in the past is the only basis for asserting a risk of sexual abuse in the future, then it follows that there is nothing (except suspicion or mere doubts) to show a risk of future sexual abuse.'
6    [1996] 1 FLR 80 at 82H–83D.

micro facts) which the judge had found. From the micro facts, he suggested, the court might have proceeded to make findings as to the probability of the macro fact. The majority rejected this approach. Yet in any assessment of the future, whether of risk or of need of one sort or another, and whether in respect of children or adult parties to proceedings, it is surely inevitable that the court will be involved in consideration of a variety of 'micro facts'. Taken one by one, such facts may not be proved to the requisite standard, but taken cumulatively they amount to evidence the court cannot ignore.[1] Lord Nicholls himself[2] approved such an approach in appropriate cases:[3]

> 'It is, of course, open to a court to conclude there is a real possibility that the child will suffer harm in the future although harm in the past has not been established. There will be cases where, although the alleged maltreatment itself is not proved, the evidence does establish a combination of profoundly worrying features affecting the care of the child within the family. In such cases it will be open to a court in appropriate circumstances to find that, although not satisfied the child is yet suffering significant harm, *on the basis of such facts as are proved* there is a likelihood that he will do so in the future.'

Thus, it seems reasonable to assert that, given a sufficient preponderance of 'micro facts', even a likelihood of significant harm can be proved.

## Standard of proof in contempt proceedings

**4.39**      Committal proceedings raise different principles from other family proceedings, since, it has been held, 'proceedings for civil contempt are not ordinary civil proceedings'.[4] The liberty of the subject is involved, and this contributes to the view that the criminal standard of proof applies to contempt proceedings. As Lord Denning MR put it:[5]

> 'A contempt of court is an offence of a criminal character. A man may be sent to prison for it. It must be satisfactorily proved. To use the time-honoured phrase, it must be proved beyond reasonable doubt.'

In *Dean v Dean*,[6] the Court of Appeal considered what standard of proof was applicable when a husband was in breach of an undertaking given to the court.[7] An

---

1   See also *Khan v Khan* [1995] 2 FLR 221 where the Court of Appeal was willing to accept that a course of behaviour was sufficient to amount to conduct sufficient to enable the court to exclude a husband. Taken individually, the acts of behaviour might not be sufficient; but taken cumulatively 'There comes a time when the worm is entitled to turn' (per Hale J). The Family Law Act 1996 now requires the court to find 'significant harm'(s 33(7)) if an occupation order is to be made: see further **13.22** below.

2   The following passage is identified as 'the correct approach' by Butler-Sloss LJ in *Re M and R (Child Abuse: Evidence)* (above) at 205F.

3   [1996] 1 FLR 80 at 101C (Lord Nicholls concluded that this state of affairs did not apply to the case before the House).

4   *Dean v Dean* [1987] 1 FLR 517 at 520A, per Dillon LJ.

5   *Re Bramblevale Ltd* [1970] Ch 128 at 137A; and see *C v C (Contempt: Evidence)* [1993] 1 FLR 220 at 223B, per Butler-Sloss LJ: 'for the purpose of establishing the case the burden of proof upon the applicant is analogous to criminal proceedings and a much heavier burden than the civil burden of balance of probabilities'.

6   [1987] 1 FLR 517, CA.

7   For this purpose, undertakings and injunctive orders can be taken to be equivalent and punishable in the same way (see eg *Hussain v Hussain* [1986] 2 FLR 271). Since then, procedure for their enforcement in the county courts has been brought into line with enforcement of orders (County Court Rules 1981, Ord 29, r 1A); while Rules of the Supreme Court 1965, Ord 45, r 5

application for the husband's committal dealt with his liberty as a subject. The view of the Court of Appeal on the consequent necessary standard of proof was summarised by Dillon LJ as follows:[1]

> 'It has long been recognised that the procedure in contempt is of a criminal nature and that the case against the alleged contemnor must be proved to the criminal standard of proof.'

**4.40** Whether an approach based on the liberty of the subject (per Denning LJ) or on procedure (per Dillon LJ) is adopted, the effect is the same: the standard of proof applicable where the court is concerned with committal for breach of an injunction or undertaking is the criminal standard. That standard is based on the proposition that proof of the facts must be beyond reasonable doubt, explained by Denning J in *Miller v Minister of Pensions* as follows:[2]

> 'That degree [of proof – the criminal standard] is well settled. It need not reach certainty, but it must carry a high degree of probability. Proof beyond reasonable doubt does not mean proof beyond the shadow of a doubt. The law would fail to protect the community if it admitted fanciful possibilities to deflect the course of justice. If the evidence is so strong against a man as to leave only a remote possibility in his favour, which can be dismissed with the sentence 'of course it is possible but not in the least probable' the case is proved beyond reasonable doubt, but nothing short of that will suffice.'

Similarly, where magistrates intend to consider committal to prison for non-payment of maintenance having found that 'the default was due to the defendant's wilful neglect or culpable refusal'[3] then, before committal, the magistrates must give the defendant a chance to produce evidence before the court as to his personal circumstances and of any payments he said he had made.[4]

## Secure accommodation applications

**4.41** Principles which apply to committal proceedings also apply to applications for a secure accommodation order.[5] Such proceedings are 'family proceedings',[6] but the object of the application is that a child is held in secure accommodation, ie the application for the order deals with the liberty of the subject and, as such, the criminal standard of proof would appear to be applicable.[7]

---

(enforcement of orders) and Ord 52, r 1 (committal for contempt of court) appear to be intended to apply equally to injunctions as to undertakings. The Family Law Act 1996, s 46(1) specifically gives the court power, where it could make an occupation or non-molestation order, to accept an undertaking which is then enforceable 'as if it were an order of the court' (s 46(4)).

1   *Dean v Dean* [1987] 1 FLR 517 at 521B. Statements equivalent to this were also made by Stephen Brown and Neill LJJ in *Dean*.
2   [1947] 2 All ER 372 at 373.
3   Magistrates' Courts Act 1980, s 93(6). The same words are used, in the context of committal for non-payment of child support maintenance, in the Child Support Act 1991, s 40(3).
4   *R v Slough Magistrates' Court ex parte Lindsay* [1997] 1 FLR 695, per Sir Stephen Brown P.
5   Children Act 1989, s 25.
6   Ibid, s 92(2); and see *Oxfordshire County Council v R* [1992] 1 FLR 648, per Douglas Brown J.
7   See eg *Dean v Dean* [1987] 1 FLR 517.

# 4 COGENCY OR THE WEIGHT OF EVIDENCE

**4.42** The question of admissibility of evidence must be distinguished from the weight or credibility of that evidence. Admissibility may be determined by law, but the weight of evidence, it has been said, is a matter of fact or 'common sense'.[1] The 'best evidence rule' may be a matter of history,[2] but the fact remains that evidence on a particular subject from different witnesses, or by varying means of adducing that evidence, will bear different weight. This may be due to the court's perception of a witness's credibility, or, for example, because one witness's evidence is first-hand, while another's evidence, although admissible, remains hearsay.

## Judicial assessment of cogency

**4.43** The question of the judicial role in the weighing of evidence was considered by the Court of Appeal in *Re N (Child Abuse: Evidence)*.[3] In that case the court had admitted video-recorded evidence of an interview with a child then aged four. On an application by the father for contact, which the mother had refused, the judge heard evidence from a court welfare officer and guardian ad litem. He saw the video evidence,[4] and concluded that the father had sexually abused the daughter. He dismissed the father's application. After agreeing with the judge's findings as to the unsatisfactory nature of the mother's evidence, Ward LJ proceeded to categorise the video interview of the child as 'so tainted by pressure and leading questions as to be unreliable'.[5] The interview appeared to have been conducted by a police sergeant and social worker in the presence of the mother.[6] Of the weight to be accorded to the evidence contained in the recording, Ward LJ held that the judge should remind himself that the evidence is hearsay. Accordingly, in assessing its weight and credibility, the judge should bear in mind factors such as that the evidence was from a child and was made in response to leading questions; in addition, the judge should consider any internal inconsistencies in the evidence.[7] Ward LJ concluded as follows:[8]

---

1   See eg *Phipson* and its reference to *Lord Advocate v Blantyre* (1879) 4 App Cas 770, in which Lord Blackburn said 'The weight of evidence depends on rules of common sense' (at p 792). Civil Evidence Act 1995, s 4(2) now sets out a number of factors which the court must bear in mind in assessing the weight to be given to hearsay evidence.

2   The rule that the best evidence must be given of which the nature of the case permits: see eg *Phipson* at para 7–12.

3   [1996] 2 FLR 214, CA. This case, as regards the reception of expert evidence, was explained by Butler-Sloss LJ in *Re M and R (Child Abuse: Evidence)* [1996] 2 FLR 195 at 205G et seq. However, its assessment of the question of weight of evidence is unaffected by *Re M and R*.

4   There had been no transcript of the evidence before the judge. He and the parties only saw the video at the same time as the hearing of the application.

5   [1996] 2 FLR 214 at 224C.

6   By reference to the *Report of the Inquiry into Child Abuse in Cleveland 1987* (HMSO, 1988) and to *Re A and B (Minors) (No 1) (Investigation of Alleged Abuse)* [1995] 3 FCR 389, Ward LJ explained how unsatisfactory the interview was and how unsuitable it was that the mother should have been present.

7   See further **4.60** below on weight of hearsay evidence in children proceedings, and note that none of the aspects of the video evidence referred to by Ward LJ appear to come directly within the factors (not an exclusive list) set out in Civil Evidence Act 1995, s 4(2); for which see further **4.49** below.

8   [1996] 2 FLR 214 at 221A–B.

'[The judge] will look for any inherent improbabilities in the truth of what the child relates and will decide what part, if any, he can believe and whether stripped of embellishments of fancy or exaggeration there remains, none the less, a hard core of truth.'

As a definition of cogency, and a consideration of the judicial process in assessing it, this statement from Ward LJ contains a particularly helpful explanation of what is involved in the judicial process of weighing evidence for credibility and persuasiveness. *Re N* concerned a child's evidence, and that evidence on video; but the process of evaluation of evidence, as described by Ward LJ, is appropriate for weighing the cogency of any evidence, whether of adult or child. On the basis of his view as to the weight of the evidence and in relation to the video recording, Ward LJ concluded:[1]

'The possibility of the child's evidence having been contaminated by a very pressured, driven interview by the child protection team, the lapse of time, the absence of repeated complaint, the mother's presence, all this should have given rise to anxiety about the reliance to be placed on what [the child] was saying.'

## 5   HEARSAY EVIDENCE

**4.44**     *Cross and Tapper* defines 'hearsay' as follows:[2]

'A litigant may endeavour to prove a fact in issue by direct testimony, that is by swearing to it himself, or calling a witness to swear to it, but it sometimes happens that all he or his witness can do is to depose to what someone else was heard to say on the subject, and the rules against hearsay must then be borne in mind .... The following will suffice as a succinct statement of the rule: "an assertion other than one made by a person while giving oral evidence in the proceedings is inadmissible as evidence of the fact asserted".'

For the purposes of the Civil Evidence Act 1995, 'hearsay' is defined as:[3]

'A statement made otherwise than by a person while giving oral evidence in the proceedings which is tendered as evidence of the matters stated.'

**4.45**     The rule against hearsay in the family jurisdiction may be thought to be of minimal significance. However, it remains the case that, in family proceedings: '... if hearsay evidence is to be adduced, the source of the information on which it is based must be included or good reason given for not doing so'.[4] The Civil Evidence Act 1995 now provides that evidence shall not be excluded[5] in civil proceedings[6] because it is hearsay, although there are safeguards, such as the giving of notice to other parties of an intention to rely on hearsay evidence;[7] while in the majority of children proceedings evidence will always be admissible, despite the hearsay rules, where the

---

1     [1996] 2 FLR 214 at 226H.
2     *Cross and Tapper on Evidence* 8th edn (Butterworths, 1995) 45–46. *Cross* here quotes a
      formulation which was approved by the House of Lords in *R v Sharp* [1988] 1 WLR 7 at 11.
3     Civil Evidence Act 1995, s 1(2)(a).
4     *Practice Direction of 31 January 1995 (Case Management)* [1995] 1 WLR 332, [1995] 1 FLR
      456 at para 3.
5     Civil Evidence Act 1995, s 14 stresses that no other exclusionary rule of evidence is intended to
      be affected by the Act save for the rules relating to hearsay.
6     'Civil proceedings' may be taken to include family proceedings; see **4.46** below.
7     Civil Evidence Act 1995, s 1 (admissibility of hearsay) and s 2 (safeguards); and see below.

issue before the court relates to the 'upbringing, maintenance or welfare of a child'.[1] Children proceedings are, further, exempt from a number of rules of evidence relating to:[2] statements and other matters in the report of a guardian ad litem; statements referred to in a court welfare officer's report; and evidence in emergency protection order proceedings held by the court to be relevant.

## Hearsay evidence in family proceedings – Civil Evidence Act 1995

**4.46**　　　The Civil Evidence Act 1995 came into force on 31 January 1997. For present purposes, it deals with the admissibility of hearsay evidence and the proof of certain documentary evidence in civil proceedings. It is not easy to find a satisfactory statutory definition of 'civil proceedings'. The Act provides a form of definition, but only by providing that '"civil proceedings" means civil proceedings, before any tribunal,[3] being proceedings in relation to which the strict rules of evidence apply whether as a matter of law or by agreement of the parties'.[4] Unfortunately, this definition begs, or restates, the question: it explains where the proceedings take place and that those proceedings are such that rules of evidence apply to them. However, it does not say what the proceedings are. If the question of whether the Act applies to family proceedings is framed in the context of this definition, the questioner is none the wiser. In what follows, it will be assumed that civil proceedings are intended to include all family proceedings,[5] save for children proceedings relating to 'upbringing, maintenance or welfare of a child', which, for this purpose, have their own rules as to admissibility of hearsay evidence.[6]

**4.47**　　　The definition of the term 'hearsay'[7] applies to a 'statement'. This is defined under the Act as 'any representation of fact or opinion, however made'.[8] This is plainly intended to apply more widely than to the evidence of a witness which is committed to paper, the normal understanding of the term statement[9] in civil proceedings. The question will be: how far can the term be extended?[10] For example, most documents contain hearsay evidence, unless a witness can confirm the truth of their contents. Therefore, if the evidence is in a document which is not agreed, will it

---

1　　Children (Admissibility of Hearsay Evidence) Order 1993, SI 1993/621; and see below.
2　　Children Act 1989, ss 41(11), 7(4) and 45(7).
3　　This definition must include the magistrates exercising their jurisdiction defined by Family Proceedings Courts (Children Act 1989) Rules 1991, SI 1991/1395, Family Proceedings Courts (Matrimonial Proceedings etc) Rules 1991, SI 1991/1991 and Family Proceedings Courts (Child Support Act 1991) Rules 1993, SI 1993/1627.
4　　Civil Evidence Act, s 11. A similar definition is provided by eg Family Law Reform Act 1969, s 18(1).
5　　The term 'family proceedings' is not easy to define, either, on the basis of any statutory material available; see **1.29** et seq above.
6　　Children (Admissibility of Hearsay Evidence) Order 1993; see below.
7　　Civil Evidence Act 1995, s 1(2).
8　　Ibid, s 13.
9　　As in eg Family Proceedings Rules 1991, r 4.17 and Rules of the Supreme Court 1965, Ord 38, r 2A, both of which provide for exchange of statements in connection with proceedings; and, in respect of non family proceedings, see Civil Procedure Rules 1998, r 32.4.
10　Video evidence in proceedings relating to the welfare and upbringing of children raises different questions since this will normally be covered by the rules relating to hearsay in Children (Admissibility of Hearsay Evidence) Order 1993; see below.

be necessary to give notice of an intention to adduce the hearsay evidence in the document under s 2 of the Act?

### Hearsay in civil proceedings

**4.48**    The Civil Evidence Act 1995, s 1(1) is expressed as a double negative: evidence is not to be excluded on the ground that it is hearsay. That is to say, exclusionary rules relating to hearsay do not apply merely because the evidence is hearsay. However, the corollary does not apply: the effect of s 1(1) is not that the evidence is automatically admissible. To adduce hearsay evidence a party must give notice to other parties to the proceedings, such notice to be 'as is reasonable and practicable enabling [them] to deal with any matters arising from its being hearsay'.[1] The Rules of the Supreme Court 1965, Ord 38, Part III[2] has been amended with effect from 1 January 1997 to give effect to the new provisions in s 2 of the Civil Evidence Act 1995.[3] Rules of the Supreme Court 1965, Ord 38, rr 20–34[4] have been deleted and are replaced by Ord 38, rr 20–24. Rule 21 provides the procedural framework for giving notice under s 2. The court may, on application of the party who requires a witness's attendance, permit that person to call the witness and cross-examine him on his statement.[5]

### Credibility

**4.49**    Evidence may not be excluded on the ground that it is hearsay. However, the court will be concerned to establish to what extent the evidence is credible, that is to say, what weight should the court give to the evidence?[6] The Civil Evidence Act 1995, s 4 provides a statutory basis for considering the weight to be attached to hearsay evidence. In doing this the court must first assess 'any circumstances from which any inference can reasonably be drawn as to the reliability or otherwise of the evidence'.[7] To do this, s 4(2) provides a non-inclusive list of factors for the court to consider, including such factors as:

(a)   the extent to which it would have been 'reasonable and practicable' for the maker of the statement to come to court;

(b)   whether the statement was made contemporaneously with the events recorded in it; or

(c)   whether the statement is an edited account or is made collaboratively for a particular purpose.

**4.50**    In this consideration, there seems to be no presumption as to the weight to be attached to the evidence. Use of the words 'reliability or otherwise' would seem to preclude this. The checklist in s 4(2) lists factors which are mostly designed to temper

---

1    Civil Evidence Act 1995, s 2(1). The duty to give notice may be waived by agreement (s 2(3)).
2    Rules of the Supreme Court 1965, Ord 38 is reproduced in similar terms by County Court Rules 1981, Ord 20.
3    Civil Procedure Rules 1998, rr 33.1–33.5 deal with hearsay under the Civil Evidence Act 1995, s 2 in respect of non family proceedings.
4    Rules of the Supreme Court 1965, Ord 38, rr 20–34 dealt with evidence under Civil Evidence Act 1968, Part I of which has been repealed by Civil Evidence Act 1995.
5    Civil Evidence Act 1995, s 3 and Rules of the Supreme Court 1965, Ord 38, r 22.
6    See **4.42** et seq above, especially discussion of *Re M and R (Child Abuse: Evidence)*.
7    Civil Evidence Act 1995, s 4(1).

the court's view of the reliability of the evidence, to reduce its cogency in terms of proof of the issues before the court. However, a finding that the evidence is less than reliable does not make it inadmissible. It is merely a question of assessment of the weight of evidence, although the evidence itself still remains before the court.

## Children proceedings – Children (Admissibility of Hearsay Evidence) Order 1993

**4.51** Children (Admissibility of Hearsay Evidence) Order 1993, art 2 provides that in civil proceedings before the High Court, county court or in family proceedings,[1] or in civil proceedings under the Child Support Act 1991 before the magistrates' court, 'evidence given in connection with the upbringing, maintenance or welfare of a child shall be admissible, notwithstanding any rule of law relating to hearsay'. The Civil Evidence Act 1995, and its provisions as to hearsay evidence, do not apply if hearsay is already admissible under other provisions.[2] Thus, the application to civil and family proceedings of the Children (Admissibility of Hearsay Evidence) Order 1993 is not affected by the coming into operation of the 1995 Act.
**4.52** Part of the purpose behind the introduction of the 1993 Order was to assist the court in receiving the evidence of children without their being present in court to give evidence. The children's wishes and feelings could be represented by others, in particular by a welfare officer or guardian ad litem. For the court to receive children's evidence or evidence as to their views as hearsay from a third party will almost invariably be preferable to encouraging the parties to file statements or affidavits by children who are the subject of the application before the court.[3] However, not all children's evidence will be admissible as hearsay, whether in reports or as part of the evidence of a witness, if the proceedings do not relate to their upbringing or welfare. In *C v C (Contempt: Evidence)*, Butler-Sloss LJ said:[4]

> '... the applicant seeking to rely upon children's hearsay evidence should be required to demonstrate that the proposed evidence shows a substantial connection with the upbringing, maintenance or welfare of a child.'

**4.53** In its application to admissibility of hearsay evidence in children proceedings, the 1993 Order requires the court to consider two factors, which will now be considered in turn:

---

1   Any proceedings in the magistrates' court under the Children Act 1989 are to be treated as 'family proceedings' (Children Act 1989, s 92(2)); but the question will still arise as to whether a particular matter relates to the 'upbringing' etc of children, eg under Children Act 1989, Part X and the registration as fit persons of childminders (see consideration of this question, albeit in connection with the costs issue, by Wilson J in *London Borough of Sutton v Davis (Costs) (No 2)* [1994] 2 FLR 569, especially at 571E).
2   Civil Evidence Act 1995, s 1(3).
3   See eg *Re M (Family Proceedings: Affidavits)* [1995] 2 FLR 100 at 103C, CA: 'it is quite wrong in the normal case for the child who is the subject of the dispute to be dragged into the arena and asked to swear an affidavit' (per Butler-Sloss LJ).
4   [1993] 1 FLR 220 at 223C (proceedings for an alleged contempt of a court order which related to the protection of the mother of children, not the children themselves, apply only where the child was the applicant for the order, or the violence or other breach of an order was directed at the child); see also **4.55** below.

(1)  whether or not the proceedings apply to 'evidence given in connection with the upbringing, maintenance or welfare of a child'; and
(2)  whether the application relates to children in the types of proceedings covered by the order.

### Evidence of the 'upbringing, maintenance or welfare of a child'

**4.54**  Evidence 'in connection with the upbringing, maintenance or welfare of a child' covers a wide spectrum of proceedings in which children are involved. However, for the 1993 Order to apply the upbringing, maintenance or welfare of the children must be in issue. The proceedings must have a direct bearing on the best interests of or financial provision for the child. The contrast between family proceedings, which have a direct bearing on the best interests of the child and those, although concerned broadly with children, which do not, can be illustrated by examples from contempt proceedings and from proceedings under the Children Act 1989, Part X.

### Proceedings for committal for contempt

**4.55**  Proceedings for committal for contempt are civil proceedings and may involve the welfare of the child; but the question whether that is the case must be asked before it is decided to admit hearsay evidence. For example, in *C v C (Contempt: Evidence)*,[1] a mother had a non-molestation injunction order against the father of her four children, although the order made no specific reference to the children. She applied to the court to commit the father for breach of the order and wished to rely on the evidence of the children contained in the court welfare officer's report and an affidavit from the minister of her church. The question was whether the children's evidence, which was accepted to be hearsay, was admissible. There was no doubt that the proceedings were civil proceedings. The question then was whether they related to the 'upbringing, maintenance or welfare' of the children. Butler-Sloss LJ explained the judge's view of this as follows:[2]

> 'The judge construed [these] words ... to mean: "A proceeding which could directly have a bearing upon the upbringing or welfare of a child – where the best interests or future of the child is being considered ...", and contrasted it with the quasi-criminal contempt proceedings where the evidence was not given in connection (in this case) with the welfare of the children, but to establish whether their father is in breach of the injunctions and, if he is, what penalty he should suffer.'

Butler-Sloss LJ was clear that 'there is no good reason to exclude contempt proceedings as such from the operation of the Order, having always in mind the approach of the courts to the liberty of the subject'.[3] However, where the injunction order had been designed primarily to protect a parent, it is unlikely that the 1993 Order will affect the admissibility of hearsay evidence:

> 'In family proceedings which primarily affect the parents, it is probable that none of the three factors set out in the Order will be directly relevant and hearsay evidence

---

1    [1993] 1 FLR 220.
2    Ibid, at 222C–D.
3    Ibid, at 223B; and see **4.39** above on the question of the weight of evidence and standard of proof in contempt proceedings.

admissibility of which is based upon the Order would be likely to be excluded. This would be equally so in contempt proceedings designed to enforce orders made in such family proceedings.'[1]

*Certain children proceedings in magistrates' court*

**4.56**    While any proceedings in the magistrates' court under the Children Act 1989 are to be treated as 'family proceedings',[2] it does not necessarily follow – from the fact that they are proceedings under the Children Act 1989 – that they are proceedings which relate to the upbringing, maintenance or welfare of children. For example, under the Children Act 1989, s 71(7)–(11) a local authority may refuse to register a person as a childminder or to provide day care; and if refused registration that person may appeal under s 77(6). Do such proceedings relate to the upbringing or welfare of children? If granted registration the work of the childminder or day centre will plainly relate to the upbringing and welfare of children, but at the stage of refusal the decision is a matter of administration by the local authority. In *London Borough of Sutton v Davis*,[3] Wilson J approached the question of whether or not a childminder should remain registered under the Children Act 1989, s 71(1) on analogy with cases which dealt with the powers of a local authority to grant or refuse certain licences.[4] Further, Wilson J upheld the magistrates' order for costs against the local authority. In doing so he distinguished between the way in which the court dealt with costs in proceedings where the welfare of children was concerned, as distinct from proceedings, such as the present application, where a childminder challenged a local authority decision which she and the magistrates considered to be wrong. In the latter type of case, as in *London Borough of Sutton v Davis*, 'The proceedings were adversarial and the local authority lost the argument'.[5] Such proceedings do not relate directly to the upbringing or welfare of a child. Therefore, were hearsay evidence to be in issue in such proceedings it would be only in accordance with the rules under the Civil Evidence Act 1995.[6]

**4.57**    In *C v C (Contempt: Evidence)*,[7] Butler-Sloss LJ concluded: 'It will be a matter of the facts of each case as to whether the connection is sufficiently substantial to justify the hearsay evidence being admitted'. She compared the position with contempt proceedings by a parent where the committal application is to protect the parent. Here evidence from a child who was not directly affected 'would be unlikely to demonstrate other than an insubstantial connection'. On the other hand:[8]

> '... if the injunction said to have been breached was designed to protect the child, evidence of its breach coming from the child himself would be likely to be in connection with the welfare of the child.'

---

1    [1997] 1 FLR 220 at 223D–E, per Butler-Sloss LJ.
2    Children Act 1989, s 92(2).
3    [1994] 1 FLR 737.
4    See eg ibid, at 744H–746A.
5    *London Borough of Sutton v Davis (Costs) (No 2)* [1994] 2 FLR 569 at 571F.
6    See **4.48** above.
7    [1993] 1 FLR 220 at 223, CA; and see further **4.52** above.
8    Ibid, at 223E–F.

## The proceedings

**4.58**     The lack of a definition of 'civil proceedings' has already been mentioned.[1] For most proceedings this will create no problem. Proceedings which are not criminal may be said to be civil proceedings. This will include an application for committal for contempt, even though the standard of proof required for proof of such a standard will be higher than the civil standard.[2] The term 'family proceedings' also creates its own particular problems of definition.[3] In the context of the 1993 Order the term applies specifically only in the magistrates' court. In the High Court and county courts 'family proceedings' are included in the wider term 'civil proceedings'.[4] In the magistrates' court the term will include most applications under the Children Act 1989.[5] In addition, a number of other statutes will have applications which bear on the welfare of children: the list in the Children Act 1989, s 8(3) supplemented by the Family Law Act 1996, s 63(2) forms a useful starting point;[6] but because these two do not include the Children Act 1989, Part III it does not mean that applications for a secure accommodation order[7] are excluded from the ambit of the hearsay order.[8]

**4.59**     In the final analysis what is important is not the form of the proceedings, but whether or not the facts in each case demonstrate a connection with the upbringing, maintenance or welfare of a child which is sufficiently substantial to justify the hearsay evidence being admitted. If the facts demonstrate a sufficient connection and the proceedings are not criminal then the likelihood will be that they are proceedings (if they involve children in this way) which are covered by the 1993 Order and hearsay evidence will be admissible.

## Weight of hearsay evidence

**4.60**     Finally, it must be recalled that the court will be concerned to assess what weight is to be given to any evidence.[9] This applies to hearsay evidence as much as any other evidence. This assessment will be as relevant in relation to evidence

---

1     See **4.46** above.
2     See **4.55** above; and see eg *C v C (Contempt: Evidence)* [1993] 1 FLR 220 at 223B, per Butler-Sloss LJ.
3     See **1.29** above.
4     The 1993 Order does not make clear by what criterion it defines proceedings under the Child Support Act 1991. Most magistrates' court proceedings are dealt with under the Family Proceedings Courts (Child Support Act 1991) Rules 1993; however, reference here may be to applications for committal for failure to pay arrears of child support maintenance (Child Support Act 1991, s 40) which are dealt with by way of complaint under Magistrates' Court Rules 1981, SI 1981/552, r 97(1) (warrant for commitment).
5     For exceptions to this statement, see **4.56** above.
6     Family Law Act 1996, s 63(1) and (2) prescribes, as 'family proceedings', proceedings under the inherent jurisdiction of the High Court in relation to children and proceedings under the Family Law Act 1996, Parts II (when in force) and IV, the Matrimonial Causes Act 1973, the Adoption Act 1976, the Domestic Proceedings and Magistrates' Courts Act 1978, Matrimonial and Family Proceedings Act 1984, Part III, Children Act 1989, Parts I, II and III, and Human Fertilisation and Embryology Act 1990, s 30.
7     Children Act 1989, s 25, which is included in Part III of the Act.
8     By Children Act 1989, s 92(2), all proceedings under the Act are treated as family proceedings in relation to the magistrates' court; and see *Oxfordshire County Council v R* [1992] 1 FLR 648, per Douglas Brown J.
9     For weight of evidence, see **4.42** et seq above.

admitted under the Children (Admissibility of Hearsay Evidence) Order 1993 or the Civil Evidence Act 1995, s 1 as to any other evidence. Concerning a video-recorded interview[1] of a child, Ward LJ commented:[2]

> 'The recording is admitted as a form of hearsay evidence. It is for the judge to decide its weight and credibility. He will accordingly have regard to the fact that the evidence from the child is elicited in response to leading questions, under some pressure. He will judge the internal consistency and inconsistency of the story. He will look for any inherent improbabilities in the truth of what the child relates and will decide what part, if any, he can believe and whether stripped of embellishments of fancy or exaggeration there remains, none the less, a hard core of truth.'

The Civil Evidence Act 1995, s 4(2) contains a list of factors which the court can have in mind when assessing the weight of hearsay evidence.[3] In the context of proceedings relating to the welfare of children these may be of only passing relevance to that assessment. However, wider questions, such as those raised by Ward LJ above, may arise for consideration by the court where children's evidence is concerned. This will be especially so when an issue to be considered is how, and by whom, a child's evidence was obtained.

---

1    In a challenge to video evidence, it was held in *B v B (Court Bundles: Video Evidence)* [1994] 2 FLR 323, Wall J, at para 15 to the Practice Note appended to the judgment, that if there is to be a challenge 'to the technique used or debate as to the interpretation of what the child or interviewer has said' transcripts of the interview should be available to the court. On video evidence, see Hershman and McFarlane *Children: Law and Practice* (Family Law) at [1401]–[1410] (interviews with children).

2    *Re N (Child Abuse: Evidence)* [1996] 2 FLR 214, CA; and see further consideration of this case in the context of weight of evidence at **4.43** above.

3    See **4.49** above for a consideration of s 4(2).

# Chapter 5

## OPINION EVIDENCE

### 1 INTRODUCTION

**5.1**    'Opinion', in the context of rules of evidence, means an inference drawn by a witness from observed facts, although in practice this may occasionally mean inferences from facts observed by others.[1] The general rule is that a witness gives evidence as to fact. The judge then draws inferences from those facts. However, an expert[2] witness may express an opinion based upon, or derived from, the facts, since:[3]

> 'The law recognises that, so far as matters calling for special knowledge are concerned, judges ... are not necessarily equipped to draw the inferences from the facts stated by the witnesses. A witness is therefore allowed to state his opinion with regard to such matters provided he is expert in them.'

**5.2**    The object of expert evidence is that the expert should assist the court impartially in areas where the judge is not expected to be knowledgeable. The concept of assistance to the court is stressed by the Civil Procedure Rules 1998: r 35.3(1) provides that 'It is the duty of an expert to help the court on matters within his expertise'; and by r 35.3(2) 'This duty overrides any obligation to the person from whom he has received the instructions and by whom he is paid.'[4] As Ward LJ explained: 'The court has no expertise of its own, other than legal expertise ... The expert advises, but the judge decides'.[5] However, the expert is entitled to speak only from his expertise, and must, therefore, be wary of giving opinions which go beyond that expertise.

### Mutuality

**5.3**    Since the expert has evidence which will go into areas which are not familiar to the courts or to the parties, court rules are framed so as to ensure mutuality between the parties and to ensure that they have notice of expert evidence to be called by other

---

1    For example, Doctor A, writing a report of his assessment of the injuries to a child, derived from the notes of Doctor B and from police photographs, will not be giving his opinion from facts observed by him.
2    A curious aside on developments under the Children Act 1989 is that it seems that 'many medical practitioners, including experienced practitioners, were said to feel uncomfortable with the concept of setting themselves up as "experts" ' (Dame Margaret Booth *Avoiding Delay in Children Act Cases* (July 1996), para 3.6.3).
3    *Cross and Tapper on Evidence* 8th edn (Butterworths, 1995).
4    *Practice Direction – Experts and Assessors* (CPR Pt 35) para 1.1 requires that an expert's report be addressed to the court not to the party who commissioned their evidence.
5    *Re B (Care: Expert Witness)* [1996] 1 FLR 667 at 670C–D, CA.

parties.[1] This general statement of principle may often be eroded, first, in children cases, where it may be necessary to save children from excessive assessment or examination,[2] and, secondly, where the court, on application by the parties, appoints an expert,[3] in which case a party may call only one expert on the question considered by the court's expert.[4]

## Woolf and the expert

**5.4** In his criticism of the cost and delay in litigation, Lord Woolf[5] identified the use of the expert as particularly insidious:[6]

> 'The need to engage experts was a source of excessive expense, delay and, in some cases, increased complexity through the excessive or inappropriate use of experts. Concern was also expressed [during Lord Woolf's consultative process] as to their failure to maintain their independence from the party by whom they had been instructed.'

Perhaps the ills described in the civil jurisdiction by Lord Woolf are not generally so prevalent among family lawyers;[7] but there is evidence of similar concern among those concerned with family courts, especially in regard to expense[8] and delay.[9] The extent to which the Civil Procedure Rules 1998 (made following the Woolf reports) remains to be seen and will be considered at the end of this chapter in relation to expert evidence.[10]

---

1    Rules of the Supreme Court 1965, Ord 38, r 36; in respect of non family proceedings, see Civil Procedure Rules 1998, r 35.4; and see **5.16** et seq below.
2    See eg Family Proceedings Rules 1991, r 4.18 and comments in *Report of the Inquiry into Child Abuse in Cleveland 1987* (HMSO, 1988) at para 13: 'Second opinions requested by parents need to be carefully considered. Children ought not to be subjected to repeated examinations in support of a search by parents or a medical view with which they could agree'. These words are repeated almost verbatim in *The Children Act 1989 Guidance and Regulations, Volume 1, Court Orders* (HMSO, 1991) para 3.48.
3    Rules of the Supreme Court 1965, Ord 40; Civil Procedure Rules 1998, rr 35.7–35.9 (see further **5.24** et seq below). The fact that parties jointly instruct an expert, whether by agreement or as ordered by the court, does not prevent a party then calling his own expert on the issue; see **5.33** below.
4    Rules of the Supreme Court 1965, Ord 40, r 6; and see *Abbey National Mortgagees plc v Key Surveyors Nationwide Ltd and Others* [1996] 1 WLR 1534, CA.
5    Lord Woolf MR *Access to Justice: Interim Report* (HMSO, June 1995) ch 23; and Lord Woolf MR *Access to Justice: Final Report* (HMSO, July 1996), ch 14.
6    *Access to Justice: Interim Report* (HMSO, June 1995) ch 23, para 1.
7    Per contra see eg comments of Thorpe J in *F v F (Ancillary Relief: Substantial Assets)* [1995] 2 FLR 45.
8    See eg *Children Act Advisory Committee Annual Report 1993/4* at p 13: 'the way forward is for the courts to exercise a more robust control of their existing powers [to contain the proliferation of experts]'.
9    The position in children cases is summarised in Booth *Avoiding Delay in Children Act Cases* (July 1996), paras 2.6 and 3.8, although Dame Margaret sees evidence of improvement in increased joint instruction of experts (para 3.6.7).
10   See **5.48** et seq below.

## 2   RULES CONCERNING OPINION EVIDENCE

**5.5**      The rules of evidence which apply to opinion evidence are, strictly, a branch of hearsay evidence; but since the meaning of that term has reduced since the coming into operation of the Civil Evidence Act 1995[1] and since, in the field of family and child law, hearsay has been of only limited relevance (at least in practice), opinion evidence is categorised as being a form of secondary evidence.[2]

### Meaning of 'opinion'

**5.6**      The term 'opinion' in the law of evidence means an inference from observed facts based on the witness's expertise. The former rule that witnesses can speak only from facts observed by them has been relaxed to the extent that experts will frequently base their opinions on secondary and tertiary evidence[3] such as medical notes, photographs of evidence, a firm's accounts (secondary evidence) and textbooks (tertiary evidence). Such opinions are admissible provided they are relevant to the issues before the court[4] and subject to the agreement of the parties or the leave of the court.[5] The Civil Procedure Rules 1998, in respect of non family proceedings, prefer to limit the terminology of opinion evidence to 'expert evidence';[6] although the rules fail to define 'expert', preferring a definition which merely restates the question: an 'expert' is 'an expert ... instructed to give or prepare evidence' for court proceedings.[7]

### The exclusionary rules

**5.7**      Four exclusionary rules exist at common law as to opinion evidence. These can most conveniently be set out as questions, after which each will be explained:

(1)   Is the witness qualified to give an opinion on the facts before the court?
(2)   Is the particular case one calling for expertise?
(3)   If the case may be one for opinion evidence, what is the extent of the need for such evidence and the weight to be given to it by the judge?
(4)   Is the expert being called upon to express an opinion on the ultimate issue before the court?

#### *Qualification to give an opinion on the facts before the court*

**5.8**      Both the witness and the advocate challenging him must be clear about the range of an individual's expertise and be sure that that expertise is not exceeded. Where a witness is not truly qualified, his opinion evidence in a particular field may be challenged, for example where an accountant strays into the area of actuarial valuation, or where a paediatrician strays into the field of child psychology. The

---

1      For a consideration of hearsay and the Civil Evidence Act 1995, see **4.44** et seq above.
2      See **3.7** above.
3      For consideration of secondary and tertiary evidence, see **3.7** et seq above.
4      And, in respect of non family proceedings, see the Civil Procedure Rules 1998, r 35.1 (duty to restrict expert evidence to 'that which is reasonably required').
5      See further **5.17** below.
6      Civil Procedure Rules 1998, r 35.2.
7      Ibid, r 35.2.

corollary to this is that the person who gives evidence or expresses an opinion on a subject on which he is not qualified to express an opinion must expect his evidence to be discounted or ignored.[1] Where a party believes that opinion evidence in a report for the court is intended to be given by someone who is not expert, he may challenge the report by taking out a summons or issuing notice of application on an interlocutory basis; or, if there is no time to issue such an application, the objector can apply at the hearing for deletion of that part of the evidence not covered by the witness's expertise.

## Cases not calling for expertise

**5.9**      It is only necessary to call expert evidence on matters with which the court is unfamiliar. It has been held that: 'If on the proven facts a judge . . . can form [his] own conclusions without help, then the opinion of an expert is unnecessary'.[2] If a witness's opinion, however well qualified, is not relevant to the issues in the case, the judge is entitled to say so. This question is then bound up with judicial notice:[3] what does the judge know and on what does he need help from an expert? The experienced family judge may have knowledge about certain aspects of paediatric medicine, but he will rarely be qualified to express an opinion on other than the more elementary of medical questions. A district judge may live in a particular town, but he would generally be unwise to take a view on valuation of property other than on the most rudimentary of bases; and if he intends to do so he should tell the parties.[4]

## The weight to be given to the opinion

**5.10**      Although particular opinion evidence may be admissible, there remains the question of the weight to be attached to it.[5] In *Re M and R (Child Abuse: Evidence)*[6] Butler-Sloss LJ explained the position thus: 'The modern view is to regulate [reception of expert evidence] by way of weight, rather than admissibility'. With respect to Butler-Sloss LJ, it is first necessary to determine admissibility according to whether or not evidence is relevant[7] (a point which she confirms a few lines earlier in her judgment). Relevance will then determine admissibility of the evidence. This leads to the question of the weight of evidence, and this will depend on the extent of the relevance of the evidence to the issues and on the expertise and credibility[8] of the witness. If the evidence is 'arguably relevant but in [the judge's] view ultimately unhelpful he can generally prevent its reception' because the evidence 'would carry little weight with him'.[9] In this way the judge's reception of evidence, which may be

---

1    *Edmonds v Edmonds* [1990] 2 FLR 202, CA (husband's opinion evidence on valuation of the
     former matrimonial home discounted in the face of the evidence of a professional valuer).
2    *R v Turner* [1975] QB 834 at 841, per Lawton LJ; and see *Brown v Gould and Swayn* (1996)
     unreported, 24 January, where the Court of Appeal held that it was perfectly well qualified to
     understand a solicitor's practice in conveyancing, without expert opinion upon it from a
     practising solicitor, for the purposes of a professional negligence claim.
3    See further **3.33** above.
4    On analogy with *Norbrook Laboratories (GB) Ltd v Health & Safety Executive* [1998] TLR 96,
     (1998) *The Times*, 23 February, QBD.
5    For further consideration of weight of evidence, see **4.42** above.
6    [1996] 2 FLR 195 at 211B, CA.
7    And see Civil Procedure Rules 1998, r 35.1.
8    For a discussion of credibility, see **5.43** below.
9    *Re M and R (Child Abuse: Evidence)* (above) at 211B, per Butler-Sloss LJ.

regarded as of only peripheral relevance, is determined by its cogency rather than by its relevance.[1]

### *Opinion on the ultimate issue*

**5.11**    The rule at common law is that a witness cannot be asked to express an opinion on the ultimate issue before the court:[2] it is for the judge, not the witness, to decide the main issues being tried. In practice, it is often difficult for an expert to avoid comment on the main issue. Accordingly, the Civil Evidence Act 1972 specifically provides that a witness's 'opinion on any relevant matter on which he is qualified to give expert evidence shall be admissible in evidence';[3] and 'relevant matter' here 'includes an issue in the proceedings in question'.[4] This effectively brings the ultimate issue rule to an end,[5] but it leaves intact the principle that, although the expert may express an opinion (including a view on the main issue before the court), it is for the judge finally to decide.[6] He may take a different course from that recommended by an expert, but, if he does so, he should explain why.[7]

## 3   LAW AND PROCEDURE

### Civil Evidence Acts

**5.12**    The Civil Evidence Act 1995, s 1(1), which came into force on 31 January 1997, provides that 'evidence shall not be excluded on the ground that it is hearsay';[8] and, in the Act, 'references to hearsay include hearsay of whatever degree'.[9] The Act repeals Part I of the Civil Evidence Act 1968 and ss 1 and 2(1) and (2) of the Civil Evidence Act 1972 which, respectively, dealt with hearsay generally and (the 1972 Act) with expert evidence specifically. The object of the 1995 Act remains to ensure that, where possible, notice is given of a party's intention to adduce hearsay evidence.

**5.13**    It must be assumed that the new Act is intended to apply to opinion evidence. However, no attempt is made in any of the three Civil Evidence Acts to define

---

1    Butler-Sloss LJ left open her view as to whether or not a judge may refuse to hear evidence at all, even though that evidence is admissible. The court was 'clearly of opinion that the judge in proceedings such as these should have such a power' to exclude ([1996] 2 FLR 195 at 213C).

2    In children proceedings, this rule is blatantly ignored much of the time; court welfare officers and guardians ad litem are positively encouraged by most judges to make recommendations to the court which, by most definitions of the term, must involve an opinion on the 'ultimate issue'.

3    Civil Evidence Act 1972, s 3(1).

4    Ibid, s 3(3).

5    The unremarkable, but clear, provisions of Civil Evidence Act 1972, s 3 were overlooked – or not referred to the court – in *Re S and B (Minors) (Child Abuse: Evidence)* [1990] 2 FLR 489, CA and *Re N (Child Abuse: Evidence)* [1996] 2 FLR 214, CA; but, following a discussion of the background to s 3, Butler-Sloss LJ explained the applicability of the section in family proceedings in *Re M and R (Child Abuse: Evidence)* [1996] 2 FLR 195 at 205G et seq, CA.

6    See eg *Re CB and JB (Care Proceedings: Guidelines)* [1998] 2 FLR 211, Wall J at 219B–H.

7    See eg *Re B (Care: Expert Witness)* [1996] 1 FLR 667, CA: 'It ... is necessary for a judge to give reasons for disagreeing with experts' conclusions or recommendations. ... A Judge cannot substitute his views for the views of the experts without some evidence to support what it is he concludes' (at 674G, per Butler-Sloss LJ).

8    For further consideration of hearsay, see **4.44** above.

9    Civil Evidence Act 1995, s 1(2)(b).

'opinion', 'expert' or 'expert evidence', although the 1972 Act, for example, uses all those terms. The reference in the 1995 Act to the fact that hearsay includes 'hearsay of whatever degree' is brief to the point, almost, of meaninglessness. The Act repealed two sections of the 1972 Act which dealt with statements of opinion, while it leaves intact the Civil Evidence Act 1972, s 2(3) et seq which deal with provision for rules of court on opinion evidence. Commentators regarded opinion evidence as a branch of hearsay. *Cross and Tapper*[1] regard the rules relating to opinion evidence as having 'originated in the same doctrine as that to which the rule against hearsay can be traced'; while the explanation in *Phipson*[2] suggests a rather more tenuous relationship between the two. On this basis it would be by no means clear that opinion evidence could unequivocally be described as 'hearsay of whatever degree'; but given the repeals which have been effected it seems likely that opinion evidence was intended to be included in the provisions of the new Act.

**5.14**    The Rules of the Supreme Court, Ord 38, rr 34–43 and the County Court Rules, Ord 20, rr 25–28 provide the procedural structure for opinion and expert evidence in accordance with the Civil Evidence Act 1972, s 2. In what follows, we shall refer only to Ord 38, since Ord 20 effectively adopts the relevant part of Ord 38 in its entirety for civil proceedings in the county courts. In the Civil Procedure Rules 1998, Part 35 deals with the evidence of experts in respect of non family proceedings.

## Privilege and experts' reports

**5.15**    While s 2 of the Civil Evidence Act 1972 provides the machinery for disclosure of reports, it does not affect the general rule of law that reports obtained for the purpose of contemplated or pending proceedings or for the purpose of giving legal advice are privileged from disclosure,[3] (although privilege can be waived by the person whose privilege it is). The privilege does not operate in reverse: a doctor, for example, has a duty to inform the relevant authorities in the event of suspicions of abuse to children.[4]

## Family proceedings and Rules of the Supreme Court 1965, Ord 38

**5.16**    The Rules of the Supreme Court 1965 apply in family proceedings insofar as they are inconsistent with the Family Proceedings Rules 1991.[5] Rules which relate to opinion or expert evidence appear rarely in the Family Proceedings Rules 1991: r 4.18[6] contains special – and very important – rules on the examination of children for the purpose of preparation of a court report;[7] but there is little else on the subject.

---

1    *Cross and Tapper on Evidence* 8th edn (Butterworths, 1995) p 546.
2    *Phipson on Evidence* 14th edn (Sweet & Maxwell, 1990) para 22-06.
3    See **7.20** et seq below; but for exceptions to the rule, see *Re L (Police Investigation: Privilege)* [1996] 2 WLR 395, [1996] 1 FLR 731, HL; and see discussion of this case and the question of disclosure of adverse evidence in children cases at **7.17** et seq below.
4    *Working Together Under the Children Act 1989: a guide to arrangements for inter-agency co-operation for the protection of children from abuse* (HMSO, 1991).
5    Family Proceedings Rules 1991, r 1.3(1). For the extent to which the Civil Procedure Rules 1998 apply in respect of family proceedings, see **1.31** et seq above and Chapter 15.
6    And its equivalent in Family Proceedings Courts (Children Act 1989) Rules 1991, SI 1991/1395, r 18.
7    See further **11.88** et seq below.

Consequently, procedure concerning opinion evidence in family proceedings is governed almost entirely by the Rules of the Supreme Court 1965, Ord 38.[1] However, to supplement the dearth in Family Proceedings Rules 1991, an array of Practice Directions and recommendations governing practice and procedure in relation to opinion evidence has been set out by the judiciary, for example in relation to the identification and instruction of experts.[2]

### Leave or agreement to adduce expert evidence

**5.17**    An essential feature of expert evidence is the requirement of fairness and mutuality between the parties – a party who is unable to respond to the opinion of an expert, because he does not know of the opinion in advance of the hearing, may be prejudiced. The rules reflect this by providing that expert evidence cannot be adduced except:

(a)   by leave of the court;
(b)   by agreement of the parties;
(c)   by affidavit in appropriate circumstances; or
(d)   in accordance with court directions.[3]

A party who fails to comply with these rules may be prevented from relying upon his expert evidence, save, perhaps, where the welfare of a child might be affected by omitting the evidence (here public policy in ensuring mutuality might have to be balanced against the needs of the child). The court has power to limit the number of experts to be called,[4] and if the application for leave is made late the court has an inherent jurisdiction to refuse leave where to grant it might delay the trial.[5]

**5.18**    It may be the case that these general rules on leave to adduce experts' reports do not apply in children proceedings. Whether or not entirely by the intention of the draughtsman, a distinction has been developed by the Family Proceedings Rules 1991 (so far as they relate to children proceedings) between: (a) written statements of oral evidence, which must be disclosed and filed at court; and (b) 'expert's reports', which are classed as 'documents' and which must also be filed at court and served on all parties.[6] There is no express requirement, within these rules, that the court's leave be obtained to adduce expert evidence. The requirement of the Family Proceedings Rules 1991 that evidence which is to be relied upon be filed at court does not of itself dispense with the requirement of Rules of the Supreme Court 1965, Ord 38, r 36 for leave; but the implication must surely be there. There is an imprecision in this area of

1    And see Civil Procedure Rules 1998, Part 35.
2    See eg *Re M (Minors) (Care Proceedings: Child's Wishes)* [1994] 1 FLR 749, per Wall J; *Re G (Minors) (Expert Witness)* [1994] 2 FLR 291, per Wall J; *Re C (Expert Evidence: Disclosure: Practice)* [1995] 1 FLR 204, per Cazalet J; *Re FS (Child Abuse: Evidence)* [1996] 2 FLR 158; *Re CS (Expert Witnesses)* [1996] 2 FLR 115; *Children Act Advisory Committee Annual Report 1994/5* (with draft letter of instruction).
3    Rules of the Supreme Court 1965, Ord 38, r 36; County Court Rules 1981, Ord 20, r 27; and, in respect of non family proceedings, see Civil Procedure Rules 1998, r 35.4.
4    Rules of the Supreme Court 1965, Ord 38, r 4; and, in respect of non family proceedings, see Civil Procedure Rules 1998, r 35.4.
5    *Winchester Cigarette Machinery Ltd v Payne* (1993) *The Times*, 19 October, CA.
6    Family Proceedings Rules 1991, r 4.17(1); r 4.14(1)(b) impliedly describes experts' reports as 'documents'.

the rules. Given that, on the one hand, Ord 38 is framed deliberately so as to avoid prejudice to parties, and that this area of Family Proceedings Rules 1991 is designed to protect the welfare of children, this imprecision is unfortunate.

## Substance of evidence

**5.19**    As with witness statements generally in children proceedings,[1] rules require 'that the *substance* of the evidence be disclosed'[2] (emphasis added). It has been held that use of the word 'substance' means evidence that a witness will give at the trial, not all the evidence he could give on the subject.[3]

## Partial disclosure

**5.20**    The court is able to order disclosure of only part of an expert's report.[4] Partial disclosure may be ordered on grounds that full disclosure would be 'undesirable'.[5] This provision will need to be treated with caution. If it is to be relied upon, the important principle of public policy of ensuring full disclosure as between the parties will need to be born in mind; and in children cases this public policy consideration will be balanced against the need to protect the child.[6]

## Meeting of experts

**5.21**    The court, of its own motion, may 'direct that there be a meeting "without prejudice"' of experts involved in the case, 'for the purpose of identifying the parts of their evidence which are in issue'.[7] They may then produce a joint statement identifying points agreed and any points which remain in issue. In children cases, experts should be invited to hold such a meeting which can be coordinated by the guardian ad litem or the child's solicitor.[8] The aim of this direction is to clarify areas of agreement, and to identify the areas of disagreement which will have to be resolved at the hearing. The result, it is hoped, will be to reduce expense and shorten the length of the hearing. For example: property valuers may be able to agree aspects of their evidence which are mutually accepted (such as comparable properties used in the valuation of a particular property);[9] accountants could meet to agree the basis for their

---

1    See eg Family Proceedings Rules 1991, r 4.17(1)(a): 'written statements of the substance of the oral evidence which the party intends to adduce'.
2    Rules of the Supreme Court 1965, Ord 38, r 37.
3    *Derby & Co v Weldon (No 9)* [1990] TLR 712.
4    Rules of the Supreme Court 1965, Ord 38, r 39.
5    Where a party objects to disclosure, the court can order production to itself of any document, including an expert's report, so that consideration can be given to the question of partial disclosure.
6    See eg *Re G (Minors) (Welfare Report: Disclosure)* [1993] 2 FLR 293, CA: partial disclosure of welfare report only where real harm to children if disclosure ordered.
7    Rules of the Supreme Court 1965, Ord 38, r 38; in respect of non family proceedings, see Civil Procedure Rules 1998, r 35.12. Family Proceedings Rules 1991, r 2.74(1)(b)(ii) (Ancillary Relief Pilot Scheme) suggests that a procedure akin to this be directed by the district judge on the first appointment. See approval of this procedure in Woolf *Access to Justice: Final Report* (HMSO, July 1996), ch 13, para 42 et seq.
8    *Re C (Expert Evidence: Disclosure: Practice)* [1995] 1 FLR 204, per Cazalet J.
9    A meeting of valuers was commended eg by Booth J in *Evans v Evans* [1990] 1 FLR 319, [1990] 2 All ER 147 and by Cazalet J in *Re C (Expert Evidence: Disclosure: Practice)* [1995] 1 FLR 204.

valuation of a business even though they might not agree the final figure; and medical witnesses could meet to attempt to agree, for example, the causes of a child's injuries. There is no reason why experts should not meet to discuss their views provided that their conclusions are recorded in some way, however briefly.[1]

**5.21A**    In *Re CB and JB (Care Proceedings: Guidelines)*,[2] Wall J clearly considers that it is the duty of the lawyers and the guardian ad litem to identify circumstances where an experts' meeting might be appropriate.[3] He gave some helpful guidance on the subject of meetings of experts, as follows:

–    where experts disagree there is no need for them to meet face to face-to-face where a telephone conference can be held between them and provided that such a conference has a proper agenda;
–    careful consideration must be given to the purpose of the meeting[4] and to whom should therefore attend. For example, where the issue is the cause of a child's injuries it would be inappropriate, normally, for psychiatrists to join a meeting;
–    expert's meetings must have a clear agenda and should, probably, be chaired by the guardian ad litem's solicitor;
–    there should be a record of the meeting prepared, perhaps, by the guardian ad litem; and the result of the meeting distilled into a statement by the experts involved at the meeting.

### Expert not to be called as a witness

**5.22**    In appropriate cases, application can made for receiving an expert's evidence solely in writing because he 'cannot or should not be called as a witness'.[5] The court can then decide, in relation to that report, whether it is to be received in evidence as it stands,[6] or whether it must be treated as being adduced like any other hearsay evidence.[7] The effect of the Children Act 1989, s 45(7) is to exclude Rules of the Supreme Court 1965, Ord 38, r 41 in applications for an emergency protection order. Section 45(7) enables the court, 'regardless of any . . . rule of law which would otherwise prevent it from doing so', to take account of 'any statement contained in any report' concerned with the proceedings and no leave under Ord 38, r 41 is therefore necessary. Thus, a doctor's statement relating to a child's injuries, for example, may be presented and relied upon, even though the doctor is not at court to be cross-examined on his report.

---

1    *Re CB and JB (Care Proceedings: Guidelines)* [1998] 2 FLR 211, Wall J at 224H.
2    [1998] 2 FLR 211 Wall J at 226C–229A.
3    In respect of non family proceedings, see Civil Procedure Rules 1998, r 35.12(1) plainly envisages the court as having a discretion to order meetings of experts; though presumably parties could apply for an order in appropriate circumstances.
4    Under Civil Procedure Rules 1998, r 35.12(2), the court in non family proceedings can, in effect, set the agenda for the meeting.
5    Rules of the Supreme Court 1965, Ord 38, r 41.
6    See also *Society of Lloyds v Clementson* [1996] CLC 1205: expert witness excused attendance at court because he had other more 'important work'.
7    For hearsay evidence, see Civil Evidence Act 1995, Rules of the Supreme Court 1965, Ord 38, Part III; and, in respect of non family proceedings, see Civil Procedure Rules 1998, Part 33 and **4.44** et seq above.

*Report disclosed by another party*

**5.23** A party may use, as part of his evidence, a report disclosed by another party.[1]

## Court-appointed expert

**5.24** The court has power to appoint an expert, but this power is exercisable in two separate ways: appointment of a court expert on the application of a party to the proceedings; and appointment of welfare officers in children cases.

### Court expert

**5.25** The High Court may appoint an expert[2] 'on the application of any party' to the proceedings before the court.[3] The function of the expert is 'to inquire and report upon any question of fact or opinion not involving questions of law or of construction'.[4] If possible, the expert should be a person agreed between the parties, and the question to be put to him should be agreed between them, failing which the court will appoint and settle instructions to him.[5] The expert's report is sent to the court and then to the parties who, if they wish to cross-examine the expert, must seek leave.[6] The court fixes the expert's fee which is payable by the parties, who are jointly and severally liable for it subject to any order for costs the court may make in the cause or application.[7] With notice to other parties a party may call evidence on the question to be reported on to the court, for which there appears to be no requirement for leave.[8]

### Appointment on application

**5.26** Without citing any precedent for his observation, Lord Macnaghten expressed the view that the court can call in its own expert.[9] If a judge sees an issue he would like resolved or wishes to try to discourage a proliferation of experts, it would seem attractive for him to be able to call upon his own expert. It is possible that a judge in the High Court has power to adopt this course under the court's inherent jurisdiction. The county court, by contrast, is an entirely statutory creation and has no

---

1   Rules of the Supreme Court 1965, Ord 38, r 42; in respect of non family proceedings, see Civil Procedure Rules 1998, r 35.11.
2   Or, as it was put by Saunders J in 1554: 'If matters arise in our law which concern other sciences or faculties we commonly apply for the aid of that science or faculty which it concerns. This is a commendable thing in our law' in *Buckley v Rice-Thomas* (1554) 1 Plowd 118 at 124, quoted in *Cross and Tapper on Evidence* 8th edn (Butterworths, 1995), p 555.
3   Rules of the Supreme Court 1965, Ord 40, r 1(1); and, in respect of non family proceedings, see Civil Procedure Rules 1998, rr 35.7 and 35.8 which create a more robust regime, considered below. There is no equivalent rule in the county courts.
4   Rules of the Supreme Court 1965, Ord 40, r 1(1).
5   Ibid, Ord 40, r 1(2) and (3).
6   Ibid, Ord 40, r 4.
7   Ibid, Ord 40, r 5.
8   Ibid, Ord 40, r 6; although, where applicable, an issue might arise on costs, especially where a party has agreed the expert and his terms of reference.
9   In *Colls v Home and Colonial Stores Ltd* [1904] AC 179 at 192, where he said: 'I do not put [these practical suggestions] forward as carrying any authority; ... but I have often wondered why the Court does not more frequently avail itself of the power of calling in a competent adviser to report to the Court upon the question'. In the case under consideration he considered that 'the Court ought to have obtained such a report for its own guidance'. The Civil Procedure Rules 1998 still do not give the judge power to call his own opinion evidence (see eg r 35.7(1)).

such thing as an inherent jurisdiction; and an equivalent of the Rules of the Supreme Court 1965, Ord 40 does not exist in the County Court Rules 1981. However, two difficulties arise for any court in exercising such a jurisdiction.

(1) Ord 40, r 1(1) can be brought into operation only 'on the application of any party'. On the two recent reported examples of Ord 40 being used it is not clear that, in either case, a party to the proceedings had so applied;[1]

(2) the funding of the appointment can be by the parties only, and it must be very doubtful whether the court has an inherent jurisdiction to require a party to pay costs incurred by the court – as distinct from that party's own costs and disbursements.

*Rules of the Supreme Court 1965, Ord 40 and case management*

**5.27** Support for a scheme along the line of Ord 40 but operated by the court on its own motion is advocated by Woolf.[2] On appeal from the Official Referees Court, Sir Thomas Bingham MR upheld the judge's 'novel' direction under Ord 40 upon the following bases:[3]

– 'exhortations to trial judges[4] to be interventionist and managerial' should be heeded by making orders of this sort, while the court must 'be constantly alert to the paramount requirements of justice' to both parties;

– to avoid the 'fact' that expert witnesses, if called by a party, tend 'to espouse the cause of those instructing them', while a court-appointed expert may, by contrast, 'prove a reliable source of expert opinion'; and

– regard for the costs, relative to the values of the properties concerned, of giving leave to each party to adduce the evidence of individual experts in each case.

The case involved a large number of properties, but the principles set out by the Master of the Rolls is as applicable to children cases with a variety of experts, or financial relief cases where successive efforts are made by the parties to secure a valuation report favourable to their cause.[5]

## Welfare officers

**5.28** The reports of welfare officers in children cases are in a wholly different category from the court-appointed expert under the Rules of the Supreme Court 1965, Ord 40. For present purposes the term 'welfare officer' is used loosely to include a guardian ad litem, a court welfare officer, the Official Solicitor[6] and a local authority social worker. Part of the welfare officer's role is to report on facts found by him; but

---

1    *Re K (Contact: Psychiatric Report)* [1995] 2 FLR 432, CA; *Abbey National Mortgagees plc v Key Surveyors Nationwide Ltd and Others* [1996] 1 WLR 1534, CA; and see Burrows 'Order in a Psychiatric Report' [1996] Fam Law 305.

2    *Access to Justice: Final Report* (HMSO, July 1996) ch 13, para 16 et seq.

3    *Abbey National Mortgagees plc v Key Surveyors Nationwide Ltd and Others* (above).

4    Ie in case management, Practice Directions such as, in the Family Division, *Practice Direction of 31 January 1995 (Case Management)* [1995] 1 WLR 332, [1995] 1 FLR 456.

5    See eg the comments of Anthony Lincoln J on the questions of over-valuing of a business and the expense of such efforts in *B v B (Financial Provision)* [1989] 1 FLR 119.

6    The role of the Official Solicitor is hybrid: solicitor, guardian ad litem/representative of the child and welfare officer. Here he is acting as a reporting officer and, thus, in this context, as a welfare officer.

much of his function is to express an opinion to the court based on those facts and on his experience of dealing with children and families.[1] In giving an opinion he may be said to do so from the standpoint of an expert. Yet the principle of mutuality rarely exists in this context as the court has made plain its dislike of independent welfare reports.[2] The function of the welfare officer in this context arises in three distinct ways: the court welfare officer, the guardian ad litem and the social worker.

### Court welfare officer

**5.29**      The court has the power to order a welfare report which may be compiled by a probation officer or someone appointed by the local authority.[3] This appointment is very much akin to the appointment of an expert under Rules of the Supreme Court 1965, Ord 40. Indeed, the terminology of s 7(1) is strikingly similar to Ord 40, r 1: where 'a court is considering *any question* with respect to a child' (emphasis supplied) it may require a court welfare officer 'to report to the court on such matters relating to the welfare of that child as are required to be dealt with'. However, s 7(1) differs from Ord 40 in at least two crucial respects:

(1)   the court orders the report of its own motion and does not depend on the application of the parties. In consequence, welfare officers are paid for by the taxpayer not by the parties;

(2)   while a party is technically entitled to call his own welfare officer,[4] the practice is not officially sanctioned by the rules, as it is by Ord 40, r 6 in the case of court-appointed experts.

### Guardians ad litem and the Official Solicitor

**5.30**      The term 'guardian ad litem' is used in four distinct ways in family proceedings:

(1)   as the person named to defend proceedings taken against a person under a disability (including children),[5] as distinct from a child's 'next friend' who acts on the child's behalf to bring proceedings.[6] With his agreement the Official Solicitor may act in this capacity;[7]

(2)   as guardian ad litem appointed in 'specified proceedings'[8] from the panel of guardians ad litem. In exceptional cases the Official Solicitor might take this role

---

1    See also consideration of experts expressing an opinion on the ultimate issue at **5.11** above.
2    *Practice Direction of 24 March 1983 (Family Division – Independent Welfare Reports)* [1983] 1 WLR 416, (1983) FLR 450 plainly inhibits the appointment of an 'independent reporter'; and Family Proceedings Rules 1991, r 4.18 may now be regarded, by analogy, as preventing independent welfare reports without leave of the court.
3    Children Act 1989, s 7.
4    Although the practice is very strongly discouraged by the courts: see **5.26** above.
5    See eg Rules of the Supreme Court 1965, Ord 80, r 2 and Family Proceedings Rules 1991, r 9.2. The Civil Procedure Rules 1998, Part 21 in respect of non family proceedings has introduced a different regime into the rules, employing similar concepts to previously but no longer using guardians ad litem.
6    Which could include taking over an application commenced by a child under the Family Proceedings Rules 1991, r 9.2A(1).
7    Ibid, r 9.5(1).
8    Which are almost entirely public law proceedings as defined in Children Act 1989, s 41(6). This is the sense in which 'guardian ad litem' is used in Legal Aid Act 1988, s 15(3A)(c) preventing

where no guardian ad litem has been appointed or the issues are exceptionally complex;[1]

(3)  as guardian ad litem or reporting officer in adoption proceedings (where the guardian ad litem is involved more to report to the court – as with the court welfare officer – than to represent the child as guardian ad litem in (1) or (2) above);

(4)  the Official Solicitor as guardian ad litem where he acts both as a solicitor, to a limited extent,[2] and as a form of court welfare officer reporting to the court in more difficult cases. Other parties may be required to pay his fees.

**5.31**     The role of guardians ad litem (as in (1) and (3) above) in this context differs from that of court welfare officers in that the former represent the child and they are thus partisan to that extent. However, if the views of a guardian ad litem in Children Act 1989 proceedings and those of the child diverge, it is the guardian's own views that he must present to the court. He is to that extent both representative of a party and reporting officer. Where, as in specified proceedings, the child also has a solicitor he will represent the child where he considers the child to be 'able, having regard to his understanding, to give ... instructions on his own behalf'.[3] Where the child is represented by the Official Solicitor and differs in his views from the Official Solicitor, he can apply to the court for the Official Solicitor to be released from acting for him.

*Local authority social workers*
**5.32**     From an evidential point of view the role of the social worker is as follows:

(1)  as court-appointed welfare officer under the Children Act 1989, s 7 he is in the same position as the court welfare officer and reports to the court;

(2)  as a social worker involved in care proceedings he is the local authority's witness and represents the views of his social services department. Much of his evidence will be from the standpoint of a witness; while an appreciable part of his evidence will be based on his opinion.

## Restrictions on evidence to be called

**5.33**     It is an essential principle of English civil law that a party is entitled to adduce such relevant evidence as he chooses, subject to rules relating to confidentiality and to leave being obtained to adduce opinion evidence.[4] Thus, any attempt by the courts to restrict a party's rights to call evidence (eg where district judges purport

---

legal aid being available for guardians ad litem in specified proceedings, not denying legal aid for guardians ad litem in the sense of (1) or (2).

1     Children Act 1989, s 41(8); and see *Practice Note of 8 September 1995 (The Official Solicitor: Appointment in Family Proceedings)* [1995] 2 FLR 479.

2     He does not, for example, take it upon himself to elicit a child's views or represent those views in court.

3     Family Proceedings Rules 1991, r 4.12(1)(a).

4     This view of the law of England and Wales is not shared by the Civil Procedure Rules 1998 which purport to allow courts to restrict the evidence to be called: in respect of non family proceedings, see Civil Procedure Rules 1998, r 32.1; and see **1.35** above.

to order parties to agree one valuer[1]) would appear to be *ultra vires*, save where it is sanctioned by the rules.[2] Further, there are sanctions in terms of costs and legal aid which may place certain disincentives in the way of parties in calling expert evidence not sanctioned by the court.

## Rules

**5.34**    Certain rules place a limit, for practical purposes, upon the opinion evidence which a party may call, for example:

–    the Rules of the Supreme Court 1965, Ord 38, r 36 and the Civil Procedure Rules 1998, r 35.4(1), in respect of non family proceedings impose a limit on the right to call evidence, in that the court's leave must be obtained (in the absence of agreement) for the calling of expert evidence;

–    the Family Proceedings Rules 1991, r 4.18 reduces the extent to which a child may be examined for the purpose of adducing evidence to a court;

–    the Family Proceedings Rules 1991, r 4.23 reduces the extent to which documents may be disclosed, such as for the purpose of obtaining an opinion upon them;

–    in all cases it is open to the court to restrict the number of expert witnesses[3] to be called by a party.[4]

## Costs

**5.35**    The award of costs is a matter entirely at the discretion of the court,[5] but costs orders can be a potent weapon for the court to show its disapproval of a particular party's actions. Thus, if a party to proceedings has behaved disproportionately in adducing evidence or has sought to adduce evidence in excess of that for which leave is granted[6] he may be penalised to the extent that any order for costs against another party may exclude the cost of the opinion evidence, or such expenditure may not be allowed on taxation of costs.[7]

---

1    In *Evans v Evans* [1990] 1 FLR 319, [1990] 2 All ER 147, Booth J was more tentative than ordering the appointment of an agreed valuer, directing only that parties attempt to agree a valuer, failing which each would have to appoint his own.

2    Eg Rules of the Supreme Court 1965, Ord 38, r 4 which enables the court to limit the number of witnesses to be called by each party; and see Civil Procedure Rules 1998, r 32.1, considered at **1.13** above.

3    The power to restrict the number of witnesses does not enable the court to exclude expert evidence altogether (*Sullivan v West Yorkshire Passenger Transport Executive* [1985] 2 All ER 134, CA).

4    Rules of the Supreme Court 1965, Ord 38, r 4. While *Practice Direction of 24 March 1983 (Independent Welfare Report)* [1983] 1 WLR 416, (1983) FLR 450 inhibits the appointment of an 'independent reporter' (and see **5.28** above), it does not prevent it.

5    Supreme Court Act 1981, s 51(1); Civil Procedure Rules 1998, r 44.3(1).

6    See eg Civil Procedure Rules 1998, r 44.3(4).

7    The criterion for taxation of costs on 'the standard basis' is that the costs were 'proportionate to the matters in issue' with any doubt being resolved in favour of the paying party; Civil Procedure Rules 1998, r 44.4(2)); while costs on 'the indemnity basis' are taxed on the basis of whether or not they were reasonably incurred with any doubt being resolved in favour of the receiving party (Civil Procedure Rules 1998, r 44.4(3)); and see *F v F (Duxbury Calculation: Rate of Return)* [1996] 1 FLR 833, per Holman J for an explanation of the meaning of indemnity basis for costs).

## *Legal aid*

**5.36** Where a party to proceedings has a legal aid certificate, all expenditure on a case has to be justified on taxation of the solicitor's bill of costs, save where prior authority has been obtained from the Legal Aid Board for a particular item of expenditure.[1] In children proceedings, the Board has indicated that where leave of the court is required for a child to be medically examined,[2] prior authority from the Board[3] for payment of expert's fees will be granted only once such leave has been granted by the court.[4] Thus, where a party has a legal aid certificate he will at all times be particularly conscious of whether or not expenditure on expert evidence will be authorised by the Board or, if authority is not obtained, whether the expenditure will be allowed on legal aid taxation.

## 4 CHARACTERISTICS OF OPINION EVIDENCE

**5.37** In looking at what we have characterised as opinion evidence, it is necessary to distinguish between the partisan opinion and the opinion of the independent expert. Thus, a witness giving evidence for his employer, such as a social worker in a care case, will be entitled to express an opinion, but that cannot, by definition, be impartial in the same way that the evidence of an independent expert should be.

### Partisan opinion evidence

**5.38** A local authority social worker is entitled to give an opinion based on his expertise, but he is not expected to be impartial in the sense considered below. For example, the local authority (his employers) may decide on a course with which the social worker does not agree, yet he is expected to adhere to the employer's line in court, whatever his personal views may be, and tailor his opinions accordingly. An inevitable consequence of this is that the credibility of the social worker's opinion evidence may be tainted by his partiality in a way which the evidence of the guardian ad litem and the court welfare officer will not be, although in many respects the expertise of each will be much the same.

### Impartial expert evidence

**5.39** The essence of the evidence of the independent expert is its impartiality, and this should be so, by whomsoever he may be instructed.[5] The expert is instructed by a party, but this is on the basis implied by the rules of evidence – that the expert is required to assist the court impartially in areas where the court is inexpert and needs help; this assistance should be impartial regardless of who is his paymaster. In

---

1 Civil Legal Aid (General) Regulations 1989, SI 1989/339, reg 63(1); and see regs 59–61 for the obtaining of authorities from the Board.
2 Family Proceedings Rules 1991, r 4.18.
3 For grant of prior authority from the Board, see Civil Legal Aid (General) Regulations 1989, reg 60.
4 Note for Guidance No 7–18(d) issued by the Legal Aid Board (*Legal Aid Handbook* (Sweet & Maxwell)).
5 See also the criticisms by Thorpe LJ of the partiality of experts involved in *Vernon v Bosley (Expert Evidence) (Note)* [1998] 1 FLR 297, CA.

*Whitehouse v Jordan and Another*[1] the problem was expressed by Lord Wilberforce as follows:

> '... expert evidence presented to the court should be, and should be seen to be, the independent product of the expert, uninfluenced as to form or content by the exigencies of litigation. To the extent that it is not, the evidence is likely to be not only incorrect, but self-defeating.'

Again, in *Note: Re R (A Minor) (Experts' Evidence)*,[2] Cazalet J stated the position thus:

> 'Expert witnesses are in a privileged position; indeed, only experts are entitled to give an *opinion* in evidence.[3] Outside the legal field the court itself has no expertise and for that reason frequently has to rely on the evidence of experts. Such experts must express only opinions which they genuinely hold and which are not biased in favour of one particular party.'

**5.40**    From this it follows that the expert must not join in the adversarial process;[4] and he should state to the court equally facts which support, and facts which do not support, the case of the person who commissioned this evidence. If an expert advances a hypothesis which he knows to be controversial he must tell the court and put forward any material which contradicts his hypothesis.[5]

## Extent to which court follows expert evidence

**5.41**    However, the court is not bound by the opinion of an expert.[6] The court is entitled to question the expert's credibility,[7] although in view of the role of the independent witness in court – to help the judge in areas where the court is not expert – the court is likely to be strongly influenced by expert opinion, especially where pitted against that of a layman.[8] The court should give its reasons where it departs from the opinion of a welfare officer,[9] although the final decision is that of the judge,[10] who will take account of the weight of the opinion evidence and the extent of its relevance to the issues before the court. However, the judge should not hesitate to depart from the recommendations of the expert where, for example, he believes that the welfare of a child demands that he do so.[11]

---

1    [1981] 1 WLR 246, HL quoted with approval by Wolf *Access to Justice: Final Report* (HMSO, July 1996), ch 13, para 29.
2    [1991] 1 FLR 291 at 292C.
3    This may not be entirely fair to the 'partisan' witness referred to at **5.38** above who may also be entitled to express an opinion based on social work expertise.
4    See comments of Lord Wilberforce in *Whitehouse v Jordan and Another* [1981] 1 WLR 246, HL; and see per Wall J in *Re JC (Care Proceedings: Procedure)* [1995] 2 FLR 77 considered further at **3.23** above.
5    *Re A and B (Minors) (No 2)* [1995] 1 FLR 351, per Wall J.
6    *Collier v Simpson* (1831) 5 C & P.
7    See eg *Rochdale Borough Council v A* [1991] 2 FLR 192, per Douglas Brown J.
8    *Edmonds v Edmonds* [1990] 2 FLR 202, CA: valuation evidence for one party was contradicted by lay evidence from the other party; when the lay evidence turned out to be correct, leave to appeal out of time was still refused as expert evidence could and should have been called at the original hearing.
9    *W v W (A Minor: Custody Appeal)* [1988] 2 FLR 505.
10   See also **5.11** above.
11   *J v C* [1970] AC 668.

## Duties of expert witnesses

**5.42**    In *The Ikarian Reefer*,[1] Cresswell J, drawing on the *dicta* of Cazalet J in *Note: Re R (A Minor) (Expert's Evidence)*,[2] summarised the duties and responsibilities of the expert as follows:

- expert evidence should be the independent product of the expert uninfluenced as to form or content by the surrounding litigation;[3]
- an expert should provide independent assistance to the court by means of objective opinion on matters within his expertise, but without in any way assuming the role of advocate for a point of view or for a party to the proceedings;[4]
- an expert should state the facts or assumptions on which his opinions are based, and should not omit facts which could detract from his stated opinion;
- an expert should state when a question falls outside his expertise;
- where an opinion is based on provisional data, or the opinion is qualified in any way, the expert must say so;
- if an expert changes his mind on reading another expert's report he should say so as soon as possible, through legal representatives.

## Credibility

**5.43**    The essence of any evidence is that it must be relevant to the issue before the court and that it must be credible. The more essential to the case the evidence, the more important that it be credible. In many family cases there is relatively little dispute about the primary evidence: the means of parties, for example that a party owns a particular property or a defined number of shares in a private company; or that a child has particular injuries or has behaved in a particular way at school. Fundamental issues before the court will then be the value of the assets or an explanation of the child's injuries or behaviour, both of which are essentially in the arena of opinion evidence. Expert evidence may thus become central to a decision on the issues before the court. The following principles may be enunciated to deal with the question of credibility of an expert. In part, they are derived from *Rochdale Borough Council v A*[5] and *Note: Re R (A Minor) (Experts' Evidence)*;[6] and, although these cases are children cases, the observations of the judges in both are applicable to expert evidence generally.

### *Expertise based on an acknowledged qualification*

**5.44**    An expert should not give evidence beyond or outside his expertise, nor, by extension, should he be tempted to give an opinion on facts or hypotheses for which he is not properly prepared. If he does so, he should stress to the court his awareness of the limits of his expertise. An accountant may be the only financial expert in court and

---

1    [1993] 2 Lloyd's Rep 69 at 81.
2    [1991] 1 FLR 291.
3    Per Lord Wilberforce in *Whitehouse v Jordan* (see **5.39** above).
4    Similarly, if an expert advances a hypothesis which is controversial, he must say so (*Re AB (Child Abuse: Expert Witnesses)* [1995] 1 FLR 181, per Wall J).
5    [1991] 2 FLR 192, per Douglas Brown J.
6    [1991] 1 FLR 291, per Cazalet J.

may be willing to give tentative assistance on actuarial matters, but in so doing he should explain the limit of such knowledge as he may have and its source (eg discussions with a colleague, personal interest etc). If an expert knows that his opinion is controversial, he must say so.[1]

### Express opinion only from known sources

**5.45**    In *Rochdale Borough Council v A*,[2] Douglas Brown J was critical of the relatively inexperienced doctor who gave evidence by means of 'vague citation'. The doctor spoke of sources indicating certain factors, but at best she was referring to secondary sources and had not read the primary literature to which she was referring. Where an expert relies on sources he should be specific in his citation and be sure that he has considered the sources in the original or from reliable syntheses.

### Avoidance of partiality

**5.46**    One of the easiest ways for an expert to taint his evidence, sometimes even fatally, will be for him to show partiality to one or other witness (as already discussed above). The temptation to call the witness recommended by the client (his accountant, for example, or the local authority's preferred child psychiatrist) should therefore be avoided unless such witnesses can be certain to express their opinions without partiality.

### Avoidance of personal prejudices and obsessions

**5.47**    It is important that the expert avoids personal prejudices, although witnesses may not always recognise them in themselves – a self-evident truth to one person may be a prejudice to another. It may be the object of the party who has called the witness to use his particular line of expertise – some might say his obsession – to assist in establishing his case.[3] From the adviser's point of view such witnesses must be treated with caution as, if their adoption of a line of argument is regarded by the court as unbalanced, the weight of their evidence will be reduced.

---

1    *Re AB (Child Abuse: Expert Witnesses)* [1995] 1 FLR 181, per Wall J.
2    [1991] 2 FLR 192 at 218E.
3    One of the more striking recent examples of this was Dr Marietta Higgs in Cleveland: see *Report of the Inquiry into Child Abuse in Cleveland 1987* (HMSO, 1988). *Rochdale Borough Council v A* also provides an example of witnesses being 'so obsessed with their own beliefs in what the children were saying' ([1991] 2 FLR 192 at 212E, per Douglas Brown J).

# Chapter 6

---

## DISCOVERY AND DISCLOSURE

## 1 INTRODUCTION

### Disclosure

**6.1** The duty of disclosure requires a party to an action to provide to other parties and to the court information relevant to an action.[1] The courts have held that a duty of disclosure arises from the wording of certain statutes: for example 'the duty of the court ... to have regard to all the circumstances of the case'[2] in an application for matrimonial financial relief has been held to give rise to a duty of 'full and frank disclosure'.[3] In children cases the extent to which a duty of disclosure exists is an issue which is very much alive:[4] where leave has been given to disclose confidential documents to an expert witness for preparation of a report, that report must be filed and disclosed to all parties;[5] while different rules as to the extent of disclosure may apply to local authorities as compared to other parties.[6] Disclosure of the facts on which a party bases his case, whether by statement, affidavit or sworn statement, is now a feature of all jurisdictions.[7]

### Disclosure and the inquisitorial process

**6.2** One of the reasons the family jurisdiction has developed the concept of a duty of disclosure – almost unknown in other jurisdictions, it seems,[8] save in the arena of the interlocutory injunction[9] – relates to the quasi-inquisitorial function which statute imposes upon family judges, and to which the judiciary is increasingly adapting itself. This is an aspect of the family jurisdiction considered by the House of Lords in *Re L*

---

1   The Civil Procedure Rules 1998 adopt the terminology of family proceedings, using 'disclosure of documents' to replace the term 'discovery'. However, the concept of disclosure of information as understood by family lawyers does not seem to apply to civil procedure yet.
2   Matrimonial Causes Act 1973, s 25(1).
3   *Livesey (formerly Jenkins) v Jenkins* [1985] AC 424, [1985] FLR 813, HL.
4   See **6.5** and **7.15** et seq below.
5   *Re L (Police Investigation: Privilege)* [1996] 2 WLR 395, [1996] 1 FLR 731, HL.
6   *R v Hampshire County Council ex parte K* [1990] 2 QB 71, [1990] 1 FLR 330, Div Ct.
7   The Civil Procedure Rules 1998, although not applicable to family proceedings, adopt the terminology of disclosure: see **15.11** below.
8   For example in *Phipson on Evidence* 14th edn (Sweet & Maxwell, 1990) para 10–30 et seq and *Cross and Tapper on Evidence* 8th edn (Butterworths, 1995) pp 270–272 the topic receives only cursory attention, mostly in relation to the requirement that the prosecution disclose witness statements in advance of a trial.
9   See **13.14** below.

*(Police Investigation: Privilege)*,[1] and behind such developments as the Ancillary Relief Pilot Scheme.[2] The inquisitorial function of the court has been explained by Thorpe J as follows:[3]

> 'I think that it is timely to stress that ancillary relief applications in this Division are not purely adversarial proceedings. The court has an independent duty to discharge the function imposed by statute. The court has from that duty the power to investigate and the power to ensure compliance with the duty of full and frank disclosure owed by the litigants.'

## Discovery

**6.3**     Where disclosure has not been provided by a party, whether of documents or facts, discovery[4] may be sought against that party or interrogatories raised.[5] This may be by order for discovery, interrogatories, or other questionnaire under the relevant rules. Each of these remedies will be considered in due course.[6] However, two important components of the discovery process are its exclusionary rules. First, a variety of documents are privileged from discovery. The subject of privilege is dealt with in a separate chapter.[7] The question of whether a fact can be disclosed or an admission made 'without prejudice' will also be considered there.[8] Secondly, many documents may be excluded by the fact that they are not relevant, or insufficiently relevant, to the issues before the court.[9]

## Evidence from third parties

**6.4**     Evidence from third parties may be voluntary, in which case normal rules as to the relevance of their evidence apply. However, where their evidence is not given voluntarily, it may be necessary to issue a subpoena (or witness summons in the county court) to secure third parties' attendance at court; or where their evidence relates to documents which they are to produce, those documents – but no more – may be sought in advance of the final hearing by application for a production appointment which the third parties will be required to attend with the documents concerned.

---

1     [1996] 2 WLR 395, [1996] 1 FLR 731, HL; and see **7.18** below.
2     See further **10.35** below.
3     *F v F (Ancillary Relief: Substantial Assets)* [1995] 2 FLR 45 at 70A.
4     Whilst the Civil Procedure Rules 1998 may have rejected the term 'discovery' (see n 1 to **6.1** above), the term has been retained for family proceedings as recently as April 1998 in the Family Proceedings Rules 1991, r 2.73(3) (prohibition of discovery of documents after filing of Form A): see further **10.40** below.
5     In the Civil Procedure Rules 1998, the term 'interrogatory' in relation to non family proceedings has now gone, to be replaced by a power in the court – not apparently available on application of a party – to order a party to provide further information under r 18.1.
6     See **6.26** et seq below.
7     See Chapter 7.
8     See **7.33** below.
9     See **6.26** below; and for further consideration of relevance, see **4.44** et seq above.

## 2    DISCLOSURE

### Duty of disclosure[1]

**6.5**    The duty of disclosure may be said to arise in family proceedings from the quasi-inquisitorial role of the court within this jurisdiction. That role derives from what has been seen for many years as the paternalistic jurisdiction of the family courts. For example, in *Edgar v Edgar*,[2] Ormrod LJ referred back to earlier cases as authority for the proposition that a wife could not preclude the courts from adjudicating upon a claim for financial relief.[3] In *Hildebrand v Hildebrand*[4] Waite J explained this aspect of the family jurisdiction as follows:

> 'There is another important feature in the context of discovery which it is relevant to mention as applying in family cases. The jurisdiction is a paternal one, and, where financial proceedings are involved, the court is exercising not merely a paternal but also, in appropriate instances, an inquisitorial jurisdiction. Underlying the whole basis of the court's discretion under the amended s 25 of the Matrimonial Causes Act 1973 is the duty of both sides to provide the court with information about all the circumstances of the case, including, amongst other things, the particular matters specified in s 25.'

**6.6**    The majority of the earlier developments in the field of disclosure in the family jurisdiction have been in the field of financial relief.[5] The overriding duty the parties have to the court – not just to each other – to give full disclosure was enunciated by Lord Brandon of Oakbrook in *Livesey (formerly Jenkins) v Jenkins*:[6]

> '... each party concerned in claims for financial provision and property adjustment (or other forms of ancillary relief not material in the present case) owes a duty to the court to make full and frank disclosure of all material facts to the other party and to the court.'

### 'Full relevant disclosure'[7]

**6.7**    Lord Brandon in *Livesey (formerly Jenkins) v Jenkins* went on to describe the 'principle of full and frank disclosure' as explained by the duty upon the court to

---

1    The important subject of disclosure upon *ex parte* and interlocutory injunctions is dealt with at **13.14** below.

2    [1981] 1 WLR 1410, (1981) FLR 19, CA.

3    *Hyman v Hyman* [1929] AC 601, HL; and *Wright v Wright* [1970] 1 WLR 1219, CA considered by Ormrod LJ in *Edgar v Edgar* (1981) FLR 19 at 23A–F. The proposition considered in *Edgar* has a statutory basis in Matrimonial Causes Act 1973, s 34(1) which makes void any provision in a maintenance agreement which seeks 'to restrict any right to apply to a court for an order containing financial arrangements'.

4    [1992] 1 FLR 244 at 247F–G.

5    For example, as recently as March 1993, Douglas Brown was able to hold that proceedings under the Children Act 1989 were not paternal or administrative. Therefore, there was no duty to disclose a document covered by legal professional privilege (*Barking and Dagenham London Borough Council v O and Another* [1993] 2 FLR 651 at 655D–E). This position has since been radically altered by eg *Oxfordshire County Council v M* [1994] Fam 151, [1994] 1 FLR 175, CA; and *Re L (Police Investigation: Privilege)* [1996] 2 WLR 395, [1996] 1 FLR 731, HL (see further **7.18** et seq below).

6    [1985] AC 424, [1985] FLR 813, HL at 823B.

7    Lord Hailsham of St Marylebone LC preferred the term 'full relevant disclosure' ([1985] FLR at 815F) which, in the context of the rules of evidence (see relevant evidence at **4.4** et seq above) is

exercise its discretion under the Matrimonial Causes Act 1973, s 25[1] to which he had earlier referred:[2]

> '... in proceedings [for financial relief, the parties] must provide the court with information about all the circumstances of the case [including the matters specified in s 25(2)]. Unless they do so, directly or indirectly, and ensure that the information provided is correct, complete and up-to-date, the court is not equipped to exercise, and cannot therefore lawfully and properly exercise, its discretion in the manner ordained by s 25(1).'

With the greatest respect to Lord Brandon, an analysis of the Matrimonial Causes Act 1973, s 25 does not entirely bear out his analysis. That full disclosure is necessary for the court to exercise its discretion is beyond doubt. The duty can be implied only by Lord Brandon's own reading of s 25. The duty is not express within the terms of the section. Indeed, read literally, the duty is imposed upon the court to look at the circumstances of the case.[3] This imposes on the court the dual role in which it not unusually finds itself in family proceedings: on the one hand, discharging an essentially inquisitorial function[4] (ie to investigate the justice of a case, whether after a contested hearing or on considering a consent application); while on the other being required, within an adversarial process, to evaluate evidence and to adjudicate on issues between the parties.

**6.8** Lord Brandon's interpretation of s 25 has enabled him to create a totally new doctrine in the field of ancillary relief on marital breakdown.[5] That a party must give full relevant disclosure of all information material to an assessment of all the factors in s 25 may well be a logical inference from the section; but until *Livesey v Jenkins* this requirement had not been so clearly enunciated. New law was created, and the family jurisdiction began to develop a distinctive direction which begins necessarily to undermine doctrines relating to confidentiality and the, sometimes obstructive, secrecy of litigation privilege.

## Disclosure and the duty not to mislead the court

**6.9** In *Vernon v Bosley (No 2)*,[6] the Court of Appeal looked at disclosure in the context of a duty to the court. The court considered the question of whether a party to litigation has a duty to disclose a material change of circumstances known to him – and, in that case, known also to his counsel and solicitors – which occurred between close of his case and delivery of judgment. The case involved a claim based on the personality change suffered by the plaintiff as a result of his having witnessed the death of his children. In separate children proceedings, concerning the plaintiff's

---

to be preferred to the more generally used 'full and frank disclosure'; but it is probably too late to adopt Lord Hailsham's terminology in place of the more common terminology.

1　Similar terminology to s 25 can be found in Inheritance (Provision for Family and Dependants) Act 1975, s 3(1) in respect of claims under that Act so it may be assumed that a similar duty of disclosure falls on parties to applications under that Act.

2　[1985] AC 424, [1985] FLR 813, HL at 822B–C.

3　'It shall be the duty of the court in deciding whether to exercise its powers under section 23, 24 or 24A above and, if so, in what manner, to have regard to all the circumstances of the case ...'

4　See eg *dicta* of Waite J in *Hildebrand* [1992] 1 FLR 244 and Thorpe J in *F v F* [1995] 2 FLR 45.

5　It is striking that the duty of disclosure in civil proceedings applies only to documents, but that now it lasts 'until the proceedings are concluded' (Civil Procedure Rules 1998, r 31.11(1)).

6　[1997] 3 WLR 683, CA, Stuart-Smith and Thorpe LJJ, Evans LJ dissenting.

surviving children, a family court had received evidence that the plaintiff's psychological state had improved dramatically. Those proceedings took place between the judgment at first instance in the personal injury case and the hearing of the defendant's appeal. The defendant's counsel received a copy of the judgment in the children proceedings anonymously. The question arose, in the Court of Appeal, as to whether the plaintiff or his advisers should have disclosed their knowledge of the improved prognosis before judgment in the Court of Appeal. The issue of disclosure was approached on the basis of a duty not to mislead the court, a duty which rested on legal advisers and lay client alike.

### A party's duty not to mislead

**6.10** The duty of a party to proceedings not to mislead the court was explained by Stuart-Smith LJ as follows:[1]

> 'It is the duty of every litigant not to mislead the court or his opponent. He will obviously mislead the court if he gives evidence which he knows to be untrue. But he will also do so if, having led the court to believe a fact to be true, he fails to correct it when he discovers it to be false. This duty continues in my opinion until the judge has given judgment.'

He went on to explain the essential distinction between the entitlement of a party to call only such evidence as assists his case, as distinct from the duty of a party and his advisers 'to correct an incorrect appreciation which the court will otherwise have as a result of their conduct of the case hitherto'.[2] The first is a passive role, which enables a party to adversarial proceedings to omit evidence from a witness which does not assist his case, but prevents him from deliberately giving a misleading impression. Thus, there is no duty on a defendant to disclose previous convictions in a criminal trial, but he may not claim to be of good character, since that would be positively untrue. Similarly, as the law now stands,[3] a parent in children proceedings is not obliged to disclose to the court details of a psychiatric history which may have a bearing on the court's decision; but nor may that parent suggest, in evidence, that he has no history of psychiatric treatment if he knows that this is not the case.

### Legal adviser's duty not to mislead

**6.11** Legal representatives are in a precisely analogous position to a party to proceedings. Thus, solicitors and counsel alike have a duty not to mislead the court. For the solicitor the duty is expressed as follows: 'Solicitors who act in litigation, whilst under a duty to do their best for their client, must never deceive or mislead the court'.[4] Counsel's duty to the court was explained by Denning LJ in *Tombling v Universal Bulb Co Ltd*:[5]

> 'The duty of counsel to his client in a civil case – or in defending an accused person – is to make every honest endeavour to succeed. He must not, of course, knowingly mislead the

---

1     [1997] 3 WLR 683, at 698E.
2     Ibid, at 699G.
3     But see *Re L (Police Investigation: Privilege)* [1996] 2 WLR 395, [1996] 1 FLR 731, HL; and discussion at **7.18** below.
4     *The Guide to the Professional Conduct of Solicitors*, Principle 22.01 (The Law Society).
5     [1951] 2 TLR 289 at 297.

court, either on the facts or on the law, but, short of that, he may put such matters in evidence or omit such others as in his discretion he thinks will be most to the advantage of his client ... he is only the advocate of the client to speak for him and present his case, and he must do it to the best of his ability, without making himself the judge of its correctness, but only of its honesty.'

Thus, if another party does not unearth an inconvenient fact of which the plaintiff is aware, then in adversarial proceedings there is no duty on the plaintiff to disclose it. Similarly, a legal representative cannot stand by while a client deliberately misleads the court. However, *Vernon v Bosley (No 2)* takes the law further, providing that if there are facts of which the plaintiff and his advisers are aware, they may not allow the judge to proceed on a set of facts or assumptions which they know not to be the truth. In such circumstances the adviser's duty is to withdraw from the case if his client will not accept advice to disclose information to the court which will correct the error.

### *Legal adviser's duty to disclose on withdrawal from the case*

**6.12**    A final question arises as to what duty a legal adviser who withdraws owes to the court. Does he have any duty to disclose the information to the court, without which the court will have been misled? At the conclusion of his judgment in *Vernon v Bosley (No 2)*,[1] Thorpe LJ expressed the following view regarding:

'... counsel's obligation if his client demurs in the communication of necessary material to the judge. If counsel's duty goes no further than requiring his withdrawal from the case there seems to me to be a remaining risk of injustice. Of course such an event leads to speculation. But more than one inference is there to be drawn. I would hold that in those circumstances counsel has a duty to disclose the relevant material to his opponent and, unless there be agreement between the parties otherwise, to the judge.'

These remarks were made *obiter*. There is a certain logic to them, especially as to the judge's concern to avoid the 'remaining risk of injustice'. However, with the greatest respect to Thorpe LJ, he overlooked two fundamental factors: first, once he has withdrawn from the case a legal adviser is no longer on the court record as acting for the client – he has no further part in the proceedings; secondly, and far more important, Thorpe LJ ignored the whole doctrine of confidentiality and privilege,[2] ie that the advocate is no more than the client's *alter ego*. If the law were as Thorpe LJ suggested, the majority of the rules relating to privilege would need to be re-evaluated.

## Disclosure of documents obtained illegally ('self-help')

**6.13**    What happens where a party takes documents belonging to another party, an exercise known by some ancillary relief lawyers as 'self-help'? In *T v T (Interception of Documents)*,[3] the wife, in anticipation of the husband failing to disclose information, had opened his post and broken into his office to obtain information. In fact the husband did not make full disclosure and, in these circumstances, Wilson J took the view that it was reasonable for the wife to take documents without the use of

---

1    [1997] 3 WLR 683 at 723F.
2    See eg *R v Derby Magistrates' Court ex parte B* [1996] AC 487, [1996] 1 FLR 513, HL; and see further **7.8** below.
3    [1994] 2 FLR 1083, per Wilson J.

force and to take copies of those documents.[1] However, it was wrong that she used force, that she kept original documents and that she opened the husband's mail. Further, in relation to discovery the judge held[2] as follows:

> 'The original and copy documents which she had taken were discoverable documents and all those that she had in her possession at the discovery stage of the litigation should have been disclosed at that time, ie at the time of the delivery of her questionnaire, or earlier upon request. Those coming into her possession at a later stage should have been disclosed forthwith.'

**6.14** In the present context, the term 'discovery stage of the litigation' is imprecise. If the documents were discoverable – and of that there can be no doubt – then in this jurisdiction they should have been disclosed as soon as possible after exchange of affidavits by the wife to the husband; and that duty to disclose continued up to the date of trial.[3] In this particular case, any failure to disclose documents by Mr T should have been reasonably clear by comparing the documents obtained by the wife, to those documents disclosed by Mr T already or exhibited to his affidavit of means.

## Proceeding with only partial *inter partes* disclosure

**6.15** It is possible for the court to direct that material which might be damaging to a child shall not be disclosed to another party to the proceedings,[4] but such a direction will be obtained only where there are exceptional circumstances and where the welfare of a child demands it.[5] A direction will only rarely be made on the principle that, save in exceptional circumstances, a party to proceedings must always know the case against him and be heard upon it.[6] This was explained by Lord Mustill[7] as follows:

> '... it is a first principle of fairness that each party to a judicial process shall have an opportunity to answer by evidence and argument any adverse material which the tribunal may take into account when forming its opinion. This principle is lame if the party does not know the substance of what is said against him (or her), for what he does not know he cannot answer.'

---

1    It is not permissible to raise questions on documents in a party's possession which seek to trick the party questioned into answering questions to which the questioner already knows the answer (*Hildebrand v Hildebrand* [1992] 1 FLR 244, Waite J).
2    [1994] 2 FLR 1083 at 1085E–F.
3    *Livesey (formerly Jenkins) v Jenkins* [1985] AC 424, [1985] FLR 813, HL.
4    The Civil Procedure Rules 1998 seem only to restrict inspection or disclosure of a document where application is made to the court for the withholding of disclosure 'on the ground that disclosure would damage the public interest': r 31 19(1). No grounds on which a party may apply to the court are set out.
5    *Official Solicitor v K* [1965] AC 201, HL; followed in *Re B (A Minor) (Disclosure of Evidence)* [1993] 1 FLR 191, CA.
6    In a very different context, this right was explained by Lord Denning thus: 'If the right to be heard is to be a real right which is worth anything, it must carry with it a right in the accused man to know the case against him. He must know what evidence has been given and what statements have been made affecting him: and then he must be given a fair opportunity to correct or contradict them' (*Kanda v Government of Malaya* [1962] AC 322, HL).
7    *Re D (Adoption Reports: Confidentiality)* [1995] 2 FLR 687 at 689D–E, HL; and see further *dictum* to this effect at p 700G.

The question of whether or not information should be withheld is one for the judge to decide. In doing so, the judge will balance the need to do justice as between the parties, against the risk of detriment to the welfare of the child if evidence is fully disclosed. This conclusion was reached by Lord Evershed in *Official Solicitor v K* in the following terms:[1]

> 'When [this] situation arises ... there may well indeed have to be ... a "balancing" of the generally accepted right of a properly interested party, particularly a parent, to disclosure of information submitted to the judge upon which he proposes in some measure to base his conclusion (on the one hand) and the paramount interest of the ward of court (on the other hand). It may, however, be that, in such a situation, the latter consideration upon the balance should outweigh the former [subject to the judge being] well satisfied that the confidential information to which he proposes to pay regard is in truth reliable. ... The interest of the infant is the paramount interest and purpose of the jurisdiction. Disclosure or no disclosure therefore must in the end remain a matter for the judge's discretion ...'

**6.16**      The principles applicable to judicial limiting of disclosure has been considered more recently in the House of Lords, here in the context of adoption proceedings.[2] Lord Mustill considered the balancing exercise that the judge must conduct between 'the requirement of openness',[3] on the one hand, with, as he termed, the fact that 'pulling in the other direction is an impulse towards the confidentiality of sensitive information'.[4] He examined these two conflicting principles in the context of the Adoption Rules 1984, r 53[5] (custody, inspection and disclosure of documents and information). Rule 53(2) enables 'a party who is an individual and is referred to in a confidential report' to inspect 'that part of [a confidential] report which refers to him, subject to any direction given by the court' as to partial or total non-disclosure or disclosure only to legal advisers. Lord Mustill characterises this sub-rule as reflecting 'the tension between the two principles to which I have referred, but leaves it to be resolved by the court according to the circumstances of the individual case'.[6] He then set himself the task of reconciling 'the conflict between the two conflicting policies', while recognising that complete reconciliation was impossible.[7] He started from the following presumption:[8]

> 'For my part I have no hesitation in saying that a strong presumption in favour of disclosing to a party any material relating to him or her is the point at which the judge should start. It is true, as frequently emphasised, that the requirements of natural justice are not invariable, and that circumstances must alter cases. Nevertheless the opportunity to know about and respond to adverse materials is at the heart of a fair hearing.'

Having started from this presumption, Lord Mustill proceeded to analyse *Official Solicitor v K* and to draw attention to one of the conclusions of that case: that disclosure should be withheld from a party or parent only 'in rare cases and where [the

---

1      [1965] AC 201 at 219 and 220.
2      *Re D (Adoption Reports: Confidentiality)* [1995] 2 FLR 687.
3      A requirement which Lord Mustill regarded as 'particularly important in proceedings for adoption' (ibid, at 689E).
4      Ibid, at 689E and 689G.
5      SI 1984/265.
6      Ibid, at 691F.
7      Ibid, at 694E.
8      Ibid, at 694F.

judge] is fully satisfied judicially that real harm to the infant must otherwise ensue'.[1] He concluded his speech by suggesting that the test for withholding disclosure, certainly in adoption cases, should be not as high as suggested by Lord Evershed in *Official Solicitor v K*, but that it should remain high:[2]

'The presumption in favour of disclosure is strong indeed, but not so strong that it can be withheld only if the judge is satisfied that real harm to the child *must* otherwise ensue.'

### Test in *Official Solicitor v K* in Children Act 1989 proceedings

**6.17**   In *Re B (A Minor) (Disclosure of Evidence)*,[3] the Court of Appeal was confronted by a case in which a 15-year-old girl had made allegations of sexual abuse against her stepfather. She was afraid that if he found out he would kill her. Her mother applied to terminate his contact with her and sought an order that her affidavit not be disclosed to the stepfather. The Court of Appeal refused her application but, in so doing, it looked at the question of whether the principles in *Official Solicitor v K* applied only in wardship or to other children proceedings. Glidewell LJ held that those principles applied equally in proceedings under the Children Act 1989. He referred in particular to *Re C (A Minor: Irregularity of Practice)*[4] where the Court of Appeal had held, as he saw it, as follows:[5]

'... it was permissible for a judge in the exercise of his discretion and acting in the paramount interests of the child, to see a court welfare officer privately in his chambers during a trial, and that there was no absolute objection to the receipt of a confidential report, but that the judge should only exercise his discretion to adopt either of these courses in exceptional circumstances.'

Consequently, he went on to hold that:[6]

'In my opinion, therefore, a court which is considering an application for an order under ss 8 and 10 of the Children Act 1989 has the power, in its discretion, to receive and act on evidence adduced by one party, or emanating from a welfare officer, which is not disclosed to another party.'

### Disclosure denied: only in 'exceptional circumstances'

**6.18**   In reaching the above conclusion, Glidewell LJ stressed the need for a judge, when exercising his discretion in accordance with *Official Solicitor v K*, to exclude disclosure from one party only in 'exceptional circumstances'. Balcombe LJ supported this criterion for limiting disclosure:[7] 'The jurisdiction should only be exercised in exceptional circumstances, and then only for the shortest period possible consonant with preserving the welfare of the child'. In *Re M (Minors) (Disclosure of*

---

1    *Official Solicitor v K* [1965] AC 201 quoted by Lord Mustill in *Re D (Adoption Reports: Confidentiality)* [1995] 2 FLR 687 at 696C.
2    [1995] 2 FLR 687 at 699H.
3    [1993] 1 FLR 191, CA.
4    [1991] 2 FLR 438, CA – a case under the Guardianship of Minors Act 1971.
5    [1993] 1 FLR 191 at 200H–201A.
6    Ibid, at 201C.
7    Ibid, at 201D and 203E. In this case, the Court of Appeal rejected the mother's application that the court should deal with the case without the father seeing evidence against him.

*Evidence),*[1] Butler-Sloss LJ concurred with the views expressed in *Re B*, that the principles set out in *Official Solicitor v K* applied to Children Act 1989 proceedings. In *Re M* the judge below had taken the view that he could exclude parts of a report if to fail to do so might pose a significant risk to the children. Butler-Sloss LJ held that this was not a sufficiently stringent test, preferring the test of whether disclosure would cause a possibility of 'real harm' to the child.[2]

### Disclosure and the mature child

**6.19**    In *Re C (Disclosure)*,[3] Johnson J was confronted by the question of whether or not information given by a 16-year-old (C) to the guardian ad litem in care proceedings could be withheld from her mother. The guardian suggested that only the mother's solicitor should receive the information on terms that it was not passed on to the client. The solicitor said that his instructions did not permit this. It was then a matter of whether or not the court could deny disclosure of the information to the mother but allow the care application to proceed. Johnson J approached the question in the light of *Official Solicitor v K*. He considered that C was of an age and understanding within the terms of *Gillick*[4] and that 'were it not for her involvement in these proceedings there could be no compulsion upon her to disclose this information to her mother'.[5] This being the case, the approach he adopted was to consider the importance of the relationship between C and the guardian ad litem and her social workers. If that were destroyed it would damage C. C did not want the information disclosed, however important it might be objectively. Johnson J therefore concluded:[6]

> '. . . it is my view that such disclosure would destroy C's faith in those who are seeking to help her and it is for this reason that I have concluded that disclosure would most probably result in real harm to C.'

### Partial disclosure after Re D

**6.20**    In *Re C (Disclosure)*,[7] Johnson J quoted both from *Re D (Adoption Reports: Confidentiality)* (above) and *Official Solicitor v K*, and based his conclusions on *dicta* from both cases, citing first a section from the speech of Lord Jenkins in *Official Solicitor v K*,[8] which concluded that 'any attempt to formulate general pronouncements applicable to all cases will be likely to create more difficulties than it solves'. *Re D* applied to adoption proceedings, while *Official Solicitor v K* applied to a wardship summons. Glidewell LJ approved the *Official Solicitor v K* principles to Children Act 1989 applications. Johnson J applied both cases to a later Children Act 1989 case. For most purposes, in the context of children proceedings generally, it would seem to be a sterile argument to distinguish levels of applicability of both cases. It may be that, because of the special nature of adoption proceedings – that the parental tie can be

---

1    [1994] 1 FLR 760, CA.
2    Ibid, at 764D.
3    [1996] 1 FLR 797.
4    *Gillick v West Norfolk and Wisbech Area Health Authority and Another* [1986] 1 AC 112, [1986] 1 FLR 224, HL.
5    [1996] 1 FLR 797 at 804B.
6    Ibid, at 803H.
7    Ibid, at 801G–803F.
8    Ibid, at 801H (from *Official Solicitor v K* [1965] AC 201 at 232E).

broken irrevocably – a higher test applies. However, in the final analysis, the test is 'real harm' to the child set against the presumption that disclosure should be generally ordered. As Johnson J held in *Re C*, 'real harm' must be the probable – not the inevitable – result of disclosure;[1] and it is for the judge, in his discretion, to decide, on the facts of the particular case and the particular information concerned, whether the probability of harm to the child outweighs the presumption in favour of disclosure.

## Remedies for material non-disclosure[2]

**6.21** The High Court has an inherent jurisdiction to set aside its orders made where there has been fraud, mistake or material non-disclosure.[3] No such inherent jurisdiction exists in the county court (for example under the County Courts Act 1984, s 38) since by the County Court Rules 1981, Ord 37, r 1 a statutory route is provided.[4] This rule provides that a judge has power to order a rehearing 'where no error of the court at the hearing is alleged';[5] that is to say, the decision whether or not to set aside an order is a matter for the discretion of the judge.

### *'No error of the court'*

**6.22** The classic explanation of what is meant by an 'error of the court' was provided by Lord Merriman P in *Peek v Peek*:[6]

'Is the allegation which is being made against the decision an allegation that the court went wrong on the materials before it, or is it an allegation that the court went wrong because evidence on a vital matter was concealed from the court?'

If the allegation is that the court 'went wrong on the materials before it' then the remedy is by way of appeal to the appropriate appellate court;[7] whereas if it is said that the court did not have the information in the first place, for example because disclosure was not complete, then the application is to set aside the original order.[8] These two options for rehearing – appeal or set aside – must be distinguished from the

---

1     [1996] 1 FLR 797 at 803H (quoted at **6.19** above).
2     This subject will be considered in more detail at **13.15** et seq in relation to orders for financial relief.
3     See eg *de Lasala v de Lasala* [1980] AC 546, (1979) FLR Rep 223, HL especially at 561C and 232E, per Lord Diplock.
4     See the careful analysis of this question by Richard Anelay QC (sitting as a deputy judge of the High Court) in *T v T (Consent Order: Procedure to Set Aside)* [1996] 2 FLR 640, especially at 656C–661B.
5     County Court Rules 1981, Ord 37, r 1(1).
6     [1948] P 46 at 60 (affirmed by the Court of Appeal at [1948] 2 All ER 297, CA).
7     Eg district judge to circuit judge (County Court Rules 1981, Ord 37, r 6; Family Proceedings Rules 1991, r 8.1(1)); judge to the Court of Appeal (Rules of the Supreme Court 1965, Ord 59).
8     It is beyond the scope of this book to consider procedure in any detail. In his cerebral treatment of the subject, Ward J explains the procedure in *B-T v B-T (Divorce: Procedure)* [1990] 2 FLR 1; but many practitioners may prefer (with the greatest respect to Ward J) the more straightforward

further questions of: (1) applications to the appellate court to receive fresh evidence;[1] and (2) applications for leave to appeal out of time.[2]

### *Material non-disclosure*

**6.23**     For present purposes, the essence of whether or not an order may be set aside turns on whether or not the non-disclosure was material to the decision of the court: did the court go wrong 'because evidence on a *vital* matter was concealed from' it? (to paraphrase Lord Merriman P). Thus, it will be necessary for an applicant seeking to set aside an order to show not only that relevant evidence was not disclosed, but that evidence would have had a bearing on the court's decision. This was explained by Lord Brandon in *Livesey (formerly Jenkins) v Jenkins*[3] as follows:

> 'I would end with an emphatic word of warning. It is not every failure of frank and full disclosure which would justify a court in setting aside an order of the kind concerned in this appeal. On the contrary, it will only be in cases when the absence of full and frank disclosure has led to the court making, either in contested proceedings or by consent, an order which is substantially different from the order which it would have made if such disclosure had taken place that a case for setting aside can possibly be made good.'

If the failure to disclose is only of 'some relatively minor matter . . . which would not have made any substantial difference to the order', any application to set aside is likely to be dismissed with costs. Thus, for example, evidence concerning a child may be relevant to an issue before the court, in strict evidential terms; but on any application to set aside its order the court will go further than looking only at the relevance of the evidence withheld from it. It will consider the questions: if this evidence had been put before us would it substantially have altered the decision which was made; would it have altered the way in which the court's discretion was exercised when the original order was made? If the answers to these questions are 'no' or 'probably not', it is unlikely that the court will exercise its discretion to set aside the original order.

**6.24**     If the failure to disclose is fraudulent,[4] different principles are likely to apply. It will still be necessary to show that the failure to disclose was material to the decision of the court, but the onus which the applicant will have to discharge is likely to be greater than in cases of innocent or negligent failure to disclose.[5] In explaining his decision to order the setting aside of a seven-year-old order, Richard Anely QC (sitting as a High Court judge) held that he was 'particularly influenced by the fact that by reason of the husband's fraudulent non-disclosure the court was prevented from properly exercising its powers under Matrimonial Causes Act 1973, s 25'.[6]

---

approach to the subject suggested by Thorpe J in *Re C (Financial Provision: Leave to Appeal)* [1993] 2 FLR 799.

1     *Ladd v Marshall* [1954] 1 WLR 1489, [1954] 3 All ER 745, CA; *Mulholland v Mitchell* [1971] AC 666, HL; and see **14.27** et seq below.

2     *Barder v Barder (Caluori Intervening)* [1988] AC 20, [1987] 2 FLR 480, HL.

3     [1985] AC 424, [1985] FLR 813 at 830E, HL.

4     See eg *de Lasala v de Lasala* [1980] AC 546, and see **6.21**.

5     For an example of an adoption order set aside on grounds of fraud or mistake, see *Re M (A Minor)* (1990) *Adoption and Fostering* 48.

6     *T v T (Consent Order: Procedure to Set Aside)* [1996] 2 FLR 640 at 664G.

## Disclosure and the Child Support Act 1991

**6.25**    Disclosure in the context of the Child Support Act 1991 can be considered only as a postscript as the law now stands. The scheme set up by the Act and the regulations under it comply, at present, with principles of confidentiality which those familiar with social security legislation will know, but is totally at odds with the concept of full disclosure recognised by family lawyers. Thus, on the making of an assessment, minimal information will be provided to the parties as to the other's means. On an appeal to the Child Support Appeal Tribunal, this information will be fleshed out a little, but it is necessary to file notice of appeal to obtain the information. As between the parties and the Child Support Agency (CSA), there is no continuing duty of disclosure. However, where an absent parent seeks information as to the basis on which the CSA has arrived at its decision – which he considers may be erroneous – that the person with care should receive benefit, there is at present no basis on which he can obtain disclosure of the information from the CSA.[1]

## 3   DISCOVERY AND PRE-TRIAL IDENTIFICATION OF RELEVANT EVIDENCE

### Identification of relevant documents

**6.26**    The principle of discovery[2] imposes upon parties to proceedings the duty to identify relevant documentary material to one another. In family proceedings, formal discovery will rarely be given by parties in the way which is the norm in other civil proceedings;[3] or, where it is required by a party, it will be by formal request.[4] However, rare though formal discovery may be in family proceedings, Wall J has reminded practitioners[5] of the availability of the pre-trial discovery procedure which may be invoked in all family proceedings.[6] While discovery is limited to identifying relevant documents, the pre-trial process of identification of evidence extends also to interrogatories, questionnaires and the production appointment; and it will be convenient to consider each of these aspects of evidence here since they are all part of similar pre-trial procedures and governed by similar principles. It is not the intention of what follows to consider procedure in any detail, but procedural aspects of the subject and reference to the relevant rules will, from time to time, be inevitable. Before looking at pre-trial identification of evidence, a number of preliminary points need to be made.

---

1    This question is the subject of an application for judicial review by an absent parent which awaits adjudication by the High Court.
2    Now 'disclosure' of documents under the Civil Procedure Rules 1998 in relation to non family proceedings, Part 31: see **6.3** above.
3    Rules of the Supreme Court 1965, Ord 24: see **6.30** et seq below.
4    See eg Family Proceedings Rules 1991, rr 2.63 and 2.73(4)(a).
5    *Re JC (Care Proceedings: Procedure)* [1995] 2 FLR 77 at 83D.
6    By virtue of Family Proceedings Rules 1991, r 1.3(1), Rules of the Supreme Court 1965, Ord 24 will apply in family proceedings to the extent to which the Order is not inconsistent with the Family Proceedings Rules 1991; but see **1.34** above.

## Relevance of evidence

**6.27** Some of the more astringent comments from the bench in recent years have derived from the frequent inability (or so it seems) of some lawyers to distinguish relevant documents from those which are irrelevant or, at best, only barely relevant.[1] A theme running through what follows will be the question of paying careful attention to relevance of the evidence which is requested by one party, while, of course, the same attention to relevance is necessary for that party in the presentation of his evidence.

## Discretionary remedy

**6.28** Discovery is an equitable remedy, derived from the jurisdiction of the Court of Chancery. To order discovery is therefore a matter of the court's discretion in each case.[2] In the context of the relevance of evidence[3] consideration has already been given to the extent to which the court may refuse to order that evidence be provided: for example on the grounds that to order the production of the documents or information requested would be oppressive, insufficiently relevant to the issues before the court or not justified on the grounds of cost.[4] These principles will require reconsideration in the context of pre-trial preparation, and may prove pivotal from the point of view of the judiciary in its management of cases.[5]

## Privilege

**6.29** Essential to the question of discovery and pre-trial identification of evidence are the rules relating to privilege, confidentiality and public interest immunity. These rules enable the court – sometimes as a matter of law or public policy, sometimes as a matter of discretion – to exclude evidence from disclosure, and are the subject of separate treatment in Chapter 7.

---

1   See eg the comments of Ward LJ at the conclusion of *G v G (Periodical Payments: Jurisdiction)* [1997] 1 FLR 368 at 383E, CA: 'We were presented with a cardboard carton of six arch-lever files containing about 1200 pages of material totally irrelevant on this appeal ... Such copying represents a total waste ... It is now time that practitioners take note of *The Supreme Court Practice* ... paras 59/9/16–59/9/18 and the taxing master's powers to disallow costs of unnecessary copying. I shall invite him to consider such a course in this case'.

2   Under the Civil Procedure Rules 1998 in respect of non family proceedings, there is no express reference to the sorts of equitable terminology in the old rules ('necessary ... for disposing fairly of the cause or matter': Rules of the Supreme Court 1965, Order 24, r 8), save in respect of the overriding principle of the case being dealt with in ways 'proportionate' to the issues (Civil Procedure Rules 1998, rr 1.1(2)(c) and 31.3(2)).

3   See **4.4** et seq above.

4   Rules of the Supreme Court 1965, Order 24, r 8; and see principle that cases be dealt with in a way proportionate to the issues in Civil Procedure Rules 1998, r 1.1(2)(c) and r 31.3(2).

5   This was explained by Hoffmann J in *Arab Monetary Fund v Hashim (No 5)* [1992] 2 All ER 911 at 913 (in the context of a fraud case) as follows: 'The function of the judge [at the interlocutory stage of an action] is not so much to decide or even define the issues between the parties as to supervise an investigation by the plaintiff [eg] requiring defendants to permit searches for evidence, demanding documents and information from third parties'.

# Discovery

## *Discovery defined*

**6.30**     Discovery applies to documents and to the right of a party to any application to the court to have sight of all documents relevant to that application. It has been judicially defined by Dunn J in the context of divorce proceedings as follows:[1]

> 'A party to a suit must disclose [ie give discovery of] all the documents in his possession, custody or power which are relevant to the matters in issue. The court has a discretion whether or not to order him to make disclosure [ie discovery] ... The discretion is a judicial discretion, and in exercising it the court will have regard to all the circumstances.'

Thus, Dunn J stressed the discretionary nature of the remedy; and 'all the circumstances' to which he referred will include such matters as whether the discovery requested is 'necessary for the disposing fairly of the cause or matter or for saving costs'.[2]

## *Discovery by order*

**6.31**     The rules relating to discovery are now set out in the Rules of the Supreme Court 1965, Ord 24.[3] Rule 3[4] provides that:

> 'The court may order a party to a cause or matter (whether begun by writ, originating summons or otherwise) to make and serve on any other party a list of the documents which are or have been in his possession, custody or power relating to any matter in question in the cause or matter.'

Thus, where documents are not disclosed voluntarily, discovery can be ordered by the court. Discovery of documents may be ordered, or a party may seek disclosure of facts (as distinct from documents) by interrogatories.[5] Special rules apply in connection with matrimonial financial relief,[6] although, in financial relief proceedings covered by the Ancillary Relief Pilot Scheme, discovery is restricted only to such specific discovery as is ordered by the court.[7] Discovery applies only as between parties to an application, and continues until the date of judgment.[8] The evidence of third parties may be obtained by witness summons or subpoena by production appointment.[9]

---

1    *B v B (Matrimonial Proceedings: Discovery)* [1978] Fam 181 at 193, [1979] 1 All ER 801 at 811.
2    Rules of the Supreme Court 1965, Ord 24, r 8; and see further **6.30** et seq below.
3    The equivalent rules in the county courts are County Court Rules 1981, Ord 14, rr 1–10; in respect of non family proceedings, see Civil Procedure Rules 1998, Part 31.
4    The equivalent rule to this is County Court Rules 1981, Ord 14, r 1; in respect of non family proceedings, see Civil Procedure Rules 1998, r 31.12.
5    For interrogatories, see **6.37** et seq below.
6    Family Proceedings Rules 1991, r 2.63 enables a party to matrimonial financial relief proceedings to seek information, lists of documents and discovery; see further **10.12** below. (In proceedings for financial provision for children under Children Act 1989, Sch 1, where facts about a parent's financial circumstances are requested, there is no equivalent to Family Proceedings Rules 1991, r 2.63 and, as such, it appears that interrogatories must be raised.)
7    Family Proceedings Rules 1991, r 2.73(3) and (4)(a); and see **10.40** below.
8    *Vernon v Bosley (No 2)* [1997] 3 WLR 683, CA; and, in respect of non family proceedings, see Civil Procedure Rules 1998, r 31.11(1) (cf **6.9** et seq above).
9    For the evidence of third parties, see **6.40** et seq below.

Documents obtained on discovery can be used only for the purposes of the case, and there is an implied undertaking to this effect.[1] In children proceedings, documents may be disclosed to third parties only with leave of the court, save as set out in the rules.[2] The term 'document' can include not only information on paper or copies of such documents, but also information stored on computer[3] and information on video.[4]

### Documents in 'possession, custody or power'

**6.32**    The reference to 'documents in his possession, custody or power'[5] extends not only to documents which are still held by a party, but also those relevant to the case which have been held by him and those which others (eg his solicitor, his accountant or a member of his staff) hold for him. Thus, in *T v T (Consent Order: Procedure to Set Aside),*[6] the husband failed to disclose accounts and correspondence between a firm of which he was a director and a prospective purchaser relating to a period when, had they been disclosed, the wife's advisers would have realised what was happening in relation to the future acquisition of his company. He had a duty to disclose the documents, or at least the information they contained; but had he been subjected to an order for formal discovery within the terms of Rules of the Supreme Court 1965, Ord 24, r 3 the accounts would have been discoverable.[7]

**6.33**    Formally, documents are required to be listed and the lists exchanged.[8] If a party wishes 'to claim that any documents are privileged from production', the documents must still be listed and the reason for claiming privilege set out.[9] If a party wishes to challenge whether or not a document is privileged, it will be necessary to apply to the court by summons or notice of application for a determination on that preliminary issue.[10]

---

1    *Home Office v Harman* [1983] AC 280, [1983] 1 All ER 532, HL.
2    Family Proceedings Rules 1991, r 4.23; Family Proceedings Courts (Children Act 1989) Rules 1991, SI 1991/1395, r 23.
3    *Derby & Co Ltd v Weldon (No 9)* [1991] 1 WLR 652, [1991] 2 All ER 901.
4    See eg *B v B (Court Bundles: Video Evidence)* [1994] 2 FLR 323, per Wall J (orse *Practice Note (11 November 1993)* para 15); *Re R (Child Abuse: Video Evidence)* [1995] 1 FLR 451, per Johnson J).
5    Rules of the Supreme Court 1965, Ord 24, r 3(1); County Court Rules 1981, Ord 14, r 1(1); and, in respect of non family proceedings, see Civil Procedure Rules 1998, r 31.8(1).
6    [1996] 2 FLR 640 at 649G–651H, per Richard Anelay QC sitting as a deputy judge of the High Court; and see further consideration of this case at **6.24** above.
7    It is possible that the correspondence to which he had access as a director of the company would not have been discoverable (*B v B (Matrimonial Proceedings: Discovery)* [1978] Fam 181, [1979] 1 All ER 801, per Dunn J).
8    Rules of the Supreme Court 1965, Ord 24, r 5(1); County Court Rules 1981, Ord 14, r 1(1); and, in respect of non family proceedings, see Civil Procedure Rules 1998, r 31.10(2).
9    Rules of the Supreme Court 1965, Ord 24, r 5(2); County Court Rules 1981, Ord 14, r 5(1)(a) and 8; and, in respect of non family proceedings, see Civil Procedure Rules, r 31.10(4). See Chapter 7 for a further consideration of the subject of privilege.
10    See eg *Re C (Expert Evidence: Disclosure: Practice)* [1995] 1 FLR 204 where Cazalet J explains the procedure for the local authority to adopt when seeking public interest immunity; and now, in respect of non family proceedings, see Civil Procedure Rules 1998, r 31.19.

### *Necessary for disposing fairly of the proceedings or for the saving of costs*

**6.34**    The Rules of the Supreme Court 1965, Ord 24, r 8 provides that an application for discovery should be dismissed if it is regarded by the court as not necessary; and the court:[1]

> 'shall in any case refuse to make an [order for discovery] if and so far as it is of the opinion that discovery is not necessary either for disposing fairly of the cause or matter or for saving costs.'

This rule is drafted in almost identical terms to Ord 26, r 1(1) (interrogatories); and certain of the principles which apply to interrogatories can be considered in relation to the necessity for discovery.[2] In particular, in relation to discovery, the following will not be allowed: (a) discovery of documents which are not relevant, or not sufficiently relevant, to the issues before the court;[3] and (b) discovery which is regarded as oppressive.[4]

**6.35**    The question of saving of costs is likely to gain increasing prominence as the climate generated by *Woolf* bears fruit.[5] Already, it has been suggested that in the interests of 'reducing the cost and delay of civil litigation' the court should 'exercise its discretion to limit – (a) discovery'.[6] Where the court's brake on discovery has not held, costs thrown away as a result of indiscriminate or unnecessary discovery are likely to be lost.[7]

### *Court bundles*

**6.36**    It is not intended here to consider the preparation of court bundles in any detail;[8] but it is plainly very important that practitioners bear in mind the relevance – in terms of the rules of evidence – of disclosed material when bundles are prepared.

---

1   Rules of the Supreme Court 1965, Ord 24, rr 8 and 13(1); County Court Rules 1981, Ord 14, r 8. There is no equivalent provision in the Civil Procedure Rules 1998.
2   For a full note on this subject, see *The Supreme Court Practice 1999* (Sweet & Maxwell) paras 26/1/2–26/1/7.
3   See eg *Thyssen-Bornemisza v Thyssen-Bornemisza (No 2)* [1985] FLR 1069, CA; and see **4.17** above.
4   See eg *Hildebrand v Hildebrand* [1992] 1 FLR 244, per Waite J and *Thyssen-Bornemisza v Thyssen-Bornemisza (No 2)* (above); and see **4.17** above.
5   Lord Woolf MR *Access to Justice: Final Report* (HMSO, July 1996). See also costs savings as one of the objects of the Ancillary Relief Pilot Scheme (Family Proceedings Rules 1991, rr 2.74 (1) and 2.76); Burrows *Ancillary Relief Pilot Scheme – A Practice Guide* (Family Law, 1997) paras 1.10 and 7.7 et seq; and see **10.35** below; and see Civil Procedure Rules 1998, r 1.1.
6   *Practice Direction of 31 January 1995 (Case Management)* [1995] 1 WLR 332, [1995] 1 FLR 456, at paras 1 and 2.
7   See eg the comments of Ward LJ in *G v G (Periodical Payments: Jurisdiction)* [1997] 1 FLR 368, CA, quoted at n 1 to **6.27** above; and see Civil Procedure Rules 1998, r 44.3(5) (the court's powers to take account of a party's conduct in assessment of costs).
8   Wall J makes extensive suggestions for preparation of bundles in *B v B (Court Bundles: Video Evidence)* [1994] 1 FLR 323. Directions for preparation of bundles for the Court of Appeal are dealt with in *Practice Direction of 26 July 1995 (Court of Appeal: Procedure)* [1995] 3 WLR 1191, [1995] 3 All ER 850, at Part II; and see *Practice Direction (Court of Appeal: Revised Procedure)* [1997] 1 WLR 1013 (which further limits bundles of documents).

Disclosed documents, after 'rigorous pruning of unnecessary material',[1] should be prepared for the hearing[2] or as directed by the court; and documents appropriate for a 'proper understanding of the case' should be easily identifiable.[3] The question of over-burdening a case with documents has led to the exceptional provision in the Ancillary Relief Pilot Scheme forbidding all discovery after issue of proceedings save by request to the court.[4]

## Interrogatories

**6.37**    In view of the other remedies available for raising questions of other parties in parts of the family jurisdiction[5] and of the lack of defined pleadings as against other civil proceedings, interrogatories[6] are likely to feature little in family proceedings. Indeed, in *Hildebrand v Hildebrand*,[7] Waite J left open the question of whether interrogatories applied at all in the matrimonial financial relief jurisdiction in view of the 'very wide scope of [Family Proceedings Rules 1991, r 2.63]'.[8] However, that said interrogatories may be raised in defended divorce proceedings[9] (hardly a significant intrusion into the family jurisdiction); and it would seem that interrogatories are the only way in which enquiries can be made, for example, in proceedings for financial relief for children under the Children Act 1989, s 17 and Sch 1.[10]

### *Applicability of interrogatories in family proceedings*

**6.38**    While this treatment does not pretend to be the academic debate to which Waite J consigned interrogatories in financial relief proceedings,[11] it is relevant to consider briefly the subject of interrogatories in the present context. Interrogatories may be raised in the High Court under the Rules of the Supreme Court 1965, Ord 26 and in the county courts under the County Court Rules 1981, Ord 14, r 11;[12] and these rules will apply to family proceedings covered by the Family Proceedings Rules

---

1    *B v B (Court Bundles: Video Evidence)* (above), otherwise *Practice Note of 11 November 1993*, at para 10, per Wall J.
2    *Practice Direction of 31 January 1995 (Case Management)* [1995] 1 FLR 456, at para 5.
3    Ibid, at para 8.
4    Family Proceedings Rules 1991, r 2.73(3) and (4)(a). This provision, which is anyway of doubtful legitimacy, is unlikely to find its way into any final version of the new scheme.
5    See eg the questionnaire under Family Proceedings Rules 1991, r 2.63 (requests for further information in ancillary relief proceedings, applicable also in proceedings under the Family Law Act 1996, Part IV: Family Proceedings Rules 1991, r 3.9, considered further at **10.30** below).
6    In respect of non family proceedings, see Civil Procedure Rules 1998, Part 18 (requests for further information).
7    [1992] 1 FLR 244; and see further consideration of this case at **6.5** above.
8    Ibid, at 247E.
9    Family Proceedings Rules 1991, r 2.21; and see eg *Butterworth v Butterworth* [1997] 2 FLR 336, CA.
10   Family Proceedings Rules 1991, r 2.63 applies only to 'any party to an application for ancillary relief'.
11   'I am content to leave [the question of whether or not interrogatories apply in ancillary relief proceedings] to be debated by the academics until it is decided in some case where it arises directly for consideration' (*Hildebrand v Hildebrand* [1992] 1 FLR 244, at 247E).
12   Order 14, r 11 does little more than apply the provisions of Rules of the Supreme Court 1965, Ord 26 in the county courts; and, in respect of non family proceedings, see Civil Procedure Rules 1998, Part 18 (Further Information) and Practice Direction PD 18 which sets out the procedures to be followed by parties in seeking further information.

1991[1]. The only obvious advantages of interrogatories over the Family Proceedings Rules 1991, r 2.63 questionnaire is that the replies must be made on oath[2] (unless the court otherwise directs); and the remedies for non-compliance with interrogatories are relatively prompt and, where necessary, punitive.[3]

**6.39** The object of interrogatories is to enable a party to proceedings ('the applicant') to seek information:[4]

> 'relating to any matter in question between the applicant and [another party to] the cause or matter which are necessary either – (a) for disposing fairly of the cause or matter, or (b) for saving costs.'

As with discovery generally, a discretion is vested in the court over whether or not to order interrogatories which have not been answered voluntarily. The interrogatories must not only relate to matters which are relevant to the issues between the parties, but they must also be 'necessary' for the disposing of the matter fairly.[5] The main bases for present purposes for the refusal of interrogatories relate to: whether or not they are relevant to the issues before the court; whether the answering of the interrogatories will be to save costs;[6] whether the interrogatories are oppressive;[7] and whether the information sought by the interrogatory is privileged.[8] Further, as with any enquiry for further information, the applicant for the information must recall that the party of whom information is to be sought will be present at trial to be cross-examined. To identify as much pre-trial information may be generally desirable, but to do so at unnecessary expense may be counter-productive.[9]

## 4 EVIDENCE FROM THIRD PARTIES

### Witnesses: subpoena and the witness summons

**6.40** Where evidence is required from a third party which will not be given voluntarily, it will be necessary to issue a witness summons (in the county court) or a subpoena (in the High Court).[10] For hearings in chambers in the High Court, leave is

---

1 By virtue of Family Proceedings Rules 1991, r 1.3(1), Ord 26 will apply in family proceedings to the extent to which they are not inconsistent with the Family Proceedings Rules 1991.
2 Rules of the Supreme Court 1965, Ord 26, r 2(2).
3 Ibid, Ord 26, r 6.
4 Ibid, Ord 26, r 1.
5 The principles upon which interrogatories may be administered or will be ordered by the court are set out in *The Supreme Court Practice 1999* (Sweet & Maxwell) paras 26/1/2–26/1/7.
6 See eg *Thyssen-Bornemisza v Thyssen-Bornemisza (No 2)* [1995] FLR 1069, CA; considered at **4.17** above.
7 For the question of oppressive enquiry, see eg *Frary v Frary and Another* [1993] 2 FLR 696, CA; considered further at **4.15** above.
8 The subject of privilege is considered at Chapter 7.
9 See eg principle No 3(a) in *The Supreme Court Practice 1999* (Sweet & Maxwell) at para 26/1/4: '(a) Interrogatories will not generally be allowed where the object is to obtain an admission of a fact which can be proved by a witness who will in any case be called at the trial, and therefore the interrogatory will not save but add to costs'.
10 In non family proceedings, Civil Procedure Rules 1998, Part 34 deals with issue of a witness summons (the term 'subpoena' disappears).

required for issue of a subpoena.[1] Otherwise – ie for hearings in open court and for all hearings in the county court (save in the unlikely event that a witness is required at a directions appointment)[2] – a subpoena or witness summons issues as of right[3] provided the correct formalities are complied with.[4] However, a witness may apply to the court which issued the subpoena or witness summons, for it to be set aside on the grounds analogous to refusal of discovery or interrogatories,[5] for example that it is oppressive[6] or that it is regarded by the court as irrelevant to the issues or too speculative.[7]

## The production appointment

### *Ancillary to subpoena duces tecum*

**6.41**    The production appointment is not a free-standing remedy, but one which is ancillary to the court's powers to issue a subpoena *duces tecum*. This was explained thus by Ralph Gibson LJ in *Frary v Frary and Another*:[8]

> 'The effect of r 2.62(7) [of the Family Proceedings Rules 1991] is to bring forward the time at which a witness may be required to attend. . . . The new rule prescribes an order for production – that is to say, an order in the nature of subpoena *duces tecum* to be made to operate before the hearing but limited by r 2.62(8) to the production of documents which could be compelled at the hearing. Thus, if the court would issue a subpoena *duces tecum* or make an order for the production of documents at trial, it can make that order for production at a production appointment under the rule.'

The important component of the rule is, therefore, the question of whether or not the court would order production of documents or permit a subpoena *duces tecum* to be complied with by a witness: this was the issue under consideration in *Frary*.[9] Secondary to this is the question of whether or not a production appointment should be ordered in respect of documents from a particular witness.[10]

---

1    Rules of the Supreme Court 1965, Ord 32, r 7: the party requiring attendance of the witness must produce to the court office 'a note from a judge or [district judge] authorising issue of the writ [of subpoena]'.
2    County Court Rules 1981, Ord 20, r 12(8).
3    Rules of the Supreme Court 1965, Ord 38, r 14; County Court Rules 1981, Ord 20, r 12; and, in respect of non family proceedings, see Civil Procedure Rules 1998, r 34.3(1).
4    *Senior v Holdsworth ex parte Independent Television News Ltd* [1976] QB 23.
5    For further consideration of refusal of discovery and interrogatories, see **4.11** et seq above.
6    *Morgan v Morgan* [1977] Fam 122, per Watkins J; and see further at **4.13** above.
7    *Senior v Holdsworth ex parte Independent Television News Ltd* (above).
8    [1993] 2 FLR 696 at 702H–703A, CA.
9    In *Frary* the application for production against a husband's cohabitant was refused on grounds that the order was oppressive and unnecessary; and see further at **4.15** above.
10   This question is considered under relevance of evidence at **4.4** above; and, since hitherto the production appointment is used most in the ancillary relief jurisdiction, the secondary question will be considered there; see **10.32** et seq below.

### *Production appointments and Khanna hearings*

**6.42**    Although new in its introduction specifically to the Family Proceedings Rules 1991[1] the concept of the production appointment is derived from the Rules of the Supreme Court 1965, Ord 38, r 13[2] where it had existed long before the 1991 Rules. The production appointment procedure has been taken a step further by Sir Donald Nicholls V-C in *Khanna v Lovell White Durrant (A Firm)*,[3] in which he followed *Williams v Williams*[4] (a matrimonial financial relief case). In that case, Sir John Donaldson MR regretted the fact that he could not require a bank to produce documents in advance of the hearing[5] and then went on:[6]

> 'If [the bank documents] are only discoverable by means of a *subpoena duces tecum* calling on the appropriate officer of the bank to attend the hearing, I see no reason why the court should not order that the hearing should begin on a specified day and, so far as that day is concerned, be confined to receiving the documents, the remainder of the hearing standing adjourned to a date to be fixed.'

Sir Donald Nicholls V-C took up this suggestion in *Khanna* and adopted the course suggested in *Williams*. The difference between the *Khanna* appointment and the production appointment[7] is that the former can be fixed on issue of the subpoena, without the need for the preliminary appointment at which an order for production is sought.[8]

## Discovery from third parties

**6.43**    On occasion, parties may require evidence from public bodies for purposes of family proceedings, particularly care proceedings. The courts are concerned to ensure that all that is possible is done to enable the court to reach a decision with all relevant evidence relating to a child's welfare being available.[9] Thus, in *Nottinghamshire County Council v H*,[10] Johnson J held that where the local authority sought disclosure from the Crown Prosecution Service of documents relating to forthcoming criminal proceedings, discovery of documents relating to a child held by the police might be ordered – as on the facts of this case – where it was sought, essentially, to enable the local authority to make a more informed decision about the future of the children in its interim care. Discovery was limited to providing the documents to the local authority in the first instance; although if they were to be relied on in the care proceedings they would have to be disclosed to all parties subject to any leave of the

---

1    Family Proceedings Rules 1991, r 2.62 is derived from Matrimonial Causes Rules 1977, SI 1977/1247, r 77. Rule 77 did not include any provision for a production appointment.
2    In respect of non family proceedings, see Civil Procedure Rules 1998, r 31.17 (orders for disclosure against a person not a party).
3    [1995] 1 WLR 121.
4    [1988] 1 FLR 455, CA.
5    He does not appear to have been referred to Ord 38, r 13.
6    [1988] 1 FLR 455 at 461A.
7    Under either Rules of the Supreme Court 1965, Ord 38, r 13 or Family Proceedings Rules 1991, r 2.62(7)–(9).
8    The procedure for application for a production appointment is considered in *B v B (Production Appointment: Procedure)* [1995] 1 FLR 913, per Thorpe J.
9    See eg *Re S (Contact: Evidence)* [1998] 1 FLR 798, CA (considered further below).
10   [1995] 1 FLR 115.

court or rule excluding their discovery. Similarly, in *Re R (Child Abuse: Video Evidence)*,[1] Johnson J expressed the hope that police and hospitals would release video evidence to solicitors, on the solicitors' undertakings not to copy the evidence, save to expert witnesses. If police and hospitals refused to help in this way, application could be made to the court; and, in appropriate cases, such applications might attract an award of costs.

**6.44**     Where video evidence could be said to have an important effect on the future welfare of a child, it was right that the judge should see it. Thus, in a contact application, where the father sought leave for production of a video of a police interview of a child, it was proper that this should be available to the court.[2]

## Discovery to third parties

**6.45**     It is possible for third parties, such as the police, to seek leave[3] of the court for discovery to them of confidential documents or of otherwise privileged evidence arising in family (mostly children) proceedings.[4] The court may also give leave to a party in criminal proceedings to use confidential documents in his defence.[5] In considering disclosure of confidential information to third parties, such as the police, the court will consider the importance of the police being able to work, for example, with the local authority. In *Re W (Disclosure to Police)*[6] the Court of Appeal considered that where the police were investigating serious allegations, a family judge should be slow to refuse leave to an authority to pass on important information; and this was especially so where social workers and police were working co-operatively on the same case.

**6.46**     Where leave is needed to bring material arising in litigation relating to a child to the attention of a case conference, it may be necessary to seek leave of the court to disclose reports arising in the litigation.[7] If such application is made, it is not a reason for refusing to disclose that information to health trust personnel at the case conference where the material might alert them to a claim by (in this case) the mother in professional negligence.[8]

---

1    [1995] 1 FLR 451.
2    *Re S (Contact: Evidence)* [1998] 1 FLR 798, CA.
3    Leave is sought pursuant to Family Proceedings Rules 1991, r 4.23.
4    See eg *Re EC (Disclosure of Material)* [1996] 2 FLR 725, CA.
5    *Re D (Minors) (Wardship: Disclosure)* [1994] 1 FLR 346, CA.
6    [1998] 2 FLR 135, CA. This case also raised the issue of whether a social services department needed leave of the court to pass on documents which contained confidential information to the police, where the documents themselves were not filed at court in children proceedings. On this point, Butler-Sloss LJ drew attention to *Working Together Under the Children Act 1989* (HMSO, 1991) (which deals with inter-agency co-operation in the investigation of child abuse) and to the need for agencies to work together as closely as possible in investigating alleged crimes in the field of child protection. She pointed out that Family Proceedings Rules 1991, r 4.23 deals only with documents filed at court: there was no need for a local authority to seek leave to disclose confidential documents held by it and not filed at court.
7    Administration of Justice Act 1960, s 12(1).
8    *Re M (Disclosure)* [1998] 1 FLR 734, CA.

# Chapter 7

## PRIVILEGE

### 1 INTRODUCTION

**7.1** Documents may be excluded or exempted from discovery,[1] or evidence prevented from being given in court, on grounds that such documents or evidence are privileged from discovery.[2] In the fields of family and child law, privilege will attach to documents or other evidence in the following categories[3] of circumstance:[4]

(1) professional confidences;
(2) 'without prejudice' correspondence;
(3) incriminating questions.

#### Waiver of privilege

**7.2** The privilege is that of the client (not, for example, of his legal representative). Thus, only the person to whom the privilege attaches can waive the protection of that privilege. For example, a client is entitled to open – ie to disclose to the court – a letter which was written 'without prejudice',[5] or a party to proceedings may be willing to give evidence as to what advice he was given by his legal representative. In both these cases, but for the waiver, the 'without prejudice' letter or the evidence as to advice would be privileged.

#### Privilege and admissibility[6]

**7.3** It follows from the fact that privilege can be waived that, while a document may be privileged from disclosure, this does not mean that it is inadmissible once the privilege is waived. Professor Tapper states[7] the position as follows:

---

1  See Chapter 6 for consideration of rules relating to discovery.
2  Lord Woolf MR *Access to Justice: Final Report* (HMSO, July 1996) ch 12, para 37 misleadingly prefers the term 'disclosure' for what has hitherto been known as discovery: 'the process for discovery of documents (which I now recommend should be called 'disclosure')'. For the family lawyer the term 'disclosure' has a particular meaning distinct from 'discovery': explained at **6.1** and **6.3** above. 'Disclosure' is dealt with in the Civil Procedure Rules 1998 at Part 31.
3  This list, suitably amended for family law purposes, has been taken from *Phipson on Evidence* 14th edn (Sweet & Maxwell, 1990) para 20-02.
4  To the list of categories of document excluded from disclosure could be added those excluded by public interest immunity. This category of document is considered at **11.47** et seq below.
5  For consideration of 'without prejudice' correspondence, see **7.29** et seq below.
6  For a consideration of admissibility, see **4.5** above.
7  Tapper 'Evidential privilege in cases involving children' [1997] CFLQ 1.

'A crucial distinction needs to be drawn between the rules of privilege and rules of admissibility. A rule of privilege in its classical form does no more than prevent compulsory disclosure or production. It is essentially a shield for the holder of the piece of evidence and should be distinguished from a rule of admissibility, which in its classical form prevents the use in court of a piece of evidence.'

Thus, where privilege is waived by a party to proceedings, a document can be put before the court and is admissible, if relevant[1], as part of that party's evidence. Similarly, where an offer is put forward in correspondence as part of negotiations for settlement of a matter, the document containing that offer is privileged,[2] except where the offer is accepted, when the privilege goes and the document is admissible by either party as part of his evidence.[3]

## Privileged information received by other parties

**7.4**	If a privileged document, or other privileged information, is obtained by another party to the proceedings whether by mistake – for example the document being sent in error to that other party by the client's solicitors – or by some form of impropriety,[4] this does not necessarily prevent the document being admissible.[5] However, it seems highly likely that an injunction will lie against the party who has obtained the documents to enjoin use of the documents.[6] Application for an injunction should be made in the proceedings, and there should be no unreasonable delay in seeking the injunction.[7] However, where confidential information arises in separate proceedings that information should be disclosed. It is not covered by privilege in the separate proceedings.[8] *Vernon v Bosley (No 2)*[9] concerned findings contained in a judgment in children proceedings perused separately from the plaintiff's personal injury appeal. Information about the findings in the children proceedings which differed from the findings of the first instance judge in the personal injury proceedings should have been disclosed to the Court of Appeal. Such information was not covered by any rule relating to confidentiality nor by any form of litigation privilege.[10]

**7.5**	Where a party or his solicitor has received the document and 'realises that he has received the document only by reason of an obvious mistake' the court has power

---

1	For consideration of relevance and admissibility, see **4.5** et seq above.
2	*Rush & Tompkins Ltd v GLC* [1988] 3 All ER 201, CA; and see **7.30** below.
3	*Walker v Wilsher* (1889) 23 QBD 335, CA.
4	In *T v T (Interception of Documents)* [1994] 2 FLR 1083, it was held that a wife's behaviour in taking her husband's correspondence and other documents was not 'conduct' in the context of Matrimonial Causes Act 1973, s 25(2)(g) but could be reflected in a costs order against her.
5	*Calcraft v Guest* [1898] 1 QB 759; *Goddard v Nationwide Building Society* [1987] QB 670, CA. On the other hand, see the Civil Procedure Rules 1998, r 31.20 which applies 'where a party inadvertently allows a privileged document to be inspected'; then the party who has seen the document may only use it 'with the permission of the court'.
6	*Webster v James Chapman & Co* [1989] 3 All ER 939; and see *Goddard v Nationwide Building Society* [1987] QB 670.
7	*Guinness Peat Properties Ltd v Fitzroy Robinson Partnership* [1987] 1 WLR 1027, per Slade LJ.
8	*Vernon v Bosley (No 2)* [1997] 3 WLR 683, CA; and see **7.16** for discovery in these circumstances.
9	[1997] 3 WLR 683, [1998] 1 FLR 304.
10	*Re L (Police Investigation: Privilege)* [1996] 1 FLR 731, HL; and see further **7.18** below.

to intervene and 'should ordinarily intervene' save in cases of 'inordinate delay'.[1] The Bar Council Code of Conduct, r 7 provides:

> 'If a barrister comes into possession of a document belonging to another party by some means other than the normal and proper channels (eg by mistake) he should ... unless satisfied that the document has been properly obtained in the ordinary course of events at once return the document unread to the person entitled to possession of it.'

No comparable rule appears to exist for solicitors. In view of the distaste with which the Court of Appeal seemed to view the actions of the solicitors concerned in *Derby & Co Ltd v Weldon (No 8)*[2] and of the fact that solicitors' professional rules require them to act towards others with fairness, that is to say, other than 'in a way which is fraudulent, deceitful or otherwise contrary to their position as solicitors',[3] it must be the rule that the solicitors' profession should be expected to adhere to a rule similar to that of the Bar. This view seems to be supported by the fact that an injunction is likely to be granted by the courts in almost all circumstances where documents become available to a solicitor by the mistake of another party or his solicitor.

## 2 PROFESSIONAL CONFIDENCES

**7.6** Professional confidences can be divided into those between legal adviser and client, on the one hand, and communications between the legal adviser (or client) and a third party in contemplation of litigation, on the other. This second category has been further divided in the case of children proceedings between those where 'litigation privilege' applies and those where the privilege is lost because, to obtain the information from the third party (normally a report from a medical expert) it has been necessary to obtain leave from the court to disclose to the expert confidential court documents;[4] and it is a condition of the court granting that leave that the resulting report be filed at court.[5]

## Legal adviser

**7.7** Privilege depends on the communication having been made to a 'legal adviser'. The term applies at common law to solicitors and barristers, but may now be taken to extend to solicitors' staff.[6] The terminology preferred by the Courts and Legal

---

1    *Guinness Peat Properties Ltd v Fitzroy Robinson Partnership* [1987] 1 WLR 1027 at 1045–1046, per Slade J; approved in *Derby & Co Ltd v Weldon (No 8)* [1991] 1 WLR 73 at 97H, per Dillon LJ and at 100E, per Butler-Sloss LJ, CA.
2    [1991] 1 WLR 73 at 97, per Dillon LJ, and at 100, per Butler-Sloss LJ. The defendant's solicitors requested disclosure of documents knowing that discovery of them had been given in error.
3    Solicitors' Practice Rules 1990, r 18.01.
4    Under Family Proceedings Rules 1991, r 4.23; Family Proceedings Courts (Children Act 1989) Rules 1991, SI 1991/1395, r 23.
5    *Re L (Police Investigation: Privilege)* [1996] 2 WLR 395, [1996] 1 FLR 731, HL; and see further **7.14** et seq below.
6    *Crompton (Alfred) Amusement Machines Ltd v Customs and Excise Commissioners* [1972] 2 QB 102, CA.

Services Act 1990 is 'legal or other representative'[1] which may have more significance under litigation privilege, but which, in this context, means: 'In relation to a party to proceedings ... any party person exercising a right of audience or to conduct litigation on his behalf'.[2] The Courts and Legal Services Act 1990, s 119(1) defines 'right to conduct litigation' as the right to commence process on behalf of a client and 'to perform any ancillary functions in relation to proceedings'; while the term is also connoted with 'litigation services' which, perhaps more significantly in the present context, means:

> 'Any services which it would be reasonable to expect a person who is exercising, or contemplating exercising, a right to conduct litigation in relation to any proceedings, or contemplated proceedings, to provide.'

The Courts and Legal Services Act 1990, s 63 extends legal professional privilege to communications made 'to or by a person who is not a barrister or solicitor' when that person is acting as advocate or providing litigation services.[3] It probably applies to mediators, but they will rarely give legal advice.[4]

## Communications with a client

**7.8**     A lawyer's client cannot be compelled to disclose, or give evidence as to, communications passing between lawyer and client. Similarly, a legal representative may not disclose or give evidence concerning those communications, or be compelled to do so by the courts.[5] The rule is based on the necessity for full confidentiality between lawyer and client if the lawyer's assistance is to be as fully effective as possible, and on the public interest in preserving this.[6] As the Lord Chief Justice put the proposition in *R v Derby Magistrates' Court ex parte B*,[7] and after his exhaustive review of authorities stretching back to the sixteenth century:

> 'no exception should be allowed to the absolute nature of legal professional privilege, once established [for it] is much more than an ordinary rule of evidence, limited in its application to the facts of a particular case. It is a fundamental condition on which the administration of justice as a whole rests.'

**7.9**     The essentially liberal view of the Lord Chief Justice contrasts with that of *Cross and Tapper*[8] which speaks of privilege as depriving a 'tribunal of relevant evidence [so that] powerful arguments are required to justify their existence'. Those words were written before *R v Derby Magistrates' Court ex parte B*; but Professor Tapper took the opportunity to criticise that case subsequently.[9] This criticism was

---

1     See eg Courts and Legal Services Act 1990, ss 4, 111 and 112 (each of which amend the wasted costs jurisdictions in the civil courts and the criminal courts).
2     Supreme Court Act 1981, s 51(13), as inserted by Courts and Legal Services Act 1990, s 4(1).
3     Courts and Legal Services Act 1990, s 63(1)(a).
4     See further **7.36** below.
5     This principle was clearly endorsed by the House of Lords in *R v Derby Magistrates' Court ex parte B* [1995] 3 WLR 681, [1996] 1 FLR 513 (considered further at **7.17** below); but see reservations of Tapper at **7.9** below. A possible exception may arise in wardship where a solicitor may be compelled to release information from his file relating to an abducting client's address (*Re B (Abduction: Disclosure)* [1995] 1 FLR 774, CA).
6     *Guide to Professional Conduct of Solicitors 1996* 7th edn (The Law Society) App 16B.
7     [1997] AC 487, [1996] 1 FLR 513 at 528F and 527H, HL, per Lord Taylor CJ.
8     *Cross and Tapper on Evidence* 8th edn (Butterworths, 1995), p 451.
9     Tapper 'Prosecution and Privilege' (1996) *The International Journal of Evidence and Proof*, October, 1.

levelled at privilege, essentially from the standpoint of advice in criminal proceedings, rather than in family or child law proceedings. He spoke disapprovingly of the House of Lords choosing 'to exalt the doctrine of legal professional privilege into an absolute right' which, he suggested, 'betrays conceptual confusion [which] can be justified neither in principle nor on authority'.[1] These must sound harsh words to any reader of the Lord Chief Justice's speech in which he explained his speech by means of extensive reference to legal authority. In the process, he re-stated a well-known and clear legal principle. The only area where, at present, the concept of legal professional privilege remains in question is where it may conflict with the welfare of children.[2]

## Client's privilege

**7.10** The rules relating to legal professional privilege exist to protect the client, not the lawyer. Thus, privilege may be waived by the client, or on his instructions, but not by the legal adviser save to the extent that he has the authority implied by his retainer to do so. Privilege attaches only to information given to a legal adviser, and not to information given to, for example, doctors or social workers.[3]

**7.11** The corollary to the rule that the privilege is the client's, is that the legal adviser therefore owes a duty to the client not to disclose confidential information.[4] This is subject to the exception where solicitors, 'in truly exceptional circumstances',[5] may breach their duty of confidentiality, such as in circumstances where children are at risk of serious harm or where a crime (such as child abduction) may be committed.[6] Further, where a lawyer acts for two parties (for example, a child and her parents in proceedings for contact under the Children Act 1989) and a conflict of interest emerges, then in an action by one party against the solicitor the privilege can be overriden where the other party can be shown to have acted in bad faith.[7]

## Privilege and the mature child

**7.12** Where a solicitor is acting for a mature child, the child is the client and, like any other client, is owed an absolute duty of confidentiality. The *Solicitors Family*

---

1 Ibid, p 24.
2 See **7.15** et seq below. Tapper touches on this as an area in which legal professional privilege can be overridden, at p 20; and develops his ideas on the question in 'Evidential privilege in cases involving children' [1997] CFLQ 1 at 20.
3 *D v National Society for the Prevention of Cruelty to Children* [1978] AC 171, [1977] 1 All ER 589, HL; and see *GMC Guidance on Confidentiality* (October 1995) and *Working Together Under the Children Act 1989: a Guide to Arrangements for Inter-agency Co-operation for the Protection of Children from Abuse* (HMSO, 1991), especially para 3.10 et seq which, under the heading 'Exchange of Information' (perhaps a little euphemistic) deals with the requirement of medical, nursing and social work agencies to disclose to social services departments information about child abuse.
4 Per Thorpe LJ in *Vernon v Bosley (No 2)* [1997] 3 WLR 683, CA; considered further at **6.9** above.
5 *Guide to Professional·Conduct of Solicitors 1996* 7th edn (The Law Society), App 16B (b)(iii).
6 Perhaps on analogy with *W v Egdell* [1990] 1 All ER 835 (consultant psychologist released report where a patient was to be released and he feared that the patient might then commit further offences).
7 *Nationwide Building Society v Various Solicitors* (1998) *The Times*, 5 February, Blackburne J.

*Law Association Guide to Good Practice when Acting for Children* considers the question as follows:[1]

> '(1) Where information leads to a strong suspicion that a crime is to be committed by the child (eg. as a young abuser), then confidentiality is overridden and information can be passed to a third party.
>
> (2) The solicitor's duty to the client may be overridden where the welfare of a child is concerned and if a solicitor is ordered by the court (as officer of the court) to disclose otherwise privileged information ( *Re B (Abduction: Disclosure)* [1995] 1 FLR 774, CA).[2]
>
> (3) Where a mature child is being abused, the duty of absolute confidentiality applies, save where the solicitor has information that younger siblings (or others) are also subject to abuse or where the child client is in fear of his life or of serious injury. The solicitor should advise the client where to go for help and should try to persuade the child to report the abuse.'

### Communications in course of employment

**7.13**　　　The communications between solicitor and client are privileged provided they are made in the course of the client's employment of the solicitor, or of their relationship as solicitor and client;[3] but not, for example, where a lay person merely talks to someone who happens to be a solicitor. Thus, it is not necessary for there to be litigation underway or in contemplation[4] for the privilege to attach to the communication.

## Communications in contemplation of litigation – litigation privilege

**7.14**　　　Communications between a client and his legal adviser attract absolute privilege as explained above; whereas communications between a client or his legal adviser and a third party (eg to obtain a report and expert opinion on a feature of the case or proposed case) attract privilege only where the dominant purpose of the document is that it should be used in litigation or contemplated litigation.[5] Thus, where an expert's report is obtained prior to or during the course of proceedings it is privileged from disclosure: for example, an adverse valuation report may be withheld in financial relief proceedings (although this does not prevent the other spouse obtaining the evidence by calling the witness himself). However, if the report is obtained for separate proceedings, it will not be covered by litigation privilege in the instant proceedings, and should be discovered to other parties and disclosed to the court.[6] In family proceedings, this is subject to the important exception of medical evidence in children proceedings where leave has been granted to disclose confidential documents.[7]

---

1　　4th edn (SFLA, 1997) para I.4 which considers the question by reference also to *The Guide to Professional Conduct of Solicitors 1996* 7th edn (The Law Society), at Annex 16B, para A.

2　　There may be doubt as to whether this case survives *R v Derby Magistrates' Court ex parte B* [1995] 3 WLR 681, [1996] 1 FLR 513, HL. On the other hand, in its inherent jurisdiction the High Court has wide powers, even in the case of privilege: see eg *Re D (Minors) (Conciliation: Privilege)* [1993] 1 FLR 932, CA (considered further at **7.30** below).

3　　*Greenough v Gaskell* (1833) 1 My & K 98, per Lord Brougham.

4　　Cf litigation privilege at **7.14** below where communications must be in contemplation of litigation in order to be privileged.

5　　*Waugh v British Railways Board* [1980] AC 521, HL.

6　　*Vernon v Bosley (No 2)* [1998] 1 FLR 304, CA.

7　　See **7.17** below.

## 3 PRIVILEGE IN CHILDREN PROCEEDINGS

**7.15** The law and rules of evidence on the subject of legal professional privilege and duty of disclosure in children cases is in a state of development.[1] It demonstrates the tension between the adversarial and inquisitorial systems of justice and the conflicts they can throw up when they are treated as existing side by side.[2] The dilemma over privilege in children cases exists most starkly for a parent's legal representative in public law proceedings, although it may as easily arise when a solicitor is acting for any party to children proceedings, whether under the Children Act 1989, Part II (private law) or Parts IV and V (public law).[3] The areas of privilege, each of which will be considered in turn, can be categorised as follows:

(a)  reports received from expert witnesses where leave has been given by the court to a party to disclose confidential documents;
(b)  communications received from third parties, whether oral or in writing, where no question of leave of the court arises; and
(c)  communications direct with the client.

### Privilege and 'full relevant disclosure'

**7.16** Before considering privilege in children proceedings, it is important to dispose of one area of possible misunderstanding: that disclosure of confidential information in children proceedings is akin to the duty of full relevant disclosure in financial relief proceedings.[4] With respect to any who may adhere to the proposition, it is precisely because facts relating to the parties' financial circumstances are not privileged or confidential that there is a duty of disclosure.[5] The need for rules relating to confidential information or privilege is because a client may have to confide in a legal adviser and be given confidential advice; and, in English law, he is treated as being entitled to do so to ensure proper preparation of his case.[6] By contrast, it has been held that the terminology of the Matrimonial Causes Act 1973, s 25(1) – 'the

---

1   As Lord Jauncey of Tullichettle observed in *Re L (Police Investigation: Privilege)* [1996] 2 WLR 395 at 403H, [1996] 1 FLR 731, HL the question of an absolute bar to legal professional privilege in children cases where the information affects the welfare of a child remains at large (despite the *obiter dicta* of Wall and Thorpe JJ considered below).
2   See consideration of Lord Nicholls' speech in *Re L* (above) at **7.19** below; and see **1.25** above for a discussion of the question of the inquisitorial function of the court.
3   For contrasting points of view on this subject, see eg District Judge Brasse 'The Duty of Disclosure in Children Cases' [1996] Fam Law 358; and Burrows 'Disclosure in Children Cases' [1996] Fam Law 566.
4   In matrimonial financial relief proceedings, there is a duty on both parties to provide 'full relevant disclosure': *(Livesey (formerly Jenkins)) v Jenkins* [1985] AC 424, [1985] FLR 813, HL; confirmed by *Practice Direction of 31 January 1995 (Case Management)* [1995] 1 WLR 332, [1995] 1 FLR 456 at para 4; and see **6.5** above. Ward J (as he then was) suggested a relationship between this and children proceedings in *Oxfordshire County Council v P* [1995] Fam 161, [1995] 1 FLR 552 at 557E (cited without comment by Lord Jauncey in *Re L (Police Investigation: Privilege)* [1996] 2 WLR 395, [1996] 1 FLR 731 at 740D, HL); and Singer J has been heard to concur with the similarity of children and matrimonial financial relief proceedings.
5   See further **6.7** et seq above.
6   *R v Derby Magistrates' Court ex parte B* [1996] AC 487, [1996] 1 FLR 513, HL.

duty of the court to consider all the circumstances' of the case – requires full disclosure.[1] Thus, if facts about financial matters can ever be said to be confidential – in the same way that information considered in most children proceedings is confidential – statute has been held to provide that any confidentiality is overridden. Thus, to connote financial disclosure in ancillary relief proceedings with legal professional privilege relating to confidential information – whether in children or any other proceedings – is to confuse two different aspects of the rules of evidence.

## Reports where leave of the court is obtained

**7.17** The debate on the subject of privilege and the report obtained from an expert with leave of the court[2] was brought into full relief by *Oxfordshire County Council v M*.[3] Although that case has largely been overtaken by *Re L (Police Investigation: Privilege)*,[4] Lord Jauncey in the later case relied extensively upon the President's judgment in *Oxfordshire*, in particular by citing it as authority for the kinship of wardship and Children Act 1989 proceedings. However, the true *ratio* of the *Oxfordshire* decision – which is also the *ratio* of the decision in *Re L* – is to be sought in the shorter judgments of Steyn and Kennedy LJJ, who sat with the President, and who both stressed that they limited their decision to the question of reports on children obtained after the court had given leave to disclose confidential documents to an expert. Specifically in rejection of a speculative view expressed by Wall J in *Re DH (A Minor) (Child Abuse)*,[5] Steyn LJ made the following comment:[6]

'... I restrict my conclusion to the point before us. It does not mean that legal professional privilege has no role to play. For example, the promotion of the welfare of the child does not require that communications between a client and a lawyer should be disclosed: such advice is not material which could arguably affect the judgment of the court.'

This *dictum* is a reminder of the later *R v Derby Magistrates' Court ex parte B*[7] and of the stress which that case lays on 'the absolute nature of legal professional privilege' and its fundamental position within the English system of justice.

## Privilege and the non-adversarial system of justice

**7.18** The decision in *Re L (Police Investigation: Privilege)*[8] was based on the assumption that children proceedings are non-adversarial. Lord Jauncey proceeded on the simple premise that Children Act 1989 proceedings are akin to wardship, that is, they are largely non-adversarial. Then, calling in aid the judgment of Sir Stephen Brown in *Oxfordshire County Council v M*, he asserted that 'the role of the court under

1　*Livesey (formerly Jenkins) v Jenkins* [1985] AC 424: the *dicta* of the House of Lords applying to Matrimonial Causes Act 1973, s 25(1) and the question of disclosure are considered at **6.7** et seq above.
2　Family Proceedings Rules 1991, r 4.23 and Family Proceedings Courts (Children Act 1989) Rules 1991, r 23, both of which prohibit disclosure of any 'document ... held by the court and relating to [children] proceedings ... without leave of the judge or district judge/the justices' clerk or the court'.
3　[1994] Fam 151, [1994] 1 FLR 175, CA.
4　[1996] 2 WLR 395, [1996] 1 FLR 731, HL.
5　[1994] 1 FLR 679, per Wall J, whose words are quoted in full at **7.27** below.
6　*Oxfordshire County Council v M* [1994] Fam 151, [1994] 1 FLR 175 at 188E.
7　[1996] AC 487, [1996] 1 FLR 513, HL; considered further at **7.8** above.
8　[1994] 1 FLR 175, CA.

the Act does not differ significantly from its role in wardship proceedings'.[1] From this bald assertion he concluded that litigation privilege has no part in 'non-adversarial' proceedings and that therefore the *Oxfordshire* case should be followed. If this reasoning is incorrect then, said Lord Jauncey, where proceedings 'are [adversarial], litigation privilege must continue to play its normal part. If they are not, different considerations may apply.'[2] In his strong support for Lord Jauncey, Professor Tapper points to 'revolutionary changes in legal proceedings in modern times' and concludes:[3]

> 'The whole thrust of these changes is to promote a system in which litigation is conducted not only with all the cards on the table, but face up for all to see except where the very nature of adversarial procedure demands concealment.[4] The majority is surely right to deny the inclusion in such a category where the welfare of children is required to be the paramount consideration ...'

## Privilege: Lord Nicholls and the classical view

**7.19**    In his dissenting speech in *Re L (Police Investigation: Privilege)* Lord Nicholls began by referring to the House of Lords decision in the *Derby Magistrates'* case[5] and then moved on to consider the statutory nature of Children Act 1989 proceedings:[6]

> 'Clear words ... or a compelling context are needed before Parliament can be taken to have intended that the privilege should be ousted in favour of another interest. The Children Act contains neither. There is no express abrogation of the privilege. Nor do the provisions in the Act, designed to promote the welfare of children, carry with them an implication that in future parents who become involved in court proceedings are not to have the normal freedom to consult lawyers and potential witnesses, and to do so confidentially.'

He went on to consider the meanings of adversarial, non-adversarial and 'the bewitching label of inquisitorial' and to point out that, however much parties may seek to be non-adversarial and to assist the court to reach a conclusion which will best promote the welfare of the child, there will be features of the case which are adversarial. What is required, after all, is a fair hearing.[7] He concluded that if the normal adversarial model is to be changed in Children Act 1989 proceedings then Parliament should say so. It should not be left to the courts to create or superimpose a court model where none was intended by Parliament.[8]

---

1    [1996] AC 16, [1996] 1 FLR 731 at 738E.
2    Ibid, at 737E.
3    Tapper 'Evidential privilege in cases involving children' [1997] CFLQ 1 at 16.
4    This comment is made in response to, and in criticism of, the speech of Lord Nicholls; yet a feature of this disappointing article is that Professor Tapper (like Lord Jauncey on this issue, but unlike Lord Nicholls) does not provide clear premises to the conclusions he reaches.
5    *R v Derby Magistrates' Court ex parte B* [1996] AC 487, [1996] 1 FLR 513, HL; and see **7.8** above.
6    [1996] AC 16, [1996] 1 FLR 731 at 741D–E.
7    Ibid, at 743.
8    Although Lord Nicholls was in a minority in the House of Lords there is much that he said on privilege generally (ie outside the main issue) which remains worthy of careful reading. He analysed the problem by looking at the subject of privilege as a whole; and he had no difficulty in concluding that legal professional privilege in general (aside from reports obtained after leave to disclose) remained intact.

## Communications from third parties – no leave of the court required

**7.20**   Where a report has been obtained from a third party, such as a medical witness, legal principle is clear although views may differ widely as to the correct practice. The issue may arise, for example, in private law children proceedings – such as for a residence order – where a parent's legal representatives commission a medical report on their client from (say) a psychiatrist who has been treating him. It is not necessary, in this instance, to seek leave of the court to disclose confidential documents:[1] in any event, at this stage, proceedings have not yet started. However, when the report comes back, it contains information which has a clear bearing on the client's ability to care for a child. What does the legal representative do with the report in the event that the client presses for continuation of the proceedings or for issue of an application? The following factors arise as the law now stands.

### Dominant purpose of the communication

**7.21**   A preliminary consideration will be whether the dominant purpose[2] of the report was the contemplated court proceedings. If not (and this will be unlikely in family proceedings, especially in the example quoted above) the report must be disclosed, according to the strict rules of discovery.[3]

### Does legal professional privilege apply?

**7.22**   The question of whether legal professional privilege applies in the above example is the subject of differing, and often strongly held, views among certain members of the judiciary.[4] However, as the law now stands,[5] such reports are covered by the rules relating to legal professional privilege and are therefore exempt from disclosure, however much the information may impinge on the welfare of a child concerned in the proceedings (and whatever may be the personal view of the lawyer concerned). This was a question deliberately left unresolved by the House of Lords in *Re L (Police Investigation: Privilege)*:[6] Lord Jauncey specifically said that he was not willing to adjudicate upon the point, holding only that litigation privilege did not apply where the court has given leave to disclose confidential documents. Thus, without the permission of his client, a solicitor is not at liberty to disclose the information in the communication, subject to the exceptions considered above as to the commission of an anticipated criminal offence[7] and to a solicitor's duty not to mislead the court.[8]

---

1    Ie in the terms of Family Proceedings Rules 1991, r 4.23.
2    *Waugh v British Railways Board* [1980] AC 521, HL; and see **6.26** above.
3    *Wheeler v Le Marchant* (1881) 17 ChD 675, CA; although it may be doubted whether this rule would apply strictly in family proceedings.
4    For example, contrast the views of Wall and Thorpe JJ (at **7.27** below) with the speech of Lord Nicholls in *Re L (Police Investigation: Privilege)* [1996] 2 WLR 395, [1996] 1 FLR 731, HL (considered at **7.18** above).
5    Now that the Civil Procedure Act 1997 is in force the Lord Chancellor can by statutory instrument alter rules of evidence as they apply in civil courts (Sch 1, para 4).
6    [1996] AC 16, [1996] 1 FLR 731 at 739H–740E, per Lord Jauncey .
7    See **7.12** above.
8    See **6.9** et seq below and **7.23** above.

### Duty not to mislead the court

#### (1) Solicitors

**7.23**    As officers of the court, solicitors 'whilst under a duty to do their best for their client, must never deceive or mislead the court'.[1] If a solicitor allows a client to put forward information which he knows to be false, and with the intention of misleading the court, that solicitor 'takes part in a positive deception of the court'.[2] It is an implied duty of the solicitor's retainer by the client that he will carry out his duties within the rules of professional conduct; and if required to go outside these rules (eg to mislead the court) then the client must be asked to modify his instructions or the solicitor must cease to act.[3] Thus, if the solicitor has the information from a report or other communication and the client wants to give evidence to the court which conflicts with the report, the solicitor must withdraw; although there is still no professional duty to breach the client's privilege and disclose how the client is misleading the court.

#### (2) Barristers

**7.24**    A similar duty attaches to a member of the Bar. This was explained by Denning LJ in *Tombling v Universal Bulb Co Ltd*[4] as follows:

> 'The duty of counsel in a civil case    or in defending an accused person – is to make every honest endeavour to succeed. He must not, of course, knowingly mislead the court, either on the facts or on the law, but, short of that, he may put such matters in evidence or omit such others as in his discretion he thinks will be most to the advantage of his client.'

This *dictum* is cited with approval in *Vernon v Bosley (No 2)*.[5] That case is considered more fully in the context of discovery;[6] but for present purposes it will be sufficient to say that the case involved a judge's findings concerning medical evidence in children proceedings in which, as a parent, the plaintiff was a party. Contemporaneously, his damages claim, which also turned on medical information about him, was subject to an appeal to the Court of Appeal. Findings in the family court were very different from those in the civil proceedings at first instance. Those findings, if disclosed to the defendants, might have had a significant effect on the damages awarded. Plaintiff's counsel advised the plaintiff that the findings need not be disclosed. However, by a route still not known, the judgment found its way to counsel for the defendants. The question here is whether or not medical information in separate proceedings was privileged from disclosure. The Court of Appeal, by a majority,[7] held that litigation privilege did not apply and therefore the report should have been discovered to the defendants and disclosed to the court. The majority in the Court of Appeal went on to hold that counsel should have ensured that the plaintiff was advised as to disclosure. Indeed, Thorpe LJ went further. He held – without citing any authority for his proposition – that where counsel has the information and, because the plaintiff will

---

1    *Guide to the Professional Conduct of Solicitors 1996* 7th edn (The Law Society) para 22.01.

2    Ibid, Annex 22C; and see *Vernon v Bosley (No 2)* [1997] 3 WLR 683, CA, considered fully at **6.9** above.

3    *Cordery on Solicitors* (Butterworths) para F[705].

4    [1951] 2 TLR 289 at 297.

5    [1997] 3 WLR 683 at 699C, CA.

6    See **6.9** above.

7    Stuart-Smith and Thorpe LJJ; Evans LJ dissenting.

not disclose, he (counsel) has had to withdraw from a case, then in those circumstances he should 'disclose the relevant material to his opponent and, unless there be argument between the parties otherwise, to the judge'.[1]

## Law reform

**7.25**    The above is an unsatisfactory and artificial state of affairs which seems to call for reform. In most instances the party who is denied access to the report can subpoena the expert witness concerned. In many children cases the witness will be seen by the court welfare officer or guardian ad litem who will obtain the information for which the solicitor seeks privilege. It is submitted that it is preferable that rules be issued[2] to clarify the position, rather than that a High Court seek to amend fundamental rules by judicial fiat. While it is possible to have sympathy for Mr Vernon's counsel in his assessment of the then law on litigation privilege and the lack of a duty to disclose (as distinct from the duty not to mislead the court) to a layman the proposition that one court can decide a case concerning the same individual based on two completely different assessments of his health must surely appear absurd.

## Communications direct with the client

**7.26**    In view of the ringing endorsement of the rule that communications between lawyer and client are absolutely privileged in the *Derby Magistrates' case*,[3] it can perhaps be assumed that (for the foreseeable future, at any rate) such communications will remain privileged from disclosure absolutely. This absolute privilege is subject to three qualifications.

(1) In 'truly exceptional circumstances'[4] solicitors may breach their duty of confidentiality, for example where children are at risk of serious harm or where a crime (such as child abduction) may be committed. Bearing in mind the assessment of the law set out above concerning the limited duty to disclose reports which are subject to 'litigation privilege'[5] a lawyer who takes it upon himself to pass on confidential information out of a personal concern for the welfare of a child risks severe criticism for breaching client confidentiality.
(2) A solicitor may not allow a client to mislead the court.[6]
(3) It is possible that in wardship the court has an inherent jurisdiction to order a solicitor to disclose confidential information.[7]

---

1    Such a proposition would seem to contradict Lord Taylor LCJ's leading speech in *R v Derby Magistrates' Court ex parte B* [1996] AC 481, [1996] 1 FLR 513, HL.
2    Under Civil Procedure Act 1997, Sch 1, para 4 the Lord Chancellor can change rules of evidence by statutory instrument.
3    *R v Derby Magistrates' Court ex parte B* [1995] AC 481, [1996] 1 FLR 513, HL; and see **7.9** above.
4    *Guide to Professional Conduct of Solicitors 1996* (The Law Society), at App 16B (b)(iii); and see **7.23** above. The Guide carefully considers a number of possible dilemmas which may confront a solicitor where he has information from a client (child or adult) which suggests that a crime may be committed.
5    See **7.22** above.
6    See **6.10** above.
7    *Re B (Abduction: Disclosure)* [1995] 1 FLR 774, CA, where a solicitor was required by the court to give his client's address where a child had been abducted.

## The abolition of privilege in children proceedings?

**7.27**    As already mentioned, two Family Division judges have allied themselves with the view that in children proceedings there should be no such thing as legal professional privilege. Thus, Wall J allied himself with the *obiter dictum* of Thorpe J (as he then was) in the following terms:[1]

> 'For what it is worth, and accepting that what I say is plainly obiter, I respectfully align myself with the decision of Thorpe J in [the *Essex* case[2]], where he said:
>
>> "For my part, I would wish to see case-law go yet further and to make it plain that the legal representatives in possession of such material relevant to determination but contrary to the interests of their client, not only are unable to resist disclosure by reliance on legal professional privilege, but have a positive duty to disclose to the other parties and to the court ..."'

**7.28**    However, until Parliament says otherwise, it seems, with respect, that it cannot be said that normal legal professional privilege is altered by the Children Act 1989. Rules provide that confidential material can be disclosed only with leave of the court. This is statutory sanction for enabling it to be said – indeed the House of Lords has said it[3] – that, as a condition of grant of that leave, the court can insist that the reports be disclosed. That is very different from saying, without sanction from Parliament and in an arena created by statute, that the courts should by order override legal professional privilege. As has been observed:

> 'Should the child lawyer carry a warning for his or her child law clients, whether child, parent or other potential party to proceedings: 'Think before you speak to me'? To pose the last question surely provides the answer [to the question of the extent to which legal professional privilege should be further eroded in children proceedings]?'[4]

Put that way the necessity for the near absolute nature of privilege for communications between solicitor and client perhaps becomes clearer. While it is possible to have sympathy with judges who would see full disclosure of all otherwise confidential information which impinges on the welfare of the child disclosed to the court (in line with the views of Professor Tapper quoted above),[5] the need for a core of confidentiality for the private client surely remains.

## 4    NEGOTIATIONS AND 'WITHOUT PREJUDICE' CORRESPONDENCE

**7.29**    If the purpose of litigation is to seek a court adjudication upon the parties' differences, the negotiated agreement (whereby submission to the final adjudication of the court is avoided) must be at least as important to most parties.[6] The evidence which forms the basis of such negotiations, whether they succeed or whether the

---

1    *Re DH (A Minor) (Child Abuse)* [1994] 1 FLR 679 at 703F.
2    *Essex County Council v R* [1993] 2 FLR 826.
3    *Re L (Police Investigation: Privilege)* [1996] 2 WLR 395, [1996] 1 FLR 731; considered above.
4    See Burrows 'Disclosure in Children Cases' [1996] Fam Law 566 at 569.
5    See **7.9** above.
6    For a lay view on these questions, see Davis, Cretney and Collins *Simple Quarrels* (Clarendon Press, 1994).

dispute still goes to a final court hearing, forms an important component in the process of a case. It will be convenient here to consider the subject as follows:

(1)   privilege and 'without prejudice' correspondence; and
(2)   mediation and the negotiated agreement, which itself involves an assessment of the law as it seems likely to be when and if the Family Law Act 1996 comes into operation.

## Privilege and 'without prejudice' correspondence

**7.30**     It is public policy that litigants be encouraged to negotiate and attempt to settle their differences rather than contest such differences through the courts to a final hearing.[1] From this has developed the view that without prejudice[2] communications are privileged from disclosure;[3] and, in that the rule probably applies to all who endeavour to assist parties in achieving a settlement (such as mediators or court welfare officers), it is wider than the rule relating to legal professional privilege. All negotiations, whether oral or in writing, are privileged, as is any document which is part of the negotiations. If genuinely part of negotiations a letter marked 'without prejudice' will be so privileged; but so too will any other document – whether or not marked 'without prejudice' – which is part of the negotiations. Similarly, evidence on discussions with a view to settlement will be privileged, even though 'without prejudice', or similar words, are not used;[4] and this principle probably applies also to mediation (conciliation)[5] whether the issue concerns children[6] or money.[7] In the case of children, this is subject to the important rider that where statements are made in the course of conciliation or mediation that indicate that the maker has in the past caused, or may in the future cause, serious harm to a child, that statement may be admitted to the court at the discretion of the trial judge.[8]

## Waiver of privilege

**7.31**     As with other branches of privilege, the privilege attaching to without prejudice correspondence is that of the individual who made the communication, or of the client. Thus, only the individual who made the communication – the writer of the 'without prejudice' letter, for example – can waive the privilege. If a solicitor wrote the letter, only the client can waive privilege.[9] Once privilege is waived, the document

1     See eg *Cutts v Head* [1984] Ch 290, [1984] 1 All ER 597, CA.
2     The Glossary to Civil Procedure Rules 1998 offers a definition of 'without prejudice' as follows: 'Negotiations with a view to a settlement are usually conducted "without prejudice" which means that the circumstances in which the content of those negotiations may be revealed to the court are very limited' – more a comment on the concept of privilege rather than a precise legal definition.
3     *Rush & Tomkins Ltd v Greater London Council* [1989] AC 1280, [1988] 3 All ER 737, HL.
4     *Chocoladafabriken Lindt v Nestle* [1978] RPC 287.
5     *McKenzie v McKenzie* [1971] P 33, [1971] 3 All ER 1034, CA
6     *Re D (Minors) (Conciliation: Privilege)* [1993] 1 FLR 932, CA.
7     But see consideration of the mediated 'memorandum of understanding' at **7.36** below.
8     *Re D (Minors) (Conciliation: Privilege)* (above); and see *Working Together Under the Children Act 1989* (HMSO, 1991) for the duties of professionals where given otherwise confidential information concerning harm to children (**7.10** above).
9     *Calcraft v Guest* [1898] 1 QB 759, CA.

or the evidence as to the negotiations are admissible as evidence, although because one party waives privilege does not mean that evidence of both sides of the negotiations then becomes admissible.

## Acceptance of without prejudice offer

**7.32**    An offer contained in a without prejudice communication is capable of acceptance and, if accepted, the communication ceases to be privileged.[1] This will depend, however, on the acceptance of terms as a whole: a party cannot accept certain terms but not others and then claim admissibility of the totality of the without prejudice communications. Ordinary contract principles would seem to apply: to form a contract the acceptance cannot be conditional on other counter-proposals being accepted.[2] If an offer is accepted unconditionally and the privilege is lost, the correspondence as a whole is admissible. Whether or not the parties are then held to their agreement will be subject to *Edgar*[3] principles.

## Admissions made 'without prejudice'

**7.33**    An admission or a statement of existing facts or of the strength of a party's case, even although marked 'without prejudice', is not privileged and can be referred to at any hearing.[4] Thus, where, during negotiations, a party admits the existence of financial information not hitherto disclosed, evidence as to that admission can be adduced in evidence,[5] although it will be for the party alleging the admission to prove it. To allow otherwise would be to permit a party to fail to give the full relevant disclosure on which the financial relief jurisdiction is based,[6] yet purport to hide behind the cloak of privilege information as to his means which should be in the open domain of the evidence before the court. On this question, a mediator would be compellable, although as a first step the party to whom the admission was made should give notice to admit facts to the party who made the admission.[7]

**7.34**    Whether a district judge on a financial dispute-resolution appointment would be compellable is a more difficult question. This may be thought to revolve, in part, upon a distinction between the role of the mediator in mediation and the district judge in the very different forum of the financial dispute-resolution appointment: the first facilitates the parties in reaching an agreement; the second has a more directive role in suggesting solutions. It may be that their roles are different. However, that is not the whole answer since it may be argued that the question truly depends on whether or not a district judge, at a financial dispute-resolution appointment, is acting

---

1    It is probably necessary to exclude from this assessment of the parties' agreement to terms the mediated 'memorandum of understanding'; see **7.36** below.

2    The counter-offer has the effect of creating a fresh set of proposals and, in law, the original set of proposals is not capable of acceptance (*Hyde v Wrench* (1840) 3 Beav 334).

3    *Edgar v Edgar* [1981] 1 WLR 1410, (1981) FLR 19, , CA; and see further **7.37** below.

4    *Buckinghamshire County Council v Moran* [1989] 2 All ER 225, CA.

5    To this extent *Practice Direction of 16 June 1997 (Ancillary Relief Procedure: Pilot Scheme)* [1997] 2 FLR 304 which states that 'evidence ... of any admission made in the course of a FDR appointment will not be admissible in evidence' appears to be wrong.

6    *Livesey (formerly Jenkins) v Jenkins* [1985] AC 424, [1985] FLR 813, HL; and see **6.7** above.

7    Rules of the Supreme Court 1965, Ord 27, r 2; County Court Rules 1981, Ord 20, r 2; and, in respect of non family proceedings, see Civil Procedure Rules 1998, r 32.18 (Notice to admit facts).

'in relation to his judicial functions' because, as a judge, it is probable that he is not compellable.[1] Whether a district judge in the role of mediator at a financial dispute-resolution appointment can properly be said to be acting 'in relation to his judicial functions' is altogether another question.[2]

## *Calderbank* correspondence

**7.35** Not only is it public policy to encourage negotiation, but, especially in the ancillary relief field, parties are being encouraged more and more to set out in correspondence terms on which they will settle.[3] A particular reason for without prejudice correspondence in the ancillary relief jurisdiction is a *Calderbank*[4] letter, which is written without prejudice but subject to the proviso that it may be referred to the court on the issue of costs. The principles derived from *Calderbank* have now been incorporated into the Rules[5] so that the importance of without prejudice correspondence in this context is emphasised.[6] However, a *Calderbank* letter may not be referred to the court, 'until the question of costs falls to be decided',[7] unless, presumably, the party who writes the letter decides to waive privilege.[8] A *Calderbank* letter can be written before issue of proceedings,[9] a proposition which is confirmed by the Civil Procedure Rules 1998.[10]

## Mediation and the negotiated agreement: Family Law Act 1996

**7.36** The Family Law Act 1996 introduces, in a somewhat unfocussed way, a variety of terms which may or may not connote agreement, for example the 'financial arrangement' and the 'negotiated agreement', referred to first in the Family Law Act 1996, s 9(2). Nowhere in the Act are the terms clearly defined. To this confusion can now be added the terminology of the mediation movement: the 'memorandum of understanding'. Before looking at this variety of terms it is necessary to consider the present law, much of which is likely to survive the coming into force of the new Act.

---

1    *Warren v Warren* [1996] 2 FLR 777 at 785, per Lord Woolf MR, CA: '... it is my view that no judge in relation to his judicial functions is a compellable witness'.

2    Considered further at **10.53** below.

3    This is one of the features which the reformers had in mind in the setting-up of the Ancillary Relief Pilot Scheme; and see eg *Gojkovic v Gojkovic (No 2)* [1992] Fam 40, [1991] 2 FLR 233, CA; *A v A (Costs: Appeal)* [1996] 1 FLR 14, per Singer J.

4    *Calderbank v Calderbank* [1976] Fam 93, [1975] 3 All ER 333, CA. A *Calderbank* letter is effective only where there has been full disclosure of both parties' means (*Gojkovic v Gojkovic (No 2)* (above)).

5    See eg Rules of the Supreme Court 1965, Ord 22, r 14 (*Calderbank* letters); Ord 62, r 9 (effect of *Calderbank* correspondence on awards of costs); and see Civil Procedure Rules 1998, r 36.20 (considered below).

6    The equivalent to the *Calderbank* letter in the Civil Procedure Rules 1998 is the Part 36 offer. The Civil Procedure Rules 1998, Part 36 sets out a series of rules dealing with the payment into court ('Part 36 payment') and the Part 36 offer alongside one another. Where an applicant 'fails to obtain a judgment which is more advantageous than a Part 36 offer' a presumption operates that he should have his costs 'unless [the court] considers it unjust to do so' (r 36.20(1)(b) and (2)).

7    Rules of the Supreme Court 1965, Ord 22, r 14; County Court Rules 1981, Ord 11, r 10; and, in respect of non family proceedings, see Civil Procedure Rules 1998, r 36.19.

8    For waiver of privilege, see **7.2** above.

9    *Butcher v Wolfe and Another* [1999] 1 FLR 334, CA.

10   Civil Procedure Rules 1998, r 36.10.

## *Edgar* and the agreement 'fairly arrived at'

**7.37**    The starting point for any consideration of the status of agreements and their approval so far as the court is concerned is *Edgar v Edgar*.[1] That case concerned a settlement which included an agreement by the wife, given by her against legal advice, not to claim further capital provision from her husband. In subsequent divorce proceedings, she sought capital provision. This was awarded by the judge at first instance. Allowing the husband's appeal, Ormrod LJ reviewed earlier authorities and, with Oliver LJ, came to the following conclusions.

(1)    The terminology of the Matrimonial Causes Act 1973, s 25 places the court in the same position as it was under earlier legislation: spouses may not, by their own agreement, preclude the courts from exercising jurisdiction over their financial arrangements.[2] This will remain the position under the Family Law Act 1996.

(2)    That said, Oliver LJ held that:[3]

'... in a consideration of what is just to be done in the exercise of the court's powers under the [Matrimonial Causes Act 1973] in the light of the conduct of the parties, the court must, I think, start from the position that a solemn and freely negotiated bargain ... ought to be adhered to unless some clear and compelling reason, such as, for instance, a drastic change of circumstances, is shown to the contrary.'

(3)    Thus, while an agreement cannot bind the court, what weight should be given to it and to events leading to it as factors in the parties' conduct? In answering this question, Ormrod LJ set out – in a passage which has frequently been relied upon since – the basis upon which, he considered, judges should approach agreements between the parties:[4]

'It is not necessary in this connection to think in formal legal terms, such as misrepresentation or estoppel, *all* the circumstances as they affect each of two human beings must be considered in the complex relationship of marriage. So, the circumstances surrounding the making of the agreement are relevant. Undue pressure by one side, exploitation of a dominant position to secure an unreasonable advantage, inadequate knowledge, possibly bad legal advice, an important change of circumstances, unforeseen or overlooked at the time of making the agreement, are all relevant to the question of justice between the parties. Important too is the general proposition that, formal agreements, properly and fairly arrived at with competent legal advice, should not be displaced unless there are good and substantial grounds for concluding that an injustice will be done by holding the parties to the terms of their agreement.'

**7.38**    Since *Edgar*, the courts have relatively consistently followed this approach[5] making allowances for, for example, a wife who had submitted to an agreement on the

---

1    [1980] 1 WLR 1410, (1981) 2 FLR 19, CA, affirmed by *Xydhias v Xydhias* [1999] 1 FLR 683, CA.

2    *Hyman v Hyman* [1929] AC 601, HL; *Wright v Wright* [1970] 1 WLR 1219, CA.

3    (1981) 2 FLR 19 at 31H. Further, both Oliver and Ormrod LJ (at 24H) stressed that reaching an agreement was a factor to be taken into account as conduct within the terms of s 25(2) (as it now is).

4    Ibid, 25C.

5    See eg *H v H (Financial Relief: Non-disclosure: Costs)* [1994] 2 FLR 94, where Thorpe J reversed a district judge's decision to alter the financial arrangements set out in a separation deed. The husband had spent recklessly by the time the ancillary relief claim came on. While finding that the district judge's order might reflect reality, the judge held that the court should ensure that the parties' agreement should be honoured by the husband. In *N v N (Consent Order:*

basis of manifestly bad legal advice,[1] and a husband who, in a very short period after the agreement, had fallen on hard times while his former wife had maintained her share of the matrimonial assets intact.[2]

**7.39**    Exceptions to the general (*Edgar*) rule can occur, but they will be in only exceptional circumstances, turning on such issues as the standard of legal advice,[3] exceptional changes of circumstances,[4] or, more obviously, a failure fully to disclose means or material information.[5]

## Mediation and the 'memorandum of understanding'

**7.40**    To this muddled statutory thinking, the mediators have now added the 'memorandum of understanding'. In this context, it may be assumed that the 'understanding' is no more than the equivalent of a form of words agreed between the parties which remains privileged from disclosure until it has been considered and approved by the parties' solicitors. The memorandum in probative terms – save where facts are stated in it[6] – is of limited use, although, as a means for the parties to avoid expensive litigation and further disharmony, the mediated memorandum is an undoubted boon. That said, however, it remains fundamental to the process in evidential terms that full disclosure be provided to the mediator.[7] Whether or not disclosure is made, the memorandum remains a document which is privileged from disclosure.

## 5    DOCUMENTS OR INFORMATION TENDING TO INCRIMINATE

**7.41**    The Civil Evidence Act 1968, s 14(1) exempts a person from answering questions or providing documents which would 'tend to expose that person [or their spouse] to proceedings for an offence or for the recovery of a penalty'. Thus, a party to

    *Variation)* [1993] 2 FLR 868, CA, a wife was held to her agreement (in a side letter which accompanied an order for periodical payments) that she would seek no further order. In *Benson v Benson (Deceased)* [1996] 1 FLR 692, the husband was held to his agreement (recorded in a consent order *inter vivos* and subsequently varied by agreement with the wife's personal representatives following her death).

1    *Camm v Camm* (1983) FLR 577, CA.
2    *Beach v Beach* [1995] 2 FLR 160, Thorpe J.
3    See eg *B v B (Consent Order: Variation)* [1995] 1 FLR 9, Thorpe J: where a wife with a history of psychiatric disturbance had agreed, on the basis of poor legal advice, to a termination after seven years of her periodical payments, it would be manifestly unjust to uphold that agreement.
4    See eg *Beach v Beach* [1995] 2 FLR 160.
5    *Livesey (formerly Jenkins) v Jenkins* [1985] AC 424, [1985] FLR 813, HL
6    See **7.33** above.
7    This assessment takes no account of doubts that have been expressed about the requirement to seek mediation as a condition of grant of legal aid (Family Law Act 1996, s 29) and anxieties concerning the lack of a statutory code for mediators and of their failure, on occasion, to ensure full relevant disclosure from both parties. An adviser will also be in a difficult position where a mediator has negotiated an 'understanding' that appears prejudicial to his client; but that is a subject beyond the scope of this book.

proceedings may claim privilege from discovery for documents which might reasonably be expected to expose him to criminal proceedings.

**7.42** This principle has been overridden, to an extent, in children proceedings where a party may be able to claim immunity from prosecution as a result of giving evidence, in the children proceedings, about a crime.[1] This is justified on the ground that there is a public interest in individuals being encouraged to talk frankly, and without prosecution on the basis of what they have said, about what has given rise to the state of affairs concerning a child (for example, unexplained injuries which she has suffered). That is not say that information arising in proceedings cannot be passed on to the police.[2] The distinction is that the police are entitled, if given leave by the court, to use the information released by the family court to assist them with their inquiries and ensured, in *Re EC (Disclosure of Material)*,[3] that a proper inquiry was carried out into her sister's death; but the prosecution may not rely on what a parent may have said in the course of a child protection investigation or in court proceedings as evidence in subsequent criminal proceedings.

---

1   Children Act 1989, s 98(2).
2   *Re EC (Disclosure of Material)* [1996] 2 FLR 725, CA.
3   Ibid.

# Chapter 8

## PARENTAGE

### 1   INTRODUCTION

#### Direction for tests

**8.1**    Where an issue of paternity arises in civil proceedings,[1] the Family Law
Reform Act 1969[2] provides that any party may apply to the court for a direction for
blood tests[3] to seek to establish whether or not a party 'is or is not thereby excluded[4]
from being the father' of the person or child concerned in the proceedings. The
purpose of the test will be to establish evidence for use in existing civil proceedings,
and the direction will be ancillary to existing proceedings. Where there are no
proceedings, or no way for a parent to bring the issue of paternity before the court, a
person may be able to make application for a declaration under the Rules of the
Supreme Court 1965, Ord 15, r 16.[5]

#### Civil proceedings

**8.2**    Tests are available in 'civil proceedings', a term which is not defined in the
Family Law Reform Act 1969. The term may be taken, therefore, to exclude criminal
proceedings, but includes family proceedings in all jurisdictions: the High Court,
county courts and family proceedings courts. Indeed, family proceedings are likely to
form the majority in which a blood test direction is used. Procedure is governed by the
Rules of the Supreme Court 1965, Ord 112 and the County Court Rules 1981, Ord 47,
r 5.[6] Blood test directions are made alongside existing proceedings, and therefore,
formally, applications in family proceedings will be covered by the rules as originally
drafted[7] whereas applications in such proceedings as under the Inheritance (Provision
for Family and Dependants) Act 1975 will be covered by the new-style Rules of the

---

1    The Government has issued a consultation paper dated March 1998 in which it seeks views on
     the law relating to paternity and parental responsibility with a view to considering legislation –
     mostly procedural in cases of paternity.
2    Section 20(1).
3    Now generally DNA tests.
4    Strictly speaking, tests can only exclude a person from paternity; but see **8.8** below and,
     especially, the comments of Waite LJ in *Re A (A Minor) (Paternity: Refusal of Blood Test)*
     [1994] 2 FLR 463, CA, considered there.
5    See an explanation of this in *T v Child Support Agency and Another* [1997] 2 FLR 875,
     especially at 884D–886A, per Cazalet J. This is essentially a procedural matter, but may prove to
     be significant for the small minority of parents who cannot have a question of paternity otherwise
     brought before the court.
6    These rules, as Ord 112, remain in force following the coming into operation of the Civil
     Procedure Rules 1998.
7    See explanation at **1.31** above.

Supreme Court 1965, Ord 112. For practical purposes, the difference in forms of application will be minimal.


## 2   THE DIRECTION

### Discretion to direct

**8.3**      Whether or not to order a direction is a matter for the discretion of the court, which discretion should be exercised only in the interests of the child concerned.[1] In *Re H (Paternity: Blood Test)*,[2] the Court of Appeal reviewed the basis for directing tests. In that case, a man had undergone a vasectomy. His wife subsequently had sexual relations with another man (B) and became pregnant. The child was registered in the husband's name. B applied for contact and, if this were opposed, for DNA tests. The mother opposed the tests. The judge held that there should be tests, and the Court of Appeal upheld that decision. In the course of his judgment, Ward LJ reviewed recent authorities and the background to the scheme set up by the Family Law Reform Act 1969, ss 20–23, and considered the questions which must be asked when the court exercises its discretion to make a direction,[3] among which are the following.

#### *Is the mother's refusal to submit to a test determinative of whether a test should be ordered?*

**8.4**      In *Re H (Paternity: Blood Test)*, the judge below was confronted by conflicting authorities. In *Re CB (A Minor) (Blood Tests)*,[4] Wall J stated that the question could be determinative; whereas Mr Michael Horowitz QC (sitting as a deputy judge of the High Court) in *Re G (A Minor) (Blood Test)*[5] stated that it need not be determinative. Ward LJ pointed out that the court could do no more than direct a blood test, since a sample 'shall not be taken from [any] person except with his consent'[6] for compliance with a direction. Subject to that proviso, and in the knowledge that a party might refuse to comply with the direction, the court was entitled to make the direction.[7] The court could then draw any appropriate inference from the refusal to comply with the direction.

---

1     *S v S; W v Official Solicitor* [1972] AC 24, [1970] 3 All ER 107, HL; and see *Re F (A Minor) (Blood Tests: Paternal Rights)* [1993] Fam 314, CA.
2     [1996] 2 FLR 65, CA.
3     Ward LJ proposed a form of words for the direction (at 83D) as follows:
       'It is directed pursuant to s 20(1) of the Family Law Reform Act 1969:
       (a) that blood tests (including DNA tests) be used to ascertain whether such tests show that [Mr A] is or is not excluded from being the father of [child B] born on [date]; and
       (b) that for that purpose blood samples be taken on or before [date] from the following persons: [Mr A], [Mrs X (mother of child B)] and [child B]; and
       (c) that the person appearing to the court to have care and control of [child B], who is under the age of 16, is [Mrs X];
       (d) that such tests be carried out by [Mr CD of [address]]'.
4     [1994] 2 FLR 762.
5     [1994] 1 FLR 495.
6     Family Law Reform Act 1969, s 21(1); and see *S v S; W v Official Solicitor* [1972] AC 24.
7     [1996] 2 FLR 65 at 75D.

### Can an adverse inference be drawn only if compliance is refused after a direction is made?

**8.5**    The Family Law Reform Act 1969, s 23(1)[1] provides that where a direction has been given refusal to comply may enable the court to draw such inferences 'as appear proper in the circumstances'. In *Re H (Paternity: Blood Test)*, the question arose as to whether an inference could be drawn if the refusal was made in advance of the direction being made. Ward LJ held that, although refusal of a direction was 'more eloquent testimony':[2]

> 'Common sense seems to me to dictate that if the truth can be established with certainty,[3] a refusal to produce the certainty justifies some inference that the refusal is made to hide the truth, even if the inference is not as strong as when the court's direction is flouted.'

Refusal in advance of the direction can thus give rise to an adverse inference if a parent clearly indicates an intention not to comply with any direction which the court makes.

### To what extent does the welfare of the child influence the decision?

**8.6**    If a test can be shown to be against the child's interests, it should not be directed. Ward LJ cited[4] with approval a *dictum* of Lord Reid in *S v S; W v Official Solicitor*[5] that 'the court ought to permit a blood test ... unless satisfied that that would be against the child's interests'. However, interests of others may be involved – such as one or other of the parents or other parties to the proceedings – so that the child's welfare is not necessarily paramount. Again, Ward LJ quoted[6] from *S v McC*,[7] this time from Lord Hodson: 'The interests of other persons are involved in ordinary litigation. The infant needs protection but that is no justification for making his rights superior to those of others'. In this case, Ward LJ held that 'every child has a right to know the truth unless his welfare clearly justifies the cover-up'.[8]

### How does the prospect of success in the proceedings influence the decision?

**8.7**    The outcome of the proceedings in which the direction is sought is not, alone, a factor in deciding whether to make a direction; the paternity question is a free-standing application to be decided on its merits. Any gain to a child in not being disturbed by the application must be balanced against the benefit to him in knowing his parentage.[9] Thus, in *Re H*, although it seemed to the judge that it was unlikely that B would secure an order for contact, if a parent, he was 'entitled to

---

1    See further **8.7** below.
2    [1996] 2 FLR 65 at 77A and D.
3    Scientific testing now makes this 'virtually inescapable': *Re A (A Minor) (Paternity: Refusal of Blood Test)* [1994] 2 FLR 463 at 473B, per Waite LJ, CA.
4    [1996] 2 FLR 65 at 77F.
5    [1972] AC 24 at 45D, [1970] 3 All ER 107, HL.
6    [1996] 2 FLR 65 at 77G.
7    [1972] AC 24 at 58G.
8    [1996] 2 FLR 65 at 80G.
9    Ibid, at 78G–H.

apply' for contact;[1] so that parentage must be decided before the application can even get to the stage of being considered and, perhaps, dismissed by the court.

## Inferences from failure to comply with a direction

**8.8**    Originally, blood tests had the effect of excluding[2] paternity; tests could not prove paternity beyond any possible doubt. In absolute terms, DNA is the same, but the narrowing of the probabilities against paternity are reduced to an infinitesimal amount. Where a person is required to comply with a direction for tests, the Family Law Reform Act 1969, s 23(1) provides that where a direction has been given:

> 'And [where] any person fails to take any step required of him for the purpose of giving effect to the direction, the court may draw such inferences, if any, from the fact as appear proper in the circumstances.'

The question of the scientific probability and of the inferences which the courts may now safely draw, was explained by Waite LJ in *Re A (A Minor) (Paternity: Refusal of Blood Test)*[3] as follows:

> 'Against that background of law and scientific advance, it seems to me to follow, both in justice and in common sense, that if a mother makes a claim against one of the possible fathers, and he chooses to exercise his right not to submit to be tested, the inference that he is the father of the child should be virtually inescapable.'

**8.9**    In *Re A*, Waite LJ reviewed[4] the legislative history of the Family Law Reform Act 1969, the advances in scientific testing and the advent of the Children Act 1989, and concluded that the Family Law Reform Act 1969, s 23 'was untouched by the Children Act'.[5]

> 'The result is that all issues of paternity now fall to be resolved within the framework of the Children Act by courts which are given statutory freedom (at all levels of the family court jurisdiction) to deal with the evidence at large, and (specifically) to reach their own determination as to the significance to be attached to, and the inferences to be drawn from, the circumstances that a person has refused to consent to a scientific test directed by the court under [Family Law Reform Act 1969, s 20].'

### *The inference in* Re A

**8.10**    *Re A* involved a man (G) who had had sexual relations with the mother of a child at a time when the mother had been having sexual relations with two other men – as subsequently reported in the *News of the World*. The mother claimed periodical payments (pre-Child Support Act 1991) from G. He denied paternity, but, when a direction for DNA testing was made, he refused to comply, essentially on the ground that there were others who might also be the father. Waite LJ rejected G's appeal insofar as it was based on the allegation that others might also be the father. He held that a child has a legal claim to be maintained by his father:[6]

---

1    Children Act 1989, s 10(4) – parent's entitlement to apply for s 8 orders.
2    See terminology of Family Law Reform Act 1969, s 20(1), quoted at **8.1** above.
3    [1994] 2 FLR 463 at 473B, CA.
4    Ibid, at 469D–F.
5    Ibid, at 469G.
6    Ibid, at 473E–F.

'G was given the opportunity to have it established by submission to a blood test that he was – or was not – that man. He has chosen to reject that opportunity. The fact that there are others to whom the same opportunity might have been afforded is in my view irrelevant to the inference that now has to be drawn from his own refusal. That inference is inescapable. The court should find proven forensically what G, by his refusal, has prevented from being established scientifically – namely the fact that he is [the child's] father.'

## Standard of proof

**8.11** In *Re A*, Waite LJ considered the question of 'degree of proof' in cases of paternity and summarised the effect of the authorities on the subject as being that paternity raises a serious issue requiring that the 'balance of probability has to be established to a degree of sureness in the mind of the court which matches the seriousness of the issue'. However, the process of assessment of balance of probability to any degree is likely to be taken over by the precision of the scientific testing. As to any inference under the Family Law Reform Act 1969, s 23(1), the combined effect of scientific testing, on the one hand, and the cases of *Re A* and *Re H*, on the other, must make it almost impossible for anyone directed to take part in tests to escape inferences against him if he refuses to do so.

# Chapter 9

## MATRIMONIAL CAUSES

### 1 INTRODUCTION

**9.1** Divorce is one of the only areas of mainstream family law, at first instance, where procedures remain rooted in civil procedural rules. However, this applies only to the handful of defended divorces which are dealt with by the courts each year. Petitions for nullity, whether or not defended, are very rare. The combination of these factors means that matrimonial causes will be dealt with only cursorily in the present edition.

**9.2** That said, it remains the case that the 'special procedure'[1] contains some singular aspects from an evidential point of view which require brief consideration before it is consigned to history by the procedure set up under the Family Law Act 1996.[2]

### 2 MATRIMONIAL CAUSES

#### Cause commenced by petition

**9.3** Of all the forms of family proceedings, the main suit in a matrimonial cause approximates most closely to a conventional civil action, save that it is one of the rare surviving instances of a process which is commenced by filing a petition.[3] The petition for divorce, judicial separation or nullity which begins any matrimonial cause is required to contain certain formal information set out in the Family Proceedings Rules 1991.[4] This information is followed, first, by the assertion that the marriage has irretrievably broken down (in cases of divorce) and, secondly, the fact under the Matrimonial Causes Act 1973, s 1(2) relied upon (in cases of divorce or judicial separation) or the ground in the case of other petitions. Next, the petition is required to contain 'brief particulars of the individual facts relied on *but not the evidence by which*

---

1 Family Proceedings Rules 1991, rr 2.24(3) and 2.36, characterised by Ormrod LJ as 'a complete misnomer. It is no longer the "special procedure"; it is now the ordinary procedure for dealing with undefended causes of all kinds' (*Day v Day* [1980] Fam 29, (1980) FLR 341 at 344(iv), CA).
2 The special procedure will not survive the Family Law Act 1996 for nullity petitions as it does not, at present, apply to them. Family Proceedings Rules 1991, r 2.24(3) applies only to petitions for divorce and judicial separation.
3 Family Proceedings Rules 1991, r 2.2(1).
4 Ibid, r 2.3 provides that 'unless otherwise directed' a petition shall contain the information set out in App 2 to the Rules, such as date of marriage, addresses and occupation of the parties, names and dates of birth of children, etc.

*they are to be proved*' (emphasis added)[1] and concludes with a prayer (hence the name 'petition') for the relief sought.

## Evidence on the main suit

**9.4**      It is not intended here to consider divorce procedure,[2] but it is necessary to review the evidence required and the way it is dealt with by the court. In a defended divorce, the evidence required to establish facts pleaded, for example unreasonable behaviour,[3] may have to be as precisely proved as in any contested civil trial;[4] whereas the evidence required to support an undefended cause under the special procedure is as rudimentary as it can be.

## The petition

### *Proof of marriage*

**9.5**      Proof of the parties' marriage is established by filing their certified marriage certificate.[5] The importance of this document cannot be overstated, since it is the foundation of the entire jurisdiction. Without a marriage, the provisions of the Matrimonial Causes Act 1973 cannot be invoked and the financial relief available to the parties to a relationship is very limited.[6]

### *Grounds and facts*

**9.6**      In the case of a married person seeking a divorce, there is a single ground: 'that the marriage has broken down irretrievably'.[7] The Matrimonial Causes Act 1973 is phrased negatively, by providing that this ground cannot be proved save by establishing one or more of the facts set out in s 1(2): adultery, unreasonable behaviour, desertion for two years, two years' living apart with consent and five years' living apart.[8] By contrast, for all other petitions the grounds are the facts themselves:

---

1      Family Proceedings Rules 1991, App 2, para (1)(m). This complies with the standard rule of pleading (see eg Rules of the Supreme Court 1965, Ord 18, r 7(1); and see Chapter 2 for further consideration of pleading).
2      See Family Proceedings Rules 1991, rr 2.9–2.51 and the procedural guide in *The Family Court Practice 1999* (Family Law).
3      Matrimonial Causes Act 1973, s 1(2)(b); and see *Butterworth v Butterworth* [1997] 2 FLR 336, CA.
4      See eg *Butterworth v Butterworth* (ibid); considered at **9.9** below.
5      Family Proceedings Rules 1991, r 2.6(2). In the case of a foreign marriage, a certificate or register entry relating to that marriage will be evidence (Family Proceedings Rules 1991, r 10.14 (1)), but these documents should be accompanied by a certified translation (r 10.14(2)).
6      See eg *dicta* of Millet J in *Windeler v Whitehall* [1990] 2 FLR 505 at 506; but see provisions of Inheritance (Provision for Family and Dependants) Act 1975, s 1(1)(e), which may enable a cohabitant to set up a dependency after the death of her partner.
7      Matrimonial Causes Act 1973, s 1(1).
8      Ibid, s 1(2)(a)–(e).

judicial separation consists of proving that one of the facts in s 1(2) exists;[1] and nullity necessitates proving facts to set up a series of different grounds which differ according to whether the petitioner seeks to prove the marriage void or voidable.[2]

## Evidence for a decree of divorce, judicial separation or nullity

**9.7** The Matrimonial Causes Act 1973, s 1(3) and (4) (in the case of divorce) and s 17(2) (judicial separation) provide that it is 'the duty of the court to inquire, so far as it reasonably can, into the facts alleged by the petitioner and into any facts alleged by the respondent'; and (for divorces) 'if the court is satisfied on the evidence of any such fact as is mentioned in [s 1(2)], then, unless it is satisfied on all the evidence that the marriage has not broken down irretrievably, it shall ... grant a decree of divorce'. Generally, save in the case of the small minority of defended divorces and petitions for nullity, this duty is discharged by a district judge considering the relevant papers placed before him under the special procedure.

### *Special procedure list*

**9.8** The special procedure is brought into operation by the petitioner filing a prescribed affidavit[3] whereupon the cause (if undefended and for divorce or judicial separation) will be entered in the special procedure list by the district judge (subject to any other direction).[4] Once entered in the special procedure list the district judge 'shall consider the evidence filed by the petitioner'.[5] If the district judge is satisfied[6] as to the evidence of irretrievable breakdown, he will sign a certificate under the special procedure;[7] or if the district judge is not satisfied, the petitioner may have an opportunity to file further evidence.[8] In an undefended cause, this is the nearest the court approaches to its duty to 'inquire ... into any facts alleged by the petitioner',[9] since, essentially, the court adopts a declaratory role in dealing with petitions (as with its role in dealing with adoption orders), rather that assuming its normal role of adjudicating upon disputed issues.

### *Defended causes*

**9.9** Once a cause becomes defended a different set of rules, many of them based on, or incorporating directly, the Rules of the Supreme Court 1965, become effective,

---

1  Matrimonial Causes Act 1973, s 17(1).
2  Ibid, ss 11 (void) and 12 (voidable).
3  Family Proceedings Rules 1991, r 2.24(3)(a).
4  Ibid, r 2.24(3).
5  Ibid, r 2.36(1). In this context the term 'petitioner' can be taken to imply 'respondent' where the cause is proceeding on the respondent's answer.
6  In satisfying himself as to the evidence, it has been held that there is no room for over-meticulousness or over-technicality by a district judge: (*R v Nottinghamshire County Court ex parte Byers* [1985] FLR 695, per Latey J).
7  Family Proceedings Rules 1991, r 2.36(1)(a).
8  Ibid, r 2.36(1)(b).
9  Matrimonial Causes Act 1973, ss 1(3) and 17(2).

ie many aspects of the range of civil procedures come into operation.[1] It has been held:[2]

> '... the present state of the English law of divorce gives the respondent to a divorce petition the right to oppose it and to have the allegations made in the petition against him properly proved to the satisfaction of the court to the civil standard of the balance of probabilities.'

Thus, in *Butterworth v Butterworth*,[3] a wife filed a petition which contained only allegations which 'were brief in the extreme with an absence of information, with an absence of particulars, most importantly [of violence, as alleged]'.[4] The recorder decided the case solely on the evidence he heard on the day of the trial, rather than relying on pleadings which had been properly prepared. For this, he was criticised in the Court of Appeal:[5]

> 'All respondents are entitled to pleadings if they wish to defend a divorce. ... [They] are entitled to have their cases properly tried and if it is a defended divorce, I have to say, properly tried by a judge.'

In conclusion, the Court of Appeal took the view – which it found totally unsatisfactory – that the recorder, and the district judge who had given directions, had failed to ensure that the husband knew the case he was due to meet; and that the recorder had 'to use a colloquialism, "ditched" the petition and made findings on generalised allegations proved in a form which the husband did not have an opportunity properly to meet'.[6]

**9.10**      Accordingly, once a cause becomes defended, the grant of a decree ceases to be a question of a declaration of the fact that a marriage has broken down irretrievably or that a couple be judicially separated. Instead, it becomes a question of trial of a serious issue properly pleaded and to proper standards of proof. It is perhaps ironic that *Butterworth v Butterworth* should have been a reminder of this in the dying days of the old law.[7]

### Undefended causes in open court

**9.11**      Where a district judge is not prepared to include a case in the special procedure list or where the cause is not for divorce or judicial separation (ie almost entirely, in nullity causes), the cause will be listed for trial in open court before a judge. In the case of petitions for nullity, there is provision for medical examination in certain circumstances.[8]

---

1    Family Proceedings Rules 1991, rr 2.11–2.21 and 2.28–2.35: exchange and filing of pleadings, amendment, service etc (rr 2.11–2.19); discovery (r 2.20) and interrogatories (r 2.21); evidence at the trial (r 2.28); evidence by deposition (r 2.29), by subpoena or witness summons (r 2.30); and trial (rr 2.32–2.33).
2    *Butterworth v Butterworth* [1997] 2 FLR 336 at 339G, per Butler-Sloss LJ; for standard of proof to civil standard, see **4.26** above.
3    Ibid, at 336, CA.
4    Ibid, at 337G.
5    Ibid, at 339C–D.
6    Ibid, at 340B.
7    Proof required for a divorce or separation order under the Family Law Act 1996 will be based on a matter of proof of expiry of time, not irretrievable breakdown based on a number of facts.
8    Family Proceedings Rules 1991, rr 2.22 and 2.23.

# Chapter 10

## FINANCIAL RELIEF

### 1 INTRODUCTION

#### Matrimonial ancillary relief

**10.1**     Most evidential principles which apply to claims for financial relief generally are derived from the matrimonial ancillary relief jurisdiction,[1] but it should not be forgotten that many of the principles which apply in that jurisdiction apply equally, for example, to proceedings for financial relief under the Inheritance (Provision for Family and Dependants) Act 1975 and under the Children Act 1989, s 17 and Sch 1. For the most part the principles which are described in the context of matrimonial ancillary relief may be taken also to apply to these other financial relief provisions.

**10.2**     Procedure within the matrimonial ancillary relief jurisdiction has been extensively altered by the Ancillary Relief Pilot Scheme[2] which operates in a limited number of county courts. This Scheme sets up a number of procedural alterations which are not the direct concern of this book. However, these procedural alterations have a number of important consequences in evidential terms and for pre-trial case preparation, such as in relation to discovery, questionnaires and privilege. These variations will be considered separately[3] from the section dealing with the main principles relating to ancillary relief; but, given the success of the Scheme, it seems likely that it will be adopted in some similar form in all courts from June 2000.

#### Equity and financial relief

**10.3**     As already mentioned, much of the family jurisdiction derives from equitable principles,[4] and in many ways the ancillary relief jurisdiction has many of the hallmarks of the sixteenth century origins of equity derived from the concept of judges exercising a discretion based on conscience.[5] This, in turn, can be said to give the court a paternalistic role which, in its turn, imposes on the judge an inquisitorial

---

1     Matrimonial Causes Act 1973, Part II (soon to be amended by Family Law Act 1996, Sch 2).
2     Now incorporated into Family Proceedings Rules 1991, SI 1991/1247, at rr 2.71–2.77.
3     See **10.35** et seq below.
4     A short essay on this subject appears at **1.18** above; and see Cretney and Masson *Principles of Family Law* 6th edn (Sweet & Maxwell, 1996) p 123 et seq and *Snell's Equity* 29th edn (Sweet & Maxwell, 1990) p 533 et seq.
5     See eg Baker *Spelman's Reports, Vol II* (Selden Society, 1978) pp 37–41 and 80–82; *Christopher St German on Chancery and Statute* (Selden Society, 1985) pp 71–73.

function, for example a duty imposed by statute to have regard to all the circumstances of the case.[1] This duty does not always sit easily with the adversarial system within which litigation in England and Wales is conducted.[2] In the ancillary relief jurisdiction the tension between the inquisitorial – even paternalistic[3] – role of the court and the adversarial mode of disposal of cases can, in many ways, be seen in its most developed form. This tension has left the procedural rules often lacking in precision;[4] and the Ancillary Relief Pilot Scheme has so far done little to clarify this imprecision.[5] From the stand-point of a family lawyer, the Civil Procedure Rules 1998 do little to increase the inquisitorial nature of family procedure[6] save in one or two vital respects.[7]

## Discretion and the financial relief jurisdiction

**10.4**      Pre-eminently, the financial relief jurisdiction is discretionary and the legislation is framed in terms which often imply an inquisitorial role for the court.[8] This leaves the very real potential for uncertainty between the parties' rights to call what evidence they choose and the court's duty to make enquiry as to the parties' financial circumstances. In practice, it is left to the parties to present their case and in the way that they wish, subject to full disclosure being given. However, in theory, there would be nothing to prevent a district judge or judge directing one or other party to provide documents or other evidence on particular facts which neither party had, until then, called evidence, or to which they had not even addressed their minds. In practice the tension between the parties' right to call evidence and the right of the district judge to investigate has been managed, but the Ancillary Relief Pilot Scheme will (rightly, it may be said) throw these tensions into higher relief.

## Property: equity and the law

**10.5**      Family law as a subject may be said to include a variety of equitable aspects of property law: from the doctrine of notice and the equity to set aside[9] through to implied trusts and proprietary estoppel. In that the last of these – implied trusts and proprietary estoppel – may form the only basis on which a non-owning cohabitant can claim a share in a couple's former home, they are very much within the ambit of family law. However, in procedural and evidential terms these aspects of the equitable jurisdiction are outside the ambit of conventional family proceedings rules;[10] and the

---

1    See eg Matrimonial Causes Act 1973, s 25(1).
2    See further **1.25** above.
3    See comments of Waite J in *Hildebrand v Hildebrand* [1992] 1 FLR 244; considered at **6.5** above.
4    See eg Family Proceedings Rules 1991, r 2.68; considered at **10.35** et seq.
5    See Burrows *Ancillary Relief Pilot Scheme – A Practice Guide* (Family Law, 1997), especially at para 9.14.
6    And see further **10.57** et seq below.
7    Considered at **1.31** above.
8    See eg the 'the duty of the court ... to have regard to all the circumstances of the case' (Matrimonial Causes Act 1973, s 25(1)); 'the duty of the court to consider whether it would be appropriate' to impose a financial clean break on the parties (s 25A(1)).
9    Eg against a bank, as in *Barclays Bank v O'Brien* [1994] 1 FLR 1, HL and a variety of succeeding cases.
10   Proceedings in respect of each of these topics would be covered by the Civil Procedure Rules 1998.

extent to which the courts exercise a discretion over disposal and an inquisitorial function are more narrowly defined. To embark upon an investigation of the evidential principles applicable to such proceedings (for the few who regard them as part of family law) is beyond the scope of this book.

## 2  GENERAL PRINCIPLES

### Discretion and the duty of disclosure

**10.6**     As has been seen, it can be argued that where the court is exercising its discretion in disposal of issues between the parties, there is a higher duty of disclosure[1] than where disposal is based on law alone.[2] Thus, in *Livesey (formerly Jenkins) v Jenkins*,[3] the leading case on the subject and authority for the propositions to be advanced here, a wife had failed to inform her husband and the court of the fact that she was shortly to remarry at a time when she and the husband were submitting to a consent order. The terms of that order were that she was to take a transfer of the husband's share in the former matrimonial home in full settlement of all financial claims between them. On the wife's remarriage the husband applied to set aside the order on grounds of the wife's non-disclosure of her intention to remarry; on appeal to the House of Lords, the husband was successful and the order was ultimately set aside. Lord Brandon, in a well-known passage, clearly relates the question of disclosure to the discretion the judge or district judge must exercise in disposing of an application for ancillary relief:[4]

> '... the terms of [the Matrimonial Causes Act 1973, s 25(1)][5] ... are, in my opinion, of crucial importance in relation to the questions raised by this appeal. The scheme which the legislature enacted by [the Matrimonial Causes Act 1973, ss 23, 24 and 25] was a scheme under which the court would be bound, before deciding whether to exercise its powers under ss 23 and 24, and, if so, in what manner, to have regard to all the circumstances of the case. ... It follows that, in proceedings in which the parties invoke the exercise of the court's powers under ss 23 and 24, they must provide the court with information about all the circumstances of the case, [including the matters specified in s 25(2)]. Unless they do so, directly or indirectly, and ensure that the information provided is correct, complete and up-to-date, the court is not equipped to exercise, and cannot therefore lawfully and properly exercise, its discretion in the manner ordained by s 25(1).'

**10.7**     From this passage, Lord Brandon links the question of disclosure closely with the duty of the court ('the court would be bound ... to have regard etc') to have

---

1     For a consideration of the duty of disclosure, see **6.7** above.
2     Cf consideration of legal professional privilege at **7.8** above; and disposal of the appeal in *Vernon v Bosley (No 2)* [1998] 1 FLR 304, CA; considered at **6.9** above.
3     [1985] AC 424, [1985] FLR 813, HL.
4     Ibid, at 822A–C.
5     Matrimonial Causes Act 1973, s 25(1): 'It shall be the duty of the court in deciding whether to exercise its powers under ss 23, 24 and 24A above and, if so, in what manner, to have regard to all the circumstances of the case, first consideration being given to the welfare while a minor of any child of the family who has not attained the age of eighteen'.

regard to all the circumstances of the case to enable the judge to exercise his discretion in disposal of the application, whether on a contested or a consent order basis.

## Disclosure and other forms of financial relief

**10.8**      Since the duty of disclosure derives from the court being bound to consider all the circumstances of the case, it is a short step to import the same duty into any financial relief legislation where a similar duty can be inferred from the statutory provisions under which the court exercises its powers. Indeed, such a duty was perhaps suggested by Lord Brandon himself when he stated:[1]

> 'It follows necessarily from [the fact that the court must be provided with correct, complete and up-to-date information] that each party concerned in claims for financial provision and property adjustment (*or other forms of ancillary relief not material in the present case*) owes a duty to the court to make full and frank disclosure of all material facts to the other party and the court.' (emphasis added)

Such provisions where the court has a duty to consider all the circumstances of a case, including certain prescribed matters, include the Children Act 1989, Sch 1, para 4(1),[2] the Inheritance (Provision for Family and Dependants) Act 1975, s 3(1)[3] and the Matrimonial and Family Proceedings Act 1984, s 18(1) and (2).[4]

## Disclosure and the 'clean break'

**10.9**      In his short speech in *Livesey (formerly Jenkins) v Jenkins*, Lord Scarman[5] linked the duty of disclosure to 'the justice of the clean break';[6] but, unfortunately, said no more on the subject than this. The Matrimonial Causes Act 1973, s 25A(1) imposes on the court a duty, when making orders for financial relief:

> '... to consider whether it would be appropriate so to exercise [its] powers that the financial obligations of each party towards the other will be terminated as soon after the grant of the decree [of divorce or nullity] as the court considers just and reasonable.'

Again, the word 'duty' is used which raises the concept of a discretion vested in the judge who must decide whether to adopt one course or another. Perhaps it is indeed possible to imply into these provisions a duty of full disclosure, although to debate the question further is probably unnecessary, since to arrive at s 25A(1) the court must already have had the full disclosure which is required to exercise its discretion under

---

1    *Livesey (formerly Jenkins) v Jenkins* [1985] FLR 813 at 823C.
2    'In deciding whether to exercise its powers under paragraph 1 or 2, and if so in what manner, the court shall have regard to all the circumstances ... '
3    Where the court is considering whether to make an order under s 2 of the Act 'the court shall ... in determining whether and in what manner it shall exercise its powers under that section, have regard to the following matters ... '
4    'In deciding whether to exercise its powers under s 17 [of the Act] and, if so, in what manner ... the court shall have regard to all the circumstances ...'
5    [1985] FLR 813 at 815G–816A.
6    A concept developed by Lord Scarman himself in *Minton v Minton* [1979] AC 593, [1979] 1 All ER 79, HL and now provided for, to an extent, by statute in Matrimonial Causes Act 1973, s 25A(1).

s 25(1) and (2). By definition, therefore, full disclosure should already have preceded the court's consideration of its duty under s 25A(1).

## Disclosure, mediation and negotiated agreements

**10.10**     It is by now trite law that any agreement incorporated into a court order derives its enforceability from the order, not from the agreement which preceded it.[1] However, where parties reach agreement through mediation or by other negotiated means and provided they are at arm's length and separately advised, that agreement is likely to be upheld by the courts.[2] With the increased interest in mediation, and financial dispute-resolution under the Ancillary Relief Pilot Scheme, the question of full disclosure in the mediation process becomes as important as in any other context where financial relief is under consideration.[3] Failure to disclose in respect of a consent order gives a party aggrieved a basis for applying to set aside the order;[4] but where the failure to disclose is in relation to a negotiated agreement or one reached following mediation then recourse to the courts can only be on the basis of contractual remedies, such as misrepresentation and mistake.[5]

## Disclosure and professional negligence

**10.11**     It is well known that a failure properly to investigate a spouse's financial circumstances can give rise to a claim in professional negligence against the solicitor who has failed properly to seek discovery.[6] Further, it has been held that a solicitor's firm has a case to answer in negligence where it has failed to ensure a full valuation of a former matrimonial home which subsequently sells for more than was anticipated at the time of a consent order.[7] The difficulty for many practitioners is in being able to identify how far a legal representative is reasonably required to go in pressing for discovery – the question of steering between the 'Scylla' of dissipating assets in costs as against the 'Charybdis' of failing to protect a client's interests.[8]

## Discovery: a discretionary remedy

**10.12**     In the field of inquiry under the financial relief jurisdiction, equitable principles are again significant since, as has already been discussed, discovery is a discretionary remedy. This therefore gives the court a wide choice in deciding whether to require a party to provide discovery,[9] and this discretionary approach can

---

1     *De Lasala v de Lasala* [1980] AC 546, [1979] 3 WLR 390, HL; *Edgar v Edgar* [1981] 1 WLR 1410, (1981) FLR 19, CA.
2     *Edgar v Edgar* (ibid); and see eg *Smith v McInerney* [1994] 2 FLR 1077, per Thorpe J.
3     Disclosure in the context of mediation and the negotiated agreement is considered at **7.39** above.
4     See **6.21** above.
5     See eg Cheshire, Fifoot and Furmston *Law of Contract* (Butterworths, 1991) chs 8 and 9.
6     *Dickinson v Jones Alexander & Co* [1993] 2 FLR 521, per Douglas Brown J.
7     *B v Miller & Co* [1996] 2 FLR 23, per McKinnon J (QBD). Now see *Kelley v Corston* [1998] 1 FLR 986, CA which may enable solicitors in circumstances such as *B v Miller & Co* to claim advocates' immunity from suit; but see disapproval of both these cases in *Hall & Co v Simmons et al* [1999] 1 FLR 536, CA. The narrowing of the field of advocate's immunity from suit proposed by the Lord Chief Justice in the *Hall & Co* case is probably the most authoritative summary of the current state of the law.
8     *Dutfield v Gilbert H Stephens and Sons* [1988] Fam Law 474, per Anthony Lincoln J.
9     Rules of the Supreme Court 1965, Ord 24, r 8 (see **6.26** above).

be seen operating in the court's approach to the answering of questions[1] and ordering third parties to provide evidence.[2] With the increasing concern of the judiciary and government over the cost of litigation,[3] it is inevitable that the courts will become increasingly vigilant as to the necessity of particular lines of inquiry pursued by one or other party to a financial relief application. This question has already been considered in the context of the oppressive inquiry.[4] In the context of financial relief, it will now be appropriate to consider inquiries in the context of relevance of evidence.

## Relevance: defining the issues in a discretionary jurisdiction

**10.13**    Under the Ancillary Relief Pilot Scheme in particular, and in family proceedings generally, a clear concern for definition of issues by the parties is emerging.[5] This goes immediately to the relevance of evidence since, without a definition of the issues, it is impossible to define the evidence which is relevant to the court's consideration of those issues. In this area, it is possible again to detect the tension between the inquisitorial role implied by a discretionary jurisdiction and the pursuit of family litigation by adversarial processes. What one district judge and a wife think is irrelevant in one case, another district judge and the husband in the same case might think is highly relevant. Until a more co-operative role between judiciary and parties in case preparation can be developed – and a definition of the issues to be tried by the court is at the centre of this – such tension will persist.[6]

**10.14**    The conflict in approach to relevance of evidence can be seen in the differing judicial approaches to the issue of the means of a party's cohabitant. The court is required to have regard to the 'financial resources' which a party 'has or is likely to have in the foreseeable future'.[7] Among the information which must be provided to the court when the parties seek a consent order is a statement as to 'whether either party . . . has any present intention . . . to cohabit with another person'.[8] That provision was framed in the aftermath of *Livesey (formerly Jenkins) v Jenkins*[9]

---

1    Rules of the Supreme Court 1965, Ord 26, r 1; Family Proceedings Rules 1991, r 2.63 and 2.74 (1)(a)(i) (see **10.30** below); and see consideration of the court's role by Waite J in *Hildebrand v Hildebrand* [1992] 1 FLR 244 (see **6.34** above); and see Civil Procedure Rules 1998, r 18.1 (power of the court to order provision of further information).

2    Rules of the Supreme Court 1965, Ord 38, r 13 and Family Proceedings Rules 1991, r 2.62(7)–(9) (production appointments: see **10.32** above); Rules of the Supreme Court 1965, Ord 38, r 14 and *Morgan v Morgan* [1977] Fam 122, per Watkins J (*subpoena duces tecum*: see **6.40** above).

3    Lord Woolf MR *Access to Justice: Final Report* (HMSO, July 1996); and see Thorpe LJ's introduction to the original Ancillary Relief Pilot Scheme (SFLA and FLBA, August 1996).

4    See **6.28** and **6.37** above. The terminology preferred by the Civil Procedure Rules 1998 in this context is that a request for disclosure is 'proportionate' to the issues before the court (r 1.1(2)(c)); and see **1.34** above.

5    Family Proceedings Rules 1991, r 2.73(4)(c) (and see further **10.45** below); *Practice Direction of 31 January 1995 (Case Management)* [1995] 1 WLR 332, [1995] 1 FLR 456, paras 2 and 4(a). The Civil Procedure Rules 1998 stress the importance of definition of issues as part of the Rules' 'overriding objective' (r 1.4(2)): to 'identify the issues at an early stage', to 'decide promptly which issues need full investigation' and to decide in which order issues are to be resolved.

6    See consideration of co-operative case preparation at **1.25** above; and see Civil Procedure Rules 1998, r 1.4(2) and references to 'issues' set out in n 6 above.

7    Matrimonial Causes Act 1973, s 25(2)(a). Similar words to this appear in Children Act 1989, Sch 1, para 4(1)(a) and Inheritance (Provision for Family and Dependants) Act 1975, s 3(1)(a).

8    Family Proceedings Rules 1991, r 2.61(1)(d).

9    [1985] AC 424, [1985] FLR 813, HL; and see **10.6** above.

which involved remarriage, but the framer of the rule[1] was plainly concerned at the possibility not only of remarriage, but also cohabitation, including future cohabitation. By contrast, Ralph Gibson LJ expressed his own personal distaste at the involvement of cohabitants in matrimonial financial relief proceedings in *Frary v Frary and Another*[2] by citing with approval Bridge LJ in *Wynne v Wynne and Jeffers*[3] when he said:

> 'It will only be in the rarest cases where it will be possible to say that full information about the property and income of the third party, whether the third party is a new spouse, a new mistress, a new lover, a rich uncle or a mother or any other friend or relation from whom one of the spouses has expectations, will be relevant to the issue which the court has to consider under s 25 of the Matrimonial Causes Act 1973.'

## 3 MATRIMONIAL ANCILLARY RELIEF

**10.15** The procedural framework for evidence in matrimonial financial relief is provided by the Family Proceedings Rules 1991, rr 2.58–2.77; but in parts the framework is rudimentary.[4] On the other hand, the procedural framework of the Ancillary Relief Pilot Scheme is very detailed, as it applies to evidence. It is therefore necessary to supplement the Scheme provided by the Family Proceedings Rules 1991 by reference to the Rules of the Supreme Court 1965[5] and to case-law. The original, or existing, Scheme set up by the Family Proceedings Rules 1991, rr 2.52–2.70 will be considered here, followed by a consideration of the Pilot Scheme under rr 2.71–2.77.

### Originating process

#### *Evidence in support of the application*

**10.16** Commencement of the ancillary relief process is based loosely on the originating summons procedure set out in the Rules of the Supreme Court 1965, Ord 28: an application to the court supported, in the first instance, by affidavit[6] evidence. Specifically, under the ancillary relief process, an application is required to be supported by an affidavit by the applicant[7] which contains 'full particulars of his property and income, and stating the facts relied on in support of the application'.[8] A respondent to such an application 'shall file an affidavit in answer containing full particulars of his (sic)[9] property and income'.[10] By implication, this requires an

---

1   Originally, Matrimonial Causes Rules 1977, r 76A.
2   [1993] 2 FLR 696 at 703E, CA.
3   [1981] 1 WLR 69 at 74H, CA.
4   See eg Family Proceedings Rules 1991, r 2.58; considered at **10.16** below.
5   Family Proceedings Rules 1991, r 1.3(1).
6   Rules relating to affidavit evidence are in Rules of the Supreme Court 1965, Ord 41; and see **3.13** above.
7   The sparseness of the requirements of Family Proceedings Rules 1991, r 2.58(2) and (3) contrasts with the requirements of r 2.73 and Form E under the pilot scheme (see **10.37** below).
8   Ibid, r 2.58(2).
9   Notwithstanding the inevitability of marital relationships – that applicant and respondent will be different genders – the draftsperson relies faithfully on the Interpretation Acts to make both parties masculine unless the contrary is shown.
10  Family Proceedings Rules 1991, r 2.58(3).

applicant and respondent to prepare affidavits with the Matrimonial Causes Act 1973, s 25(1) and (2) in mind; but the rule does not say so. Still less does the rule require a person to give full disclosure of his means. Family lawyers familiar with *Livesey (formerly Jenkins) v Jenkins*[1] will know what is expected of their clients; but a layman who reads only r 2.58 can surely be forgiven – when asked to give facts 'in *support* of the application' (emphasis supplied) – for failing to draw attention, for example, to his pension expectations, his planned remarriage or his interest in expectancy in a substantial trust fund.

### *'Investigation by district judge' of the application*

**10.17**     The Family Proceedings Rules 1991, r 2.62 preserves the terminology of investigation[2] of the facts of an application by a district judge. It gives him power to 'order the attendance of any person for the purpose of being examined or cross-examined and order the discovery and production of any document or require further affidavits',[3] and 'to give directions as to the filing and service of pleadings and as to the further conduct of the proceedings'.[4] The power to give directions is well known, but few district judges would recognise powers to call further evidence as among those which they use as a matter of general practice. They are content, as a rule, to leave it to the parties to marshall their evidence before them in accordance with general adversarial principles.

## Evidence and the ancillary relief application

**10.18**     It is broadly true to say that it is a matter for the parties to choose their evidence, and to call that evidence in the order they wish,[5] on an ancillary relief application, subject to the theoretical power of the district judge to 'investigate' and to the normal rules as to relevance, hearsay and opinion evidence.[6] However, a number of judicial pronouncements and Practice Directions have explained ways in which case preparation and presentation[7] of the evidence should – or should not – be dealt with.

### *Marshalling the evidence – relevance*

**10.19**     Careful consideration of the relevance of evidence to issues before the court is one of the more important aspects of any case preparation. This is stressed by the overriding objectives of the Civil Procedure Rules 1998; and it has been emphasised judicially on a number of occasions. For example, in *P v P (Financial Provision)*,[8] Anthony Lincoln J considered the claim of a wife against a husband who

---

1     [1985] AC 424, [1985] FLR 813, HL; and see **10.6** et seq above.
2     Family Proceedings Rules 1991, r 2.62(4).
3     Ibid, r 2.64(2).
4     Ibid, r 2.64(3).
5     But see the Civil Procedure Rules 1998, r 32.1, which appears to give the court powers to control evidence, to exclude otherwise admissible evidence and to limit cross-examination (considered further at **1.35** above).
6     See **4.4** et seq and **4.44** et seq above, and Chapter 5.
7     On the question of case management specifically, see *Practice Direction of 31 January 1995 (Case Management)* [1995] 1 WLR 332, [1995] 1 FLR 456.
8     [1989] 2 FLR 241.

owned a successful haulage business. The parties owned a house with an equity value of £260,000. The wife had acquired shares in the business and wanted the company to buy out those shares. The judge rejected that approach. Both parties had commissioned reports from accountants who had placed very different figures on the company's worth. Anthony Lincoln rejected the usefulness of such valuations:[1]

> '... in my view the circumstances here require the court to adopt the approach enunciated by Dunn LJ in *Potter v Potter*,[2] namely that there should be a broad and general consideration of the resources of the parties and, against this backcloth, the court should proceed to assess the wife's reasonable requirements and the husband's ability to meet them in one way or another. This case, in my view, should be approached in the same way. It is no different. All that is needed is the broadest evaluation of the company's worth. This enables the court to decide what are the wife's reasonable requirements. If there is liquidity in the company which could be realized to meet her requirements, then the final order will take that liquidity into account. If there is none ... then the court must look elsewhere.'

Thus, so far as Anthony Lincoln J was concerned, a valuation of the company – other than 'the broadest evaluation' – was of only the most marginal relevance, whereas what was required here was a realistic estimate of the husband's liquidity. The real issue was how much the husband realistically could afford to pay to the wife and, with this figure in mind, what the wife needed to meet her reasonable requirements. The company was not to be sold. Therefore the important question (the relevant evidence) for the judge was what the husband could afford to borrow to pay to his wife.

*Relevance of evidence in Evans v Evans*
**10.20**    In *Evans v Evans*,[3] Booth J, with the concurrence of the President of the Family Division, gave what amounts to a Practice Direction[4] setting out the then views on case management. She also looked critically at the relevance of the evidence adduced before her. In *Evans*, the principle assets consisted of two modest properties and the husband's small business. Relative to the assets in the case and the issues involved, considerable sums had been expended in legal costs,[5] especially in valuation of the husband's business and assessment of the wife's contribution to the company. Booth J dealt with the relevance of the latter issue to what she had to decide as follows:[6]

> 'It is convenient at this point to refer to another issue which was raised, challenged and pursued at great and unprofitable length. That issue related to the contribution by the wife to the running of the husband's businesses.'

Each party asserted a different version of events: the wife alleged a virtual partnership, while the husband said little more than that she helped out 'occasionally'.

---

1    [1989] 2 FLR 241 at 243H–244A; and see *B v B (Financial Provision)* [1989] 1 FLR 119, per Anthony Lincoln J.
2    (1983) FLR 331; and see **4.14** above.
3    [1990] 1 FLR 319.
4    Considered at **10.22** below.
5    Booth J ended her judgment ([1990] 1 FLR 319 at 329C): 'This is and was at all times an essentially straightforward case and if they are united in nothing else this husband and wife must be united in bitterly regretting the dissipation of their assets which has so unfortunately occurred'.
6    [1990] 1 FLR 319 at 323F–324A.

Numerous affidavits were filed and witnesses were called and cross-examined. The judge then continued:

> 'As I endeavoured to point out during the hearing, the whole issue was, in the context of this case, irrelevant. The husband has never challenged the fact that the wife is and always has been a good mother ... *The assets are simply not available fully to satisfy the wife's reasonable needs and those of the husband,* so that there can be no question of any enhanced award to the wife by reason of her contribution to the business. It was, therefore, to my mind totally unnecessary to investigate this issue at all as it cannot in any way promote her case. The wife was a full-time mother who I have no doubt helped out as and when she was needed in a way which was compatible with her responsibilities to the children.' (emphasis added)

**10.21**     Practitioners may object that judicial hindsight is a wonderful thing. Could the judge's comments have been predicted during the course of preparation of the case? Should it have been possible to foresee that the evidence of the wife's alleged contribution would ultimately prove irrelevant? If, at the outset, the wife's legal advisers (in particular) had asked themselves: what are the assets, what are the reasonable needs of the parties and how can they be dealt with? (to which Booth J alludes in the passage emphasised above and as Anthony Lincoln J asked in *P v P (Financial Provision)*[1]) then it should have been possible to avoid many of the evidential excesses; and a substantial proportion of the extra costs incurred in *Evans* might have been saved. As ever, the question must first be to define the issues in the case. Here, the issue was the wife's reasonable requirements balanced against the husband's ability to provide for them. Secondly, to deal with those issues (assuming the business was not to be sold) involved an assessment of what the husband could reasonably afford to pay, ie his liquidity.

*'Guidelines' in Evans*

**10.22**     Booth J's practice note, described as 'general guidelines to be followed by the practitioner in the preparation of a substantial ancillary relief case',[2] is of importance at this stage to the extent that it stressed the need for evaluation of what is relevant evidence, for example:[3]

> '(1) Affidavit evidence should be confined to relevant facts and should not be prolix or diffuse. ...[4]
>
> (4) While it may be necessary to obtain a broad assessment of the value of a share holding in a private company it is inappropriate to undertake an expensive and meaningless exercise to achieve a precise valuation of a private company which will not be sold: *P v P (Financial Provision)* [1989] 2 FLR 241. ...
>
> (6) Care should be taken in deciding what evidence, other than professional evidence, should be adduced and emotive issues which are not material to the case should be avoided. ...

---

1    [1989] 2 FLR 241 at 243H; considered at **10.19** above.

2    [1990] 1 FLR 319 at 321C. The guidelines are at pp 321C–322B of the judgment.

3    See definition of issues and financial dispute-resolution under Ancillary Relief Pilot Scheme; considered at **10.45** and **10.50** below.

4    This guideline recalls Rules of the Supreme Court 1965, Ord 41, rr 5 and 6: 'An affidavit may contain only such facts as the deponent is able of his own knowledge to prove' (r 5(1)); and 'any matter which is ... irrelevant or otherwise oppressive' may be struck out of an affidavit (r 6).

(9) In a substantial case it may be desirable to have a pre-trial review to explore the possibility of settlement and to define the issues . . .'.

*Court bundles*

**10.23**    Relevance of documentary evidence, so far as the court hearing is concerned, centres on the court bundle prepared by the parties' solicitors. This is referred to in the *Evans* guidelines[1] as follows:

'(7) Solicitors on both sides should together prepare bundles of documents for use at the hearing and should reach agreement as to what should be included and what excluded: duplication of documents should always be avoided.'

Were this guideline written today, it would probably be in more stringent terms.[2] For example, in dealing with bundles of documents *Practice Direction: Case Management (31 January 1995)*,[3] at para 5 concludes: 'Where documents are copied unnecessarily or bundled incompetently the cost will be disallowed'. The courts are at pains to cut the unnecessary cost of incompetent preparation of bundles or where bundles have been prepared without proper or any regard to the relevance of the evidence which the documents represent.

## Opinion evidence

**10.24**    Proceedings for financial relief are no exception to the range of proceedings where there has been judicial concern at the overuse of experts.[4] Most evidence in the financial relief field will come from accountants, surveyors and, increasingly, actuaries. In her guidelines in *Evans*, Booth J proposed the following in connection with opinion evidence:[5]

'(3) Wherever possible, valuations of properties should be obtained from a valuer jointly instructed by both parties. Where each party instructs a valuer then reports should be exchanged and the valuers should meet in an attempt to resolve any differences between them and to narrow the issues . . .[6]

(5) All professional witnesses should be careful to avoid a partisan approach[7] and should maintain proper professional standards.'

**10.25**    With expert evidence in this context, there are two pre-eminent factors: is it necessary to instruct independent valuers or other experts; and, if so, to what extent

---

1    Of the documents in the *Evans* case, Booth J commented (at p 324B–C) as follows:
'The conduct of this case has resulted in an enormous amount of documentation much of which has been copied and incorporated into bundles which have served little useful purpose. A large bundle of copy bank statements has not been opened and two bundles of correspondence have barely received a passing glance. From the other large bundles it has been easy to extract the small number of relevant documents . . . All this has led to the most appalling waste of money. . . .'
2    See eg the comments of Ward LJ in *G v G (Periodical Payments: Jurisdiction)* [1997] 1 FLR 368 at 383E, CA; referred to at **6.27** above.
3    [1995] 1 WLR 332, [1995] 1 FLR 456.
4    See eg *Potter v Potter* (1983) FLR 331, CA; *B v B (Financial Provision)* [1989] 1 FLR 119, per Anthony Lincoln J; *Evans v Evans* [1990] 1 FLR 319, per Booth J.
5    It will be seen that Booth J also refers to the subject of valuation evidence at para (4) of her guidelines (see **10.22** above).
6    Note also that the court has power to compel such meetings under Rules of the Supreme Court 1965, Ord 38, r 38; considered further at **5.21** above.
7    On the importance of impartiality in opinion evidence, see **5.39** above.

will their evidence be relevant to the issues between the parties? For the average urban house, for example, it ought to be possible to agree a valuer;[1] but with more complicated rural or commercial property it may be possible for there to be relatively wide views which may justify separate instruction. If valuation of a business is contemplated, it is essential that the party who instructs the valuer is clear as to why he wants the valuation, since, as has been said many times (including by Booth J at para (4) of her guidelines)[2] if the valuation is sought in respect of an asset which is not to be sold, then a relatively precise figure obtained at substantial cost, perhaps at appreciable expense to both parties, is of little or no value to them or to the courts.

## Inferences from the evidence

### Orders on the basis of assets not actually shown to exist

**10.26** In a wide discretionary jurisdiction, there is scope occasionally for the court to draw wide inferences from the evidence before it and to act accordingly. Waite LJ explained this discretion as follows:[3]

> '... the judges who administer this jurisdiction have traditionally accepted the Shakespearian principle that 'it is excellent to have a giant's strength but tyrannous to use it like a giant'. The precise boundaries of that judicial self-restraint have never been rigidly defined – nor could they be, if the jurisdiction is to retain its flexibility. But certain principles emerge from the authorities. One is that the court is not obliged to limit its orders exclusively to resources of capital or income which are shown actually to exist. The availability of unidentified resources may, for example, be inferred from a spouse's expenditure or style of living ... Another is that where a spouse enjoys access to wealth but no absolute entitlement to it[4] ([eg] a beneficiary under a discretionary trust or someone who is dependant on the generosity of a relative) ... '

Thus, in *Thomas v Thomas*,[5] the husband was joint managing director of a successful family company; he was also a name at Lloyd's and had a substantial pension fund. His share holding in the family company was estimated as worth £600,000. The family home, valued at £250,000, was used as security for loans and guarantees of nearly that sum. His income from the company was relatively low since it was company policy to plough back profits into the business. The judge ordered the husband to pay the wife a lump sum of £158,000 and to provide the wife and children with income which would have left him with a deficiency on his stated income. The judge made the order on the assumption that the husband could increase his income by procuring a change in company policy as to payment of management salaries.[6] The Court of Appeal agreed with the judge.

---

1   Note the dangers of agreeing valuation (as distinct from the valuer to be instructed) (*B v Miller & Co* [1996] 2 FLR 23, per McKinnon J, QBD).
2   For examples, see **10.19** and **10.22** et seq above.
3   *Thomas v Thomas* [1995] 2 FLR 668 at 670E–G, CA.
4   See also eg *Browne v Browne* [1989] 1 FLR 291, CA (a wife who had easy access to funds in a substantial discretionary trust was ordered to pay a lump sum to her former husband). Where a company is the husband's alter ego, an order could be made effectively against the company (*Green v Green* [1993] 1 FLR 326, per Connell J); but not where minority interests might be infringed by the order (*Nicholas v Nicholas* [1984] FLR 285, CA).
5   [1995] 2 FLR 668, CA.
6   The court is entitled to take account of any increase in earning capacity 'which it would in the opinion of the court be reasonable to expect a party to take steps to acquire' (Matrimonial Causes Act 1973, s 25(2)(a)).

**10.27** On appeal, the husband argued that the court below had acted improperly in that it had assumed, without adequate evidence, that alternative arrangements could be made by him for substitute security. Thus, the husband had an order made against him merely, it might be said, because he failed to prove a negative, namely that there was no other security available to support the loans and guarantee. Further, he said, it placed unfair pressure on him to rely on his mother and brother (the other company directors) to raise income.

*Inference where there is failure to disclose*

**10.28** Case reports are rife with situations where the courts have been unable to accept the evidence of a party – normally a husband – and have proceeded in the best way possible.[1] In *Newton v Newton*,[2] for example, the court found that the husband's income was impossible to ascertain with any certainty, but that there was a fundamental gap in his evidence when he dealt with his liquidity. He had failed to tell the court what his own bank was likely to say to an approach for further funding. The issue was put by Sir Roualeyn Cumming-Bruce in the Court of Appeal as follows:[3]

'.. faced with the absence of any evidence as to the reaction of credit houses to a further credit advance, I take the view that the judge was justified in holding that it was reasonably practicable for the husband to find a way to pay the lump sum and to discharge his current obligations by obtaining further credit.'

*Proof of a negative*

**10.29** Cases such as *Newton* and *Thomas* are on the cusp of what may be permissible on evidence – or lack of it – before the court. Waite LJ was careful, in the opening words of his judgment,[4] to explain the extent to which, in appropriate cases, the courts could permissibly exercise their wide discretion, even in the absence of clear evidence, for propositions on which they intended to proceed. However, the fact remains that the general rule is that there is an onus on the applicant to prove what he asserts;[5] and in neither of those cases did the applicant (the wife) seem to have been required to prove what she asserted, namely that the husband could borrow (in *Newton*) or find essential alternative security for his debts (in *Thomas*). Indeed, in *Newton* the Court of Appeal seemed expressly to take the view that it was for the

---

1  Recent examples include: *W v W (Periodical Payments: Pensions)* [1996] 2 FLR 480, per Connell J (the 'devious conduct' of the husband – an able businessman – who was not 'genuinely concerned to assist the court to a proper understanding of his financial arrangements' made it impossible for the court to make a 'clean break' order); *Hellyer v Hellyer* [1996] 2 FLR 579, CA where the court felt able to make a substantial lump sum order against a husband, who was apparently insolvent in England, but who had a young son who had substantial business interests in the Isle of Man.

2  [1990] 1 FLR 33, CA.

3  Ibid, at 45C – to cope with any actual liquidity problem the court gave the husband 18 months to find the money he was ordered to pay.

4  See **10.26** above.

5  See eg *Re H (Sexual Abuse: Standard of Proof)* [1996] 2 WLR 8, [1996] 1 FLR 80, HL; considered at **4.21** above.

husband to disprove an unproved assertion. Cases of this sort have the potential to turn the rules of evidence on their head; but practitioners should be wary of assuming that a court will proceed in the absence of evidence of positive evidence, for example from an accountant, banker or some other financier, as to a husband's liquidity.[1]

## Questionnaires[2]

**10.30**	In her 'guidelines' in *Evans v Evans*,[3] Booth J suggested:

> '(2) Inquiries made under [the Family Proceedings Rules 1991, r 2.63] should, as far as possible, be contained in one comprehensive questionnaire and should not be made piecemeal at different times.'

In *Hildebrand v Hildebrand*,[4] Waite J left open the question of whether in financial relief proceedings interrogatories were available, given the availability of the r 2.63 questionnaire. For present purposes, it need only be recalled that ordering inquiries is discretionary. Inquiries will not be ordered if they are regarded as irrelevant, or not sufficiently relevant, to the decision-making process of the court;[5] or if they are held to be oppressive, within the terms of the Rules of the Supreme Court 1965, Ord 26, r 1.[6] However, if a party presses for information the court can order that if the replies prove to be irrelevant, the cost of providing them should fall on that party.[7]

**10.31**	In *G v G (Financial Provision: Discovery)*,[8] the issues considered by Bracewell J were first, whether r 2.63 included providing information, as distinct from information only from documents, and, secondly, whether the court could order the discovery of documents not yet in existence, in this case confirmation of certain information about the husband's partnership arrangements as a solicitor.[9] Bracewell J had no difficulty in finding[10] that the rule intends that:

> '... all relevant information is available to the court for the fair disposal of applications for ancillary relief. ... The information which can be sought under this rule is not limited to documents.'

Further, she held[11] (in words reminiscent of the Rules of the Supreme Court 1965, Ord 24, r 8 and Ord 26, r 1(1)[12]) that she could order the husband to 'use his best

---

1	See eg *Potter v Potter* (1983) 4 FLR 331, CA; *P v P (Financial Provision)* [1989] 2 FLR 241, per Anthony Lincoln J; considered at **10.19** above.
2	Family Proceedings Rules 1991, r 2.63.
3	[1990] 1 FLR 319; and see references **10.20** et seq above.
4	[1992] 1 FLR 244 at 247E; and see further **6.37** above.
5	*Thyssen-Bornemisza v Thyssen-Bornemisza (No 2)* [1985] FLR 1069, CA; and see **4.17** above.
6	*Hildebrand v Hildebrand* [1992] 1 FLR 244, per Waite J; and see **4.11** above.
7	*Practice Direction* [1981] 1 WLR 1010, [1981] 2 All ER 642.
8	[1992] 1 FLR 40.
9	To the husband's initial objection that, as a solicitor of the Supreme Court, 'his integrity was being impugned by the request' the judge held (at 41E): 'That argument does not appeal to me at all. The husband, as a solicitor ... is in no different position, and has no different responsibilities and obligations, than any other litigant in this type of case'.
10	[1992] 1 FLR 40 at 41H.
11	Ibid, at 42B and C.
12	Dealing with orders for discovery and interrogatories; see **6.30** and **6.37** above.

endeavours' to obtain a letter from his firm which gave the information requested by his wife:

> '... the information which [the wife] seeks in this case is, in my view, proper and necessary information in order to ensure the fair disposal of the case, and I am satisfied that there is jurisdiction to make the order.'

## Production appointment[1]

### *Use of the production appointment*

**10.32**     It will be recalled that a production appointment has the effect of bringing forward to a pre-trial stage the time when a third party can be required to produce documents,[2] ie it is equivalent to a pre-trial appointment for giving effect to a subpoena *duces tecum*.[3] The procedure for obtaining a production appointment was explained by Thorpe J in *B v B (Production Appointment: Procedure)*.[4] The use of the production appointment in appropriate cases is theoretically wide. However, as with the questionnaire or interrogatories, the ordering of a production appointment is discretionary, and will not be ordered where the documents requested are regarded by the court as irrelevant[5] or oppressive of the witness.[6]

### *Confidential documents*

**10.33**     In *D v D (Production Appointment)*,[7] Thorpe J considered his powers to order production of confidential documents,[8] in this case documents held by an accountant who, with the wife in the case, was an executor of the wife's late father's estate. The accountant (Mr M), did not help himself by giving minimal assistance to the court. Thorpe J, in the particular circumstances, had no difficulty in finding that he had jurisdiction to override the privilege which might normally attach to the confidential documents held by Mr M: 'orders should be made to ensure that full and frank disclosure is achieved, if not voluntarily, then by compulsion'.[9] As to the extent and the effect of the production order which he was able to make, Thorpe J held as follows:[10]

> 'It seems to me that where there is manifest evidence and inference of an avoidance of the duty of full and frank disclosure, the exercise of discretion as to the bounds of production

---

1     Family Proceedings Rules 1991, r 2.62(7)–(9).
2     *Frary v Frary and Another* [1993] 2 FLR 696, CA. This production appointment is the same as under Rules of the Supreme Court 1965, Ord 38, r 13; considered at **6.41** above.
3     Cf the *Khanna* appointment (after *Khanna v Lovell White Durrant (A Firm)* [1995] 1 WLR 121, per Sir Donald Nicholls V-C); and see **6.42** above.
4     [1995] 1 FLR 913, in which Thorpe J confirmed that the procedure set out in *The Family Court Practice 1999* (Family Law) is the correct procedure.
5     *Frary v Frary and Another* [1993] 2 FLR 696.
6     *Morgan v Morgan* [1977] Fam 122, (1977) FLR Rep 473 per Watkins J (and see **4.13** above); *Frary v Frary and Another* (above).
7     [1995] 2 FLR 497.
8     It has been held that a bank does not breach confidentiality to a customer where it produces bank statements when ordered so to do (*Robertson v Canadian Imperial Bank of Commerce* [1994] 1 WLR 1493, PC).
9     [1995] 2 FLR 497 at 500F.
10    Ibid, at 499H–500B.

should be broad rather than narrow. If the boundary is set narrow, then it encourages the perpetuation of the obstructive strategy. . . . If the boundary is set wide, the worst that can happen is that costs may be unnecessarily incurred in the disclosure of irrelevant material.'

To the objection that the husband might see documents relative to the affairs of third parties, Thorpe J concluded:[1]

'. . . in reality the production order is implemented not by the husband, not even by his legal team, but by Mr S, who is the investigative accountant instructed on his behalf. If Mr S sees a document or material that relates to third parties he will quickly exclude it and return it as being irrelevant to his purposes.'

**10.34**      Thorpe J, it may be said, took the use of the production appointment considerably beyond the limits of the order envisaged by the Court of Appeal in *Frary v Frary*.[2] There, it was stressed that the production appointment merely brought forward the date upon which documents could be produced by a third party to the court. Thorpe J made no attempt to equate the production appointment in *D v D* with the subpoena *duces tecum*, but viewed it in the context of the court's 'duty to carry out the s 25 exercise as between the husband and the wife'.[3] If the appointment is approached more as part of the court's discretionary armoury to ensure full relevant disclosure, as Thorpe J approached it, and if it is stripped of the oppressive elements which did nothing to assist Mrs Frary's application, it is possible to see it as having a wider application than was envisaged by the Court of Appeal in *Frary*.

## 4   PROCEEDINGS UNDER THE PILOT SCHEME

### Court control and the inquisitorial function

**10.35**      The Ancillary Relief Pilot Scheme (the Scheme) started life as a 'draft rule' annexed to a President's Direction dated 25 July 1996[4] which was published as a judicial guide and, to the profession, a practitioner's guide (the Guide).[5] It is limited to a specific number of courts[6] and applies to all ancillary relief applications issued in those courts since 1 October 1996. The President's Direction defined the 'objective' of the Scheme, as then drafted, as follows:

'To reduce delay, facilitate settlements, limit costs incurred by the parties to the proceedings and provide the court with much greater control over the conduct of proceedings than exists at present.'

Consideration has already been given to the tension between the court's investigative powers in performing its duties under the Matrimonial Causes Act 1973, s 25(1)[7] and

---

1       [1995] 2 FLR 497 at 500C.
2       [1993] 2 FLR 696, CA; considered in detail at **4.15** above.
3       [1995] 2 FLR 497 at 500B.
4       Now incorporated formally into the Family Proceedings Rules 1991 by the Family Proceedings (Amendment No 2) Rules 1997, SI 1997/1056.
5       Lord Chancellor's Advisory Group on Ancillary Relief *Ancillary Relief Pilot Scheme: Practitioner's Guide* (SFLA and FLBA, August 1996).
6       Family Proceedings Rules 1991, r 2.71(2).
7       'It shall be the duty of the court in deciding whether to exercise its powers . . . to have regard to all the circumstances of the case . . . '; and see the assessment of the meaning of these words in

the exercise of those powers in a court process which remains essentially adversarial in form. However, the rules give no clear guidance for the parties or the judiciary in explanation of the court's inquisitorial function.[1] The High Court judiciary is beginning to envisage a more inquisitorial role for the court; and this can be seen developing with the introduction of the Civil Procedure Rules 1998 for civil proceedings.[2] The words of Thorpe J,[3] in *F v F (Ancillary Relief: Substantial Assets)*,[4] summarise this process:[5]

> '... I think that it is timely to stress that ancillary relief applications in this Division are not purely adversarial proceedings. The court has an independent duty to discharge the function imposed by statute. The court has from that duty the power to investigate and the power to ensure compliance with the duty of full and frank disclosure owed by the litigants.'

**10.36**      Procedure and the marshalling of evidence have been designed under the Scheme to ensure a relatively high degree of court control. This will be considered here in some detail, since the Scheme is due to be implemented in all courts during 2000.

## Statement in Form E

**10.37**      The statement in Form E[6] is the document in which both parties set out their financial circumstances and exchange information about their means and the basis of their applications. One of the objects of Form E is to restrict the extent to which each party sets out his evidence.[7] Meanwhile, Family Proceedings Rules 1991, r 2.73(3) seeks to restrict discovery as between the parties.

### Form E – the document

**10.38**      Form E is intended to replace the affidavit of means, to limit disclosure to the factors set out in r 2.73(2) and to form the principle means by which the court is provided with the information it needs to exercise its discretion under the Matrimonial Causes Act 1973, s 25. However, it should be recalled that by the use of the words 'in particular' the legislature intended the list to be illustrative only of the main factors to be considered: not all factors are relevant to each case and 'all the circumstances'

---

the context of disclosure as between the parties by Lord Brandon in *Livesey (formerly Jenkins) v Jenkins* [1985] AC 424, [1985] FLR 813, HL; and see further **10.6** above.

1    Save in the little used Family Proceedings Rules 1991, r 2.62(4).
2    See eg, rr 1.4 and 32.1, also considered at **1.31** above and in Chapter 15.
3    As he then was.
4    [1995] 2 FLR 45. The *dictum* quoted follows immediately upon a brief description by Thorpe J of the meetings of what was shortly to become the Lord Chancellor's Advisory Group on Ancillary Relief under the judge's chairmanship.
5    Ibid, at 70A; and see eg the approach of Wilson J to joinder of trustees in a case involving substantial funds transferred by a husband to a discretionary trust whose objects excluded the wife in *T v T and Others (Joinder of Third Parties)* [1996] 2 FLR 357 at 365F and 366E: 'A crucial matter for my determination ... will be to evaluate the real control over the assets of this trust ... a *duty* has been imposed upon the court in these proceedings. I have to get to the bottom of the reality behind this trust'.
6    Prescribed by Family Proceedings Rules 1991, r 2.73(2).
7    For the extent to which the rule as drawn can restrict the extent of evidence which a party can call, see **10.40** below.

means that other factors outside the list can be considered. Form E cannot, therefore, be regarded as limiting parties only to the evidence prescribed in the Form and in r 2.73(2).

**10.39**     Form E is described as 'a statement'[1] which is signed and sworn by the spouse who makes the statement, and contains certain prescribed information.[2] However, it differs radically from an affidavit of means:[3] there, subject to rules of evidence and pre-eminently the rules relating to admissibility of relevant evidence, a deponent sets out facts and claims according to no prescribed formula. By contrast, the Scheme sets out what information is to be provided both in r 2.73(2) and, usually in tabular form, in Form E.[4] It will be seen that the information required by the rule is not always the same as prescribed by Form E.[5] Where that occurs and the two are inconsistent, the rule must take precedence over the Form. Further, Form E sometimes takes a party a long way from the requirements of the Matrimonial Causes Act 1973, s 25(2).[6]

## Limitations on further investigation and discovery

**10.40**     A significant object of the Scheme is to endeavour to keep discovery within sensible bounds.[7] Time and again, as is well known, judges have been critical of the extent to which parties and their advisers indulge in excessive discovery. Rules exist which, when used by the courts, can curb these excesses: from wasted costs orders,[8] through restrictions on taxation of costs,[9] to a variety of practice directions.[10] What the Scheme seeks to do, as part of its aim to 'provide the court with much greater control over the conduct of proceedings than exists at present',[11] is to limit discovery save where documents accompany Form E or as directed by the district judge[12] and to control the extent to which parties can raise questionnaires. It remains the case, however, that although the Family Proceedings Rules 1991, r 2.63 has been disapplied under the Scheme,[13] nothing has been done to prevent a party raising interrogatories.[14]

---

1     Although it may be noted that the Civil Procedure Rules revert to the use of the term 'affidavit': Civil Procedure Rules 1998, r 32.15.
2     Family Proceedings Rules 1991, r 2.73(1).
3     See **10.16** above.
4     Family Proceedings Rules 1991, r 2.73(1) and App 1A.
5     Eg in relation to details of insurance policies required by r 2.73(2)(f)(iv) and Form E.
6     Eg in relation to a party's health: cf s 25(2)(e) and the wider references to health in Form E.
7     'Proportionate' in terms of Civil Procedure Rules 1998, r 1.1.
8     Supreme Court Act 1981, s 51(7) and Rules of the Supreme Court 1965, Ord 62, r 11, as explained in *Ridehalgh v Horsefield* [1994] Ch 205, [1994] 2 FLR 194, CA; and see *Practice Direction of 31 January 1995 (Case Management)* [1995] 1 WLR 332, [1995] 1 FLR 456, at para 5.
9     See eg *G v G (Periodical Payments: Jurisdiction)* [1997] 1 FLR 368 at 383E, per Ward LJ; considered at **6.27** above.
10    See eg *Practice Direction of 31 January 1995 (Case Management)* [1995] 1 WLR 332, [1995] 1 FLR 456, at paras 2(a) (power of court to limit discovery), 4(a) (duty of legal representatives to confine evidence to what is reasonably essential) and 5 (disallowance of costs for incompetent preparation of bundles); *B v B (Court Bundles: Video Evidence)* [1994] 2 FLR 323, per Wall J (Practice note especially para 10 concerning 'rigorous pruning of unnecessary material').
11    *Ancillary Relief Pilot Scheme: Practitioner's Guide* (SFLA and FLBA, August 1996).
12    Family Proceedings Rules 1991, rr 2.73(3)(a) and (4)(b) and 2.74(1)(a)(ii).
13    Ibid, r 2.71(3)(a).
14    Rules of the Supreme Court 1965, Ord 26, r 1; considered further at **6.37** above.

### Questionnaire seeking further information and schedule seeking documents

**10.41** The Scheme directs that a questionnaire setting out further information sought shall be filed and served together with a 'schedule setting out the documents' required of the other party.[1] As already considered, where a questionnaire or request for documents is being drafted, the usual rules as to relevance to the issues and oppressive enquiry will be born in mind.[2] Where a questionnaire is been filed the district judge will 'determine . . . the extent to which [it] shall be answered'.[3] Thus, the district judge can refuse to require a question to be answered. The factors the court has in mind in exercising its discretion as to the ordering of replies remain the same: is the answer to the question likely to be relevant, or sufficiently relevant, to the issues before the court,[4] and is the request likely to be oppressive of a party?[5] If a party presses for information the court can order that, if the replies prove to be irrelevant, the cost of providing them should fall on that party.[6]

### Evidence 'to be adduced'

**10.42** At the first appointment the district judge 'shall give directions as to . . . (iii) any evidence sought to be adduced by each party'.[7] It remains to be seen whether this provision is intended to be used; just as it remains to be seen to what extent powers to limit evidence will be used in proceedings covered by the Civil Procedure Rules 1998.[8] Further, it should be born in mind that the evidence put forward in Form E is limited by the form and will almost certainly need to be supplemented in all but the most routine of cases. For example, where some explanation as to the history of a marriage, or of a person's present financial state (whether good or bad), is relevant, a further affidavit by that party is likely to be necessary if lengthy examination-in-chief and unnecessary surprises are to be avoided at the final hearing.

### Documentary evidence: discovery

**10.43** At the first appointment the district judge considers the extent to which 'documents requested under Rule 2.73[(4)(b)] shall be produced and give directions for the production of such further documents as may be necessary'.[9] The normal rule in ancillary relief cases is that parties are required to give full relevant disclosure of information relating to their applications.[10] Under the Scheme the object is only to limit *inter partes* discovery[11] first, to what is necessarily annexed to Form E, and, secondly, to such documents as may be directed to be disclosed by the district judge. While it is always a matter for the court's discretion as to what is ordered to be

---

1    Family Proceedings Rules 1991, r 2.73(4)(a) and (b). These sub-rules, it will be noted, are mandatory.
2    See **4.4** (relevance) and **4.10** (oppressive enquiry) above.
3    Family Proceedings Rules 1991, r 2.74(a)(i).
4    See eg *Thyssen-Bornemisza v Thyssen-Bornemisza (No 2)* [1985] FLR 1069, CA; and see **4.17** above.
5    And see *Hildebrand v Hildebrand* [1992] 1 FLR 244, per Waite J; considered at **4.11** above.
6    *Practice Direction* [1981] 1 WLR 1010, [1981] 2 All ER 642.
7    Family Proceedings Rules 1991, r 2.74(1)(b)(iii).
8    Civil Procedure Rules 1998, r 32.1; and see **15.6** below.
9    Family Proceedings Rules 1991, r 2.74(1)(a).
10   *Livesey (formerly Jenkins) v Jenkins* [1985] AC 424, [1985] FLR 813, HL.
11   Family Proceedings Rules 1991, r 2.73(3).

discovered, the effect of the Scheme is to enable the district judge to exercise a much closer control over the extent of disclosure. In particular, it will be noted that the district judge specifically has a duty to direct production of such other documents 'as may be necessary'. This will involve the district judge, at the directions stage, in considering what documents will be required for the exercise of the court's discretion at any final hearing.

### Valuation evidence

**10.44**      Rule 2.74(1)(b)(i) and (ii) requires the district judge to give directions on valuations and expert evidence. The extent to which opinion evidence may be called – save where it is agreed by the parties – has always been a matter for the court.[1] If the expert is seeking to give opinion evidence on a matter on which the court already has expertise (some aspect of accountancy, for example) the court would be entitled to exclude the evidence.[2] There is nothing in r 2.74(1) which suggests that the courts should depart from the Rules of the Supreme Court, Ord 38.[3] The Scheme specifically implies 'joint instruction of independent experts',[4] as an object of the Scheme is to save costs; and there is recent evidence of judicial approval of appointment of a court expert.[5] The court, of its own motion, may 'direct that there be a meeting "without prejudice" of experts involved in the case, 'for the purpose of identifying the parts of their evidence which are in issue'.[6] They may then produce a joint statement identifying points agreed and any points which remain in issue.

## A concise statement of the issues between the parties

**10.45**      As part of its concern to clarify the relevance of the evidence to be called and thereby to reduce cost, the Scheme requires that parties file, at the first appointment, 'a concise statement of the issues between the parties'.[7] As has already been seen, the classic definition of the issues is those matters for decision by the court to be distilled from the pleadings.[8] For the lawyer dealing with ancillary relief under the Scheme the only pleading, properly so called, is the originating application Form A.[9] Form E is evidence, although there is no doubt that it is from Form E that the issues between the parties are to be deduced. In family cases the issues can often be occurring as the case proceeds,[10] or they may emerge with discovery. It is not always easy, therefore, to state the issues with too much certainty long in advance of the final

---

1    See **5.16** above.
2    See eg *Bown v Gould and Swayn* [1996] PNLR 130.
3    For consideration of the Rules of the Supreme Court 1965, Order 38, rr 34–43 see **5.16** above; and see Civil Procedure Rules 1998, Part 35 for a comparison of the new rules concerning expert evidence in civil proceedings.
4    Family Proceedings Rules 1991, r 2.74(1)(b)(i).
5    Appointed under Rules of the Supreme Court 1965, Ord 40 (even though at present this provision may only be available in the High Court); and see *Re K (Contact: Psychiatric Report)* [1995] 2 FLR 432, CA and *Abbey National Mortgagees plc v Key Surveyors Nationwide Ltd and Others* [1996] 1 WLR 1534, CA.
6    Rules of the Supreme Court 1965, Ord 38, r 38; Civil Procedure Rules 1998, r 35.12; and see approval of this procedure in *Evans v Evans* [1990] 1 FLR 319, per Booth J (**10.24** above) and in Lord Woolf MR *Access to Justice: Final Report* (HMSO, July 1996) ch 13, para 42 et seq.
7    Family Proceedings Rules 1991, r 2.73(4)(c).
8    See **2.3** above.
9    Family Proceedings Rules 1991, r 2.72(1).
10   See consideration of this question by Burrows and Parker at [1993] Fam Law 156.

hearing. That said, an attempt must be made to define the issues, not only to satisfy r 2.73(4)(c), but also to be able to define the relevance of evidence – the extent to which questionnaires are to be answered and documents ordered to be disclosed.

### '*The issues'– a definition*

**10.46**     The rules do not attempt to define the term 'statement of issues'. Issues may be said to fall into two main categories: first, primary issues, ie issues which require, or are capable of, resolution by the court by court order; and, secondary or evidential issues, ie issues arising from the evidence on which the court may or may not need to make a finding in order to resolve one or more of the primary issues.

*Primary issues*

**10.47**     A primary issue will be a question on which the court can make an order,[1] for example:

–     whether or not the former matrimonial home should be sold;
–     if sold, in what proportions the proceeds should be divided;
–     if not sold (so that the wife stays in the house), whether there should be a charge-back in favour of the husband;
–     whether the wife should have periodical payments;
–     if so, how much, for how long and whether there should be an order under the Matrimonial Causes Act 1973, s 28(1A);
–     whether there should be a clean break.

*Evidential issues*

**10.48**     Evidential issues surrounding the above primary issues might include:

–     the availability of alternative property which the wife could buy;
–     the extent to which the wife is or is not realising her earning capacity;
–     the husband's need for capital;
–     the extent to which both have other assets and either has a pension fund (for definition of quantum of the charge-back or lump sum, if a sale is ordered).

### '*A concise statement of the issues'*

**10.49**     The primary issues are the issues which must be set out in the statement for the purposes of r 2.73(4)(c),[2] that is, the aspects of the case on which a district judge can assist with mediation or on which he is able to make an order (as distinct from making findings on the evidence) if the case goes to a final hearing. However, it would clearly be helpful to the court if the evidential issues could also be set out.

## Financial dispute-resolution

**10.50**     The financial relief dispute appointment (FDR) may be seen as the centrepiece of the Scheme in achieving settlement of cases and thereby of saving costs.[3] Before the FDR can be effective there must be full relevant disclosure by both

---

1     Note the reminder in *Dinch v Dinch* [1987] 2 WLR 252, [1987] 1 FLR 162, HL that the court can make orders only in accordance with their powers under the Matrimonial Causes Act 1973.
2     It is accepted that this is not how the position is shown in the *Commentary*: but nor is it clear on the basis of what definition of the term 'issues' the authors of the *Commentary* worked.
3     Family Proceedings Rules 1991, r 2.74(1)(c) and (f)(ii).

sides, since settlement without full disclosure leaves the party who does not disclose open to an application to set aside any order obtained,[1] whether by settlement of the case or following a contested hearing. Negotiations with a view to settlement are meaningless without full disclosure; just as a *Calderbank* letter cannot properly be so called until discovery has been given and disclosure is complete.[2] From an evidential point of view there are two prerequisites which are essential to the FDR: first, all requirements as to disclosure must be complete; and, secondly, the entirety of both parties' *Calderbank* correspondence must be available to the court.

### Requirements as to disclosure complete

**10.51**      Prior to the FDR it is essential, at the very least, that Form E is completed with the information required by the Family Proceedings Rules 1991, r 2.73(2),[3] documents are provided, questionnaires are completed, and any other evidence (including expert evidence) is provided in accordance with directions given by the court. Without this the FDR can be only partially useful (for example, as a means of narrowing the issues between the parties), and without full relevant disclosure settlement of the case is impossible.[4]

### Calderbank correspondence

**10.52**      Before the FDR appointment the applicant is required to file all offers and proposals, together with responses which have passed between the parties.[5] These documents will then be returned to the parties at the end of the FDR: they will not be retained on the court file.[6] This openness before the district judge, it is to be hoped, will assist in moving towards settlement and may be part of the public policy rule that parties be encouraged to settle their differences rather than litigate to the finish.[7] A district judge who deals with the FDR can then take no further part in the proceedings, save to give directions.[8]

### Admissions made 'without prejudice'

**10.53**      An admission or statement of existing facts or of the strength of a party's case, even though stated to be 'without prejudice', is not privileged and can be treated as admissible evidence at any hearing.[9] Thus, for example, where a party admits (in the course of negotiations or during the FDR) the existence of financial information not previously disclosed, evidence as to that admission can be adduced in subsequent court proceedings,[10] although the onus will be on the party alleging the admission to

---

1    *Livesey (formerly Jenkins) v Jenkins* [1985] AC 424, [1985] FLR 813, HL; *T v T (Consent Order: Procedure to Set Aside)* [1996] 2 FLR 640, per Richard Anelay QC as deputy High Court judge; and see further **6.21** above.
2    *Gojkovic v Gojkovic (No 2)* [1992] Fam 40, [1991] 2 FLR 233, CA; and see **7.35** above.
3    See **10.37** et seq above.
4    See further **6.7** above.
5    Family Proceedings Rules 1991, r 2.75(1)(b).
6    Ibid, r 2.75(1)(b).
7    *Cutts v Head* [1984] Ch 290, [1984] 1 All ER 597, CA; and see **7.30** above.
8    Family Proceedings Rules 1991, r 2.75(1)(a) and (d).
9    *Buckinghamshire County Council v Moran* [1989] 2 All ER 225, CA; and see further **7.33** et seq above.
10   But see *Practice Direction of 16 June 1997 (Ancillary Relief Procedure: Pilot Scheme)* [1997] 2 FLR 304; considered further at **10.55** below.

prove it. On this question a mediator would be compellable. Whether a district judge on an FDR appointment would be compellable may be more contentious. In his capacity as a judge, it is probable that a district judge is not compellable.[1] However, whether a district judge in the role of mediator can properly be said to be acting 'in relation to his judicial functions' is altogether another question. The fact that he is subsequently precluded from exercising a judicial function in relation to the case in hand and that privilege is removed from documents placed before him, suggests strongly that he cannot be said to be performing a judicial function in any accepted sense of the term. Accordingly, in relation to any admission made before him in the course of the FDR, the district judge may be compellable.

### Notice to admit facts

**10.54**    Before the burden of proving the admission needs be considered or the debate on whether or not a district judge is compellable needs to be engaged, the first step for the party to whom the admission was made should be to give notice to admit the facts of the admission to the party who made it.[2] In the context of the Scheme and its concern for costs, the notice to admit facts is particularly important: if the fact of the admission is admitted costs will be saved; if it is not admitted, but subsequently proved, the costs of proving the admission will fall in any event on the person who fails to admit.[3]

### Admissions according to the Practice Direction

**10.55**    Since the coming into operation of the Scheme the President has issued *Practice Direction of 16 June 1997 (Ancillary Relief Procedure: Pilot Scheme).*[4] This Practice Direction is designed to enable parties to discuss matters openly at the FDR without fear that things said in mediation would then be repeated at a subsequent court hearing. The question is considered in the context of *Re D (Minors) (Conciliation: Privilege).*[5] In that case, it was held that evidence of statements made in conciliation meetings concerning children could not be given in subsequent proceedings save with leave of the court, and only then where such statement makes it clear that the maker has in the past, or is likely in the future, to cause harm to the child. The Practice Direction goes much wider than *Re D* and relates the narrow issue dealt with there, which essentially relates to children proceedings, to the FDR in ancillary relief proceedings. Public policy requires that parties are able to negotiate and put forward proposals on a basis which secures privilege for their negotiation; but the Practice Direction seeks to make admissions made in the course of negotiations privileged, which is a different matter altogether.[6]

1    *Warren v Warren* [1996] 2 FLR 777 at 785, per Lord Woolf MR, CA: 'It is my view that no judge in relation to his judicial functions is a compellable witness'.
2    Rules of the Supreme Court 1965, Ord 27, r 2; County Court Rules 1981, Ord 20, r 2.
3    Rules of the Supreme Court 1965, Ord 62, r 6(7) (r 6(8) if admission of documents is requested).
4    [1997] 2 FLR 304.
5    [1993] Fam 23, [1993] 1 FLR 932, CA.
6    See **10.53** above which is believed to be a correct statement of the law. If it is correct, the Practice Direction leaves open the question of whether a Practice Direction can be used to change the law.

**10.56**      This leaves at large the question: if an admission relates to something which should have been disclosed in any event, can that admission be privileged? In *Re D*, Sir Thomas Bingham MR set out his conclusions[1] very tentatively and stressed the limitations of what he was saying. The judgment does not deal with admissions of fact (eg 'my mother is holding £10,000 for me' or 'I have been offered £150,000 for my family company shares'). The Practice Direction appears (perhaps unwittingly) to extend privilege to such admissions of fact[2] and thereby in part to undermine the principle of full relevant disclosure. The answer to the question at the beginning of this paragraph must be: No. The cloak of privilege cannot hide a wrongdoing, namely failure to disclose a fact material to the proceedings; and it would be most unfortunate if a fact disclosed in an FDR, which could not be examined at the time of the ancillary relief proceedings, could found a subsequent application to set aside any order made subsequently in those proceedings.

---

1      [1993] 1 FLR 932 at 938D–G.
2      See para 3 of the Practice Direction.

# Chapter 11

## EVIDENCE IN CHILDREN PROCEEDINGS

### 1 INTRODUCTION

#### The scope of children proceedings since 1989

**11.1** The Children Act 1989 introduced a new recognition of rights of children and parents, and a restructuring of the courts at every level. It established what has been described as a 'concurrent system of jurisdiction for a wide range of family proceedings in new magistrates' family proceedings courts, county courts and the High Court'.[1] Within the system, there is scope for flexibility and the smooth transfer of cases between one tier and another.[2] Most cases concerning children are now brought under the Children Act 1989, two obvious exceptions being wardship and child abduction cases.[3] Under the Children Act 1989, children proceedings may be commenced within 'family proceedings' which are defined as 'any proceedings under the inherent jurisdiction of the High Court in relation to children' and as proceedings under the enactments listed in s 8(4).[4] All proceedings under the Act in magistrates' courts are treated as 'family proceedings', by virtue of s 92(2).[5]

**11.2** Proceedings under the Children Act 1989 are now begun by a standard form application for each child. The Act enables private law remedies to be sought by a parent or relative, for parental responsibility under s 4, and for residence, contact, a prohibited steps order or a specific issue order under s 8. Local authority applications for care or supervision orders are made under s 31, and secure accommodation orders under s 25. Child protection duties of local authorities are given legal scope by child assessment orders under s 43, orders for the emergency protection of children under s 44, and the recovery of abducted children under s 50. Parents have the right to make applications in relation to children in care under s 34, and for the discharge of care or supervision orders under s 37.

---

1   *The Children Act 1989 Guidance and Regulations, Volume 1: Court Orders* (HMSO 1991) at p 2.
2   Children (Allocation of Proceedings) Order 1991, SI 1991/1677.
3   See **11.3** below for wardship.
4   Children Act 1989, s 8(3) and (4). The enactments set out in s 8(4) are Parts I, II and IV of the Children Act 1989, the Matrimonial Causes Act 1973, the Domestic Violence and Matrimonial Proceedings Act 1976, the Adoption Act 1976, the Domestic Proceedings and Magistrates' Court Act 1978 and Part III of the Matrimonial and Family Proceedings Act 1984. Proceedings on an application by a local authority for leave under s 100(3) are specifically excluded from the definition of 'family proceedings'.
5   Applications for secure accommodation in the magistrates' courts are therefore 'family proceedings' (*Oxfordshire County Council v R* [1992] 1 FLR 648).

## High Court applications: wardship

**11.3**　　　Some children applications are still made in the High Court. Historically, the wardship jurisdiction in relation to children was exercised by the High Court in private disputes over children, but was increasingly harnessed by the local authorities as a way of taking children into care in complex or difficult cases, or where swift protective action was necessary. Since the Children Act 1989, s 100(2), local authorities have been applying for the public law remedies available under the Act. The right of private individuals to apply under the wardship jurisdiction has not, technically, been curtailed by statute; but the Court of Appeal has held that the wardship jurisdiction should be invoked only in exceptional circumstances, 'where a question concerning the child's upbringing or property could not be resolved under the Act of 1989 so as to secure his best interests'.[1]

## High Court applications: the inherent jurisdiction

**11.4**　　　The High Court retains its inherent jurisdiction to make decisions about children. This is a power specific only to the High Court and is exercisable whether or not a child is a ward of court. Through the exercise of its inherent powers, the High Court provides a necessary forum for the determination of complex issues, for example those with a foreign element, issues concerning consent to medical treatment, applications by a child for leave to make an application, and applications for an injunction to safeguard a child which would run counter to the principle of press freedom. The High Court may also hear children cases which lie outside the Children Act 1989, such as some adoption proceedings, and cases involving child abduction under the Hague or the European Conventions. Local authorities require the leave of the court under s 100(3) of the Act to invoke the inherent jurisdiction of the High Court (eg to restrain harmful publicity about a child, to prevent a violent father discovering a child's whereabouts, or to obtain leave to carry out abortion, sterilisation or other controversial medical treatment[2]).

## 2　CHARACTERISTICS OF CHILDREN PROCEEDINGS

### Evidence in children proceedings

**11.5**　　　The role and function of evidence within children proceedings is shaped by the particular characteristics of those proceedings.[3] These may be summarised as follows.

(1)　*The welfare principal* – the welfare of the child rather than other factors, such as the wishes and rights of the parents, is the focus of the decision-making process within the court.

---

1　　*Re CT (A Minor) (Wardship: Representation)* [1993] 2 FLR 278, CA; *sub nom Re T (A Minor) (Child: Representation)* [1994] Fam 49.

2　　White, Carr and Lowe *A Guide to the Children Act 1989* (Butterworths, 1990), pp 132–134; see also White, Carr and Lowe *The Children Act in Practice* (Butterworths, 1995), pp 278–280.

3　　See also HHJ Nigel Fricker QC 'Family law is different' [1995] Fam Law 306.

(2) *The tribunal* – many of the issues raised within children courts may be quasi-criminal in their seriousness and implications, but unlike the criminal courts, children cases are tried by judges (and lay magistrates), not juries.

(3) *Inquisitorial not adversarial* – the traditional wardship jurisdiction was inquisitorial. The Children Act 1989 introduced a new system of children hearings. The consensus in decided cases is that the High Court hearing Children Act cases has inherited some of the powers of the wardship jurisdiction; at this level, children cases are inquisitorial not adversarial.[1]

(4) *Standard of proof* – the standard of proof is the civil standard, although in certain circumstances the weight of evidence needed to satisfy the balance of probabilities may be greater, commensurate with the seriousness of the allegations to be tried, or the proximity of the offender to the victim.[2]

(5) *The inclusionary rule* – the practice of the courts in children cases in relation to evidence is distinctive. The general law of evidence applies in principle to all cases concerning children. However, the Children Act 1989 has provided for statutory exceptions, in other words, evidence normally inadmissible in other proceedings may be received (subject to relevance[3]) in evidence in children proceedings.[4] The task for the court is then to decide what weight should be placed upon it.

## *The welfare principle*

**11.6**    The opening provisions of the Children Act 1989 set out what has been described as 'the overarching welfare provisions to be applied in all proceedings under the Act'.[5] Section 1(1) requires the court to consider a 'child's welfare [as its] paramount consideration'. The importance of the welfare principle, whether statutorily defined as 'first and paramount',[6] 'paramount' or 'first consideration'[7] has implications for what can and should be admitted as evidence in children courts. In the criminal courts, where the purpose of the proceedings is the fair trial of the individual, evidence which is unfair to the defendant, such as hearsay evidence, which cannot be properly tested by cross-examination, or evidence of previous convictions, which is plainly prejudicial, are examples of evidence which are normally and properly excluded from the proceedings. Where the directed objective of the proceedings is the welfare of the child, it is axiomatic that all evidence which is relevant should be before the court. There is therefore a presumption of admissibility and an extensive duty of disclosure – what may be described as the inclusionary rule.

---

1    See consideration of the adversarial system at **11.7** below.
2    See further at **11.10** and **11.15** below (standard of proof).
3    See further at **4.4** et seq above (relevance of evidence).
4    The exception of exclusionary rules for children is not so prominent since the passing of the Civil Evidence Act 1995; see **4.46** et seq above.
5    *The Children Act 1989 Guidance and Regulations, Volume 1: Court Orders* (**11.1**, n 1), at p 1.
6    As was the case under the old Guardianship of Minors Act 1971 which the Children Act 1989 repealed and replaced.
7    Adoption Act 1976, s 6.

### *Inquisitorial not adversarial*

**11.7**      The inquisitorial jurisdiction of the High Court in wardship cases was founded on the concept of *parens patriae*, where the court, by delegation of the sovereigns duties, had a quasi-parental relationship with the ward of court, and assumed protective responsibility towards the ward.[1] When a child became a ward of court, the parent effectively surrendered parental responsibility to the High Court, which exercised it on behalf of the sovereign.

**11.8**      The High Court in Children Act 1989 proceedings behaves differently from the wardship jurisdiction in that it does not abrogate to itself parental responsibility. Early decisions following the implementation of the Act emphasised the contrast with wardship and the adversarial nature of the new process.[2] There remains an adversarial element within children proceedings in that it is the duty of each party to subject the case of an opponent to rigorous forensic cross-examination. However, the paramountcy of the welfare principle and the central importance of the child in Children Act 1989 proceedings has meant that the High Court, in practice, has restated the inquisitorial role of the tribunal. For example, in *Re G (A Minor) (Care Proceedings)*,[3] a local authority and a father agreed that a care order should be made on a child but, nevertheless, the local authority sought findings of fact against the father in respect of physical and sexual abuse and neglect. Wall J emphasised that no agreement between parties could deprive the court of its duty to satisfy itself that the threshold criteria were indeed met; the court had a duty to investigate, and make such findings of fact as were appropriate,[4] although the High Court has disapproved of the practice of justices proceeding to hear lengthy evidence in respect of a consent agreement, or of the court departing from such agreement without giving the advocates the opportunity to deal with outstanding issues.[5] Similar thinking on the adversarial nature of children proceedings – this time in the areas of privilege and confidentiality – can be seen in *Re L (Police Investigation: Privilege)*[6] where the House of Lords expressed the view (following a comment made by Sir Stephen Brown in *Oxfordshire County Council v M*[7]) that Children Act cases, like wardship, were non-adversarial.[8]

---

1    Pearce *Wardship: The Law and Practice* (Fourmat Publishing, 1986) pp 1–4; Levy *Wardship Proceedings* (Longman, 1987) pp 5–6.

2    For example, *Barking and Dagenham v O and Another* [1993] 3 WLR 49, where Douglas Brown J found that Children Act cases were adversarial, in contrast to wardship. This case has now been reversed by a series of decisions culminating in *Re L (Police Investigation: Privilege)* [1996] 2 WLR 395, [1996] 1 FLR 731, HL.

3    [1994] 2 FLR 69.

4    This decision has now effectively been reversed by *Re B (Agreed Findings of Fact)* [1998] 2 FLR 968.

5    *Devon County Council v S and Others* [1992] 2 FLR 244. The practice of submitting draft orders to the bench was commended as a means of ensuring genuine consent among the parties, and to help the justices define, with greater precision, points at which they may decide to depart from the agreed package.

6    [1996] 2 WLR 395, [1996] 1 FLR 731, HL.

7    [1994] Fam 151, [1994] 1 FLR 175, CA.

8    The subject of privilege in children proceedings (with which *Re L* is primarily concerned) is considered fully at **7.17–7.24** above and **11.34–11.46** below.

### The nature of the tribunal – the judge as finder of fact

**11.9**     In common with most other civil proceedings, findings and decisions in children cases have been exclusively the province of the judge or lay justices: there has never been any role for a jury in children cases. Children cases are heard either by a professional judiciary at High Court or county court level, or by magistrates who sit in family proceedings courts and have received special training since the Children Act 1989. Some evidence might be highly prejudicial to a defendant if known to a jury in a criminal trial. Although potentially harmful to a parent or a local authority in children proceedings, the welfare principle dictates that relevant evidence should be before the court; a professional judiciary and a trained bench with the assistance of a legally qualified court clerk will deal with such evidence in an appropriate way.

### The burden and standard of proof

**11.10**     The burden of proof in children proceedings lies, as in other areas of civil law, with the person making the application or other assertion of fact – a point stressed by Lord Nicholls in *Re H (Sexual Abuse: Standard of Proof)*.[1] The Children Act 1989, however, has introduced a complexity to this process, by virtue of several criteria which require to be sequentially proved, or on which the court must be satisfied,[2] before an order is made. A local authority applicant seeking a care or supervision order in care proceedings will have to satisfy the 'threshold criteria' as set out in s 31(2) of the Act:

> 'A court may only make a care or supervision order if it is satisfied –
> (a)   that the child concerned is suffering, or is likely to suffer, significant harm: and
> (b)   that the harm, or likelihood of harm, is attributable to –
>   (i)   the care given to the child, or likely to be given to him if the order were not made, not being what it would be reasonable to expect a parent to give him; or
>   (ii)   the child's being beyond parental control.'

The entire burden is not discharged at this stage however, since s 1(5) of the Act imposes a further burden in that the court is prohibited from making orders under the Act 'unless it considers that doing so would be better for the child than making no order at all'. If s 1(5) is satisfied, the court then has to consider in applications for s 8 orders which are contested, and in applications for care and supervision orders, the 'welfare checklist' as set out in s 1(3). The court reaches its decision mindful of the paramountcy of the welfare principle as enshrined in s 1(1), and the principle that delay is prejudicial to that welfare in s 1(2).

### The operation of 'presumptions'

**11.11**     The Children Act 1989 enshrines a deep-rooted and fundamental principle: that the welfare of children is paramount in the court's consideration of an application relating to children. In addition, there are certain presumptions which are statutorily enshrined in the Act, such as the presumption against delay in s 1(2), and the 'no

---

1     [1996] AC 563; *sub nom Re H and R (Child Sexual Abuse: Standard of Proof)* [1996] 1 FLR 80, HL; and see **4.21** above.

2     See Lord Nicholls again in *Re H (Sexual Abuse: Standard of Proof)* (ibid), at 95F–G (considered further at **4.25** above).

order' principle in s 1(5). These and a number of other presumptions may operate on the burden of proof in certain instances.

*A presumption of contact*

**11.12** There may be said to be a presumption that a child should have contact with both parents. This is based on the principle that, in general, a child should have a relationship with both parents, wherever possible, and that it is therefore to the advantage of the child to have contact.[1] The strength of this presumption is likely to mean in effect that, in a contested hearing over contact to a child, it is for the party opposing contact to establish the grounds for the opposition, effectively shifting the burden of proof to that party, who may in fact be the respondent in the proceedings.[2]

*A presumption in favour of the status quo*

**11.13** The importance of the welfare principle in children proceedings can also lead to an increased burden on an applicant who applies to the court to vary a residence order and thus to alter the status quo. The court must consider the s 1(3) welfare checklist, including the requirement to consider the likely effect on the child of 'any change in his circumstances'.[3] On this basis, it is unlikely that an adequate parent, who has cared for a child for a number of years, will be displaced as carer; and this may be so even though the applicant parent, if given the opportunity to care, might be able better to provide for the child's welfare. The more settled the child, the heavier the burden upon the applicant who wishes to change arrangements for his care.

**11.14** The presumption in favour of the status quo also operates in interim hearings. Where satisfactory arrangements concerning the care of the child are in place, applications to change a child's residence or schooling are unlikely to succeed pending the careful consideration of a final hearing. In public law cases, the sharing of parental responsibility with the local authority under an interim care order is difficult to displace, and the legal arrangements established at the early hearings are likely to prevail for the duration of the proceedings, although seen as neutral and bestowing no advantage to any side.[4]

*The standard of proof*

**11.15** The standard of proof[5] which is applied by children courts in all cases involving the welfare of children is the ordinary civil standard. This is proof on the balance of probabilities, defined by Denning J in *Miller v Ministry of Pensions* as follows: 'if the evidence is such that the tribunal can say "We think it more probable than not", the burden is discharged but, if the probabilities are equal, it is not'.[6]

---

1    See for example *Re R (A Minor) (Contact)* [1993] 2 FLR 762 at 767; *Re H (Minors) (Access)* [1992] 1 FLR 148 at 153A.
2    See Parker and Eaton 'Opposing Contact' [1994] Fam Law 36.
3    Children Act 1989, s 1(3)(c).
4    *Hampshire County Council v S* [1993] 1 FLR 559; *Re G (Minors) (Interim Care Order)* [1993] 2 FLR 839; *Re W (A Minor) (Interim Care Order)* [1994] 2 FLR 892, CA.
5    See further **11.10** et seq above.
6    [1947] 2 All ER 372.

*Proof in sexual abuse cases*

**11.16**    In cases of sexual abuse or where the allegations are otherwise serious the current state of the law is expressed by a majority of the House of Lords in *Re H (Sexual Abuse: Standard of Proof).*[1] The court must be satisfied on the balance of probabilities that the occurrence of abuse was more likely than not. Their Lordships' view was that the more serious the allegation in any particular case, the less likely it was that the event occurred, and therefore the stronger the evidence needed to establish the allegation on the balance of probabilities. This does not mean that the more serious the allegation, the higher the standard of proof which is required; rather, 'the more improbable the event, the stronger must be the evidence that it did occur before, on the balance of probability, its occurrence will be established'.[2] Earlier decisions in the lower courts suggesting that a higher degree of probability is necessary where a father is alleged to have been guilty of sexual misconduct with his child,[3] or where there is only a single possible perpetrator,[4] have been expressly disapproved by the House of Lords, as it 'would risk causing confusion and uncertainty'.[5] The civil standard of the balance of probabilities is to be applied in the same way to allegations of non-accidental injury or serious physical abuse.[6]

*Admissibility and judicial discretion – the inclusionary rule*

**11.17**    By contrast, for example, with criminal proceedings, the rules of evidence in children proceedings are inclusionary rather than exclusionary. The roots of this lie in the wardship jurisdiction: wardship proceedings with regard to children have long been held to be subject to an inquisitorial, rather than an adversarial process. The court has a duty to enquire into the well-being of a child, rather than to adjudicate upon a gladiatorial contest between opposing parties. Where the welfare of a child is at issue, it is proper that all relevant issues are brought to the attention of the court. Accordingly, hearsay evidence,[7] from sources which in other civil proceedings would be subject to the claims of privilege (perhaps), or which are protected by public interest immunity, may nevertheless be admissible in children cases.[8] Evidence deriving from covert video surveillance, even where it may be improperly or illegally obtained, has been held to be admissible in children cases.[9] In children proceedings, evidence filed in written form or given orally is therefore fully before the court, without the filter of judicial discretion which exists in criminal proceedings.

---

1    [1996] AC 563; *sub nom Re H and R (Child Sexual Abuse: Standard of Proof)* [1996] 1 FLR 80, HL (considered fully at **4.33** et seq above).

2    *Re H and R* (ibid), at 96E. The House of Lords approved recent decisions in the Court of Appeal, including *Re W (Minors) (Sexual Abuse: Standard of Proof)* [1994] 1 FLR 419, CA; *Re B (Child Sexual Abuse: Standard of Proof)* [1995] 1 FLR 904; *Re L (Sexual Abuse: Standard of Proof)* [1996] 1 FLR 116, [1995] Fam Law 451, CA.

3    *Re G (No 2) (A Minor) (Child Abuse: Evidence)* [1988] 2 FLR 314; *Re G (A Minor) (Child Abuse: Standard of Proof)* [1987] 1 WLR 1461.

4    *Re W (Minors) (Sexual Abuse: Standard of Proof)* [1994] 1 FLR 419, CA.

5    *Re H and R (Child Sexual Abuse: Standard of Proof* (above), at 97C.

6    *Re M (A Minor) (Appeal) (No 2)* [1994] 1 FLR 59, CA; followed in *Re P (A Minor) (Care: Evidence)* [1994] 2 FCR 751.

7    The subject of hearsay in children proceedings is considered fully at **11.24** et seq below.

8    For discussions on privilege, see **11.34**, and on public interest immunity, see **11.47**.

9    *Re DH (A Minor) (Child Abuse)* [1994] 1 FLR 679.

**11.18**      Certain evidence may need especially meticulous testing by the tribunal. Children's disclosures of sexual abuse have given particular difficulty, being potentially probative, but also highly prejudicial to the parent or party implicated.[1] In *Re E (A Minor) (Child Abuse: Evidence)*,[2] Scott Baker J set out his analysis of the proper general approach to disclosures by children:

'. . . very great caution is necessary in evaluating what weight is attached to each child's evidence. I bear in mind the following:

1. Where a child has been interviewed more than once, second and subsequent interviews are likely to be of diminishing, if not negligible, value.

2. These children are all of very tender years.

3. Great care must be taken in assessing the reliability of the adults who report what the children said.

4. I have to look at the climate in which the children made their disclosures, and decide whether the children may have been influenced in what they have said by the adults' words or behaviour.

5. I have to consider what the children are reported as having said is likely to be fact or fiction or a mixture of the two.

6. I have to consider the consistency of each child's accounts.

7. I have to consider whether each child's behaviour, before and after the disclosures, is consistent with the truth of them.

8. I have to look for reliable independent evidence to corroborate what the children said.'

**11.19**      Where ritual or satanic abuse has been alleged, it has been held that for the allegation to be proved it is necessary to establish that what the children have said has been recorded in a reliable form, and that such evidence has been correctly and accurately analysed.[3] Evidence admissible under the twin criteria of relevance and the welfare principle is therefore properly submitted to the full exercise of judicial discretion. Evidence which appears ostensibly to be highly prejudicial in isolation will be weighed and tested against other evidence, and indeed may be mitigated in its effect by this process.

*Res judicata and issue estoppel in Children Act proceedings*

**11.20**      Issue estoppel[4] creates a bar on the subsequent litigation of all decided issues whose resolution was essential to the determination of earlier proceedings, as well as preventing the raising of other issues which should have been brought forward in those proceedings, but were not so raised.[5] This means that, where an issue has been formally determined upon by a court and a specific finding of fact made by the judge, it cannot be raised again for redetermination.

**11.21**      There is a tension in the application of such concepts to children cases. Children proceedings are essentially concerned with an immediate and current situation. Circumstances may change during the minority of a child. Other

---

1      See *Report of the Inquiry into Child Abuse in Cleveland 1987* (HMSO, 1988), especially paras 12.1–12.69.

2      [1991] 1 FLR 420 at 425; [1991] Fam Law 222, CA.

3      *Rochdale Borough Council v A and Others* [1991] 2 FLR 192.

4      Considered further at **11.22** below.

5      *Arnold v National Westminster Bank plc* [1991] 2 AC 93 at 104; *Fidelitas Shipping Co Ltd v V/O Exportchleb* [1966] 1 QB 630 at 643, cited in *C v Hackney London Borough Council* [1996] 1 FLR 427 at 429E–F.

arrangements become more appropriate at a later date. On the other hand, certain children proceedings may have a quasi-criminal element to them, when specific findings of fact, in respect of parental conduct, are made. In such circumstances, it may be appropriate to apply issue estoppel to prevent old issues being re-litigated. When it comes to applying a rule of issue estoppel, it has been suggested by Hale J in *Re B (Children Act Proceedings) (Issue Estoppel)* that 'the weight of Court of Appeal authority is against the existence of any strict rule of issue estoppel which is binding upon any of the parties in children's cases'.[1] The wide discretion of judges in family cases means that application of the doctrine of estoppel is entirely a matter for the court. It is for the judge to decide on the admissibility or otherwise of evidence, and thus the scope of the doctrine of *res judicata*.

*Application of issue estoppel*

**11.22**    The context in which issue estoppel is likely to operate may be summarised as follows:

(1)   where a specific issue of fact has been previously decided[2] – this must be expressed as a specific finding, not just 'worrying signs and real possibilities';[3]

(2)   where the finding has been by a court of competent jurisdiction for the purpose of children cases, including the family proceedings court, as part of the common jurisdiction in family cases;[4]

(3)   where the parties in the earlier and the later action are the same, at least in relation to the central allegation;[5]

(4)   where the issues the court is invited to determine are the same as in the previous litigation;[6]

(5)   where the judge in the previous proceedings has made a finding on the merits, having heard the witnesses cross-examined, and has conducted a full forensic enquiry, rather than made a decision of the papers;[7]

(6)   where the finding has been final and conclusive.[8]

**11.23**    *Re B (Children Act Proceedings) (Issue Estoppel)*[9] was a case of care proceedings relating to two boys where sexual abuse by a man was alleged. The local authority sought to rely on a finding of fact against the same man in earlier proceedings that involved different children. The matter came before Hale J as a preliminary issue and she concluded:

'It follows that the answer to the question [whether or not issue estoppel applies] is "not necessarily". The local authority will obviously wish to assert that the father has sexually abused two other children. It will be for the trial judge to decide how this is to be proved. He will no doubt wish to consider whether there appears to be some real reason to cast

---

1    [1997] 1 FLR 285 at 295D.
2    *B v Derbyshire County Council* [1992] 1 FLR 538 at 544E.
3    *Re S, S and A (Care Proceedings)* [1995] 2 FLR 244 at 249E.
4    *K v P (Children Act Proceedings: Estoppel)* [1995] 1 FLR 248 at 253H: the High Court should take account of properly made findings in the family proceedings court.
5    Ibid, at 253H–254A.
6    Ibid, at 254B.
7    *Re S, S and A (Care Proceedings)* [1995] 2 FLR 244 at 249C.
8    *K v P (Children Act Proceedings: Estoppel)* [1995] 1 FLR 248 at 253H.
9    [1997] 1 FLR 285.

doubt upon the earlier findings. That is a matter which has not been addressed before me for the purpose of this preliminary ruling. But if it is to be pursued, it would no doubt be appropriate for the whole case to be transferred to be heard by a High Court judge.'

## 3    THE INCLUSIONARY RULE – HEARSAY EVIDENCE

### Hearsay and the Children Act 1989

**11.24**      The coming into operation of the Children Act 1989 confirmed the extent to which hearsay evidence was admissible in children proceedings. Section 96(3) enabled the Lord Chancellor to make provision for the admissibility of evidence, which would not otherwise be admissible under any rule of law relating to hearsay. Any order under s 96(3) may only be made with respect to civil proceedings, and relates to 'evidence in connection with the upbringing, maintenance or welfare of a child.'[1]

### Admissibility of hearsay evidence orders

**11.25**      Pursuant to s 96(3), two successive Children (Admissibility of Hearsay Evidence) Orders[2] have been made. The current Order is the Children (Admissibility of Hearsay Evidence) Order 1993.[3] The present state of the law is that in civil proceedings before the High Court or a county court, and in family proceedings and in civil proceedings under the Child Support Act 1991 in a magistrates' court, 'evidence given in connexion with the upbringing, maintenance or welfare of a child shall be admissible notwithstanding any rule of law relating to hearsay'.[4] Proceedings for a secure accommodation order in respect of a child in the magistrates' court are family proceedings, and hearsay is therefore admissible.[5]

**11.26**      The effect of the Order is that for the first time the law and practice with regard to hearsay in all civil courts dealing with children is unified. Where evidence is being heard relating to a child's upbringing, maintenance or welfare, either in the area of public or private law, hearsay is admissible.

### *Forms of hearsay admissible*

**11.27**      A clear advantage of the Order is that it permits the evidence of children to be placed before civil courts, without the need for the child to give evidence orally and be cross-examined upon it, although there would, in theory, be nothing to stop a party issuing a witness summons to compel the attendance of the child. It is not only the evidence of a child which becomes admissible, but that of any person relevant to the proceedings. The evidence which may be admitted under the Order is not confined to first-hand hearsay, but may be second-hand or even more remote. The wording of the order does not limit the type or origin of admissible hearsay in any way. Thus, medical or scientific records, such as charts showing paediatric measurements, are also

---

1      Children Act 1989, s 96(4)(a).
2      See further **4.51** et seq above.
3      SI 1993/621.
4      Children (Admissibility of Hearsay Evidence) Order 1993, SI 1993/621 in force 5 April 1993.
5      *Oxfordshire County Council v R* [1992] 1 FLR 648.

admissible. The expert responsible for the compiling of the measurements may be needed to give oral evidence as to their interpretation, but will not be required to prove their provenance.

## Cogency and relevance of hearsay evidence

**11.28**    The admissibility of hearsay within children proceedings does not, of course, absolve the court of its duty to consider and assess the appropriate weight to be placed upon evidence received by it. The question of relevance arises at every stage and in relation to every piece of evidence. The courts are aware that in the interests of justice to all the parties concerned, hearsay evidence has to be handled carefully, with due consideration of the extent to which it can be relied upon.[1] By direction of the President of the Family Division, where hearsay evidence is adduced, 'the source of the information must be declared or good reason given for not doing so'.[2] The proper approach to hearsay evidence is therefore to address the extent to which surrounding circumstances indicate the accuracy or otherwise of the statement received in evidence: whether the maker of the statement was a credible witness, or had any reason to conceal or to misrepresent, and whether the statement was made contemporaneously or as close as possible to the events alleged to have occurred.

### *Admissibility of hearsay evidence in applications for emergency protection orders*

**11.29**    The Children Act 1989 also provides for specific relaxations of the normal rules of evidence, other than the provision for the admissibility of hearsay. An emergency protection order entitles the applicant immediately to remove a child from his carer where there is reasonable cause to believe that the child is likely to suffer significant harm.[3] The paramount need to protect the welfare of the child in an emergency provides an example of how strict rules of evidence may be subordinate to welfare considerations in children cases. Accordingly, the Children Act 1989, s 45(7) provides as follows:

> '(7) Regardless of any enactment or rule of law which would otherwise prevent it from doing so, a court hearing an application for, or with respect to, an emergency protection order may take account of –
> (a) any statement contained in any report made to the court in the course of, or in connection with, the hearing; or
> (b) any evidence given during the hearing,
> which is, in the opinion of the court, relevant to the application.'

It is consistent with the aims of the Act that emergency protection orders can be made quickly; and s 45(7) ensures that this can be done without the need for first-hand oral evidence of the facts relied upon. The rights of parents are however recognised by the prohibition against the renewal of the order on more than one occasion, and the right to apply for the discharge of the order after 72 hours.[4]

---

1    *Re W (Minors) (Wardship: Evidence)* [1990] 1 FLR 203 at 227; *R v B County Council ex parte P* [1991] 2 All ER 65 at 72J.
2    *Practice Direction of 31 January 1995 (Case Management)* [1995] 1 WLR 332, [1995] 1 FLR 456, at para 3.
3    Children Act 1989, s 44(1).
4    Ibid, s 44(6) and (9).

## Admissibility of hearsay evidence in reports of the guardian ad litem

**11.30**    The Children Act 1989 provides for further statutory exceptions in respect of evidence in a guardian ad litem's report. Guardians in children proceedings are intended to be seen independent of the conflicting interests of parent and local authority. Their power is quasi-inquisitorial in that there is a requirement upon the guardian to make such investigations as are necessary, and to bring to the attention of the court 'all such records and documents which may in his opinion assist in the proper determination of the proceedings'.[1] The special position of the guardian is underlined by statutory exceptions relating to the admissibility of his evidence. Thus, the Children Act 1989, s 41(11) provides:

> 'Regardless of any enactment or rule of law which would otherwise prevent it from doing so, the court may take account of –
> (a)  any statement contained in a report made by a guardian ad litem who is appointed under this section for the purpose of the proceedings in question; and
> (b)  any evidence given in respect of the matters referred to in the report,
> in so far as the statement or evidence is, in the opinion of the court, relevant to the question which the court is considering.'

This section covers 'any statement', not just one made personally by the guardian; as such, anything told to the guardian by (for example) a health visitor or school teacher who may not have provided statements within the proceedings immediately becomes admissible. Further, the statutory exception provided by s 41(11) does not attach to statements contained within reports prepared by another guardian in earlier or different proceedings; but such statements would become admissible in any event by the alternative route of the Children (Admissibility of Hearsay Evidence) Order 1993.[2]

## Hearsay evidence and local authority records

**11.31**    Further, the Children Act 1989 provides for the widest possible admissibility of material contained within local authority records which relate to the child. The guardian has the right to 'examine and take copies of' local authority records;[3] and a copy of such a record taken by a guardian is 'admissible as evidence of any matter referred to in any report which the Guardian makes to the court, or evidence which he gives in the proceedings'.[4] Therefore, it seems likely that the court is entitled to treat records repeated within the guardian's report as evidence of the truth of the matters contained within them.[5]

---

1    Family Proceedings Rules 1991, SI 1991/1247, r 4.11(9)(b); Family Proceedings Courts (Children Act 1989) Rules 1991, SI 1991/1395, r 11(9)(b).
2    See **11.25** above.
3    Children Act 1989, s 42(1).
4    Ibid, s 42(2). The guardian has a primary duty to safeguard the welfare of the child. Even where public interest immunity might be claimed by a local authority to protect its records, it could not prevail over the express provisions of s 42; see *Re T (A Minor) (Guardian ad Litem: Case Record)* [1994] 1 FLR 632.
5    Hershman and McFarlane *Children Law and Practice* (Family Law) at D[1346].

## Admissibility of hearsay evidence in the reports of the court welfare officer

**11.32**     The position of the court welfare officer in private law cases is, to an extent, analogous to that of the guardian ad litem in public law cases, although, in contrast to the guardian, the court welfare officer is not a party to the proceedings, and is not legally represented. Some of the special provisions relating to evidence contained within a guardian's report apply also to a court welfare officer's report. Therefore, regardless of any enactment or rule of law which would otherwise prevent it from doing so, the court may take account of 'any statement contained in the report, and any evidence given in respect of matters referred to in the report', subject to whether, in the opinion of the court, the statement or evidence is relevant to the question which it is considering.[1]

## 4   PRIVILEGE, PUBLIC INTEREST IMMUNITY AND CONFIDENTIALITY

### Privilege from discovery

**11.33**     There are three particular aspects of the rules of evidence which may apply to admissibility in children proceedings: exclusion of evidence on grounds of privilege, public interest immunity and confidentiality. One of these bases may be raised by a party who resists the disclosure[2] of confidential material. The importance of the welfare principle since the Children Act 1989, and perhaps the extent to which the court is willing to adopt an inquisitorial role, has seen the erosion of principles of confidentiality in children cases.[3]

### Privilege and disclosure

#### *Disclosure of social work records*

**11.34**     A local authority has a high duty in law on the grounds of general fairness, but also in the interests of the welfare of the child, to disclose 'all relevant material', save that covered by public interest immunity, to parties in care proceedings.[4] Judicial guidance has been given on what categories of social work documents ought normally to be disclosed within children proceedings.

---

1     Children Act 1989, s 7(4). This is analogous to s 41(11) relating to guardian ad litem, but there is no equivalent provision for court welfare officers to have the right to examine and copy local authority records.

2     See also Chapter 6 (disclosure) and Chapter 7 (privilege) above.

3     For a discussion of the extent of the duty to disclose in children cases, see Brasse 'The Duty of Disclosure in Children's Cases' [1996] Fam Law 358; Walsh 'Beyond Legal Professional Privilege' [1996] Fam Law 412; Burrows 'Disclosure in Children's Cases' [1996] Fam Law 566.

4     *R v Hampshire County Council ex parte K and Another* [1990] 1 FLR 330 – a judicial review of the refusal of a local authority to disclose medical reports relating to a child to parents who were respondents in care proceedings under the Children and Young Persons Act 1969. The absence of a procedure for discovery in juvenile court care proceedings was remedied by Family Proceedings Rules 1991, r 4.17(1) and Family Proceedings Courts (Children Act 1989) Rules 1991, r 17(1).

**11.35** *Re A and Others (Minors) (Child Abuse: Guidelines)*[1] was a wardship case involving allegations of ritual and sexual abuse to a number of children by members of the extended family. The local authority freely disclosed notes made by social workers and foster-parents, continuation sheets and NSPCC form Vs, which have the function of a day-to-day log, and minutes of case conferences and reviews. This was approved by Hollings J, who held that a local authority should provide discovery of original material recording matters of fact in relation to children, parents or other relevant persons, especially transcripts and records of matters in issue. However, he recognised that notes or records of case conferences or meetings where opinions were given were in a different category: those attending should be able to express opinions freely, without having to look over their shoulder. (This argument is also the classic justification for public interest immunity.) The judge also held that it was open to the local authority to waive the privilege attaching to those documents.

**11.36** The present practice in relation to disclosure is that local authorities often recognise that parents who are parties in children proceedings need to have access to social work records in order to address allegations made against them, and may volunteer disclosure, despite the cost in time and money in copying records, which may be voluminous, difficult to read and of varying degrees of relevance. Specifically, in care proceedings, a local authority has a duty to disclose all relevant material which may assist parents in rebutting allegations made against them, and which modifies or cast doubts upon its case [2]. Where there are likely to be factual issues arising out of social work records, parties should apply their minds to pre-trial discovery, to avoid unnecessary delay during trial while material is obtained and distributed to the parties.[3] However, it is not the position that in every case there be 'carte blanche disclosure of social work notes and records',[4] as, in each case, a proper case for discovery must be made out.

## Disclosure of medical records and reports

**11.37** The preservation of the confidence which exists between a patient and the doctors, nurses and other medical staff who may have dealings with him, is a matter of fundamental principles, and enshrined within the codes of conduct which govern the medical profession. A doctor must refrain from voluntarily disclosing information about a patient to a third party. Medical records are therefore prima facie privileged. They may also be subject to public interest immunity. There is, nevertheless, a recognition that, exceptionally, the professional obligations of confidence may be overridden where disclosure is in the public interest. A doctor owes a duty to his patient to preserve confidentiality; but he owes a duty to the public which may be greater than his duty to his patient. In particular, where a doctor has reason to believe that a child is being physically or sexually abused, it is permissible for a doctor to disclose information to a third party; it is the view of the General Medical Council that there is a positive duty upon the doctor to do so.[5]

---

1    [1991] 1 WLR 1026.
2    *Re C (Expert Evidence: Disclosure: Practice)* [1995] 1 FLR 204.
3    *Re JC (Care Proceedings: Procedure)* [1995] 2 FLR 77 at 82C.
4    Ibid, at 83C.
5    See General Medical Council *Annual Report 1987*, cited in *Working Together under the Children Act 1989 – A guide to inter-agency cooperation for the protection of children from abuse* (HMSO, 1991) p 12.

**11.38** The trend towards disclosure is reflected in *Re C (A Minor) (Evidence: Confidential Information)*[1] in which proposed adopters sought to rely upon an affidavit deposed by the mother's former general practitioner which was adverse to her. Sir Stephen Brown P held that the affidavit was admissible: the public interest in the restricted disclosure of relevant confidential material concerning the mother's medical condition might, having regard to the special circumstances, prevail over the public interest in the need to maintain confidentiality between doctor and patient. Any prohibition against the voluntary disclosure of information nevertheless envisages that, at the request of a court, such information will be forthcoming, since it has always been accepted that doctors are obliged to answer questions put to them in court about their own patients.[2]

*Disclosure of video evidence*

**11.39** Doctors may also be obliged to disclose material including video recordings to parties in children proceedings. Such disclosure may be partial. In *B v B (Child Abuse: Evidence)*,[3] Johnson J considered a submission by the Hospital for Sick Children, Great Ormond Street, that video recordings of interviews with a child in which allegations of sexual abuse by the father were made, were confidential to the child, and should be disclosed only to the doctors and lawyers involved, and should not be seen by the parents. It was held that the disputed material was not privileged, but should not, in any event, be shown to the parents,[4] because of the potential damage to the child that might flow from such a disclosure.

**11.40** It is now accepted practice that legal advisers, and doctors instructed by them, should have access to police videos, and videos made in hospitals. The practice followed by some police forces and hospitals of declining to permit tapes or copies of tapes to leave their premises has been disapproved by the High Court. Travel costs to view videos can add disproportionately to the legal aid bill, and experts may be inhibited from having free access to such material. Solicitors should be permitted custody of tapes, on the receipt of specific undertakings as to their use.[5]

*Partial disclosure*

**11.41** In *Re C (Disclosure)*,[6] Johnson J considered the question of the extent to which the court can order disclosure of only part of the evidence to one party.[7] In that case he was referred to, and cited with approval, *Official Solicitor v K*:[8]

'In *Official Solicitor v K* Lord Jenkins (at 226A) referred to Upjohn LJ's approval of a practice which in my own experience is now often followed when this kind of problem arises. Lord Jenkins said:

"... the ... Lord Justice commended as an excellent and commonplace practice a form

---

1    [1991] 2 FLR 478, CA.
2    Kingham 'Medical Confidentiality' [1991] Fam Law 506.
3    [1991] 2 FLR 487.
4    This decision overlooks the difficulty that a legal adviser's knowledge is that of his client; for without the client the legal adviser has no existence in relation to the information.
5    *Re R (Child Abuse: Video Evidence)* [1995] 1 FLR 451.
6    [1996] 1 FLR 797, per Johnson J.
7    See also consideration of this question at **6.14** above.
8    [1965] AC 201.

of procedure whereby the judge declares his willingness to disclose the contents of the confidential reports to the parties' legal advisers provided they are not disclosed to the parties themselves, and said he had never known any objection to it until the mother took the objection in the present case."

I was told that the mother's solicitor had stated that his instructions did not permit him to take part in that practice. Accordingly it seemed to me there was no point in his being invited to travel 200 miles to attend the hearing before me because without knowing what the information is he could scarcely be expected to contribute to the decision or take effective steps on his client's behalf.'

**11.42**      Although of practical good sense, this practice can create difficulties for the legal representative, since in the context of court proceedings the legal representative does not have an existence independent from his client and, as such, information possessed by the adviser should always be communicated to the client.

### Duty on parties to disclose their own adverse material

*Wardship*
**11.43**      Occasionally an issue may arise as to the admissibility of expert evidence which is adverse to a party to the proceedings, although it is highly relevant to the question of the welfare of the child. The welfare principle comes directly into opposition with the principle that information given by a party to his solicitor, or evidence collected on his instructions for the advancement of his case, is privileged. In *Re A (Minors) (Disclosure of Material)*,[1] a wardship case, a mother was suspected of causing the death of one of her children by deliberate suffocation. She failed to file a report from a paediatric pathologist instructed on her behalf. Johnson J referred to the parental, administrative and non-adversarial character of the wardship jurisdiction, and held that the High Court did have the power, in appropriate cases, to override the legal professional privilege which attached to such a report. That power, however, was to be exercised 'only rarely, and only when the court is satisfied that it is necessary for it to be exercised in order to achieve the best interests of the child involved'.[2] As the law then stood the judge declined to find, as a matter of principle, that an implied term of leave being given to instruct an expert should be that any resulting report should be submitted to the court and the other parties.

*Children Act 1989 cases*
**11.44**      The attempts in recent years to use the power of the wardship court to set aside legal and professional privilege has been extended into Children Act 1989 cases. A number of reported cases have grappled with the question of the disclosure by a party to children proceedings of expert reports commissioned on the instructions of that party which turn out to be adverse to his interests. However, the position has

---

1      [1991] 2 FLR 473.
2      *Re A (Minors: Disclosure of Material)* [1991] 2 FLR 473 at 477B.

stabilised since the House of Lords' decision in *Re L (Police Investigation: Privilege)*.[1] The rule, following *Re L*,[2] is that where a party to children proceedings has been given leave to disclose confidential material[3] to a third party to obtain a report, that report must be filed at court and served on all parties.

### The decision in Re L

**11.45**    In *Re L* the police, supported by the guardian ad litem, applied in children proceedings for the disclosure of a report by a chemical pathologist in relation to a child admitted to hospital. The admission was on the basis of a belief that the child had consumed methadone. The police were considering criminal proceedings against the parents. The report had been obtained on the application of the parents, and although it differed from the account of events given by the mother, it was nevertheless filed by her following a direction of the court in children proceedings. The mother's subsequent appeal to the House of Lords against disclosure of the document was dismissed by a 3:2 majority.[4]

### The modern law of privilege in children proceedings

**11.46**    The current state of the law may thus be stated as follows. Solicitor–client communications, including those prior to the commissioning of an expert's report, remain privileged, and are thus also confidential. The letter of instruction to the expert,[5] and the report itself, are not privileged and will be ordered to be filed and served where leave has been given to disclose confidential material for a report to be prepared. The position for solicitors, who may handle and receive damaging material in their preparation of children cases, and the question of whether there is a duty placed upon all parties to children proceedings to make voluntary disclosure of all matters relevant to the child's welfare, remains uncertain following the decision in *Re L*. The House of Lords specifically did not resolve the point. The advocate has a duty not to mislead the court,[6] but the positive duty placed upon the advocate to disclose relevant matters to the court, even where such disclosure is against the interests of the client, as urged in *Essex County Council v R*,[7] appears not to exist.

## Public interest immunity

### The principles of public interest immunity

**11.47**    Public interest immunity is a doctrine developed to enable the courts to protect information from disclosure, on the ground that the public interest requires it. Documents or information coming into existence at the highest level of government and policy-making will not be disclosed where the public interest requires

---

1    [1996] 2 WLR 395, [1996] 1 FLR 731, HL.

2    Privilege following *Re L* is considered fully at **7.17** et seq above.

3    Under Family Proceedings Rules 1991, r 4.23; Family Proceedings Courts (Children Act 1989) Rules 1991, r 23.

4    See further **7.19** et seq above.

5    *Re DH (Child Abuse)* [1996] 1 FLR 679, per Wall J; *Re CS (Expert Witnesses)* [1996] 2 FLR 115, per Bracewell J; *Vernon v Bosley (Expert Evidence) (Note)* [1998] 1 FLR 297, CA.

6    Considered further at **7.23** above; and see *Vernon v Bosley (No 2)* [1998] 1 FLR 304, [1997] 3 WLR 683, CA.

7    [1993] 2 FLR 826, per Thorpe J.

non-disclosure, irrespective of the hardship occasioned to a litigant who may wish to rely upon them. On the other hand, information or documents of a routine administrative nature may be subject to successful applications for disclosure.

**11.48**     Public interest immunity therefore attaches primarily to documents held by public bodies, such as local authorities in pursuance of their social services functions or, for example, by the NSPCC. It may be in the public interest that such documents are not disclosed. The justification for this principle has been explained in *Re D:*[1] Harman LJ held that disclosure of such documents was contrary to public policy, 'because these records must not be kept by people looking over their shoulders in case they should be attacked for some opinion they may feel it their duty to express'.[2] A public authority with a statutory duty to keep records would find it difficult to perform that public duty, if it were under the apprehension that such material might come under public scrutiny in a court of law.[3] It is therefore customary for social workers to contend that material within their files relating to children in their care is subject to an absolute assurance of confidentiality and should not be disclosed in order to protect children and third party sources. Other bodies such as the Probation Service may also claim the shield of public interest immunity in relation to documents held by them.[4]

### Public interest immunity and waiver

**11.49**     Historically, one of the defining features of public interest immunity, and one which precisely distinguishes it from privilege, is that it cannot be waived. However, it has been held that public interest immunity is capable of being waived in respect of documents dealing with matters of day-to-day administration and record-keeping, rather than matters of central government policy.[5]

### Public interest immunity in children cases

**11.50**     Circumstances may arise within children proceedings where a party seeks to advance his case by the disclosure of documents covered by public interest immunity. For example, in *Re M (A Minor) (Disclosure of Material)*,[6] a father applied for general discovery of social work records relating to his elder daughter, which contained allegations of rape and incest against him, in wardship proceedings relating to a younger half-sister. Refusing the father's appeal, the Court of Appeal held that social work documents were covered by public interest immunity, although there was no absolute rule against disclosure. An application for specific documents was possible, but the party making the discovery must establish the need for the production of the specific document. It was for the court to perform the balancing exercise between the competing public interests of immunity and disclosure, but it should inspect the documents only where there were definite grounds for expecting to find material of real importance.[7]

---

1     [1970] 1 WLR 599, [1970] 1 All ER 1088.
2     Ibid, at 601E.
3     Similar reason was applied in *Gaskin v Liverpool City Council* [1980] 1 WLR 1549.
4     *Re M (Minors) (Confidential Documents)* [1987] 1 FLR 47, [1986] Fam Law 336.
5     *Campbell v Tameside MBC* [1982] QB 1065, CA.
6     [1990] 2 FLR 36, CA.
7     Ibid, at 44C; and see the approach of the court to discovery in *R v Reading Justices ex parte Berkshire County Council* [1996] 1 FLR 149; considered at **11.53** below.

## *Application of public interest immunity to documents*

**11.51**      In *Re C (Expert Evidence: Disclosure: Practice)*,[1] Cazalet J considered the role of public interest immunity and set out the following guidelines to be considered when deciding whether immunity applied to a particular document or class of documents in care proceedings.

–      A local authority has a duty to disclose all relevant information which might assist parents to rebut allegations made against it, save for documents which might be protected by public interest immunity.

–      It was then for the party seeking disclosure to show the reasons why the document should be produced, but it was for the court to decide whether documents covered by public interest immunity should be disclosed.

–      The local authority is under a duty to disclose relevant documents, not protected by public interest immunity, which modify or cast doubt on its case.[2]

–      If a relevant document appears to be protected by public interest immunity, the local authority should draw the existence of the document to the notice of the other parties. The local authority should prepare a précis of the information, which would be disclosed if ordered.

–      The local authority should draw the guardian's attention to any matters of concern within the documents. Moreover, if in the course of inspecting social services files, the guardian finds relevant records which have not been disclosed, he should invite disclosure by the local authority. The guardian is not, however, entitled to disclose documents covered by public interest immunity.

The main feature which emerges from these guidelines is the general duty on the local authority to give discovery of documents. The local authority may claim public interest immunity, in which case the onus then shifts to the party seeking the documents to persuade the court that they should be discovered. It is then for the court to decide whether public interest immunity should apply.

## *Public interest immunity in criminal cases*

**11.52**      Where criminal charges are laid alleging the abuse, neglect or physical assault of children, parallel material may be held in social services files, as well as documentary evidence filed at court in care proceedings. Defence lawyers in criminal prosecutions involving children may apply within children proceedings for the disclosure of documents held by social services.[3] In these circumstances, it has been recommended that the question of disclosure should be left to the trial judge in the criminal proceedings: 'he alone will be in a position to assess the relevance and likely effect of the disclosure of any material which might be contained in the documents'.[4] The family court should not therefore make an order or ruling binding the judge

---

1      [1995] 1 FLR 204.

2      See also **11.34** above on the local authority's duty of disclosure.

3      *Re D (Minors) (Wardship: Disclosure)* [1994] 1 FLR 346, CA; *R v K(DT) (Evidence)* [1993] 2 FLR 181, CA; *Re K (Minors) (Care Proceedings: Disclosure)* [1994] 1 FLR 377; *R v Reading Justices ex parte Berkshire County Council* [1996] 1 FLR 149 are examples of applications within children proceedings for discovery of documents for use in criminal proceedings.

4      *Re H (Criminal Proceedings: Disclosure of Adoption Records)* [1995] 1 FLR 964, per Sir Stephen Brown P.

conducting a criminal trial. Application is made directly to the criminal court by subpoena[1] to the local authority social services department for public interest immunity to be set aside, and for material held by social services to be disclosed.

### Guidelines in R v Reading Justices

**11.53**      Applications in criminal proceedings for the disclosure of social services documents relating to children are now governed by *R v Reading Justices ex parte Berkshire County Council*.[2] This case involved an application for documents to the magistrates' court under the Magistrates' Court Act 1980, s 97, but the principles deriving from the judgment have been expressly approved by Lord Taylor LCJ in *R v Derby Magistrates' Court ex parte B*,[3] and are therefore relevant to applications made directly to the Crown Court. The *Reading Justices* case establishes that only 'material evidence' should be disclosed. The principles are as follows:[4]

> '(i) to be material evidence, documents must not be only relevant to the issues arising in the criminal proceedings, but also documents admissible as such in evidence;
> (ii) documents which are desired merely for the purpose of possible cross examination are not admissible in evidence and, thus, are not material for the purposes of s 97;
> (iii) whoever seeks production of documents must satisfy the justices with some material that the documents are "likely to be material" in the sense indicated, likelihood for this purpose involving a real possibility, although not necessarily a probability;
> (iv) it is not sufficient that the applicant merely wants to find out whether or not the third party has such material documents. This procedure must not be used as a disguised attempt to obtain discovery.'

### Inadmissibility and immateriality

**11.54**      Applications to gain sight of material to use solely in cross-examination should fail, because such documents are not admissible in their own right. Hearsay and opinions of social workers and other third parties are not admissible in criminal proceedings, save by virtue of statutory exceptions.[5] Under the Criminal Justice Act 1988, s 24, a statement in a document received or supplied by a person in the course of a profession (such as social work) shall be admissible, subject to the discretion of the trial judge. However, s 24 does not provide for the admissibility of the document itself, and the criminal courts are now bound by the *Reading Justices* principles. It is also open for the local authority to argue the immateriality of the documents or information sought, because their contents are irrelevant to the defence case.

### Applicability of public interest immunity

**11.55**      Once a judge decides that documents are material, by virtue of their relevance and admissibility, the question of public interest immunity falls to be

---

1      The subpoena is issued under the Criminal Procedure (Attendance of Witnesses) Act 1965, s 2(1), requiring the person to whom it is directed 'to attend before the court and give evidence or produce any document or thing likely to be material evidence'.
2      [1996] 1 FLR 149, [1996] 1 Cr App R 239.
3      [1995] 4 All ER 526 at 535.
4      [1996] 1 FLR 149 at 156D–E.
5      For example, s 23 of the Criminal Evidence Act 1988 provides for the admissibility of hearsay evidence where hearsay is made in a document, and the author of the statement could have given direct oral evidence of the facts contained within it, but is prevented from doing so by specified

considered. The local authority must then argue that disclosure should not be ordered, by asserting public interest immunity. In reality, once the court is satisfied that documents are material, disclosure will then be ordered, subject to performing the 'balancing exercise' of weighing the need of the defendant to defend himself, against the public interest in maintaining confidentiality. The Court of Criminal Appeal has held that it is not necessary for the trial judge to read the social services files in order to determine an application for disclosure: the judge may properly accept the assurances of 'an independent competent member of the Bar that the documents requested were irrelevant'.[1] The Court of Appeal envisaged that counsel for the local authority would determine which documents were relevant, by reading them through, in the light of the particulars in the summons. The judge could accept that submission and order disclosure, or could go on to read them himself. The obligation upon a local authority engaged in a search through its own files is only to indicate the relevance of documents to the questions asked in the summons, not to cure any defect in that summons. Public interest immunity must then be asserted, and cannot be waived by the local authority; the formal setting-aside of public interest immunity remains a matter for the judge.

## Confidential evidence

### *Scope*

**11.56**      Questions of confidentiality[2] as between parties to the proceedings and their advisers arise in the context of children proceedings in three principal areas:

(1)   between the parties to proceedings and the outside world;
(2)   between the parties to proceedings and professionals, including statutory agencies; and
(3)   among the parties and within proceedings.

### *Confidentiality and the outside world: documentary evidence:*

**11.57**      There is a statutory requirement of confidentiality in children cases. In the family courts, the rules provide as follows:[3]

'Notwithstanding any rule of court to the contrary, no document, other than a record of an order, held by the court and relating to proceedings to which this Part applies shall be disclosed, other than to –
(a)   a party,
(b)   the legal representative of a party,
(c)   the guardian ad litem,
(d)   the Legal Aid Board, or
(e)   a welfare officer,
without leave of the judge or district judge.'

---

circumstances. Section 24 lets in a document created by a person in the course of a trade or business where there is a reasonable inference that that person has a personal knowledge of the facts in question.
1      *R v W(G); R v W(E)* [1996] Crim LR 904.
2      See further 'Professional confidences' at **7.6** et seq above.
3      Family Proceedings Rules 1991, r 4.23(1); Family Proceedings Courts (Children Act 1989) Rules 1991, r 23.

Thus, disclosure of any document (other than court orders) relating to children proceedings and filed at court may not be disclosed to third parties save with leave of the court. This continues the practice in wardship that leave must be requested to disclose evidential documents to persons who are not parties; unauthorised disclosure in wardship is potentially a contempt of court, even where it is to an expert whose views would have been helpful to the court.[1]

**11.58**      The prohibition against disclosure in the Family Proceedings Rules 1991, r 4.23 can be narrow in its scope. For example, in *Re G (Social Worker: Disclosure)*[2] the Court of Appeal held by a majority that the leave requirement applied only to documents actually filed at court.[3] A social worker does not need leave to disclose information recorded in case files or a report which, for whatever reason, has never reached the court; and, where the document is created in contemplation of proceedings, leave is not needed in the interests of promoting co-operation between professionals (eg police and social workers) in dealing with allegations of child abuse.[4] However, it has also been held that there is no doubt that the use by a party or legal representative in other proceedings of information (as distinct from documents) acquired in family proceedings requires the leave of the court because information acquired in children proceedings is, like documents, confidential.[5] Similarly, a local authority requires leave of the court under r 4.23 for disclosure of a guardian ad litem's report to a family centre, even though the centre is part of the local authority social services department. The report is confidential to the court and the court is entitled to decide to whom the report is to be disseminated.[6]

### Disclosure among professionals

**11.59**      Confidentiality should not inhibit the proper exchange of information between multiple agencies jointly concerned in child protection work. These frequently include the police, and other bodies which are not parties to the proceedings. A strict interpretation of the rule which prohibits disclosure of court documents to non-parties without leave of the court would actively hamper the necessary close working relationships between professionals in the child care field, which was the most important recommendation to come out of the Cleveland Enquiry.[7] *Re G* (above) restated the Cleveland principles that multi-disciplinary agencies engaged in child protection must not be fettered in the free exchange of information through formal channels such as a case conference, or informal communications; and this principle has been confirmed by *Re W (Disclosure to Police)*[8] in respect of documents and information in existence where proceedings are pending.

---

1    *Practice Direction* [1987] 3 All ER 640.
2    [1996] 1 FLR 276.
3    Ibid, at 282G; *Oxfordshire County Council v P (A Minor)* [1995] 1 FLR 552, disapproved on this point.
4    *Re W (Disclosure to Police)* [1998] 1 FLR 135, CA.
5    *Re A (Criminal Proceedings: Disclosure)* [1996] 1 FLR 221 at 224A, per Butler-Sloss LJ.
6    *Re C (Guardian ad Litem: Disclosure of Report)* [1996] 1 FLR 61, per Sir Stephen Brown P.
7    *Report of the Enquiry into Child Abuse in Cleveland 1987* (HMSO, 1988).
8    [1998] 1 FLR 135, CA.

### *Duty of statutory bodies to provide information*

**11.60**    Statutory bodies have a duty to disclose information to a local authority where its staff believe that a child may be suffering significant harm.[1] This duty extends to the education and housing authorities, to health authorities and anyone else authorised by the Secretary of State.[2] To this extent, therefore, confidentiality as between professionals is reduced. Such information may relate to a child, or to an adult, such as an alleged perpetrator. Material obtained in this way could then be disclosed in subsequent children proceedings. Further, their discovery could be compelled (subject to issues of public interest immunity),[3] and the guardian ad litem would have access to the information obtained under s 47.[4] A similar responsibility to assist the local authority can be imputed to the police in appropriate circumstances.[5]

### *Oral admissions*

**11.61**    It follows from the above that a social worker is free to pass on spoken admissions which have implications for child protection. Admissions made to social workers and recorded in writing in the social work file are not governed by the Family Proceedings Rules 1991, r 4.23. However, oral admissions to a guardian ad litem may be treated differently to those received by social workers, because the function of the guardian is defined by the court proceedings. Thus, for example, a guardian should seek leave of the court before disclosing information to the police.[6]

### *Children Act 1989, s 98*

**11.62**    The Children Act 1989, s 98 seeks to enable parties to proceedings to avoid self-incrimination. It provides as follows:

> '(1) In any proceedings in which a court is hearing an application for an order under Part IV or V, no person shall be excused from –
>    (a)   giving evidence on any matter; or
>    (b)   answering any question put to him in the course of his giving evidence,
> on the ground that doing so might incriminate him or his spouse of an offence.
> (2) A statement or admission made in such proceedings shall not be admissible in evidence against the person making it or his spouse in proceedings for an offence other than perjury.'

Thus, in proceedings for care, supervision or child protection orders, no person shall be excused from giving evidence on any matter, or answering any question put to him in the course of giving evidence, on the grounds of self-incrimination or that of a spouse. However, statements or admissions made in such proceedings shall not be

---

1    Children Act 1989, s 47(1).
2    Ibid, s 47(9) and (11).
3    Rules of the Supreme Court 1965, Ord 24; *Re JC (Care Proceedings: Procedure)* [1995] 2 FLR 77, per Wall J; and see **11.36** et seq above.
4    Children Act 1989, s 42(2); and see **11.30** above.
5    See eg *Nottinghamshire County Council v H* [1995] 1 FLR 115, per Johnson J where the local authority sought disclosure from the Crown Prosecution Service of documents relating to forthcoming criminal proceedings. Disclosure might be ordered – as on the facts of this case – where it is sought, essentially, to enable the local authority to make a more informed decision about the future of the children in its interim care.
6    *Oxfordshire County Council v P* [1995] Fam 161, [1995] 1 FLR 552, per Ward J.

admissible in evidence against the maker or his spouse, in prosecutions in the criminal courts, for offences other than perjury.[1] This is to encourage witnesses in children cases to be frank with the local authority and with the courts, and to facilitate further investigations and assessments. The protection offered by s 98(2) protects only against statements and other evidence being admissible in evidence in criminal proceedings (other than for an offence of perjury). There is no promise of confidentiality generally. An admission protected by s 98(2), so far as evidence in court is concerned, may nevertheless be disclosed to the police to assist them with their investigations.[2]

### Disclosure to the police to assist investigations

**11.63**      Applications by the police for disclosure of information may be divided into categories of information which is required prior to a final hearing and evidence given at the trial of an application for a care order. The first may be a question of confidentiality, the second may or may not be covered by the Children Act 1989, s 98.

### Information arising in connection with children proceedings

**11.64**      Police will be refused sight of medical records and other information only rarely.[3] Recent applications by the police within Children Act 1989 cases have raised not only issues as to confidentiality, but also the question of the limitations of solicitor–client privilege and the privilege against self-incrimination. The current state of the law is represented by the majority judgment of the House of Lords in *Re L (Minors) (Police Investigation: Privilege)*.[4] It is now clear that the courts have jurisdiction to hear applications for the disclosure of documents by a body, such as the police, who were not parties in care proceedings. The court has an unfettered discretion in dealing with such applications, but the judge must exercise his discretion judicially, by considering the interests of the child concerned, the public interest in encouraging frankness by preserving confidentiality, and the public interest in upholding the legal process by providing evidence for use in other proceedings.[5]

### Privilege against self-incrimination

**11.65**      Where a party to care proceedings, for example a parent of the child concerned, makes an admission in evidence which is covered by the Children Act 1989, s 98(1), the police may still seek leave of the court to use that evidence as part of their inquiries. Guidelines as to the matters which a judge will consider when deciding whether to give leave for the evidence to be made available to the police were set out by Swinton Thomas LJ in *Re EC (Disclosure of Material)*[6] as follows:[7]

(1)   the welfare and interests of the child or children concerned in the care proceedings;

---

1      But see consideration of *Re EC (Disclosure of Material)* [1996] 2 FLR 725, CA at **11.65** above.
2      *Re EC (Disclosure of Material)* (ibid).
3      Cazalet J in *A County Council v W (Disclosure* [1997] 1 FLR 574 at 587E.
4      [1996] 2 WLR 395, [1996] 1 FLR 731, HL; and see **11.44** and Chapter 7 (privilege) above.
5      *Oxfordshire County Council v L and F* [1997] 1 FLR 235 at 241E–F.
6      [1996] 2 FLR 725, CA.
7      This approach was approved by the Court of Appeal in *Re W (Disclosure to Police)* [1998] 2 FLR 135 at 144B, per Butler-Sloss, CA.

(2)  the welfare and interests of other children generally;

(3)  the maintenance of confidentiality in children cases;

(4)  the importance of encouraging frankness in children cases;

(5)  the public interest in the administration of justice;

(6)  the public interest in the prosecution of serious crime and the punishment of offences;

(7)  the gravity of the alleged offence and the relevance of the evidence to it;

(8)  the desirability of co-operation between the various child protection agencies;

(9)  where s 98(2) applies, the fact that an admission would not be admissible against him in criminal proceedings, fairness to a person who has incriminated himself and any danger of oppression would also be relevant;

(10) whether any other material disclosure has taken place.

The Court of Appeal recognised that disclosure may not be ordered if the welfare of the affected child is likely to be adversely affected in a serious way, or if the evidence has little or no bearing upon a police investigation. However, the strong public interest in making available to the police material relevant in the prosecution of persons involved in violent or sexual offences against children is likely to be a very important factor in whether or not to order release of information to police.[1] Where there is an admission of culpability for the death of a child (as in *Re EC*), the case for disclosure is likely to be strong.

## *Disclosure to other public bodies*

**11.66**     A balance in favour of disclosure where the welfare of children is concerned has also been clearly stated in connection with applications for disclosure of material filed in care proceedings. For example, the General Medical Council has been successful in obtaining the disclosure[2] where there was a finding in care proceedings that a registered medical practitioner had sexually abused his daughter. It was held that the welfare of the children in the case was a major factor in the exercise of the court's discretion, and the welfare of the children would not be promoted by disclosure. However, there was an overwhelming and overriding public interest in disclosure to the General Medical Council because of the risk to the community from the father, subject to the provision maintaining the anonymity of the child in any ensuing disciplinary hearing against the father.

## *Confidentiality: disclosure and confidentiality between parties*

**11.67**     It is a fundamental principle that a court should not make findings or draw conclusions upon evidence or information which a party to legal proceedings has not seen, and is therefore not in a position to deal with. Occasionally, in children proceedings, a party may wish to rely upon material in court which he wishes to keep confidential. Another party may not then know of its existence or content. In *Official Solicitor v K*,[3] the House of Lords held that, within the wardship jurisdiction, confidential reports might exceptionally be submitted to the court but withheld from

---

1    *Re EC (Disclosure of Material)* [1996] 2 FLR 725, CA at 734C.

2    *A County Council v W and Others (Disclosure)* [1997] 1 FLR 574, per Cazalet J.

3    [1965] AC 201; and see **6.15** et seq above for full consideration of the question of partial disclosure.

the parties; the test is whether the material is reliable, and whether 'real harm' to the child might otherwise ensue.

**11.68**      The importance of disclosure to a party has been justified by Art 6(1) of the European Convention of Human Rights, which states that 'everyone is entitled to a fair and public hearing within a reasonable time by an independent and impartial tribunal established by law'. The European Court of Human Rights has ruled unanimously that the withholding of social work documents filed in care proceedings relating to a child from the mother of the child was a violation of Art 6(1) of the European Convention on Human Rights.[1] A practice direction has further stressed the duty of full relevant disclosure in all family proceedings.[2]

### Welfare reports, welfare officers and confidentiality

**11.69**      Welfare reports have been distinguished particularly as documents to which confidentiality attaches. Reports filed in High Court proceedings must be endorsed with a direction as to the confidentiality of their contents; and this is now common practice in the lower courts.[3] The confidentiality attaching to a court welfare report is not absolute: subject to the leave of the court, information contained within it may be used in other proceedings.[4] Welfare officers are also affected by the principle that there should be full disclosure to all parties, as there should be to the court. A welfare officer should not give a judge his views on a confidential and private basis without giving parties an opportunity to deal with them in cross-examination; a decision resting on private and confidential advice from a welfare officer may be set aside on appeal as a material irregularity.[5]

### Confidentiality of statements during conciliation and mediation

**11.70**      Evidence may not be given of statements made by one or other parties in the course of meetings held, or communications made, for the purpose of conciliation, 'save in the very unusual case where a statement is made clearly indicating that the maker has in the past caused or is likely in the future to cause serious harm to the well-being of the child'.[6]

### Disclosure to parties for use in other proceedings

**11.71**      The courts have the power to grant an application by a party to children proceedings for the disclosure of material for use in other proceedings. Such proceedings may be civil, such as actions in negligence, or criminal, with an obvious nexus with the circumstances giving rise to Children Act 1989 proceedings. In *Re D (Minors) (Wardship: Disclosure)*,[7] it was held that a judge in the exercise of his

---

1      *McMichael v United Kingdom* [1995] 2 FCR 718.
2      *Practice Direction of 31 January 1995 (Case Management)* [1995] 1 WLR 332, [1995] 1 FLR 456, at para 3; and see also Brasse 'The Duty of Disclosure in Children's Cases' [1996] Fam Law 358; Burrows 'Disclosure in Children's Cases [1996] Fam Law 566.
3      *Practice Direction* [1984] 1 All ER 827, [1984] FLR 356.
4      *Brown v Matthews* [1990] 1 Ch 662, CA.
5      *Re C (A Minor) (Confidential Information)* [1991] FCR 308, CA.
6      *Re D (Minors) (Conciliation: Disclosure of Information)* [1993] Fam 231; Cretney *Comment* [1993] Fam Law 410; see also **11.64** above.
7      [1994] 1 FLR 346, CA.

discretion must balance the importance of confidentiality in wardship proceedings and the need for frankness by persons giving evidence in the wardship court, against the public interest in seeing that justice is done:[1]

> 'In relation to criminal proceedings it is clear that the wardship court should not, as it were, seek to erect a barrier which will prejudice the operation of another bench of the judicature.'

**11.72** In *Re Manda (Wardship: Disclosure of Evidence)*,[2] the Court of Appeal held that where disclosure is sought to assist in any other area of litigation: 'the public interest in the administration of justice required that all relevant information should be available for use in those proceedings'. In that case the parents of an elective mute won the right to disclose wardship papers to an expert for the purpose of a proposed claim in negligence against a local authority, health authority and a consultant paediatrician. The child also indicated a wish to pursue a similar action: the court would have to decide where the interests of a minor lay, although the older the child, the more relevant his views. A child who had achieved his majority was entitled to decide what were in his own interests, and, by implication, such interests might outweigh the principle of confidentiality.[3] Leave has been given for disclosure for use in an immigration appeal before a special adjudicator, where the father was claiming that he was likely to be executed if sent back to Angola. It was held that all the written documents were to be disclosed, as the value of disclosure to assist the adjudicator in doing justice in the immigration proceedings outweighed the possibility of any harm to the children resulting from such disclosure.[4]

*Disclosure in criminal proceedings*

**11.73** Parties also commonly seek disclosure of relevant but confidential material, where they are not only parties to children proceedings, but are defendants in criminal proceedings, with obvious implications for the liberty of the individual. The approach of the Court of Appeal in relation to wardship in *Re D (Minors) (Wardship: Disclosure)*[5] has been extended to apply to Children Act 1989 cases. In *Re K(Minors) (Care Proceedings: Disclosure)*[6] a father charged with the rape of his two children applied for the disclosure of statements made by the mother, transcripts of video recorded interviews with the children filed within the care proceedings, and for leave for defence counsel in the criminal proceedings to see all documents filed within the care proceedings. Booth J held that the production of the material would not be to the detriment of the children concerned: 'it is in fact greatly in their interests that their father should have a fair trial and greatly in the interests of justice that there should be

---

1    [1994] 1 FLR 346 at 351, per Sir Stephen Brown P.
2    [1993] Fam 183, [1993] 2 WLR 161, [1993] 1 FLR 205.
3    This decision contrasts with the restrictive approach of the High Court in *Re X, Y, and Z (Wardship: Disclosure of Material)* [1992] 1 FLR 84, where the court declined to disclose wardship material relating to children in the Cleveland child abuse cases to a newspaper which wished to use unspecified material in defending a libel action brought by two paediatricians. It was held that such disclosure was potentially damaging, not for the children, but for the wardship jurisdiction, which relied upon the help of relatives and professionals, given in the context of confidentiality.
4    *Re F (A Minor) (Disclosure: Immigration)* [1994] 2 FLR 958.
5    [1994] 1 FLR 346, CA (and see above).
6    [1994] 1 FLR 377, [1994] 3 All ER 230; *sub nom Kent County Council v K* [1994] 1 WLR 912.

no impediment to this'. Leave of the court is necessary even for the disclosure of factual information which is held within material filed in children cases, where this may be relevant to assist a defendant in the cross-examination of criminal witnesses.[1]

**11.74**     On the other hand, courts have been critical of defence lawyers who seek information from children files as a routine trawl of all documents and other evidence available; and this may be both by a party to children proceedings and by third parties who consider that material on social services files may be of assistance in their defence. For example, in *R v Reading Justices ex parte Berkshire County Council*,[2] the Divisional Court held that a party[3] seeking the production of documents from a third party (in this case a local authority and its director of social services) had to satisfy the justices (who, in that case, were requested to give leave) that the documents were 'likely to be material evidence'.[4] The central principles to be derived from the statute and the authorities when considering the question of discovery by a third party in such circumstances were:

(1)   to be material evidence documents must not only be relevant to the issues arising in the criminal proceedings, but also be documents admissible in evidence;
(2)   documents desired merely for the purpose of possible cross-examination are not admissible in evidence;
(3)   anyone who seeks production of documents must satisfy the court that the documents are likely to be material – the likelihood to involve real possibility, although not necessarily probability;
(4)   the procedure must not be used as a disguised attempt to obtain discovery.

### Confidentiality in adoption proceedings

**11.75**     The concept of the welfare of the child is also treated differently under the Adoption Act 1976 by comparison with the Children Act 1989. The Adoption Act 1976, s 6 provides that in reaching any decision relating to the adoption of a child a court or adoption agency shall 'have regard to all the circumstances, first consideration being given to the need to safeguard and promote the welfare of the child'.[5] The successful placing of a child for adoption and the subsequent making of an adoption order is one of the most sensitive areas of family law. The court must be aware continually of the need to balance the provision of information to adopters, and to natural parents, against the risks to the child of destabilising a placement.

### Disclosure of confidential material filed in children proceedings to adopters

**11.76**     It may be of assistance to a local authority in the search for potential adopters, particularly where independent adoption agencies are being consulted, to be able to disclose hitherto confidential information. Once the prospective adopters have been identified and matched to the child, disclosure will be necessary to assist them

---

1     *Re A (Criminal Proceedings: Disclosure)* [1996] 1 FLR 221.
2     [1996] 1 FLR 149 (and see **11.53** above under public interest immunity).
3     In this case, police officers, who were alleged to have abused children.
4     Within the meaning of Magistrates' Courts Act 1980, s 97(1).
5     The welfare of the child in adoption proceedings does not prevail over other considerations, in contrast to the paramountcy principle of Guardianship of Minors Act 1971, s 1, and Children Act 1989, s 1. See Jones *Adoption Manual* 2nd edn (Sweet & Maxwell, 1997), p 11.

and their lawyers in preparing their case, which may be opposed by the natural parents (unless the child is already free for adoption). A local authority will need to seek leave under the Family Proceedings Rules 1991, r 4.23 for the disclosure of papers filed in Children Act 1989 proceedings to the prospective adopters. This follows the previous practice in wardship.[1] Such leave might be sought in the final hearing of a care application: specific directions as to the timing and limitation of the disclosure should be given by the court.

### Disclosure in adoption proceedings

**11.77**     Once adoption proceedings are underway the rules provide that the court has the power to direct that sight of a report by a person named in it be limited as follows:[2]

> 'A party who is an individual and is referred to in a confidential report supplied to the court by an adoption agency, a local authority, a reporting officer or a guardian ad litem may inspect, for the purposes of the hearing, that Part of any such report which refers to him, subject to any direction given by the court that:
> (a)    no Part of one or any of the reports shall be revealed to that party, or
> (b)    the Part of one or any of the reports referring to that party shall be revealed only to that party's legal advisers, or
> (c)    the whole or any other Part of one or any of the reports shall be revealed to that party.'

Thus, no part of such a report, confidential to the court, may be revealed to that party, subject to any limiting direction given by the court. In considering applications for disclosure under the Adoption Rules 1984, r 53(2), the court must balance the risk to the child in destabilising his placement against the general desirability of openness, explained by Butler-Sloss LJ in *Re S (A Minor) (Adoption)*[3] as follows:[4]

> 'There should not be unnecessary secrecy ... but it is a question of balancing the provision of information against the risk to the child of identification of his placement and destabilisation of his future home.'

### Confidentiality and Re D

**11.78**     The tendency of the courts to give weight to the wishes and feelings of the child has been reconsidered by the House of Lords in *Re D (Minors) (Adoption Reports: Confidentiality)*.[5] A mother contesting the adoption of her two children wanted to inspect sections of the guardian ad litem's report which dealt with the wishes and feelings of the children in relation to her. Her application was refused at first instance, and by the Court of Appeal, on the basis that the guardian's report was confidential. The House of Lords recognised the potential for conflict between the

1    *Practice Direction (Ward of Court: Disclosure of Wardship Papers to Prospective Adopters)* [1989] 1 All ER 169.
2    Adoption Rules 1984, SI 1984/265, r 53(2); there is no equivalent provision under Magistrates' Courts (Adoption) Rules 1984, SI 1984/611.
3    [1993] 2 FLR 204, CA.
4    Ibid, at 210C.
5    [1996] 2 FLR 687; and see consideration of this case in the context of disclosure generally at **6.15** above.

principle that each party to a judicial process should have the opportunity to answer any adverse material before the court, and the need for confidentiality in relation to sensitive, private information, which is a characteristic of adoption proceedings. However, it concurred in the conclusion that the confidential nature of the adoption process must not be taken to extremes:[1]

> 'Plainly, where it is suggested that disclosure may harm the child the court will take the matter very seriously, but it should look closely at both the degree of likelihood that harm will occur, and the gravity of the harm if it does in fact occur. To say that harm must be certain would ... pitch the test too high, since future events cannot be predicted with complete confidence, but a powerful combination of likelihood and seriousness of harm will be required before the requirements for a fair trial can be overridden.'

After a review of recent authorities, Lord Mustill (with the concurrence of the remainder of the House) concluded that 'non-disclosure should be the exception, not the rule' and set out the following principles governing confidentiality:[2]

> 'It is a fundamental principle of fairness that a party is entitled to the disclosure of all materials which may be taken into account by the court when reaching a decision adverse to that party. This principle applies with particular force to proceedings designed to lead to an order for adoption, since the consequences of such an order are so lasting and far-reaching.
>
> When deciding whether to direct that notwithstanding r 53(2) of the Adoption Rules 1984 a party referred to in a confidential report supplied by an adoption agency, a local authority, a reporting officer or a guardian ad litem shall not be entitled to inspect the part of the report which refers to him or her, the court should first consider whether disclosure of the material would involve a real possibility of significant harm to the child.
>
> If it would, the court should next consider whether the overall interests of the child would benefit from non-disclosure, weighing on the one hand the interest of the child in having the material properly tested, and on the other both the magnitude of the risk that harm will occur and the gravity of the harm if it does occur.
>
> If the court is satisfied that the interests of the child point towards non-disclosure, the next and final step is for the court to weigh that consideration, and its strength in the circumstances of the case, against the interest of the parent or other party in having an opportunity to see and respond to the material. In the latter regard the court should take into account the importance of the material to the issues in the case.
>
> Non-disclosure should be the exception and not the rule. The court should be rigorous in its examination of the risk and gravity of the feared harm to the child, and should order non-disclosure only when the case for doing so is compelling.'

### *Judicial discretion to withhold discovery*

**11.79**    In adoption proceedings as in other children cases, questions of confidentiality may arise where a guardian receives information from a child, which the child wishes to be withheld from the parent. The question of the disclosure of such information remains, again, a matter of judicial discretion. Older children should be told that the judge will be made aware of their preference for confidentiality, but ultimately it is for the court to decide how to deal with the information.[3] In serial number adoption proceedings, all information is to be regarded as confidential to the

---

1    [1995] 2 FLR 687 at 694G.
2    Ibid, at 700G–701B.
3    *Re D (Adoption Reports: Confidentiality)* [1995] 1 FLR 631, CA.

court until disclosure is ordered.[1] Thus, a parent has the right to participate in the proceedings, but does not have a right to receive information save with leave of the court.

### *Confidentiality of information post-adoption*

**11.80**    The Adoption Act 1976, s 50 provides that the Adopted Children's Register, kept by the Registrar General, should be confidential. Information thus held is available only to adopted persons in strictly defined circumstances.[2] The test to be applied in determining applications for disclosure of information under s 50(5) is whether the applicant has made out a case of sufficient weight and justification, so as to persuade the court of the reasonableness of the order sought. It is necessary to show a need or benefit which relates to the adopted person, rather than the desire of a birth relative to seek information about an adopted child. The need to pass on information about a deteriorating genetic condition has been held to satisfy this test.[3]

## 5   EXPERT EVIDENCE[4] IN CHILDREN CASES

### Function and scope

**11.81**    Many children cases inevitably involve allegations of physical, emotional or sexual abuse to or of children. There may be factual disputes about what has happened to a child, or argument about the capacity of a mother or father to provide adequate parenting. Parties may wish to adduce evidence from a variety of medical, psychiatric or other expert witnesses. Frequently, courts will be assisted by an appropriate expert, and it is the function of that expert to assist in the proving of the factual sub-stratum, not just to provide opinion evidence. However, judicial concern has been expressed about the proper and effective use of experts in children cases, and this has led to best practice guidance from the Children Act Advisory Committee.[5]

**11.82**    Expert evidence in children proceedings may be summarised as follows:

–    admissible evidence of facts observed by the expert;
–    explanation and interpretation of evidence of fact adduced by another witness or by the expert himself;
–    opinion evidence.

Thus, it is important to be clear that the expert may be both a witness of fact (eg giving a description of the physical injuries to a child) and of opinion (eg giving an explanation to the court of whether the bruises were accidental and, if they were not, how they may have occurred).

---

1    *Re K (Adoption: Disclosure of Information)* [1997] 2 FLR 74.
2    Adoption Act 1976, ss 50(5) and 51.
3    *Re H (Adoption: Disclosure of Information)* [1995] 1 FLR 236; *D v The Registrar General* [1997] 1 FLR 715, CA.
4    See also Chapter 5 on opinion evidence.
5    *Children Act Advisory Committee Handbook of Best Practice in Children Act Cases* (set out eg as *Best Practice Guidance June 1997* in Part VI of *The Family Court Practice 1999* (Family Law)) at Section 5 which deals with experts and the courts.

## The expert and the judge

**11.83**    The function of the expert in children proceedings – as in any other – is wholly different from that of the judge. It is for the expert to conduct an assessment and express an opinion within the particular area of his expertise. While the court is likely to be heavily dependent upon the skill, knowledge and intellectual integrity of the expert, he cannot usurp the function of the judge, who must decide the particular issues of each case.[1] An expert's opinion on the ultimate issue is admissible by virtue of the Civil Evidence Act 1972.[2] This is subject to the overriding requirement of the relevance of that opinion which, together with questions of weight, is a matter for the judge. The final decision is for the judge alone.[3]

## Admissibility of expert evidence: *Re M and R* and the Civil Evidence Act 1972, s 3

**11.84**    It had been held[4] that expert opinion as to the truth or otherwise of a witness's evidence is inadmissible, because it usurps the function of the judge. In *Re M and R (Child Abuse: Evidence)*,[5] the Court of Appeal drew attention to the conflict between the earlier cases and the Civil Evidence Act 1972, s 3. This provides as follows:

'(1) Subject to any rules of court made in pursuance of Part I of the Civil Evidence Act 1968 or this Act, where a person is called as a witness in any civil proceedings, his opinion on any relevant matter on which he is qualified to give expert evidence shall be admissible in evidence.

(2) It is hereby declared that where a person is called as a witness in any civil proceedings, a statement of opinion by him on any relevant matter on which he is not qualified to give expert evidence, if made as a way of conveying relevant facts personally perceived by him, is admissible as evidence of what he perceived.

(3) In this section "relevant matter" includes an issue in the proceedings in question.'

Thus, by virtue of s 3, the opinion of an expert is admissible in evidence where relevant.

### Final decision with the judge

**11.85**    Despite the provisions of s 3, the final decision remains with the judge, and expert evidence which is admissible under s 3 may still be rejected because it lacks weight or relevance. In *Re M and R* (above), Butler-Sloss LJ explained this as follows:

---

1    For guidance on medical evidence about children, including guidance as to the duties of a medical expert, see *Re C (Minors) (Wardship: Medical Evidence)* [1987] 1 FLR 418; *Re R (A Minor) (Experts' Evidence) (Note)* [1991] 1 FLR 291; *sub nom Re J (Child Abuse: Expert Evidence)* [1991] FCR 193 (full report); *Re M (Minors) (Sexual Abuse: Evidence)* [1993] 1 FLR 822; *B v B (Child Abuse: Contact)* [1994] 2 FLR 713; *Re AB (Child Abuse: Expert Witnesses)* [1995] 1 FLR 181; *Manchester City Council v B* [1996] 1 FLR 324 (as to the limits on the value of medical research and the need for experts to have relevant expertise); *Note: Vernon v Bosley (Expert Evidence)* [1998] 1 FLR 297, CA.

2    See also **11.84** below.

3    *Re M and R (Child Abuse: Evidence)* [1996] 2 FLR 195, CA.

4    See eg *Re S and B (Minors) (Evidence)* [1990] 2 FLR 459, CA; *Re N (Child Abuse: Evidence)* [1996] 2 FLR 214, CA.

5    [1996] 2 FLR 195, CA.

'Many if not all family law cases involving children feature expert opinion evidence. Recently the proper limits of such evidence have been the subject of a number of decisions. A conflict exists between obiter dicta of this court in *Re S and B (Minors) (Child Abuse: Evidence)*[1] (since followed – also obiter – by two other Court of Appeal decisions) and the Civil Evidence Act 1972 – which was not cited to the court in any of those three decisions. ... In cases involving children, expert medical and psychiatric evidence from paediatricians and allied disciplines is often quite indispensable to the court. As Parker LCJ said in *Director of Public Prosecutions v A and BC Chewing Gum Ltd*,[2] when dealing with children, the court needs "all the help it can get". But that dependence in no way compromises the fact that the final decision in the case is the judge's and his alone.'

## Judicial assessment of expert evidence

**11.86**    The court is therefore entitled to reject even the unanimous opinions of experts and guardians ad litem, and there is 'no rule that the judge suspends judicial belief simply because the evidence is given by an expert'.[3] The task of the judge has been expressed as follows: 'I have to remind myself that the question is whether I believe the child, not whether I believe those who believe her'.[4] Because it is for the judge alone to decide whether a child should be believed, evidence from the expert should be couched in terms of consistency or inconsistency of a fact in relation to the event which is alleged to have occurred.[5]

**11.87**    Similarly, the judge by definition is not an expert in the field about which an expert may be giving evidence: 'the court has no expertise of its own other than legal expertise ... the expert advises but the judge decides'.[6] It is permissible for the judge to decline to follow the opinion of the experts (and the guardian ad litem), as long as the findings are not against the weight of the evidence as a whole. The court should always give reasons for departing from the recommendations of the instructed expert. The judge should not become involved in controversy between experts, except where such controversy is itself an issue in the case, and the judge has to make an assessment of it for the proper resolution of the proceedings.

## Procedure in relation to expert evidence

**11.88**    The convention within the wardship jurisdiction that a child should not be examined without leave of the court[7] has been retained and extended following the introduction of the Children Act 1989. The Family Proceedings Rules 1991, r 4.18[8] provides as follows:

---

1    [1990] 2 FLR 489.
2    [1968] 1 QB 159 at 165A.
3    *Re B (Care: Expert Witnesses)* [1996] 1 FLR 667 at 670E.
4    *Re FS (Minors) (Care Proceedings)* [1996] 2 FLR 158, CA at 169A, per Butler-Sloss LJ.
5    *Re N (Child Abuse: Evidence)* [1996] 2 FLR 214 at 221F–222F.
6    *Re B (Care: Expert Witnesses)* [1996] 1 FLR 667 at 670, CA.
7    See also comments on over-examination of children in *Report of the Inquiry into Child Abuse in Cleveland 1987* (HMSO, 1988).
8    Family Proceedings Courts (Children Act 1989) Rules 1991, r 18 is in precisely similar terms as r 4.18. *The Family Court Practice 1999* (Family Law) contains a very full note on r 4.18; and we are indebted to the editor and contributors of *The Family Court Practice 1999* for much of what follows on this subject.

'(1) No person may, without the leave of the court, cause the child to be medically or psychiatrically examined, or otherwise assessed, for the purpose of the preparation of expert evidence for use in the proceedings.

(2) An application for leave under paragraph (1) shall, unless the court otherwise directs, be served on all parties to the proceedings and on the guardian ad litem.

(3) Where the leave of the court has not been given under paragraph (1), no evidence arising out of an examination or assessment to which that paragraph applies may be adduced without the leave of the court.'

Thus, no one, without leave of the court, may have a child medically examined for the purpose of obtaining a report for use in the proceedings; and this applies, it need hardly be added, for children in all family proceedings and whether in public or in private law. Leave can be sought by application in Form C2 by use of the directions procedure under the rules.[1] The order or directions sought should be described clearly, together with brief reasons why the application has been made.

## Principles governing grant of leave

**11.89**      The grant of leave will depend upon the circumstances of the case. The court may take the strict view that the Children Act 1989, s 1(1) does not apply to the decision – any judge is certain to pay great attention to the welfare of the child. It will also consider the interests of the parties, the need for a fair hearing at which the issues can properly be determined, and the delay principle. In considering whether to grant leave, the court should seek to identify the issue which forms the basis of the local authority's application, and consider whether it would be usefully addressed by the proposed evidence. Leave to obtain expert evidence can be refused on the ground that the evidence does not bear sufficiently on the issue that falls for determination.[2]

### *Limitation of number of experts*

**11.90**      Where leave for an examination is given, the court will usually try to limit the number of examinations to which the child is subjected.[3] Wherever possible, the examination should be conducted by one expert who is agreed upon by all parties (in default of agreement the Official Solicitor holds a list of experts and could nominate an appropriate person). Alternatively, the court may grant leave solely to the guardian ad litem to arrange an examination or assessment.

## Practice and court directions on leave applications

**11.91**      In *Re G (Minors) (Expert Witnesses)*,[4] Wall J issued what amounts to a practice direction to govern the grant of leave and consequential directions for expert evidence in children cases. Further assistance can also be gained from other cases

---

1    Family Proceedings Rules 1991, r 4.14; Family Proceedings Courts (Children Act 1989) Rules
     1991, r 14.
2    *H v Cambridgeshire County Council* [1996] 2 FLR 566.
3    The dangers of the court granting a general leave, rather than leave for the instruction of a
     particular expert or experts, can be seen from *Note: Re B (Child Sexual Abuse: Standard of
     Proof)* [1995] 1 FLR 904 in which, following the grant of leave in general terms without
     limitations, 11 psychiatrists/psychologists became involved in the proceedings.
4    [1994] 2 FLR 291.

such as *Re C (Expert Evidence: Disclosure: Practice)*[1] (which contains detailed specimen directions which should normally be given), *Re R (Child Abuse: Video Evidence)*,[2] *Re A and B (Minors) (No 2)*,[3] *Re T and E (Proceedings: Conflicting Interests)*[4]and *Re CS (Expert Witnesses)*.[5] The following propositions are derived principally from *Re G*, but with additions from the other authorities, in which case this is specifically noted.

– Generalised orders giving leave for the papers to be shown to 'an expert' or 'experts' should never be made. In each case, the expert or area of expertise should be identified.
– As part of the process of granting or refusing leave, either for the child to be examined or for papers in the case to be shown to an expert, the advocates have a positive duty to place all relevant information before the court, and the court has a positive duty to inquire into that information and in particular into the following matters:
  (i) the category of expert evidence which the party in question seeks to adduce;
  (ii) the relevance of the expert evidence sought to be adduced to the issues arising for decision in the case;
  (iii) whether or not the expert evidence can properly be obtained by the joint instruction of one expert by two or more of the parties;
  (iv) whether or not expert evidence in any given category may properly be adduced by only one party (eg by the guardian ad litem) or whether it is necessary for experts in the same discipline to be instructed by more than one party.
– A party proposing to apply for leave should supply to all the other parties and file with the court at least 10 days before the application date a written explanation of the area of expertise of the proposed expert, with reasons why the court should grant leave.[6]
– Where the court exercises its discretion to grant leave for the papers to be shown to a particular expert, the court should, where possible, give directions as to:
  (i) the availability for each expert and each party of copies of all the letters of instruction to experts and lists of documents supplied to those experts;[7]
  (ii) the timescale in which the evidence should be produced;
  (iii) the disclosure of any expert report both to the parties and to the other experts in the case;
  (iv) discussions between experts following mutual disclosure of reports;
  (v) the filing of further evidence by the experts or parties stating the areas of agreement and/or disagreement between the experts.
– Where it is impractical to give such directions at the time leave to disclose the papers is granted, the court should set a date for a further directions appointment at which the appropriate directions can be given.

---

1   [1995] 1 FLR 204, per Cazalet J.
2   [1995] 1 FLR 451.
3   [1995] 1 FLR 351.
4   [1995] 1 FLR 581.
5   [1996] 2 FLR 115.
6   *Re C (Expert Evidence: Disclosure: Practice)* [1995] 1 FLR 204.
7   Ibid.

–    Where it is necessary to consider the estimated length of the hearing at a
     directions appointment, the number of expert witnesses and the likely length of
     their evidence should be considered carefully.[1]
–    Where local authorities wish to carry out an assessment, the court should set out
     carefully the timescale within which it is to be completed and fix an early
     directions appointment following the date set for completion to consider the
     further conduct of the case, including the necessity for expert evidence. If
     possible, a date should be set for final hearing prior to completion of the
     assessment, but it is probable that this cannot be done until the assessment is
     complete and the issues in the case emerge. The fact that the timetable set may
     need to be revised will not necessarily be a reason not to timetable.[2]

**11.92**     It follows that advocates who seek the leave of the court to disclose papers
to an expert must apply their minds at an early stage of the proceedings to the issues in
the case to which medical evidence will be relevant. Applications for leave to instruct
experts should be made at as early a stage in the proceedings as possible,
commensurate with the state of the evidence. Advocates must come to the directions
appointment at which the application is to be decided prepared to satisfy the tribunal
as to the need for expert evidence of the specified type sought. Given the pressures of
work on expert witnesses, particular experts should be identified and instructed at the
earliest possible moment and, whenever possible, an inquiry should be made of the
expert concerned to ensure that he can meet the likely timetable of the case.

## Instructions to experts[3]

**11.93**     In *Re M (Minors) (Care Proceedings: Child's Wishes)*,[4] Wall J pointed out
the following.
(a)   It is important that medical experts who are asked to give reports or opinions in
      child cases are fully instructed. The letter of instruction should always set out the
      context in which the expert's opinion is sought and define carefully the specific
      questions the expert is being asked to address.
(b)   Careful thought should be given to the selection of the papers to be sent to the
      expert; they should be relevant and sufficient for the expert to venture a sound
      opinion. The letter of instruction should always list the documents sent.[5]
(c)   The letter of instruction should always be disclosed to the other parties and
      included in the bundle of documents to be used in court.
(d)   Doctors and other experts should not hesitate to request further information and
      ask for additional documentation.

---

1    *Re MD and TD (Minors) (Time Estimates)* [1994] 2 FLR 336, per Wall J; *President's Direction
     of 22 November 1993* [1994] 1 FLR 108.
2    *E v Humberside County Council and S* [1996] Fam Law 444.
3    *The Family Court Practice 1999* (Family Law) contains a 'Procedural checklist for instructing
     experts'.
4    [1994] 1 FLR 749; and see also *Re MD and TD (Minors) (Time Estimates)* (above).
5    In *Re CS (Expert Witnesses)* [1996] 2 FLR 115, Cazalet J points out that the expert should never
     be provided with an unsorted pile of papers and, to assist him, should have an agreed chronology
     and background history.

(e) Doctors who have had other clinical experience of the child outside the litigation (for example, if they have treated him before) should ensure that all their clinical material is available for inspection by the court and by other experts, including all medical notes, hospital records, photographs, correspondence and X-rays.

(f) Experts who are going to give evidence at the trial should be kept up to date on relevant developments and any expert whose evidence goes to the disposal of the case or to the issues raised in the guardian ad litem's report should read the guardian ad litem's report before giving evidence.[1]

(g) Experts should always be invited to confer with each other before the trial in an attempt to reach agreement or limit the issues.[2]

(h) Careful (and early) co-operative planning between lawyers for the different parties should be undertaken to ensure the experts' availability and that they can be called to give evidence in a logical sequence. Consideration should be given to collecting expert evidence of a particular type together, irrespective of the fact that the witnesses are called for different parties, for example having a paediatricians' day so that each can listen to the others' evidence and comment on it.

(i) Where an expert's opinion is uncontentious and he is not required for cross-examination, that fact should be established as early as possible in the preparations for trial and the expert notified accordingly.

## Evidence obtained in disregard of r 4.18(1)

**11.94** There is no absolute bar on the use of material obtained pursuant to an unauthorised examination or assessment, and there may be circumstances in which it is in the interests of the child that such evidence be admitted despite the breach of the rules.[3] However, breach of the Family Proceedings Rules 1991, r 4.18(1) is likely to be treated as a very serious matter and the court will require a full explanation of how it came about before being prepared to grant leave for the evidence to be adduced.

## 6   CHILDREN IN CHILDREN PROCEEDINGS

### Age and understanding

**11.95**   Since *Gillick v West Norfolk and Wisbech Area Health Authority*,[4] lawyers have developed the term '*Gillick*-competent' to describe children of age and

---

1   *Re T and E (Proceedings: Conflicting Interests)* [1995] 1 FLR 581.

2   *Re C (Expert Evidence: Disclosure: Practice)* [1995] 1 FLR 204 suggests a direction that letters of instruction should point out as a condition of instructing the expert the requirement to prepare, after discussion with the other experts, a joint document setting out the areas of agreement and dispute. *Re R (Child Abuse: Video Evidence)* [1995] 1 FLR 451 suggests that it would be good practice for the solicitor for one of the parties, usually for the guardian, to be responsible for convening the meeting between the experts. A coordinator, normally the guardian ad litem or the local authority, should collate the experts' reports and produce a schedule for the court (*Re C (Expert Evidence: Disclosure: Practice)* (above)).

3   *R v Nottinghamshire County Council* [1993] 1 FCR 576, [1993] Fam Law 625 provides an example of a local authority being given leave to adduce evidence despite having breached directions as to filing statements.

4   [1986] AC 112, [1986] 1 FLR 224, HL.

understanding, or mature children, and the case itself remains an important authority (even though much of its approach has now been incorporated into the Children Act 1989). In terms of child development, as Lord Scarman observed:[1]

> 'If the law should impose on the process of "growing up" fixed limits where nature knows only a continuing process, the price would be artificiality and a lack of realism in an area where the law must be sensitive to human development and social change.'

There is no arbitrary age at which understanding develops; and understanding of some issues will develop earlier than of others.[2]

> 'The Act of 1989 enables and requires a judicious balance to be struck between two considerations. First is the principle, to be honoured and respected, that children are human beings in their own right with individual minds and wills, views and emotions, which should command serious attention. A child's wishes are not to be discounted or dismissed simply because he is a child. He should be free to express them and decision-makers should listen. Second is the fact that a child is, after all, a child. ... Everything of course depends on the individual child ... [Under] the Act, a babe in arms and a sturdy teenager on the verge of adulthood are both children, but their positions are quite different: for one the second consideration will be dominant, for the other the first principle will come into its own.'

## Children taking proceedings in their own right

**11.96**     Consistent with their aim of taking account of the wishes and feelings of the mature child, the Family Proceedings Rules 1991 have developed a procedure to enable children to commence their own court process in children proceedings.[3] Thus, a minor[4] is entitled to begin, prosecute or defend proceedings in his own right without next friend or guardian ad litem if: (a) he has leave of the court; or (b) a solicitor considers that he is of sufficient understanding to give instructions and the solicitor is willing to act.[5] The application is for leave pursuant to the Children Act 1989, s 10(8) and is made in the High Court.[6] In a consideration of the merits of the application for the grant of leave, the judge must have in mind the likelihood of success of the application, but must not fetter a child's statutory right to seek an order in appropriate circumstances.[7]

## The child as a party to proceedings

**11.97**     Where a child is represented in proceedings, he should be joined as a party.[8] In specified (public law) proceedings, the child is automatically a party to the

---

1    *Gillick v West Norfolk and Wisbech Area Health Authority* [1986] 1 AC 112, [1986] 1 FLR 224 at 250.
2    *Re S (A Minor) (Independent Representation)* [1993] 2 FLR 437 at 448E, per Sir Thomas Bingham MR, CA.
3    Family Proceedings Rules 1991, r 9.2A.
4    'Minor' is the terminology anomalously preserved by the rules.
5    Family Proceedings Rules 1991, r 9.2A(1).
6    *Practice Direction of 22 February 1993 (Children Act 1989 – Applications by Children)* [1993] 1 FLR 668.
7    *Re SC (A Minor) (Leave to Seek Residence Order)* [1994] 1 FLR 96, per Booth J.
8    *L v L (Minors) (Separate Representation)* [1994] 1 FLR 156.

proceedings. The rules direct that as soon as practicable after the commencement of such proceedings, the court shall appoint a guardian ad litem, whose function it is to 'give such advice to the child as is appropriate having regard to his understanding', and to instruct the solicitor representing the child.[1]

## Conflict between mature child and the guardian

**11.98** Circumstances may arise with respect to an older child where the views of the child as to his welfare are different from those of the guardian ad litem. In these circumstances the solicitor may take instructions direct from the child[2] and must then act in accordance with the child's instructions, having regard to the child's understanding, and taking into account the views of the guardian and any directions given by the court. Difficulties may arise where a teenager, ostensibly old enough to instruct, may nevertheless lack sufficient understanding because of mental disability, emotional disturbance or a psychiatric condition. The opinion of an expert already instructed in the case should be sought as to the child's ability to instruct directly.[3] Where the child is capable of conducting proceedings on his own behalf, the guardian ad litem must bring the matter to the attention of the court at the first opportunity. The guardian will be required to continue to perform all the duties required by the Children Act 1989, except that there will be no requirement to appoint a solicitor for the child. Where the guardian informs the court that the child has or intends to instruct his own solicitor, the court may give leave for the guardian ad litem to be separately represented.[4]

## Removal of the guardian

**11.99** Cases may arise where the views of the guardian ad litem and the child diverge to such an extent that the child may seek the removal of the guardian. Accordingly, a child may apply to the court for leave to remove the guardian ad litem (or next friend); and the application shall be granted, where the court considers that the minor 'has sufficient understanding to participate as a party in the proceedings', without a guardian or next friend.[5] This rule has been used successfully to remove the Official Solicitor as guardian ad litem, where his view diverged from that of a 15-year-old boy as to where the boy's best interests lay.[6]

## The child as a party in specified proceedings: reading the documents

**11.100** Where a child is separately represented in specified proceedings, he becomes entitled to have access to and read all the documents filed in the proceedings.

---

1   Family Proceedings Rules 1991, r 4.11(2)(a) and (b); Family Proceedings Courts (Children Act 1989) Rules 1991, r 11(2)(a) and (b).
2   Family Proceedings Rules 1991, r 4.12(1)(a); Family Proceedings Courts (Children Act 1989) Rules 1991, r 12(1)(a).
3   *Re H (A Minor) (Care Proceedings: Child's Wishes)* [1993] 1 FLR 440.
4   *Re M (Minors) (Care Proceedings: Children's Wishes)* [1994] 1 FLR 749.
5   Family Proceedings Rules 1991, r 9.2A(4) and (6); and see Bennett and Dunford 'The Child as Client – "sacking" the Guardian' [1993] Fam Law 354.
6   *Re H (A Minor) (Role of the Official Solicitor)* [1993] 2 FLR 552, *sub nom In re H (A Minor) (Guardian ad Litem: Requirement)* [1994] Fam 11. In such cases, the Official Solicitor may be invited to assist the court as *amicus curiae*; see also *Re S (A Minor) (Independent*

Some statements and expert reports may contain material which it would not be in the child's interests to read, or which may be positively harmful to the child. Solicitors are under a duty to facilitate access by the lay client to documents filed in legal proceedings. However, this is subject to the exception where the document would adversely affect the client's physical or mental condition. The guidance of the guardian or expert instructed in the proceedings should be sought.[1] In *Re M (Minors) (Disclosure of Evidence)*,[2] the test for withholding the disclosure of information to a party is 'real harm', not the lesser test of 'significant harm'; and this criterion may be helpful when considering the question of whether documents should be withheld from child parties. Where a child has sufficient understanding to be separately represented, there is in any event a duty upon solicitors to advise the child of the contents of documents served upon him.[3]

## Attendance of the child at court

**11.101** Family Proceedings Rules 1991, r 4.16(2) provides as follows:

'Proceedings or any part of them shall take place in the absence of any party, including the child, if –
(a)  the court considers it in the interests of the child, having regard to the matters to be discussed or the evidence likely to be given, and
(b)  the party is represented by a guardian ad litem or solicitor;
and when considering the interests of the child under sub-paragraph (a) the court shall give the guardian ad litem, the solicitor for the child and, if he is of sufficient understanding, the child an opportunity to make representations.'

Thus, the child, if he is a party, is required to be at court, unless the court otherwise directs, although in practice this provision is ignored: the general position is that the child is not at court for hearings or directions appointments.

**11.102** The attitude of the court towards the attendance of children has consistently been a cautious one. In *Re C (A Minor) (Care: Child's Wishes)*,[4] the subject of a care order application, a 13-year-old girl, who was young for her years, had been present throughout the majority of the hearing before the judge and throughout the appeal hearing. The judge commented that it would be a pity if the presence of children as young as this at the hearing of High Court appeals from magistrates in family proceedings were to be allowed to develop unquestioningly into a settled practice, and that listening to lawyers debating one's future was not an experience that should in normal circumstances be wished upon any young child.[5]

Representation) [1993] 2 WLR 801, [1993] 2 FLR 437, CA; *Re CT (A Minor) (Wardship: Representation)* [1993] 2 FLR 278, CA; *sub nom Re T (A Minor) (Child: Representation)* [1994] Fam 49, [1993] 4 All ER 518, CA.
1   *Guide to the Professional Conduct of Solicitors 1993; Guidance on Acting for Children in Private Law Proceedings under the Children Act 1989* (The Law Society, July 1992).
2   [1993] Fam 142, [1993] 1 FLR 191.
3   Family Proceedings Rules 1991, r 4.12(2); Family Proceedings Courts (Children Act 1989) Rules 1991, r 12(2)
4   [1993] 1 FLR 832 (appeal from a magistrates' court to the High Court).
5   See also *Re M (Family Proceedings: Affidavits)* [1995] 2 FLR 100, CA which stresses that it is quite wrong in the normal case for a child (in that case, a child aged 12 to 13) who is the subject of a dispute between parents in family proceedings to be 'dragged into the arena' and asked to swear an affidavit.

Where guardians ad litem are proposing to arrange for young children to be present at an appeal, they should give that question very careful thought beforehand and be prepared, if necessary, to explain their reasons to the court. In *Re W (Secure Accommodation Order: Attendance at Court)*,[1] Ewbank J said that attending court is likely to be harmful for a child and should be permitted only if the court is satisfied that it is in the child's interests. The fact that the child would need to be physically restrained during the hearing in order to control him (as in *Re W*) would, in itself, be sufficient ground for refusing to allow the child to be in court.[2]

## The child as a witness

**11.103**     The common law rule is that, in principle, a child may give sworn evidence. The possibility that children might give evidence was within the contemplation of the draughtsmen of the Children Act 1989. Section 96 provides as follows:

'(1) Subsection (2) applies in any civil proceedings where a child who is called as a witness in any civil proceedings does not, in the opinion of the court, understand the nature of an oath.
(2) The child's evidence may be heard by the court if, in its opinion –
(a) he understands that it is his duty to speak the truth; and
(b) he has sufficient understanding to justify his evidence being heard.'

Thus, s 96(1) and (2) allows a child who does not understand the oath to give unsworn evidence providing he understands the duty to speak the truth and has sufficient understanding to justify his evidence being heard. A child can give sworn evidence or, if he does not understand the nature of the oath but comes within s 96(2), unsworn evidence. In either of these situations, he is theoretically compellable.[3]

**11.104**     For example, in *Re P (Witness Summons)*,[4] parties to care proceedings (the mother and stepfather) applied for leave to appeal the refusal to permit the issue of a witness summons under the County Court Rules 1991, Ord 20, r 12 to secure the attendance to give oral evidence and to be cross-examined, of N, a 12-year-old child who had made allegations that the stepfather had abused her and the child who was the subject of the care proceedings. The principle applicable to the witness summons application was that the judge could decline to issue the summons if to do so would be oppressive of the witness;[5] and the child's welfare would inevitably be of great relevance – although not determinative – in consideration of this question. Wilson J,

---

1     [1994] 2 FLR 1092.
2     *Re C (Residence: Child's Application for Leave)* [1995] 1 FLR 927 contains further reference to the disadvantages of a child being present during a hearing.
3     *R v B County Council ex parte P* [1991] 1 WLR 221, [1991] 1 FLR 470. See Magistrates' Courts Act 1980, s 97 which applies to relevant proceedings in a family proceedings court and a summons can therefore, technically, be issued to secure the attendance of an unwilling but competent child as a witness. However, the court said that the use of a s 97 summons (or, by analogy, a witness summons or subpoena) for this purpose is inappropriate in care proceedings in view of the procedure permitting the admission of hearsay evidence in such cases.
4     [1997] 2 FLR 447.
5     As to the undesirability of a child giving evidence, see also *W v W and Hampshire County Council* (1981) FLR 68; and *Re M (Family Proceedings: Affidavits)* [1995] 2 FLR 100, CA; see also *Re A (Care: Discharge Application by Child)* [1995] 1 FLR 599 (the question of a child applicant in public law proceedings giving evidence).

in *Re P*, referred to the damage that can be caused by questioning a child complainant and said that he would expect that, in most cases concerning a child of N's age, or younger, the court would favour the absence of oral evidence despite the weakening of the evidence against the adult.

### Children and hearsay evidence

**11.105**    In practice, in Children Act 1989 cases, indirect evidence of what a child has said is often introduced in relation to allegations of child abuse, as the Children (Admissibility of Hearsay Evidence) Order 1993 permits. For example, an adult to whom the child has made an allegation may be called to give evidence of what the child has said, and the guardian ad litem or welfare officer may convey to the court the child's wishes and feelings. Because this evidence cannot be tested in cross-examination the court must[1] consider carefully the extent to which it can be relied on.

### Child's compellability under the Children Act 1989, Parts IV and V

**11.106**    The Children Act 1989, s 95(1) enables the court to require the attendance of the child concerned in a Part IV or Part V application. However, it may be preferable to rely on provisions more specifically designed for the purpose of requiring the attendance of witnesses by means of subpoena or witness summons, in particular:

–    Magistrates' Courts Act 1980, s 97 as applied by the Family Proceedings Courts (Children Act 1989) Rules 1991, r 33 in relation to magistrates' court proceedings;
–    Family Proceedings Rules 1991, r 2.30 in relation to matrimonial causes pending in a divorce county court or the High Court;
–    County Court Rules 1981, Ord 20, r 12 as applied by the Family Proceedings Rules 1991, r 1.3 in relation to non-matrimonial proceedings in the county court;
–    Rules of the Supreme Court 1965, Ord 38, rr 14–19 with regard to non-matrimonial proceedings in the High Court.

Where a parent wishes to call a willing child to give evidence, he may apparently be prevented from doing so in an appropriate case by means of a specific issue order.[2]

## Child understanding the nature of the oath

**11.107**    The question of whether a child understands the nature of the oath was considered in *R v Hayes*.[3] In that case, it was held that a child could give evidence on oath if he had a sufficient appreciation of the solemnity of the occasion and the added responsibility to tell the truth which is involved in taking the oath, over and above the duty to tell the truth which is an ordinary duty of normal social conduct. The court took the view that the dividing line between children who are competent to give sworn evidence and those who are not is normally between the ages of 8 and 10. Whether a child gives sworn or unsworn evidence, he may be cross-examined. It is for the court

---

1    As is stressed by *R v B County Council ex parte P* [1991] 1 WLR 221, [1991] 1 FLR 470.
2    Children Act 1989, s 8(1); and see Cousins 'Child's Evidence: Specific Issue Order' [1992] Fam Law 278.
3    [1977] 1 WLR 234, [1977] 2 All ER 288.

to determine whether the child is competent to give evidence, whether sworn or unsworn, and, where a child is found to be competent, he will also be a compellable witness. There is a balance to be maintained between upholding the rights of child parties to participate and be heard in the proceedings, and the need to protect them from the potentially damaging experience of attending court and of hearing evidence in the case which is prejudicial to their welfare.[1]

## Expression of a child's views

**11.108** The preferred means for a child's evidence to be received or his wishes and feelings to be expressed to the court is through a court welfare officer, or a guardian ad litem. Where a child is of sufficient understanding, a guardian may append a verbatim report of the child's views to his report, despite the existence of ' conflict between child and guardian. Attempts by parents in private law proceedings to place the evidence of children before the court by way of sworn affidavits have been deprecated by the courts. For example, Butler-Sloss LJ has stated:[2]

> '... it is not the practice in the Family Division to allow children to intervene in family proceedings between their parents, and for very good reason. It is not fair on children that they should be dragged into the arena, that they should be asked specifically to choose between two parents, both of whom they love, and they ought not to be involved in the disputes of their parents.'

## Child seeing the judge

**11.109** While the Children Act 1989, s 1(3)(a)[3] has given greater prominence to children's views, it is a matter for the judge to decide whether or not personally to interview a child; and it is, above all, a question for the exercise of judicial discretion. Certainly, the judge is under no obligation to see a child in private.[4] The judge will decide who should be present during an interview with a child, but he cannot promise the child absolute confidentiality, and he must tell the parties what the child has said to him so that they may deal with it.[5] *B v B (Minors) (Interviews and Listing Arrangements)*[6] contains guidance on the subject of seeing children, including the following.

– The discretion to see children in private must be exercised cautiously and it should not be automatic or routine.

– It should be done only after hearing submissions from the parties, and there must be a good reason for the judge to see a child. The judge must consider that it is in the interests of the child to see him. The ascertainment of the child's wishes and feelings is, where relevant, normally the province of the court welfare officer or

1   *Re A (Care: Discharge Application by Child)* [1995] 1 FLR 539.
2   *Re M (Family Proceedings: Affidavits)* [1995] 2 FLR 100, CA.
3   Children Act 1989, s 1(3)(a) requires the court to have particular regard to the 'ascertainable wishes and feelings of the child concerned (considered in the light of his age and understanding)'.
4   *Re R (A Minor) (Residence: Religion)* [1993] 2 FLR 163.
5   *H v H (Child: Judicial Interview)* [1974] 1 WLR 595, [1974] 1 All ER 1145; *Elder v Elder* [1986] 1 FLR 610; *Dickinson v Dickinson* (1983) Fam Law 174.
6   [1994] 2 FLR 489, CA.

the guardian ad litem, who can be questioned by or on behalf of the parties in the normal way.
– If a judge does see a child, it is preferable for the interview to take place once the evidence in the case has been completed, but before speeches. Then, if necessary, there can be further evidence, or counsel can take instructions and address the court on any issues arising from it.
– It is of the utmost importance for judge to make it clear to the child that the responsibility for the ultimate decision is the court's, not the child's.

**11.110** If the judge sees a child, this should be at court.[1] Further, the judge should make it clear to the child that the court may not be able to do what the child wants because the judge has to take an overall view of the child's welfare. The judge in *B v B* (above) was said to have:

> '... directed himself impeccably ... by making it clear to the children that he could not promise them that he would not disclose to their parents what they said to him; indeed, he went further and told the children that there could be no secrets relating to what they talked about and that he would have to tell both parents what had been said.'[2]

*Gillick v West Norfolk and Wisbech Area Health Authority*[3] began the process of judicial listening to children, which the Children Act 1989, especially s 1(3)(a), has built upon; but judges remain cautious – perhaps understandably – of too often listening to children, even relatively mature children.

---

1    *L v L (Access: Contempt)* [1991] FCR 547, (1991) 135 SJ 152.
2    [1994] 2 FLR 489, CA at 494G.
3    [1986] 1 AC 112, [1986] 1 FLR 224.

# Chapter 12

## CHILD ABDUCTION

### 1 INTRODUCTION

#### The Hague and European Conventions and non-Convention proceedings

**12.1** The vast majority of cases concerning child abduction in civil proceedings involve countries which are signatories to the two main Conventions to which the United Kingdom is also a signatory, namely the Hague Convention on the Civil Aspects of International Child Abduction 1980 ('the Hague Convention'),[1] and the European Convention of Recognition and Enforcement of Decisions Concerning Custody of Children 1980 ('the European Convention').[2] At 1 May 1999, there were some 49 signatories to the Hague Convention and 20 signatories to the European Convention. Applications under either of these Conventions will be determined pursuant to the provisions of the Child Abduction and Custody Act 1985. Since such applications constitute family proceedings, procedure is governed by the Family Proceedings Rules 1991, Part IV; and thus they are exempt from the Civil Procedure Rules 1998.

**12.2** If one of the States concerned is not a signatory to either of the Conventions then the application for the return of a child is usually made in wardship proceedings[3] or in proceeedings under the Children Act 1989 brought in the High Court.

#### Family Law Act 1986

**12.3** Where the application involves a Convention or non-Convention State, it may be necessary, in addition, to refer to the provisions of the Family Law Act 1986. This will be so, particularly if the whereabouts of the child is unknown and the court needs to exercise its powers to order the disclosure of where the child is living,[4] to seek the recovery of a child,[5] or to make directions in relation to the possible surrender of passports.[6]

**12.4** It should not be forgotten that child abduction is a criminal offence under the provisions of the Child Abduction Act 1984, although consideration of the relevant criminal procedures is beyond the intended scope of this book.

---

1 See Sch 1 to Child Abduction and Custody Act 1985.
2 Ibid, Sch 2.
3 Family Proceedings Rules 1991, Part V.
4 Family Law Act 1986, s 33.
5 Ibid, s 34.
6 Ibid, s 37.

## 2   EVIDENCE IN CHILD ABDUCTION PROCEEDINGS

### Proceedings under the Child Abduction and Custody Act 1985

**12.5**      Proceedings under the Child Abduction and Custody Act 1985 may be characterised, first, by the speed at which they are conducted and, secondly, by the fact that oral evidence is extremely rare. The stated objects of the Hague Convention at Article 1(a) are 'to secure the prompt return of children wrongfully removed to or retained in any contracting State'; and, whilst such emphasis also applies in applications involving non-Convention States,[1] Family Proceedings Rules 1991, r 6.10 specifically provides that a Convention application may be adjourned for a period not exceeding 21 days at any one time: that is to say, the case must come back before the court within 21 days of the last order being made.

**12.6**      The proceedings are summary in nature. Thus, the preparation of the case, whether for the plaintiff or the defendant, must be conducted speedily. Considerations relating to liaising with a party who lives overseas and contacting witnesses, foreign lawyers and so on, in different time zones and, quite possibly, in different languages, must be borne in mind at the outset.

### *Application by originating summons*

**12.7**      Applications under the Hague or European Conventions are made by originating summons and issued at the Principal Registry in London.[2] The originating summons must contain the information specified by Family Proceedings Rules 1991, r 6.3 and must be accompanied by all the relevant documents as specified in either Article 8 of the Hague Convention or Article 13 of the European Convention. There is no requirement for an order determining the custody of a child as the Hague Convention is concerned with enforcement of 'rights of custody'.[3] Thus, a State which gives effect to the concept of parental responsibility, which concept itself does not require the existence of an order,[4] is likely to give effect to the provisions of the Hague Convention. The original application from the requesting State must be in the original language of that State and must be accompanied by a translation into English.[5]

### *Evidence on application and defence*

**12.8**      Family Proceedings Rules 1991, r 6.7 deals with evidence on an application under the Hague or the European Conventions. It provides as follows:

'(1)   The plaintiff, on issuing an originating summons under the Hague Convention or the European Convention, may lodge affidavit evidence in the principal registry in support of his application and serve a copy of the same on the defendant with the originating summons.

(2)   A defendant to an application under the Hague Convention or the European Convention may lodge affidavit evidence in the principal registry and serve a copy of

---

1    *Re P (Abduction: Non-Convention Country)* [1997] 1 FLR 780.
2    Family Proceedings Rules 1991, r 6.2.
3    See Article 3 of the Hague Convention.
4    See, for example, in respect of England and Wales, Children Act 1989, s 2.
5    Child Abduction and Custody Act 1985, Sch 1, art 24.

the same on the plaintiff within seven days after service of the originating summons on him.

(3) The plaintiff in an appliction under the Hague Convention or the European Convention may within seven days thereafter lodge in the principal registry a statement in reply and serve a copy thereof on the defendant.'

**12.9** It should be noted that it is not an absolute requirement to file an affidavit with the originating summons at the outset of the case. It is, however, usual to do so in order to ensure compliance with the provisions of Article 8 of the Hague Convention or Article 13 of the European Convention.[1] Where instructions have come from the Lord Chancellor's Department (as will normally be the case; this ensures that non means- and non merits-tested legal aid is granted to the foreign plaintiff),[2] it is usual to exhibit the letter of instruction and the application from the Convention State (together with any necessary translations). Care will be needed to ensure that any references in the documemnt which may not be helpful to the plaintiff's case are explained in the applicant's affidavit.

### *Defence affidavit*

**12.10** A defendant has seven days from the date upon which he is served with the originating summons to file his affidavit of evidence. Almost without exception, he will be served with an order preventing removal of the child from the jurisdiction and/or from a specified address and directing the delivery up of passports and travel documents of the child to the High Court Tipstaff or his agents. Because of the summary nature of the proceedings and the fact that oral evidence is very rare (see below), the affidavit must set out and explain any defence upon which the defendant will rely; for example:

(a) if the contention is that one of the elements which must be made out in order to rely upon the provisions of the Hague Convention is missing, for example the plaintiff does not have, or was not exercising his or her rights of custody, then all the relevant detail must be contained in the affidavit;

(b) if the defendant intends to rely upon one of the defences in Article 13 of the Hague Convention, for example that the plaintiff had acquiesced in the alleged wrongful removal or retention, then again all the particulars must be given. This is particularly so as any gaps cannot be plugged or inconsistencies explained by a party later through the giving of oral evidence;

(c) in a case where the defendant attempts to establish the defence of 'consent' under Article 13(a) of the Hague Convention then:

'the evidence for establishing consent needs to be clear and compelling. In normal circumstances, such consent will need to be in writing or at the very least evidenced by documentary material. Moreover, unlike acquiescence, I find it difficult to conceive of circumstances in which consent could be passive: there must in my judgment be clear and compelling evidence of a positive consent to the removal of the child from the jurisdiction of his habitual residence.'[3]

---

1    See **12.7** above.
2    Civil Legal Aid (General) Regulations 1989, reg 14.
3    Per Wall J in *Re W (Abduction: Procedure)* [1995] 1 FLR 378 at 888.

Furthermore, the burden of proof to establish the defence is upon the defendant.[1]

## Oral evidence

**12.11**　　The rule that there is no right to call oral evidence to supplement affidavit evidence in Convention cases is referred to in *Re E (A Minor) (Abduction)*[2] by Balcombe LJ, when he confirmed that, in proceedings commenced by originating summons and by affidavit, 'there is no right on which the party can insist to supplement that evidence by oral evidence'. However, the court has a discretion to admit oral evidence in such cases, though such discretion has only been exercised rarely. His Lordship also envisaged cases in which the deponent of an affidavit might be cross-examinaed on his affidavit, and then re-examined orally in reply.

**12.12**　　In *Re F (A Minor) (Child Abduction)*,[3] Butler-Sloss LJ said:

> 'There is a real danger that if oral evidence is generally admitted in Convention cases, it would become impossible for them to be dealt with expeditiously and the purpose of the Convention might be frustrated.'

In *Re F*, there were irreconcilable issues exposed in the affidavit but no application to call oral evidence was made to the trial judge. Butler-Sloss went on to say[4] that some limited oral evidence relevant to the issue which was disputed in the affidavit would clearly be helpful in certain cases. However, 'the admission of oral evidence in Convention cases should be allowed sparingly'.[5]

**12.13**　　In *Re W*,[6] where both parties in their affidavits had put forward a credible case on the question of consent, Wall J said that it would be appropriate that the court should hear oral evidence, since this was available. In cases where one party is available and not the other, oral evidence is unlikely to resolve the issue.

## Evidence by court welfare officer

**12.14**　　Bearing in mind the summary nature of child abduction proceedings and that oral evidence is the exception, it is more common to find oral evidence being given by a court welfare officer and/or expert witnesses. If the defendant asks to argue, pursuant to Article 13 of the Hague Convention, that the child objects to being returned and has attained an age and degree of maturity at which it is appropriate to take account of his view, the task of ascertaining those views and assessing the age and degree of maturity is likely to fall to a court welfare officer who may then be asked to give oral evidence to the court.

## Evidence of 'grave risk'

**12.15**　　If the defence is based on Article 13(b), ie, that there is a grave risk that the child's return would expose him or her to physical or psychological harm or otherwise place the child in an intolerable situation then expert evidence may be required to assist the court in determining the gravity of the risk, especially in relation to

---

1　　*Re C (Abduction: Consent)* [1996] 1 FLR 414.
2　　[1989] 1 FLR 135, CA at 142.
3　　[1992] 1 FLR 548, CA at 553.
4　　Ibid.
5　　Ibid.
6　　*Re W (Abduction: Procedure)* [1995] 1 FLR 878.

psychological harm. In *N v N (Abduction: Article 13 Defence)*,[1] where the children's objections and grave risk of psychological harm were both in issue before the court, oral evidence was heard from the court welfare officer, a consultant adult psychiatrist and two consultant child psychiatrists. However, the rule is that oral evidence is rare and the onus on solicitors and counsel to ensure that the affidavit evidence contains all relevant matters and issues to be raised before the court is a high one.

**12.16**    Where a child has been found and given over to the requesting parent, there is no power to order a person to give evidence.[2]

### *Disclosure of information*

**12.17**    Family Proceedings Rules 1991, r 6.16 reinforces the provisions of the Child Abduction and Custody Act 1985, s 24A, which enables the court, where adequate information as to the child's whereabouts is not available, to order any person who it has reason to believe may have relevant information to disclose it.[3] A person is not excused from complying with an order under s 24A by reason that to do so may incriminate him or his spouse of an offence.[4] A statement or admission made in compliance with such an order will not be admissible in evidence against the person or his spouse in proceedings for any offence other than perjury. The court has power to order the attendance of a witness who may be able to give information about the whereabouts of the child.[5] Where an order for disclosure is made, the form of order should provide for the disclosure of 'all information possessed by [the named person/s] as to the past movements and present whereabouts of the child or of the defendant'.[6]

## Proceedings in non-Convention cases

### *Paramountcy of a child's welfare*

**12.18**    Where it is alleged that a child has been abducted into England and Wales from a non-Convention country, the court will have jurisdiction if the child is physically present within England and Wales; or where there are continuing proceedings for divorce, judicial separation or nullity of marriage.[7] Whereas the child's welfare will be paramount, the court will adhere to the Convention principles, which are that the best interests of the child will normally be served by having any decisions made as to that child's welfare and upbringing in his or her country of habitual residence, and by looking to see whether any of the provisions relevant to Article 13 of the Hague Convention apply.

**12.19**    The ambit of the discretion as to whether or not a child should return in a non-Convention case is wider than in a Convention case and welfare considerations may involve the preparation of reports by a court welfare officer. Evidence may well be required as to the operation and effect of the domestic laws which will be applied to

1    [1995] 1 FLR 107.
2    *Re D (A Minor) (Child Abduction)* [1989] 1 FLR 97.
3    This may include a solicitor. *Re B (Abduction: Disclosure)* [1995] 1 FLR 774.
4    Child Abduction and Custody Act 1985, s 24A(2).
5    And see *Re D (A Minor) (Child Abduction) (Note)* [1989] 1 FLR 97.
6    Ibid, at 100.
7    Family Law Act 1986, ss 2 and 2A.

determine the child's position in the event that an order for a return is made. However, in *Re JA (Child Abduction: Non-Convention Country)*[1] the Court of Appeal upheld a decision of Singer J not to return a two-year-old child to the United Arab Emirates. The court held that the decision to return the child must be justified by more than an adoption, by analogy, of the Hague Convention approach. It would be:

> 'an abdication of responsibility and an abnegation of the duty of the court for a ward under its protection to surrender the determination of its ward's future to a foreign court whose regime might be inimical to the child's welfare.'[2]

### Welfare considerations: the affidavit evidence

**12.20**      In *Re JA*, the father was a national of the United Arab Emirates and the mother was English. In *T v T (Abduction: Non-Convention Country)*,[3] the Court of Appeal upheld a decision of Mr Horowitz QC (sitting as a Deputy Judge of the High Court) where he had ordered the summary return of two children to the United Arab Emirates having heard argument based upon welfare considerations. A defendant is likely to raise issues relating to welfare of children upon an application for the return of a child to a non-Convention country. The affidavit in support of the application should therefore deal at length with questions relating to a child's welfare and the application of the welfare test in the relevant foreign court. Unless the court is satisfied that the welfare test will apply, it cannot be satisfied that it is in the best interests of the child to return it to that court for it to resolve the disputed question. However, the onus will be upon the defendant to adduce evidence of disimilarity.[4]

## 3   CASE PREPARATION

### Skeleton arguments

**12.21**      In Hague and European Convention cases, a defendant should file a short statement setting out the nature of the defence upon which he intends to rely and again, as per Wall J in *Re W (Abduction: Procedure)*:[5]

> '... if a specific defence was going to be raised to an application under the Hague Convention it was desirable that it should appear in the affidavits or that notice of such intention should be given. ... I found counsel for the father's succinct skeleton response extremely helpful in concentrating my mind and the minds of the parties, on the relevant issues of the case.'

---

1    [1998] 1 FLR 231.
2    Ibid, at 243.
3    [1998] 2 FLR 1110.
4    *Re JA (Child Abduction: Non Convention Country)* [1998] 1 FLR 231, per Ward LJ at 241.
5    *Re W (Abduction: Procedure)* [1995] 1 FLR 878 at 892.

## Bundles

**12.22**    In *Re W (Abduction: Procedure)*,[1] Wall J gave helpful directions as to the duty upon solicitors and counsel to prepare and lodge properly indexed trial bundles[2] with the court, and a warning concerning the possible disallowing of taxation costs where the poor presentation of a case and the absence of bundles has had an adverse effect upon the timing of a case. He stressed that it was wrong to think that bundles were required only in long cases and that, the less time available for a case, the more important it was that the bundle was properly prepared.

---

1    [1995] 1 FLR 878.
2    And see *Practice Direction of 31 January 1995 (Case Management)* [1995] 1 FLR 456, [1995] 1 WLR 332, para 5.

# Chapter 13

# INJUNCTIONS

## 1    INTRODUCTION

**13.1**    All injunction orders, across the spectrum from a non-molestation order[1] through to the rare *Anton Piller*[2] order, have features in common when it comes to such questions as standard of proof and enforcement, just as they have clear distinguishing features in terms of the object for which they are designed and the procedure by which they are obtained. All injunctions and undertakings given to the court may be enforced by committal and other penalties.

**13.2**    The Family Law Act 1996, Part IV and the Protection from Harassment Act 1997 raise particular questions in relation to evidence because of the relative clarity of factual issues involved, and because allegations will be made by an applicant which must lead the court to make findings of fact. Further, such injunctions may often be the sole end of the proceedings in which they are granted, whereas the origin of an injunction is that it is generally a remedy which is interlocutory to other proceedings which have, as their main object, enforcement, protection or establishment of a substantive right by the plaintiff.

**13.3**    Reference is made here to the Protection from Harassment Act 1997 since that Act creates what amounts, by most standards, to a remedy in family proceedings, although it may also be used in circumstance far removed from the family jurisdiction. Meanwhile, an occupation and non-molestation order under the Family Law Act 1996, Part IV, an order under the Matrimonial Causes Act 1973, s 37(2) and a prohibited steps order are recognisably part of a family law process with their procedure being governed by the Family Proceedings Rules 1991;[3] whereas applications under the Protection from Harassment Act 1997 are in tort, procedure is governed by the Civil Procedure Rules 1998 and an applicant can seek damages from the defendant.[4] Applications under the Matrimonial Causes Act 1973, s 37(2) have long been a part of the family jurisdiction (importing many of the features of the more recent *Mareva*[5] injunction), while the *Anton Piller* order makes only occasional appearances in the family jurisdiction.

---

1    Family Law Act 1996, s 42.
2    *Anton Piller KG v Manufacturing Processes Ltd* [1976] Ch 55, [1976] 2 WLR 162; now provided for by Civil Procedure Act 1997, s 7.
3    SI 1991/1247, as amended by the Family Proceedings (Amendment) (No 3) Rules 1997.
4    Protection from Harassment Act 1997, s 3(2).
5    *Mareva Cia Naviera SA v International Bulkcarriers SA, The Mareva* [1980] 1 All ER 213, [1975] 2 Lloyd's Rep 509, CA.

## 2  INJUNCTIONS AND UNDERTAKINGS

### Origin of injunctions

**13.4**      Injunctions are an equitable remedy rooted in the earliest development of the equitable jurisdiction in the late Middle Ages. Their modern derivation is statutory, but they preserve their equitable basis in the extent to which – even where based on a statutory foundation – the court remains vested with extensive discretion over the grant of injunctions. Accordingly, the Supreme Court Act 1981, s 37(1) provides:

> 'The High Court may by order (whether interlocutory or final) grant an injunction . . . in all cases in which it appears to the court to be just and convenient to do so.'

The same jurisdiction is available in the county courts as 'if the proceedings were in the High Court'.[1] This wording thus gives the court a discretion whether to grant in individual cases, and an inherent jurisdiction to make an order where justice and convenience require it.[2]

### Undertakings

**13.5**      A formal undertaking given to the court by a party to proceedings has the same effect as an injunction.[3] It must be drawn up and served upon the party giving the undertaking by the court[4] and be endorsed with a penal notice if it is to be enforced by committal.[5] It can then be enforced in the same way as an injunction.[6] Confusion over the term arises in the matrimonial financial relief jurisdiction. In reality, the term in that context creates a different form of commitment which is more akin to recording before the court an agreement between the parties or an assurance to the court that certain steps will be taken by a party. The order recording the undertaking is not served personally and therefore cannot lead to committal.[7]

### Types of injunction

**13.6**      Injunctions can be categorised as prohibitory or mandatory: to order someone not to do something (eg not to molest the applicant or not to move money from a particular account); or to require them to perform an act (eg to leave the parties' home). Further, they can be categorised as 'perpetual', ie final, or interlocutory. An interlocutory injunction will last until the conclusion of the proceedings, and its object is to maintain the status quo pending the final order of the court on the application (for example, a *Mareva* injunction or an order under the Matrimonial Causes Act 1973,

---

1    County Courts Act 1984, s 38(1).
2    See eg *Shipman v Shipman* [1991] 1 FLR 250, where Anthony Lincoln J felt unable to make an order under Matrimonial Causes Act 1973, s 37(2) but was still willing to make an order under the inherent jurisdiction of the High Court.
3    Save that eg in occupation/non-molestation order proceedings under Family Law Act 1996, Part IV it cannot be attached with a power of arrest (s 46(2)).
4    County Court Rules 1981, Ord 29, r 1(2), as amended by r 1A(a).
5    Ibid, Ord 29, r 1(2), as applied by r 1A.
6    See eg *Gandolfo v Gandolfo* [1981] QB 359.
7    See further Burrows ' "Undertakings" and Consent Orders' [1998] Fam Law 158.

s 37(2)). Whereas the final injunction is the primary or only object of the application (eg a non-molestation or occupation order[1]) it may not, in fact, last for ever: for example, the period for which occupation orders may last are statutorily prescribed.[2]

## Forms of order

**13.7**    For the purpose of what follows the following orders will be considered.

| Order/injunction | Statutory basis | Procedure | Documents in support |
|---|---|---|---|
| Order in the inherent jurisdiction of the High Court | Supreme Court Act 1981, s 37 | CPR 1998, Part 25[3] | Affidavit |
| Wardship and the inherent jurisdiction | Supreme Court Act 1981, s 37; Children Act 1989, s 100 | FPR 1991, r 5.1 | Affidavit |
| *Anton Piller* | Civil Procedure Act 1997, s 7 | CPR 1998, Part 25[4] | Affidavit |
| *Mareva* | Supreme Court Act 1981, s 37 – inherent jurisdiction | FPR 1991 application interlocutory to existing ancillary relief proceedings[5] | Affidavit |
| Restraint of disposal[6] | Matrimonial Causes Act 1973, s 37(2)(a) | FPR 1991 – application interlocutory to existing ancillary relief proceedings | Affidavit |
| Avoidance of disposition | Matrimonial Causes Act 1973, s 37(2)(b) | FPR 1991 – application interlocutory to existing ancillary relief proceedings and see FPR 1991, r 2.59(3)(b) | Affidavit |
| Prohibited steps order | Children Act 1989, s 8 | FPR 1991, r 4.4 | Statement |

---

1    These orders used to be regarded as interlocutory to family proceedings, normally divorce: for analysis of this point see eg *Richards v Richards* [1984] FLR 11 at 29E–H, per Lord Scarman, HL. Since the coming into operation of Family Law Act 1996, Part IV there is no doubt that the orders and their continuance can be independent of divorce proceedings and can continue independently of any orders in proceedings alongside which they are issued.

2    Family Law Act 1996, ss 33(10), 35(10), 36(10) etc.

3    County courts can make orders in the inherent jurisdiction of the High Court (County Courts Act 1984, s 38) except orders which they are prevented from making either under County Courts Act 1984, s 38(3) (orders on judicial review) or under County Courts Remedies Regulations 1991, SI 1991/1222 (eg *Anton Piller* orders: see below).

4    An *Anton Piller* order cannot be obtained in the county courts (County Courts Remedies Regulations 1991, reg 2(a)).

5    In the county courts, a *Mareva* injunction can be obtained only in family proceedings (County Courts Remedies Regulations 1991, reg 3(3)(a)).

6    A jurisdiction exactly equivalent exists for: (a) restraint of disposal; and (b) avoidance of disposition under Matrimonial and Family Proceedings Act 1984, s 23(2), and similar powers under Inheritance (Provision for Family and Dependants) Act 1975, ss 10 and 11.

| Order/injunction | Statutory basis | Procedure | Documents in support |
|---|---|---|---|
| Exclusion requirement | Children Act 1989, ss 38A and 44A | FPR 1991, r 4.4 alongside proceedings under Children Act 1989, ss 38 and 44[1] | Statement |
| Occupation order | Family Law Act 1996, s 33(3) | FPR 1991, r 3.9 | Sworn statement |
| Non-molestation order | Family Law Act 1996, s 42 | FPR 1991, r 3.9 | Sworn statement |
| Prevention of harrassment | Protection from Harassment Act 1997 | CPR 1998, Part 25 | Affidavit |

## Evidence in support of an injunction

**13.8**     The grant of an injunction is a discretionary remedy. Nevertheless, principles have been set down for consideration by the courts when considering granting injunctions, some of which are statutory[2] and some which are defined by the courts themselves.[3] In considering the evidence required to support an injunction, it is necessary to look first at general principles applicable to the grant of an interlocutory injunction; and then to look at specific orders. By their nature, many injunctions will be urgent and, in some cases, will be required on an *ex parte* basis. These orders and the evidential basis for their grant will be considered separately.

## Interlocutory injunctions – general principles

**13.9**     Formerly, the onus lay on the applicant for an interlocutory injunction to show that the order he claimed was in support of a prima facie case. This burden on the applicant was eased by the House of Lords in *American Cyanamid Co v Ethicon Ltd*,[4] where general principles were set by which courts might consider the grant of an interlocutory injunction.[5]

### *'Serious question to be tried'*

**13.10**     The applicant must produce affidavit evidence to show that 'there is a serious question to be tried' by the court. He must show an issue for which there is supporting material and which gives rise to a real question for trial by the court: for example, in the case of an application to restrain publicity in respect of a child,

---

1     Children Act 1989, ss 38 (interim care order) and 44 (emergency protection order).
2     See eg Family Law Act 1996, s 33(6) and (7) (and see **13.22** below).
3     See eg the *American Cyanamid Co v Ethicon Ltd* [1975] AC 396, [1975] 1 All ER 504, HL (discussed below).
4     [1975] AC 396, [1975] 1 All ER 504, HL.
5     In *Polly Peck International plc v Nadir (No 2)* [1992] 4 All ER 769, CA, Lord Donaldson of Lymington MR stated that the *American Cyanamid* case had 'as such, no application to the grant or refusal of a *Mareva* injunction'; although his reasons for saying this are not entirely clear. For present purposes, it will be assumed that the general principles set out in the *American Cyanamid* case will be applicable as guidelines for the vast majority of interlocutory injunctions under consideration.

whether there is evidence of an intention to publish material concerning the child;[1] or, in the case of an application under the Matrimonial Causes Act 1973, s 37(2)(a), whether there is evidence of an intention to dispose of assets to which the applicant may reasonably be said to have a claim. If the applicant can show no such prima facie claim the matter ends there. If such a claim is shown the court goes on to look at the balance of convenience.

### *Balance of convenience*

**13.11**     The Supreme Court Act 1981, s 37(1) gives the court a discretion to grant an injunction where it is 'just and convenient' to do so. Accordingly, the *American Cyanamid* case proposed a test based on the balance of convenience as between the applicant and the respondent: should the court exercise its discretion in favour of the applicant having regard to the respective circumstances of the parties? For example, it might be asked whether the husband's need for a fund of money pending the final hearing of the application, perhaps to restore his ailing business, is greater than the wife's need to have the fund protected from possible dissipation of the money by the husband's business;[2] or whether the husband's funds should be preserved within the jurisdiction pending the outcome of the wife's financial relief application, for her convenience, or whether he should be allowed to take money abroad to the possible prejudice of the wife.[3]

### *Status quo*

**13.12**     'Where other factors appear to be evenly balanced it is a counsel of prudence to take such measures as are calculated to preserve the status quo.'[4] Thus, unless the respondent can show loss to himself by the grant of the injunction which outweighs the potential loss to the applicant (eg the inability to develop a business opportunity) the tendency would be for an order to be made to preserve the status quo.[5]

## Ex parte applications

**13.13**     Many injunction applications will be *ex parte* or made on an urgent basis when there will be little opportunity for the respondent to reply in any detail. By definition, the *Anton Piller* order application will be made in this way, as will many initial *Mareva* applications, non-molestation order applications and some prohibited steps order applications. In most cases the evidence to be adduced will be dictated by the nature of the application; occasionally, it may be dictated by statute.[6] An

---

1     See eg *Re Z (A Minor) (Freedom of Publication)* [1996] 1 FLR 191, CA.
2     This dilemma was considered by Lord Diplock in the *American Cyanamid* case ([1975] AC 396 at 408) where he pointed out that there might be a difference between enjoining a respondent from commencing a course of action, and interrupting 'him in the conduct of an established enterprise [which] would cause much greater inconvenience'.
3     *Shipman v Shipman* [1991] 1 FLR 250 at 253E, per Anthony Lincoln J: 'As in all such cases of injunctive process [here a wife sought to prevent a husband taking money abroad], the balance of convenience has to be considered'.
4     *American Cyanamid Co v Ethicon Ltd* [1975] AC 396 at 408, per Lord Diplock.
5     A course favoured, for example, by Anthony Lincoln J in *Shipman v Shipman* [1991] 1 FLR 250.
6     See eg Family Law Act 1996, s 45(2).

application made *ex parte* imposes particular duties on the applicant, the most important of which will be to give full relevant disclosure of all material aspects of the case to the court.[1]

## Duty of full relevant disclosure[2]

**13.14**    In support of an *ex parte* application the applicant must make full disclosure of all matters known to him which may be material for the judge to know. This was explained by Warrington LJ in *R v Kensington Income Tax Commissioners ex parte Princess Edmond de Polignac*[3] as follows:

> 'It is perfectly well settled that a person who makes an *ex parte* application to the court –
> that is to say, in the absence of the person who will be affected by that which the court is
> asked to do – is under an obligation to the court to make the fullest possible disclosure of
> all the material facts within his knowledge, and if he does not make the fullest possible
> disclosure, then he cannot obtain any advantage from the proceedings.'

This disclosure extends to and includes any weaknesses in the applicant's case and points which it might be thought the defendant would raise in opposition if the application had been dealt with *inter partes*. Disclosure on this basis was explained by Douglas Brown J in an interim care application in wardship (pre-Children Act 1989) as follows:[4]

> 'Affidavits, particularly affidavits for use in an ex parte hearing, should be drawn with
> care and should be accurate, balanced and fair, and, by analogy with *Mareva* or *Anton
> Piller* applications, ex parte affidavits should contain material, if known, which militates
> against the relief sought.'

The duty to disclose extends to facts which could have been found out by reasonable enquiry.[5] It may be assumed that if a legal adviser knows of the facts which should be disclosed he will be guilty of misleading the court if, on an *ex parte* application, facts known to the legal adviser are not disclosed.[6] The relevance of what facts are material to its decision is to be decided by the court, not the applicant; and the court will ensure that a party who fails to disclose is deprived of any advantage thereby gained.[7] A party who is not frank with the court may find himself required to pay the respondents costs on an indemnity basis.[8]

## Effects of non-disclosure[9]

**13.15**    An *ex parte* injunction which has been made without full disclosure is likely to be set aside:[10]

---

1    *Lazard Brothers & Co v Midland Bank Ltd* [1933] AC 289, HL.
2    See further consideration of the duty of relevant disclosure at **6.7** above.
3    [1917] 1 KB 486.
4    *Rochdale Borough Council v A* [1991] 2 FLR 192 at 231H.
5    *Bank Mellat v Nikpour* [1985] FSR 85.
6    See further **6.9** above on duties of the legal adviser not to mislead the court.
7    *Brink's-Mat Ltd v Elcombe* [1988] 1 WLR 1350, [1988] 3 All ER 188, CA.
8    *Burgess v Burgess* [1996] 2 FLR 34 at 41F–G, per Waite LJ, CA: 'Hale J was fully entitled to
      take account of the total lack of any evidence at the final hearing' to assume that the 'application
      had been made without justification' and to order costs on an indemnity basis.
9    Cf setting aside of orders for non-disclosure: **6.21** above.
10   *Bank Mellat v Nikpour* (above), per Lord Denning MR.

'The principle that no injunction obtained *ex parte* shall stand if it has been obtained in circumstances in which there was a breach of the duty to make the fullest and frankest disclosure is of great antiquity. Indeed it is so well enshrined in the law that it is difficult to find authority for the proposition; we all know it; it is trite law.'

Despite a failure to disclose the court retains a discretion to extend the injunction, especially where the failure to disclose was innocent or an injunction would have been made had there been full material disclosure.[1]

## 3   STANDARD OF PROOF ON INJUNCTION APPLICATIONS

**13.16**    The standard of proof[2] applicable in injunction applications will depend on three factors, some of which are interrelated:

(1)    whether or not the application is dealt with on affidavits, statement or sworn statement evidence or on a combination of these and of live evidence;
(2)    whether or not the order sought is interlocutory or final;
(3)    the seriousness of the issue being tried before the court.

These factors can be analysed, however, by resolving questions of standard of proof by considering whether the order sought is interlocutory or final: this will be the essential criterion by which standard of proof is considered.

### Interlocutory orders

**13.17**    Almost invariably an interlocutory order will be dealt with on affidavit evidence alone. The *American Cyanamid* appeal turned on the weight of evidence required for the obtaining of such an injunction.[3] *American Cyanamid* dealt with this question as follows:[4]

'... in the context of the exercise of a discretionary power to grant an interlocutory injunction ... [t]he court ... must ... be satisfied that the claim is not frivolous or vexatious; in other words, that there is a serious question to be tried.

It is no part of the court's function at this stage of the litigation to try to resolve conflicts of evidence on affidavit as to facts on which the claims of either party may ultimately depend nor to decide difficult questions of law which call for detailed argument and mature considerations. These are matters to be dealt with at the trial.'

From this it can be seen that a relatively low standard of proof – 'a serious question to be tried' – is required for the grant of an interlocutory injunction. One reason for this is that the court will be trying the main issue in full at a final hearing, and it can, in most jurisdictions, seek from the applicant certain undertakings as to damages which form, in a sense, a *quid pro quo* for the lower standard of proof demanded.

**13.18**    However, damages in the family jurisdiction is an unusual concept. There is no provision for such a concept, for example, in the Matrimonial Causes Act 1973, s 37(2), and it would be inconceivable in applications for an occupation or

---

1    *Brink's-Mat Ltd v Elcombe* [1988] 1 WLR 1350.
2    For full consideration of standard of proof, see **4.21** et seq above.
3    *American Cyanamid Co v Ethicon Ltd* [1975] AC 396 at 405E.
4    Ibid, at 407G, per Lord Diplock.

non-molestation order, or in children proceedings. Even where he granted an injunction in his inherent jurisdiction in *Shipman v Shipman*,[1] Anthony Lincoln J refused to support the view that an injunction in the financial relief jurisdiction could be accompanied by 'the many restrictions and safeguards surrounding the use of worldwide *Mareva* injunctions' and stated his view that 'the matrimonial field calls for a different approach'.[2]

### Interlocutory injunctions – 'a serious question to be tried'

**13.19**    In the *American Cyanamid* case, Lord Diplock in the House of Lords described the standard of proof for interlocutory injunctions generally in predominantly negative terms:[3]

> 'The use of such expressions as "a probability", "a prima facie case", or "a strong prima facie case" in the context of the exercise of a discretionary power to grant an interlocutory injunction leads to confusion as to the object sought to be achieved by this form of temporary relief.'

He then went on to characterise the standard required as to satisfy the court 'that there is a serious question to be tried'.[4]

### The Mareva standard – 'a good arguable case'

**13.20**    This question was raised again in the Court of Appeal in *Derby & Co Ltd and Others v Weldon and Others*,[5] where Parker LJ considered the question of evidence on application for a *Mareva* order and stressed the need for the court to find only a 'good arguable case' which should 'be decided on comparatively brief evidence'.[6] Parker LJ went on, somewhat opaquely, to stress his view that:[7]

> '. . . the difference between an application for an ordinary injunction and a *Mareva* lies only in this, that in the former case the plaintiff need only establish that there is a serious question to be tried, whereas in the latter the test is said to be whether the plaintiff shows a good arguable case. This difference, which is incapable of definition, does not however affect the applicability of Lord Diplock's observations to *Mareva* cases.'

## Final orders

**13.21**    The final order, it will be recalled, is the issue to be decided by the court, and it is not interlocutory to some other application (even though a non-molestation order application may have been made, for example, alongside divorce proceedings). Save when such an order is obtained on an *ex parte* basis, it will be dealt with on a combination of sworn statements, affidavits or statements, with the parties' evidence

---

1    [1991] 1 FLR 250.
2    Ibid, at 253E.
3    [1975] AC 396 at 407G.
4    Ibid.
5    [1989] 2 WLR 276.
6    Ibid, at 283. Here the Court of Appeal was highly critical of a *Mareva* hearing which lasted 27 days and involved 'several thousand pages of affidavits and evidence'.
7    Ibid, at 283E.

being called as need be. Accordingly, the standard of proof is the usual civil standard – 'the preponderance of probability'[1] – with reference to the severity of the issues raised.[2]

## 4 DOMESTIC ORDERS – OCCUPATION OF THE FAMILY HOME AND NON-MOLESTATION

**13.22** The Family Law Act 1996, Part IV creates a series of occupation orders[3] and the non-molestation order.[4] The Protection from Harassment Act 1997, by contrast, creates only the tort of harassment[5] which will enable the applicant, if claiming damages under the Act, to seek an injunctive relief interlocutory to the proceedings in tort. Both Acts provide for enforcement of an order by application for a warrant.[6] In both types of proceedings, application to commit can be made in the absence of a warrant having been issued;[7] and in the case of occupation and non-molestation orders, a power of arrest can attach to an order[8] (although not an undertaking[9]).

### Application for an order: pleadings and evidence

**13.23** Application for an injunction under the Family Law Act 1996, Part IV can be made[10] in existing 'family proceedings'.[11] The application, whether for an occupation order[12] or a non-molestation order[13] (or both), is commenced by filing a prescribed form.[14] The application is supported by 'a statement which is signed . . . and . . . sworn to be true'.[15] The facts and information to be set out in the prescribed form are extensive; but, as in so many family proceedings, it is the statement which performs the true role of setting out the allegations, which (insofar as they are disputed) will define the issues between the parties.

**13.24** Occupation orders have been described as a 'Draconian remedy' and, in *Richards v Richards*,[16] Lord Brandon of Oakbrook spoke of their 'potentially serious

---

1   *Re H (Sexual Abuse: Standard of Proof)* [1996] AC 563; *sub nom Re H and R (Child Sexual Abuse: Standard of Proof)* [1996] 1 FLR 80, HL.
2   See further consideration of standard of proof at **4.21** above.
3   Family Law Act 1996, ss 33 and 35–38.
4   Ibid, s 42.
5   Protection from Harassment Act 1997, s 3(1). There are those who say that a tort of harassment already existed which s 3(1) merely confirms; and see *Burris v Azadani* [1996] 1 FLR 266, CA.
6   Family Law Act 1996, s 47(8); Protection from Harassment Act 1997, s 3(3).
7   Rules of the Supreme Court 1965, Ord 45, r 5; County Court Rules 1981, Ord 29, r 1.
8   Family Law Act 1996, s 47(2).
9   Ibid, s 46(2).
10  Family Proceedings Rules 1991, r 3.8(3).
11  As defined by Family Law Act 1996, s 63(1) and (2).
12  Family Law Act 1996, ss 33–39.
13  Ibid, s 42.
14  Family Proceedings Rules 1991, r 3.8(1).
15  Ibid, r 3.8(4).
16  [1984] FLR 11 at 32F.

effect' on the party excluded. There are clear statutory criteria for their grant.[1] The standard of proof for evidence called may depend on the nature of the remedy sought, with more cogent proof being required for the more finely balanced occupation order application. Where medical evidence is sought to be adduced in support of the application, it will be important to bear in mind the need to seek leave to call the evidence.[2]

## 5   FINANCIAL ORDERS – RESTRAINT OF DISPOSAL

**13.25**      The terms 'restraint of disposal' and 'avoidance of disposition' are taken loosely from the Matrimonial Causes Act 1973, s 37(2), but for present purposes may be taken to refer to the following:

(1)  applications pursuant to the Matrimonial Causes Act 1973, s 37(2):
    (a)   to restrain future disposals or dealings with property (s 37(2)(a)[3]), and
    (b)   for avoidance of disposition (s 37(2)(b) and (c));[4]
(2)  applications within the inherent jurisdiction of the court to grant injunctions (now provided for by the Supreme Court Act 1981, s 37(1)–(3)):[5]
    (a)   to prevent a respondent dealing with his assets,
    (b)   applications for *Mareva*[6] injunctions, and
    (c)   applications for *Anton Piller*[7] orders;
(3)  applications to prevent an application for financial relief after an overseas divorce under the Matrimonial and Family Proceedings Act 1984, s 24.

Applications under (1) above can be made only in matrimonial proceedings; but applications under (2) above can be made in all financial relief proceedings including,

---

1    Now set out in Family Law Act 1996, s 33(7) and (8); and in similar terms for other categories of party to the application (ss 35–38).
2    Rules of the Supreme Court 1965, Ord 38, r 36; Civil Procedure Rules 1998, r 35.4(1); and see **5.16** et seq above.
3    For the court's powers to restrain disposal of matrimonial property abroad, see *Hamlin v Hamlin* [1986] 1 FLR 61, CA.
4    In appropriate courts, these applications are covered by the Ancillary Relief Pilot Scheme in view of the definition of ancillary relief in Family Proceedings Rules 1991, r 1.2(1); but see Burrows *Ancillary Relief Pilot Scheme – A Practice Guide* (Family Law, 1997) at 8.8 and 8.9 for difficulties in pleading such applications under the scheme.
5    Supreme Court Act 1981, s 37(1)–(3), which provides:
    '(1)  The High Court may by order (whether interlocutory or final) grant an injunction . . . in all cases in which it appears to the court to be just and convenient to do so.
    (2)  Any such order may be made either unconditionally or on such terms and conditions as the court thinks just.
    (3)  The power of the High Court under subsection (1) to grant an interlocutory injunction restraining a party to any proceedings from removing from the jurisdiction of the High Court, or otherwise dealing with, assets located within that jurisdiction shall be exercisable in cases where that party is, as well as in cases where he is not, domiciled, resident or present within that jurisdiction.'
6    *Mareva Cia Naviera SA v International Bulkcarriers SA, The Mareva* [1980] 1 All ER 213, [1975] 2 Lloyd's Rep 509.
7    *Anton Piller KG v Manufacturing Processes Ltd* [1976] Ch 55, [1976] 2 WLR 162. *Anton Piller* orders are now provided for by statute under Civil Procedure Act 1997, s 7.

for example, the Married Women's Property Act 1882, s 17 and the Trusts of Land and Appointment of Trustees Act 1996, s 14.

**13.26** All of the above applications in family proceedings are injunctions, or have the same effect as an injunction, interlocutory to financial relief proceedings, which must either be underway or about to be commenced.[1] The powers of the High Court can be exercised to a limited degree by the county courts.[2]

## Pleadings

**13.27** As so often with family proceedings, the pleadings, properly so-called, are rudimentary.[3] Thus, much of the case, and information as to the issues involved in it, will be in the affidavits. As has been seen, in preparation of the application and the affidavit in support, certain factors in proof of the application must be set out, certain guidelines must be born in mind and certain principles as to disclosure must be observed.[4] The pleadings[5] will consist of the notice of application (or cross-application) for financial relief and an application for the form of injunction sought.[6]

## General principles for grant

**13.28** The principles applicable to the grant of injunctions in the field of financial relief are, essentially, no different from that already described in general terms above;[7] and in the event of an *ex parte* application the need for full disclosure[8] cannot be stressed too strongly. In terms of the standard of proof applicable for the obtaining of an interlocutory injunction, it will be recalled that it has been suggested that in order to obtain a *Mareva* injunction the applicant must prove a 'good arguable case'; whereas for other injunctions the standard is 'a serious question to be tried'.[9]

---

1    In the case of proceedings about to be commenced, suitable undertakings as to commencement must be given to the court; and see Civil Procedure Rules 1998, r 25.2(4).

2    County Courts Act 1984, s 38: this section enables the county courts to make 'any order which could be made by the High Court if the proceedings were in the High Court' subject to certain exceptions (s 38(1)). Those exceptions or 'orders of a prescribed kind' (s 38(3)(b)) for present purposes would exclude the orders under consideration here save for County Court Remedies Regulations 1991, reg 3(3)(a), the effect of which is to enable the county court to grant such injunctions.

3    See Chapter 2 above.

4    See **13.14** et seq above.

5    Those looking for draft pleadings will be assisted by Fricker (ed) *Emergency Remedies and Procedures* (Family Law).

6    In all cases, it is assumed that the necessary application for financial relief under Matrimonial Causes Act 1973 or other Act has been filed with such affidavit or other evidence in support as may be appropriate. In cases of urgency, an undertaking as to filing of the main application and supporting affidavit etc can be given.

7    See **13.9** above.

8    See **13.14** above.

9    **13.20** and **13.19** (respectively) above.

# Chapter 14

## APPEALS AND JUDICIAL REVIEW

### 1 GENERAL PRINCIPLES

#### Evidence on appeal

**14.1** The question of the admissibility of 'fresh evidence'[1] on appeal, while couched in terms regarding the 'need for finality in litigation' and the 'disapproval of allowing litigants a second chance at trial', is in actuality governed by the *dicta* offered by Lord Wilberforce in 1971:[2]

> 'Positively, . . . it may be expected that courts will allow fresh evidence when to refuse it would affront common sense, or a sense of justice.'

**14.2** Appellate courts considering appeals in family matters have been much more lenient in allowing fresh evidence in matters involving children. The *dicta* of Waite LJ in *Re G (A Minor) (Care Evidence)*[3] is instructive:

> '. . . procedural requirements [in cases involving children] generally are commonly relaxed to take account of the demands, always predominant, of the welfare of the child concerned. This does not mean, however, that the adoption of a relaxed and flexible procedure renders the principle of natural justice of less account in family proceedings than in others. . . .
>
> Given that the jurisdiction has these special characteristics, there are bound to be occasions when, often through no one's fault and for the highest of motives, corners are cut, or routine evidential or procedural rules broken, in what are perceived as the higher interests of speed or urgency or some other factor making it imperative to reach an early conclusion for the sake of the child concerned. It was no doubt in recognition of this, as well as for less obvious good reasons, that the principle was developed that the rule in

---

1    Fresh evidence is defined here as evidence not adduced at the trial or hearing below. Courts have used the term interchangeably to apply both to matters occurring before trial, yet not adduced at trial, as well as those matters occurring after trial. See *Ladd v Marshall* [1954] 3 All ER 745, CA; *Mulholland v Mitchell* [1971] AC 666; *Vernon v Bosley (No 2)* [1998] 1 FLR 304. Evidence of matters occurring after final hearing is treated in a different manner to evidence of matters occurring before the final hearing. The latter is admissible only on 'special grounds'. Evidence of matters that have occurred after a final hearing are admissible upon the unfettered discretion of the Court of Appeal (*Murphy v Stone-Wallwork (Charlton) Ltd* [1969] 1 WLR 1023 at 1036).
2    *Mulholland v Mitchell* [1971] AC 666 at 680.
3    [1994] 2 FLR 785 at 797, CA. See *G v G (Minors: Custody Appeal)* [1985] 2 All ER 225 at 228, [1985] FLR 894, HL where Lord Fraser said:
> '. . . evidence dealing with events that have occurred since the hearing in the court below is readily admitted, especially in custody cases where the relevant circumstances may change drastically in a short period of time.'
But see *B v P (Access)* [1992] 2 FCR 576, per Booth J.

*Ladd v Marshall* [1954] 1 WLR 1489 regarding the admission of fresh evidence on appeal is applied less rigorously in children cases than in others.'

**14.3** With that *caveat*, the general rule regarding the admission on appeal (whether to the High Court or Court of Appeal) of evidence of matters occurring before final hearing is this: further evidence is admissible on appeal only where such evidence:

(a)  could not have been obtained at the trial with reasonable diligence;[1]
(b)  would or might, if believed, have a very important effect on the mind of the tribunals; and
(c)  is of a sort which inherently is not improbable.[2]

The Court of Appeal has unfettered discretion whether to admit evidence of events occurring after the final hearing.[3]

**14.4** In private law residence matters under the Children Act 1989, the Court of Appeal will admit fresh evidence on appeal under the general guidelines noted above. Where a decision at first instance relating to custody is unassailable on the evidence before the judge, the Court of Appeal may, in the light of fresh evidence, remit the matter to the judge to review his decision.[4]

**14.5** It was held in the case of *Re W (Care: Leave to Place Outside Jurisdiction)*[5] that where fresh evidence became available after the final hearing where a care order had been made in favour of the local authority, the proper course for the parents was to appeal against the care order and seek to adduce the fresh evidence, not to bring a fresh application for a discharge of the care order.

**14.6** In cases involving enforcement of orders of the court, leave to adduce fresh evidence will ordinarily be given to a contemnor in an appeal against a committal order for contempt, if it is necessary or expedient in the interests of justice.[6]

**14.7** Evidence relevant to the question of costs is admissible in the Court of Appeal even if not previously adduced.[7]

## The proper court

**14.8** Appeals in family matters from a district judge in the county court lie in first instance to a judge, and thence to the Court of Appeal and, exceptionally, to the House of Lords. Appeals from a district judge of the Family Division lie to a High Court judge, and from there to the Court of Appeal and, exceptionally, to the House of Lords. Appeals from High Court judges lie to the Court of Appeal and thence – again, only in exceptional cases – to the House of Lords. Appeals from magistrates lie to the High Court, either by appeal pursuant to s 94 of the Children Act 1989, or by way of case stated. Appeals heard in the county court or High Court are governed by the

---

1   *Skone v Skone* [1971] 2 All ER 582, HL.
2   *Croydon London Borough Council v A and Others* [1992] Fam 169 (appeal from magistrates to High Court judge under Children Act 1989); *Ladd v Marshall* [1954] 1 WLR 1489, [1954] 3 All ER 745, CA; *Roe v Robert McGregor & Sons* [1968] 1 WLR 925.
3   *G v G* [1985] 2 All ER 225; Civil Procedure Rules 1998, Sch 1 RSC, Ord 59, r 10(2).
4   *M v M* [1987] 1 WLR 404, CA; *A v A* [1988] 1 FLR 193; cf *Re G* (1988) 152 JPN 382, CA.
5   [1994] 2 FLR 1087.
6   *Irtelli v Squatriti* [1992] 3 All ER 294, [1992] 3 WLR 218, CA.
7   *Computer Machinery Co Ltd v Drescher* [1983] 1 WLR 1379.

Family Proceedings Rules 1991 and the old Rules of the Supreme Court 1965; appeals to the Court of Appeal and applications for judicial review are both covered by new-style Rules of the Supreme Court 1965 (as amended).[1]

### *Permission to appeal*

**14.9**     Appeals to the Court of Appeal in all matters involving the residence of a child, contact with a child, or the education and welfare of a child require permission by either the court at first instance or the Court of Appeal.[2] A decree absolute and nullity are treated as final for the purposes of appeal to the Court of Appeal. An order by a judge relating to ancillary relief in matrimonial proceedings, including a property adjustment order, an order for the payment of a lump sum and any other order making or relating to financial provision, whether capital or income, is treated as interlocutory, and therefore requires permission of the judge or the Court of Appeal. Appeals made out of time also require permission.[3] The application for permission outside the time limits must be made to the Court of Appeal, and will be heard by the Registrar of Civil Appeals, a single Lord Justice, or the full court.[4]

**14.10**     An appeal of an order made pursuant to the Children Act 1989 by a family proceedings court may be appealed without permission to the High Court, Family Division.[5]

**14.11**     Appeals against committal orders and secure accommodation orders do not require permission to appeal.[6]

## 2   APPEALS FROM DISTRICT JUDGES

### Interim orders

**14.12**     An appeal from a district judge in a county court in family proceedings lies to a judge in chambers unless the judge otherwise directs.[7] Appeals from interim orders by district judges are discouraged.[8] An appeal from an *ex parte* order will not normally be necessary because an application can be made to the district judge or judge to set the order aside or to discharge or vary it. The order would be only for an interim period in any event, and ordinarily the matter would be properly argued on an *inter partes* basis a short time after the *ex parte* order had been made. Nevertheless,

---

1   See further **1.31** et seq, above and Chapter 15. One effect of the dichotomy is that certain terminology differs according to whether the old or new style Rules of the Supreme Court apply. For example, the term 'leave' has been replaced in the new Rules of the Supreme Court by 'permission'.
2   Civil Procedure Rules 1998, Sch 1 RSC, Ord 59, r 1B(3).
3   Ibid, Sch 1 RSC, Ord 59, r 15.
4   Ibid, Sch 1 RSC, Ord 59, r 14.
5   Children Act 1989, s 94.
6   Civil Procedure Rules 1998, Sch 1 RSC, Ord 59, r 1B(1)(a).
7   Family Proceedings Rules 1991, SI 1991/1247, r 8.1(5).
8   *Re H (Minors) (Interim Custody)* [1991] FCR 564, [1991] Fam Law 394, CA (no appeal unless interim situation 'intolerable'); *Re J (A Minor) (Interim Custody Appeal)* [1989] 2 FLR 304, [1989] Fam Law 375, CA.

there are instances where the Court of Appeal has entertained appeal from an *ex parte* order.[1]

**14.13**    An appeal from a decision of a district judge sitting in a county court in proceedings where periodical payments, a lump sum or property adjustment order is in issue must be transferred to the High Court, whether on application by a party or otherwise, where it appears to the district judge that the appeal raises a difficult or important question of law.[2]

**14.14**    If appeal is sought from a decree nisi pronounced by a district judge, and no error of that judge is alleged, an application for rehearing should be made to that district judge. If error is alleged, appeal lies to a judge,[3] as noted. Appeal will lie from the grant or refusal of a decree nisi by a judge to the Court of Appeal without permission.[4] No appeal will lie from a decree absolute of divorce or nullity in favour of any party who, having had time and opportunity to appeal, has not appealed from that decree.[5]

## Final orders – ancillary relief

**14.15**    All orders by district judges in the county court regarding applications for ancillary relief are deemed 'final' for the purposes of the County Court Rules 1981, Ord 37, r 6, and therefore require full grounds of appeal to be set out with any notice of appeal. This includes any orders or decisions granting or varying an order (or refusing to do so) on an application for ancillary relief, including the following:

(1)    applications for failing to provide reasonable maintenance under the Matrimonial Causes Act 1973, s 27;

(2)    applications for alterations of maintenance agreements under the Matrimonal Causes Act 1973, s 35;

(3)    applications for alteration of maintenance agreements after the death of a party;

(4)    applications under the Married Women's Property Act 1882, s 17;

(5)    applications under ss 1, 9 of, and Sch 1 to the Matrimonial Homes Act 1983.

No leave is required to appeal the district judge's decision to a judge. The judge is not fettered by the discretion of the district judge,[6] and the Court of Appeal on any further appeal will treat the substantial discretion as that of the judge, even where the judge has adopted the order of the district judge.

**14.16**    The appeal is not considered to be a complete rehearing, and the judge must pay attention to the district judge's reasoning based on the evidence. The judge must interfere only for good and sufficient reasons.[7] There is no absolute right to admit evidence of matters occurring before the date of the final hearing, and the decision

1    See *WEA Records Ltd v Visions Channel 4 Ltd* [1983] 2 All ER 589, setting out the general rules; and *G v G* (1989) *The Times*, 23 November, CA. In the latter case, no judge was available to whom the application could have been made to vary the *ex parte* order.

2    *Practice Direction of 5 June 1992 (Family Division: Distribution of Business)* [1992] 1 WLR 586, [1992] 2 FLR 87, at para 4.

3    *Peek v Peek* [1948] 2 All ER 297, CA; County Court Rules 1981, Ord 37, r 1.

4    Supreme Court Act 1981, s 18(1)(h)(v).

5    Ibid, s 18(1)(d); *McCarney v McCarney* [1986] 1 FLR 312, [1986] Fam Law 102, CA; *Crosby v Crosby* [1987] 1 FLR 1, [1986] Fam Law 328, CA.

6    Family Proceedings Rules 1991, r 8.1(3); and see *Marsh v Marsh* [1993] 1 WLR 744, CA.

7    *Marsh v Marsh* [1993] 1 WLR 744, CA.

whether to admit fresh evidence is discretionary, and will be reversed on appeal or if that discretion is wrongly exercised.[1] Evidence of matters that have transpired since the final hearing before the district judge are, however, admissible. Otherwise, the court would not be given 'correct, complete and up-to-date' information necessary to enable it to carry out its mandate under s 25 of the Matrimonial Causes Act 1973.[2]

**14.17**    Rule 8.1 of the Family Proceedings Rules 1991 (which governs appeals from district judges) applies only in the county court. Thus, a notice of appeal from a district judge in a county court must be issued within 14 days.[3] The notice must be served not less than 14 clear days before the date fixed for hearing of the appeal.[4] A notice of appeal from a decision by a district judge in the High Court must be filed within five days of the decision appealed against, or within seven days where the case is proceeding in a district registry. Appeals to a High Court judge amount to a rehearing, although assisted by the notes of evidence and judgment below. The judge is not fettered by the way in which the district judge arrived at his decision.[5] A notice of appeal does not stay the district judge's order.[6]

**14.18**    A note of judgment must be prepared by the appellant and agreed by the respondent. The note must then be submitted to the district judge for approval. The note should be lodged with the judge at least 21 days before the hearing.[7] If it is believed that the district judge's notes of evidence are required, a certificate to that effect must be lodged with the district judge within 21 days of filing and serving of the notice of appeal. The appellant must therefore file and serve:

(1)  the notice of appeal;
(2)  the order appealed against;
(3)  the agreed note of judgment or reasons.

## Rehearings

**14.19**    The district judge (and the judge) has the power under the County Court Rules 1981 to order a rehearing in certain limited circumstances. A rehearing may be ordered where there has been no error alleged on the part of the judge, but:

(1)  documents or other evidence have not been disclosed;[8]
(2)  there has been misconduct by an officer of the court; or
(3)  the parties have been absent; or
(4)  there has been misconduct by the opposite party; or
(5)  a witness has committed perjury or made a mistake; or
(6)  there has been a surprise which has caused a miscarriage of justice.[9]

To determine whether an error of the court is alleged, the test is as follows:[10]

---

1   *Marsh v Marsh* [1993] 1 WLR 744, CA.
2   *Jenkins v Livesey (formerly Jenkins)* [1985] AC 424 at 437, per Lord Brandon.
3   Family Proceedings Rules 1991, r 8.1(4).
4   Family Proceedings Rules 1991, r 8.1(4). But see Rules of the Supreme Court 1965, Ord 58, r 1(3), stating that a notice must be served within five days after issue.
5   Rules of the Supreme Court 1965, Ord 58, r 1(3), (4) and r 3(2); *Evans v Bartlam* [1937] AC 473.
6   Ibid, Ord 59, r 13 (High Court); Family Proceedings Rules 1991, r 8.1(6) (county courts).
7   *Practice Direction* [1985] 1 WLR 361, [1985] 1 All ER 896.
8   See eg *Jenkins v Livesey (formerly Jenkins)* [1985] AC 424.
9   County Court Rules 1981, Ord 37, r 2.
10  *Peek v Peek* [1948] 2 All ER 297 at 303.

'Is the allegation which is made against the decision an allegation that the court went wrong on the materials before it, or is it an allegation that the court went wrong because evidence on a vital matter was concealed from the court.'

If the allegation is that the court went wrong on the materials before it, this is an allegation that there was an error by the court. If the appellant alleges that vital material was concealed from the court, however, this allegation should be made at first instance to the district judge (or judge) who heard the matter.[1] Where both concealment and error are alleged, the proper course is appeal.[2] It has been held that the power of the county court to order a rehearing is limited to where there has been non-disclosure of material information which a party had a duty to place before the court. Ward J distinguished that situation with the one ordinarily faced by parties, ie where fresh evidence has become available, not because of any improper conduct, but simply because the parties did not have the information before them when the matter was first heard.[3] In the latter situation, the proper course is appeal.

**14.20** If appeal is from a district judge in the High Court, the appeal by the High Court judge amounts to a rehearing, assisted by the notes of evidence and judgment below.[4] There is unfettered discretion on the part of the High Court judge hearing the appeal to admit fresh evidence, whether of matters occurring before or after the hearing below.[5]

## Final orders – Children Act 1989

**14.21** Appeals under the Children Act 1989 lie from a district judge (High Court and county court) to a judge of the court in which the decision is made. The notice must be filed, in both the county court and High Court, within seven days of making the order if the appeal is brought pursuant to s 38(1) of the Act, relating to interim care and supervision orders. In all other cases the notice must be filed within 14 days after the order or decision sought to be overturned. The judge may extend the time for appeal.[6]

**14.22** All notices of appeal must be served no less than 14 days before hearing. The notice must state the grounds of appeal clearly. The notice must be served on all parties to the proceedings, and on any guardian ad litem.

**14.23** All notices of appeal must also be accompanied by a certified copy of the summons or application and a certified copy of the order appealed against, or any order staying its execution. The notice must also be accompanied by a copy of any notes of evidence and any reasons given for the decision.[7]

**14.24** A respondent who wishes to contend that the decision should be varied either in any event or if the appeal is allowed in whole or in part, or a respondent who contends the decision should be affirmed on the grounds other than those relied on by

---

1   *T v T (Consent Order: Procedure to Set Aside)* [1996] 2 FLR 640, per Richard Anelay QC sitting as a High Court judge.
2   *Re B (Minors) (Custody)* [1991] 1 FLR 137. The Court of Appeal might set aside the order complained of and order a rehearing, or admit the fresh evidence and consider the matter on appeal.
3   *B-T v B-T* [1990] 2 FLR 1.
4   Rules of the Supreme Court 1965, Ord 58, r 1.
5   Ibid; *Evans v Bartlam* [1937] AC 473; *Krakauer v Katz* [1954] 1 All ER 244.
6   Family Proceedings Rules 1991, r 4.22(3).
7   Ibid, r 4.22(2).

the district judge, or a respondent who contends by cross-appeal that the decision of the court below was wrong in whole or in part, must serve a notice on all of the parties to the appeal within 14 days after receipt of the notice of appeal. In this respondent's notice, the respondent must set out the grounds upon which that party relies.[1] The procedure set out in the preceding paragraphs also applies to an appeal from a district judge against his decision under the Children Act 1989 to transfer back to the magistrates a case which had been transferred by the magistrates to the county court. An appeal against this decision lies to a designated circuit judge under the Children (Allocation of Proceedings) (Appeals) Order 1991.[2] No right of appeal against other transfer decisions under the Act is permitted.

**14.25**     A Practice Direction[3] sets out what must also be done by both parties' representatives following entry of notice of appeal from a district judge of the Family Division.

(1)   Where the appellant is represented and either party wishes to bespeak a copy of the district judge's notes of evidence, the appellant's solicitors shall:

    (a)   within 21 days from the date of lodging the appeal certify that either the appellant or the respondent considers that the notes of evidence taken before the district judge are necessary for the purpose of the appeal and that notes of evidence will be lodged; and

    (b)   if it is so certified, not less than 21 days prior to the hearing of the appeal, lodge a copy of the notes of evidence and of judgment. The notes of evidence might be bespoken from the district judge, and the notes of judgement will be notes prepared by the appellant's solicitor, and, if the respondent is represented, agreed to by his legal advisers and approved by the district judge.

(2)   Where the appellant is acting in person and the respondent is represented, the respondent's solicitor shall comply with the obligations noted above, except as to agreement on the notes of judgment. The respondent's solicitor shall inform the appellant of the lodging of the notes and (if required) supply to the appellant a copy of the notes on payment of the usual charge.

(3)   Where either party is represented but neither party wishes to bespeak a copy of the district judge's notes of evidence a copy of the notes of judgment shall be prepared by the appellant's solicitor. If the respondent is represented, his solicitor should agree the notes of the judgment. If the appellant is not represented, the respondent's solicitors should prepare the note of judgment. In any case, the note of judgment should be approved by the district judge in not less than 21 days prior to the hearing; a copy of the notes shall be lodged by the solicitor who prepared them.

(4)   Where both parties to the appeal are acting in person, the appellant shall notify the district judge of the appeal and the district judge shall, where possible, make a note for the assistance of the judge hearing the appeal. The district judge shall furnish each party with a copy of that note or certify that no note can be made.

---

1    Family Proceedings Rules 1991, r 4.22(4).
2    SI 1991/1801.
3    *Practice Direction (Matrimonial Causes: Registrar: Appeal)* [1985] 1 WLR 361, [1985] 1 All ER 896; see Family Proceedings Rules 1991, r 4.22(2).

## 3  APPEALS FROM COUNTY COURT AND HIGH COURT TO THE COURT OF APPEAL

**14.26**　　An appeal from an order of a judge (county court or High Court) in family proceedings will lie to the Court of Appeal in the manner provided by the Rules of the Supreme Court 1965, Ord 59.[1] Permission of the judge or of the Court of Appeal will be required if the order appealed against is an interlocutory order.[2] Permission is also required if the appeal is from a decision or order of the Divisional Court heard as an appeal to the High Court.[3]

### Fresh evidence

**14.27**　　The Court of Appeal will admit fresh evidence as a matter of justice in children cases.[4] Permission to adduce fresh evidence will also ordinarily be given to the contemnor in an appeal against a committal order for civil contempt, if it is necessary or expedient in the interests of justice.[5] An appellant has a duty to disclose fresh evidence arising between the hearing at first instance and the appeal:[6] the court must not be misled by parties or advocates. If fresh evidence is available on appeal but ought to be tested in order to establish primary facts, the Court of Appeal will remit the case to the judge to test the fresh evidence. The judge is ordinarily directed to review his decision in the light of this evidence.[7]

**14.28**　　Where the appeal is from an interlocutory judgment or order, the Court of Appeal may receive further evidence on questions of fact. The court may receive either oral or affidavit evidence, or evidence from depositions taken before an examiner.[8]

**14.29**　　The Court of Appeal has unfettered discretion to receive fresh evidence where there has been no trial or hearing on the merits in the court below, or where the evidence sought to be adduced relates to matters which have occurred after the date of trial or hearing.[9] An application for permission to adduce further evidence should be made in the first instance by summons to the Registrar of Civil Appeals, supported by an affidavit giving the facts relied on in support of the application.

**14.30**　　An application to the Court of Appeal to admit fresh evidence must set out, by statement of affidavit of the potential witness, the evidence sought to be adduced,

---

1　Ie Civil Procedure Rules 1998, Sch 1 RSC, Ord 59; see County Courts Act 1984, s 77.

2　All appeals regarding ancillary relief made to the Court of Appeal require permission.

3　Supreme Court Act 1981, s 18(1)(e).

4　*Re G (A Minor) (Care: Evidence)* [1994] 2 FLR 785, CA.

5　*Irtelli v Squatriti* [1992] 3 All ER 294, CA. The Court of Appeal will ordinarily apply by analogy the Criminal Appeal Act 1968, s 23(1), which provides that the power to receive fresh evidence on appeal is completely unfettered. Cases decided under that Act, however, have in fact shown the court often warning about the mischief that would result if ordinarily it received fresh evidence without some explanation as to why it had not been adduced below. See *Stafford v Director of Public Prosecutions* [1968] 3 All ER 752.

6　*Vernon v Bosley (No 2)* [1998] 1 FLR 304, CA.

7　*A v A (Custody: Appeal)* [1988] 1 FLR 193, [1988] Fam Law 57, CA; *M v M (Transfer of Custody Appeal)* [1987] 1 WLR 404, [1987] 2 FLR 146, CA.

8　Civil Procedure Rules 1998, Sch 1 RSC, Ord 59, r 10(2). Where a judge has made an interlocutory decision for reasons which are not plainly wrong, the appellate court is ordinarily slow to interfere. See *Ashmore v Court of Lloyds* [1992] 1 WLR 466, [1992] 2 All ER 486, HL.

9　*Mulholland v Mitchell* [1971] AC 666, [1971] 1 All ER 307, HL.

and an explanation why the evidence could not be obtained at the trial or hearing.[1] The Court of Appeal has held that it is not acceptable to ask the court to order a new trial simply because a potential witness might give certain evidence if compelled to do so.[2]

**14.31** The Court of Appeal ordinarily will refuse to order a new trial or rehearing where the ground of appeal is misdirection, improper admission or rejection of evidence, if the appellant court considers that no substantial wrong or miscarriage of justice has occurred.[3]

**14.32** In *Buckinghamshire County Council v M*,[4] a local authority sought to adduce fresh evidence on appeal, where the court below had made no order because the judge disagreed with the authority's care plan. Thorpe J stated in his judgment that, in this situation, fresh evidence should not be heard on appeal but should be heard by the judge below in what actually amounts to a rehearing ordered by the Court of Appeal. The court held in *Buckinghamshire County Council v M* that when the judge disagreed with a care plan at a final hearing, yet believed that the child was at risk of significant harm, the proper order was an interim care order. The fresh evidence might then be heard by the judge at the next interim hearing.[5]

**14.33** Applications for permission to appeal should include, where necessary, any application to extend time for appealing. It should be made *ex parte* in writing, setting out the reasons why permission should be granted and, if the time for appealing has expired, the reasons why the application was not made within the appropriate time period. The application for permission should therefore include a brief statement of the factual background of the case, the order below, the reasons in law why the order should not have been made, and the proper order that should have been made. The application should state briefly what the contentions on appeal by the appellant would be.[6]

**14.34** The notice of appeal must specify the grounds of appeal and the precise form of the order sought from the Court of Appeal.[7] The notice must also specify the list of appeals where the appellant proposes that the matter will be set down.[8] The notice must be served on all parties affected by the appeal, whether or not those parties actually appeared and participated at the hearing below.[9]

---

1    Civil Procedure Rules 1998, Sch 1 RSC, Ord 59, r 10(2); *Mulholland v Mitchell* [1971] AC 666, [1971] 1 All ER 307, HL.
2    *Sutcliffe v Pressdram Ltd* [1990] 2 WLR 271, [1991] 1 All ER 269, CA.
3    Civil Procedure Rules 1998, Sch 1 RSC, Ord 59, r 11(2). See *Dimino v Dimino* [1989] 1 FLR 297, CA, where the Court of Appeal held that an irregularity of practice in a county court may have given rise to an inference that the judge had prejudged the case. However, on the facts, the Court of Appeal found that there was no miscarriage of justice and refused a rehearing.
4    [1994] 2 FLR 506.
5    See also *Re W (Care: Leave to Place Outside Jurisdiction)* [1994] 2 FLR 1087, where it was stated *obiter dicta* that when a care order has been made and later the parents seek to present fresh evidence, the proper course is not to apply to discharge the order, but to seek leave to appeal out of time.
6    *RG Carter Ltd v Clarke* [1990] 1 WLR 578, CA; Rules of the Supreme Court 1965, Ord 59, r 14.
7    Civil Procedure Rules 1998, Sch 1 RSC, Ord 59, r 3(1) and (2).
8    Ibid, Ord 59, r 3(4), ie Family Division – Final List; or county courts – Interlocutory List.
9    Ibid, Ord 59, r 3(5); *Gillooly v Gillooly* [1950] 2 All ER 1118. The notice must also be served on any other party directed to be served by the Court of Appeal (Ord 59, r 8(1)).

## Procedure in the Court of Appeal

**14.35**    The Court of Appeal has now set out explicit directions (backed by sanctions) for the serving and filing of skeleton arguments and other documents. The Practice Direction is set out in full in Appendix 1.

**14.36**    The Practice Direction is, in a certain sense, a substantive direction. The Court of Appeal, according to the note, believes the Bar has demonstrated 'basic misconceptions as to the purpose of the civil appeal system and the different roles played by the appellate courts and courts of first instance.'[1] The court makes this accusation because 'many appeals and applications for [permission] to appeal are made which are quite hopeless.'[2] Therefore, the court believes it necessary to issue guidance as to when permission to appeal should be sought. The court therefore clearly seeks a change in perception by the Bar as to when an application for leave should be the appropriate advice.

**14.37**    The court first notes in the Practice Direction that the question of permission should, in most instances, be raised immediately after judgment has been given, in order to assure that the judge who gave judgment might then consider the question of permission.

**14.38**    The Practice Direction then provides 'guidance' as to the substantive question of when permission should be granted. The test remains as it has been for many years in other circumstances, and since 1991, as it has been in Children Act matters:

> '[Permission] will be given unless an appeal would have no real prospect of success. A fanciful prospect is insufficient. [Permission] may also be given in exceptional circumstances even though the case has no real prospect of success if there is an issue which, in the public interest, should be examined by the Court of Appeal. Examples are where a case raises questions of great public interest or questions of general policy, or where authority binding on the Court of Appeal may call for reconsideration.'

**14.39**    The Practice Direction then sets out the basic rules arising from this overall policy.

(1)    Where the question for appeal is solely a *point of law*, permission should not be sought (or granted) unless the question involves a point of law which will materially alter the outcome of the case. The Practice Direction then notes that the usual method of turning a fact question into a point of law (that the finding was not substantiated by the evidence and was therefore wrong as a matter of law) should only be used when there is no evidence to support a finding. It is not enough, in other words, merely to contend that the findings are against the great weight of the evidence.

(2)    *Questions of fact* are ordinarily left to the trial judge, unless the challenge is to the inference which the judge has drawn from the primary facts, or where the judge has not received any particular benefit from having seen the witness give evidence.

(3)    If the appeal concerns a question where the judge is ordinarily given a *discretion* with regard to his or her decision, the burden for the appellant is heavy.

---

1    See Appendix 2: Practice Direction, para 2.1.3.
2    Ibid.

**14.40**    The Practice Direction also sets out requirements for skeleton arguments, with skeletons now being required for applications for permission on the papers. Three copies of the skeleton must accompany the bundle of documents which the applicant's solicitors lodge with the Court of Appeal. The skeletons should be lodged with, but not form a part of, the bundles on appeal.

**14.41**    The respondent's skeleton argument must be lodged within 14 days of receipt of the applicant's bundle. Advocates should note this is a change in the rules by the court, which previously allowed the skeletons to be received by the court shortly before the hearing date.

**14.42**    The Practice Direction also sets out the procedure to be used by the court for determining appeals in family matters. When an application for permission is referred to the single Lord Justice on the papers alone, and the Lord Justice decides to grant permission, there will be no change from the present practice, save that the Lord Justice may now give directions for the subsequent process of the appeal.

**14.43**    If permission is refused, the single Lord Justice must give reasons. A letter from the court will be sent, along with the reasons, confirming that the disappointed applicant has a right to an oral hearing. The request for oral hearing must be received within 14 days. If no application is received within that time, the application for permission will be determined in open court without further reference to the applicant.

## Powers of the Court of Appeal

**14.44**    This book is not intended to deal exhaustively with matters other than pleadings and evidence, and the following is therefore not intended to be a complete listing of the Court of Appeal's broad powers. However, any consideration of pleadings and evidence must deal, at least in passing, with the court's powers especially as they derive from the evidence considered by the court.

**14.45**    The Court of Appeal may draw any inference of fact, give any judgment and make any order which ought to have been given or made. It may make such further or other order as it believes the case may require. The court may make any order on such terms as it thinks just to ensure the determination on the merits of the real question and controversy between the parties. The court may do this even where any ground for allowing the appeal or varying the decision below is not specified in the notice of appeal. The court may do so even if no notice of appeal had been given in respect of the particular part of the decision involved.[1]

**14.46**    The Court of Appeal, if it believes it is necessary, will order a rehearing before another judge where the court finds the trial or hearing to have been irregular, for example where a judge has intervened before the closing argument.[2] The Court of Appeal may also substitute an order which is just and equitable or an order which has ceased to be just and equitable. In *Hope-Smith v Hope-Smith*,[3] the court substituted for a lump sum which had been devalued by reason of delay a fixed percentage of the proceeds of sale. The court was satisfied that the delay had been attributable to the respondent's conduct.

---

1    Civil Procedure Rules 1998, Sch 1, Ord 59, r 10(4).
2    *Wiegeld v Wiegeld* (1982) CA Bound Transcript 411; *Barclays Bank v Kennedy* [1989] 1 FLR 359, [1989] Fam Law 143, CA; County Courts Act 1984, s 81(2), (3).
3    [1989] 2 FLR 56.

**14.47**　　　The Court of Appeal will exercise its power to substitute an appropriate order most readily in children cases.[1] The appeal will be against a decision whereby the finder of fact is empowered to utilise his discretion. The court in cases under the Children Act 1989 will therefore apply the following test: '[Was] the solution preferred by the judge ... plainly or blatantly wrong? [Counsel for appellant] must point to an error or errors by the judge and then establish that the error or errors result in the clear conclusion that the judge's decision was wrong'.[2] The Court of Appeal may allow an appeal and quash an order of the court below and make no other order, declining to remit the application for rehearing. The court may also dismiss the appeal when no useful purpose would be served by allowing the appeal and ordering a rehearing.[3] In *Buckinghamshire County Council v M*,[4] the Court of Appeal had before it the appeal of a local authority where the judge below had refused to make any order on an application for a care order. The judge accepted that the child was at risk of significant harm, but disagreed with the care plan of the local authority. (The judge believed that rehabilitation with mother was possible; the local authority wanted adoption.) The Court of Appeal held that the proper order was an interim care order. The court also refused to allow the local authority to adduce fresh evidence on appeal, holding that in this instance the evidence should be adduced at the next interim hearing.[5]

**14.48**　　　In children cases, the Court of Appeal has often stated that where oral evidence has been heard by a judge and that judge's assessment of the witness has influenced his decision, the Court of Appeal should be reluctant to interfere.[6] This is the primary reason advanced for not allowing fresh evidence where it is alleged on appeal that the witness now recants.[7] The Court of Appeal is therefore reluctant to hear fresh evidence where witnesses have given evidence below and have been assessed by the trier of fact. Similarly, the court has often stated that it will not allow argument on a

---

1　　*Re A (A Minor)* (1991) 155 JPN 458, CA.
2　　*May v May* [1986] 1 FLR 325 at 330, per Ackner LJ.
3　　See *H v H (Child Abuse: Evidence)* [1990] Fam 86, CA; *Johnson v Walton* [1991] 1 FLR 350, [1990] Fam Law 260, CA.
4　　[1994] 2 FLR 506.
5　　But see *Re W (Care: Leave to Place Outside Jurisdiction)* [1994] 2 FLR 1087 where, in the opposite situation (a care order being made, and the parents sought to present fresh evidence), the Court of Appeal stated that the proper course for the parents was to appeal the care order and seek to adduce the fresh evidence on appeal, rather than make a fresh application to discharge the care order.
6　　*Re F (A Minor) (Wardship: Appeal)* [1976] Fam 238, [1976] 1 All ER 417, CA; *Re T (A Minor: Wardship)*; *T v T (Ouster Order)* [1987] 1 FLR 181, [1986] Fam Law 298, CA; *Scott v Scott* [1986] 2 FLR 320, [1986] Fam Law 301, CA.
7　　*Ladd v Marshall* [1954] 3 All ER 745.

fresh point which has not been argued below, where the appeal is on a matter involving an exercise of discretion by the lower court.[1]

**14.49** With regard to committals made in family proceedings, the Court of Appeal has an unfettered discretion to substitute its own committal order for any irregular committal order made by the court below.[2] The court also has the power to order a rehearing of the committal proceedings.[3]

## 4 'LEAPFROG' APPEALS – THE HIGH COURT TO THE HOUSE OF LORDS

**14.50** In certain exceptional cases, direct appeal of a decision by the High Court, including the Divisional Court, is available to the House of Lords. A certificate of the High Court must first be obtained by the appellant.[4] The appellant must make the application for a certificate immediately after judgment.[5] The appellant must convince the judge that a point of law of general public importance is involved in the decision, and that the point of law relates either wholly or mainly to the construction of an enactment or of a statutory instrument and has been fully argued in the proceedings, or is a point in respect of which the judge is bound by a decision of the Court of Appeal or of the House of Lords in previous proceedings, and was fully considered in the judgments given by either court.[6] No certificate may be granted if the decision could not have been appealed to the Court of Appeal, or from the Court of Appeal, or if the decision appealed from is made by the judge within the jurisdiction of punishing a contempt of court.[7]

**14.51** If a certificate is granted by the High Court, any party may apply to the House of Lords for permission to appeal. The appeal must be made within one month of the date the certificate was granted, unless the time is extended by the House of Lords.[8] The procedure to be followed is set out in the House of Lords Directions as to Procedure, Dir 6.

---

1  *Taylor v Taylor* [1987] 1 FLR 142 at 146, per Arnold P, CA. See also *Burgess v Stafford Hotel Ltd* [1990] 3 All ER 222, CA.
2  Administration of Justice Act 1960, s 13(3); *Linett v Coles* [1986] QB 555, [1986] 3 All ER 652, CA.
3  *Duo v Duo* [1992] 1 WLR 611, [1992] 3 All ER 121, CA.
4  Administration of Justice Act 1969, s 12(1).
5  Ibid, s 12(4). The rules state that a certificate might be granted any time within 14 days of judgment.
6  Ibid, s 12(3).
7  Ibid, s 15(1), (2) and (4).
8  Ibid, s 13(1).

## 5 APPEALS FROM MAGISTRATES' COURTS

### Children Act 1989

**14.52** Any party interested, aggrieved or prejudicially affected by a decision of the family proceedings court has a right to appeal.[1]

**14.53** Magistrates have no power to order a rehearing, and limited power to correct an error in an order. Any order relating to children, however, except an adoption order, is capable of being altered by a subsequent decision made on a subsequent application made in accordance with the rules of court. Where the complaint is that the order was wrongly made, however, the aggrieved party must appeal rather than make a new application.[2]

**14.54** An appeal lies to the High Court against any order made by magistrates under the provisions of the Children Act 1989.[3] Appeals to the High Court from an order of the family proceedings court made under the Act must be made in accordance with the Family Proceedings Rules 1991, r 4.22. The appellant must file and serve on the parties to the proceedings in the court below a notice of the appeal in writing, setting out the grounds upon which the appellant relies. The notice should state what facts should have been found or what error in law has been made.[4] Any misdirection and any wrongful rejection or admission of evidence should be specified. The notice must state why the order was not in the best interests of the child. Most importantly, the notice must state precisely what the magistrates should have done.[5]

**14.55** The appellant must file a certified copy of the summons or application and of the order appealed against, and of any order staying its execution. The appellant must also file and serve a copy of any notes of the evidence, and a copy of any reasons given for the decision. The notice of appeal must be filed and served within 14 days after the determination against which the appeal is brought or, in the case of an appeal under s 38(1) of the Children Act 1989 (the making of an interim care or supervision order), within seven days after the making of the order. If appeal requires leave of court, and leave has been obtained, that court or judge may direct new time limits for the filing of documents.[6] Where the respondent wishes to contend on appeal that the decision of the court below should be varied, or that the decision should be affirmed on grounds other than those relied upon, or that the decision was wrong in whole or in part, the respondent must file and serve on all other parties a notice in writing within 14 days. The notice shall set out the grounds upon which the respondent relies.[7] No notice by a respondent may be filed or served in an appeal against an order under s 38.[8] Where the appellant seeks to withdraw the appeal, have the appeal dismissed with the consent of all parties, or amend the grounds of appeal, the appellant should make an

---

1   Children Act 1989, s 94; *Re M (Prohibited Steps Order: Application for Leave)* [1933] 1 FLR 275, per Johnson J holding that s 94 of the Children Act 1989 does not limit the class of persons who may appeal. The position is therefore analogous to Rules of the Supreme Court 1965, Ord 59, r 3.
2   Children Act 1989, s 94.
3   Ibid.
4   *Johnson v Johnson* [1969] 2 All ER 722.
5   *Practice Direction of 31 January 1992 (Children Act 1989 – Appeals)* [1992] 1 FLR 463.
6   Family Proceedings Rules 1991, r 4.22.
7   Ibid, r 4.22(5).
8   Ibid, r 4.22(6).

application to a district judge in the Principal Registry.[1] All appeals under s 94 shall be heard and determined by a single judge, unless the President of the Family Division directs otherwise.[2]

**14.56**     The appellant must apply to the justices for a signed copy of the clerk's notes of evidence.[3] If no notes are available, or if they are inadequate, the court may proceed to hear the appeal on any other evidence or statement of what occurred in the proceedings as appears to the court to be sufficient.[4] All reports and statements must also be filed and served.[5]

**14.57**     The normal rule regarding the introduction of evidence of matters occurring before the final hearing is applicable to appeals under the Children Act 1989. Fresh evidence may be adduced only with leave and in exceptional circumstances, and the court will not interfere with the exercise of the justices' discretion unless it considers that the decision was plainly wrong or that the justices had erred in principle.[6] When receiving further evidence, the court should consider the decision of the magistrates and then superimpose the fresh evidence heard on the appeal.[7] The High Court will entertain fresh evidence if the evidence relates to circumstances occurring after the final hearing by the magistrates.[8] The High Court will look at the fresh evidence to determine whether the magistrates' decision has been invalidated or undermined by subsequent developments. If the decision is found to be wrong in the light of the material before the court at the time, the appeal will be allowed on that ground. The fresh evidence will not normally affect the result.[9]

**14.58**     Unless the court directs otherwise, the notes, or an affidavit of any person present at the proceedings, cannot be used in evidence unless previously submitted to the justices.[10] If the clerk's notes are not available, the matter may be remitted back to the magistrates' court for a rehearing.[11] The notes must also be provided in 'legible typescript'.[12]

---

1    Family Proceedings Rules 1991, r 4.22(7).
2    Ibid, r 4.22(8).
3    Ibid, r 4.22(2).
4    Ibid, r 8.2(5). Any notes should contain the names of parties who appeared, who was represented, and all statements considered: *Leicestershire County Council v G* [1994] 2 FLR 329.
5    *Re U(T) (A Minor) (Care Order: Contact)* [1993] 2 FCR 565.
6    *Croydon London Borough Council v A and Others* [1992] Fam 169. But see *Re G (A Minor) (Care: Evidence)* [1994] 2 FLR 785, CA, where the Court of Appeal noted that because Children Act 1989 cases often involve shortened procedures, leave to adduce fresh evidence is more readily given in cases under the Act. See also *B v P (Access)* [1992] 2 FCR 576, where Booth J held that on an application to admit fresh evidence on appeal to the Divisional Court, the fresh evidence should be filed in a sealed envelope not to be opened until the court is satisfied that it is proper to do so.
7    *Hereford and Worcester County Council v EH* [1985] FLR 975.
8    Rules of the Supreme Court 1965, Ord 55, r 7(2).
9    *Croydon London Borough Council v A (No 2) (Note)* [1992] 2 FLR 348. The new evidence might be relevant to the High Court's decision whether to remit the case to the magistrates for rehearing or decide the matter itself pursuant to Rules of the Supreme Court 1965, Ord 55, r 7(5).
10   Family Proceedings Rules 1991, r 8.2(5).
11   *Gray v Gray* [1987] 1 FLR 16.
12   *Re W and S (Contact)* [1992] 2 FCR 665, [1992] Fam Law 358.

## Adoption Act 1976

**14.59**     An appeal lies to the High Court from any order by a magistrates' court hearing any application under the Adoption Act 1976, except appeal against a refusal to make an order on the grounds that the High Court would be a more convenient venue to hear the application.[1] The child and his guardian ad litem have no right of appeal. If an appeal is brought by another party, however, the guardian ad litem will act as such for the purposes of the appeal.[2] Although the High Court has been silent on this issue, it is likely that the usual rule will apply on appeals of adoption orders with regard to the admission of evidence of matters occurring before the original final hearing.

## Appeals against fines or committals

**14.60**     Appeals against committal orders or fines by magistrates are governed by the Administration of Justice Act 1960, s 13, and the Family Proceedings Rules 1991, r 8.2.[3] An appeal is by way of originating motion to the Divisional Court.[4] Unless the court gives leave to the contrary, there shall be no more than four clear days between the date on which the order was made and the hearing of the appeal.[5] A separate application for a stay of the committal order must be made, either to the magistrates' court or the Divisional Court.[6]

**14.61**     The appeal of an order of committal is by way of rehearing, as that term is used in the Rules of the Supreme Court 1965, Ord 55, r 3(1). The judge will review all the evidence and the way the magistrates carried out the balancing exercise. The court has power to receive further evidence on questions of fact, whether orally, by way of affidavit, by deposition taken before an examiner, or in any other manner.[7]

## Domestic Proceedings and Magistrates' Courts Act 1978

**14.62**     Appeals under the Domestic Proceedings and Magistrates' Courts Act 1978 lie to the Divisional Court of the Family Division. Appeal is entered by lodging three copies of the notice of motion (the notice of appeal) in the principal registry. The notice must be served, and the appeal entered, within six weeks after the date of the order appealed against.[8] Notice of the motion may be served in accordance with the Rules of the Supreme Court 1965, Ord 65, r 5, which provides that proper service may be effected by first-class post or by fax.

**14.63**     If the clerk's notes of the evidence are not produced, the court may hear and determine the appeal on any other evidence or statement of what occurred in the proceedings before the magistrates' court as appears to the court to be sufficient.[9]

---

1     Adoption Act 1976, s 63(3).
2     *Re S (An Infant) (Practice Note)* [1959] 2 All ER 675.
3     Family Proceedings Rules 1991, r 8.3; inserted by SI 1991/2113.
4     Rules of the Supreme Court 1965, Ord 109, rr 1 and 2.
5     Ibid, r 2(5).
6     Ibid, Ord 55, r 3(3).
7     Ibid, Ord 55, r 7(2).
8     Family Proceedings Rules 1991, r 8.2.
9     Ibid, r 8.2(5).

## 6 JUDICIAL REVIEW

**14.64**    Judicial review is 'a remedy invented by the judges to restrain the excess or abuse of power'.[1] The jurisdiction therefore covers the proceedings of inferior courts, tribunals and other bodies performing public acts and duties. This includes the magistrates' courts, county courts (for some purposes) and crown courts (save for trial on indictment) and, of course, local authorities exercising their duties under the Children Act 1989, as well as a host of other legislative enactments.

**14.65**    Judicial review is concerned with reviewing the decision-making process of the inferior tribunal or authority, and its stated purpose is to ensure that the individual has been given fair treatment by that tribunal or public authority. Where the tribunal or public authority has acted illegally, irrationally or improperly, the High court will quash, by an order of *certiorari*, the offending order or judgment.[2] It is not the intention of this work to set out all the principles of judicial review.[3]

**14.66**    Applications for judicial review require permission of a single judge of the High Court.[4] The application for permission is made *ex parte* to a judge by filing in the Crown Office a notice in the prescribed form and an affidavit. Except where permission is granted all evidence on judicial review is on affidavit and other documentary evidence.

**14.67**    The Crown Office has set out recommended precedents for use in judicial review proceedings.

**14.68**    Applications for permission to proceed with a judicial review application are *ex parte*, and are considered in one of two ways: on paper, or in open court. The applicant must formally request a hearing; otherwise, a single judge of the High Court, Queen's Bench Division will consider the application. If decided on paper, the court will notify the applicant on Form JRJ. If permission is refused, an applicant may review the application to a three-judge Divisional Court (if the matter is criminal), or to a single judge in open court (if the matter is civil, including children and family cases).

### After permission is granted

**14.69**    Where permission is granted, the applicant or his solicitor must serve a notice of motion in Form 86A,[5] the order granting permission and supporting affidavit on all persons directly affected. The applicant must then enter a copy in the Crown Office, together with an affidavit of service. The service affidavit must give the names, addresses and details of service of all respondents.[6] The affidavit of service must state the reason for failing to serve any party directly affected by the application.

**14.70**    A respondent may file an affidavit in reply within 56 days of service.[7]

---

1    *R v Secretary of State for the Home Department ex parte Brind* [1991] 1 AC 696 at 751B, per Lord Templeman.
2    *Council of Civil Service Unions and Others v Minister for Civil Service* [1984] 1 All ER 935.
3    See, generally, Fordham, *Judicial Review Handbook* (Wiley Chancery Law Publishing, 1993), and updates. *The Supreme Court Practice 1999* (Sweet & Maxwell) contains a useful introduction to the subject alongside Ord 53.
4    Supreme Court Act 1981, s 31(3); and Civil Procedure Rules 1998, Sch 1 RSC, Ord 53, r 3(1).
5    *The Supreme Court Practice 1999* (Sweet & Maxwell), para 1A–89.
6    Civil Procedure Rules 1998, Sch 1 RSC, Ord 53, r 5(5), (6).
7    *Practice Note: Affidavit in Reply* [1989] 1 WLR 358.

## The bundles for hearing

**14.71** Applicants must follow the *Practice Direction (Evidence: Documents)*.[1] If the Direction is not followed, the application may be struck out, and the applicant or his solicitor made liable for the costs.[2] The bundles must be lodged in the Crown Office at least five working days before the hearing. The bundles must include:

(1) Form 86A;
(2) affidavit in support;
(3) forms showing permission has been granted;
(4) notice of motion;
(5) the decision complained of;
(6) any further affidavit evidence;
(7) any relevant correspondence between parties;
(8) all orders made during the proceedings.[3]

The applicant must also file and serve a skeleton argument at least five clear working days before the hearing. The skeleton must:

(1) quote the Crown Office number and the fixed date for the hearing;
(2) give a time estimate;
(3) give a list of issues;
(4) list the propositions of law to be advanced, with authorities;
(5) give a chronology, properly cross-referenced;
(6) identify essential documents for reading;
(7) list and identify all persons playing a role.

## Procedure at hearing

**14.72** The applicant's counsel will open, basing arguments on the skeleton and the affidavit evidence. The respondent's counsel will proceed next. The applicant's counsel then has a right of reply. No evidence is taken. (Indeed, where evidence is disputed, judicial review is likely and an appropriate remedy in any event.)

**14.73** Fresh evidence (that is, evidence either gathered or occurring after the decision complained of) will be allowed in judicial review proceedings in three circumstances:

(1) to show the nature of the material before the decision-making authority;
(2) to determine a fact upon which jurisdiction depended, or whether essential procedural requirements were observed;
(3) to prove misconduct or bias or fraud or perjury.[4]

## Appeal of judicial review orders

**14.74** Any appeal from an order in a judicial review requires permission, from either the High Court or the Court of Appeal (if appeal from a single judge) or the

---

1   [1983] 1 WLR 922.
2   *R v Secretary of State for the Home Department ex parte Meyer-Wulff* [1986] Imm AR 258.
3   *Practice Direction (Crown Office List: Preparation for Hearings)* [1994] 1 WLR 1551.
4   See *R v Secretary of State for the Environment ex parte Powis* [1981] 1 WLR 584; Gordon QC (ed) *Judicial Review and Crown Office Practice* (Sweet & Maxwell, 1998), p 264.

House of Lords (if the appeal is from the Divisional Court).[1] The High Court should be asked for permission immediately; the Court of Appeal can be asked for permission within four weeks of the judgment sought to be appealed.[2]

## Fresh evidence on appeal

**14.75**   The same general rules for admitting fresh evidence in appeal apply for appeals from judgments for judicial review.

## 7   APPEALS FROM THE COURT OF APPEAL

**14.76**   Appeal from any order or judgment of the Court of Appeal lies to the House of Lords.[3] Permission must be obtained either from the Court of Appeal or the House of Lords.[4] Application for permission must first be made to the Court of Appeal, either at the hearing or thereafter by a notice of motion.[5] If the Court of Appeal refuses to grant permission, an application must be made to the House of Lords by petition.[6] Permission of the Court of Appeal or House of Lords must be granted for any cross-appeal.[7] The cross-appeal must be filed within six weeks of the original appeal.[8] The petition for permission to appeal must be lodged in the Judicial Office within one month from the date of the order appealed against, unless the petitioner has applied for legal aid. In that case, the one-month period runs from the issue, or refusal, of legal aid.[9] A petition lodged after the prescribed time-limit has expired must be drafted as out of time.[10] A petition for permission to appeal out of time should first set out the reasons why the petition was not lodged within the time-limit.[11] A petition for permission to appeal should briefly set out the facts and points of law involved in the appeal. It should conclude with a summary of the reasons why permission to appeal should be granted. Supporting documents will be accepted only in exceptional circumstances.

**14.77**   If permission to appeal is granted, the appellants must prepare a statement of the facts and issues involved in the appeal. The appellants are directed to draw up the statement and submit it to the respondent for discussion. Wherever possible, the statement lodged should be a single document agreed between the parties. If the parties are unable to adopt an agreed statement, the respondents may prepare their own statement. This response should be appended to that of the appellants under the title 'Respondent's statement of facts and issues'.[12] The statement should not set out

---

1    Civil Procedure Rules 1998, Sch 1 RSC, Ord 59, r 1(b), 1(c).
2    Ibid, Ord 59, r 4.
3    Appellate Jurisdiction Act 1876, s 3.
4    Administration of Justice (Appeals) Act 1932, s 1.
5    Civil Procedure Rules 1998, Sch 1 RSC, Ord 59, r 14(1).
6    Appellate Jurisdiction Act 1876, s 4; House of Lords Directions as to Procedure, Dir 1.2.
7    Ibid, Dir 26.1.
8    Ibid, Dir 26.3. The form of the cross-appeal is the same as for the original petition (Dir 1.2).
9    Ibid, Dir 2.1.
10   Ibid, Dir 2.2.
11   Ibid, Dir 2.3.
12   House of Lords Directions as to Procedure, Dir 12.1 and 12.2.

or summarise the judgments of the lower courts, set out statutory provisions, or contain an account of the proceedings below.[1]

**14.78**    The appellants must also lodge an appendix containing documents used in evidence in the proceedings below. This must be done in consultation with the respondents, and the contents must be agreed between the parties. The cost of preparing the appendix is borne in the first instance by the appellants, although ultimately the cost will be subject to the decision of the House of Lords.[2]

**14.79**    The appendix should contain only those documents or extracts necessary for the support and understanding of the argument of the appeal. Documents not used in evidence or not recording proceedings relevant to the action in the court below may not be included. Any documents disputed between the parties, and any documents which are not included in the appendix but which may be required at the hearing, should be held in readiness and, subject to permission being given, may be introduced at an appropriate moment. Six copies are required. The other parties must be given notice of any documents held in readiness at the hearing.[3]

**14.80**    As soon as cases have been exchanged, and in any event not later than one week before the date of hearing, the appellants must lodge 15 bound volumes containing:[4]

(1)   the petition of appeal;
(2)   the petition of cross-appeal, if any;
(3)   the statement of facts and issues;
(4)   the appellants' and respondents' cases;
(5)   part I of the appendix;
(6)   respondents' additional documents.

---

1    Ibid, Dir 12.3; see also *MV Yorke Motors v Edwards* [1982] 1 WLR 444, [1982] 1 All ER 1024. See Dir 37 for form of statement.
2    Ibid, Dir 13.2.
3    Ibid, Dir 13.3 and Dir 13.7.
4    Ibid, Dir 17.1. For form of the bound volumes, see Dir 37.

# Chapter 15

---

# EVIDENCE AND PLEADING AFTER WOOLF

## 1 INTRODUCTION

### Family proceedings and Civil Procedure Rules 1998

**15.1**    The Civil Procedure Rules 1998 came into operation on 26 April 1999. They were made following the publication of the two Woolf reports entitled *Access to Justice*[1] and are made pursuant to the Civil Procedure Act 1997, s 1. They are set out as a series of Parts[2] (similar in form to Orders in the present rules). They do not apply to family proceedings[3] as narrowly defined by the Matrimonial and Family Proceedings Act 1984, s 32;[4] but, on a broader definition, there are a small number of forms of process which most family lawyers would say were 'family proceedings' and are to be considered here: for example, proceedings under the Inheritance (Provision for Family and Dependants) Act 1975, the Protection from Harassment Act 1997 and the Trusts of Land and Appointment of Trustees Act 1996, s 14.

### Case management and the overriding objective

**15.2**    A primary object of the Civil Procedure Rules 1998 is to enable the court fully to manage the progress of cases; and with Parts 18 and 31 to 35, the new rules deal with the management of evidence. For the applicability of the rules to evidence, as in all other aspects, it is necessary to bear in mind the overriding objective in r 1.1(2). Where it is concerned with evidence, the overriding objective will impinge, in particular, with the saving of expense and proportionality in relation to the complexity of the issues. It remains to be seen whether proportionality will prove more restrictive as a measure of admissibility than relevance to the issues before the court.[5]

**15.3**    Meanwhile, the new rules preserve a concern for conciseness in pleading, as did the old rules.[6] Thus, the Civil Procedure Rules 1998, r 16.2(1)(a) requires that the

---

1    *Access to Justice: Interim Report* by Lord Woolf MR (HMSO, June 1995) and *Access to Justice: Final Report* by Lord Woolf MR (HMSO, July 1996).

2    In place of a definition rule or order, the Rules end with a 'glossary' and 'words [throughout the] Rules which are included in the glossary are followed by "(GL)"': Civil Procedure Rules 1998, r 2.2(2).

3    Save in the case of the costs jurisdiction under Civil Procedure Rules 1998, Parts 43, 44, 47 and 48: Family Proceedings (Miscellaneous Amendment) Rules 1999.

4    **1.31** et seq above.

5    See **4.4** et seq above (relevance and admissibility) and **15.5** below (proportionality and admissibility).

6    See **2.1–2.5** above.

claim form (by which a claim is commenced[1]) should 'contain a concise statement of the nature of the claim'. Where particulars of claim are served separately (as distinct from the claim being included in the claim form[2]) then they 'must include a concise statement of the facts on which the claimant relies'.[3]

## Discretion and the new rules

**15.4**      The Civil Procedure Rules 1998 give greater emphasis than hitherto to case management.[4] The more inquisitorial system of justice which the rules set up has lead to a greater role for judicial discretion and for court initiative in control of individual cases. The rules of evidence already provide a field where discretion plays an important role, since the court's jurisdiction on a variety of aspects of the rules of evidence – discovery and the subpoena are two examples – is based on equitable principles.

## 2   EVIDENCE AND CIVIL PROCEDURE RULES 1998

## Proportionality and relevance

**15.5**      It will be recalled that the present rule is that admissibility is tested against the relevance of the evidence to an issue before the court.[5] The overriding objective in r 1.1(2)(c) provides that 'dealing with a case justly includes . . . dealing with [that] case in ways which are proportionate' to such factors as 'the complexity of the issues'.[6] It is likely that there will be instances where this objective will be the predominant factor in determining whether particular evidence will be admitted by the court,[7] as against the less restrictive principles which dictate admissibility of evidence based on its relevance to the issues to the court. It is possible to imagine evidence which is relevant to an issue but which is not proportionate to the 'complexity of the issues'. If relevance were the criterion for admissibility, the judge would hear the evidence; but on the basis of proportionality to the issues[8] evidence might yet be excluded.

## Exclusion of evidence

**15.6**      The Civil Procedure Rules 1998, Part 32, which deals with 'Evidence', begins with the startling proposition[9] that courts may exclude evidence and decide the issues upon which evidence is to be called. The rule reads as follows:

---

1      Civil Procedure Rules 1998, rr 7.2 and 8.2.
2      Ibid, 7.4.
3      Ibid, 16.4(1)(a).
4      Ibid, Part 3 deals with 'The Court's Case Management Powers'; and cf *Practice Direction of 31 January 1995 (Case Management)* [1995] 1 FLR 456, [1995] 1 WLR 332 (by which family judges are given greater case management powers even apart from the Civil Procedure Rules 1998).
5      See further **4.4** above.
6      Civil Procedure Rules 1998, r 1.1(2)(c)(iii); and see **2.10** and **2.13** above.
7      And see consideration of Civil Procedure Rules 1998, r 32.1 at **15.6** below.
8      Ibid, r 1.1(2)(e) (allotment of court resources to a case) and r 32.1 (power to exclude evidence: **15.5** below) might also lead to exclusion of evidence.
9      But now see *Grobbelaar v Sun Newspapers Ltd* (1999) *The Times*, 12 August.

**'32.1 Power of court to control evidence**

(1) The court may control the evidence by giving directions as to –

    (a)    the issues on which it requires evidence;

    (b)    the nature of the evidence which it requires to decide those issues; and

    (c)    the way in which the evidence is to be placed before the court.

(2) The court may use its power under this rule to exclude evidence that would otherwise be admissible. ...'

It is said that the power to make this rule derives from Civil Procedure Act 1997, Sch 1, para 4 which reads:

'Civil Procedure Rules may modify the rules of evidence as they apply to proceedings in any court within the scope of the rules.'

**15.7**    It is questionable whether r 32.1 is an amendment to a 'rule of evidence' (as provided for under para 4) at all; or whether, in reality, it repesents a change to a more fundamental right. And does this change shift our judicial system away from the adversarial to a more inquisitorial form of case disposal? It is beyond question that a judge is entitled to refuse to hear evidence on grounds of it not being relevant, or insufficiently relevant, to the issues before the court.[1] Whether the court has power 'to exclude' otherwise admissible evidence and to define the issues and evidence which it wants to hear must be more open to doubt. In *Re M and R (Child Abuse: Evidence)*,[2] Butler-Sloss LJ considered, obiter, the question of whether the court had power to exclude relevant evidence, as follows:

'Lastly we consider s 5 of the Civil Evidence Act 1972:

**"Interpretation, application to arbitrations etc and savings**

. . .

(3) Nothing in this Act shall prejudice –

    (a)  any power of a court, in any civil proceedings, to exclude evidence (whether by preventing questions from being put or otherwise) at its discretion; ..."

We take that subsection to assume that the court has a discretionary power to exclude admissible (ie relevant) evidence. But the statute does not define what that power is. *Phipson on Evidence* (Sweet & Maxwell, 14th edn, 1990), p 705 states that:

"The courts have on occasions disclaimed any general discretion in civil cases to exclude evidence."

... While this is not the occasion to find that the court has such a power, still less to define it, in our judgment there plainly should be some such power in the court, particularly in the modern era of the interventionist judge, and a fortiori in non-adversarial proceedings such as these.'

With the greatest respect to the judge, so unspecific a reference to 'any power of a court' would not seem to justify the presumption that such a power exists. The provision for 'any power of a court', which may exist predicates also the possibility that the power does not exist.

## Statements and affidavits

**15.8**    Much of the remainder of the Civil Procedure Rules 1998, Part 32 deals with formalities for preparation, filing and service of witness statements, witness

---

1    See **4.4** above.

2    [1996] 2 FLR 195, CA at 212.

summaries and affidavits.[1] The Practice Direction ('Written evidence') para 3 et seq deals with the formalities for preparation of an affidavit whilst para 17 et seq deals with formalities for statements. Statements must be verified by a statement of truth.[2]

## Hearsay evidence

**15.9**    In all proceedings, evidence which is hearsay must either be agreed, or notice of intention to rely on that evidence should be given. The position for proceedings covered by the Civil Procedure Rules 1998 will be as for other family proceedings as regards substantive law.[3] Part 33 deals with notices under the Civil Evidence Act 1995, s 2(1) where notice of an intention to rely on hearsay may be required.

## Witness summonses and other evidence

**15.10**    The term subpoena is one of the casualities of Woolf plain English. The term 'witness summons' has been preferred. Accordingly, Part 34 of the Rules deals with circumstances in which a person can be required to give evidence in court or to produce a document, both by witness summons,[4] and for evidence to be produced at the hearing such as by deposition or, by examination prior to the trial or by letter of request where a person is outside the jurisdiction.[5]

## 3  DISCLOSURE

### 'Disclosure' in the context of civil proceedings

**15.11**    In the Civil Procedure Rules 1998, 'disclosure' is defined as a party 'stating that [a] document exists or has existed.[6] Thus, disclosure, in the context of civil proceedings, applies to documents and, it seems, to nothing else. This will create confusion between the civil and the family jurisdiction;[7] for in the family jurisdiction 'disclosure' means disclosure of facts,[8] whether this be in the form of documents or of any other fact relevant to assessment of the circumstances of the case. Thus, Mrs Livesey (the former Mrs Jenkins) had a duty to tell Mr Jenkins of her plans to marry;[9]

---

1    Despite the Latin origin of the term 'affidavit', it survives in Civil Procedures Rules 1998 and is defined in the glossary to the rules as a 'sworn statement'.

2    Civil Procedure Rules 1998, r 22.1(1)(c).

3    Civil Evidence Act 1995, s 1; and see **4.46** above.

4    Civil Procedure Rules 1998, r 34.2.

5    Ibid, rr 34.8, 34.9 and 34.13.

6    Civil Procedure Rules 1998, r 31.2.

7    For a full consideration of 'disclosure' in the family jurisdiction see Chapter 6.

8    *Livesey (formerly Jenkins) v Jenkins* [1985] AC 424, [1985] FLR 813, HL: 'Each party concerned in claims for financial provision and property adjustment (or other forms of ancillary relief not material in the present case) owes a duty to the court to make full and frank disclosure of all material facts to the other party and to the court.' Per Lord Brandon of Oakbrook [1985] FLR 813 at 823B.

9    *Livesey (formerly Jenkins) v Jenkins* (above).

yet it is unlikely that any document evidencing the plans for marriage would have existed.

## Standard disclosure

**15.12** Disclosure in civil proceedings centres on the process of 'standard disclosure'.[1] This is provided for as follows:

> 'Standard disclosure requires a party to disclose only
> (a) the documents on which he relies; and
> (b) the documents which –
>   (i) adversely affect his own case;
>   (ii) adversely affect another party's case; or
>   (iii) support another party's case; and
> (c) the documents which he is required to disclose by a relevant practice direction.'[2]

Further, there is a duty of 'reasonable search for documents falling within rule 31.6(b) or (c)'.[3] The thrust in the Civil Procedure Rules 1998, as with some family proceedings,[4] is to inhibit disclosure; but the duty of 'standard disclosure' unquestionably remains. The duty of disclosure under the new rules 'continues until the proceedings are concluded',[5] which may be taken to include any appeal.[6]

**15.13** A document which is disclosed may be used only 'for the purpose of the proceedings in which it is disclosed, except where ... (b) the court gives permission' or by agreement of the person whose document it is and the person who disclosed the document.[7] This concept is well known in children proceedings; and in respect of non-parties is well known in other family proceedings.[8]

## Disclosure against a third party

**15.14** The court has a discretion to make an order 'for disclosure by a person who is not a party to the proceedings',[9] but only where:[10]

> '(a) the documents of which disclosure is sought are likely to support the case of the applicant or adversely affect the case of one of the other parties to the proceedings; and (b) disclosure is necessary in order to dispose fairly of the claim or to save costs.'[11]

---

1 Civil Procedure Rules 1998, r 31.6.
2 The Practice Direction ('Disclosure and Inspection') does not so far deal with any documents which must specifically be disclosed.
3 Civil Procedure Rules 1998, r 31.7(1).
4 See eg the rigid control on 'discovery' dictated by the rules under the Ancillary Relief Pilot Scheme (Family Proceedings Rules 1991, r 2.73(3); and see **10.40** above).
5 Civil Procedure Rules 1998, r 31.11(1).
6 *Vernon v Bosley (No 2)* [1998] 1 FLR 304; [1997] 3 WLR 683, CA.
7 Civil Procedure Rules 1998, r 31.22(1).
8 See eg *S v S (Inland Revenue: Tax Evasion)* [1997] 2 FLR 774, Wilson J and *R v R (Disclosure to Revenue)* [1998] 1 FLR 922, Wilson J where, in both cases, the Inland Revenue sought leave – in the first unsuccessfully, in the second, successfully – to use a judgment in an ancillary relief case for their investigations.
9 Civil Procedure Rules 1998, r 31.17(1).
10 Ibid, r 31.17(3).
11 'to dispose fairly of the claim or to save costs': this is the same basis as for an application for discovery of documents or for interrogatories under Rules of the Supreme Court 1965, Ord 24,

This rule replaces the Rules of the Supreme Court 1965, Ord 38, r 13. It gives the court powers similar to those it has to order production of documents in ancillary relief proceedings.[1] The applicant must show that the documents are 'likely to support' or adversely affect the case and that disclosure is necessary as under (b) above; whereas the basis for a production appointment must also be that the third party 'could be compelled to produce [the document] at the trial of [the] cause or matter'.[2] Under r 31.17(3) the basis for disclosure is more liberal: to decide whether a document is 'likely to support' the case, it will be necessary in many instances at least to see that document, where a reasonable case can be put forward for that likelihood. It remains to be seen whether that more liberal approach will find its way into the court's exercise of its discretion in applications for production of documents by third parties in ancillary relief proceedings.

## Privilege and public interest immunity

**15.15**    A party's list of documents 'must indicate . . . those documents in respect of which the party claims a right or a duty to withhold inspection';[3] and a party has a right to inspection of all disclosed documents save, amongst others, documents in respect of which a party 'has a right or duty to withhold inspection of it',[4] that is, documents which are privileged from disclosure. This includes 'without prejudice' correspondence and documents for which public interest immunity is claimed. Where a party wants to uphold their claim to public interest immunity in respect of documents, application can be made for an order 'permitting him to withhold disclosure';[5] or application can be made by the party from whom documents are withheld.[6] Such claims are dealt with on the basis of an assumption that there should be disclosure[7] balanced against any higher principle such as the welfare of a child involved in the proceedings.[8]

## Relevance of disclosure: proportionality

**15.16**    As with all aspects of evidence, especially where a discretionary remedy such as disclosure is in issue, the question of relevance to the issues plays an important part. This question becomes more significant still when considered in the light of 'proportionality':[9] for example, it will be recalled that 'dealing justly' with a case

---

r 2(5) and Ord 26, r 1(1). If applicable, the law under those rules will still remain relevant for definition of r 31.17(3)(b).

1    Family Proceedings Rules 1991, r 2.58(7)–(9).
2    Rules of the Supreme Court 1965, Ord 38, r 13(2); and see the restrictive approach to this question in the Court of Appeal in ancillary relief proceedings in *Frary v Frary and Another* [1993] 2 FLR 696, CA.
3    Civil Procedure Rules 1998, r 31.10(4)(a).
4    Ibid, r 31.3(1).
5    Ibid, r 31.19(1); and see *Re C (Expert Evidence: Disclosure: Practice)* [1995] 1 FLR 204, Cazelet J for procedure in children proceedings.
6    'It is a first principle of fairness that each party to a judicial process shall [see] any adverse material which the tribunal may take into account in forming its opinion.' *Re D (Adoption Reports: Confidentiality)* [1995] 2 FLR 687, HL per Lord Mustill at 689D.
7    Civil Procedure Rules 1998, r 31.19(5).
8    *Official Solicitor v K* [1965] AC 201, (1963) FLR Rep 520, HL; and see **6.15** et seq.
9    Civil Procedure Rules 1998, r 1.1(2)(c); and see **15.5** above.

includes having regard to 'the amount of money involved' and 'the complexity of the issues'.[1] Thus, a party to civil proceedings may refuse inspection on grounds that to require it 'would be disproportionate to the issues'.[2]

**15.17**    The question of proportionality, it can be said, goes further, potentially much further, than relevance. For example, it might be argued that a document, or a series of documents, is relevant to an issue before the court; although, proportionate to the complexity of the issues involved in dealing with that particular aspect of the case, to order disclosure cannot be justified. It remains to be seen whether courts consider disclosure on grounds of relevance alone, taking into account such factors only as oppressive enquiry[3] and the saving of costs, or whether, in fact, they adopt an approach which is more akin to proportionality.

## 4   OPINION EVIDENCE

### Impartiality

**15.18**    Civil Procedure Rules 1998, Part 35 deals with expert evidence. That evidence should 'be restricted to that which is reasonably required to resolve the proceedings'.[4] One of the major factors in Lord Woolf's reports arose from his concern that, in his view, expert witnesses were often partisan, forming up with one or other 'litigation team'.[5] Accordingly, the Civil Procedure Rules 1998, r 35.3 stresses the overriding duty of the expert to the court as follows:

'**35.3 Experts – overriding duty to the court**
(1) It is the duty of an expert to help the court on the matters within his expertise.
(2) This duty overrides any obligation to the person from whom he has received instructions or by whom he is paid.'

This restates the common law position (often forgotten in modern litigation[6]) that the expert's role is intended to be impartial:[7] his or her evidence is given to the court regardless of who is responsible for payment of the expert's fee.

**15.19**    Accordingly, the expert's report is required to be addressed to the court rather than to the party who delivered instructions.[8] It must conclude with a statement that the expert understands his or her 'duty to the court' and that the report complies with that duty.[9] The expert's evidence will, in any event, be by written report, unless

---

1    Civil Procedure Rules 1998, r 1.1(2).
2    Ibid, r 31.2(2).
3    See *The Supreme Court Practice* (Sweet & Maxwell, 1999) n 26/4/1 et seq; and eg *Hildebrand v Hildebrand* [1992] 1 FLR 244, Waite J.
4    Civil Procedure Rules 1998, r 35.1.
5    *Access to Justice: Interim Report* Lord Woolf MR (HMSO, June 1995), p 182; *Access to Justice: Final Report* by Lord Woolf MR (HMSO, July 1996) pp 139–140.
6    See eg comments of Thorpe LJ *Vernon v Bosley (Expert Evidence) (Note)* [1998] 1 FLR 297, CA; and see **5.2** and **5.39** above.
7    See explanation of this role by Cazelet J in *Re C (Expert Evidence: Disclosure: Practice)* [1995] 1 FLR 204.
8    Practice Direction ('Experts and Assessors') para 1.1. Paragraph 1 generally gives details of the form which the expert's report should take.
9    Civil Procedure Rules 1998, r 35.10(2).

the court directs otherwise.[1] Where an expert has been instructed by a party, other parties may put written questions to that expert, once only and within 28 days of service of the report.[2] Any expert may ask the court, direct and without notice to the parties, for directions.[3]

## Evidence with permission

**15.20**　　　Civil Procedure Rules 1998, r 35.4 enables a party only to 'call expert evidence or to put in evidence an expert's report' with permission of the court.[4] The party who applies for permission to put in opinion evidence must identify 'the field in which he wishes to rely on expert evidence' and, if possible, the expert concerned.[5] This creates a very different climate than that fostered by the old rules, where concern was primarily with mutuality:[6] that, if one party had a witness with particular expertise, then other parties should not be taken by surprise and should be able to reply with their own witness with similar expertise. This concept is only implied by the present rules, the understandable concerns of which are more with emphasising the impartiality of expert evidence and the expert's primary duty to the court (as already considered).

**15.21**　　　No grounds upon which the court might refuse permission are suggested. Room for the court's exercise of its discretion is therefore wide. Lord Woolf's *Final Report* considered expert evidence at some length, although gives little specific help on the subject of permission in this context. A factor which is mentioned is Lord Woolf's concern that there are instances of parties using expert evidence to secure a tactical advantage:

> 'The purpose of the adversarial system is to achieve just results. All too often it is used by one party or the other to achieve something which is inconsistent with justice by taking advantage of the other side's lack of resources or ignorance of relevant facts or opinions. Expert evidence is one of the principal weapons used by litigators who adopt this approach.'[7]

Lord Woolf was concerned to ensure that any imbalance in availability of expert evidence should be corrected by the court; and this is a factor which the courts may bear in mind when considering permission under r 35.4(1). Such an approach would be consistent also with the overriding objective that the court ensures 'that the parties are on an equal footing'.[8] These considerations will be of more relevance to the civil litigator; but they may have some resonance for the lawyer representing parents in care proceedings. Whatever may be the merit of a parent's case, there are times when the sheer weight of expert evidence produced by the guardian ad litem and local

---

1　　　Civil Procedure Rules 1998, r 35.5(1).
2　　　Ibid, r 35.6.
3　　　Ibid, r 35.14(1) and (2). It will be a matter for the court whether the parties are served with a copy of the request for directions and any response.
4　　　Ibid, r 35.4(1).
5　　　Ibid, 35.4(2).
6　　　Rules of the Supreme Court 1965, Ord 38, r 34 et seq.
7　　　*Final Report*, p 138.
8　　　Civil Procedure Rules 1998, r 1.1(2)(a); and see **2.8** above.

authority can be daunting. Sometimes the availability of expert assistance merely to interpret the evidence would be welcome.[1]

## Single joint experts

**15.22** A further concern of Lord Woolf was with the partisan nature of expert evidence and the number of experts called. One solution he suggested was the single court-appointed expert.[2] He encountered resistance to his original idea (although he clearly anticipates greater use, as time goes on, of the single expert). The rule now is that where two or more parties 'wish to submit expert evidence on a particular issue, the court may direct that the evidence on that issue is to be given by one expert only'.[3] The rule requires, not that a party apply (as with Rules of the Supreme Court 1965, Ord 40), but only that two parties each want to call evidence on a particular issue. The court then has a discretion to limit that evidence to one expert; and if the parties cannot agree who that expert is to be then the court can chose either from a list chosen by them, or by such other means as the court decides.[4]

## Discussions between experts

**15.23** Consistent with the new case management techniques, the new rules[5] provide the court with powers, much more extensive than under the old rules,[6] to direct the 'issues which the experts must discuss' and to require them to:

'... prepare a statement for the court showing –
(a) those issues on which they agree; and
(b) those issues on which they disagree and a summary of their reasons for disagreeing.'

## 5 FURTHER INFORMATION

**15.24** Part 18 of the new rules combines, in succinct form, the old rules about further and better particulars of pleading and interrogatories by providing that:

'(1) The court may at any time order a party to –
(a) clarify any matter which is in dispute in the proceedings; or
(b) give additional information in relation to any such matter,
whether or not the matter is contained or referred to in a statement of case.'[7]

The important feature about this rule, consistent with Woolf case management techniques, is that it not only enables a party to apply for the further information, but

---

1 Strictly speaking, even if Civil Procedure Rules 1998 were to apply to care proceedings, permission would not be needed for this under r 35.4; although leave to disclose confidential documents to the consultant expert would be needed under Family Proceedings Rules 1991, r 4.23.
2 Limited powers exist under Rules of the Supreme Court 1965, Ord 40 to appoint a court expert on application by a party; and see *Re K (Contact: Psychiatric Report)* [1995] 2 FLR 432, CA for a family case where an appointment was made.
3 Civil Procedure Rules 1998, r 35.7(1). Rule 35.8 deals with procedure for instruction.
4 Ibid, r 35.7(3).
5 Civil Procedure Rules 1998, r 35.12(2) and (3).
6 See **5.21** above.
7 Civil Procedure Rules 1998, r 18.1.

also, notably, it gives the court the power to seek information of parties on its own initiative. These are features which are not yet known within the family jurisdiction. However, they are, perhaps, consistent with a more inquisitorial approach to procedure which is believed already to exist in family courts, especially in children proceedings.

# Appendices

# Appendix 1

## STATUTORY MATERIALS

# CIVIL EVIDENCE ACT 1972

(1972 c 30)

## ARRANGEMENT OF SECTIONS

*An Act to make, for civil proceedings in England and Wales, provision as to the admissibility in evidence of statements of opinion and the reception of expert evidence; and to facilitate proof in such proceedings of any law other than that of England and Wales*

[12 June 1972]

## 1. Application of Part I of Civil Evidence Act 1968 to statements of opinion

(1) Subject to the provisions of this section, Part I (hearsay evidence) of the Civil Evidence Act 1968, except section 5 (statements produced by computers), shall apply in relation to statementsof opinion as it applies in relation to statements of fact, subject to the necessary modifications and in particular the modification that any reference to a fact stated in a statement shall be construed as a reference to a matter dealt with therein.

(2) Section 4 (admissibility of certain records) of the Civil Evidence Act 1968, as applied by subsection (1) above, shall not render admissible in any civil proceedings a statement of opinion contained in a record unless that statement would be admissible in those proceedings if made in the course of giving oral evidence by the person who originally supplied the information from which the record was compiled; but where a statement of opinion contained in a record deals with a matter on which the person who originally supplied the information from which the record was compiled is (or would if living be) qualified to give oral expert evidence, the said section 4, as applied by subsection (1) above, shall have effect in relation to that statement as if so much of subsection (1) of that section as requires personal knowledge on the part of that person were omitted.

## 2. Rules of court with respect to expert reports and oral expert evidence

(1) If and so far as rules of court so provide, subsection (2) of section 2 of the Civil Evidence Act 1968 (which imposes restrictions on the giving of a statement in evidence by virtue of that section on behalf of a party who has called or intends to call as a witness the maker of the statement) shall not apply to statements (whether of fact or opinion) contained in expert reports.

(2) In so far as they relate to statements (whether of fact or opinion) contained in expert reports, rules of court made in pursuance of subsection (1) of section 8 of the Civil Evidence Act 1968 as to the procedure to be followed and the other conditions to be fulfilled before a statement can be given in evidence in civil proceedings by virtue of section 2 of that Act (admissibility of out-of-court statements) shall not be subject to the requirements of subsection (2) of the said section 8 (which specifies certain matters of procedure for which provision must ordinarily be made by rules of court made in pursuance of the said subsection (1)).

(3) Notwithstanding any enactment or rule of law by virtue of which documents prepared for the purpose of pending or contemplated civil proceedings or in connection with the obtaining or

giving of legal advice are in certain circumstances privileged from disclosure, provision may be made by rules of court—

(a) for enabling the court in any civil proceedings to direct, with respect to medical matters or matters of any other class which may be specified in the direction, that the parties or some of them shall each by such date as may be so specified (or such later date as may be permitted or agreed in accordance with the rules) disclose to the other or others in the form of one or more expert reports the expert evidence on matters of that class which he proposes to adduce as part of his case at the trial; and

(b) for prohibiting a party who fails to comply with a direction given in any such proceedings under rules of court made by virtue of paragraph (a) above from adducing in evidence by virtue of section 2 of the Civil Evidence Act 1968 (admissibility of out-of-court statements), except with the leave of the court, any statement (whether of fact or opinion) contained in any expert report whatsoever in so far as that statement deals with matters of any class specified in the direction.

(4) Provision may be made by rules of court as to the conditions subject to which oral expert evidence may be given in civil proceedings.

(5) Without prejudice to the generality of subsection (4) above, rules of court made in pursuance of that subsection may make provision for prohibiting a party who fails to comply with a direction given as mentioned in subsection (3)(b) above from adducing, except with the leave of the court, any oral expert evidence whatsoever with respect to matters of any class specified in the direction.

(6) Any rules of court made in pursuance of this section may make different provision for different classes of cases, for expert reports dealing with matters of different classes, and for other different circumstances.

(7) References in this section to an expert report are references to a written report by a person dealing wholly or mainly with matters on which he is (or would if living be) qualified to give expert evidence.

(8) Nothing in the foregoing provisions of this section shall prejudice the generality of ... section 75 of the County Courts Act 1984, section 144 of the Magistrates' Courts Act 1980 or any other enactment conferring power to make rules of court; and nothing in section 75(2) of the County Courts Act 1984 or any other enactment restricting the matters with respect to which rules of court may be made shall prejudice the making of rules of court in pursuance of this section or the operation of any rules of court so made.

### 3. Admissibility of expert opinion and certain expressions of non-expert opinion

(1) Subject to any rules of court made in pursuance of Part I of the Civil Evidence Act 1968 or this Act, where a person is called as a witness in any civil proceedings, his opinion on any relevant matter on which he is qualified to give expert evidence shall be admissible in evidence.

(2) It is hereby declared that where a person is called as a witness in any civil proceedings, a statement of opinion by him on any relevant matter on which he is not qualified to give expert evidence, if made as a way of conveying relevant facts personally perceived by him, is admissible as evidence of what he perceived.

(3) In this section 'relevant matter' includes an issue in the proceedings in question.

Note: amended by the Supreme Court Act 1981, s 152(4), Sch 7; the County Courts Act 1984, s 148(1), Sch 2, Pt V, para 43; and the Magistrates' Courts Act 1980, s 154, Sch 7, para 114.

### 4. Evidence of foreign law

(1) It is hereby declared that in civil proceedings a person who is suitably qualified to do so on account of his knowledge or experience is competent to give expert evidence as to the law of any country or territory outside the United Kingdom, or of any part of the United Kingdom other than England and Wales, irrespective of whether he has acted or is entitled to act as a legal practitioner there.

(2) Where any question as to the law of any country or territory outside the United Kingdom, or of any part of the United Kingdom other than England and Wales, with respect to any matter has been determined (whether before or after the passing of this Act) in any such proceedings as are mentioned in subsection (4) below, then in any civil proceedings (not being proceedings before a court which can take judicial notice of the law of that country, territory or part with respect to that matter)—

    (a) any finding made or decision given on that question in the first-mentioned proceedings shall, if reported or recorded in citable form, be admissible in evidence for the purpose of proving the law of that country, territory or part with respect to that matter; and

    (b) if that finding or decision, as so reported or recorded, is adduced for that purpose, the law of that country, territory or part with respect to that matter shall be taken to be in accordance with that finding or decision unless the contrary is proved:

Provided that paragraph (b) above shall not apply in the case of a finding or decision which conflicts with another finding or decision on the same question adduced by virtue of this subsection in the same proceedings.

(3) Except with the leave of the court, a party to any civil proceedings shall not be permitted to adduce any such finding or decision as is mentioned in subsection (2) above by virtue of that subsection unless he has in accordance with rules of court given to every other party to the proceedings notice that he intends to do so.

(4) The proceedings referred to in subsection (2) above are the following, whether civil or criminal, namely—

    (a) proceedings at first instance in any of the following courts, namely the High Court, the Crown Court, a court of quarter sessions, the Court of Chancery of the county palatine of Lancaster and the Court of Chancery of the county palatine of Durham;

    (b) appeals arising out of any such proceedings as are mentioned in paragraph (a) above;

    (c) proceedings before the Judicial Committee of the Privy Council on appeal (whether to Her Majesty in Council or to the Judicial Committee as such) from any decision of any court outside the United Kingdom.

(5) For the purposes of this section a finding or decision on any such question as is mentioned in subsection (2) above shall be taken to be reported or recorded in citable form, if, but only if, it is reported or recorded in writing in a report, transcript or other document which, if that question had been a question as to the law of England and Wales, could be cited as an authority in legal proceedings in England and Wales.

### 5. Interpretation, application to arbitrations etc and savings

(1) In this Act 'civil proceedings' and 'court' have the meanings assigned by section 18(1) and (2) of the Civil Evidence Act 1968.

(2) Subsections (3) and (4) of section 10 of the Civil Evidence Act 1968 shall apply for the purposes of the application of sections 2 and 4 of this Act in relation to any such civil proceedings as are mentioned in section 18(1)(a) and (b) of that Act (that is to say civil

proceedings before a tribunal other than one of the ordinary courts of law, being proceedings in relation to which the strict rules of evidence apply, and an arbitration or reference, whether under an enactment or not) as they apply for the purposes of the application of Part I of that Act in relation to any such civil proceedings.

(3) Nothing in this Act shall prejudice—

   (a) any power of a court, in any civil proceedings, to exclude evidence (whether by preventing questions from being put or otherwise) at its discretion; or
   (b) the operation of any agreement (whenever made) between the parties to any civil proceedings as to the evidence which is to be admissible (whether generally or for any particular purpose) in those proceedings.

## 6.   Short title, extent and commencement

(1) This Act may be cited as the Civil Evidence Act 1972.

(2) This Act shall not extend to Scotland or Northern Ireland.

(3) This Act, except sections 1 and 4(2) to (5), shall come into force on 1 January 1973, and sections 1 and 4(2) to (5) shall come into force on such day as the Lord Chancellor may by order made by statutory instrument appoint; and different days may be so appointed for different purposes or for the same purposes in relation to different courts or proceedings or otherwise in relation to different circumstances.

# CIVIL EVIDENCE ACT 1995

## (1995 c 38)

### ARRANGEMENT OF SECTIONS

*Admissibility of hearsay evidence*

*An Act to provide for the admissibility of hearsay evidence, the proof of certain documentary evidence and the admissibility and proof of official actuarial tables in civil proceedings; and for connected purposes*

[8 November 1995]

*Admissibility of hearsay evidence*

## 1. Admissibility of hearsay evidence

(1) In civil proceedings evidence shall not be excluded on the ground that it is hearsay.

(2) In this Act—

(a) 'hearsay' means a statement made otherwise than by a person while giving oral evidence in the proceedings which is tendered as evidence of the matters started; and

(b) references to hearsay include hearsay of whatever degree.

(3) Nothing in this Act affects the admissibility of evidence admissible apart from this section.

(4) The provisions of sections 2 to 6 (safeguards and supplementary provisions relating to hearsay evidence) do not apply in relation to hearsay evidence admissible apart from this section, notwithstanding that it may also be admissible by virtue of this section.

*Safeguards in relation to hearsay evidence*

**2.   Notice of proposal to adduce hearsay evidence**

(1) A party proposing to adduce hearsay evidence in civil proceedings shall, subject to the following provisions of this section, give to the other party or parties to the proceedings—

(a)  such notice (if any) of that fact, and

(b)  on request, such particulars of or relating to the evidence,

as is reasonable and practicable in the circumstances for the purpose of enabling him or them to deal with any matters arising from its being hearsay.

(2) Provision may be made by rules of court—

(a)  specifying classes of proceedings or evidence in relation to which subsection (1) does not apply, and

(b)  as to the manner in which (including the time within which) the duties imposed by that subsection are to be complied with in the cases where it does apply.

(3) Subsection (1) may also be excluded by agreement of the parties; and compliance with the duty to give notice may in any case be waived by the person to whom notice is required to be given.

(4) A failure to comply with subsection (1), or with rules under subsection (2)(b), does not affect the admissibility of the evidence but may be taken into account by the court—

(a)  in considering the exercise of its powers with respect to the course of proceedings and costs, and

(b)  as a matter adversely affecting the weight to be given to the evidence in accordance with section 4.

**3.   Power to call witness for cross-examination on hearsay statement**

Rules of court may provide that where a party to civil proceedings adduces hearsay evidence of a statement made by a person and does not call that person as a witness, any other party to the proceedings may, with the leave of the court, call that person as a witness and cross-examine him on the statement as if he had been called by the first-mentioned party and as if the hearsay statement were his evidence in chief.

**4.   Considerations relevant to weighing of hearsay evidence**

(1) In estimating the weight (if any) to be given to hearsay evidence in civil proceedings the court shall have regard to any circumstances from which any inference can reasonably be drawn as to the reliability or otherwise of the evidence.

(2) Regard may be had, in particular, to the following—

    (a) whether it would have been reasonable and practicable for the party by whom the evidence was adduced to have produced the maker of the original statement as a witness;

    (b) whether the original statement was made contemporaneously with the occurrence or existence of the matters stated;

    (c) whether the evidence involves multiple hearsay;

    (d) whether any person involved had any motive to conceal or misrepresent matters;

    (e) whether the original statement was an edited account, or was made in collaboration with another or for a particular purpose;

    (f) whether the circumstances in which the evidence is adduced as hearsay are such as to suggest an attempt to prevent proper evaluation of its weight.

*Supplementary provisions as to hearsay evidence*

## 5. Competence and credibility

(1) Hearsay evidence shall not be admitted in civil proceedings if or to the extent that it is shown to consist of, or to be proved by means of, a statement made by a person who at the time he made the statement was not competent as a witness.

For this purpose 'not competent as a witness' means suffering from such mental or physical infirmity, or lack of understanding, as would render a person incompetent as a witness in civil proceedings; but a child shall be treated as competent as a witness if he satisfies the requirements of section 96(2)(a) and (b) of the Children Act 1989 (conditions for reception of unsworn evidence of child).

(2) Where in civil proceedings hearsay evidence is adduced and the maker of the original statement, or of any statement relied upon to prove another statement, is not called as a witness—

    (a) evidence which if he had been so called would be admissible for the purpose of attacking or supporting his credibility as a witness is admissible for that purpose in the proceedings; and

    (b) evidence tending to prove that, whether before or after he made the statement, he made any other statement inconsistent with it is admissible for the purpose of showing that he had contradicted himself.

Provided that evidence may not be given of any matter of which, if he had been called as a witness and had denied that matter in cross-examination, evidence could not have been adduced by the cross-examining party.

## 6. Previous statements of witnesses

(1) Subject as follows, the provisions of this Act as to hearsay evidence in civil proceedings apply equally (but with any necessary modifications) in relation to a previous statement made by a person called as a witness in the proceedings.

(2) A party who has called or intends to call a person as a witness in civil proceedings may not in those proceedings adduce evidence of a previous statement made by that person, except—

    (a) with the leave of the court, or

    (b) for the purpose of rebutting a suggestion that his evidence has been fabricated.

This shall not be construed as preventing a witness statement (that is, a written statement of oral evidence which a party to the proceedings intends to lead) from being adopted by a witness in giving evidence or treated as his evidence.

(3) Where in the case of civil proceedings section 3, 4 or 5 of the Criminal Procedure Act 1865 applies, which make provision as to—

(a)  how far a witness may be discredited by the party producing him,

(b)  the proof of contradictory statements made by a witness, and

(c)  cross-examination as to previous statements in writing,

this Act does not authorise the adducing of evidence of a previous inconsistent or contradictory statement otherwise than in accordance with those sections.

This is without prejudice to any provision made by rules of court under section 3 above (power to call witness for cross-examination on hearsay statement).

(4) Nothing in this Act affects any of the rules of law as to the circumstances in which, where a person called as a witness in civil proceedings is cross-examined on a document used by him to refresh his memory, that document may be made evidence in the proceedings.

(5) Nothing in this section shall be construed as preventing a statement of any description referred to above from being admissible by virtue of section 1 as evidence of the matters stated.

## 7.  Evidence formerly admissible at common law

(1) The common law rule effectively preserved by section 9(1) and (2)(a) of the Civil Evidence Act 1968 (admissibility of admissions adverse to a party) is superseded by the provisions of this Act.

(2) The common law rules effectively preserved by section 9(1) and (2)(b) to (d) of the Civil Evidence Act 1968, that is, any rule of law whereby in civil proceedings—

(a)  published works dealing with matters of a public nature (for example, histories, scientific works, dictionaries and maps) are admissible as evidence of facts of a public nature stated in them,

(b)  public documents (for example, public registers, and returns made under public authority with respect to matters of public interest) are admissible as evidence of facts stated in them, or

(c)  records (for example, the records of certain courts, treaties, Crown grants, pardons and commissions) are admissible as evidence of facts stated in them,

shall continue to have effect.

(3) The common law rules effectively preserved by section 9(3) and (4) of the Civil Evidence Act 1968, that is, any rule of law whereby in civil proceedings—

(a)  evidence of a person's reputation is admissible for the purpose of proving his good or bad character, or

(b)  evidence of reputation or family tradition is admissible—

(i)   for the purpose of proving or disproving pedigree or the existence of a marriage, or

(ii)  for the purpose of proving or disproving the existence of any public or general right or of identifying any person or thing,

shall continue to have effect in so far as they authorise the court to treat such evidence as proving or disproving that matter.

Where any such rule applies, reputation or family tradition shall be treated for the purposes of this Act as a fact and not as a statement or multiplicity of statements about the matter in question.

(4) The words in which a rule of law mentioned in this section is described are intended only to identify the rule and shall not be construed as altering it in any way.

*Other matters*

## 8. Proof of statements contained in documents

(1) Where a statement contained in a document is admissible as evidence in civil proceedings, it may be proved—

(a) by the production of that document, or

(b) whether or not that document is still in existence, by the production of a copy of that document or of the material part of it,

authenticated in such manner as the court may approve.

(2) It is immaterial for this purpose how many removes there are between a copy and the original.

## 9. Proof of records of business or public authority

(1) A document which is shown to form part of the records of a business or public authority may be received in evidence in civil proceedings without further proof.

(2) A document shall be taken to form part of the records of a business or public authority if there is produced to the court a certificate to that effect signed by an officer of the business or authority to which the records belong.

For this purpose—

(a) a document purporting to be a certificate signed by an officer of a business or public authority shall be deemed to have been duly given by such an officer and signed by him; and

(b) a certificate shall be treated as signed by a person if it purports to bear a facsimile of his signature.

(3) The absence of an entry in the records of a business or public authority may be proved in civil proceedings by affidavit of an officer of the business or authority to which the records belong.

(4) In this section—

'records' means records in whatever form;

'business' includes any activity regularly carried on over a period of time, whether for profit or not, by any body (whether corporate or not) or by an individual;

'officer' includes any person occupying a responsible position in relation to the relevant activities of the business or public authority or in relation to its records; and

'public authority' includes any public or statutory undertaking, any government department and any person holding office under Her Majesty.

(5) The court may, having regard to the circumstances of the case, direct that all or any of the above provisions of this section do not apply in relation to a particular document or record, or description of documents or records.

## 10. Admissibility and proof of Ogden Tables

(1) The actuarial tables (together with explanatory notes) for use in personal injury and fatal accident cases issued from time to time by the Government Actuary's Department are admissible in evidence for the purpose of assessing, in an action for personal injury, the sum to be awarded as general damages for future pecuniary loss.

(2) They may be proved by the production of a copy published by Her Majesty's Stationery Office.

(3) For the purposes of this section—

(a) 'personal injury' includes any disease and any impairment of a person's physical or mental condition; and

(b) 'action for personal injury' includes an action brought by virtue of the Law Reform (Miscellaneous Provisions) Act 1934 or the Fatal Accidents Act 1976.

*General*

## 11. Meaning of 'civil proceedings'

In this Act 'civil proceedings' means civil proceedings, before any tribunal, in relation to which the strict rules of evidence apply, whether as a matter of law or by agreement of the parties.

References to 'the court' and 'rules of court' shall be construed accordingly.

## 12. Provisions as to rules of court

(1) Any power to make rules of court regulating the practice or procedure of the court in relation to civil proceedings includes power to make such provision as may be necessary or expedient for carrying into effect the provisions of this Act.

(2) Any rules of court made for the purposes of this Act as it applies in relation to proceedings in the High Court apply, except in so far as their operation is excluded by agreement, to arbitration proceedings to which this Act applies, subject to such modifications as may be appropriate.

Any question arising as to what modifications are appropriate shall be determined, in default of agreement, by the arbitrator or umpire, as the case may be.

## 13. Interpretation

In this Act—

'civil proceedings' has the meaning given by section 11 and 'court' and 'rules of court' shall be construed in accordance with that section;

'document' means anything in which information of any description is recorded, and 'copy', in relation to a document, means anything onto which information recorded in the document has been copied, by whatever means and whether directly or indirectly;

'hearsay' shall be construed in accordance with section 1(2);

'oral evidence' includes evidence which, by reason of a defect of speech or hearing, a person called as a witness gives in writing or by signs;

'the original statement', in relation to hearsay evidence, means the underlying statement (if any) by—

(a) in the case of evidence of fact, a person having personal knowledge of the fact, or

(b) in the case of evidence of opinion, the person whose opinion it is; and

'statement' means any representation of fact or opinion, however made.

## 14. Savings

(1) Nothing in this Act affects the exclusion of evidence on grounds other than that it is hearsay.

This applies whether the evidence falls to be excluded in pursuance of any enactment or rule of law, for failure to comply with rules of court or an order of the court, or otherwise.

(2) Nothing in this Act affects the proof of documents by means other than those specified in section 8 or 9.

(3) Nothing in this Act affects the operation of the following enactments—

(a) section 2 of the Documentary Evidence Act 1868 (mode of proving certain official documents);

(b) section 2 of the Documentary Evidence Act 1882 (documents printed under the superintendence of Stationery Office);

(c) section 1 of the Evidence (Colonial Statutes) Act 1907 (proof of statutes of certain legislatures);

(d) section 1 of the Evidence (Foreign, Dominion and Colonial Documents) Act 1933 (proof and effect of registers and official certificates of certain countries);

(e) section 5 of the Oaths and Evidence (Overseas Authorities and Countries) Act 1963 (provision in respect of public registers of other countries).

## 15. Consequential amendments and repeals

(1) The enactments specified in Schedule 1 are amended in accordance with that Schedule, the amendments being consequential on the provisions of this Act.

(2) The enactments specified in Schedule 2 are repealed to the extent specified.

## 16. Short title, commencement and extent

(1) This Act may be cited as the Civil Evidence Act 1995.

(2) The provisions of this Act come into force on such day as the Lord Chancellor may appoint by order made by statutory instrument, and different days may be appointed for different provisions and for different purposes.

(3) An order under subsection (2) may contain such transitional provisions as appear to the Lord Chancellor to be appropriate; and subject to any such provision, the provisions of this Act shall not apply in relation to proceedings begun before commencement.

(4) This Act extends to England and Wales.

(5) Section 10 (admissibility and proof of Ogden Tables) also extends to Northern Ireland.

As it extends to Northern Ireland, the following shall be substituted for subsection (3)(b)—

'(b) "action for personal injury" includes an action brought by virtue of the Law Reform (Miscellaneous Provisions) (Northern Ireland) Act 1937 or the Fatal Accidents (Northern Ireland) Order 1977.'

(6) The provisions of Schedules 1 and 2 (consequential amendments and repeals) have the same extent as the enactments respectively amended or repealed.

# SCHEDULES

## SCHEDULE 1

Section 15(1)

### CONSEQUENTIAL AMENDMENTS

*Army Act 1955 (c 18)*

1. For section 62 of the Army Act 1955 (making of false documents) substitute—

**'62 Making of false documents**

   (1)  A person subject to military law who—

      (a)  makes an official document which is to his knowledge false in a material particular, or

      (b)  makes in any official document an entry which is to his knowledge false in a material particular, or

      (c)  tampers with the whole or any part of an official document (whether by altering it, destroying it, suppressing it, removing it or otherwise), or

      (d)  with intent to deceive, fails to make an entry in an official document,

is liable on conviction by court-martial to imprisonment for a term not exceeding two years or any less punishment provided by this Act.

   (2)  For the purposes of this section—

      (a)  a document is official if it is or is likely to be made use of, in connection with the performance of his functions as such, by a person who holds office under, or is in the service of, the Crown; and

      (b)  a person who has signed or otherwise adopted as his own a document made by another shall be treated, as well as that other, as the maker of the document.

   (3)  In this section "document" means anything in which information of any description is recorded.'.

*Air Force Act 1955 (c 19)*

2. For section 62 of the Air Force Act 1955 (making of false documents) substitute—

**'62 Making of false documents**

   (1)  A person subject to air-force law who—

      (a)  makes an official document which is to his knowledge false in a material particular, or

      (b)  makes in any official document an entry which is to his knowledge false in a material particular, or

      (c)  tampers with the whole or any part of an official document (whether by altering it, destroying it, suppressing it, removing it or otherwise), or

      (d)  with intent to deceive, fails to make an entry in an official document,

is liable on conviction by court-martial to imprisonment for a term not exceeding two years or any less punishment provided by this Act.

(2)  For the purposes of this section—

    (a)  a document is official if it is or is likely to be made use of, in connection with the performance of his functions as such, by a person who holds office under, or is in the service of, the Crown; and

    (b)  a person who has signed or otherwise adopted as his own a document made by another shall be treated, as well as that other, as the maker of the document.

(3)  In this section "document" means anything in which information of any description is recorded.'.

### *Naval Discipline Act 1957 (c 53)*

3. For section 35 of the Naval Discipline Act 1957 (making of false documents) substitute—

**'35 Falsification of documents**

(1)  A person subject to this Act who—

    (a)  makes an official document which is to his knowledge false in a material particular, or

    (b)  makes in any official document an entry which is to his knowledge false in a material particular, or

    (c)  tampers with the whole or any part of an official document (whether by altering it, destroying it, suppressing it, removing it or otherwise), or

    (d)  with intent to deceive, fails to make an entry in an official document,

is liable to imprisonment for a term not exceeding two years or any less punishment authorised by this Act.

(2)  For the purposes of this section—

    (a)  a document is official if it is or is likely to be made use of, in connection with the performance of his functions as such, by a person who holds office under, or is in the service of, the Crown; and

    (b)  a person who has signed or otherwise adopted as his own a document made by another shall be treated, as well as that other, as the maker of the document.

(3)  In this section "document" means anything in which information of any description is recorded.'.

### *Gaming Act 1968 (c 65)*

4. In section 43 of the Gaming Act 1968 (powers of inspectors and related provisions), for subsection (11) substitute—

'(11) In this section—

"document" means anything in which information of any description is recorded, and "copy", in relation to a document, means anything onto which information recorded in the document has been copied, by whatever means and whether directly or indirectly.'.

### *Vehicle and Driving Licences Act 1969 (c 27)*

5.—(1) Section 27 of the Vehicle and Driving Licences Act 1969 (admissibility of records as evidence) is amended as follows.

(2) For subsection (2) substitute—

'(2) In subsection (1) of this section—

"document" means anything in which information of any description is recorded;
"copy", in relation to a document, means anything onto which information recorded in the
    document has been copied, by whatever means and whether directly or indirectly; and
"statement" means any representation of fact, however made.'.

(3) In subsection (4)(b), for the words from 'for the references' to the end substitute 'for the
definitions of "document", "copy" and "statement" there were substituted "document" and
"statement" have the same meanings as in section 17(3) of the Law Reform (Miscellaneous
Provisions) (Scotland) Act 1968, and the reference to a copy of a document shall be construed
in accordance with section 17(4) of that Act, but nothing in this paragraph shall be construed as
limiting to civil proceedings the references to proceedings in subsection (1)".'.

### *Taxes Management Act 1970 (c 9)*

6. In section 20D of the Taxes Management Act 1970 (interpretation of ss 20 to 20CC), for
subsection (3) substitute—

'(3) Without prejudice to section 127 of the Finance Act 1988, in sections 20 to 20CC above
"document" means, subject to sections 20(8C) and 20A(1A), anything in which information
of any description is recorded.'.

### *Civil Evidence Act 1972 (c 30)*

7.—(1) Section 5 of the Civil Evidence Act 1972 (interpretation and application of Act) is
amended as follows.

(2) For subsection (1) (meaning of 'civil proceedings' and 'court') substitute—

'(1) In this Act "civil proceedings" means civil proceedings, before any tribunal, in relation
to which the strict rules of evidence apply, whether as a matter of law or by agreement, of the
parties; and references to "the court" shall be construed accordingly.'.

(3) For subsection (2) (application of High Court or county court rules to certain other civil
proceedings) substitute—

'(2) The rules of court made for the purposes of the application of sections 2 and 4 of this Act
to proceedings in the High Court apply, except in so far as their application is excluded by
agreement, to proceedings before tribunals other than the ordinary courts of law, subject to
such modifications as may be appropriate.

Any question arising as to what modifications are appropriate shall be determined, in
default of agreement, by the tribunal.'.

### *International Carriage of Perishable Foodstuffs Act 1976 (c 58)*

8. In section 15 of the International Carriage of Perishable Foodstuffs Act 1976 (admissibility
of records as evidence), for subsection (2) substitute—

'(2) In this section as it has effect in England and Wales—

"document" means anything in which information of any description is recorded;
"copy", in relation to a document, means anything onto which information recorded in the
    document has been copied, by whatever means and whether directly or indirectly; and
"statement" means any representation of fact, however made.'.

(2A) In this section as it has effect in Scotland, "document" and "statement" have the same
meanings as in section 17(3) of the Law Reform (Miscellaneous Provisions) (Scotland) Act

1968, and the reference to a copy of a document shall be construed in accordance with section 17(4) of that Act.

(2B) In this section as it has effect in Northern Ireland, "document" and "statement" have the same meaning as in section 6(1) of the Civil Evidence Act (Northern Ireland) 1971, and the reference to a copy of a document shall be construed in accordance with section 6(2) of that Act.

(2C) Nothing in subsection (2A) or (2B) above shall be construed as limiting to civil proceedings the references to proceedings in subsection (1) above.'.

### Police and Criminal Evidence Act 1984 (c 60)

9.—(1) The Police and Criminal Evidence Act 1984 is amended as follows.

(2) In section 72(1) (interpretation of provisions relating to documentary evidence), for the definition of 'copy' and 'statement' substitute—

> '"copy", in relation to a document, means anything onto which information recorded in the document has been copied, by whatever means and whether directly or indirectly, and "statement" means any representation of fact, however made; and'.

(3) In section 118(1) (general interpretation), in the definition of 'document', for 'has the same meaning as in Part I of the Civil Evidence Act 1968' substitute 'means anything in which information of any description is recorded.'.

### Companies Act 1985 (c 6)

10. In section 709 of the Companies Act 1985 (inspection, &c of records kept by registrar), in subsection (3) (use in evidence of certified copy or extract), for the words from 'In England and Wales' to the end substitute—

> 'In England and Wales this is subject, in the case of proceedings to which section 69 of the Police and Criminal Evidence Act 1984 applies, to compliance with any applicable rules of court under subsection (2) of that section (which relates to evidence from computer records).'.

### Finance Act 1985 (c 54)

11.—(1) Section 10 of the Finance Act 1985 (production of computer records, &c) is amended as follows.

(2) In subsection (1) (general scope of powers conferred in relation to assigned matters within meaning of Customs and Excise Management Act 1979), for the words from 'were a reference' to the end substitute 'were a reference to anything in which information of any description is recorded and any reference to a copy of a document were a reference to anything onto which information recorded in the document has been copied, by whatever means and whether directly or indirectly'.

(3) In subsection (3) (documents within powers conferred by subsection (2)), for the words ', within the meaning of Part I of the Civil Evidence Act 1968,' substitute ', within the meaning given by subsection (1) above,'.

(4) In subsection (5) (scope of offences relating to false documents, &c), for 'the same meaning as in Part I of the Civil Evidence Act 1968' substitute 'the meaning given by subsection (1) above'.

(5) Omit subsection (7) (adaptation of references to Civil Evidence Act 1968).

*Criminal Justice Act 1988 (c 33)*

12. In Schedule 2 to the Criminal Justice Act 1988 (supplementary provisions as to documentary evidence), for paragraph 5 (application of interpretation provisions) substitute—

'5.—(1) In Part II of this Act—

"document" means anything in which information of any description is recorded;
"copy", in relation to a document, means anything onto which information recorded in the document has been copied, by whatever means and whether directly or indirectly; and
"statement" means any representation of fact, however made.

(2) For the purposes of Part II of this Act evidence which, by reason of a defect of speech or hearing, a person called as a witness gives in writing or by signs shall be treated as given orally.'.

*Finance Act 1988 (c 39)*

13.—(1) Section 127 of the Finance Act 1988 (production of computer records, &c) is amended as follows.

(2) In subsection (1) (general scope of powers conferred by or under Taxes Acts), for the words from 'were a reference' to the end substitute 'were a reference to anything in which information of any description is recorded and any reference to a copy of a document were a reference to anything onto which information recorded in the document has been copied, by whatever means and whether directly or indirectly'.

(3) In subsection (3) (documents within powers conferred by subsection (2)), for the words ', within the meaning of Part I of the Civil Evidence Act 1968,' substitute ', within the meaning given by subsection (1) above,'.

(4) Omit subsection (5) (adaptation of references to Civil Evidence Act 1968).

*Housing Act 1988 (c 50)*

14. In section 97 of the Housing Act 1988 (information, &c for applicant), for subsection (4) substitute—

'(4) In this section "document" means anything in which information of any description is recorded; and in relation to a document in which information is recorded otherwise than in legible form any reference to sight of the document is to sight of the information in legible form.'.

*Road Traffic Offenders Act 1988 (c 53)*

15. In section 13 of the Road Traffic Offenders Act 1988 (admissibility of records as evidence), for subsection (3) substitute—

'(3) In the preceding subsections, except in Scotland—

"copy", in relation to a document, means anything onto which information recorded in the document has been copied, by whatever means and whether directly or indirectly;
"document" means anything in which information of any description is recorded; and
"statement" means any representation of fact, however made.

(3A) In Scotland, in the preceding subsections "document" and "statement" have the same meanings as in section 17(3) of the Law Reform (Miscellaneous Provisions) (Scotland) Act 1968, and the reference to a copy of a document shall be construed in accordance with section

17(4) of that Act; but nothing in this subsection shall be construed as limiting to civil proceedings the references to proceedings in subsection (2) above.'.

### *Children Act 1989 (c 41)*

16. In section 96(7) of the Children Act 1989 (evidence given by, or with respect to, children: interpretation), for the definition of 'civil proceedings' and 'court' substitute—

' "civil proceedings" means civil proceedings, before any tribunal, in relation to which the strict rules of evidence apply, whether as a matter of law or by agreement of the parties, and references to "the court" shall be construed accordingly;'.

### *Leasehold Reform, Housing and Urban Development Act 1993 (c 28)*

17. In section 11(9) of the Leasehold Reform, Housing and Urban Development Act 1993 (right of qualifying tenant to certain information: interpretation), for the definition of 'document' substitute—

' "document" means anything in which information of any description is recorded, and in relation to a document in which information is recorded otherwise than in legible form any reference to sight of the document is to sight of the information in legible form;'.

### *Finance Act 1993 (c 34)*

18. In Schedule 21 to the Finance Act 1993 (oil taxation: supplementary provisions as to information), in paragraph 14(1) (meaning of 'document'), for the words from 'has the same meaning' to the end substitute 'means anything in which information of any description is recorded'.

### *Vehicle Excise and Registration Act 1994 (c 22)*

19. In section 52 of the Vehicle Excise and Registration Act 1994 (admissibility of records as evidence), for subsections (3) to (5) substitute—

'(3) In this section as it has effect in England and Wales—

"document" means anything in which information of any description is recorded;
"copy", in relation to a document, means anything onto which information recorded in the document has been copied, by whatever means and whether directly or indirectly; and
"statement" means any representation of fact, however made.'.

(4) In this section as it has effect in Scotland, "document" and "statement" have the same meanings as in section 17(3) of the Law Reform (Miscellaneous Provisions) (Scotland) Act 1968, and the reference to a copy of a document shall be construed in accordance with section 17(4) of that Act.

(5) In this section as it has effect in Northern Ireland, "document" and "statement" have the same meanings as in section 6(1) of the Civil Evidence Act (Northern Ireland) 1971, and the reference to a copy of a document shall be construed in accordance with section 6(2) of that Act.

(6) Nothing in subsection (4) or (5) limits to civil proceedings the references to proceedings in subsection (1).'.

### *Value Added Tax Act 1994 (c 23)*

20. In section 96(1) of the Value Added Tax Act 1994 (general interpretative provisions), at the appropriate places insert—

' "document" means anything in which information of any description is recorded; and "copy", in relation to a document, means anything onto which information recorded in the document has been copied, by whatever means and whether directly or indirectly.'.

## SCHEDULE 2

Section 15(2)

### REPEALS

| Chapter | Short title | Extent of repeal |
|---------|-------------|------------------|
| 1938 c 28 | Evidence Act 1938 | Sections 1 and 2 |
| | | Section 6(1) except the words from ' "Proceedings" ' to 'references' |
| | | Section 6(2)(b) |
| 1968 c 64 | Civil Evidence Act 1968 | Part I |
| 1971 c 33 | Armed Forces Act 1971 | Section 26 |
| 1972 c 30 | Civil Evidence Act 1972 | Section 1 |
| | | Section 2(1) and (2) |
| | | In section 2(3)(b), the words from 'by virtue of section 2' to 'out-of-court statements)' |
| | | In section 3(1), the words 'Part I of the Civil Evidence Act 1968 or' |
| | | In section 6(3), the words '1 and', in both places where they occur |
| 1975 c 63 | Inheritance (Provisions for Family and Dependants) Act 1975 | Section 21 |
| 1979 c 2 | Customs and Excise Management Act 1979 | Section 75A(6)(a) |
| | | Section 118A(6)(a) |
| 1980 c 43 | Magistrates' Courts Act 1980 | In Schedule 7, paragraph 75 |
| 1984 c 28 | County Courts Act 1984 | In Schedule 2, paragraphs 33 and 34 |
| 1985 c 54 | Finance Act 1985 | Section 10(7) |
| 1986 c 21 | Armed Forces Act 1986 | Section 3 |
| 1988 c 39 | Finance Act 1988 | Section 127(5) |
| 1990 c 26 | Gaming (Amendment) Act 1990 | In the Schedule, paragraph 2(7) |
| 1994 c 9 | Finance Act 1994 | Section 22(2)(a) |
| | | In Schedule 7, paragraph 1(6)(a) |
| 1994 c 23 | Value Added Tax Act 1994 | Section 96(6) and (7) |
| | | In Schedule 11, paragraph 6(6)(a) |
| 1995 c 4 | Finance Act 1995 | In Schedule 4, paragraph 38. |

## CIVIL PROCEDURE RULES 1998

## SI 1998/3132

## (EXTRACTS)

## PART 1

### OVERRIDING OBJECTIVE

#### 1.1   The overriding objective

(1) These Rules are a new procedural code with the overriding objective of enabling the court to deal with cases justly.

(2) Dealing with a case justly includes, so far as is practicable—

- (a)  ensuring that the parties are on an equal footing;
- (b)  saving expense;
- (c)  dealing with the case in ways which are proportionate—
    - (i)   to the amount of money involved;
    - (ii)  to the importance of the case;
    - (iii) to the complexity of the issues; and
    - (iv)  to the financial position of each party;
- (d)  ensuring that it is dealt with expeditiously and fairly; and
- (e)  allotting to it an appropriate share of the court's resources, while taking into account the need to allot resources to other cases.

#### 1.2   Application by the court of the overriding objective

The court must seek to give effect to the overriding objective when it—

- (a)  exercises any power given to it by the Rules; or
- (b)  interprets any rule.

#### 1.3   Duty of the parties

The parties are required to help the court to further the overriding objective.

#### 1.4   Court's duty to manage cases

(1) The court must further the overriding objective by actively managing cases.

(2) Active case management includes—

- (a)  encouraging the parties to co-operate with each other in the conduct of the proceedings;
- (b)  identifying the issues at an early stage;
- (c)  deciding promptly which issues need full investigation and trial and accordingly disposing summarily of the others;
- (d)  deciding the order in which issues are to be resolved;
- (e)  encouraging the parties to use an alternative dispute resolution (GL) procedure if the court considers that appropriate and facilitating the use of such procedure;
- (f)  helping the parties to settle the whole or part of the case;
- (g)  fixing timetables or otherwise controlling the progress of the case;
- (h)  considering whether the likely benefits of taking a particular step justify the cost of taking it;
- (i)  dealing with as many aspects of the case as it can on the same occasion;

(j)  dealing with the case without the parties needing to attend at court;

(k)  making use of technology; and

(l)  giving directions to ensure that the trial of a case proceeds quickly and efficiently.

PART 2

APPLICATION AND INTERPRETATION OF THE RULES

**2.1  Application of the Rules**

(1) Subject to paragraph (2), these Rules apply to all proceedings in—

(a)  county courts;

(b)  the High Court; and

(c)  the Civil Division of the Court of Appeal.

(2) These Rules do not apply to proceedings of the kinds specified in the first column of the following table (proceedings for which rules may be made under the enactments specified in the second column) except to the extent that they are applied to those proceedings by another enactment—

| *Proceedings* | *Enactments* |
| --- | --- |
| 1. Insolvency proceedings | Insolvency Act 1986, ss 411 and 412 |
| 2. Non-contentious or common form probate proceedings | Supreme Court Act 1981, s 127 |
| 3. Proceedings in the High Court when acting as a Prize Court | Prize Courts Act 1894, s 3 |
| 4. Proceedings before the judge within the meaning of Part VII of the Mental Health Act 1983 | Mental Health Act 1983, s 106 |
| 5. Family proceedings | Matrimonial and Family Proceedings Act 1984, s 40 |

**2.2  The glossary**

(1) The glossary at the end of these Rules is a guide to the meaning of certain legal expressions used in the Rules, but is not to be taken as giving those expressions any meaning in the Rules which they do not have in the law generally.

(2) Subject to paragraph (3), words in these Rules which are included in the glossary are followed by '(GL)'.

(3) The words 'counterclaim', 'damages', 'practice form' and 'service', which appear frequently in the Rules, are included in the glossary but are not followed by '(GL)'.

**2.3  Interpretation**

(1) In these Rules—

'child' has the meaning given by rule 21.1(2);

'claim for personal injuries' means proceedings in which there is a claim for damages in respect of personal injuries to the claimant or any other person or in respect of a person's death, and 'personal injuries' includes any disease and any impairment of a person's physical or mental condition;

'claimant' means a person who makes a claim;

'CCR' is to be interpreted in accordance with Part 50;

'court officer' means a member of the court staff;

'defendant' means a person against whom a claim is made;

'defendant's home court' means—

(a) if the claim is proceeding in a county court, the county court for the district in which the defendant's address for service, as shown on the defence, is situated; and

(b) if the claim is proceeding in the High Court, the district registry for the district in which the defendant's address for service, as shown on the defence, is situated or, if there is no such district registry, the Royal Courts of Justice;

(Rule 6.5 provides for a party to give an address for service)

'filing', in relation to a document, means delivering it, by post or otherwise, to the court office;

'judge' means, unless the context otherwise requires, a judge, Master or district judge or a person authorised to act as such;

'jurisdiction' means, unless the context requires otherwise, England and Wales and any part of the territorial waters of the United Kingdom adjoining England and Wales;

'legal representative' means a barrister or a solicitor, solicitor's employee or other authorised litigator (as defined in the Courts and Legal Services Act 1990) who has been instructed to act for a party in relation to a claim.

'litigation friend' has the meaning given by Part 21;

'patient' has the meaning given by rule 21.1(2);

'RSC' is to be interpreted in accordance with Part 50;

'statement of case'—

(a) means a claim form, particulars of claim where these are not included in a claim form, defence, Part 20 claim, or reply to defence; and

(b) includes any further information given in relation to them voluntarily or by court order under rule 18.1;

'statement of value' is to be interpreted in accordance with rule 16.3;

'summary judgment' is to be interpreted in accordance with Part 24.

(2) A reference to a 'specialist list' is a reference to a list (GL) that has been designated as such by a relevant practice direction.

(3) Where the context requires, a reference to 'the court' means a reference to a particular county court, a district registry, or the Royal Courts of Justice.

. . .

# PART 16

## STATEMENTS OF CASE

### 16.2   Contents of the claim form

(1) The claim form must—

(a) contain a concise statement of the nature of the claim;

(b) specify the remedy which the claimant seeks;

. . .

### 16.4   Contents of the particulars of claim

(1) Particulars of claim must include—

(a) a concise statement of the facts on which the claimant relies;

. . .

PART 18

FURTHER INFORMATION

## 18.1 Obtaining further information

(1) The court may at any time order a party to—

    (a) clarify any matter which is in dispute in the proceedings; or

    (b) give additional information in relation to any such matter,

whether or not the matter is contained or referred to in a statement of case.

(2) Paragraph (1) is subject to any rule of law to the contrary.

(3) Where the court makes an order under paragraph (1), the party against whom it is made must—

    (a) file his response; and

    (b) serve it on the other parties,

within the time specified by the court.

(Part 22 requires a response to be verified by a statement of truth)

## 18.2 Restriction on the use of further information

The court may direct that information provided by a party to another party (whether given voluntarily or following an order made under rule 18.1) must not be used for any purpose except for that of the proceedings in which it is given.

---

## PRACTICE DIRECTION – FURTHER INFORMATION

### THIS PRACTICE DIRECTION SUPPLEMENTS CPR PART 18

*Attention is also drawn to Part 22 (Statements of Truth)*

## 1. Preliminary Request for Further Information or Clarification

1.1 Before making an application to the court for an order under Part 18, the party seeking clarification or information (the first party) should first serve on the party from whom it is sought (the second party) a written request for that clarification or information (a Request) stating a date by which the response to the Request should be served. The date must allow the second party a reasonable time to respond.

1.2 A Request should be concise and strictly confined to matters which are reasonably necessary and proportionate to enable the first party to prepare his own case or to understand the case he has to meet.

1.3 Requests must be made as far as possible in a single comprehensive document and not piecemeal.

1.4 A Request may be made by letter if the text of the request is brief and the reply is likely to be brief; otherwise the Request should be made in a separate document.

1.5 If a Request is made in a letter, the letter should, in order to distinguish it from any other that might routinely be written in the course of a case,

(1)  state that it contains a Request made under Part 18, and

(2)  deal with no matters other than the Request.

1.6  (1)  A Request (where made by letter or in a separate document) must—

  (a)  be headed with the name of the court and the title and number of the claim,

  (b)  in its heading state that it is a Request made under Part 18, identify the first party and the second party and state the date on which it is made,

  (c)  set out in a separate numbered paragraph each request for information or clarification,

  (d)  where a Request relates to a document, identify that document and (if relevant) the paragraph or words to which it relates,

  (e)  state the date by which the first party expects a response to the Request,

(2)  (a)  A Request which is not in the form of a letter may, if convenient, be prepared in such a way that the response may be given on the same document.

  (b)  To do this the numbered paragraphs of the Request should appear on the left hand half of each sheet so that the paragraphs of the response may then appear on the right.

  (c)  Where a Request is prepared in this form an extra copy should be served for the use of the second party.

## 2.  Responding to a Request

2.1  A response to a Request must be in writing, dated and signed by the second party or his legal representative.

2.2  (1)  Where the Request is made in a letter the second party may give his response in a letter or in a formal reply.

(2)  Such a letter should identify itself as a response to the Request and deal with no other matters than the response.

2.3  (1)  Unless the Request is in the format described in paragraph 1.6(2) and the second party uses the document supplied for the purpose, a response must:

  (a)  be headed with the name of the court and the title and number of the claim,

  (b)  in its heading identify itself as a response to that Request,

  (c)  repeat the text of each separate paragraph of the Request and set out under each paragraph the response to it,

  (d)  refer to and have attached to it a copy of any document not already in the possession of the first party which forms part of the response.

(2)  A second or supplementary response to a Request must identify itself as such in its heading.

2.4  The second party must when he serves his response on the fist party serve on every other party and file with the court a copy of the Request and of his response.

## 3.  Statements of Truth

Attention is drawn to Part 22 and to the definition of a statement of case in Part 2 of the rules; a response should be verified by a statement of truth.

## 4.  General Matters

4.1  (1)  If the second party objects to complying with the Request or part of it or is unable to do so at all or within the time stated in the Request he must inform the first party promptly and in any event within that time.

(2)    He may do so in a letter or a separate document (a formal response), but in either case he must give reasons and, where relevant, give a date by which he expects to be able to comply.

4.2    (1)    There is no need for a second party to apply to the court if he objects to a Request or is unable to comply with it at all or within the stated time. He need only comply with paragraph 4.1(1) above.

(2)    Where a second party considers that a Request can only be complied with at disproportionate expense and objects to comply for that reason he should say so in his reply and explain briefly why he has taken that view.

## 5.   Applications for Orders under Part 18

5.1    Attention is drawn to Part 23 (Applications) and to the Practice Direction which supplements that Part.

5.2    An application notice for an order under Part 18 should set out or have attached to it the text of the order sought and in particular should specify the matter or matters in respect of which the clarification or information is sought.

5.3    (1)    If a Request under paragraph 1 for the information or clarification has not been made, the application notice should, in addition, explain why not.

(2)    If a Request for clarification or information has been made, the application notice or the evidence in support should describe the response, if any.

5.4    Both the first party and the second party should consider whether evidence in support of or in opposition to the application is required.

5.5    (1)    Where the second party has made no response to a Request served on him, the first party need not serve the application notice on the second party, and the court may deal with the application without a hearing.

(2)    Sub-paragraph (1) above only applies if at least 14 days have passed since the Request was served and the time stated in it for a response has expired.

5.6    Unless paragraph 5.5 applies the application notice must be served on the second party and on all other parties to the claim.

5.7    An order made under Part 18 must be served on all parties to the claim.

5.8    Costs:

(1)    Attention is drawn to the Costs Practice Direction and in particular the court's power to make a summary assessment of costs.

(2)    Attention is also drawn to rule 43.5(5) which provides that if an order does not mention costs no party is entitled to costs relating to that order.

## PART 22

## STATEMENTS OF TRUTH

### 22.1   Documents to be verified by a statement of truth

(1) The following documents must be verified by a statement of truth—

(a) a statement of case;
(b) a response complying with an order under rule 18.1 to provide further information; and
(c) a witness statement.

(2) Where a statement of case is amended, the amendments must be verified by a statement of truth unless the court orders otherwise.

(Part 17 provides for amendments to statements of case)

(3) If an applicant wishes to rely on matters set out in his application notice as evidence, the application notice must be verified by a statement of truth.

(4) Subject to paragraph (5), a statement of truth is a statement that—

(a) the party putting forward the document; or
(b) in the case of a witness statement, the maker of the witness statement, believes the facts stated in the document are true.

(5) If a party is conducting proceedings with a litigation friend, the statement of truth in—

(a) a statement of case;
(b) a response; or
(c) an application notice,

is a statement that the litigation friend believes the facts stated in the document being verified are true.

(6) The statement of truth must be signed by—

(a) in the case of a statement of case, a response or an application—
    (i) the party or litigation friend; or
    (ii) the legal representative on behalf of the party or litigation friend; and
(b) in the case of a witness statement, the maker of the statement.

(7) A statement of truth which is not contained in the document which it verifies, must clearly identify that document.

(8) A statement of truth in a statement of case may be made by—

(a) a person who is not a party; or
(b) by two parties jointly,

where this is permitted by a relevant practice direction.

### 22.2 Failure to verify a statement of case

(1) If a party fails to verify his statement of case by a statement of truth

(a) the statement of case shall remain effective unless struck out; but
(b) the party may not rely on the statement of case as evidence of any of the matters set out in it.

(2) The court may strike out (GL) a statement of case which is not verified by a statement of truth.

(3) Any party may apply for an order under paragraph (2).

### 22.3 Failure to verify a witness statement

If the maker of a witness statement fails to verify the witness statement by a statement of truth the court may direct that it shall not be admissible as evidence.

### 22.4 Power of the court to require a document to be verified

(1) The court may order a person who has failed to verify a document in accordance with rule 22.1 to verify the document.

(2) Any party may apply for an order under paragraph (1).

## PRACTICE DIRECTION – STATEMENTS OF TRUTH

### THIS PRACTICE DIRECTION SUPPLEMENTS CPR PART 22

**1. Documents to be verified by a statement of truth**

1.1 Rule 22.1(1) sets out the documents which must be verified by a statement of truth. The documents include:

(1) a statement of case,

(2) a response complying with an order under rule 18.1 to provide further information, and

(3) a witness statement.

1.2 If an applicant wishes to rely on matters set out in his application notice as evidence, the application notice must be verified by a statement of truth.[1]

1.3 An expert's report should also be verified by a statement of truth. For the form of the statement of truth verifying an expert's report (which differs from that set out below) see the practice direction which supplements Part 35.

1.4 In addition, a notice of objections to an account being taken by the court should be verified by a statement of truth unless verified by an affidavit or a witness statement.[2]

1.5 The statement of truth may be contained in the document it verifies or it may be in a separate document served subsequently, in which case it must identify the document to which it relates.

**Form of the statement of truth**

2.1 The form of the statement of truth verifying a statement of case, a response, an application notice or a notice of objections should be as follows:

'[I believe] [the (*claimant or as may be*) believes] that the facts stated in this [*name document being verified*] are true.'

2.2 The form of the statement of truth verifying a witness statement should be as follows:

'I believe that the facts stated in this witness statement are true'

2.3 Where the statement of truth is contained in a separate document, the document containing the statement of truth must be headed with the title of the proceedings and the claim number. The document being verified should be identified in the statement of truth as follows:

(1) claim form: 'the claim form issued on [*date*]',

(2) particulars of claim: 'the particulars of claim issued on [*date*]',

(3) statement of case: 'the [*defence or as may be*] served on the [*name of party*] on [*date*]',

(4) application notice: 'the application notice issued on [*date*] for [*set out the remedy sought*]',

---

1    See Rule 22.1(3).
2    See the Accounts and Enquiries practice direction supplementing Part 40 (judgments and orders).

(5)   witness statement: 'the witness statement filed on [*date*] or served on [*party*] on [*date*]'.

## Who may sign the statement of truth

3.1   In a statement of case, a response or an application notice, the statement of truth must be signed by:

(1)   the party or his litigation friend,[1] or

(2)   the legal representative[2] of the party or litigation friend.

3.2   A statement of truth verifying a witness statement must be signed by the witness.

3.3   A statement of truth verifying a notice of objections to an account must be signed by the objecting party or his legal representative.

3.4   Where a document is to be verified on behalf of a company or other corporation, subject to paragraph 3.7 below, the statement of truth must be signed by a person holding a senior position[3] in the company or corporation. That person must state the office or position he holds.

3.5   Each of the following persons is a person holding a senior position:

(1)   in respect of a registered company or corporation, a director, the treasurer, secretary, chief executive, manager or other officer of the company or corporation, and

(2)   in respect of a corporation which is not a registered company, in addition to those persons set out in (1), the mayor, chairman, president or town clerk or other similar officer of the corporation.

3.6   Where the document is to be verified on behalf of a partnership, those who may sign the statement of truth are:

(1)   any of the partners, or

(2)   a person having the control or management of the partnership business.

3.7   Where a party is legally represented, the legal representative may sign the statement of truth on his behalf. The statement signed by the legal representative will refer to the client's belief, not his own. In signing he must state the capacity in which he signs and the name of his firm where appropriate.

3.8   Where a legal representative has signed a statement of truth, his signature will be taken by the court as his statement:

(1)   that the client on whose behalf he has signed has authorised him to do so,

(2)   that before signing he had explained to the client that in signing the statement of truth he would be confirming the client's belief that the facts stated in the document were true, and

(3)   that before signing he had informed the client of the possible consequences to the client if it should subsequently appear that the client did not have an honest belief in the truth of those facts (see rule 32.14).

3.9   The individual who signs a statement of truth must print his full name clearly beneath his signature.

---

1   See part 21 (children and patients).

2   See rule 2.3 for the definition of legal representative.

3   See rule 6.4(4).

3.10 A legal representative who signs a statement of truth must sign in his own name and not that of his firm or employer.

## Consequences of failure to verify

4.1   If a statement of case is not verified by a statement of truth, the statement of case will remain effective unless it is struck out,[1] but a party may not rely on the contents of a statement of case as evidence until it has been verified by a statement of truth.

4.2   Any party may apply to the court for an order that unless within such period as the court may specify the statement of case is verified by the service of a statement of truth, the statement of case will be struck out.

4.3   The usual order for the costs of an application referred to in paragraph 4.2 will be that the costs be paid by the party who had failed to verify in any event and forthwith.

## Penalty

5. Attention is drawn to rule 32.14 which sets out the consequences of verifying a statement of case containing a false statement without an honest belief in its truth.

PART 25

INTERIM REMEDIES

### 25.1   Orders for interim remedies

(1) The court may grant the following interim remedies—

(a) an interim injunction (GL);
(b) an interim declaration;
(c) an order—
    (i)   for the detention, custody or preservation of relevant property;
    (ii)  for the inspection of relevant property;
    (iii) for the taking of a sample of relevant property;
    (iv)  for the carrying out of an experiment on or with relevant property;
    (v)   for the sale of relevant property which is of a perishable nature or which for any other good reason it is desirable to sell quickly; and
    (vi)  for the payment of income from relevant property until a claim is decided;
(d) an order authorising a person to enter any land or building in the possession of a party to the proceedings for the purposes of carrying out an order under sub-paragraph (c);
(e) an order under section 4 of the Torts (Interference with Goods) Act 1977 to deliver up goods;
(f) an order (referred to as a 'freezing injunction' (GL))—
    (i)  restraining a party from removing from the jurisdiction assets located there; or
    (ii) restraining a party from dealing with any assets whether located within the jurisdiction or not;
(g) an order directing a party to provide information about the location of relevant property or assets or to provide information about relevant property or assets which are or may be the subject of an application for a freezing injunction (GL);
(h) an order (referred to as a 'search order') under section 7 of the Civil Procedure Act 1997 (order requiring a party to admit another party to premises for the purpose of preserving evidence etc);
(i) an order under section 33 of the Supreme Court Act 1981 or section 52 of the County Courts Act 1984 (order for disclosure of documents or inspection of property before a claim has been made);

---

1     See rule 22.2(1).

(j) an order under section 34 of the Supreme Court Act 1981 or section 53 of the County Courts Act 1984 (order in certain proceedings for disclosure of documents or inspection of property against a non-party);

(k) an order (referred to as an order for interim payment) under rule 25.6 for payment by a defendant on account of any damages, debt or other sum (except costs) which the court may hold the defendant liable to pay;

(l) an order for a specified fund to be paid into court or otherwise secured, where there is a dispute over a party's right to the fund;

(m) an order permitting a party seeking to recover personal property to pay money into court pending the outcome of the proceedings and directing that, if he does so, the property shall be given up to him; and

(n) an order directing a party to prepare and file accounts relating to the dispute.

(Rule 34.2 provides for the court to issue a witness summons requiring a witness to produce documents to the court at the hearing or on such date as the court may direct)

(2) In paragraph (1)(c) and (g), 'relevant property' means property (including land) which is the subject of a claim or as to which any question may arise on a claim.

(3) The fact that a particular kind of interim remedy is not listed in paragraph (1) does not affect any power that the court may have to grant that remedy.

(4) The court may grant an interim remedy whether or not there has been a claim for a final remedy of that kind.

### 25.2 Time when an order for an interim remedy may be made

(1) An order for an interim remedy may be made at any time, including—

(a) before proceedings are started; and
(b) after judgment has been given.

(Rule 7.2 provides that proceedings are started when the court issues a claim form)

(2) However—

(a) paragraph (1) is subject to any rule, practice direction or other enactment which provides otherwise;

(b) the court may grant an interim remedy before a claim has been made only if—
 (i) the matter is urgent; or
 (ii) it is otherwise desirable to do so in the interests of justice; and

(c) unless the court otherwise orders, a defendant may not apply for any of the orders listed in rule 25.1(1) before he has filed either an acknowledgment of service or a defence.

(Part 10 provides for filing an acknowledgment of service and Part 15 for filing a defence)

(3) Where the court grants an interim remedy before a claim has been commenced, it may give directions requiring a claim to be commenced.

(4) In particular, the court need not direct that a claim be commenced where the application is made under section 33 of the Supreme Court Act 1981 or section 52 of the County Courts Act 1984 (order for disclosure, inspection etc before commencement of a claim).

### 25.3 How to apply for an interim remedy

(1) The court may grant an interim remedy on an application made without notice if it appears to the court that there are good reasons for not giving notice.

(2) An application for an interim remedy must be supported by evidence, unless the court orders otherwise.

(3) If the applicant makes an application without giving notice, the evidence in support of the application must state the reasons why notice has not been given.

(Part 3 lists general powers of the court)

(Part 23 contains general rules about making an application)

**25.4   Application for an interim remedy where there is no related claim**

(1) This rule applies where a party wishes to apply for an interim remedy but—

    (a) the remedy is sought in relation to proceedings which are taking place, or will take place, outside the jurisdiction; or

    (b) the application is made under section 33 of the Supreme Court Act 1981 or section 52 of the County Courts Act 1984 (order for disclosure, inspection etc before commencement) before a claim has been commenced.

(2) An application under this rule must be made in accordance with the general rules about applications contained in Part 23.

  (The following provisions are also relevant—

    – Rule 25.5 (inspection of property before commencement or against a non-party)
    – Rule 31.16 (orders for disclosure of documents before proceedings start)
    – Rule 31.17 (orders for disclosure of documents against a person not a party))

**25.5   Inspection of property before commencement or against a non-party**

(1) This rules applies where a person makes an application under—

    (a) section 33(1) of the Supreme Court Act 1981 or section 52(1) of the County Courts Act 1984 (inspection etc of property before commencement);

    (b) section 34(3) of the Supreme Court Act 1981 or section 53(3) of the County Courts Act 1984 (inspection etc of property against a non-party).

(2) The evidence in support of such an application must show, if practicable by reference to any statement of case prepared in relation to the proceedings or anticipated proceedings, that the property—

    (a) is or may become the subject matter of such proceedings; or

    (b) is relevant to the issues that will arise in relation to such proceedings.

(3) A copy of the application notice and a copy of the evidence in support must be served on—

    (a) the person against whom the order is sought; and

    (b) in relation to an application under section 34(3) of the Supreme Court Act 1981 or section 53(3) of the County Courts Act 1984, every party to the proceedings other than the applicant.

**25.6   Interim payments – general procedure**

(1) The claimant may not apply for an order for an interim payment before the end of the period for filing an acknowledgment of service applicable to the defendant against whom the application is made.

  (Rule 10.3 sets out the period for filing an acknowledgment of service)

  (Rule 25.1(1)(k) defines an interim payment)

(2) The claimant may make more than one application for an order for an interim payment.

(3) A copy of an application notice for an order for an interim payment must—

(a) be served at least 14 days before the hearing of the application; and
(b) be supported by evidence.

(4) If the respondent to an application for an order for an interim payment wishes to rely on written evidence at the hearing, he must—

(a) file the written evidence; and
(b) serve copies on every other party to the application,

at least 7 days before the hearing of the application.

(5) If the applicant wishes to rely on written evidence in reply, he must—

(a) file the written evidence; and
(b) serve a copy on the respondent,

at least 3 days before the hearing of the application.

(6) This rule does not require written evidence—

(a) to be filed if it has already been filed; or
(b) to be served on a party on whom it has already been served.

(7) The court may order an interim payment in one sum or in instalments.

(Part 23 contains general rules about applications)

### 25.7 Interim payments – conditions to be satisfied and matters to be taken into account

(1) The court may make an order for an interim payment only if—

(a) the defendant against whom the order is sought has admitted liability to pay damages or some other sum of money to the claimant;
(b) the claimant has obtained judgment against that defendant for damages to be assessed or for a sum of money (other than costs) to be assessed;
(c) except where paragraph (3) applies, it is satisfied that, if the claim went to trial, the claimant would obtain judgment for a substantial amount of money (other than costs) against the defendant from whom he is seeking an order for an interim payment; or
(d) the following conditions are satisfied—

   (i) the claimant is seeking an order for possession of land (whether or not any other order is also sought); and
   (ii) the court is satisfied that, if the case went to trial, the defendant would be held liable (even if the claim for possession fails) to pay the claimant a sum of money for the defendant's occupation and use of the land while the claim for possession was pending.

(2) In addition, in a claim for personal injuries the court may make an order for an interim payment of damages only if—

(a) the defendant is insured in respect of the claim;
(b) the defendant's liability will be met by—
   (i) an insurer under section 151 of the Road Traffic Act 1988; or
   (ii) an insurer acting under the Motor Insurers Bureau Agreememnt, or the Motors Insurers Bureau where it is acting itself; or
(c) the defendant is a public body.

(3) In a claim for personal injuries where there are two or more defendants, the court may make an order for the interim payment of damages against any defendant if—

(a) it is satisfied that, if the claim went to trial, the claimant would obtain judgment for substantial damages against at least one of the defendants (even if the court has not yet determined which of them is liable); and

(b) paragraph (2) is satisfied in relation to each of the defendants.

(4) The court must not order an interim payment of more than a reasonable proportion of the likely amount of the final judgment.

(5) The court must take into account—

(a) contributory negligence; and

(b) any relevant set-off or counterclaim.

### 25.8 Powers of court where it has made an order for interim payment

(1) Where a defendant has been ordered to make an interim payment, or has in fact made an interim payment (whether voluntarily or under an order), the court may make an order to adjust the interim payment.

(2) The court may in particular—

(a) order all or part of the interim payment to be repaid;

(b) vary or discharge the order for the interim payment;

(c) order a defendant to reimbuse, either wholly or partly, another defendant who has made an interim payment.

(3) The court may make an order under paragraph (2)(c) only if—

(a) the defendant to be reimbursed made the interim payment in relation to a claim in respect of which he has made a claim against the other defendant for a contribution (GL), indemnity (GL) or other remedy; and

(b) where the claim or part to which the interim payment relates has not been discontinued or disposed of, the circumstances are such that the court could make an order for interim payment under rule 25.7.

(4) The court may make an order under this rule without an application by any party if it makes the order when it disposes of the claim or any part of it.

(5) Where—

(a) a defendant has made an interim payment; and

(b) the amount of the payment is more than his total liability under the final judgment or order,

the court may award him interest on the overpaid amount from the date when he made the interim payment.

### 25.9 Restriction on disclosure of an interim payment

The fact that a defendant has made an interim payment, whether voluntarily or by court order, shall not be disclosed to the trial judge until all questions of liability and the amount of money to be awarded have been decided unless the defendant agrees.

### 25.10 Interim injunction to cease if claim is stayed

If—

(a) the court has granted an interim injunction (GL); and

(b) the claim is stayed (GL) other than by agreement between the parties, the interim injunction (GL) shall be set aside (GL) unless the court orders that it should continue to have effect even though the claim is stayed.

### 25.11   Interim injunction to cease after 14 days if claim struck out

(1) If—

(a) the court has granted an interim injunction (GL); and

(b) the claim is struck out under rule 3.7 (sanctions for non-payment of certain fees),

the interim injunction shall cease to have effect 14 days after the date that the claim is struck out unless paragraph (2) applies.

(2) If the claimant applies to reinstate the claim before the interim injunction ceases to have effect under paragraph (1), the injunction shall continue until the hearing of the application unless the court orders otherwise.

---

## PRACTICE DIRECTION – INTERIM INJUNCTIONS

### THIS PRACTICE DIRECTION SUPPLEMENTS CPR PART 25

**Jurisdiction**

1.1   High Court Judges and any other Judge duly authorised may grant 'search orders'[1] and 'freezing injunctions.'[2]

1.2   In a case in the High Court, Masters and district judges have the power to grant injunctions:

(1)   by consent,

(2)   in connection with charging orders and appointments of receivers,

(3)   in aid of execution of judgments.

1.3   In any other case any Judge who has jurisdiction to conduct the trial of the action has the power to grant an injunction in that action.

1.4   A Master or district judge has the power to vary or discharge an injunction granted by any Judge with the consent of all the parties.

**Making an Application**

2.1   The application notice must state:

(1)   the order sought, and

(2)   the date, time and place of the hearing.

2.2   The application notice and evidence in support must be served as soon as practicable after issue and in any event not less than 3 days before the court is due to hear the application.[3]

2.3   Where the court is to serve, sufficient copies of the application notice and evidence in support for the court and for each respondent should be filed for issue and service.

---

1   Rule 25.1(1)(g).

2   Rule 25.1(1)(f).

3   Rule 23.7(1) and (2) and see rule 23.7(4) (short service).

2.4 Whenever possible a draft of the order sought should be filed with the application notice and a disk containing the draft should also be available to the court. This will enable the court officer to arrange for any amendments to be incorporated and for the speedy preparation and sealing of the order. The current word processing system to be used is WordPerfect 5.1.

**Evidence**

3.1 Applications for search orders and freezing injunctions must be supported by affidavit evidence.

3.2 Applications for other interim injunctions must be supported by evidence set out in either:

(1) a witness statement, or

(2) a statement of case provided that it is verified by a statement of truth,[1] or

(3) the application provided that it is verified by a statement of truth,

unless the court, an Act, a rule or a practice direction requires evidence by affidavit.

3.3 The evidence must set out the facts on which the applicant relies for the claim being made against the respondent, including all material facts of which the court should be made aware.

3.4 Where an application is made without notice to the respondent, the evidence must also set out why notice was not given.

(See Part 32 and the practice direction that supplements it for information about evidence.)

**Urgent Applications and Applications without Notice**

4.1 These fall into two categories;

(1) applications where a claim form has already been issued, and

(2) applications where a claim form has not yet been issued,

and, in both cases, where notice of the application has not been given to the respondent.

4.2 These applications are normally dealt with at a court hearing but cases of extreme urgency may be dealt with by telephone.

4.3 Applications dealt with at a court hearing after issue of a claim form:

(1) the application notice, evidence in support and a draft order (as in 2.4 above) should be filed with the court two hours before the hearing wherever possible,

(2) if an application is made before the application notice has been issued, a draft order (as in 2.4 above) should be provided at the hearing, and the application notice and evidence in support must be filed with the court on the same or next working day or as ordered by the court, and

(3) except in cases where secrecy is essential, the applicant should take steps to notify the respondent informally of the application.

4.4 Applications made before the issue of a claim form:

(1) in addition to the provisions set out at 4.3 above, unless the court orders otherwise, either the applicant must undertake to the court to issue a claim form immediately or the court will give directions for the commencement of the claim,[2]

1 See Part 22.
2 Rule 25.2(3).

(2)    where possible the claim form should be served with the order for the injunction,

(3)    an order made before the issue of a claim form should state in the title after the names of the applicant and respondent 'the Claimant and Defendant in an Intended Action'.

4.5    Applications made by telephone:

(1)    where it is not possible to arrange a hearing, application can be made between 10.00 am and 5.00 pm weekdays by telephoning the Royal Courts of Justice on 0171 936 6000 and asking to be put in contact with a High Court Judge of the appropriate Division available to deal with an emergency application in a High Court matter. In county court proceedings, the appropriate county court should be contacted.

(2)    where an application is made outside those hours the applicant should either—

(a)    telephone the Royal Courts of Justice on 0171 936 6000 where he will be put in contact with the clerk to the appropriate Duty Judge in the High Court (or the appropriate area Circuit Judge where known), or

(b)    the Urgent Court Business Officer of the appropriate Circuit who will contact the local Duty Judge.

(3)    where the facility is available it is likely that the Judge will require a draft order to be faxed to him,

(4)    the application notice and evidence in support must be filed with the court on the same or next working day or as ordered, together with two copies of the order for sealing;

(5)    injunctions will be heard by telephone only where the applicant is acting by counsel or solicitors.

## Orders for Injunctions

5.1    Any order for an injunction, unless the court orders otherwise, must contain:

(1)    an undertaking by the applicant to the court to pay any damages which the respondent(s) (or any other party served with or notified of the order) sustain which the court considers the applicant should pay,

(2)    if made without notice to any other party, an undertaking by the applicant to the court to serve on the respondent the application notice, evidence in support and any order made as soon as practicable.

(3)    if made without notice to any other party, a return date for a further hearing at which the other party can be present,

(4)    if made before filing the application notice, an undertaking to file and pay the appropriate fee on the same or next working day, and

(5)    if made before issue of a claim form—

(a)    an undertaking to issue and pay the appropriate fee on the same or next working day, or

(b)    directions for the commencement of the claim.

5.2    An order for an injunction made in the presence of all parties to be bound by it or made at a hearing of which they have had notice, may state that it is effective until trial or further order.

5.3   Any order for an injunction must set out clearly what the respondent must do or not do.

## FREEZING INJUNCTIONS

### Orders to restrain disposal of assets worldwide and within England and Wales

6      Examples of Freezing Injunctions are annexed to this practice direction.

## SEARCH ORDERS

### Orders for the preservation of evidence and property

7.1   The following provisions apply to search orders in addition to those listed above.

### The Supervising Solicitor

7.2   The Supervising Solicitor must be experienced in the operation of search orders. A Supervising Solicitor may be contacted either through the Law Society or, for the London area, through the London Solicitors Litigation Association.

7.3   Evidence:

   (1)   the affidavit must state the name, firm and its address, and experience of the Supervising Solicitor, also the address of the premises and whether it is a private or business address, and

   (2)   the affidavit must disclose very fully the reason the order is sought, including the probability that relevant material would disappear if the order were not made.

7.4   Service:

   (1)   the order must be served personally by the Supervising Solicitor, unless the court otherwise orders, and must be accompanied by the evidence in support and any documents capable of being copied,

   (2)   confidential exhibits need not be served but they must be made available for inspection by the respondent in the presence of the applicant's solicitors while the order is carried out and afterwards be retained by the respondent's solicitors on their undertaking not to permit the respondent—

      (a)   to see them or copies of them except in their presence, and

      (b)   to make or take away any note or record of them,

   (3)   the Supervising Solicitor may be accompanied only by the persons mentioned in the order,

   (4)   the Supervising Solicitor must explain the terms and effect of the order to the respondent in every day language and advise him of his right to—

      (a)   legal advice, and

      (b)   apply to vary or discharge the order,

   (5)   where the Supervising Solicitor is a man and the respondent is likely to be an unaccompanied woman, at least one other person named in the order must be a woman and must accompany the Supervising Solicitor, and

   (6)   the order may only be served between 9.30 am and 5.30 pm Monday to Friday unless the court otherwise orders.

7.5 Search and custody of materials:

(1)   no material shall be removed unless clearly covered by the terms of the order,

(2)   the premises must not be searched and no items shall be removed from them except in the presence of the respondent or a person who appears to be a responsible employee of the respondent,

(3)   where copies of documents are sought, the documents should be retained for no more than 2 days before return to the owner,

(4)   where material in dispute is removed pending trial, the applicant's solicitors should place it in the custody of the respondent's solicitors on their undertaking to retain it in safekeeping and to produce it to the court when required,

(5)   in appropriate cases the applicant should insure the material retained in the respondent's solicitors' custody,

(6)   the Supervising Solicitor must make a list of all material removed from the premises and supply a copy of the list to the respondent,

(7)   no material shall be removed from the premises until the respondent has had reasonable time to check the list,

(8)   if any of the listed items exists only in computer readable form, the respondent must immediately give the applicant's solicitors effective access to the computers, with all necessary passwords, to enable them to be searched, and cause the listed items to be printed out,

(9)   the applicant must take all reasonable steps to ensure that no damage is done to any computer or data,

(10) the applicant and his representatives may not themselves search the respondent's computers unless they have sufficient expertise to do so without damaging the respondent's system,

(11) the Supervising Solicitor shall provide a report on the carrying out of the order to the applicant's solicitors.

(12) as soon as the report is received the applicant's solicitors shall—

(a)  serve a copy of it on the respondent, and

(b)  file a copy of it with the court, and

(13) where the Supervising Solicitor is satisfied that full compliance with paragraph 7.5(7) and (8) above is impracticable, he may permit the search to proceed and items to be removed without compliance with the impracticable requirements.

## General

8.1   The Supervising Solicitor must not be an employee or member of the applicant's firm of solicitors.

8.2   If the court orders that the order need not be served by the Supervising Solicitor, the reason for so ordering must be set out in the order.

8.3   The search order must not be carried out at the same time as a police search warrant.

8.4   There is no privilege against self incrimination in Intellectual Property cases (see the Supreme Court Act 1981 s 72) therefore in those cases, paragraph (4) of the Respondent's Entitlements and any other references to incrimination in the Search Order, should be removed.

8.5  Applications in Intellectual Property cases should be made in the Chancery Division.

8.6  An example of a Search Order is annexed to this Practice Direction.

---

## PART 31

## DISCLOSURE AND INSPECTION OF DOCUMENTS

### 31.1  Scope of this Part

(1) This Part sets out rules about the disclosure and inspection of documents.

(2) This Part applies to all claims except a claim on the small claims track.

### 31.2  Meaning of disclosure

A party discloses a document by stating that the document exists or has existed.

### 31.3  Right of inspection of a disclosed document

(1) A party to whom a document has been disclosed has a right to inspect that document except where—

   (a)  the document is no longer in the control of the party who disclosed it;
   (b)  the party disclosing the document has a right or a duty to withhold inspection of it; or
   (c)  paragraph (2) applies.

   (Rule 31.8 sets out when a document is in the control of a party)

   (Rule 31.19 sets out the procedure for claiming a right or duty to withhold inspection)

(2) Where a party considers that it would be disproportionate to the issues in the case to permit inspection of documents within a category or class of document disclosed under rule 31.6(b)—

   (a)  he is not required to permit inspection of documents within that category or class; but

   (b)  he must state in his disclosure statement that inspection of those documents will not be permitted on the grounds that to do so would be disproportionate.

   (Rule 31.6 provides for standard disclosure)

   (Rule 31.10 makes provision for a disclosure statement)

   (Rule 31.12 provides for a party to apply for an order for specific inspection of documents)

### 31.4  Meaning of document

In this Part—

   'document' means anything in which information of any description is recorded; and 'copy', in relation to a document, means anything onto which information recorded in the document has been copied, by whatever means and whether directly or indirectly.

### 31.5  Disclosure limited to standard disclosure

(1) An order to give disclosure is an order to give standard disclosure unless the court directs otherwise.

(2) The court may dispense with or limit standard disclosure.

(3) The parties may agree in writing to dispense with or to limit standard disclosure.

(The court may make an order requiring standard disclosure under rule 28.3 which deals with directions in relation to cases on the fast track and under rule 29.2 which deals with case management in relation to cases on the multi-track)

### 31.6    Standard disclosure – what documents are to be disclosed

Standard disclosure requires a party to disclose only—

(a)  the documents on which he relies; and
(b)  the documents which—
    (i)   adversely affect his own case;
    (ii)  adversely affect another party's case; or
    (iii) support another party's case; and
(c)  the documents which he is required to disclose by a relevant practice direction.

### 31.7    Duty of search

(1) When giving standard disclosure, a party is required to make a reasonable search for documents falling within rule 31.6(b) or (c).

(2) The factors relevant in deciding the reasonableness of a search include the following—

(a)  the number of documents involved;
(b)  the nature and complexity of the proceedings;
(c)  the ease and expense of retrieval of any particular document; and
(d)  the significance of any document which is likely to be located during the search.

(3) Where a party has not searched for a category or class of document on the grounds that to do so would be unreasonable, he must state this in his disclosure statement and identify the category or class of document.

(Rule 31.10 makes provision for a disclosure statement)

### 31.8    Duty of disclosure limited to documents which are or have been in party's control

(1) A party's duty to disclose documents is limited to documents which are or have been in his control.

(2) For this purpose a party has or has had a document in his control if—

(a)  it is or was in his physical possession;
(b)  he has or has had a right to possession of it; or
(c)  he has or has had a right to inspect or take copies of it.

### 31.9    Disclosure of copies

(1) A party need not disclose more than one copy of a document.

(2) A copy of a document that contains a modification, obliteration or other marking or feature—

(a)  on which a party intends to rely; or
(b)  which adversely affects his own case or another party's case or supports another party's case;

shall be treated as a separate document.

(Rule 31.4 sets out the meaning of a copy of a document)

**31.10   Procedure for standard disclosure**

(1) The procedure for standard disclosure is as follows.

(2) Each party must make, and serve on every other party, a list of documents in the relevant practice form.

(3) The list must identify the documents in a covenient order and manner and as concisely as possible.

(4) The list must indicate—

  (a) those documents in respect of which the party claims a right or duty to withhold inspection; and

  (b)  (i)  those documents which are no longer in the party's control; and
       (ii) what has happened to those documents.

  (Rules 31.19(3) and (4) require a statement in the list of documents relating to any documents inspection of which a person claims he has a right or duty to withhold)

(5) The list must include a disclosure statement.

(6) A disclosure statement is a statement made by the party disclosing the documents—

  (a) setting out the extent of the search that has been made to locate documents which he is required to disclose;

  (b) certifying that he understands the duty to disclose documents; and

  (c) certifying that to the best of his knowledge he has carried out that duty.

(7) Where the party making the disclosure statement is a company, firm, association or other organisation, the statement must also—

  (a) identify the person making the statement; and

  (b) explain why his is considered an appropriate person to make the statement.

(8) The parties may agree in writing—

  (a) to disclose documents without making a list; and

  (b) to disclose documents without the disclosing party making a disclosure statement.

(9) A disclosure statement may be made by a person who is not a party where this is permitted by a relevant practice direction.

**31.11   Duty of disclosure continues during proceedings**

(1) Any duty of disclosure continues until the proceedings are concluded.

(2) If documents to which that duty extends come to a party's notice at any time during the proceedings, he must immediately notify every other party.

**31.12   Specific disclosure or inspection**

(1) The court may make an order for specific disclosure or specific inspection.

(2) An order for specific disclosure is an order that a party must do one or more of the following things—

  (a) disclose documents or classes of documents specified in the order;

  (b) carry out a search to the extent stated in the order;

  (c) disclose any documents located as a result of that search.

(3) An order for specific inspection is an order that a party permits inspection of a document referred to in rule 31.3(2).

(Rule 31.3(2) allows a party to state in his disclosure statement that he will not permit inspection of a document on the grounds that it would be disproportionate to do so)

### 31.13  Disclosure in stages

The parties may agree in writing, or the court may direct, that disclosure or inspection or both shall take place in stages.

### 31.14  Documents referred to in statements of case etc.

A party may inspect a document mentioned in—

  (a)  a statement of case;
  (b)  a witness statement;
  (c)  a witness summary;
  (d)  an affidavit(GL); or
  (e)  subject to rule 35.10(4), an expert's report.

(Rule 35.10(4) makes provision in relation to instructions referred to in an expert's report)

### 31.15  Inspection and copying of documents

Where a party has a right to inspect a document—

  (a)  that party must give the party who disclosed the document written notice of his wish to inspect it;
  (b)  the party who disclosed the document must permit inspection not more than 7 days after the date on which he received the notice; and
  (c)  that party may request a copy of the document and, if he also undertakes to pay reasonable copying costs, the party who disclosed the document must supply him with a copy not more than 7 days after the date on which he received the request.

(Rule 31.3 and 31.14 deal with the right of a party to inspect a document)

### 31.16  Disclosure before proceedings start

(1) This rule applies where an application is made to the court under any Act for disclosure before proceedings have started.

(2) The application must be supported by evidence.

(3) The court may make an order under this rule only where—

  (a)  the respondent is likely to be a party to subsequent proceedings;
  (b)  the applicant is also likely to be a party to those proceedings;
  (c)  if proceedings had started, the respondent's duty by way of standard disclosure, set out in rule 31.6, would extend to the documents or classes of documents of which the applicant seeks disclosure; and
  (d)  disclosure before proceedings have started is desirable in order to—
    (i)  dispose fairly of the anticipated proceedings;
    (ii)  assist the dispute to be resolved without proceedings; or
    (iii)  save costs.

(4) An order under this rule must—

  (a)  specify the documents or the classes of documents which the respondent must disclose; and
  (b)  require him, when making disclosure, to specify any of those documents—

    (i)  which are no longer in his control; or

    (ii)  in respect of which he claims a right or duty to withhold inspection.

(5) Such an order may—

    (a)  require the respondent to indicate what has happened to any documents which are no longer in his control; and

    (b)  specify the time and place for disclosure and inspection.

### 31.17   Orders for disclosure against a person not a party

(1) This rule applies where an application is made to the court under any Act for disclosure by a person who is not a party to the proceedings.

(2) The application must be supported by evidence.

(3) The court may make an order under this rule only where—

    (a)  the documents of which disclosure is sought are likely to support the case of the applicant or adversely affect the case of one of the other parties to the proceedings; and

    (b)  disclosure is necesssary in order to dispose fairly of the claim or to save costs.

(4) An order under this rule must—

    (a)  specify the documents or the classes of documents which the respondent must disclose; and

    (b)  require the respondent, when making disclosure, to specify any of these documents—

        (i)  which are no longer in his control; or

        (ii)  in respect of which he claims a right or duty to withhold inspection.

(5) Such an order may—

    (a)  require the respondent to indicate what has happened to any documents which are no longer in his control; and

    (b)  specify the time and place for disclosure and inspection.

### 31.18   Rules not to limit other powers of the court to order disclosure

Rules 31.16 and 31.17 do not limit any other power which the court may have to order—

    (a)  disclosure before proceedings have started; and

    (b)  disclosure against a person who is not a party to proceedings.

### 31.19   Claim to withhold inspection or disclosure of a document

(1) A person may apply, without notice, for an order permitting him to withhold disclosure of a document on the ground that disclosure would damage the public interest.

(2) Unless the court orders otherwise, an order of the court under paragraph (1)—

    (a)  must not be served on any other person; and

    (b)  must not be open to inspection by any person.

(3) A person who wishes to claim that he has a right or a duty to withhold inspection of a document, or part of a document must state in writing—

    (a)  that he has such a right or duty; and

    (b)  the grounds on which he claims that right or duty.

(4) The statement referred to in paragraph (3) must be made—

    (a)  in the list in which the document is disclosed; or

(b) if there is no list, to the person wishing to inspect the document.

(5) A party may apply to the court to decide whether a claim made under paragraph (3) should be upheld.

(6) For the purpose of deciding an application under paragraph (1) (application to withhold disclosure) or paragraph (3) (claim to withhold inspection) the court may—

(a) require the person seeking to withhold disclosure or inspection of a document to produce that document to the court; and
(b) invite any person, whether or not a party, to make representations.

(7) An application under paragraph (1) or paragraph (5) must be supported by evidence.

(8) This Part does not affect any rule of law which permits or requires a document to be withheld from disclosure or inspection on the ground that its disclosure or inspection would damage the public interest.

### 31.20 Restriction on use of a privileged document inspection of which has been inadvertently allowed

Where a party inadvertently allows a privileged (GL) document to be inspected, the party who has inspected the document may use it or its contents only with the permission of the court.

### 31.21 Consequence of failure to disclose documents or permit inspection

A party may not rely on any document which he fails to disclose or in respect of which he fails to permit inspection unless the court gives permission.

### 31.22 Subsequent use of disclosed documents

(1) A party to whom a document has been disclosed may use the document only for the purpose of the proceedings in which it is disclosed, except where—

(a) the document has been read to or by the court, or referred to, at a hearing which has been held in public;
(b) the court gives permission; or
(c) the party who disclosed the document and the person to whom the document belongs agree.

(2) The court may make an order restricting or prohibiting the use of a document which has been disclosed, even where the document has been read to or by the court, or referred to, at a hearing which has been held in public.

(3) An application for such an order may be made—

(a) by a party; or
(b) by any person to whom the document belongs.

---

## PRACTICE DIRECTION – DISCLOSURE AND INSPECTION

### THIS PRACTICE DIRECTION SUPPLEMENTS CPR PART 31

**GENERAL**

1.1 The normal order for disclosure will be an order that the parties give standard disclosure.

1.2 In order to give standard disclosure the disclosing party must make a reasonable search for documents falling within the paragraphs of rule 31.6.

1.3   Having made the search the disclosing party must (unless rule 31.10(8) applies) make a list of the documents of whose existence the party is aware that fall within those paragraphs and which are or have been in the party's control (see rule 31.8).

1.4   The obligations imposed by an order for standard disclosure may be dispensed with or limited either by the court or by written agreement between the parties. Any such written agreement should be lodged with the court.

## THE SEARCH

2.    The extent of the search which must be made will depend upon the circumstances of the case including, in particular, the factors referred to in rule 31.7(2). The parties should bear in mind the overriding principle of proportionality (see rule 1.1(2)(c)). It may, for example, be reasonable to decide not to search for documents coming into existence before some particular date, or to limit the search for documents in some particular place or places, or to documents falling into particular categories.

## THE LIST

3.1   The list should be in practice form N265.

3.2   In order to comply with rule 31.10(3) it will normally be necessary to list the documents in date order, to number them consecutively and to give each a concise description (eg letter, claimant to defendant). Where there is a large number of documents all falling into a particular category the disclosing party may list those documents as a category rather than individually eg 50 bank statements relating to account number ___ at ___ Bank, ___ 19 ___ to ___ 19 ___; or, 35 letters passing between ___ and ___ between ___ 19 ___ and ___ 19 ___

3.3   The obligations imposed by an order for disclosure will continue until the proceedings come to an end. If, after a list of documents has been prepared and served, the existence of further documents to which the order applies comes to the attention of the disclosing party, the party must prepare and serve a supplemental list.

## DISCLOSURE STATEMENT

4.1   A list of documents must (unless rule 31.10(8)(b) applies) contain a disclosure statement complying with rule 31.10. The form of disclosure statement is set out in Annex A to this practice direction.

4.2   The disclosure statement should:

(1)   expressly state that the disclosing party believes the extent of the search to have been reasonable in all the circumstances, and

(2)   in setting out the extent of the search (see rule 31.10(6)) draw attention to any particular limitations on the extent of the search which were adopted for proportionality reasons and give the reasons why the limitations were adopted eg the difficulty or expense that a search not subject to those limitations would have entailed or the marginal relevance of categories of documents omitted from the search.

4.3   Where rule 31.10(7) applies, the details given in the disclosure statement about the person making the statement must include his name and address and the office or position he holds in the disclosing party.

4.4 If the disclosing party has a legal representative acting for him, the legal representative must endeavour to ensure that the person making the disclosure statement (whether the disclosing party or, in a case to which rule 31.10(7) applies, some other person) understands the duty of disclosure under rule 31.

4.5 If the disclosing party wishes to claim that he has a right or duty to withhold a document, or part of a document, in his list of documents from inspection (see rule 31.19(3)), he must state in writing:

(1) that he has such a right or duty, and
(2) the grounds on which he claims that right or duty.

4.6 The statement referred to in paragraph 4.5 above should normally be included in the disclosure statement and must identify the document, or part of a document, to which the claim relates.

## SPECIFIC DISCLOSURE

5.1 If a party believes that the disclosure of documents given by a disclosing party is inadequate he may make an application for an order for specific disclosure (see rule 31.12).

5.2 The application notice must specify the order that the applicant intends to ask the court to make and must be supported by evidence (see rule 31.12(2) which describes the orders the court may make).

5.3 The grounds on which the order is sought may be set out in the application notice itself but if not there set out must be set out in evidence filed in support of the application.

5.4 In deciding whether or not to make an order for specific disclosure the court will take into account all the circumstances of the case and, in particular, the overriding objective described in Part 1. But if the court concludes that the party from whom specific disclosure is sought has failed adequately to comply with the obligations imposed by an order for disclosure (whether by failing to make a sufficient search for documents or otherwise) the court will usually make such order as is necessary to ensure that those obligations are properly complied with.

## CLAIMS TO WITHHOLD DISCLOSURE OR INSPECTION OF A DOCUMENT

6.1 A claim to withhold inspection of a document, or part of a document, disclosed in a list of documents does not require an application to the court. Where such a claim has been made, a party who wishes to challenge it must apply to the court (see rule 31.19(5)).

6.2 Rule 31.19(1) and (6) provide a procedure enabling a party to apply for an order permitting disclosure of the existence of a document to be withheld.

## ANNEX

### DISCLOSURE STATEMENT

I, the above named claimant [or defendant] [if party making disclosure is a company, firm or other organisation identify here who the person making the disclosure statement is and why he is the appropriate person to make it] state that I have carried out a reasonable and proportionate search to locate all the documents which I am required to disclose under the order made by the court on       day of       . I did not search:
(1) for documents predating _____,
(2) for documents located elsewhere than _____,
(3) for documents in categories other than _____.

I certify that I understand the duty of disclosure and to the best of my knowledge I have carried out that duty. I certify that the list above is a complete list of all documents which are or have been in my control and which I am obliged under the said order to disclose.

---

## PART 32

## EVIDENCE

### 32.1  Power of court to control evidence

(1) The court may control the evidence by giving directions as to—

    (a) the issues on which it requires evidence;

    (b) the nature of the evidence which it requires to decide those issues; and

    (c) the way in which the evidence is to be placed before the court.

(2) The court may use its power under this rule to exclude evidence that would otherwise be admissible.

(3) The court may limit cross-examination(GL).

### 32.2  Evidence of witnesses – general rule

(1) The general rule is that any fact which needs to be proved by the evidence of witnesses is to be proved—

    (a) at trial, by their oral evidence given in public; and

    (b) at any other hearing, by their evidence in writing.

(2) This is subject—

    (a) to any provision to the contrary contained in these Rules or elsewhere; or

    (b) to any order of the court.

### 32.3  Evidence by video link or other means

The court may allow a witness to give evidence through a video link or by other means.

### 32.4  Requirement to serve witness statements for use at trial

(1) A witness statement is a written statement signed by a person which contains the evidence which that person would be allowed to give orally.

(2) The court will order a party to serve on the other parties any witness statement of the oral evidence which the party serving the statement intends to rely on in relation to any issues of fact to be decided at the trial.

(3) The court may give directions as to—

    (a) the order in which witness statements are to be served; and

    (b) whether or not the witness statements are to be filed.

### 32.5  Use at trial of witness statements which have been served

(1) If—

    (a) a party has served a witness statement; and

    (b) he wishes to rely at trial on the evidence of the witness who made the statement, he must call the witness to give oral evidence unless the court orders otherwise or he puts the statement in as hearsay evidence.

(Part 33 contains provisions about hearsay evidence)

(2) Where a witness is called to give oral evidence under paragraph (1), his witness statement shall stand as his evidence in chief (GL) unless the court orders otherwise.

(3) A witness giving oral evidence at trial may with the permission of the court—

(a) amplify his witness statement; and
(b) give evidence in relation to new matters which have arisen since the witness statement was served on the other parties.

(4) The court will give permission under paragraph (3) only if it considers that there is good reason not to confine the evidence of the witness to the contents of his witness statement.

(5) If a party who has served a witness statement does not—

(a) call the witness to give evidence at trial; or
(b) put the witness statement in as hearsay evidence,

any other party may put the witness statement in as hearsay evidence.

### 32.6   Evidence in proceedings other than a trial

(1) Subject to paragraph (2), the general rule is that evidence at hearings other than the trial is to be by witness statement unless the court, a practice direction or any other enactment requires otherwise.

(2) A hearings other than the trial, a party may, in support of his application, rely on the matters set out in—

(a) his statement of case; or
(b) his application notice,

if the statement of case or application notice is verified by a statement of truth.

### 32.7   Order for cross-examination

(1) Where, at a hearing other than the trial, evidence is given in writing, any party may apply to the court for permission to cross-examine the person giving the evidence.

(2) If the court gives permission under paragraph (1) but the person in question does not attend as required by the order, his evidence may not be used unless the court gives permission.

### 32.8   Form of witness statement

A witness statement must comply with the requirements set out in the relevant practice direction.

(Part 22 requires a witness statement to be verified by a statement of truth)

### 32.9   Witness summaries

(1) A party who—

(a) is required to serve a witness statement for use at trial; but
(b) is unable to obtain one,

may apply, without notice, for permission to serve a witness summary instead.

(2) A witness summary is a summary of—

    (a)  the evidence, if known, which would otherwise be included in a witness statement; or

    (b)  if the evidence is not known, the matters about which the party serving the witness summary proposes to question the witness.

(3) Unless the court orders otherwise, a witness summary must include the name and address of the intended witness.

(4) Unless the court orders otherwise, a witness summary must be served within the period in which a witness statement would have had to be served.

(5) Where a party serves a witness summary, so far as practicable, rules 32.4 (requirement to serve witness statements for use at trial), 32.5(3) (amplifying witness statements), and 32.8 (form of witness statement) shall apply to the summary.

### 32.10　Consequence of failure to serve witness statement or summary

If a witness statement or a witness summary for use at trial is not served in respect of an intended witness within the time specified by the court, then the witness may not be called to give oral evidence unless the court gives permission.

### 32.11　Cross-examination on a witness statement

Where a witness is called to give evidence at trial, he may be cross-examined on his witness statement, whether or not the statement or any part of it was referred to during the witness's evidence in chief(GL).

### 32.12　Use of witness statements for other purposes

(1) Except as provided by this rule, a witness statement may be used only for the purpose of the proceedings in which it is served.

(2) Paragraph (1) does not apply if and to the extent that—

    (a)  the witness gives consent in writing to some other use of it;

    (b)  the court gives permission for some other use; or

    (c)  the witness statement has been put in evidence at a hearing held in public.

### 32.13　Availability of witness statements for inspection

(1) A witness statement which stands as evidence in chief(GL) is open to inspection unless the court otherwise directs during the course of the trial.

(2) Any person may ask for a direction that a witness statement is not open to inspection.

(3) The court will not make a direction under paragraph (2) unless it is satisfied that a witness statement should not be open to inspection because of—

    (a)  the interests of justice;

    (b)  the public interest;

    (c)  the nature of any expert medical evidence in the statement;

    (d)  the nature of any confidential information (including information relating to personal financial matters) in the statement; or

    (e)  the need to protect the interests of any child or patient.

(4) The court may exclude from inspection words or passages in the statement.

## 32.14   False statements

(1) Proceedings for contempt of court may be brought against a person if he makes, or causes to be made, a false statement in a document verified by a statement of truth without an honest belief in its truth.

(Part 22 makes provision for a statement of truth)

(2) Proceedings under this rule may be brought only—

(a) by the Attorney General; or
(b) with the permission of the court.

## 32.15   Affidavit evidence

(1) Evidence must be given by affidavit(GL), instead of or in addition to a witness statement if this is required by the court, a provision contained in any other Rule, a practice direction or any other enactment.

(2) Nothing in these Rules prevents a witness giving evidence by affidavit(GL), at a hearing other than the trial, if he chooses to do so in a case where paragraph (1) does not apply, but the party putting forward the affidavit(GL) may not recover the additional cost of making it from any other party unless the court orders otherwise.

## 32.16   Form of affidavits

An affidavit(GL) must comply with the requirements set out in the relevant practice direction.

## 32.17   Affidavit made outside the jurisdiction

A person may make an affidavit(GL) outside the jurisdiction in accordance with—

(a) this Part; or
(b) the law of the place where he makes the affidavit(GL).

## 32.18   Notice to admit facts

(1) A party may serve notice on another party requiring him to admit the facts, or the part of the case of the serving party, specified in the notice.

(2) A notice to admit facts must be served no later than 21 days before the trial.

(3) Where the other party makes any admission in response to the notice the admission may be used against him only—

(a) in the proceedings in which the notice to admit is served; and
(b) by the party who served the notice.

(4) The court may allow a party to amend or withdraw any admission made by him on such terms as it thinks just.

## 32.19   Notice to admit or produce documents

(1) A party shall be deemed to admit the authenticity of a document disclosed to him under Part 31 (disclosure and inspection of documents) unless he serves notice that he wishes the document to be proved at trial.

(2) A notice to prove a document must be served—

(a) by the latest date for serving witness statements; or

(b) within 7 days of disclosure of the document,

whichever is later.

---

## PRACTICE DIRECTION – WRITTEN EVIDENCE

### THIS PRACTICE DIRECTION SUPPLEMENTS CPR PART 32

### EVIDENCE IN GENERAL

1.1  Rule 32.2 sets out how evidence is to be given and facts are to be proved.

1.2  Evidence at a hearing other than the trial should normally be given by witness statement[1] (see paragraph 17 onwards). However a witness may give evidence by affidavit if he wishes to do so[2] (and see paragraph 1.4 below).

1.3  Statements of case (see paragraph 26 onwards) and application notices[3] may also be used as evidence provided that their contents have been verified by a statement of truth.[4]

(For information regarding evidence by deposition see Part 34 and the practice direction which supplements it.)

1.4  Affidavits must be used as evidence in the following instances:

(1)  where sworn evidence is required by an enactment,[5] Statutory Instrument, rule,[6] order or practice direction,

(2)  in any application for a search order, a freezing injunction, or an order requiring an occupier to permit another to enter his land, and

(3)  in any application for an order against anyone for alleged contempt of court.

1.5  If a party believes that sworn evidence is required by a court in another jurisdiction for any purpose connected with the proceedings, he may apply to the court for a direction that evidence shall be given only by affidavit on any pre-trial applications.

1.6  The court may give a direction under rule 32.15 that evidence shall be given by affidavit instead of or in addition to a witness statement or statement of case:

(1)  on its own initiative, or

(2)  after any party has applied to the court for such a direction.

1.7  An affidavit, where referred to in the Civil Procedure Rules or a practice direction, also means an affirmation unless the context requires otherwise.

### AFFIDAVITS

### Deponent

2  A deponent is a person who gives evidence by affidavit or affirmation.

---

1  See rule 32.6(1).
2  See rule 32.15(2).
3  See Part 23 for information about making an application.
4  Rule 32.6(2) and see Part 22 for information about the statement of truth.
5  See, eg, s 3(5)(a) of the Protection from Harassment Act 1997.
6  See, eg, RSC Ord 115, rr (2B), (14) and others (Confiscation and Forfeiture in Connection with Criminal Proceedings and RSC Ord 110, r 3 (Environmental Control Proceedings – injunctions 'in rem' against unknown Defendant).

**Heading**

3.1 The affidavit should be headed with the name and number of the proceedings and the Court or Division in which they are proceeding; where the proceedings are in more than one matter the heading should state 'In the matter of ... and other matters' but where the proceedings are between parties it is sufficient to set the heading out as follows:

A.B. (and others)                    Claimants/Applicants
C.D. (and others)                    Defendants/Respondents
                                     (as appropriate)

3.2 At the top right hand corner of the first page (and on the back sheet) there should be clearly written:

(1) the party on whose behalf it is made,

(2) the initials and surname of the deponent,

(3) the number of the affidavit in relation to that deponent,

(4) the identifying initials and number of each exhibit referred to, and

(5) the date sworn.

**Body of Affidavit**

4.1 The affidavit must, if practicable, be in the dependent's own words, the affidavit should be expressed in the first person and the deponent should:

(1) commence 'I (*full name*) of (*address*) state on oath ...',

(2) if giving evidence in his professional, business or other occupational capacity, give the address at which he works in (1) above, the position he holds and the name of his firm or employer,

(3) give his occupation or, if he has none, his description, and

(4) state if he is a party to the proceedings or employed by a party to the proceedings, if it be the case.

4.2 An affidavit must indicate:

(1) which of the statements in it are made from the deponent's own knowledge and which are matters of information or belief, and

(2) the source for any matters of information or belief.

4.3 Where a deponent:

(1) refers to an exhibit or exhibits, he should state 'there is now shown to me marked "..." the (*description of exhibit*)', and

(2) makes more than one affidavit (to which there are exhibits) in the same proceedings, the numbering of the exhibits should run consecutively throughout and not start again with each affidavit.

**Jurat**

5.1 The jurat of an affidavit is a statement set out at the end of the document which authenticates the affidavit.

5.2 It must:

(1)  be signed by all deponents,

(2)  be completed and signed by the person before whom the affidavit was sworn whose name and qualification must be printed beneath his signature,

(3)  contain the full address of the person before whom the affidavit was sworn, and

(4)  follow immediately on from the text and not be put on a separate page.

**Format of Affidavits**

6.1  An affidavit should:

(1)  be produced on durable quality A4 paper with a 3.5cm margin,

(2)  be fully legible and should normally be typed on one side of the paper only,

(3)  where possible, be bound securely in a manner which would not hamper filing, or otherwise each page should be endorsed with the case number and should bear the initials of the deponent and of the person before whom it was sworn,

(4)  have the pages numbered consecutively as a separate document (or as one of several documents contained in a file),

(5)  be divided into numbered paragraphs,

(6)  have all numbers, including dates, expressed in figures, and

(7)  give in the margin the reference to any document or documents mentioned.

6.2  It is usually convenient for an affidavit to follow the chronological sequence of events or matters dealt with; each paragraph of an affidavit should as far as possible be confined to a distinct portion of the subject.

**Inability of Deponent to read or sign Affidavit**

7.1  Where an affidavit is sworn by a person who is unable to read or sign it, the person before whom the affidavit is sworn must certify in the jurat that:

(1)  he read the affidavit to the deponent,

(2)  the deponent appeared to understand it, and

(3)  the deponent signed or made his mark, in his presence.

7.2  If that certificate is not included in the jurat, the affidavit may not be used in evidence unless the court is satisfied that it was read to the deponent and that he appeared to understand it. Two versions of the form of jurat with the certificate are set out at Annex 1 to this practice direction.

**Alterations to Affidavits**

8.1  Any alteration to an affidavit must be initialled by both the deponent and the person before whom the affidavit was sworn.

8.2  An affidavit which contains an alteration that has not been initialled may be filed or used in evidence only with the permission of the court.

**Who may administer oaths and take Affidavits**

9.1  Only the following may administer oaths and take affidavits:

(1)  Commissioners for oaths,[1]

---

1    Commissioner for Oaths Act 1889 and 1891.

(2)   Practising solicitors,[1]

(3)   other persons specified by statute,[2]

(4)   certain officials of the Supreme Court,[3]

(5)   a circuit judge or district judge,[4]

(6)   any justice of the peace,[5] and

(7)   certain officials of any County Court appointed by the Judge of that court for the purpose.[6]

9.2   An affidavit must be sworn before a person independent of the parties or their representatives.

## Filing of Affidavits

10.1   If the court directs that an affidavit is to be filed,[7] it must be filed in the court or Division, or Office or Registry of the court or Division where the action in which it was or is to be used, is proceeding or will proceed.

10.2   Where an affidavit is in a foreign language:

(1)   the party wishing to rely on it—

(a)   must have a translated, and

(b)   must file the foreign language affidavit with the court, and

(2)   the translator must make and file with the court an affidavit verifying the translation and exhibiting both the translation and a copy of the foreign language affidavit.

## EXHIBITS

## Manner of Exhibiting Documents

11.1   A document used in conjunction with an affidavit should be:

(1)   produced to and verified by the deponent, and remain separate from the affidavit, and

(2)   identified by a declaration of the person before whom the affidavit was sworn.

11.2   The declaration should be headed with the name of the proceedings in the same way as the affidavit.

11.3   The first page of each exhibit should be marked:

(1)   as in paragraph 3.2 above, and

---

1   Section 81 of the Solicitors Act 1974.
2   Section 65 of the Administration of Justice Act 1985, s 113 of the Courts and Legal Services Act 1990 and the Commissioners for Oaths (Prescribed Bodies) Regulations 1994 and 1995.
3   Section 2 of the Commissioners for Oaths Act 1889.
4   Section 58 of the County Courts Act 1984.
5   Section 58 as above.
6   Section 58 as above.
7   Rules 32.1(3) and 32.4(3)(b).

(2)   with the exhibit mark referred to in the affidavit.

## Letters

12.1 Copies of individual letters should be collected together and exhibited in a bundle or bundles. They should be arranged in chronological order with the earliest at the top, and firmly secured.

12.2 When a bundle of correspondence is exhibited, the exhibit should have a front page attached stating that the bundle consists of original letters and copies. They should be arranged and secured as above and numbered consecutively.

## Other documents

13.1 Photocopies instead of original documents may be exhibited provided the originals are made available for inspection by the other parties before the hearing and by the judge at the hearing.

13.2 Court documents must not be exhibited (official copies of such documents prove themselves).

13.3 Where an exhibit contains more than one document, a front page should be attached setting out a list of the documents contained in the exhibit; the list should contain the dates of the documents.

## Exhibits other than documents

14.1 Items other than documents should be clearly marked with an exhibit number or letter in such a manner that the mark cannot become detached from the exhibit.

14.2 Small items may be placed in a container and the container appropriately marked.

## General provisions

15.1 Where an exhibit contains more than one document:

(1)   the bundle should not be stapled but should be securely fastened in a way that does not hinder the reading of the documents, and

(2)   the pages should be numbered consecutively at bottom centre.

15.2 Every page of an exhibit should be clearly legible; typed copies of illegible documents should be included, paginated with 'a' numbers.

15.3 Where affidavits and exhibits have become numerous, they should be put into separate bundles and the pages numbered consecutively throughout.

## Affirmations

16.   All provisions in this or any other practice direction relating to affidavits apply to affirmations with the following exceptions:

(1)   the deponent should commence 'I (*name*) of (*address*) do solemnly and sincerely affirm ...', and

(2)   in the jurat the word 'sworn' is replaced by the word 'affirmed'.

## WITNESS STATEMENTS

## Heading

17.1 The witness statement should be headed with the name and number of the proceedings and the Court or Division in which they are proceeding; where the proceedings are in more than one matter the heading should state 'In the matter of ... and other matters' but where the proceedings are between parties it is sufficient to set the heading out as follows:

| | |
|---|---|
| A.B. (and others) | Claimants/Applicants |
| C.D. (and others) | Defendants/Respondents |
| | (as appropriate) |

17.2 At the top right hand corner of the first page there should be clearly written:

(1) the party on whose behalf it is made,

(2) the initials and surname of the witness,

(3) the number of the statement in relation to that witness,

(4) the identifying initials and number of each exhibit referred to, and

(5) the date the statement was made.

**Body of witness statement**

18.1 The witness statement must, if practicable, be in the intended witness's own words, the statement should be expressed in the first person and should also state:

(1) the full name of the witness,

(2) his place of residence or, if he is making the statement in his professional, business or other occupational capacity, the address at which he works, the position he holds and the name of his firm or employer,

(3) his occupation, or if he has none, his description, and

(4) the fact that he is a party to the proceedings or is the employee of such a party if it be the case.

18.2 A witness statement must indicate:

(1) which of the statements in it are made from the witness's own knowledge and which are matters of information or belief, and

(2) the source for any matters of information or belief.

18.3 An exhibit used in conjunction with a witness statement should be verified and identified by the witness and remain separate from the witness statement.

18.4 Where a witness refers to an exhibit or exhibits, he should state 'I refer to the (*description of exhibit*) marked "...".'

18.5 The provisions of paragraphs 11.3 to 15.3 (exhibits) apply similarly to witness statements as they do to affidavits.

18.6 Where a witness makes more than one witness statement to which there are exhibits, in the same proceedings, the numbering of the exhibits should run consecutively throughout and not start again with each witness statement.

**Format of witness statement**

19.1 A witness statement should:

(1) be produced on durable quality A4 paper with a 3.5 cm margin,

(2) be fully legible and should normally be typed on one side of the paper only,

(3) where possible, be bound securely in a manner which would not hamper filing, or otherwise each page should be endorsed with the case number and should bear the initials of the witness,

(4)   have the pages numbered consecutively as a separate statement (or as one of several statements contained in a file),

(5)   be divided into numbered paragraphs,

(6)   have all numbers, including dates, expressed in figures, and

(7)   give in the margin the reference to any document or documents mentioned.

19.2  It is usually convenient for a witness statement to follow the chronological sequence of the events or matters dealt with, each paragraph of a witness statement should as far as possible be confined to a distinct portion of the subject.

## Statement of Truth

20.1  A witness statement is the equivalent of the oral evidence which that witness would, if called, give in evidence; it must include a statement by the intended witness that he believes the facts in it are true.[1]

20.2  To verify a witness statement the statement of truth is as follows:

'I believe that the facts stated in this witness statement are true'

20.3  Attention is drawn to rule 32.14 which sets out the consequences of verifying a witness statement containing a false statement without an honest belief in its truth.

## Inability of witness to read or sign statement

21.1  Where a witness statement is made by a person who is unable to read or sign the witness statement, it must contain a certificate made by an authorised person.

21.2  An authorised person is a person able to administer oaths and take affidavits but need not be independent of the parties or their representatives.

21.3  The authorised person must certify:

(1)   that the witness statement has been read to the witness,

(2)   that the witness appeared to understand it and approved its content as accurate,

(3)   that the declaration of truth has been read to the witness,

(4)   that the witness appeared to understand the declaration and the consequences of making a false witness statement, and

(5)   that the witness signed or made his mark in the presence of the authorised person.

21.4  The form of the certificate is set out at Annex 2 to this Practice Direction.

## Alterations to witness statements

22.1  Any alteration to a witness statement must be initialled by the person making the statement or by the authorised person where appropriate (see paragraph 21).

22.2  A witness statement which contains an alteration that has not been initialled may be used in evidence only with the permission of the court.

## Filing of witness statements

23.1  If the court directs that a witness statement is to be filed,[2] it must be filed in the court or division, or Office or Registry of the court or Division where the action in which it was or is to be used, is proceeding or will proceed.

---

1     See Part 22 for information about the statement of truth.
2     Rule 32.4(3)(b).

23.2 Where the court has directed that a witness statement in a foreign language is to be filed:

    (1)  the party wishing to rely on it must—

        (a)  have it translated and

        (b)  file the foreign language witness statement with the court, and

    (2)  the translator must make and file with the court an affidavit verifying the translation and exhibiting both the translation and a copy of the foreign language witness statement.

### Certificate of court officer

24.1 Where the court has ordered that a witness statement is not to be open to inspection by the public[1] or that words or passages in the statement are not to be open to inspection[2] the court officer will so certify on the statement and make any deletions directed by the court under rule 28.14(4).

### Defects in affidavits, witness statements and exhibits

25.1 Where:

    (1)  an affidavit,

    (2)  a witness statement, or

    (3)  an exhibit to either an affidavit or a witness statement,

does not comply with Part 32 or this practice direction in relation to its form, the court may refuse to admit it as evidence and may refuse to allow the costs arising from its preparation.

25.2 Permission to file a defective affidavit or witness statement or to use a defective exhibit may be obtained from a Judge[3] in the court where the case is proceeding.

## STATEMENTS OF CASE

26.1 A statement of case may be used as evidence in an interim application provided it is verified by a statement of truth.[4]

26.2 To verify a statement of case the statement of truth should be set out as follows:

'[I believe] [the (*party on whose behalf the statement of case is being signed*) believes] that the facts stated in the statement of case are true'.

26.3 Attention is drawn to rule 32.14 which sets out the consequences of verifying a witness statement containing a false statement without an honest belief in its truth.

(For information regarding statements of truth see Part 22 and the practice direction which supplements it.)

(Practice directions supplementing Parts 7, 9 and 17 provide further information concerning statements of case.)

---

1    Rule 32.13(2).
2    Rule 32.13(4).
3    Rule 2.3(1); definition of judge.
4    See rule 32.6(2)(a).

## ANNEX 1

### Certificate to be used where a deponent to an affidavit is unable to read or sign it

'Sworn at ..................... this ..................... day of ..................... Before me, I having first read over the contents of this affidavit to the deponent [*if there are exhibits, add* 'and explained the nature and effect of the exhibits referred to in it'] who appeared to understand it and approved its content as accurate, and made his mark on the affidavit in my presence.

*Or*, (after, *Before me*) the witness to the mark of the deponent having been first sworn that he had read over etc. (*as above*) and that he saw him make his mark on the affidavit. (*Witness must sign*).

### Certificate to be used where a deponent to an affirmation is unable to read or sign it

'Affirmed at ..................... this ..................... day of ..................... Before me, I having first read over the contents of this affirmation to the deponent [*if there are exhibits, add* 'and explained the nature and effect of the exhibits referred to in it'] who appeared to understand it and approved its content as accurate, and made his mark on the affirmation in my presence.

*Or*, (after, *Before me*) the witness to the mark of the deponent having been first sworn that he had read over etc. (*as above*) and that he saw him make his mark on the affirmation. (*Witness must sign*).

## ANNEX 2

### Certificate to be used where a witness is unable to read or sign a witness statement

I certify that I [*name and address of authorised person*] have read over the contents of this witness statement and the declaration of truth to the witness [*if there are exhibits, add* 'and explained the nature and effect of the exhibits referred to in it'] who appeared to understand (a) the statement and approved its content as accurate and (b) the declaration of truth and the consequences of making a false witness statement, and made his mark in my presence.

---

### PART 33

### MISCELLANEOUS RULES ABOUT EVIDENCE

#### 33.1   Introductory

In this Part—

   (a)  'hearsay' means a statement made otherwise than by a person while giving oral evidence in proceedings which is tendered as evidence of the matters stated; and
   (b)  references to hearsay include hearsay of whatever degree.

#### 33.2   Notice of intention to rely on hearsay evidence

(1)  Where a party intends to rely on hearsay evidence at trial and either—

   (a)  that evidence is to be given by a witness giving oral evidence;
or
   (b)  that evidence is contained in a witness statement of a person who is not being called to give oral evidence;

that party complies with section 2(1)(a) of the Civil Evidence Act 1995 by serving a witness statement on the other parties in accordance with the court's order.

(2) Where paragraph (1)(b) applies, the party intending to rely on the hearsay evidence must, when he serves the witness statement—

(a) inform the other parties that the witness is not being called to give oral evidence; and
(b) give the reason why the witness will not be called.

(3) In all other cases where a party intends to rely on hearsay evidence at trial, that party complies with section 2(1)(a) of the Civil Evidence Act 1995 by serving a notice on the other parties which—

(a) identifies the hearsay evidence;
(b) states that the party serving the notice proposes to rely on the hearsay evidence at trial; and
(c) gives the reason why the witness will not be called.

(4) The party proposing to rely on the hearsay evidence must—

(a) serve the notice no later than the latest date for serving witness statements; and
(b) if the hearsay evidence is to be in a document, supply a copy to any party who requests him to do so.

### 33.3 Circumstances in which notice of intention to rely on hearsay evidence is not required

Section 2(1) of the Civil Evidence Act 1995 (duty to give notice of intention to rely on hearsay evidence) does not apply—

(a) to evidence at hearings other than trials;
(b) to a statement which a party to a probate action wishes to put in evidence and which is alleged to have been made by the person whose estate is the subject of the proceedings; or
(c) where the requirement is excluded by a practice direction.

### 33.4 Power to call witness for cross-examination on hearsay evidence

(1) Where a party—

(a) proposes to rely on hearsay evidence; and
(b) does not propose to call the person who made the original statement to give oral evidence,

the court may, on the application of any other party, permit that party to call the maker of the statement to be cross-examined on the contents of the statement.

(2) An application for permission to cross-examine under this rule must be made not more than 14 days after the day on which a notice of intention to rely on the hearsay evidence was served on the applicant.

### 33.5 Credibility

(1) Where a party—

(a) proposes to rely on hearsay evidence; but
(b) does not propose to call the person who made the original statement to give oral evidence; and
(c) another party wishes to call evidence to attack the credibility of the person who made the statement,

the party who so wishes must give notice of his intention to the party who proposes to give the hearsay statement in evidence.

(2) A party must give notice under paragraph (1) not more than 14 days after the day on which a hearsay notice relating to the hearsay evidence was served on him.

### 33.6   Use of plans, photographs and models as evidence

(1) This rule applies to evidence (such as a plan, photograph or model) which is not—

  (a) contained in a witness statement, affidavit (GL) or expert's report;
  (b) to be given orally at trial; or
  (c) evidence of which prior notice must be given under rule 33.2.

(2) This rule includes documents which may be received in evidence without further proof under section 9 of the Civil Evidence Act 1995.

(3) Unless the court orders otherwise the evidence shall not be receivable at a trial unless the party intending to put it in evidence has given notice to the other parties in accordance with this rule.

(4) Where the party intends to use the evidence as evidence of any fact then, except where paragraph (6) applies, he must give notice not later than the latest date for serving witness statements.

(5) He must give notice at least 21 days before the hearing at which he proposes to put in the evidence, if—

  (a) there are not to be witness statements; or
  (b) he intends to put in the evidence solely in order to disprove an allegation made in a witness statement.

(6) Where the evidence forms part of expert evidence, he must give notice when the expert's report is served on the other party.

(7) Where the evidence is being produced to the court for any reason other than as part of factual or expert evidence, he must give notice at least 21 days before the hearing at which he proposes to put in the evidence.

(8) Where a party has given notice that he intends to put in the evidence, he must give every further party an opportunity to inspect it and to agree to its admission without further proof.

### 33.7   Evidence of finding on question of foreign law

(1) This rule sets out the procedure which must be followed by a party who intends to put in evidence a finding on a question of foreign law by virtue of section 4(2) of the Civil Evidence Act 1972.

(2) He must give any other party notice of his intention.

(3) He must give the notice—

  (a) if there are to be witness statements, not later than the latest date for serving them; or
  (b) otherwise, not less than 21 days before the hearing at which he proposes to put the finding in evidence.

(4) The notice must—

  (a) specify the question on which the finding was made; and
  (b) enclose a copy of a document where it is reported or recorded.

### 33.8   Evidence of consent of trustee to act

A document purporting to contain the written consent of a person to act as trustee and to bear his signature verified by some other person is evidence of such consent.

## PART 34

## DEPOSITIONS AND COURT ATTENDANCE BY WITNESSES

### 34.1 Scope of this Part

(1) This Part provides—

    (a) for the circumstances in which a person may be required to attend court to give evidence or to produce a document; and

    (b) for a party to obtain evidence before a hearing to be used at the hearing.

(2) In this Part, reference to a hearing includes a reference to the trial.

### 34.2 Witness summonses

(1) A witness summons is a document issued by the court requiring a witness to—

    (a) attend court to give evidence; or

    (b) produce documents to the court.

(2) A witness summons must be in the relevant practice form.

(3) There must be a separate witness summons for each witness.

(4) A witness summons may require a witness to produce documents to the court either—

    (a) on the date fixed for a hearing; or

    (b) on such date as the court may direct.

(5) The only documents that a summons under this rule can require a person to produce before a hearing are documents which that person could be required to produce at the hearing.

### 34.3 Issue of a witness summons

(1) A witness summons is issued on the date entered on the summons by the court.

(2) A party must obtain permission from the court where he wishes to—

    (a) have a summons issued less than 7 days before the date of the trial;

    (b) have a summons issued for a witness to attend court to give evidence or to produce documents on any date except the date fixed for the trial; or

    (c) have a summons issued for a witness to attend court to give evidence or to produce documents at any hearing except the trial.

(3) A witness summons must be issued by—

    (a) the court where the case is proceeding; or

    (b) the court where the hearing in question will be held.

(4) The court may set aside(GL) or vary a witness summons issued under this rule.

### 34.4 Witness summons in aid of inferior court or of tribunal

(1) The court may issue a witness summons in aid of an inferior court or of a tribunal.

(2) The court which issued the witness summons under this rule may set it aside.

(3) In this rule, 'inferior court or tribunal' means any court or tribunal that does not have power to issue a witness summons in relation to proceedings before it.

### 34.5 Time for serving a witness summons

(1) The general rule is that a witness summons is binding if it is served at least 7 days before the date on which the witness is required to attend before the court or tribunal.

(2) The court may direct that a witness summons shall be binding although it will be served less than 7 days before the date on which the witness is required to attend before the court or tribunal.

(3) A witness summons which is—

(a) served in accordance with this rule; and
(b) requires the witness to attend court to give evidence,

is binding until the conclusion of the hearing at which the attendance of the witness is required.

### 34.6   Who is to serve a witness summons

(1) A witness summons is to be served by the court unless the party on whose behalf it is issued indicates in writing, when he asks the court to issue the summons, that he wishes to serve it himself.

(2) Where the court is to serve the witness summons, the party on whose behalf it is issued must deposit, in the court office, the money to be paid or offered to the witness under rule 34.7.

### 34.7   Right of witness to travelling expenses and compensation for loss of time

At the time of service of a witness summons the witness must be offered or paid—

(a) a sum reasonably sufficient to cover his expenses in travelling to and from the court; and
(b) such sum by way of compensation for loss of time as may be specified in the relevant practice direction.

### 34.8   Evidence by deposition

(1) A party may apply for an order for a person to be examined before the hearing takes place.

(2) A person from whom evidence is to be obtained following an order under this rule is referred to as a 'deponent' and the evidence is referred to as a 'deposition'.

(3) An order under this rule shall be for a deponent to be examined on oath before—

(a) a judge;
(b) an examiner of the court; or
(c) such other person as the court appoints.

(Rule 34.15 makes provision for the appointment of examiners of the court)

(4) The order may require the production of any document which the court considers is necessary for the purposes of the examination.

(5) The order must state the date, time and place of the examination.

(6) At the time of service of the order the deponent must be offered or paid—

(a) a sum reasonably sufficient to cover his expenses in travelling to and from the place of examination; and
(b) such sum by way of compensation for loss of time as may be specified in the relevant practice direction.

(7) Where the court makes an order for a deposition to be taken, it may also order the party who obtained the order to serve a witness statement or witness summary in relation to the evidence to be given by the person to be examined.

(Part 32 contains the general rules about witness statements and witness summaries)

### 34.9 Conduct of examination

(1) Subject to any directions contained in the order for examination, the examination must be conducted in the same way as if the witness were giving evidence at a trial.

(2) If all the parties are present, the examiner may conduct the examination of a person not named in the order for examination if all the parties and the person to be examined consent.

(3) The examiner may conduct the examination in private if he considers it appropriate to do so.

(4) The examiner must ensure that the evidence given by the witness is recorded in full.

(5) The examiner must send a copy of the deposition—

   (a) to the person who obtained the order for the examination of the witness; and
   (b) to the court where the case is proceeding.

(6) The party who obtained the order must send each of the other parties a copy of the deposition which he receives from the examiner.

### 34.10 Enforcing attendance of witness

(1) If a person served with an order to attend before an examiner—

   (a) fails to attend; or
   (b) refuses to be sworn for the purpose of the examination or to answer any lawful question or produce any document at the examination,

a certificate of his failure or refusal, signed by the examiner, must be filed by the party requiring the deposition.

(2) On the certificate being filed, the party requiring the deposition may apply to the court for an order requiring that person to attend, or to be sworn or to answer any question or produce any document, as the case may be.

(3) An application for an order under this rule may be made without notice.

(4) The court may order the person against whom an order is made under this rule to pay any costs resulting from his failure or refusal.

### 34.11 Use of deposition at a hearing

(1) A deposition ordered under rule 34.8 may be given in evidence at a hearing unless the court orders otherwise.

(2) A party intending to put in evidence a deposition at a hearing must serve notice of his intention to do so on every other party.

(3) He must serve the notice at least 21 days before the day fixed for the hearing.

(4) The court may require a deponent to attend the hearing and give evidence orally.

(5) Where a deposition is given in evidence at trial, it shall be treated as if it were a witness statement for the purposes of rule 32.13 (availability of witness statements for inspection).

### 34.12 Restrictions on subsequent use of deposition taken for the purpose of any hearing except the trial

(1) Where the court orders a party to be examined about his or any other assets for the purpose of any hearing except the trial, the deposition may be used only for the purpose of the proceedings in which the order was made.

(2) However, it may be used for some other purpose—

    (a) by the party who was examined;

    (b) if the party who was examined agrees; or

    (c) if the court gives permission.

### 34.13   Where a person to be examined is out of the jurisdiction – letter of request

(1) Where a party wishes to take a deposition from a person outside the jursidiction, the High Court may order the issue of a letter of request to the judicial authorities of the country in which the proposed deponent is.

(2) A letter of request is a request to a judicial authority to take the evidence of that person, or arrange for it to be taken.

(3) The High Court may make an order under this rule in relation to county court proceedings.

(4) If the government of the country to which the letter is sent allows a person appointed by the High Court to examine a person in that country, the High Court may make an order appointing a special examiner for that purpose.

(5) A person may be examined under this rule on oath or affirmation or in accordance with any procedure permitted in the country in which the examination is to take place.

(6) If the High Court makes an order for the issue of a letter of request, the party who sought the order must file—

    (a) the following documents and, except where paragraph (7) applies, a translation of them—

        (i)   a draft letter of request;

        (ii)  a statement of the issues relevant to the proceedings;

        (iii) a list of questions or the subject matter of questions to be put to the person to be examined; and

    (b) an undertaking to be responsible for the Secretary of State's expenses.

(7) There is no need to file a translation if—

    (a) English is one of the official languages of the country where the examination is to take place; or

    (b) a practice direction has specified that country as a country where no translation is necessary.

### 34.14   Fees and expenses of examiner

(1) The examiner may charge a fee for the examination.

(2) He need not send the deposition to the court unless the fee is paid.

(3) The examiner's fees and expenses must be paid by the party who obtained the order for examination.

(4) If the fees and expenses due to an examiner are not paid within a reasonable time, he may report that fact to the court.

(5) The court may order the party who obtained the order for examination to deposit in the court office a specified sum in respect of the examiner's fees and, where it does so, the examiner will not be asked to act until the sum has been deposited.

(6) An order under this rule does not affect any decision as to the party who is ultimately to bear the costs of the examination.

**34.15 Examiners of the court**

(1) The Lord Chancellor shall appoint persons to be examiners of the court.

(2) The persons appointed shall be barristers or solicitor–advocates who have been practising for a period of not less than three years.

(3) The Lord Chancellor may revoke an appointment at any time.

(Other relevant rules can be found in Schedule 1, in the following RSC O.70 (obtaining evidence for foreign court); O.79 (issue of witness summons in relation to criminal proceedings in the High Court))

---

## PRACTICE DIRECTION – DEPOSITIONS AND COURT ATTENDANCE BY WITNESSES

### THIS PRACTICE DIRECTION SUPPLEMENTS CPR PART 34

**WITNESS SUMMONS**

**Issue of witness summons**

1.1 A witness summons may require a witness to:

  (1)  attend court to give evidence,

  (2)  produce documents to the court, or

  (3)  both,

on either a date fixed for the hearing or such date as the court may direct.[1]

1.2 Two copies of the witness summons[2] should be filed with the court for sealing, one of which will be retained on the court file.

1.3 A mistake in the name or address of a person named in a witness summons may be corrected if the summons has not been served.

1.4 The corrected summons must be re-sealed by the court and marked 'Amended and Re-Sealed'.

**Witness summons issued in aid of an inferior court or tribunal**

2.1 A witness summons may be issued in the High Court or a county court in aid of a court or tribunal which does not have the power to issue a witness summons in relation to the proceedings before it.[3]

2.2 A witness summons referred to in paragraph 2.1 may be set aside by the court which issued it.[4]

2.3 An application to set aside a witness summons referred to in paragraph 2.1 will be heard:

  (1)  in the High Court by a Master at the Royal Courts of Justice or by a district judge in a District Registry, and

---

1    Rule 34.2(4).
2    In Practice Form N20.
3    Rule 34.4(1).
4    Rule 34.4(2).

(2)   in a county court by a district judge.

2.4   Unless the court otherwise directs, the applicant must give at least 2 days' notice to the party who issued the witness summons of the application, which will normally be dealt with at a hearing.

## Travelling expenses and compensation for loss of time

3.1   When a witness is served with a witness summons he must be offered a sum to cover his travelling expenses to and from the court and compensation for his loss of time.[1]

3.2   If the witness summons is to be served by the court, the party issuing the summons must deposit with the court:

(1)   a sum sufficient to pay for the witness's expenses in travelling to the court and in returning to his home or place of work, and

(2)   a sum in respect of the period during which earnings or benefit are lost, or such lesser sum as it may be proved that the witness will lose as a result of his attendance at court in answer to the witness summons.

3.3   The sum referred to in 3.2(2) is to be based on the sums payable to witnesses attending the Crown Court.[2]

3.4   Where the party issuing the witness summons wishes to serve it himself,[3] he must:

(1)   notify the court in writing that he wishes to do so, and

(2)   at the time of service offer the witness the sums mentioned in paragraph 3.2 above.

## DEPOSITIONS

### To be taken in England and Wales for use as evidence in proceedings in courts in England and Wales

4.1   A party may apply for an order for a person to be examined on oath before:

(1)   a judge,

(2)   an examiner of the court, or

(3)   such other person as the court may appoint.[4]

4.2   The party who obtains an order for the examination of a deponent[5] before an examiner of the court[6] must:

(1)   apply to the Foreign Process Section of the Masters' Secretary's Department at the Royal Courts of Justice for the allocation of an examiner.

(2)   when allocated, provide the examiner with copies of all documents in the proceedings necessary to inform the examiner of the issues, and

(3)   pay the deponent a sum to cover his travelling expenses to and from the examination and compensation for his loss of time.[7]

---

1   Rule 34.7.
2   Fixed pursuant to the Prosecution of Offences Act 1985 and the Costs in Criminal Cases General Regulations 1986.
3   Rule 34.6(1).
4   Rule 34.8(3).
5   See Rule 34.8(2) for explanation of 'deponent' and 'deposition'.
6   For the appointment of examiners of the court see rule 34.15.
7   Rule 34.8(6).

4.3 In ensuring that the deponent's evidence is recorded in full, the court or the examiner may permit it to be recorded on audiotape or videotape, but the deposition[1] must always be recorded in writing by him or by a competent shorthand writer or stenographer.

4.4 If the deposition is not recorded word for word, it must contain, as nearly as may be, the statement of the deponent; the examiner may record word for word any particular questions and answers which appear to him to have special importance.

4.5 If a deponent objects to answering any question or where any objection is taken to any question, the examiner must:

(1) record in the deposition or a document attached to it—

(a) the question,
(b) the nature of and grounds for the objection, and
(c) any answer given, and

(2) give his opinion as to the validity of the objection and must record it in the deposition or a document attached to it.

The court will decide as to the validity of the objection and any question of costs arising from it.

[...]

---

## PART 35

## EXPERTS AND ASSESSORS

### 35.1 Duty to restrict expert evidence

Expert evidence shall be restricted to that which is reasonably required to resolve the proceedings.

### 35.2 Interpretation

A reference to an 'expert' in this Part is a reference to an expert who has been instructed to give or prepare evidence for the purpose of court proceedings.

### 35.3 Experts – overriding duty to the court

(1) It is the duty of an expert to help the court on the matters within his expertise.

(2) This duty overrides any obligation to the person from whom he has received instructions or by whom he is paid.

### 35.4 Court's power to restrict expert evidence

(1) No party may call an expert or put in evidence an expert's report without the court's permission.

(2) When a party applies for permission under this rule he must identify—

(a) the field in which he wishes to rely on expert evidence; and
(b) where practicable the expert in this field on whose evidence he wishes to rely.

(3) If permission is granted under this rule it shall be in relation only to the expert named or the field identified under paragraph (2).

---

1    See rule 34.8(2) for explanation of 'deponent' and 'deposition'.

(4) The court may limit the amount of the expert's fees and expenses that the party who wishes to rely on the expert may recover from any other party.

### 35.5   General requirement for expert evidence to be given in a written report

(1) Expert evidence is to be given in a written report unless the court directs otherwise.

(2) If a claim is on the fast track, the court will not direct an expert to attend a hearing unless it is necessary to do so in the interests of justice.

### 35.6   Written questions to experts

(1) A party may put to—

   (a) an expert instructed by another party; or
   (b) a single joint expert appointed under rule 35.7,

written questions about his report.

(2) Written questions under paragraph (1)—

   (a) may be put once only;
   (b) must be put within 28 days of service of the expert's report; and
   (c) must be for the purpose only of clarification of the report;
   unless in any case,
      (i) the court gives permission; or
      (ii) the other party agrees.

(3) An expert's answers to questions put in accordance with paragraph (1) shall be treated as part of the expert's report.

(4) Where—

   (a) a party has put a written question to an expert instructed by another party in accordance with this rule; and
   (b) the expert does not answer that question,

the court may make one or both of the following orders in relation to the party who instructed the expert—

      (i) that the party may not rely on the evidence of that expert; or
      (ii) that the party may not recover the fees and expenses of that expert from any other party.

### 35.7   Court's power to direct that evidence is to be given by a single joint expert

(1) Where two or more parties wish to submit expert evidence on a particular issue, the court may direct that the evidence on that issue is to be given by one expert only.

(2) The parties wishing to submit the expert evidence are called 'the instructing parties'.

(3) Where the instructing parties cannot agree who should be the expert, the court may—

   (a) select the expert from a list prepared or identified by the instructing parties; or
   (b) direct that the expert be selected in such other manner as the court may direct.

### 35.8   Instructions to a single joint expert

(1) Where the court gives a direction under rule 35.7 for a single joint expert to be used, each instructing party may give instructions to the expert.

(2) When an instructing party gives instructions to the expert he must, at the same time, send a copy of the instructions to the other instructing parties.

(3) The court may give directions about—

(a) the payment of the expert's fees and expenses; and
(b) any inspection, examination or experiments which the expert wishes to carry out.

(4) The court may, before an expert is instructed—

(a) limit the amount that can be paid by way of fees and expenses to the expert; and
(b) direct that the instructing parties pay that amount into court.

(5) Unless the court otherwise directs, the instructing parties are jointly and severally liable (GL) for the payment of the expert's fees and expenses.

**35.9   Power of court to direct a party to provide information**

Where a party has access to information which is not reasonably available to the other party, the court may direct the party who has access to the information to—

(a) prepare and file a document recording the information; and
(b) serve a copy of that document on the other party.

**35.10   Contents of report**

(1) An expert's report must comply with the requirements set out in the relevant practice direction.

(2) At the end of an expert's report there must be a statement that—

(a) the expert understands his duty to the court; and
(b) he has complied with that duty.

(3) The expert's report must state the substance of all material instructions, whether written or oral, on the basis of which the report was written.

(4) The instructions referred to in paragraph (3) shall not be privileged (GL) against disclosure but the court will not, in relation to those instructions—

(a) order disclosure of any specific document; or
(b) permit any questioning in court, other than by the party who instructed the expert,

unless it is satisfied that there are reasonable grounds to consider the statement of instructions given under paragraph (3) to be inaccurate or incomplete.

**35.11   Use by one party of expert's report disclosed by another**

Where a party has disclosed an expert's report, any party may use that expert's report as evidence at the trial.

**35.12   Discussions between experts**

(1) The court may, at any stage, direct a discussion between experts for the purpose of requiring the experts to—

(a) identify the issues in the proceedings; and
(b) where possible, reach agreement on an issue.

(2) The court may specify the issues which the experts must discuss.

(3) The court may direct that following a discussion between the experts they must prepare a statement for the court showing—

(a) those issues on which they agree; and

(b) those issues on which they disagree and a summary of their reasons for disagreeing.

(4) The content of the discussion between the experts shall not be referred to at the trial unless the parties agree.

(5) Where experts reach agreement on an issue during their discussions, the agreement shall not bind the parties unless the parties expressly agree to be bound by the agreement.

### 35.13  Consequence of failure to disclose expert's report

A party who fails to disclose an expert's report may not use the report at the trial or call the expert to give evidence orally unless the court gives permission.

### 35.14  Expert's right to ask court for directions

(1) An expert may file a written request for directions to assist him in carrying out his function as an expert.

(2) An expert may request directions under paragraph (1) without giving notice to any party.

(3) The court, when it gives directions, may also direct that a party be served with—

(a) a copy of the directions; and

(b) a copy of the request for directions.

### 35.15  Assessors

(1) This rule applies where the court appoints one or more persons (an 'assessor') under section 70 of the Supreme Court Act 1981 or section 63 of the County Courts Act 1984.

(2) The assessor shall assist the court in dealing with a matter in which the assessor has skill and experience.

(3) An assessor shall take such part in the proceedings as the court may direct and in particular the court may—

(a) direct the assessor to prepare a report for the court on any matter at issue in the proceedings; and

(b) direct the assessor to attend the whole or any part of the trial to advise the court on any such matter.

(4) If the assessor prepares a report for the court before the trial has begun—

(a) the court will send a copy to each of the parties; and

(b) the parties may use it at trial.

(5) The remuneration to be paid to the assessor for his services shall be determined by the court and shall form part of the costs of the proceedings.

(6) The court may order any party to deposit in the court office a specified sum in respect of the assessor's fees and, where it does so, the assessor will not be asked to act until the sum has been deposited.

(7) Paragraphs (5) and (6) do not apply where the remuneration of the assessor is to be paid out of money provided by Parliament.

## PRACTICE DIRECTION – EXPERTS AND ASSESSORS

### THIS PRACTICE DIRECTION SUPPLEMENTS CPR PART 35

*Part 35 is intended to limit the use of oral expert evidence to that which is reasonably required. In addition, where possible, matters requiring expert evidence should be dealt with by a single expert. Permission of the Court is always required either to call an expert or to put an expert's report in evidence.*

### FORM AND CONTENT OF EXPERT'S REPORTS

1.1 An expert's report should be addressed to the court and not to the party from whom the expert has received his instructions.

1.2 An expert's report must:

(1) give details of the expert's qualifications,

(2) give details of any literature or other material which the expert has relied on in making the report,

(3) say who carried out any test or experiment which the expert has used for the report and whether or not the text or experiment has been carried out under the expert's supervision,

(4) give the qualifications of the person who carried out any such test or experiment, and
(i) summarise the range of opinion, and
(ii) give reasons for his own opinion,

(6) contain a summary of the conclusions reached,

(7) contain a statement that the expert understands his duty to the court and has complied with that duty (rule 35.10(2)), and

(8) contain a statement setting out the substance of all material instructions (whether written or oral). The statement should summarise the facts and instructions given to the expert which are material to the opinions expressed in the report or upon which those opinions are based (rule 35.10(3)).

1.3 An expert's report must be verified by a statement of truth as well as containing the statements required in paragraph 1.2(7) and (8) above.

1.4 The form of the statement of truth is as follows:

'I believe that the facts I have stated in this report are true and that the opinions I have expressed are correct.'

1.5 Attention is drawn to rule 32.14 which sets out the consequences of verifying a document containing a false statement without an honest belief in its truth.

(For information about statements of truth see Part 22 and the practice direction which supplements it.)

1.6 In addition, an expert's report should comply with the requirements of any approved expert's protocol.

### INFORMATION

2 Where the Court makes an order under rule 35.9 (ie where one party has access to information not reasonably available to the other party), the document to be prepared

recording the information should set out sufficient details of any facts, tests or experiments which constitute the information to enable an assessment and understanding of the significance of the information to be made and obtained.

## INSTRUCTIONS

3    The instructions referred to in paragraph 1.2(8) will not be protected by privilege (see rule 35.10(4)). But cross-examination of the expert on the contents of his instructions will not be allowed unless the court permits it (or unless the party who gave the instructions consents to it). Before it gives permission the court must be satisfied that there are reasonable grounds to consider that the statement in the report of the substance of the instructions is inaccurate or incomplete. If the court is so satisfied, it will allow the cross-examination where it appears to be in the interests of justice to do so.

## QUESTIONS TO EXPERTS

4.1    Questions asked for the purpose of clarifying the expert's report (see rule 35.6) should be put, in writing, to the expert not later than 28 days after receipt of the expert's report. (See paragraphs 1.2 to 1.5 above as to verification.)

4.2    Where a party sends a written question or questions direct to an expert and the other party is represented by solicitors, a copy of the questions should, at the same time, be sent to those solicitors.

## SINGLE EXPERT

5    Where the court has directed that the evidence on a particular issue is to be given by one expert only (rule 35.7) but there are a number of disciplines relevant to that issue, a leading expert in the dominant discipline should be identified as the single expert. He should prepare the general part of the report and be responsible for annexing or incorporating the contents of any reports from experts in other disciplines.

## ASSESSORS

6.1    An assessor may be appointed to assist the court under rule 35.15. Not less than 21 days before making any such appointment, the court will notify each party in writing of the name of the proposed assessor, of the matter in respect of which the assistance of the assessor will be sought and of the qualifications of the assessor to give that assistance.

6.2    Where any person has been proposed for appointment as an assessor, objection to him, either personally or in respect of his qualification, may be taken by any party.

6.3    Any such objection must be made in writing and filed with the court within 7 days of receipt of the notification referred to in paragraph 6.1 and will be taken into account by the court in deciding whether or not to make the appointment (s 63(5) County Courts Act 1984).

6.4    Copies of any report prepared by the assessor will be sent to each of the parties but the assessor will not give oral evidence or be open to cross-examination or questioning.

---

## PART 39

### MISCELLANEOUS PROVISIONS RELATING TO HEARINGS

**39.1    Interpretation**

In this Part, reference to a hearing includes a reference to the trial.

**39.2   General rule – hearing to be in public**

(1) The general rule is that a hearing is to be in public.

(2) The requirement for a hearing to be in public does not require the court to make special arrangements for accommodating members of the public.

(3) A hearing, or any part of it, may be in private if—

(a)  publicity would defeat the object of the hearing;
(b)  it involves matters relating to national security;
(c)  it involves confidential information (including information relating to personal financial matters) and publicity would damage that confidentiality;
(d)  a private hearing is necessary to protect the interests of any child or patient;
(e)  it is a hearing of an application made without notice and it would be unjust to any respondent for there to be a public hearing;
(f)  it involves uncontentious matters arising in the administration of trusts or in the administration of a deceased person's estate; or
(g)  the court considers this to be necessary, in the interests of justice.

(4) The court may order that the identity of any party or witness must not be disclosed if it considers non-disclosure necessary in order to protect the interests of that party or witness.

(RSC O.52, in Schedule 1, provides that a committal hearing may be in private)

---

## PRACTICE DIRECTION – MISCELLANEOUS PROVISIONS RELATING TO HEARINGS

### THIS PRACTICE DIRECTION SUPPLEMENTS CPR PART 39

**HEARINGS**

1.1   In Part 39, reference to a hearing includes reference to the trial.[1]

1.2   The general rule is that a hearing is to be in public.[2]

1.3   Rule 39.2(3) sets out the type of proceedings which may be dealt with in private.

1.4   The decision as to whether to hold a hearing in public or in private must be made by the judge conducting the hearing having regard to any representations which may have been made to him.

1.5   The hearings set out below shall in the first instance be listed by the court as hearings in private under rule 39.2(3)(c), namely:

(1)   a claim by a mortgagee against one or more individuals for an order for possession of land,

(2)   a claim by a landlord against one or more tenants or former tenants for the repossession of a dwelling-house based on the non-payment of rent,

(3)   an application to suspend a warrant of execution or a warrant of possession or to stay execution where the court is being invited to consider the ability of a party to make payments to another party,

---

1   Rule 39.1.
2   Rule 39.2(1).

(4)  a redetermination under rule 14.13 or an application to vary or suspend the payment of a judgment debt by instalments,

(5)  an application for a charging order (including an application to enforce a charging order), garnishee order, attachment of earnings order, administration order, or the appointment of a receiver,

(6)  an oral examination,

(7)  the determination of an assisted person's liability for costs under regulation 127 of the Civil Legal Aid (General) Regulations 1989;

(8)  an application for security for costs under section 726(1) of the Companies Act 1985, and

(9)  proceedings brought under the Consumer Credit Act 1974, the Inheritance (Provision for Family and Dependants) Act 1975 or the Protection from Harassment Act 1997,

(10) an application by a trustee or personal representative for directions as to bringing or defending legal proceedings.

1.6  Rule 39.2(3)(d) states that a hearing may be in private where it involves the interests of a child or patient. This includes the approval of a compromise or settlement on behalf of a child or patient or an application for the payment of money out of court to such a person.

1.7  Attention is drawn to paragraph 5.1 of the practice direction which supplements Part 27 (relating to the hearing of claims in the small claims track), which provides that the judge may decide to hold a small claim hearing in private if the parties agree or if a ground mentioned in rule 39.2(3) applies. A hearing of a small claim in premises other than the court will not be a hearing in public.

1.8  Nothing in this practice direction prevents a judge ordering that a hearing taking place in public shall continue in private, or vice-versa.

1.9  If the court or judge's room in which the proceedings are taking place has a sign on the door indicating that the proceedings are private, members of the public who are not parties to the proceedings will not be admitted unless the court permits.

1.10 Where there is no such sign on the door of the court or judge's room, members of the public will be admitted where practicable. The judge may, if he thinks it appropriate, adjourn the proceedings to a larger room or court.

1.11 When a hearing takes place in public, members of the public may obtain a transcript of any judgment given or a copy of any order made, subject to payment of the appropriate fee.

1.12 When a judgment is given or an order is made in private, if any member of the public who is not a party to the proceedings seeks a transcript of the judgment or a copy of the order, he must seek the leave of the judge who gave the judgment or made the order.

1.13 A judgment or order given or made in private, when drawn up, must have clearly marked in the title:

'Before [*title and name of judge*] sitting in Private'

1.14 References to hearings being in public or private or in a judge's room contained in the Civil Procedure Rules (including the Rules of the Supreme Court and the County Court Rules scheduled to Part 50) and the practice directions which supplement them do not restrict any existing rights of audience or confer any new rights of audience in respect of applications or proceedings which under the rules previously in force would have been heard in court or in chambers respectively.

## FAILURE TO ATTEND THE TRIAL

2.1 Rule 39.3 sets out the consequences of a party's failure to attend the trial.

2.2 The court may proceed with a trial in the absence of a party.[1] In the absence of:

    (1)   the defendant, the claimant may—

        (a) prove his claim at trial and obtain judgment on his claim and for costs, and
        (b) seek the striking out of any counterclaim,

    (2)   the claimant, the defendant may—

        (a) prove any counterclaim at trial and obtain judgment on his counterclaim and for costs, and
        (b) seek the striking out of the claim, or

    (3)   both parties, the court may strike out the whole of the proceedings.

2.3 Where the court has struck out proceedings, or any part of them, on the failure of a party to attend, that party may apply in accordance with Part 23 for the proceedings, or that part of them, to be restored and for any judgment given against that party to be set aside.[2]

2.4 The application referred to in paragraph 2.3 above must be supported by evidence giving reasons for the failure to attend court and stating when the applicant found out about the order against him.

## BUNDLES OF DOCUMENTS FOR HEARINGS OR TRIAL

3.1 Unless the court orders otherwise, the claimant must file the trial bundle not more than 7 days and not less than 3 days before the start of the trial.

3.2 Unless the court orders otherwise, the trial bundle should include a copy of:

    (1)   the claim form and all statements of case,

    (2)   a case summary and/or chronology where appropriate,

    (3)   requests for further information and responses to the requests,

    (4)   all witness statements to be relied on as evidence,

    (5)   any witness summaries,

    (6)   any notices of intention to rely on hearsay evidence under rule 32.2,

    (7)   any notices of intention to rely on evidence (such as a plan, photograph etc) under rule 33.6 which is not—

        (a) contained in a witness statement, affidavit or expert's report,
        (b) being given orally at trial,
        (c) hearsay evidence under rule 33.2,

    (8)   any medical reports and responses to them,

    (9)   any experts' reports and responses to them,

---

1     Rule 39.3(1).
2     Rule 39.3(2) and (3).

(10) any order giving directions as to the conduct of the trial, and

(11) any other necessary documents.

3.3 The originals of the documents contained in the trial bundle, together with copies of any other court orders should be available at the trial.

3.4 The preparation and production of the trial bundle, even where it is delegated to another person, is the responsibility of the legal representative[1] who has conduct of the claim on behalf of the claimant.

3.5 The trial bundle should be paginated (continuously) throughout, and indexed with a description of each document and the page number. Where the total number of pages is more than 100, numbered dividers should be placed at intervals between groups of documents.

3.6 The bundle should normally be contained in a ring binder or lever arch file. Where more than one bundle is supplied, they should be clearly distinguishable, for example, by different colours or letters. If there are numerous bundles, a core bundle should be prepared containing the core documents essential to the proceedings, with references to the supplementary documents in the other bundles.

3.7 For convenience, experts' reports may be contained in a separate bundle and cross-referenced in the main bundle.

3.8 If a document to be included in the trial bundle is illegible, a typed copy should be included in the bundle next to it, suitably cross-referenced.

3.9 The contents of the trial bundle should be agreed where possible. The parties should also agree where possible:

(1) that the documents contained in the bundle are authentic even if not disclosed under Part 31, and

(2) that documents in the bundle may be treated as evidence of the facts stated in them even if a notice under the Civil Evidence Act 1995 has not been served.

Where it is not possible to agree the contents of the bundle, a summary of the points on which the parties are unable to agree should be included.

3.10 The party filing the trial bundle should supply identical bundles to all the parties to the proceedings and for the use of the witnesses.

## SETTLEMENT OR DISCONTINUANCE AFTER THE TRIAL DATE IS FIXED

4.1 Where:

(1) an offer to settle a claim is accepted, or

(2) a settlement is reached, or

(3) a claim is discontinued,

which disposes of the whole of a claim for which a date or 'window' has been fixed for the trial, the parties must ensure that the listing officer for the trial court is notified immediately.

4.2 If an order is drawn up giving effect to the settlement or discontinuance, a copy of the sealed order should be filed with the listing officer.

---

1    For the definition of legal representative see rule 2.3.

**REPRESENTATION AT HEARINGS**

5    At any hearing, a written statement containing the following information should be provided for the court:

(1)   the name and address of each advocate,

(2)   his qualification or entitlement to act as an advocate, and

(3)   the party for whom he so acts.

**RECORDING OF PROCEEDINGS**

6.1   At any hearing, whether in the High Court or a county court, the judgment will be recorded unless the judge directs otherwise. Oral evidence will normally be recorded also.

6.2   No party or member of the public may use unofficial recording equipment in any court or judge's room without permission of the court. To do so without permission constitutes a contempt of court.[1]

**EXHIBITS AT TRIAL**

7    Exhibits which are handed in and proved during the course of the trial should be recorded on an Exhibit List and kept in the custody of the court until the conclusion of the trial, unless the judge directs otherwise. At the conclusion of the trial it is the parties' responsibility to obtain the return of those exhibits which they handed in and to preserve them for the period in which any appeal may take place.

---

## PRACTICE DIRECTION

## THE COURT OF APPEAL (CIVIL DIVISION)

## 1   INTRODUCTION

### 1.1   Jurisdiction of the Court of Appeal

1.1.1   The Court of Appeal is a superior court of record. It exercises all the jurisdiction conferred on it by the Supreme Court Act 1981. In any appeal to the Civil Division of the Court of Appeal, and in relation to the amendment, execution and enforcement of any judgment or order made on such appeal, it has the same authority and jurisdiction as the court or tribunal from which the appeal is brought. When rules of court permit, any incidental jurisdiction in any proceedings pending before the Civil Division of the Court of Appeal, not involving the determination of an appeal, may be exercised, with or without a hearing, by a single judge of that Court, or by the master.

### 1.2   Consolidated Practice Directions

1.2.1   This is a consolidation, with some amendments, of all the principal Practice Directions which apply to proceedings in the Court of Appeal (see the list at Annex A). It covers the process of instituting proceedings, documentation including skeleton arguments, the requirement for permission to appeal, judgments, case management and Alternative Dispute Resolution. It also deals with particular aspects of the current practice of the Court of Appeal,

---

1    Section 9 of the Contempt of Court Act 1981.

for example, the making of references to the European Court of Justice under Article 177 of the EC Treaty. It should be noted that permission to appeal is now required in the vast majority of cases. This consolidated Practice Direction applies equally to appeals to the Court in family cases. Further or amended directions may be issued once the new Civil Procedure Rules, governing the work of the Court of Appeal, have been made.

### 1.3    The Civil Appeals Office

1.3.1    The administrative work of the Civil Appeals Office is conducted under the direction of the Head of the Civil Appeals Office. When acting in a judicial capacity he is known as master. In this Practice Direction the term master is used with that specific meaning. Provision is also made for the appointment of deputy masters.

### 1.4    Litigants in Person

1.4.1    All of this Practice Direction may be of relevance to litigants in person but the key points of which they need to be aware will be found at section 8.

## 2    PERMISSION TO APPEAL

### 2.1    When is permission required?

2.1.1    Most appeals require the permission of the court below (the court which made the decision which is challenged) or of the Court of Appeal to bring an appeal.

2.1.2    Since 1 January 1999, permission has been required for all appeals except appeals against:

(a) committal orders;
(b) refusals to grant *habeas corpus*; and
(c) secure accommodation orders made pursuant to section 25 of the Children Act 1989.

(see RSC Order 59 r 1B(1)(a)–(c))

2.1.3    The experience of the Court of Appeal is that many appeals and applications for permission to appeal are made which are quite hopeless. They demonstrate basic misconceptions as to the purpose of the civil appeal system and the different roles played by appellate Courts and courts below. The court below has a crucial role in determining applications for permission to appeal. This guidance indicates how applicants, and courts, should approach the matter.

### 2.2    From which court should permission to appeal be sought?

2.2.1    The court which has just reached a decision is often in the best position to judge whether there should be an appeal. It should not leave the decision to the Court of Appeal. Courts below can help to minimise the delay and expense which an appeal involves. Where the parties are present for delivery of the judgment, it should be routine for the judge below to ask whether either party wants permission to appeal and to deal with the matter then and there. However, if the court below is in doubt whether an appeal would have a realistic prospect of success or involves a point of general principle, the safe course is to refuse permission to appeal. It is always open to the Court of Appeal to grant it.

2.2.2    The advantages which flow from permission being considered by the court of first instance are lost if the application cannot be listed before the judge who made the decision which is the subject of the application. Where it is not possible for the application for permission to be listed before the same judge, or where undue delay would be caused by so listing it, the Court of Appeal will be sympathetic to applicants who claim that it was impracticable for them to make their application to the court below and will not require such an application to be made.

## 2.3 Oral or paper hearings

2.3.1    Many applications to the Court of Appeal for permission to appeal are considered in the first instance by a single Lord Justice on paper, but in some cases the Court directs that the application should proceed straight to an oral hearing. Usually, only applications for permission where the applicant is legally represented are dealt with on paper. However, some applications from litigants in person may be deemed suitable to be dealt with in the same way. Following a notification that the Lord Justice is minded to refuse permission to appeal and in the absence of a request for an oral hearing being received within 14 days, the application will be determined in open court without further reference to the applicant.

2.3.2    Whether the application is dealt with on paper or at a hearing the applicant should not burden the Court with documents which are not relevant to the application. The letter from the Civil Appeals Office acknowledging entry of the application in the records of the Court sets out the Court's requirements concerning application bundles.

## 2.4 Applications for permission listed for oral hearing

2.4.1    If the single Lord Justice, on consideration of the papers, grants permission or directs an oral hearing of the application, directions may be given on paper as to (1) the maximum time to be allowed to each party for oral argument on the appeal or the oral hearing of the application for permission, as the case may be; (2) the filing and service of skeleton arguments; and (3) other directions for the progress of the case.

2.4.2    Where an application for permission to appeal is listed for oral hearing, whether initially or after a decision on paper, the following directions will apply.

2.4.3    In all cases where the application is listed for an oral hearing at which the Court has directed that other parties are to have the opportunity to attend, the applicant's solicitors (or the applicant, if acting in person) must, on receipt of notification from the Civil Appeals Office that such a hearing has been directed, immediately supply the respondent's solicitors (or the respondent, if in person) with a copy of the application bundle (including a copy of the transcript or note of judgment) in exactly the same form as the bundles filed for the use of the Court of Appeal. For the purposes only of providing the copy of the application bundle to the respondent's side photocopies of transcripts of judgment and, where relevant, evidence, may be used. The costs of provision of that bundle shall be borne by the applicant initially, but will form part of the costs of the application.

## 2.5 Time allowed for oral hearings

2.5.1    In the absence of specific directions, the Court of Appeal will expect oral argument in support of applications for permission to appeal, or renewed applications for permission to apply for judicial review, to be confined to a maximum of 20 minutes.

## 2.6 Skeleton arguments for applications for permission to appeal

2.6.1    In order to assist the Court of Appeal to deal efficiently with applications for permission to appeal, all represented applicants for permission must provide a skeleton argument and applicants in person are strongly encouraged to do so. Three copies of the skeleton argument must accompany the bundle of documents which the applicant's solicitors lodge with the Civil

Appeals Office for the application. (These copies should be filed with, but not bound in, the bundle.) Where dates are of significance in relation to the proposed appeal, a chronology should be filed and served with the applicant's skeleton argument.

2.6.2    If the application is listed for oral hearing at which the Court has directed that other parties are to have the opportunity to attend, the respondent's skeleton argument must be filed and served within 14 days of receipt of the applicant's bundle. Where an application for permission to appeal is listed for hearing, with the appeal to follow if permission is granted, the timetable for skeleton arguments will be the same as in the case of an appeal, and the amount of time allowed for oral argument will depend on the time estimate for the appeal.

### 2.7    Renewed applications for permission to apply for judicial review

2.7.1    The applicant's advocate (and where any respondent will be represented at the Court of Appeal hearing, that party's advocate) must file four copies of their skeleton arguments with the Civil Appeals Office with the application bundles.

2.7.2    This applies only to renewed applications for permission to apply for judicial review. Where permission to apply has been granted and the substantive application for judicial review has been dealt with in the High Court, any application to the Court of Appeal for permission to appeal against that decision will be governed by the general provisions for such applications.

### 2.8    The general test for permission

2.8.1    There is no limit on the number of appeals the Court of Appeal is prepared to hear. It is therefore not relevant to consider whether the Court of Appeal might prefer to select for itself which appeals it would like to hear. The general rule applied by the Court of Appeal, and thus the relevant basis for first instance courts deciding whether to grant permission, is that permission will be given unless an appeal would have no real prospect of success. A fanciful prospect is insufficient. Permission may also be given in exceptional circumstances even though the case has no real prospect of success if there is an issue which, in the public interest, should be examined by the Court of Appeal. Examples are where a case raises questions of great public interest or questions of general policy, or where authority binding on the Court of Appeal may call for reconsideration. The approach will differ depending on the category and subject matter of the decision and the reason for seeking permission to appeal, as will be indicated below. However, if the issue to be raised on the appeal is of general importance that will be a factor in favour of granting permission. On the other hand, if the issues are not generally important and the costs of an appeal will far exceed what is at stake, that will be a factor which weighs against the grant of permission to appeal.

### 2.9    A point of law

2.9.1    Permission should not be granted unless the judge considers that there is a realistic prospect of the Court of Appeal coming to a different conclusion on a point of law which will materially affect the outcome of the case. An appeal on the grounds that there is no evidence to support a finding is an appeal on a point of law, but it is insufficient to show that there was little evidence.

### 2.10    A question of fact

2.10.1    The Court of Appeal will rarely interfere with a decision based on the judge's evaluation of oral evidence as to the primary facts or if an appeal would involve examining the fine detail of the judge's factual investigation. Permission is more likely to be appropriate where what is being challenged is the inference which the judge has drawn from the primary facts, or where the judge has not received any particular benefit from having actually seen the witnesses, and it is properly arguable that materially different inferences should be drawn from the evidence. In such a case the judge, if he grants permission, should expressly indicate that this is the basis on which permission is given.

2.10.2    If a case is one which has involved considering many witnesses and/or documents, it will be especially important that the trial court considers whether to grant permission and, where it refuses permission, gives its reasons for doing so. This is because in a case of this sort the Court of Appeal is less able to assess whether an appeal is appropriate.

### 2.11    Questions of discretion

2.11.1    The Court of Appeal does not interfere with the exercise of discretion by a judge unless satisfied the judge was wrong. The burden on an appellant is a heavy one (many family cases do not qualify for permission for this reason). It will be rare, therefore, for a trial judge to give permission on a pure question of discretion. He may do so if the case raises a point of general principle on which the opinion of a higher court is required.

### 2.12    Appeals from interlocutory orders

2.12.1    An interlocutory order is an order which does not entirely determine the proceedings. Where the application is for permission to appeal from an interlocutory order, additional considerations arise:

(a) the point may not be of sufficient significance to justify the costs of an appeal;
(b) the procedural consequences of an appeal (eg loss of the trial date) may outweigh the significance of the interlocutory issue;
(c) it may be more convenient to determine the point at or after the trial.

2.12.2    In all cases under (a) permission to appeal should be refused. In the case of (b) and (c) it will be necessary to consider whether to refuse permission or adjourn the application until after trial so as to preserve the appellant's right to appeal.

### 2.13    Limited and conditional permission

2.13.1    Permission may be limited to one or more points. It may also be conditional, eg on some special order for costs. If a court grants permission on one or more issues only, it should expressly refuse permission on other issues. The reason for this is that the other issues can then only be raised with the permission of the Court of Appeal.

2.13.2    If an appellant wishes to raise additional issues for which there is no permission to appeal, written notice of this must be given to all other parties and the Court of Appeal within 28 days of permission being granted, or 28 days prior to the hearing, if this is earlier. Unless there are special reasons for making an application earlier, to avoid additional expense the application to raise an additional issue should be dealt with at the outset of the appeal and all parties should normally be prepared to argue the additional issues at that hearing. If, however, a respondent considers the additional issues will have a significant effect on the preparation necessary for, or the length of, the hearing, he may inform the appellant within 14 days of receiving the notice that he requires an application to be made prior to the hearing. An application should then be made in writing within 14 days accompanied, if necessary, by short written submissions, which should be served on the respondent. The respondent may deliver short written submissions within a further 14 days. The court will, where practicable, give its decision as to whether the additional issues can be argued prior to the hearing of the appeal.

**2.14    Reasons**

2.14.1    When permission is refused by the court below, the Court gives short reasons which are primarily intended to inform the applicant why permission is refused. Where permission is granted, reasons may be given which are intended to identify for the benefit of the parties and the Court hearing the appeal why it was thought right to give permission. There may be only one issue that the judge or judges giving permission considered it was necessary to draw to the attention of the parties and the Court hearing the appeal. It is a misconception to assume that, because only one aspect of the proposed appeal was mentioned in any reasons which were given, permission was granted under a misapprehension that there were not other issues to be determined on any appeal unless the reasons make this clear.

2.14.2    When the Lord Justice is minded to refuse permission to appeal, his or her reasons for doing so will be sent to the applicant's solicitors (or the applicant, if in person). A letter will accompany the Lord Justice's comments informing the applicant of the right to seek an oral hearing. (An example of the letter that will be sent is at **Annex B** to this Practice Direction.) The Lord Justice will direct whether the oral hearing should be before one or two Lords Justices.

**2.15    The form**

2.15.1    At **Annex C** to this Practice Direction is a generic example of the form which the judge should complete when he grants or refuses permission to appeal, giving his reasons. The reasons for the decision need only be brief, eg difficult point of law or pure question of fact. All parties will, on request, be given a copy of the form. It is the applicant's responsibility to annex the form to his notice of application where he has been refused permission, or to his notice of appeal where he has been granted permission.

**2.16    Directions**

2.16.1    When an application for permission to appeal is referred to the single Lord Justice on the papers alone and the Lord Justice decides to grant permission, the Lord Justice may give directions for the subsequent progress of the appeal.

**2.17    Legally-aided applicants**

2.17.1    In any case where the applicant is legally aided and the single Lord Justice is minded to refuse permission to appeal on paper, the applicant's solicitor must send to the relevant legal aid office a copy of the single Lord Justice's comments (together with any reasons he/she gave for refusing permission) as soon as it has been received from the Civil Appeals Office. The court will require confirmation that this has been done in any case where an application for permission to appeal is renewed before the full court on legal aid.

**2.18    Applications to set aside grant of permission to appeal to the Court of Appeal**

2.18.1    There is a heavy onus on a respondent who seeks to set aside permission. Before making such an application, the respondent must bear in mind that the fact that the appeal has no real prospect of success does not necessarily mean that permission should not have been given. The applicant will be required to establish that there was no good reason for giving permission, which may not be the same thing. In addition, it should be borne in mind, prior to making such an application, that this court is likely to be very unsympathetic to it being made if it will in effect involve the parties in exactly the same expense as determining the appeal itself, and will not necessarily save the time of the Court but risk the Court having to have two hearings when only one would be necessary had there been no application to set aside.

## 2.19   More than one level of appeal

2.19.1    Where there has already been one unsuccessful appeal to a court (not a tribunal) against the decision being challenged, for example from a District Judge to a Circuit Judge or from a Master to a High Court Judge, and the application is for permission for a further appeal to the Court of Appeal, a more restrictive approach to the test for permission to appeal should be adopted. Permission should be granted only if the case raises a point of principle or practice or the case is one which for some other compelling reason should be considered by the Court of Appeal.

## 3   SKELETON ARGUMENTS

### 3.1   Introduction

3.1.1    Skeleton arguments are, as their name implies, a very abbreviated note of the argument and in no way usurp any part of the function of oral argument in court. They are an *aide-memoire* for convenience of reference before and during the hearing.

### 3.2   When are they required?

3.2.1    Skeleton arguments are compulsory in the case of all appeals (and full-court applications) to the Civil Division of the Court of Appeal, and in the case of all applications for permission to appeal (heard by a single judge), except (i) in cases which are heard as a matter of great urgency and (ii) any individual case where the court otherwise directs. Litigants in person are strongly encouraged to provide skeleton arguments.

### 3.3   The necessity for skeleton arguments

3.3.1    Before the appeal is called on, the judges will normally have read the notice of appeal, any respondent's notice and the judgment appealed from. The purpose of this pre-reading is not to form any view of the merits of the appeal, but to familiarise themselves with the issues and scope of the dispute and thereby avoid the necessity for a lengthy, or often any, opening of the appeal.

3.3.2    This process is assisted by the provision of skeleton arguments, which are much more informative than a notice of appeal or a respondent's notice, being fuller. During the hearing of the appeal itself, skeleton arguments enable much time to be saved because they reduce or obviate the need for the judges to take a longhand note, sometimes at dictation speed, of the submissions and authorities and other documents referred to. Furthermore, in some circumstances a skeleton argument can do double duty not only as a note for the judges but also as a note from which counsel can argue the appeal. It cannot be over-emphasised that skeleton arguments are not formal documents. They are simply a tool to be used in the interests of greater efficiency.

### 3.4   Form and content

3.4.1    To facilitate filing of skeleton arguments in the Civil Appeals Office, advocates must ensure:

(a) that their names are typed at the end of their skeleton arguments; and
(b) that the correct Court of Appeal reference number is shown on the front page. Where a skeleton argument covers two or more appeals, or applications, which are due to be heard together the reference numbers for all of them must be given.

3.4.2    The skeleton arguments should contain a numbered list of the points which the advocate proposes to argue, stated in no more than one or two sentences, the object being to identify each point, not to argue it or to elaborate on it. Each listed point should be followed by full references to the material to which the advocate will refer in support of it, ie the relevant pages or passages in authorities, bundles of documents, witness statements, transcripts and the judgment under appeal. It should also contain anything which the advocate would expect to be taken down by the court during the hearing, such as propositions of law, chronologies of events, lists of dramatis personae and, where necessary, glossaries of terms. If more convenient, these can of course be annexed to the skeleton argument rather than being included in it. Both the court and the opposing advocate can then work on the material without writing it down, thus saving considerable time and labour.

## 3.5  Length

3.5.1   The purpose of a skeleton argument is to identify and summarise the points, not to argue them fully on paper. A skeleton argument should therefore be as succinct as possible. In the case of a normal length appeal against a final order (ie an appeal in the range of one to two days), skeleton arguments should not normally exceed 10 pages in the case of an appeal on law and 15 pages in the case of an appeal on fact.

3.5.2   In the case of points of law, the skeleton argument should state the point and cite the principal authority or authorities in support, with references to the particular page(s) where the principle concerned is enunciated. In the case of questions of fact, it should state briefly the basis on which it is contended that the Court of Appeal can interfere with the finding of fact concerned, with cross-references to the passages in the transcript or notes of evidence which bear on the point.

## 3.6  Chronologies

3.6.1   The court wishes to emphasise the importance of advocates for the appellant preparing a written chronology of events relevant to the appeal. If practicable the chronology should be agreed with the respondent(s). This should be a separate document in order that it can readily be consulted in conjunction with other papers. The appellant's advocate's skeleton argument must be accompanied by the written chronology of events relevant to the appeal cross-referenced to the core bundle or appeal bundle.

## 3.7  Respondent's skeleton argument

3.7.1   In the case of respondents who wish only to contend that the judgment of the court below is correct for the reasons given, the respondent's advocate can send in a letter to that effect in place of a skeleton argument. Where, however, the respondent is going to rely on any authority or refer to any evidence which is not dealt with in the judgment of the court below, a respondent's skeleton argument must be filed. The respondent's advocate must always file a skeleton argument in any case where there is a respondent's notice.

## 3.8  Skeleton arguments and litigants in person

3.8.1   In the interests of avoiding placing undue burdens on them, litigants in person are not obliged to file skeleton arguments in support of their appeals and applications, but are strongly encouraged to do so. Where the litigant in person does decide to put in a skeleton argument he/she must;

(a) file four copies of it with the Civil Appeals Office within the time limit which would apply if an advocate were acting; and

(b) provide the respondent's advocate with a copy of it no later than the date on which the copies are filed with the Civil Appeals Office.

## 3.9 Timetable for skeleton arguments

3.9.1   If any advocate does not have instructions or all necessary papers sufficiently far in advance to be able to complete and file the skeleton argument on time, he/she should write to the master immediately.

## 3.10 Applications for extensions of time to file skeleton arguments

3.10.1   Applications for extensions of time must be made by the advocate personally (not by his or her clerk, or instructing solicitor). Such applications should be made by letter or fax setting out the reasons why the prescribed timetable could not be complied with and what further time is required. Such letters should be filed with, or posted to, the Case Section Support and Documents Room (Room E307, Royal Courts of Justice, Strand, London WC2A 2LL); the fax number is 0171–936 6810. That office will then pass the letter or fax to the master or the relevant Lord Justice.

## 3.11 Skeleton arguments and time limits

3.11.1   The court expects the time limits to be strictly adhered to and extensions of time will only be granted if it is satisfied that there are good reasons for doing so.

## 3.12 Skeleton arguments and the Short Warned List

3.12.1   In the case of appeals and applications assigned to the Short Warned List, applications for extensions of time for filing skeleton arguments will normally be dealt with by the master and the letter or fax should therefore be addressed to him. Requests for cases to be removed from the Short Warned List and given a fixture will not automatically relieve advocates from the obligation to file skeleton arguments. In most instances, before deciding whether the case should be taken out of the Short Warned List, the master or supervising Lord Justice will need to see the skeleton arguments in order to assist him to determine whether the case is one which satisfies the test for being given a fixture or second fixture. Where skeleton arguments are required for that purpose, the Civil Appeals Listing Office will inform the advocates concerned.

## 3.13 Skeleton arguments for appeals and full court applications

3.13.1   Where permission to appeal is granted by the Court of Appeal, the appellant (and any respondent who has filed a skeleton argument in response to the permission application) may use the same skeleton arguments for the purposes of the appeal (subject to making any minor amendments which they consider necessary, such as changes to page references), or they may prepare fresh skeleton arguments for the purposes of the appeal.

3.13.2   The appellant's solicitors must include with the appeal bundle, or the bundle for any full court application, four copies of their skeleton argument. (These copies should be filed with, but not bound in, the bundle.) The appellant's solicitors must also include a copy of that skeleton argument with the set of bundles served on the respondent. Appellants are reminded of the obligation to serve a set of bundles on the respondent at the same time as the appeal bundles are filed with the Civil Appeals Office.

3.13.3   The respondent's solicitors must file with the Civil Appeals Office four copies of their skeleton argument within 21 days of the date on which the appellant's bundle was served on them or, if earlier, not later than 14 days before the appeal hearing. No supplemental or revised skeleton arguments may be filed without the permission of the Court. Permission will only be granted if there are good reasons for doing so.

**3.14    Application or appeals in linked or similar cases**

3.14.1    Where advocates are aware that an application or appeal in which they are instructed is linked with another case, or raises issues similar to or connected with, those raised in other applications and appeals, they should inform the master, by letter, as soon as practicable.

## 4   CASE MANAGEMENT

**4.1   Supervising Lords Justices**

· 4.1.1    A group of supervising Lords Justices maintain oversight of groups of appeals. This involves them in specific case management as well as keeping abreast of developments in their areas of litigation. They will welcome general information from the professional bodies and specialist associations about difficulties or initiatives of which the Court of Appeal should be aware. The membership of the team will change from time to time. The names of the current supervising Lords Justices and their areas of responsibility are set out in **Annex D**.

**4.2   Case management**

4.2.1    When it appears to the court that it would for any reason be advantageous to do so, the Court will invite the parties' advocates and any party acting in person to attend a directions hearing held in advance of the main hearing. Such directions hearings may be conducted by the full Court, a single Lord Justice or the master.

4.2.2    Supervising Lords Justices will give directions concerning the progress and future conduct of appeals on their own initiative wherever they think fit, and most requests from parties for expedition or for other directions to be given will be referred to the relevant supervising Lord Justice.

4.2.3    So far as possible, directions will be given on paper, in the interests of saving costs. In those cases where a hearing is necessary, it will be conducted before the supervising Lord Justice in private (unless otherwise directed) and therefore both solicitors and counsel will have a right of audience. It will rarely be necessary for more than one counsel, or, where counsel has not been briefed, for more than one solicitor to attend on behalf of any particular party.

4.2.4    Directions hearings will not be allowed to develop into satellite litigation. They are intended to be a speedy and informal means of arriving at practical solutions to unresolved problems relating to the preparation for and future conduct of the appeal. Attempts at 'point scoring' will not be tolerated. The supervising Lord Justice will have read in advance the judgment under appeal, the notice of appeal and any respondent's notice, together with any correspondence or other documents which raise or define the issues to be decided at the directions hearing. Advocates should therefore proceed straightaway to make their points about those issues briefly and without any opening or preamble. The costs of such directions hearings will be in the discretion of the Court in the usual way. Although a shorthand note of the hearing will be taken, a detailed or lengthy judgment will not normally be given.

4.2.5    To ensure that all requests for directions are centrally monitored and correctly allocated, all requests for directions or rulings (whether relating to listing or any other matters) should be made to the Civil Appeals Listing Office. Those seeking directions or rulings must not approach the supervising Lord Justice either directly, or via his or her clerk.

4.2.6    If directions are requested or needed close to the hearing date, the matter will normally be referred to the presiding Lord Justice of the court in which the appeal is due to be heard. He or she will then make the necessary directions as a single Lord Justice or refer the matter to the full court.

4.2.7   The management of the list will continue to be dealt with by the listing officer under the oversight of the master. Subject to any direction given in any individual case by the full Court or by a Lord Justice, the master and deputy masters will continue to exercise their powers to give directions.

4.2.8   The Court may at any time give directions whether in individual cases or through information leaflets in relation to the documents to be produced. It may also give directions as to the manner in which documents are to be presented and as to other matters incidental to the conduct of the appeal, as appear best adapted to secure the just, expeditious and economical disposal of the appeal.

4.2.9   Directions regarding documentation may be given without a hearing. The master may at any time issue a notice requiring the parties to an appeal or application to attend before him. Any party given notice of an appeal or application may apply at any time for an appointment before the master.

## 5   RECEIVING AND PROCESSING APPEALS AND APPLICATIONS

### 5.1   The principal features of the system

5.1.1   In the case of notices of appeal and applications which are filed by personal attendance at the Civil Appeals Office Registry, the staff on the counter will not carry out any check on whether permission to appeal is required or whether there is any other jurisdictional bar to the appeal or application being accepted. The counter staff will carry out a preliminary check on the following:

   (a)  whether the relevant time limits have been complied with;
   (b)  whether a copy of the order being appealed has been filed;
   (c)  in the case of applications (other than in time applications for permission to appeal), whether the statement of truth in the application notice has been signed and whether a witness statement or an affidavit in support of the application is included with the papers; and
   (d)  whether the correct court fee has been paid.

5.1.2   If the person dealing with the matter at the counter considers that the appeal is out of time, or that any of the other requirements listed above have not been complied with, he/she will inform the solicitor, or solicitor's clerk, of this and will not take the papers in. If the solicitor who has the conduct of the case considers that all relevant time limits and other formalities have been complied with, that solicitor (not the clerk) should telephone the Civil Appeals Office or send a letter or fax, and the matter will be referred to the master.

5.1.3   If the member of the staff at the counter considers that the time limits and other formalities have been complied with, he/she will accept the papers; but they will then be referred to an office lawyer and, if necessary, the master. If it is considered that, for any reason, the appeal or application has not been validly instituted or is one which the Court has no jurisdiction to entertain, the appellant's/applicant's solicitor (or the appellant/applicant if in person) will be informed of this, normally by letter or telephone. Any query concerning the office lawyer's decision will be referred to the master.

5.1.4   It follows from the arrangements set out above that the fact that the staff in the Civil Appeals Office have accepted the notice of appeal or application concerned must not be taken to be an indication, still less a guarantee, that the appeal or application is validly instituted or is one which the court has jurisdiction to entertain.

5.1.5   Appeals and applications filed by post will be similarly dealt with. The staff in the registry will carry out the preliminary check on time limits and formalities, and then the papers will be referred for legal scrutiny.

5.1.6   If, after the preliminary check, the appeal or application is considered to be in order, it will be set down (ie entered in the records of the Court of Appeal) and given a reference number. The appellant's/applicant's solicitors (or the appellant/applicant if in person) will then be informed by a letter from the Civil Appeals Office that the appeal/application has been set down; that letter will give the appeal/application reference number (which should be quoted when writing or telephoning) and will specify what further steps must be complied with by the appellant's/applicant's side and within what timetable. When an appeal is set down the appellant must inform the respondent of the reference number and the timetable.

5.1.7   It is important to emphasise that these procedures for vetting appeals and applications are intended to assist the court in the management of its case load and to ensure, so far as possible, that invalid appeals or applications are not accepted. They do not, however, relieve any party (whether represented or acting in person) of the obligation to comply with the requirements of all of the relevant rules and directions and that party's solicitor, or the party himself/ herself, as the case may be, will remain solely responsible for all consequences, including the costs, of any failure to comply with any relevant requirement.

5.1.8   It is unwise for solicitors, or litigants in person, to leave it until the last day, or even close to the last day, of the period concerned before posting or bringing the requisite documents to the Civil Appeals Office.

## 5.2   Notice of appeal

5.2.1   Except for appeals and decisions of the Social Security Commissioners on questions of law and appeals from certain tribunals (see RSC Order 59 rule 21 and Order 61), there is a single time limit for serving the notice of appeal of four weeks from the date on which the judgment or order of the court below was sealed or otherwise perfected, unless this limit is abridged or extended by order of the court below, the master, a Lord Justice or the Court of Appeal (see RSC Order 59 r 4(1)). Such applications are ordinarily heard by the master.

## 5.3   Contents of Notice of Appeal

5.3.1   A notice of appeal which complies fully with RSC Order 59 rule 3 will both define and confine the area of controversy on the hearing of the appeal, thus saving both time and expense to the parties.

5.3.2   The notice of appeal must contain a certificate stating which track the case is currently allocated to in the Court below.

5.3.3   There is no form of notice of appeal fixed by statute or the rules. If a notice of appeal does not contain the following suggested statement or certificate, it will not for that reason alone be invalid. However the following suggestions are recommended in order to save the parties time, trouble and expense.

(a)  On setting down an appeal to the Court of Appeal one copy of the notice of appeal should be endorsed with a certificate of the solicitors for the appellant (or the appellant himself if in person) stating the date or dates on which notice of appeal was served on the party or parties named as respondents and on the county court or tribunal as appropriate. The officer receiving the notice of appeal should satisfy himself that it was served in due time on the respondents and on the appropriate court or tribunal where required and must refuse to set the appeal down if it appears that the notice was served out of time. The copy of the notice of appeal containing the certificate as to service shall be in the custody of the officer in attendance on the Court of Appeal when the appeal comes on to be heard.

(b) Notices of appeal should contain, after the signature by the solicitor for the appellant, a statement as follows:

'No notice as to the date on which this appeal will be in the list for hearing will be given: it is the duty of solicitors to keep themselves informed as to the state of the lists. A respondent intending to appear in person should inform the Civil Appeals Office Registry, Royal Courts of Justice, WC2A 2LL, of that fact and give his address; if he does so he will be notified to the address given of the date when the appeal is expected to be heard.' The form of the notice of appeal will be found at **Annex E**.

## 5.4 The list of appeals

5.4.1 RSC Order 59 rule 3(4) requires the notice of appeal to specify the list of appeals in which the appellant proposes that the appeal shall be set down. There are final and interlocutory lists as described in **Annex F**.

## 5.5 Setting down the appeal

5.5.1 Order 59 Rule 5 requires the appellant to 'set down' the appeal within seven days after the later of (i) the date on which service of the notice of appeal was effected, or (ii) the date on which the judgment or order of the court below was sealed or otherwise perfected. The time limit is important and will be strictly enforced. 'Setting down' means filing the notice of appeal with the court, accompanied by the documents specified in RSC O.59 r 5(1). Any application to extend time for setting down must be made to the master.

## 5.6 Respondent's Notice

5.6.1 RSC O.59 r 6 makes provision for the service of a respondents' notice within 21 days after the service of the notice of appeal and its subsequent filing. The content of any such notice is as important as that of the notice of appeal and for the same reason, it defines and confines the scope of the argument on the appeal, enables the members of the Court to inform themselves in advance of the hearing of what the appeal is about and so saves both time and expense. Again the time limit is important and will be strictly enforced, any application for an extension of time must be made to the master unless the appeal is before the Court itself at the time when the application is made.

## 5.7 Amendment of notice of appeal and respondent's notice

5.7.1 It can happen that, on reflection, it is thought desirable to amend such notices. Rule 7 allows this to be done without leave at any time before the appeal first appears in the documents list. An application for permission to amend should be made to the master on notice to all other parties, unless the appeal is already before the Court for some other purpose.

## 5.8 Appearance of appeal or application in the documents list

5.8.1 Once an appeal or application appears in the document list, the appellant has fourteen days in which to file the various documents specified at paragraph 7.2. and 7.3. A notice of appeal and respondent's notice may be amended as of right before the case enters the documents list, but thereafter only with permission.

## 5.9  Constitution of Courts

5.9.1   Section 54(4) of the Supreme Court Act 1981 and the Court of Appeal (Civil Division) Order 1982, SI 1982/543, have authorised the constitution of Courts consisting of two judges instead of three in certain specified circumstances, mainly appeals from interlocutory decisions, which includes most family and divorce matters, and appeals from the county courts. It will sometimes happen that, whilst an appeal is of such a nature that there is jurisdiction for a two-judge Court to hear it, issues of complexity or general importance arise such that a three-judge Court is desirable. Should this appear to the master to be the case, he will list the appeal for hearing by a three-judge Court. In addition the parties that this is the case may apply to the master for a special listing before a three judge Court, but should not adopt this course unless there are compelling reasons for so doing.

## 5.10  Documents needed for filing an application

5.10.1   Upon filing an application, the following documents are to be filed in duplicate in addition to the relevant court fee:

(a)  the application notice;
(b)  the order under appeal;
(c)  in the case of an application for permission to appeal, the order of the court below refusing such permission and any written reasons given;
(d)  any witness statement or affidavit in support of the application. In the case of an application for permission to appeal, the statement of truth must be signed or a witness statement or affidavit be filed only if the application is made after the expiry of the time limit or if a stay of execution or other remedy is requested;
(e)  In the case of an application for permission to appeal, the draft notice of appeal or document stating the grounds of the proposed appeal.

5.10.2   The application notice must contain a certificate stating which track the case is currently allocated to in the Court below.

5.10.3   The forms of notice of application are at **Annex G**.

## 5.11  Internal appeals and referrals

5.11.1   The master has power to refer matters to a single judge and the single judge power to refer matters to the Court of Appeal. The judicial decision of the master may be appealed to a single Lord Justice and the determination of the single Lord Justice may be appealed to the full Court of Appeal. However, in respect of a determination by the master, there is no right of appeal to the Court of Appeal without the leave of that Court if the master's determination has been reviewed by the single Lord Justice.

## 5.12  Time estimates

5.12.1   In all cases where there are solicitors acting for the appellant they must file with the Civil Appeals Office within 14 days after an appeal has been entered in the records of the Court, an estimate of the length of the appeal hearing (exclusive of judgment). That time estimate must be on the form sent to the solicitors with the letter from the Civil Appeals Office acknowledging that the appeal has been entered in the records of the Court. The procedure is as follows:

(a)  form must be duly completed and signed by the appellant's advocate.

(b) Within that 14 day time limit the original of that completed form must be sent or delivered to the Civil Appeals Office and a photocopy must be sent to the respondent's advocate, either directly or through the respondent's solicitors.

(c) The respondent's advocate must consider the appellant's estimate as soon as it has been received and notify the Civil Appeals Office within 14 days (by filing the photocopy of the form with the respondent's section of it completed and signed) if his/her own estimate differs from that of the appellant's advocate. In the absence of such notification the respondent's advocate will be deemed to have accepted the estimate from the appellant's side.

5.12.2    Where the court directs that an application for permission to appeal shall be listed for hearing with the appeal to follow if permission is granted and the court has not specified what length of time is to be allowed for oral argument, the appellant's advocate must provide a certified time estimate of the length of the hearing on the assumption that permission will be granted and the court will hear argument on the appeal. The procedure is the same as in paragraph 5.12.1., except that (1) the time-limit will be 14 days after the date of the direction that the application be listed with appeal to follow, and (2) the estimate need not be on any special form.

5.12.3    A copy of the certified estimate must he placed and kept with each advocate's papers. Each time the advocate for any party is asked to give any advice or to deal with anything in connection with the appeal he/she must check whether the estimate is still correct. The fact that a time estimate has been filed in the case does not prevent the Court from allocating its own time estimate.

### 5.13   Revised estimates

5.13.1    If, for any other reason, the original estimate requires revision, the Civil Appeals Office should be informed immediately in writing by the advocate concerned.

### 5.14   Appeal bundles

5.14.1    On filing the appeal bundles with the Civil Appeals Office, the appellant's solicitors must supply the respondent's solicitors (or the respondent, if in person) with a set of the appeal bundles in exactly the same form as the bundles filed for the use of the Court of Appeal. The costs of provision of bundles for the respondent shall be borne by the appellant initially, but will form part of the costs of the appeal.

5.14.2    Appellants will not, however, be required to furnish respondents with transcripts of judgment and evidence. The appellant's solicitors (or the appellant, if in person) must notify the respondent's solicitors (or the respondent, if in person) of what transcripts have been provided for the court so that they can order transcripts for their own use and also make representations if they consider that further transcripts will be required. Respondents must order and pay for transcripts for the use of their solicitors and advocates (see Section 7 **Documentation**).

### 6   LISTING AND HEAR-BY DATES

### 6.1   Introduction

6.1.1    Listing is carried out for the whole of the Court of Appeal rather than for individual courts. In order to ensure, so far as possible, that cases are heard in their proper place in the list, each appeal is given a target date (known as its 'hear-by date'). Because some types of appeal are inherently more urgent than others (for instance, family cases) different hear-by dates are set for different species of appeals; a list of the current hear-by dates is annexed to this practice direction at **Annex H**. The aim is that appeals should be listed so that they are heard neither significantly earlier, nor significantly later, than their respective hear-by dates. In the interests of flexibility the listing officer has a discretion to fix the hearing date within a reasonable band on either side of the hear-by date. That system will not always apply to appeals assigned to the Short Warned List; such cases may be put into the list considerably earlier than their hear-by dates and may not be called on for hearing until some time thereafter.

6.1.2 In relation to applications for permission to appeal or renewed applications for permission to apply for judicial review it will not be possible, save in exceptional circumstances, to list such cases to suit advocates availability.

6.1.3 Appeals will only be expedited so as to be heard well in advance of their hear-by dates, or deferred significantly thereafter, if there is a judicial direction to that effect. Requests for expedition should be made to the master, initially by letter: see paragraph 6.6. below. Informal requests for listing significantly before the hear-by date may be made to the Listing Officer.

## 6.2 Fixtures

6.2.1 A 'fixture' means a hearing date fixed in advance: it means that the hearing is fixed to begin on a specified date or on the next following sitting day at the option of the court. Appeals (other than (a) those assigned to the Short Warned List, (b) those given second fixtures; and (c) cases where special listing directions have been given) will be given fixtures. If it does not prove to be possible for the court concerned to take the appeal on the specified date or on the following sitting day, and the Listing Office is unable to transfer the appeal to another court, the hearing date will have to be rearranged.

## 6.3 Second fixtures

6.3.1 Some appeals are designated by the court as 'second fixtures.' A second fixture is a hearing date arranged in advance on the express basis that the list is fully booked for the period in question and therefore the case will be heard only if a suitable gap occurs in the list. Any second fixture for which space does not become available will be given a first fixture on the earliest convenient date.

## 6.4 The Short Warned List

6.4.1 Cases assigned to the Short Warned List are put 'on call' from a specified date and will then be called on for hearing as and when gaps occur in the Court of Appeal list. Short Warned List cases are not called in chronological order of setting down or assignment to that list; which case will be called on will depend upon the length of the gap, the subject-matter of the case and the constitution of the court. Because the number of last-minute settlements in the Court of Appeal varies enormously, it is not possible to predict when any particular Short Warned List case will be called on for hearing.

## 6.5 Short Warned List (procedure)

6.5.1 The system applicable to cases assigned to the Short Warned List is as follows.

   (a) The parties' solicitors are notified by letter from the Civil Appeals Office that the case has been assigned to the Short Warned List.
   (b) It is the duty of the solicitors to all parties (whether appellants, or respondents) on receipt of that letter from the Civil Appeals Office to inform their advocates forthwith of the fact that the case has been assigned to the Short Warned List.

(c) The Listing Office will notify counsel's clerks by telephone of the date from which the case will be 'on call' and it will remain in the Short Warned List liable to be called on either on half a day's notice or (if the master has so directed, on 48 hours' notice). The listing officers will put Short Warned List cases 'on call' in such numbers and from such dates as the state of the list requires.

(d) It is the duty of solicitors to inform their lay clients when a case has been assigned to the Short Warned List and what the consequences of that will be. It is important that this is done so that the clients are not taken by surprise if, as is quite likely, they have to be represented at the Court of Appeal hearing by a different advocate. The supervising Lord Justice or the master will consider applications to remove appeals from the Short Warned List and give them a fixture or second fixture provided that the application is made at the correct time and on valid grounds. Any such application must be made as soon as the solicitors have been notified that the appeal has been assigned to that list (ie immediately on receipt of the letter referred to in paragraph (a) above). It is far too late to do so when, or after, the case has been put 'on call.'

6.5.2    It is not a valid ground for taking a case out of the Short Warned List that the parties' advocates of first choice may not be available to represent them at the appeal hearing. A case assigned to the Short Warned List will only be taken out of that list and given a fixture or second fixture if it is, viewed objectively, one which cannot be properly presented save by a particular advocate.

6.5.3    It follows that if any party's advocate of first choice is, for whatever reason, not available to appear on the date for which a Short Warned List case is called on, then a substitute advocate must be instructed immediately. Time should not be spent asking that the case should not be called on for that particular date because the advocate is unavailable.

6.5.4    Between 75 per cent and 80 per cent, of cases are given fixtures. The master is charged with the duty of selecting the minority of cases which, in his view, can reasonably be expected to be mastered by an advocate other than the one originally instructed on half a day's notice or, in the case of those so designated, on 48 hours' notice. These are then assigned to the Short Warned List and the assignment notified to the parties.

6.5.5    The supervising Lord Justice or the master will always consider applications to remove appeals from the Short Warned List on the grounds that they are not of the appropriate character. However, such applications must be made as soon as the parties are notified that the appeal has been assigned to that list. It is far too late to do so when, or after, notification is given that such an appeal is on call.

6.5.6    Once an appeal is 'called on for hearing' it becomes the immediate personal professional duty of the advocate instructed in the appeal to take all practicable measures with a view to ensuring that his lay client is represented at the hearing by the advocate who is fully instructed and able to argue the appeal.

6.5.7    The court has power under section 51 of the Supreme Court Act 1981, as substituted by section 4 of the Courts and Legal Services Act 1990, to order the advocate who has failed in his duty to pay any 'wasted costs.' Further or alternatively the court has power to refer counsel's conduct either personally or vicariously by his clerk, to the Bar Council for consideration of whether disciplinary proceedings should be taken.

## 6.6   Expedition

6.6.1    In the interests of saving costs the supervising Lord Justice or master decide as many requests for expedition as possible on paper without a hearing. Requests for expedition should initially be made to the master by letter (or, if time is short, by fax) setting out succinctly and in short compass the grounds on which expedition is sought, and, if it is granted, how soon the appeal needs to be heard. At the same time a copy of that letter (or fax) must be sent to the other party's solicitors so that they know at the earliest possible stage that an expedited hearing is being sought, and why.

6.6.2   Subject to the qualification referred to below, the letter to the master requesting expedition should be accompanied by a transcript or note of the judgment being appealed, draft grounds of appeal, and a realistic advocate's time estimate of the anticipated length of the appeal. Where, however, a very early hearing is needed (ie a hearing within days), the letter requesting expedition should be sent to the master (with copy to the other side) without waiting for the transcript or note of judgment and the draft grounds of appeal, so that the court has the maximum possible notice that such a high degree of expedition is sought.

6.6.3   Because of the immense pressures on its lists the Court of Appeal is no longer able to expedite as many cases as in the past. Attention is drawn to the current practice of the court as summarised in *Unilever Plc v Chefaro Proprietaries Ltd (Practice Note)* [1995] 1 WLR 243 and paragraph 6.7.

### 6.7   Orders for expedited hearing of an appeal

6.7.1   There is a time-lag between the date an appeal is set down and the date it is heard. The court has in general been sparing in its grant of applications for expedition, and has imposed a high threshold which a party must cross before its application for an expedited hearing will be granted. Where that threshold is crossed and an expedited hearing is ordered, the court will in fixing the date for that hearing give weight not to the wishes of the parties to that appeal but to the interests of other parties adversely affected by the order. It will do its utmost, for example, to avoid cancelling a fixture that has already been cancelled on a previous occasion. The greater the expedition ordered, the less regard can usually be had to the parties' preferences concerning dates.

6.7.2   Expedition will not normally be granted unless the party seeking it is willing, if necessary, to change advocate. In an appropriate case the respondent may also have to change advocate; this possible adverse consequence will cause the court to lean against the making of an order save in a clear case. In granting an application for expedition, the court may seek to mitigate the disruption caused to other parties by giving procedural directions not currently given in the ordinary run of cases with a view to ensuring that the appeal is heard in the minimum time necessary to achieve a just result.

6.7.3   The following guidance must be flexibly applied according to the facts of the particular application for expedition. However, some appeals are so urgent that justice can only be done if the appeal is heard immediately or within days. This category includes:

(a)   appeals against committal orders, particularly if the adverse finding is challenged or the sentence is short;

(b)   cases in which children are likely to suffer extraordinary prejudice (that is prejudice beyond that almost inevitably consequent on involvement in proceedings) if a decision is delayed;

(c)   cases under the 1980 Hague Convention on the Civil Aspects of Child Abduction (Cmnd.8281);

(d)   asylum appeals concerning return to third countries, where the right to return may be jeopardised by delay;

(e)   cases in which the execution of a possession order is imminent and which appear to have some merit;

(f)   cases in which a decision is about to be taken or implemented which will be irrevocable or confer rights on third parties;

(g) cases in which the publication of allegedly unlawful material is imminent;

(h) appeals against judicial decisions made in the course of continuing proceedings.

6.7.4   In all these cases, not least (e), the court will expect the parties involved to approach it as soon as they learn of the order which it is sought to challenge. When the approach is left until the eleventh hour, or the necessary materials are not provided, it may well prove impracticable to arrange a hearing.

6.7.5   The court recognises the need to try to arrange expedited hearings where it appears that, without such expedition,

(a) a party may lose its livelihood, business or home or suffer irreparable loss or extraordinary hardship;

(b) the appeal will become futile;

(c) the resolution of numerous cases turning on the outcome of a case under appeal, will be unreasonably delayed, or the orderly management of class or multi-party litigation in a lower court will be disrupted;

(d) widespread divergences of practice are likely to continue, with the prospect of multiple appeals until the correct practice is laid down;

(e) there would be serious detriment to good public administration or to the interests of members of the public not concerned in the instant appeal.

6.7.6   When these criteria are not satisfied, the court will not ordinarily grant an expedited hearing of appeals on preliminary issues, or substantial interlocutory appeals (even where this means the loss of a trial date), or appeals concerning the construction of a standard document.

# 7   DOCUMENTATION

## 7.1   Directions of the Court of Appeal concerning bundles of documents for the purposes of appeals and full court applications.

7.1.1   It is the duty of those acting for appellants to ensure that the bundles of documents filed for the use of the court comply with the relevant rules and directions. It is also their duty to file the bundles within the time limit prescribed by RSC Ord. 59, rule 9(1). Neglect of these duties may lead to the appeal or application being dismissed. For that reason, attention is drawn, in particular, to the following requirements.

## 7.2   Documents for applications

7.2.1   In general, the following are required:

(a) The document used to institute the application to the Court of Appeal.

(b) The notice of appeal or draft notice of appeal.

(c) The Order of the court below being appealed.

(d) Any order of the court below which refused permission to appeal and the form giving reasons.

(e) Any affidavit or witness statement lodged with the Civil Appeals Office in support of the application.

(f) Transcripts or notes of judgment (explained in more detail under appeals heading) save that in the case of applications for permission to appeal, in the absence of a transcript, the note of judgment does not need to be approved by the judge.

(g) Claim form, statements of case.

(h) Any application notice (or case management documentation) relevant to the subject of the appeal.

(i)  If the order or judgment arose from an appeal from or setting aside of another judge's order (eg from District Judge to Circuit judge), the first order, the reasons given and the application notice used to appeal from that order.

(j)  Relevant affidavits, witness statements, summaries, experts' reports and exhibits.

(k) Such other documents as the Court may direct.

## 7.3  Documents for appeals

7.3.1   In general, the following are required:

(a)  The notice of appeal.

(b)  Any respondent's notice.

(c)  Any supplementary notice served under rule 7.

(d)  The judgment or order of the court/tribunal below.

(e)  The document by which the proceedings in the court below were begun (for civil courts, usually a claim form).

(f)  Any application notice which led to the order which is the subject of the appeal.

(g)  The statements of case (pleadings) if any, and in Admiralty cases, the preliminary acts, if any.

(h)  The approved transcript of the judge's reasons for giving the judgment or making the order of the court/tribunal below. If that is not available, the advocates' note of the judge's reasons approved, wherever possible, by the judge.

(i)  The parts of the transcript of evidence given in the court below which are relevant to any question at issue on the appeal. In the absence of an approved transcript, the relevant parts of the judge's note of the evidence.

(j)  If the order or judgment arose from an appeal from or setting aside of another judge's order (eg from District Judge to Circuit judge), the first order, the reasons given and the application notice used to appeal from that order.

(k)  The relevant affidavits, witness statements summaries, experts' reports, exhibits or parts of exhibits, as were in evidence in the court below.

(l)  Any order, whether of the Court of Appeal or court below, granting permission to appeal and, in the case of the court below, the form giving reasons.

(m) Where permission to appeal was granted by the Court of Appeal at an oral hearing, the transcript of that decision.

## 7.4  Applications and Appeals

7.4.1   Appellants/applicants are notified of the number of judges (including in Admiralty cases, assessors) due to hear their case. The appellant/applicant must provide sufficient copies and bundles for each judge.

## 7.5  Transcripts

7.5.1   All transcripts lodged (whether of evidence or of the judgment) must be official copies provided by the shorthandwriters or transcribers. Appellants are not permitted to file photocopies which they have had taken.

7.5.2   Where proceedings in any court have been officially recorded in shorthand, by stenographic machine, or on tape, official transcripts of the judgment, and, where relevant, the evidence, must be filed with the Court of Appeal, and, unless the court otherwise directs, notes of judgment or evidence will not be accepted. Normally the court will only accept notes in place of transcripts where the case requires such an urgent hearing that there is not time to obtain them.

7.5.3    Where, however, either in any division of the High Court or in a county court, the judge handed down his/her judgment, photocopies of the text of that handed-down judgment (signed by the judge) can be lodged for the purposes of an appeal to the Court of Appeal in place of official transcripts of the judgment.

## 7.6    Transcripts of Court of Appeal judgments

7.6.1    Court of Appeal (Civil Division) transcripts are held in the Supreme Court Library. Parties requiring copies of them can obtain them from the shorthand writers or transcribers on payment of the usual charges. Advocates who propose to refer to such transcripts should satisfy themselves that arrangements are being made for copies to be available to the Court and to other advocates concerned.

## 7.7    Notes of judgment

7.7.1    In cases where the judge's judgment was not officially recorded and was not handed-down, the advocate or the solicitor who appeared for the appellant in the court below must prepare a note of the judge's judgment, agree it (if possible) with the advocate or solicitor who appeared for the respondent, and submit it to the judge for approval. If the parties' advocates (or solicitors) are not able to reach agreement about the note speedily, they should submit their rival notes of judgment to the judge, stating that they are unable to agree a note. In the case of an application for permission to appeal the applicant's advocate's note of judgment does not have to be approved by either the respondent's advocate or judge.

7.7.2    Where the note of judgment has not been received back from the judge by the time the bundles are ready to be filed, copies of the unapproved note of judgment should be filed with the bundles; the approved note of judgment should then be substituted as soon as it is to hand. In those cases where the appellant is appealing in person, advocates or solicitors for the respondent must make available their notes of judgment without charge, whether or not the appellant has made any note of the reasoned judgment.

## 7.8    County court notes of evidence

7.8.1    In county court cases, where the evidence was not officially recorded, a typed copy of the judge's notes of evidence must be obtained from the county court concerned and a photocopy of those notes must be included in each bundle. Directives have been sent to county courts asking them to arrange for the notes of evidence to be transcribed as soon as the notice of appeal has been served on the county court (unless the evidence was tape recorded). The notes should then be ready for despatch to the appellant's solicitors (or the appellant, if in person) as soon as they formally request them and make provision for the copying charges.

## 7.9    Transcripts at public expense

7.9.1    An appellant or respondent acting in person will not be required to pay for a transcript where a certificate is given under this paragraph. Otherwise, the appellant or respondent will pay for any transcript required for the Court of Appeal in the first instance. The Court may in certain circumstances certify that it is proper for the cost of a transcript to be borne by public funds. These circumstances are where it is satisfied that an appellant (or respondent) is in such poor financial circumstances that the cost of a transcript would be an excessive burden on him, and, in the case of a transcript of evidence, also that there is reasonable ground for the appeal.

7.9.2    Where the Court is of opinion that it is necessary to see a transcript of proceedings and judgment (with or without a transcript of the evidence) relating to an appellant whose financial circumstances are as described above, it may certify that transcripts or all or any part of the proceedings and judgment may properly be supplied for the use of the Court at the expense of public funds. The Court for these purposes includes both the judge (of whatever level) whose decision is under appeal, and the Court of Appeal, a single judge of the Court of Appeal or the master. An appellant for these purposes includes a person who is seeking permission to appeal to the Court of Appeal.

## 7.10   Core bundles

7.10.1   In cases where the appellant seeks to place before the court bundles of documents comprising more than 100 pages, (exclusive of the judgment appealed against) the appellant's solicitors must prepare and file with the court the requisite number of copies of a core bundle containing the documents central to the appeal.

7.10.2   In all cases where the appellant or applicant is represented only core bundles are to be filed without any trial or other bundles. Core bundles must contain only those documents which the Lords Justices will need to pre-read or to which it will be necessary to refer at the hearing, either in support of, or in opposition to, the appeal or application. As soon as the appeal or application has been filed, the appellant's or applicant's solicitors must give careful consideration (with the advice of their advocate where appropriate) to the necessary content of the core bundles. If they are in any doubt concerning the documents which the other side will need, they must consult the respondent's solicitors at an early stage.

## 7.11   Time for filing Core Bundles

7.11.1   No later than the date stated in the letter from the Civil Appeals Office acknowledging entry of the case in the court's records, the appellant's solicitors must file with the Civil Appeals Office Case Section Support and Documents Room the number of sets of core bundles specified in that letter. No other bundles are to be filed.

7.11.2   One set of the full trial bundles should be brought to the Court of Appeal hearing, but not filed in advance.

## 7.12   Contents of Core Bundles

7.12.1   Each core bundle must always include the notice of appeal, the order appealed against, any other relevant orders made in the court below, the respondent's notice (if any) and the note of judgment and notes of evidence (if relevant). If it is a case where there are transcripts of the judgment/evidence, then those should not be bound in the core bundle, but kept separate, see below. In addition, the core bundle should include such of the documents put in evidence in the court below as are central to the appeal.

## 7.13   Core Bundles and litigants in person

7.13.1   For information helpful to litigants in person see paragraph 8.2.

## 7.14   Pagination

7.14.1   Bundles must be paginated. At present, many bundles are numbered merely by document. This is incorrect. Each page must be numbered individually and consecutively, starting with page 1 at the top of the bundle and working continuously through to the end.

## 7.15   Index

7.15.1   There must be an index at the front of the bundle listing the documents and giving the page references for each. In the case of documents such as letters, invoices, bank statements etc, they can be shown in the index by a general description; it is not necessary to list every letter, invoice etc separately. But if a letter or other such document is particularly important to the case, then it should be listed separately in the index so that attention is drawn to it. In particular in the case of appeals and applications in judicial review proceedings, the letter or other document which constitutes the decision sought to be reviewed must be separately itemised in the index (whether or not it forms part of the exhibit to an affidavit). Where each set of bundles consists of more than one file or bundle, an index covering all of them should be placed at the beginning of Bundle A; there should not be separate indexes for each physical bundle comprised in the set.

### 7.16  Binding of bundles

7.16.1  All the documents (with the exception of transcripts) must be bound together in some form (eg lever-arch files, ring-binders, plastic binders, or laced through holes in the top left-hand corner).

### 7.17  Legibility

7.17.1  All documents must be legible. In particular, care must be taken to ensure that the edges of pages are not cut off by the photocopying machine or rendered illegible by the binding. If it proves impossible to produce adequate copies of individual documents, or if manuscript documents are illegible, typewritten copies of the relevant pages should also be interleaved at the appropriate place in the bundle.

### 7.18  Applications for permission to adduce further evidence

7.18.1  Where (as is often the case) the court has directed that an application for permission to adduce further evidence is to be listed for hearing at the same time as the appeal, separate bundles must nevertheless be filed in respect of that application so that the further evidence can readily be distinguished from the evidence which was before the court below.

### 7.19  Time limits for filing documents

7.19.1  Time limits must be complied with and will be strictly enforced except where there are good grounds for granting an extension.

### 7.20  Responsibility of the solicitor on the record

7.20.1  The solicitor in charge of the case must personally satisfy himself/herself, and is responsible as an officer of the court for ensuring that the documentation is in order before it is delivered to the court. London agents too have a responsibility; they should be prepared to answer any questions which may arise as to the sufficiency of the documentation.

### 7.21  Affidavits

See Practice Direction to CPR Part 32.

## 8  LITIGANTS IN PERSON (LITIGANTS WITHOUT LAWYERS)

### 8.1  Applications for permission to appeal and appeals by litigants in person

8.1.1  So that the Court of Appeal can check whether it has jurisdiction to hear an application for permission to appeal, or a full appeal, litigants in person should take or send to the Civil Appeal Office:

(a)  a copy of the order or decision by the court against which he or she seeks to appeal; and

(b)  details of his or her name, address and telephone number.

8.1.2    If the application or appeal is one where the Court of Appeal has jurisdiction, the Civil Appeals Office will provide the litigant with notes for guidance on how to proceed.

8.1.3    If the application or appeal is not one where the Court of Appeal has jurisdiction, the Civil Appeals Office will write to the litigant to explain the reasons why.

8.1.4    It is emphasised that the administrative and legal staff in the Civil Appeals Office will need time to deal with these matters. Litigants are therefore advised to make sure that they communicate with the Civil Appeals Office as soon as possible after the order or decision by the court against which they wish to appeal has been given, and *well* before the expiry of the time limit for serving notice of appeal. The provision of this information at short notice can be made only in urgent circumstances. A case will not be regarded as urgent merely because a party has left it too close to the expiry of the time limit before taking the necessary steps to make the application or file an appeal. A case will be treated as urgent only if a direction to the effect is made by the Court.

## 8.2    Appeal and application bundles

8.2.1    Information about how to prepare for applications or appeals by preparing sets or a set (bundles) of documents for the use of the Court of Appeal can be found in two leaflets, one for applications and one for appeals. The Civil Appeals Office will send a copy of the relevant leaflet to the litigant with the letter confirming the matter has entered the records of the Court of Appeal.

8.2.2    It is then the responsibility of the litigant to comply with the requirements set out in the leaflet. In particular, litigants should refer to the checklist in the leaflet, which highlights the key requirements. When the litigant is sure that his or her bundles of documents comply with the requirements in the leaflet, he or she should sign the checklist and return it to the Civil Appeals Office with the bundles.

8.2.3    In certain circumstances, the Court may require fewer documents than are required for formal bundles for an application. Except in cases which are so urgent that there is no time to do so, the Civil Appeals Office will write to litigants to tell them whether limited documentation or full bundles are required.

8.2.4    Paragraphs 7.5. and 7.9. gives details about obtaining transcripts of judgment for incorporation in the bundles. Litigants who require help with the preparation of their bundles can obtain this from the Citizens' Advice Bureau in the Royal Courts of Justice. In appropriate cases (for example, where for whatever reason the litigant is unable to prepare his or her own bundles) the Citizens' Advice Bureau may arrange for the bundles to be prepared for the litigant free of charge.

## 8.3    Skeleton arguments

8.3.1    Skeleton arguments are short written statements of the arguments in support of an application or appeal. Litigants in person are not obliged to send to the court skeleton arguments in support of their applications and appeals, but are strongly encouraged to do so. If they do, they should try to comply with the directions given in the section entitled 'skeleton arguments' (section 3). Many litigants in person find that setting out the arguments which they wish to raise in court in advance can be of great assistance when, at a hearing, the Court asks the them to explain what their case is about.

8.3.2    A litigant who wishes to prepare a skeleton argument can obtain advice on how to do this from the Citizens' Advice Bureau in the Royal Courts of Justice. In appropriate cases the Citizens' Advice Bureau will prepare the skeleton argument for the litigant free of charge.

## 9    RESERVED JUDGMENTS OF THE COURT OF APPEAL

### 9.1    Availability of handed down judgments in advance of the hearing

9.1.1    Unless the court otherwise orders – for example, if a judgment contains price-sensitive information – copies of the written judgment will now be made available in these cases to the parties' legal advisers at about 4 pm on the second working day before judgment is due to be pronounced on condition that the contents are not communicated to the parties themselves until one hour before the listed time for pronouncement of judgment. Delivery to legal advisers is made primarily to enable them to consider the judgment and decide what consequential orders they should seek. The condition is imposed to prevent the outcome of the case being publicly reported before judgment is given, since the judgment is confidential until then. Some judges may decide to allow the parties' legal advisers to communicate the contents of the judgment to their clients two hours before the listed time, in order that they may be able to submit minutes of the proposed order, agreed by their clients, to the judge before the judge comes into court, and it will be open to judges to permit more information about the result of a case to be communicated on a confidential basis to the client at an earlier stage if good reason is shown for making such a direction.

9.1.2    If, for any reason, a party's legal advisers have special grounds for seeking a relaxation of the usual condition restricting disclosure to the party itself, a request for relaxation of the condition may be made informally through the judge's clerk (or through the associate, if the judge has no clerk). A copy of the written judgment will be made available to any party who is not legally represented at the same time as to legal advisers. It must be treated as confidential until judgment is given.

9.1.3    Every page of every judgment which is made available in this way will be marked 'Unapproved judgment: No permission is granted to copy or use in court'. These words will carry the authority of the judge, and will mean what they say.

9.1.4    The time at which copies of the judgment are being made available to the parties' legal advisers has been brought forward in order to enable them to submit any written suggestions to the judge about typing errors, wrong references and other minor corrections of that kind in good time, so that, if the judge thinks fit, the judgment can be corrected before it is handed down formally in court. The parties' legal advisers are therefore being requested to submit a written list of corrections of this kind to the judge's clerk (or to the associate, if the judge has no clerk) by 12 noon on the day before judgment is handed down. If it is not possible to comply with this deadline, any later corrections approved by the judge will be included in the final text which the official shorthand writer (or the judge's clerk, in courts which lack an official shorthand writer) will incorporate into the approved official text of the judgment as soon as practicable. In divisions of the court which have two or more judges, the list should be submitted in each case to the judge who is to deliver the judgment in question. Lawyers are not being asked to carry out proof-reading for the judiciary, but a significant cause of the present delays is the fact that minor corrections of this type are being mentioned to the judge for the first time in court, when there is no time to make any necessary corrections to the text.

### 9.2    Availability of approved versions of handed down judgments

9.2.1    This course will make it very much easier for the judge to make any necessary corrections and to hand down the judgment formally as the approved judgment of the court without any need for the delay involved in requiring the court shorthand writer, in courts which have an official shorthand writer, to resubmit the judgment to the judge for approval. It will always be open to the judge to direct the shorthand writer at the time of the hearing in court to include in the text of the judgment any last minute corrections which are mentioned for the first time in court, or which it has proved impracticable to incorporate in the judgments handed down. In such an event the judge will make it clear whether the shorthand writer can publish the judgment, as corrected, as the approved judgment of the court without any further reference to the judge, or whether it should be resubmitted to the judge for approval. It will be open to judges, if they wish, to decline to approve their judgments at the time they are delivered, in which case the existing practice of submitting the judgment for their approval will continue.

### 9.3 Handing down judgment in court: availability of uncorrected copies

9.3.1 When the court hands down its written judgment, it will pronounce judgment in open court. Copies of the written judgment will then be made available to accredited representatives of the media, and to accredited law reporters who are willing to comply with the restrictions on copying, who identify themselves as such. In cases of particular interest to the media, it is helpful if requests for copies can be intimated to the judge's clerk, or the presiding Lord Justice's clerk, in advance of judgment, so that the likely demand for copies can be accurately estimated. Because there will usually be insufficient time for the judge's clerk to prepare the necessary number of copies of the corrected judgment in advance, in most cases these uncorrected copies will similarly bear the warning 'Unapproved Judgment: No permission is granted to copy or use in court.' The purpose of these arrangements is to place no barrier in the way of accredited representatives of the media who wish to report the judgments of the court immediately in the usual way, or to accredited law reporters who wish to prepare a summary or digest of the judgment or to read it for the purpose of deciding whether to obtain an approved version for reporting purposes. Its purpose is to put a stop to the dissemination of unapproved, uncorrected, judgments for other purposes, while seeking to ensure that everyone who is interested in the judgment (other than the immediate parties) may be able to buy a copy of the approved judgment in most cases much more quickly than is possible at present.

9.3.2 If any member of the public (other than a party to the case) or any law reporter who is not willing to comply with the restrictions on copying, wishes to read the written judgment of the court on the occasion when it is handed down, a copy will be made available for him or her to read and note in court on request made to the associate or to the clerk to the judge or the presiding Lord Justice. The copy must not be removed from the court and must be handed back after reading. The object is to ensure that such a person is in no worse a position than if the judgment had been read aloud in full.

### 9.4 Availability of approved judgments

9.4.1 In courts without an official shorthandwriter, the approved judgment should contain on its frontispiece the rubric 'Judgment: Approved by the court for handing down (subject to editorial corrections)', and every page of a judgment which is handed down in this form will be marked in a similar manner. There will be no embargo on copying a judgment handed down in this form, so long as its status is made clear, and at present no charge will be made for permission to copy it. In future, all judgments delivered at the Royal Courts of Justice will be published in a common format. For cases decided in the two divisions of the Court of Appeal and in the Crown Office List, copies of the approved judgment can be ordered from the official shorthand writers, on payment of the appropriate fee. In the other courts in the Royal Courts of Justice, copies of the approved judgment can be ordered from the Mechanical Recording Department, on payment of the fee prescribed for copy documents. Disks containing the judgment will also be available from the official shorthandwriters, and the Mechanical Recording Department, where relevant, on payment of an appropriate charge. It is hoped that in most cases copies of the approved judgment will be available from these sources on the same day as the judgment is handed down: they should no longer be sought from judges' clerks.

### 9.5 Restrictions on disclosure or reporting

9.5.1 Anyone who is supplied with a copy of the handed-down judgment, or who reads it in court, will be bound by any direction which the court may have given in a child case under section 39 of the Children and Young Persons Act 1933, or any other form of restriction on disclosure, or reporting, of information in the judgment.

### 9.6 Availability of approved versions of ex tempore judgments

9.6.1 Delays have also been experienced in the publication of approved versions of judgments which were not reserved, whether they are produced by the official shorthand writers or by contractors transcribing the tapes which have been mechanically recorded.

9.6.2 Sometimes the delay is caused in courts without an official shorthand writer because a transcript is bespoken by one of the parties a long time after the judgment was delivered. If a transcribed copy of such a judgment is to be required, in connection with an appeal, for example, it should be ordered as soon as practicable after judgment was delivered.

9.6.3 Delays are also sometimes caused in these cases because judgments are delivered to a judge for approval without supplying the judge with copies of the material quoted in the judgment. In future no judge should be invited to approve any such transcript unless the transcriber has been provided by the party ordering the transcript with copies of all the material from which the judge has quoted. If the transcript is ordered by a person who is not a party to the case (such as a law reporter), that person should make arrangements with one of the parties to ensure that the transcriber (and the judge) will have access to all the material quoted in the judgment.

9.6.4 From time to time delays are also caused because judges have been slow in returning approved transcripts to the transcribers. Judges should endeavour to return approved transcripts to the transcribers within two weeks of their being delivered to them for approval. If anyone encounters serious delay on this account, the relevant Head of Division should be informed.

9.6.5 Where a reserved written judgment has not been reported, reference must still be made in court to the approved official transcript (if this is available) and not to the approved transcript which is handed down, since this may have been subject to late revision after the text was prepared for handing down.

### 9.7 Advocates' fees and notes of judgments

9.7.1 Advocates' brief (or, where appropriate, refresher) fee includes

(a) remuneration for taking a note of the judgment of the court;
(b) having the note transcribed accurately;
(c) submitting the note to the judge for approval where appropriate;
(d) revising it if so requested by the judge, and
(e) providing any copies required for the Court of Appeal, instructing solicitors and lay client.

9.7.2 Accordingly, save in exceptional circumstances, there can be no justification for charging any additional fee for such work.

9.7.3    When required to attend on a later day to take a judgment not delivered at the end of the hearing, the advocate will, subject to the rules of the court, ordinarily be entitled to a further fee for such attendance. This note does not affect that entitlement.

## 10    MISCELLANEOUS DIRECTIONS

### 10.1    Citation of authority

10.1.1    When authority is cited, whether in written or oral submissions, the following practice should in general be followed.

10.1.2    If a case is reported in the official Law Reports published by the Incorporated Council of Law Reporting for England and Wales that report should be cited. These are the most authoritative reports; they contain a summary of argument; and they are the most readily available. If a case is not (or not yet) reported in the official Law Reports but is reported in the Weekly Law Reports or the All England Law Reports that report should be cited. If a case is not reported in any of these series of reports, a report in any of the specialist series of reports may be cited. Such reports may not be readily available: photostat copies of the leading authorities or the relevant parts of such authorities should be annexed to written submissions; and it is helpful if photostat copies of the frequently used series are made available in court. It is recognised that occasions arise when one report is fuller than another, or when there are discrepancies between reports. On such occasions, the practice outlined above need not be followed. It is always helpful if alternative references are given.

10.1.3    Where a reserved written judgment has not been reported, reference should be made to the official transcript (if this is available) and not the handed-down text of the judgment.If the judgment under appeal has been reported before the hearing and counsel wish to argue from the published report rather than from the official transcript, the court should be provided with photocopies of the report for the use of the judges in order that they may be able to annotate it as the argument proceeds.

10.1.4    Advocates are reminded that lists of authorities, including text which they wish to refer should be delivered to the Head Usher's office not later than 5.30 pm on the working day before the day when the hearing of the application or appeal is due to commence. Advocates should also seek confirmation that an adequate number of copies are available for the use of the court and, if this is not the case, should themselves provide an appropriate number of photocopies.

10.1.5    Where, as is often the case, one or other party chooses to provide photocopies of the principal authorities (including textbook extracts and academic articles) relied on, the benefit to the court is greatly enhanced if (i) a list of those authorities, and the photocopies, are lodged with the skeleton argument so that they can be used by the members of the court when preparing for the hearing; (ii) counsel liaise with each other so as to ensure, so far as possible, that the authorities provided are not duplicated. The photocopies need only include, for each law report, the headnote and the pages containing the particular passages relied on and, for each textbook and article, the title pages and the pages containing the particular passages relied on.

10.1.6    Permission to cite unreported cases will not usually be granted unless advocates are able to assure the court that the transcript in question contains a relevant statement of legal principle not found in reported authority and that the authority is not cited because of the phraseology used or as an illustration of the application of an established legal principle.

### 10.2    Hansard Extracts

10.2.1    *Application* – This Direction concerns both final and interlocutory hearings in which any party intends to refer to the reports of parliamentary proceedings as reported in the official reports of parliamentary proceedings as reported in the official reports of either House of Parliament, *Hansard*. No other report of parliamentary proceedings is to be cited.

10.2.2 *Documents to be served* – Any party intending to refer to any extract from *Hansard* in support of any such argument as was permitted by the decisions in *Pepper v Hart* [1993] AC 593;[1992] 3 W.L.R. 1032, and *Pickstone v Freemans plc* [1989] A.C. 66; [1988] CMLR 221, HL, or otherwise, must unless the judge otherwise directs, serve upon all other parties and the court copies of any such extract together with a brief summary of the argument intended to be based upon such report.

10.2.3 *Time for Service* – Unless the judge otherwise directs, service upon other parties to the proceedings and the court of the extract and summary of arguments referred to above is to be effected not less than five clear working days before the first day of the hearing. That applies whether or not there is a fixed date. Solicitors must keep themselves informed as to the state of the lists where no fixed date had been given.

10.2.4 *Methods of service* – A service on the court is to be effected by sending to the Court of Appeal, Civil Division, three copies to the Civil Appeals Office, Case Support Section, Room E307, Royal Courts of Justice, Strand, London WC2A 2LL.

10.2.5 *Failure to serve* – If any party fails to comply with this Practice Direction the court might make such order, relating to costs and otherwise, as is in all the circumstances appropriate.

10.3.1 Judicial Review, renewal of application for permission to apply

10.3.2 A refusal in a non-criminal cause or matter by a Divisional Court of the Queen's Bench Division or by a single judge for permission to apply for judicial review is renewable to the Court of Appeal within 7 days of the decision.

10.3.3 If, following a refusal by the Divisional Court or a single judge, the Court of Appeal grants permission to apply for judicial review, the substantive application should be made to the Divisional Court unless the Court of Appeal otherwise orders. The Court of Appeal will not normally so order unless the court below is bound by authority or for some other reason an appeal to the Court of Appeal is inevitable.

10.3.4 Where the Court of Appeal grants a renewed application for permission to apply for judicial review, except where the Court of Appeal reserves the application to itself, the application should be set down in the Crown Office list to be heard by a single judge, unless a judge nominated to try cases in that list directs that the application is to be heard by a Divisional Court of the Queen's Bench Division.

## 10.4 Dismissal of appeals/applications by consent

10.4.1 Where an appellant is of full legal capacity and does not desire to prosecute an appeal, he may present a request signed by his solicitor stating that he is of full legal capacity and asking to have the appeal dismissed, in which case (subject to the request being initialled by a judge of the court or by the master) the appeal will be dismissed and struck out of the list, and an order will, if necessary, be drawn up directing payment of the costs by the appellant, such costs to be assessed in case the parties differ. Where the parties are of full legal capacity and a settlement has been reached disposing of the appeal, they may present a request signed by the solicitors for all parties to the appeal, stating that they are of full legal capacity, including the terms of settlement and asking that the appeal be dismissed by consent, in which case (subject to the request being initialled by a judge of the court or by the master) the appeal will be dismissed and struck out of the list and an order will, if necessary, be drawn up.

10.4.2   If the appellant desires to have the appeal dismissed without costs, his request must be accompanied by a consent signed by the respondents' solicitors stating that the respondents are of full legal capacity and consent to the dismissal of the appeal without costs, in which case (subject to the request being initialled by a judge of the court or by the master) the appeal will be dismissed and struck out of the list.

10.4.3   Where any party has no solicitor on the record, any such request or consent must be signed by him personally. All other applications as to the dismissal of an appeal and all applications for an order by consent reversing or varying the order under appeal will be placed in the list and dealt with in court.

10.4.4   Forms of request appear at **Annex I**.

**10.5   Allowing appeals or applications by consent**

10.5.1   In cases where parties who are of full legal capacity seek an order to allow the appeal by consent, a copy of the proposed consent order signed by the parties' solicitors (and stating that the parties are of full legal capacity), together with a document setting out the relevant history of the proceedings and the matters relied on as justifying the proposed order, should be sent to the master who will refer them to a Lord Justice for consideration. He or she will either make the order or direct that it should be referred to two Lords Justices for hearing in open court.

**10.6   Structured Settlements and consent orders involving a party under a disability**

10.6.1   The following guidance applies in respect of settlements which require the court's approval.

10.6.2   The types of case concerned are: (1) consent orders relating to appeals and applications where one of the parties is a child or a patient; and (2) structured settlements which are agreed upon at the Court of Appeal stage.

**10.7   Procedure**

10.7.1.   The following procedure should be adopted;

 (a) In cases where a consent order needs approval because one of the parties is a child a copy of the proposed order signed by the parties' solicitors should be sent to the master, together with an opinion from the advocate acting on behalf of the child. If on consideration of the documents the court considers that the consent order should be approved, the matter will be listed, but without any party being represented, and the order will be made in open court (See *Hadfield v Knowles* [1996] 1 WLR 1003).
 (b) Where a party is a patient and the case is not covered by RSC, Ord 59, r 23, the same procedure will be adopted, but the documents filed should also include any relevant reports prepared for the Court of Protection and a document evidencing formal approval by that court where required.
 (c) The same procedure should be followed in the case of a structured settlement which has been negotiated in a case which is under appeal and the documents filed should include those which would be required in the case of a structured settlement dealt with at first instance.

10.7.2   If, in any of those categories of case, the court requires further documents before deciding whether to approve the order or settlement, the master or a member of his staff will notify the solicitors of what is required. In future the court will only list any such case for mention at a hearing to be attended by the parties' advocates if the court considers that there are problems about the proposed order or settlement which cannot be satisfactorily resolved in any other way or that, for some other special reason, such a hearing is necessary or desirable.

## 10.8 Sittings of Court of Appeal in vacation

10.8.1 The Court of Appeal will sit in vacation on such days as the Master of the Rolls may direct and may hear such appeals or applications as the court may direct. Details of the number of courts sitting in August and September will be published each year, normally before Easter.

## 10.9 Solicitor's rights of audience

10.9.1 In addition to the cases in which solicitors already have rights of audience in the Supreme Court, and without prejudice to the discretion of a judge to allow a solicitor to represent his client in open court in an emergency, a solicitor may appear in the Supreme Court in formal or unopposed proceedings, that is to say those proceedings where (a) by reason of agreement between the parties there is unlikely to be any argument and (b) the court will not be called on to exercise a discretion.

10.9.2 A solicitor may also represent his client in the Supreme Court when judgment is delivered in open court following a hearing in private at which that solicitor conducted the case for his client.

## 10.10 Admiralty Appeals: Assessors

10.10.1 The relevant practice direction has not been consolidated and will be found at [1965] 1 WLR 853.

## 10.11 Use of unofficial tape recorders in court

10.11.1 Section 9 of the Contempt of Court Act 1981 contains provisions governing the unofficial use of tape recorders in court. The relevant practice direction has not been consolidated but will be found at [1981] 1 WLR 1526.

## 11 ALTERNATIVE DISPUTE RESOLUTION (ADR)

11.1.1 A *pro bono* scheme commenced in 1997. The scheme has to take into account the fact that cases which have already been tried at first instance raise different issues, so far as ADR is concerned, to cases which have yet to be tried.

11.1.2 The scheme has recently been refined. Now in appropriate cases, as soon as an appeal set down with the Civil Appeals Office, a letter of invitation to consider ADR, signed by the Master of the Rolls, is sent to the parties' solicitors. The letter encloses an explanatory leaflet and a response form. A member of staff is available to answer queries, provide general information and help with specific cases.

11.1.3 The supervising Lords Justices responsible for particular categories of work are vigilant in their case management for those cases that appear suitable for referral to ADR. Recently a very substantial commercial appeal was compromised as result of a referral by the supervising Lord Justice. Equally, presiding Lords Justices are able to propose a referral to ADR at the determination of appeals which otherwise will lead to a re-hearing or the issue of further proceedings.

11.1.4 Legal aid covers the costs of ADR for an assisted party.

11.1.5 Further information is available from the Civil Appeals Office, Royal Courts of Justice, Strand, London, WC2A 2LL (tel 0171 936 6486)].

## 12   SUPPLY OF DOCUMENTS FROM CIVIL APPEALS OFFICE FILES

12.1.1   The Civil Procedure Rules CPR rule 5.4 makes general provision for the supply of documents from court records. This note sets out the practice of the Court of Appeal (Civil Division). Requests must usually be made in writing.

12.1.2   The person making the request should,

  (a)  cite the Court of Appeal reference number;
  (b)  explain what efforts have been made to obtain the document from another party to the appeal and state what reasons have been given by that other party for refusing to supply a copy;
  (c)  enclose the prescribed fee.

12.1.3   The master may, in the first instance, determine a request without a hearing. He may also, instead of giving permission or supplying the document, give directions regarding the supply of the document by another person. He may also refer the application to a Lord Justice or the court.

12.1.4   Requests to see skeleton arguments may alternatively be made orally to the associate in at the time of the hearing in open court.

12.1.5   Below, guidance is set out in tabular form:

| INFORMATION | CAN THE INFORMATION BE RELEASED? |
| --- | --- |
| Listing of case | Yes, but only after 1500 hrs the day before the hearing when the information is made public. Otherwise leave of the court is required. The Court list comprises the name and number of the case. Apply to the Listing Office. |
| From which court the appeal came | Yes. Apply to the case section. |
| Notice of Appeal | At the discretion of the court. In general the Court will grant requests to see notices of appeal which have been served on the respondent, and respondent's notices after they have been served on the appellant. Notices of appeal relating to cases involving children will not normally be disclosed nor other notices of appeal which assert confidentiality or the existence of a reporting restriction. |

| INFORMATION | CAN THE INFORMATION BE RELEASED? |
|---|---|
| Skeleton arguments | Yes, available in court from Court clerk. Representatives of the media or members of the public can read the skeleton arguments in the courtroom, but may not take copies away. Skeleton arguments cannot be read without the permission of the Court in any cases involving minor children or any other cases where the Court has imposed a reporting restriction. |
| Files, bundles and computer records | Documents on the Court file (other than skeleton arguments, see above) cannot be shown to anyone without the leave of the Court. |
| Court orders given or made in open court | Yes. Refer to Associates. |
| Judgment | Yes. Refer to official Shorthandwriters or Supreme Court Library. |

## 13   HEARINGS IN PRIVATE

### 13.1   Hearings in private

13.1.1   Exceptional circumstances will have to be shown before the court will be prepared to hear an application or appeal in private. Where the advocate forms the view that it is necessary, in the interests of justice, that a preliminary application or an appeal should be heard in private, he or she should approach the master indicating his or her view. The reasons should be put into writing, signed by the advocate and handed to the master. In so doing, it should be understood that the advocate is expressing his personal professional view and is not making a submission on behalf of his client. This will enable the court to make a preliminary decision as to whether the application should initially be made in private or in open court. This procedure will avoid the problem which arises where the very reasons which justify a hearing in private must themselves be put forward in private if they are to be put forward at all.

## 14   REFERENCES TO THE EUROPEAN COURT OF JUSTICE

**14.1    References to the European Court of Justice by theCourt of Appeal and the High Court under Article 177 of the EC Treaty.**

14.1.1    Before making a reference to the European Court of Justice under Article 77 of the EC Treaty the Court of Appeal should pay close attention to (a) the terms of that Article, (b) Order 114 of the Rules of the Supreme Court and (c) Practice Form 109 (at para. 1A–114 of Volume 2 of the Supreme Court Practice 1999). Close attention should also be paid to the Guidance of the European Court of Justice on References by National Courts for Preliminary Rulings: this is set out in paragraph 14.2. below.

14.1.2    It is the responsibility of the Court of Appeal, not the parties, to settle the terms of the reference. This should identify as clearly, succinctly and simply as the nature of the case permits the question to which the British court seeks an answer. It is very desirable that language should be used which lends itself readily to translation.

14.1.3    The referring court should, in a single document scheduled to the order:

   (a) identify the parties and summarise the nature and history of the proceedings;
   (b) summarise the salient facts, indicating whether these are proved or admitted or assumed;
   (c) make reference to the rules of national law (substantive and procedural) relevant to the dispute;
   (d) summarise the contentions of the parties so far as relevant;
   (e) explain why a ruling of the European Court is sought, identifying the EC provisions whose effect is in issue;
   (f) formulate, without avoidable complexity, the question(s) to which an answer is requested.

14.1.4    Where the document is in the form of a judgment, as will often be convenient, passages which are not relevant to the reference should be omitted from the text scheduled to the order. Incorporation of appendices, annexes or enclosures as part of the document should be avoided, unless the relevant passages lend themselves readily to translation and are clearly identified.

14.1.5    The referring court should ensure that the order of reference, when finalised, is promptly passed to the Senior Master of the Queen's Bench Division so that it may be transmitted to Luxembourg without avoidable delay. The title of the referring court should be Court of Appeal (Civil Division) (England & Wales).

**14.2    Guidance of the European Court of Justice on References by National Courts for Preliminary Rulings**

14.2.1    The development of the Community legal order is largely the result of co-operation between the Court of Justice of the European Communities and national courts and tribunals through the preliminary procedure under Article 177 E.C. and the corresponding provisions of the ECSC and Euratom treaties. In order to make this co-operation more effective, and so enable the Court of Justice better to meet the requirements of national courts by providing helpful answers to preliminary questions, this Note for Guidance is addressed to all interested parties, in particular to all national courts and tribunals. It must be emphasised that the Note is for guidance only and has no binding or interpretative effect in relation to the provisions governing the preliminary ruling procedure. It merely contains practical information which, in the light of experience in applying preliminary ruling procedure, may help to prevent the kind of difficulties which the Court has sometimes encountered.

14.2.2   Any court or tribunal of a Member State may ask the Court of Justice to interpret a rule of Community law, whether contained in the Treaties or in acts of secondary law, if it considers that this is necessary for it to give judgment in a case pending before it.

14.2.3   Courts or tribunals against whose decisions there is no judicial remedy under national law must refer questions of interpretation arising before them to the Court of Justice, unless the Court has already ruled on the point or unless the correct application of the rule of Community law is obvious.

14.2.4   The Court of Justice has jurisdiction to rule on the validity of acts of the Community institutions. National courts or tribunals may reject a plea challenging the validity of such an act. But where a national court (even one whose decision is still subject to appeal) intends to question the validity of a Community act, it must refer that question to the Court of Justice.

14.2.5   Where, however, a national court or tribunal has serious doubts about the validity of a Community act on which a national measure is based, it may, in exceptional cases, temporarily suspend application of the latter measure or grant other interim relief with respect to it. It must then refer the question of validity to the Court of Justice, stating the reasons for which it considers that the Community act is not valid.

14.2.6   Questions referred for a preliminary ruling must be limited to the interpretation or validity of a provision of Community law, since the Court of Justice does not have jurisdiction to interpret national law or assess its validity. It is for the referring court or tribunal to apply the relevant rule of Community law in the specific case pending before it.

14.2.7   The order of the national court or tribunal referring a question to the Court of Justice for a preliminary ruling may be in any form allowed by national procedural law. Reference of a question or questions to the Court of Justice generally involves stay of the national proceedings until the Court has given its ruling, but the decision to stay proceedings is one which it is for the national court alone to take in accordance with its own national law.

14.2.8   The order of reference containing the question or questions referred to the Court will have to be translated by the Court's translators into the other official languages of the Community. Questions concerning the interpretation or validity of Community law are frequently of general interest and the Member States and Community institutions are entitled to submit observations. It is therefore desirable that the reference should be drafted as clearly and precisely as possible.

14.2.9   The order for reference should contain a statement of reasons which is succinct but sufficiently complete to give the Court, and those to whom it must be notified (the Member States, the Commission and in certain cases the Council and the European Parliament), a clear understanding of the factual and legal context of the main proceedings.

14.2.10   In particular, it should include:

–   a statement of the facts which are essential to a full understanding of the legal significance of the main proceedings;
   an exposition of the national law which may be applicable;
–   a statement of the reasons which have prompted the national court to refer the question or questions to the Court of Justice; and
–   where appropriate, a summary of the arguments of the parties.

14.2.11   The aim should be to put the Court of Justice in a position to give the national court an answer which will be of assistance to it.

14.2.12   The order for reference should also be accompanied by copies of any documents needed for a proper understanding of the case, especially the text of the applicable national provisions. However, as the case-file or documents annexed to the order for reference are not always translated in full into the other official languages of the Community, the national court should ensure that the order for reference itself includes all the relevant information.

14.2.13 A national court or tribunal may refer a question to the Court of Justice as soon as it finds that a ruling on the point or points of interpretation or validity is necessary to enable it to give judgment. It must be stressed, however, that it is not for the Court of Justice to decide issues of fact or to resolve disputes as to the interpretation or application of rules of national law. It is therefore desirable that a decision to refer should not be taken until the national proceedings have reached a stage where the national court is able to define, if only as a working hypothesis, the factual and legal context of the question; on any view, the administration of justice is likely to be best served if the reference is not made until both sides have been heard.

14.2.14 The order for reference and the relevant documents should be sent by the national court directly to the Court of Justice, by registered post, addressed to:

The Registry
Court of Justice of the European Communities
Bell L2925, Luxembourg
(352) 43031

14.2.15 The Court Registry will remain in contact with the national court until judgment is given, and will send copies of the various documents (written observations, Report for the Hearing, Opinion of the Advocate General). The Court will also send its judgment to the national court. The Court would appreciate being informed about the application of its judgment in the national proceedings and being sent a copy of the national court's final decision.

14.2.16 Proceedings for a preliminary ruling before the Court of Justice are free of charge. The Court does not rule on costs.

## ANNEXES

### Annex A

## INDIVIDUAL PRACTICE DIRECTIONS FOR COURT OF APPEAL (CIVIL DIVISION)

(in chronological order)

1   (1926) WN 308 Statutory Orders Private or Local Acts should be supplied to the Court

2   Practice Direction (1938) WN 89

3   Practice Direction (CA: Dismissal of Appeal) (1983) 1 WLR 85

4   Practice Direction (Contents of Notice of Appeal) [1953] 2 All ER 1510, [1953] 1 WLR 1503, 30/11/53

6   Practice Note (Application for Judicial Review: Substantive Hearings) [1956] 1 WLR 430

7   Transcripts of Court of Appeal Judgments [1978] 1 WLR 600, 24/2/78

8   Use of unofficial tape recorders in court [1981] 3 All ER 848, 19/11/81

9   Practice Note (CA: practice and procedure) [1982] 3 All ER 376

10  Practice Direction (Judicial Review: Appeals) Lane LCJ, Donaldson MR [1982] 1 WLR 1375, 2/11/82

11  Practice Direction (Judicial Review: Appeals) [1990] 1 All ER 128

12  Practice Note (Hearing of Anton Piller Appeals in Camera) [1982] 3 All ER 924, 5/11/82

13  Practice Note (Skeleton Arguments) [1983] 2 All ER 34, 12/4/83

14  Practice Note (Affidavits, Exhibits and Documents) [1983] 3 All ER 33, 21/7/83

15  Practice Note (Estimate of Length of Hearing) [1983] 3 All ER 544, 28/10/83

16  Practice Direction (Court of Appeal: Applications to a Single Judge) [1985] 1 WLR 739

17  Practice Note (Skeleton Arguments) [1985] 3 All ER 384, 17/10/85

18  Practice Direction (Solicitor's Rights of Audience) [1986] 2 All ER 226, 9/5/86

19  Practice Note (Appeal where Judgment under Appeal has been Reported) [1987] 1 All ER 928, 13/3/87

20  September sittings in CA (CA Sittings in the Long Vacation) (1987) 1 All ER 1067

21  Mode of Address of Lady Justice Butler-Sloss, *Palmer v Palmer*, *The Times*, 15 June 1988

22  Practice Note (Short Warned List) [1989] 1 All ER 891, 1/3/89

23  Practice Direction (QBD: Service of Documents) [1985]

24  Practice Statement (Fee Note for Judgment) (1989) *The Times*, 12 May

25  Practice Direction (Receiving and Processing Appeals and Applications [1990] 3 All ER 981, 24/10/90

26  Practice Direction (Appeals: Short Warned Lists: Counsel's Duty where Appointments Clash) (No 2) [1992] 1 WLR 485

27  Counsel's Fee Notes of Judgments PN [1994] 1 All ER 96, 13/12/93

28  Reserved Judgments ON [1995] 3 All ER 247, 22/6/95

29  Practice Direction (Citation of Authority) 23 June 1995 [1995] 1 WLR 1096

30  26 July 1995 Bingham MR [1995] 1 WLR 1188. Practice Statement (CA: Procedural Changes) WB 59/9/36

31  Bingham MR on CA Procedure (Previous Consolidation)

32  Citation of Authorities PN [1996] 3 All ER 382

33  Practice Note sub nom *Hadfield v Knowles* [1996] 1 WLR 1003 (Structured Settlements and Consent Orders involving Party under Disability) 16/5/96

34  12 May 1997 [1997] 1 WLR 1013 (CA: Amended Procedure) WB 59/9/66

35  Orders for Expedited Hearings, *Unilever v Chefaro Proprietaries* [1995] 1 WLR 243

36  Practice Registrar (unreported PN) 5/97

37  5 November 1997 [1997] 1 WLR 1535 (CA: Procedure: Changes) (Skeleton Arguments and Procedural Changes) WB 59/9/35

38  7 November 1997, modifies PD on Skeletons

39  Practice Note [1997] 1 WLR 1538 (Grounds for Leave to Appeal) 1084 WB 59/14/19

40  Practice Statement (Supreme Court: Judgments) 22/4/98, [1998] 1 WLR 825 Bingham LCJ

41  Practice Statement (Supreme Court: Judgments) (No 2) *The Times*, 2 December 1998, 2/12/98

42   Hear-by dates; revised table of dates 10/11/98

43   11/98 Lord Woolf MR's PD on leave to appeal to CA.

44   Guidance on applications to the European Court of Justice under Article 177 EC 1/99.

## Annex B

Dear

Re:

The application for permission to appeal in this case has been assigned to a Lord Justice (a judge of the Court of Appeal), who has considered the papers filed in support of the application. On the basis of the information provided, the Lord Justice is minded to refuse the application for the reasons attached to this letter.

You have the right to seek an oral hearing of the application. The advocate or party appearing at an oral hearing would need to be prepared to deal with the reasons attached to this letter and to answer any further questions that may be asked about the application. The assigned Lord Justice has directed that any oral hearing shall be before a single Lord Justice / two Lords Justices.

Wherever possible the assigned Lord Justice will conduct the oral hearing, either sitting alone or with another Lord Justice as the case may be. The oral hearing will be conducted in public in open court, unless the Court directs otherwise.

If you wish to have an oral hearing, you must notify this Office in writing within 14 days of receiving this letter. In cases where a hearing before two Lords Justices has been directed a second set of the application bundle(s) must be lodged with that notification. If the Office has not received such notification within the 14 day time limit, the application will be dealt with on the basis of the information already submitted and without any further participation by you. It will be dealt with in open court, and you will be sent an order giving the Court's decision.

Where an applicant is legally aided, and the single Lord Justice is minded to refuse the application on the papers, the applicant's solicitor must send to the relevant Legal Aid Office a copy of this letter and its attachment as soon as they have been received. The Court will require confirmation that this has been done in any case where an application for permission to appeal proceeds to an oral hearing before the Court on legal aid.

Unrepresented litigants are advised that help with their application may be available from the Citizens' Advice Bureau at the Royal Courts of Justice.

Yours faithfully,

Listing Office

Enc

## Annex C

## IN THE COURT APPLICATION FOR PERMISSION TO APPEAL TO THE COURT OF APPEAL (CIVIL DIVISION)

Title of proceedings                                              Claim

                                                                 CA Ref

Heard/tried before (insert name of Judge):                        Court no

Nature of hearing:

Date of hearing/judgment

Results of hearing (attach copy of order):
Claimant/Defendant's application for permission to appeal*        Allowed/
Refused*

Reasons for decision (*to be completed by the Judge*):

Judge's signature:

Note to the Applicant:

When completed, this form should be filed in
the Civil Appeals Office on a renewed
application for permission to appeal or when
setting down an appeal.

*Delete as appropriate

## Annex D

Current supervising Lords Justices

| | |
|---|---|
| Butler-Sloss LJ and Thorpe LJ | Family appeals |
| Morritt LJ and Chadwick LJ | Appeals from the Chancery Division |
| Pill LJ | Appeals from the Lands Tribunal and cases involving issues relating to planning, highways, footpaths or the Countryside Act 1968 |
| Aldous LJ | Patent appeals |
| Schiemann LJ | Public law appeals (including appeals from the Immigration Appeal Tribunal) and cases involving European Community law |
| Brooke LJ and Mantell LJ | Appeals from the county courts (other than family cases) |
| May LJ | Appeals from the Queen's Bench Division and appeals relating to civil procedure rules |
| Clarke LJ | Appeals from the Commercial court |
| Mummery LJ | Appeals from tribunals (other than the Immigration Appeal Tribunal and the Lands Tribunal) |

## Annex E

**NOTICE OF APPEAL**

IN THE COURT OF APPEAL        Lower Court reference (Claim No )

ON APPEAL FROM THE [HIGH COURT
OF JUSTICE (CHANCERY or QUEEN'S
BENCH or FAMILY) DIVISION
[DIVISIONAL COURT]][or]

_____ COUNTY COURT

B E T W E E N:

_____ Claimant
                                              (Plaintiff)/Petitioner

and

_____ Defendant/Respondent

   **TAKE NOTICE** that the _____ will apply to the Court of Appeal to
appeal from the judgment/order of the Honourable Mr/Mrs Justice / His/Her Honour Judge
_____ made on the _____ day of          19_____. By that order the Judge ordered that

_____
_____
_____

The [Claimant](Plaintiff)[Defendant] proposes to ask the Court of Appeal **FOR AN ORDER**
that the judgment/order be set aside [and that judgment be entered in the above-mentioned
claim for the

_____
_____
_____
_____
_____

or alternatively that a new trial may be ordered] **AND FOR AN ORDER** that the be
ordered(adjudged) to pay to the _____ his/her costs of this appeal and the costs of the
proceedings in the court below

**AND FURTHER TAKE NOTICE** that the grounds of this appeal are that
1_____
2_____
_____

**AND FURTHER TAKE NOTICE** that the above named _____ proposes that this
appeal be assigned to the [(Chancery or Queen's Bench or Family) Division or County Courts]
Final/Interlocutory List

**I CERTIFY THAT THIS CLAIM IS CURRENTLY ALLOCATED TO THE SMALL
CLAIMS / FAST / MULTI-TRACK IN THE _____ COURT.**

**DATED** this _____ day of _____ 19_____

                    **(SIGNED)**   _____
                    (Address)     _____
                                  _____
                                  _____
                                  _____

                              (Telephone No) _____
                              (Reference No) _____

**TO** the above named
and to Messrs _____ his/her Solicitors

(Address)

_____
_____
_____

(Solicitor's Reference) _____

[and to the District Judge of the _____ County Court]

No notice as to the date on which this appeal will be in the list for hearing will be given: it is the duty of solicitors to keep themselves informed as to the state of the lists. A Respondent intending to appear in person should inform the Civil Appeals Office, Room E330, Royal Courts of Justice, Strand, London WC2A 2LL, of that fact and give his address; if he does so he will be notified to the address given of the date when the appeal is expected to be heard.

I certify that a true copy of this notice was served on the _____'s solicitors on the _____day of 19_____ [and that a true copy of this notice was served on (upon) the District Judge of the _____ County Court on the _____day of 19_____]

(Signed)

IN THE COURT OF APPEAL

ON APPEAL FROM THE [HIGH COURT OF JUSTICE (CHANCERY or QUEEN'S BENCH or FAMILY) DIVISION [DIVISIONAL COURT]][or]

_____

_____ COUNTY COURT

Claimant

(Plaintiff)/Petitioner

v

Defendant/Respondent

**Notice of Appeal**

_____

(Address) _____

(Telephone No) _____

**Annex F**

List of Court Lists

County Courts:
Final List; Interlocutory List;
Final List (Admiralty); Interlocutory List (Admiralty);

Final List (Family); Interlocutory List (Family)
Chancery Division:
Final List; Interlocutory List;
Final List (Bankruptcy); Interlocutory List (Bankruptcy);
Final List (Patents); Interlocutory List (Patents);
Final List (Revenue); Interlocutory List (Revenue)

Employment Appeal Tribunal:
Final List; Interlocutory List

Family Division:
Final List; Interlocutory List

Queen's Bench Division:
Final List; Interlocutory List;
Final List (Admiralty); Interlocutory List (Admiralty);
Final List (Commercial); Interlocutory List (Commercial);
Final List (Crown Office and Divisional Court);
Interlocutory List (Crown Office and Divisional Court)

Appeal Tribunals:

Final List (Lands Tribunal); Interlocutory List (Lands Tribunal);
Final List (Other tribunals); Interlocutory List (other tribunals);
Final List (Social Security Commissioners);
Interlocutory List, (Social Security Commissioners)]
Final List (Immigration Appeal Tribunal)

## Annex G (1) Application Notice

**IN THE COURT OF APPEAL**                Lower Court reference (Claim No)

ON APPEAL FROM THE
[HIGH COURT OF JUSTICE
(CHANCERY or QUEEN'S BENCH or FAMILY) DIVISION
[DIVISIONAL COURT]][or]
_____ COUNTY COURT

B E T W E E N :

_____ Claimant
(Plaintiff)/Petitioner

and

_____ Defendant / Respondent

### Section A

*[Complete this section in all cases]*

**TAKE NOTICE** that the Claimant (Plaintiff)/Defendant (in person) will apply to the Court of
Appeal for an order that _____
_____
_____

**AND FOR AN ORDER** that (*set out costs order applied for*)
_____

**AND FURTHER TAKE NOTICE** that the application will be heard at the Royal Courts of
Justice, Strand, London WC2A 2LL on a date and at a time to be notified by the Civil Appeals
Office*

### Section B

I(We) wish to rely on the following evidence in support of this application (*here set out the
reasons why the application should be granted*)

_____
_____
_____
_____
_____
_____
_____
_____

### STATEMENT OF TRUTH

*(I believe)(The applicant believes) that the facts stated above are true

*delete as appropriate

**Position or**

**Signed** _____     **office held** _____

(Applicant)('s Solicitor)('s litigation friend)

**Date**                                    (if signing on behalf of firm or company)

## Section C

*[Complete this section in all cases]*

**I CERTIFY THAT THIS CLAIM IS CURRENTLY ALLOCATED TO THE SMALL CLAIMS / FAST / MULTI-TRACK IN THE _____ COURT.**

**DATED** this _____ day of _____ 19

(SIGNED) _____
(Address) _____
(Telephone No) _____
(Reference No) _____

TO: Messrs _____

Solicitors for the Claimant (Plaintiff) / Defendant / Petitioner / Respondent whose address for service is :

(Address) _____
_____
_____
_____

_____

(Solicitor's Reference)

## Annex G (2)

**Application Notice for Permission to Appeal (and a Stay of Execution)**

**IN THE COURT OF APPEAL**                    Lower Court reference (Claim No)

ON APPEAL FROM THE
[HIGH COURT OF JUSTICE
(CHANCERY or QUEEN'S BENCH or FAMILY) DIVISION
[DIVISIONAL COURT]][or]

_____COUNTY COURT

B E T W E E N:

_____ Claimant
(Plaintiff)/Petitioner

and

_____ Defendant / Respondent

## Section A

*[Complete this section in all cases]*

_____ **TAKE NOTICE** that the Claimant (Plaintiff) / Defendant / Petitioner / Respondent (in person) will apply to the Court of Appeal for an order that he/she be granted permission to appeal from the order of

_____

dated _____ 19_____ (and that, if permission is granted, execution of the said order should be stayed pending the hearing of the Claimant's (Plaintiff's) / Defendant's / Petitioner's / Respondent's appeal).

**AND FURTHER TAKE NOTICE** that the grounds of the proposed appeal are as set out in the draft Notice of Appeal attached

_____

## Section B

[*To be completed only in cases where the application for permission to appeal is being made after the time for appealing has expired or where a stay of execution is applied for*]

I(We) wish to rely on the following evidence in support of this application (*here set out the reasons why the application was not made before the expiry of the time for appealing and/or why a stay of execution should be granted*)

_____
_____
_____
_____
_____
_____
_____

## STATEMENT OF TRUTH

*(I believe)(The applicant believes) that the facts stated above are true
**delete as appropriate*

**Position or office**
**Signed** _____  **held** _____
(Applicant)('s Solicitor)('s litigation friend)  (if signing on behalf of firm or company)

**Date**

## Section C

[*Complete this section in all cases*]

**I CERTIFY THAT THIS CLAIM IS CURRENTLY ALLOCATED TO THE SMALL CLAIMS/FAST/MULTI-TRACK IN THE _____ COURT.**

**DATED** this _____ day of _____ 19_____

                         **(SIGNED)**_____
                         (Address)

_____
_____

_____  (Telephone No) _____
_____  (Reference No) _____

TO: Messrs _____

Solicitors for the Claimant (Plaintiff) / Defendant / Petitioner / Respondent
whose address for service is:

(Address) _____

_____

_____

_____

(Solicitor's
Reference) _____

(Solicitor's
Reference) _____

## Annex H

### *Hear-by Dates*

The current Hear-by Dates are set out in the table below. They apply to all cases entered in the
Court's records on or after 1 December 1998.

|  | TYPE OF CASE | HEAR-BY DATE |
|---|---|---|
| **Family** | Child cases | 3 months |
|  | Financial and other | 6 months |
| **Crown Office Cases and Immigration appeals** | Immigration Appeals and Crown Office Interlocutory | 3 months |
|  | Other Crown Office final orders | 9 months |
| **High Court** | Order 14 | 3 months |
|  | Other interlocutory orders* | 5 months |
|  | Bankruptcy and Directors' Disqualification cases | 5 months |
|  | Limitation as a preliminary issue in | 5 months |
|  | personal injury cases |  |
|  | All other preliminary issues | 8 months |
|  | Personal injury final orders | 12 months |
|  | Other final orders | 15 months |
| **County Court** | Interlocutory orders | 4 months |
|  | Possession | 4 months |

|  | TYPE OF CASE | HEAR-BY DATE |
|---|---|---|
| All preliminary issues | 4 months | |
| | Personal injury final orders | 8 months |
| Other final orders | 12 months | |
| **Tribunals (other than immigration appeals)** | | 12 months |

*Includes appeals confined to RSC Order 14A. For appeals referring to Order 14A and another issue, the Hear-by Date will be determined by the other issue.

It should be noted that expedition continues to be available in accordance with *Unilever v Chefaro Ltd (Practice Note)* (CA) [1995] 1 WLR 246. In addition, from 16 November 1998 very serious or distressing personal injury cases will be treated as being in the category of urgent appeals set out in that *Practice Note*.

## Annex I (1)

**REQUEST FOR DISMISSAL OF AN APPEAL**

**PLEASE NOTE**: SECTION A IS TO BE COMPLETED WHERE THERE IS NO RESPONDENT'S NOTICE AND THE APPEAL IS BEING DISMISSED WITH COSTS; IN THAT CASE, ONLY THE APPELLANT'S SOLICITOR (OR THE APPELLANT, IF ACTING IN PERSON) NEED SIGN.

IN ALL OTHER CASES SECTION B MUST BE COMPLETED AND IT MUST BE SIGNED BY THE SOLICITORS FOR ALL PARTIES (AND BY ANY PARTY ACTING IN PERSON).

IN THE COURT OF APPEAL                                          Appeal No

ON APPEAL FROM

BETWEEN:

Claimant
(Plaintiff)/Appellant
Petitioner/Respondent

and

Defendant/Appellant
Respondent/Respondent

Section A

WE, the solicitors* for the above-named Appellant, who is of full legal capacity, REQUEST the dismissal of the appeal in the above matter with costs.

DATED this                    day of                    19

(Signed)_____

*(Solicitor for Appellant)

Section B

WE, the solicitors* for the above-named Respondent and Appellant, who are of full legal capacity, REQUEST the dismissal of the appeal [*and respondent's notice*] † in the above matter with no order as to costs [*or specify other costs order required*].

DATED this            day of            19

(Signed)_____
*(Solicitor for Appellant)

(Signed)_____
*(Solicitor for Respondent)

*If any party is acting in person, please*
*modify the wording as appropriate.*
*†Delete where not applicable.*

### Annex I (2)

**GENERAL FORM OF REQUEST FOR DISMISSAL OF AN APPLICATION**

**PLEASE NOTE**: SECTION A IS TO BE COMPLETED WHERE THE APPLICATION IS BEING DISMISSED WITH COSTS; IN THAT CASE, ONLY THE APPLICANT'S SOLICITOR (OR THE APPLICANT, IF ACTING IN PERSON) NEED SIGN.

IN ALL OTHER CASES SECTION B MUST BE COMPLETED AND IT MUST BE SIGNED BY THE SOLICITORS FOR ALL PARTIES (AND BY ANY PARTY ACTING IN PERSON).

IN THE COURT OF APPEAL                              Application No
ON APPEAL FROM
BETWEEN:

Claimant
(Plaintiff)/Appellant
Petitioner/Respondent

and

Defendant/Applicant
Respondent/Respondent

---

Section A

WE, the solicitors* for the above-named Applicant, who is of full legal capacity, REQUEST the dismissal of the application in the above matter with costs.

DATED this            day of            19

(Signed)_____
*(Solicitor for Applicant)

Section B

WE, the solicitors* for the above-named Respondent and Applicant, who are of full legal capacity, REQUEST the dismissal the application in the above matter with no order as to costs [or specify other costs order required].

DATED this            day of            19

(Signed)_____
*(Solicitor for Applicant)

(Signed)_____
*(Solicitor for Respondent)

*If any party is acting in person, please modify the wording as appropriate.*

## Annex I (3)

**REQUEST FOR A DISMISSAL OF AN APPLICATION WHICH HAS NOT BEEN SERVED ON ANY OTHER PARTY**

THIS FORM IS FOR USE ONLY FOR AN APPLICATION WHICH HAS *NOT* BEEN SERVED ON ANY OTHER PARTY

IN THE COURT OF APPEAL                                          Application No
ON APPEAL FROM

BETWEEN:

Claimant
(Plaintiff)/Applicant
Petitioner/Respondent

and

Defendant/Applicant

---

WE, the solicitors* for the above-named Applicant, who is of full legal capacity,

(1) CERTIFY that the application in the above matter has not been served on any other party and

(2) REQUEST the dismissal of the said application with no order for costs.

DATED this          day of          19

(Signed)_____
*(Solicitor for Applicant)

*If any party is acting in person, please modify the wording as appropriate.

CPR Part 51
April 1999

# GLOSSARY

## Scope

This glossary is a guide to the meaning of certain legal expressions as used in these Rules, but it does not give the expressions any meaning in the Rules which they do not otherwise have in the law.

| *Expression* | *Meaning* |
|---|---|
| Affidavit | A written, sworn statement of evidence. |
| Alternative dispute resolution | Collective description of methods of resolving disputes otherwise than through the normal trial process. |
| Base rate | The interest rate set by the Bank of England which is used as the basis for other banks' rates. |
| Contribution | A right of someone to recover from a third person all or part of the amount which he himself is liable to pay. |
| Counterclaim | A claim brought by a defendant in response to the claimant's claim, which is included in the same proceedings as the claimant's claim. |
| Cross-examination (and see 'evidence in chief') | Questioning of a witness by a party other than the party who called the witness. |
| Damages | A sum of money awarded by the court as compensation to the claimant. |
| Aggravated damages | Additional damages which the court may award as compensation for the defendant's objectionable behaviour. |
| Exemplary damages | Damages which go beyond compensating for actual loss and are awarded to show the court's disapproval of the defendant's behaviour. |
| Defence of tender before claim | A defence that, before the claimant started proceedings, the defendant unconditionally offered to the claimant the amount due or, if no specified amount is claimed, an amount sufficient to satisfy the claim. |
| Evidence in chief (and see 'cross-examination') | The evidence given by a witness for the party who called him. |
| Indemnity | A right of someone to recover from a third party the whole amount which he himself is liable to pay. |
| Injunction | A court order prohibiting a person from doing something or requiring a person to do something. |
| Joint liability (and see 'several liability') | Parties who are jointly liable share a single liability and each party can be held liable for the whole of it. |

| | |
|---|---|
| Limitation period | The period within which a person who has a right to claim against another person must start court proceedings to establish that right. The expiry of the period may be a defence to the claim. |
| List | Cases are allocated to different lists depending on the subject matter of the case. The lists are used for administrative purposes and may also have their own procedures and judges. |
| Official copy | A copy of an official document, supplied and marked as such by the office which issued the original. |
| Practice form | Form to be used for a particular purpose in proceedings, the form and purpose being specified by a practice direction. |
| Pre-action protocol | Statements of understanding between legal practitioners and others about pre-action practice and which are approved by a relevant practice direction. |
| Privilege | The right of a party to refuse to disclose a document or produce a document or to refuse to answer questions on the ground of some special interest recognised by law. |
| Seal | A seal is a mark which the court puts on a document to indicate that the document has been issued by the court. |
| Service | Steps required by rules of court to bring documents used in court proceedings to a person's attention. |
| Set aside | Cancelling a judgment or order or a step taken by a party in the proceedings. |
| Several liability (and see 'joint liability') | A person who is severally liable with others may remain liable for the whole claim even where judgment has been obtained against the others. |
| Stay | A stay imposes a halt on proceedings, apart from taking any steps allowed by the Rules or the terms of the stay. Proceedings can be continued if a stay is lifted. |
| Strike out | Striking out means the court ordering written material to be deleted so that it may no longer be relied upon. |
| Without prejudice | Negotiations with a view to a settlement are usually conducted 'without prejudice' which means that the circumstances in which the content of those negotiations may be revealed to the court are very restricted. |

# FAMILY PROCEEDINGS RULES 1991

## SI 1991/1247

## (EXTRACTS)

**2.58 General provisions as to evidence etc on application for ancillary relief**

(1) A petitioner or respondent who has applied for ancillary relief in his petition or answer and who intends to proceed with the application before a district judge shall, subject to rule 2.67, file a notice in Form M13 and within four days after doing so serve a copy on the other spouse.

(2) Where an application is made for ancillary relief, not being an application to which rule 2.61 applies, the notice in Form M11 or M13, as the case may be, shall unless otherwise directed be supported by an affidavit by the applicant containing full particulars of his property and income, and stating the facts relied on in support of the application.

(3) Within 28 days after the service of an affidavit under paragraph (2) or within such other time as the court may fix, the respondent to the application shall file an affidavit in answer containing full particulars of his property and income.

**2.59 Evidence on application for property adjustment or avoidance of disposition order**

(1) Where an application is made for a property adjustment order or an avoidance of disposition order, the affidavit in support shall contain, so far as known to the applicant, full particulars—

  (a) in the case of an application for a transfer or settlement of property—
    (i) of the property in respect of which the application is made,
    (ii) of the property to which the party against whom the application is made is entitled either in possession or reversion;
  (b) in the case of an application for an order for a variation of settlement—
    (i) of all settlements, whether ante-nuptial or post-nuptial, made on the spouses, and
    (ii) of the funds brought into settlement by each spouse;
  (c) in the case of an applicaton for an avoidance of disposition order—
    (i) of the property to which the disposition relates,
    (ii) of the person in whose favour the disposition is alleged to have been made,

and in the case of a disposition alleged to have been made by way of settlement, of the trustees and the beneficiaries of the settlement.

(2) Where an application for a property adjustment order or an avoidance of disposition order relates to land, the notice in Form M11 or M13 shall identify the land and—

  (a) state whether the title to the land is registered or unregistered and, if registered, the Land Registry title number; and
  (b) give particulars, so far as known to the applicant, of any mortgage of the land or any interest therein.

(3) A copy of Form M11 or M13 as the case may be, together with a copy of the supporting affidavit, shall be served on the following persons as well as on the respondent to the application, that is to say—

(a)   in the case of an application for an order for a variation of settlement . . ., the trustees of the settlement and the settlor if living;

(b)   in the case of an application for an avoidance of disposition order, the person in whose favour the disposition is alleged to have been made;

and such other persons, if any, as the district judge may direct.

(4)   In the case of an application to which paragraph [(2)] refers, a copy of Form M11 or M13 as the case may be, shall be served on any mortgagee of whom particulars are given pursuant to that paragraph; any person so served may apply to the court in writing, within 14 days after service, for a copy of the applicant's affidavit.

(5)   Any person who—

(a)   is served with an affidavit pursuant to paragraph (3), or

(b)   receives an affidavit following an application made in accordance with paragraph (4),

may, within 14 days after service or receipt, as the case may be, file an affidavit in answer.

**2.60   Service of affidavit in answer or reply**

(1)   A person who files an affidavit for use on an application under rule 2.58 or 2.59 shall at the same time serve a copy on the opposite party and, where the affidavit contains an allegation of adultery or of an improper association with a named person, then, if the court so directs, it shall be endorsed with a notice in Form M14 and a copy of the affidavit or of such part thereof as the court may direct, indorsed as aforesaid, shall be served on that person by the person who files the affidavit, and the person against whom the allegation is made shall be entitled to intervene in the proceedings by applying for directions under rule 2.62(5) within seven days of service of the affidavit on him.

(2)   Rule 2.37(3) shall apply to a person served with an affidavit under paragraph (1) of this rule as it applies to a co-respondent.

**2.62   Investigation by district judge of application for ancillary relief**

(1)   On or after the filing of a notice in Form M11 or M13 an appointment shall be fixed for the hearing of the application by the district judge.

(2)   An application for an avoidance of disposition order shall, if practicable, be heard at the same time as any related application for financial relief.

(3)   Notice of the appointment, unless given in Form M11 or M13 (as the case may be), shall be given by the proper officer to every party to the application.

(4)   At the hearing of an application for ancillary relief the district judge shall, subject to rules 2.64, 2.65 and 10.10 investigate the allegations made in support of and in answer to the application, and may take evidence orally and may at any stage of the proceedings, whether before or during the hearing, order the attendance of any person for the purpose of being examined or cross-examined and order the discovery and production of any document or require further affidavits.

(5)   The district judge may at any stage of the proceedings give directions as to the filing and service of pleadings and as to the further conduct of the proceedings.

(6)   Where any party to such an application intends on the day appointed for the hearing to apply for directions, he shall file and serve on every other party a notice to that effect.

(7)     Any party may apply to the court for an order that any person do attend an appointment (a 'production appointment') before the court and produce any documents to be specified or described in the order, the production of which appears to the court to be necessary for disposing fairly of the application for ancillary relief or for saving costs.

(8)     No person shall be compelled by an order under paragraph (7) to produce any document at a production appointment which he could not be compelled to produce at the hearing of the application for ancillary relief.

(9)     The court shall permit any person attending a production appointment pursuant to an order under paragraph (7) above to be represented at the appointment.

### 2.63   Request for further information etc

Any part to an application for ancillary relief may by letter require any other party to give further information concerning any matter contained in any affidavit filed by or on behalf of that other party or any other relevant matter, or to furnish a list of relevant documents or to allow inspection of any such document, and may, in default of compliance by such other party, apply to the district judge for directions.

### 2.73   Notice in Form E

(1)     Not less than 35 days before the date of the first appointment the applicant and respondent shall simultaneously exchange with the other party and each file with the court a statement in Form E in Appendix 1A which—

    (a)   is signed by him;
    (b)   is sworn to be true, and
    (c)   contains the information set out in paragraph (2).

(2)     The information referred to in paragraph (1) is—

    (a)   the party's full name, age, date of birth and occupation;
    (b)   the party's state of health;
    (c)   the dates of marriage and separation of the parties;
    (d)   the full names and dates of birth of any children of the family, and the name and address of the person with whom they live;
    (e)   details of the party's present residence and the occupants thereof;
    (f)   a concise statement of the party's means including—
        (i)   his income and earning capacity,
        (ii)   the value of all his assets and liabilities,
        (iii)   the benefits under any pension scheme that he has or is likely to have with the most recent valuation (if any) furnished by the trustees or managers of the pension scheme pursuant to regulation 5 of, and Schedule 2 to, the Occupational Pension Schemes (Disclosure of Information) Regulations 1996, or paragraph 2(b) of Schedule 2 to the Personal Pension Schemes (Disclosure of Information) Regulations 1987, or regulation 4 of the Divorce etc (Pensions) Regulations 1996; and
        (iv)   any other resources (including any resources that he may receive in the foreseeable future such as by way of inheritance), and, where an insurance policy is included, its current surrender value and date of maturity;
    (g)   a concise statement of any loss of widow's or widower's pension that would be suffered by either party following a divorce;
    (h)   a concise statement of the present and future reasonable needs of himself and any children of the family;

(i)    details of the present and proposed educational arrangements for any children of the family;

(j)    details of any child support maintenance assessment made by the Child Support Agency, or of any agreement for child maintenance made between the parties;

(k)    a brief description of the standard of living enjoyed by the parties during the marriage;

(l)    whether either party has made a relevant contribution (within the meaning of section 25(2)(f) of the Act of 1973) and, if so, a concise statement of that contribution;

(m)  whether the other party's conduct (financial or otherwise) during the marriage is considered to be relevant, and if so, a concise statement of the issues of conduct relied on;

(n)   any other circumstances which he considers could significantly affect the extent of financial provision to be made for the applicant or any child of the family.

The statement shall annex only such documents as are necessary to explain or clarify any of the above information.

(3)    After the filing of the application for ancillary relief but before the first appointment, no discovery of documents shall be sought or given except—

(a)   insofar as documents have been annexed to the statement filed under paragraph (1); or

(b)   in accordance with paragraph (4) below.

(4)    Not later than 7 days before the hearing of the first appointment, each party shall file and serve on the other party—

(a)   a questionnaire setting out any further information sought from the other party;

(b)   a schedule setting out any documents sought from the other party;

(c)   a concise statement of the issues between the parties;

(d)   where an order for ancillary relief is sought that includes provision to be made by virtue of section 25B or 25C of the Act of 1973, confirmation that the trustees or managers of the pension scheme in question have been served and provided with the specified information in accordance with Rule 2.70(4),

and the party who served the notice in Form A in Appendix 1A shall confirm that all relevant persons have been served in accordance with rule 2.59(3) and (4).

## 2.74  The First Appointment

(1)    The first appointment shall be conducted with the objective of defining the issues and saving costs and the district judge—

(a)   shall determine—

(i)  the extent to which any questionnaire filed under Rule 2.73 shall be answered, and

(ii)  what documents requested under Rule 2.73 shall be produced,

and give directions for the production of such further documents as may be necessary;

(b)   shall give directions as to—

(i)  the valuation of assets (including, where practicable, the joint instruction of independent experts) and

(ii)  obtaining and exchanging experts' evidence (including the holding of meetings of experts);

(iii)  any evidence sought to be adduced by each party and as to any chronologies or schedules to be filed by each party;

(c)  shall (unless he decides that a referral is not appropriate in the circumstances) direct that the case be referred to a Financial Dispute Resolution ('FDR') appointment;

(d)  shall, where he decides that a referral to a FDR appointment is not appropriate, direct that—

(i)  a further directions appointment be fixed; or

(ii)  an appointment be fixed for the making of an interim order;

(iii)  the case be fixed for final hearing and, where such a direction is given, the district judge shall determine the level of judge before whom the case should be heard; or

(iv)  the case be adjourned for out-of-court mediation or private negotiation or in exceptional circumstances generally;

(e)  shall consider whether, having regard to all the circumstances (including the extent to which each party has adhered to the rules), to make an order as to the costs of the hearing;

(f)  may—

(i)  in a case of urgency, make an interim order;

(ii)  with the consent of both parties, treat the appointment (or part of it) as a FDR appointment to which Rule 2.75 applies;

(iii)  in a case where an order for ancillary relief is sought that includes provision to be made by virtue of section 25B or 25C of the Act of 1973, require any party to request a valuation under regulation 4 of the Divorce etc (Pensions) Regulations 1996 from the trustees or managers of any pension scheme under which the party has, or is likely to have, any benefits.

(2)  After the first appointment, no party shall be entitled to seek further discovery of documents except in accordance with directions given under paragraph (1)(a) above or with the leave of the court.

(3)  At any stage—

(a)  a party may apply for further directions or a FDR appointment;

(b)  the court may give further directions or direct that the parties attend a FDR appointment.

(4)  Both parties shall personally attend the appointment unless the court otherwise orders.

## 2.75  The FDR Appointment

(1)  The FDR appointment shall be treated as a meeting held for the purposes of conciliation and the following provisions shall apply—

(a)  the district judge (or judge) hearing the appointment shall have no further involvement with the application, other than to conduct any further FDR appointment;

(b)  not later than 7 days before the appointment the applicant shall file details of all such offers and proposals and responses to them and, at the conclusion of the appointment, any documents containing the same or referring thereto shall be returned to the applicant or respondent (as the case may be) and not retained on the court file;

(c)  parties attending the appointment shall use their best endeavours to reach agreement on relevant matters in issue between them;

(d)  the appointment may be adjourned from time to time, and at the conclusion thereof the court may make such consent order as may be appropriate, but otherwise shall give directions for the future course of the proceedings, including, where appropriate, fixing a final hearing date.

(2)    Both parties shall personally attend the appointment unless the court otherwise orders.

## 2.76   Costs

At every court hearing each party shall produce to the court a written estimate of the solicitor and own client costs incurred up to the date of that hearing.

## 4.17   Documentary evidence

(1)    Subject to paragraphs (4) and (5), in proceedings in which this Part applies a party shall file and serve on the parties, any welfare officer and any guardian ad litem of whose appointment he has been given notice under rule 4.10(5)—

    (a)   written statements of the substance of the oral evidence which the party intends to adduce at a hearing of, or a directions appointment in, those proceedings, which shall—

        (i)   be dated,

        (ii)  be signed by the person making the statement, ...

        (iii) contain a declaration that the maker of the statement believes it to be true and understands that it may be placed before the court; and

        [(iv) show in the top right hand corner of the first page—

           (a)   the initials and surname of the person making the statement,

           (b)   the number of the statement in relation to the maker,

           (c)   the date on which the statement was made, and

           (d )  the party on whose behalf it is filed; and

    (b)   copies of any documents, including experts' reports, upon which the party intends to rely at a hearing of, or a directions appointment in, those proceedings,

at or by such time as the court directs or, in the absence of a direction, before the hearing or appointment.

(2)    A party may, subject to any direction of the court about the timing of statements under this rule, file and serve on the parties a statement which is supplementary to a statement served under paragraph (1).

(3)    At a hearing or a directions appointment a party may not, without the leave of the court—

    (a)   adduce evidence, or

    (b)   seek to rely on a document,

in respect of which he has failed to comply with the requirements of paragraph (1).

(4)    In proceedings for a section 8 order a party shall—

    (a)   neither file nor serve any document other than as required or authorised by these rules, and

    (b)   in completing a form prescribed by these rules, neither give information, nor make a statement, which is not required or authorised by that form,

without the leave of the court.

(5)    In proceedings for a section 8 order no statement or copy may be filed under paragraph (1) until such time as the court directs.

## 4.18   Expert evidence – examination of child

(1)    No person may, without the leave of the court, cause the child to be medically or psychiatrically examined, or otherwise assessed, for the purpose of the preparation of expert evidence for use in the proceedings.

(2)     An application for leave under paragraph (1) shall, unless the court otherwise directs, be served on all parties to the proceedings and on the guardian ad litem.

(3)     Where the leave of the court has not been given under paragraph (1), no evidence arising out of an examination or assessment to which that paragraph applies may be adduced without the leave of the court.

### 4.19   Amendment

(1)     Subject to rule 4.17(2), a document which has been filed or served in proceedings to which this Part applies, may not be amended without the leave of the court which shall, unless the court otherwise directs, be requested in writing.

(2)     On considering a request for leave to amend a document the court shall either—

    (a)   grant the request, whereupon the proper officer shall inform the person making the request of that decision, or

    (b)   invites the parties or any of them to make representations, within a specified period, as to whether such an order should be made.

(3)     A person amending a document shall file it and serve it on those persons on whom it was served prior to amendment; and the amendments shall be identified.

### 4.20   Oral evidence

The court or the proper officer shall keep a note of the substance of the oral evidence given at a hearing of, or directions appointment in, proceedings to which this Part applies.

### 4.21   Hearing

(1)     The court may give directions as to the order of speeches and evidence at a hearing, or directions appointment, in the course of proceedings to which this Part applies.

(2)     Subject to directions under paragraph (1), at a hearing of, or directions appointment in, proceedings to which this Part applies, the parties and the guardian ad litem shall adduce their evidence in the following order—

    (a)   the applicant,
    (b)   any party with parental responsibility for the child,
    (c)   other respondents,
    (d)   the guardian ad litem,
    (e)   the child, if he is a party to the proceedings and there is no guardian ad litem.

(3)     After the final hearing of proceedings to which this Part applies, the court shall deliver its judgment as soon as is practicable.

(4)     When making an order or when refusing an application, the court shall—

    (a)   where it makes a finding of fact state such finding and complete Form C22; and
    (b)   state the reasons for the court's decision.

(5)     An order made in proceedings to which this Part applies shall be recorded, by the court or the proper officer, either in the appropriate form in Appendix 1 to these rules or, where there is no such form, in writing.

(6)     Subject to paragraph (7), a copy of an order made in accordance with paragraph (5) shall, as soon as practicable after it has been made, be served by the proper officer on the parties to the proceedings in which it was made [and] on any person with whom the child is living.

(7)     Within 48 hours after the making ex parte of—

    (a)  a [section 8 order], or

    (b)  an order under section 44, 48(4), 48(9) or 50,

the applicant shall serve a copy of the order in the appropriate form in Appendix 1 to these Rules on—

        (i)   each party,

       (ii)  any person who has actual care of the child or who had such care immediately prior to the making of the order, and

     (iii)  in the case of an order referred to in sub-paragraph (b), the local authority in whose area the child lives or is found.

(8)     At a hearing of, or directions appointment in, an application which takes place outside the hours during which the court office is normally open, the court or the proper officer shall take a note of the substance of the proceedings.

### 4.21A   Attachment of penal notice to section 8 order

CCR Order 29, rule 1 (committal for breach of order or undertaking) shall apply to section 8 orders as if for paragraph (3) of that rule there were substituted the following—

   '(3)     In the case of a section 8 order (within the meaning of section 8(2) of the Children Act 1989) enforceable by committal order under paragraph (1), the judge or the district judge may, on the application of the person entitled to enforce the order, direct that the proper officer issue a copy of the order, indorsed with or incorporating a notice as to the consequences of disobedience, for service in accordance with paragraph (2); and no copy of the order shall be issued with any such notice indorsed or incorporated save in accordance with such a direction.'

### 4.22  Appeals

(1)     Where an appeal lies—

    (a)  to the High Court under section 94, or

    (b)  from any decision of a district judge to the judge of the court in which the decision was made,

it shall be made in accordance with the following provisions; and references to 'the court below' are references to the court from which, or person from whom, the appeal lies.

(2)     The appellant shall file and serve on the parties to the proceedings in the court below, and on any guardian ad litem—

    (a)  notice of the appeal in writing, setting out the grounds upon which he relies;

    (b)  a certified copy of the summons or application and of the order appealed against, and of any order staying its execution;

    (c)  a copy of any notes of the evidence;

    (d)  a copy of any reasons given for the decision.

[(2A)  In relation to an appeal to the High Court under section 94, the documents required to be filed by paragraph (2) shall,—

    (a)  where the care centre listed in column (ii) of Schedule 2 to the Children (Allocation of Proceedings) Order 1991 against the entry in column (i) relating to the petty sessions area or London commission area in which the court below is situated—

        (i)  is the principal registry, or

       (ii)  has a district registry in the same place,

be filed in that registry, and

(b) in any other case, be filed in the district registry, being in the same place as a care centre within the meaning of article 2(c) of the said Order, which is nearest to the court below.]

(3) The notice of appeal shall be filed and served in accordance with paragraph (2)(a)—

(a) within 14 days after the determination against which the appeal is brought, or
(b) in the case of an appeal against an order under section 38(1), within 7 days after the making of the order, or
(c) with the leave of the court to which, or judge to whom, the appeal is to be brought, within such other time as that court or judge may direct.

(4) The documents mentioned in paragraph (2)(b) to (d) shall, subject to any direction of the court to which, or judge to whom, the appeal is to be brought, be filed and served as soon as practicable after the filing and service of the notice of appeal under paragraph (2)(a).

(5) Subject to paragraph (6), a respondent who wishes—

(a) to contend on the appeal that the decision of the court below should be varied, either in any event or in the event of the appeal being allowed in whole or in part, or
(b) to contend that the decision of the court below should be affirmed on grounds other than those relied upon by that court, or
(c) to contend by way of cross-appeal that the decision of the court below was wrong in whole or in part,

shall, within 14 days of receipt of notice of the appeal, file and serve on all other parties to the appeal a notice in writing, setting out the grounds upon which he relies.

(6) No notice under paragraph (5) may be filed or served in an appeal against an order under section 38.

(7) In the case of an appeal mentioned in paragraph (1)(a), an application to—

(a) withdraw the appeal,
(b) have the appeal dismissed with the consent of all the parties, or
(c) amend the grounds of appeal,

may be heard by a district judge.

(8) An appeal of the kind mentioned in paragraph (1)(a) shall, unless the President otherwise directs, be heard and determined by a single judge.

# RULES OF THE SUPREME COURT 1965

## SI 1965/1776

## (EXTRACTS)

### ORDER 24
### DISCOVERY AND INSPECTION OF DOCUMENTS

**1. Mutual discovery of documents (Ord 24, r 1)**

(1) After the close of pleadings in an action begun by writ there shall, subject to and in accordance with the provisions of this Order, be discovery by the parties to the action of the documents which are or have been in their possession, custody or power relating to matters in question in the action.

(2) Nothing in this Order shall be taken as preventing the parties to an action agreeing to dispense with or limit the discovery of documents which they would otherwise be required to make to each other.

**3. Order for discovery (Ord 24, r 3)**

(1) Subject to the provisions of this rule and of rules 4 and 8, the Court may order any party to a cause or matter (whether begun by writ, originating summons or otherwise) to make and serve on any other party a list of the documents which are or have been in his possession, custody or power relating to any matter in question in the cause or matter, and may at the same time or subsequently also order him to make and file an affidavit verifying such a list and to serve a copy thereof on the other party.

(2) Where a party who is required by rule 2 to make discovery of documents fails to comply with any provision of that rule, the Court, on the application of any party to whom the discovery was required to be made, may make an order against the first-mentioned party under paragraph (1) of this rule or, as the case may be, may order him to make and file an affidavit verifying the list of documents he is required to make under rule 2, and to serve a copy thereof on the applicant.

(3) An order under this rule may be limited to such documents or classes of document only, or to such only of the matters in question in the cause or matter, as may be specified in the order.

**5. Form of list and affidavit (Ord 24, r 5)**

(1) A list of documents made in compliance with rule 2 or with an order under rule 3 must be in Form No 26 in Appendix A, and must enumerate the documents in a convenient order and as shortly as possible but describing each of them or, in the case of bundles of documents of the same nature, each bundle, sufficiently to enable it to be identified.

(2) If it is desired to claim that any documents are privileged from production, the claim must be made in the list of documents with a sufficient statement of the grounds of the privilege.

(3) An affidavit made as aforesaid verifying a list of documents must be in Form No 27 in Appendix A.

**7. Order for discovery of particular documents (Ord 24, r 7)**

(1) Subject to rule 8, the Court may at any time, on the application of any party to a cause or matter, make an order requiring any other party to make an affidavit stating whether any

document specified or described in the application or any class of document so specified or described is, or has at any time been, in his possession, custody or power, and if not then in his possession, custody or power when he parted with it and what has become of it.

(2) An order may be made against a party under this rule notwithstanding that he may already have made or been required to make a list of documents or affidavit under rule 2 or rule 3.

(3) An application for an order under this rule must be supported by an affidavit stating the belief of the deponent that the party from whom discovery is sought under this rule has, or at some time had, in his possession, custody or power the document, or class of document, specified or described in the application and that it relates to one or more of the matters in question in the cause or matter.

## 8.   Discovery to be ordered only if necessary (Ord 24, r 8)

On the hearing of an application for an order under rule 3, 7 or 7A the Court, if satisfied that discovery is not necessary, or not necessary at that stage of the cause or matter, may dismiss or, as the case may be, adjourn the application and shall in any case refuse to make such an order if and so far as it is of opinion that discovery is not necessary either for disposing fairly of the cause or matter or for saving costs.

**Note:** Amended by Rules of the Supreme Court (Amendment No 4) 1971, SI 1971/1907

## 10.   Inspection of documents referred to in pleadings, affidavits and witness statements (Ord 24, r 10)

(1) Any party to a cause or matter shall be entitled at any time to serve a notice on any other party in whose pleadings, affidavits or witness statements reference is made to any document requiring him to produce that document for the inspection of the party giving the notice and to permit him to take copies thereof.

(2) The party on whom a notice is served under paragraph (1) must, within four days after service of the notice, serve on the party giving the notice a notice stating a time within seven days after the service thereof at which the documents, or such of them as he does not object to produce, may be inspected at a place specified in the notice, and stating which (if any) of the documents he objects to produce and on what grounds.

**Note:** Amended by Rules of the Supreme Court (Amendment) (No 2) 1992, SI 1992/1907

## 12.   Order for production to Court (Ord 24, r 12)

At any stage of the proceedings in any cause or matter the Court may, subject to rule 13(1), order any party to produce to the Court any document in his possession, custody or power relating to any matter in question in the cause or matter and the Court may deal with the document when produced in such manner as it thinks fit.

## 13.   Production to be ordered only if necessary, etc (Ord 24, r 13)

(1) No order for the production of any documents for inspection or to the Court, or for the supply of a copy of any document, shall be made under any of the foregoing rules unless the Court is of opinion that the order is necessary either for disposing fairly of the cause or matter or for saving costs.

(2) Where on an application under this Order for production of any document for inspection or to the Court, or for the supply of a copy of any document, privilege from such production or supply is claimed or objection is made to such production or supply on any other ground, the

Court may inspect the document for the purpose of deciding whether the claim or objection is valid.

**Note:** Amended by Rules of the Supreme Court (Amendment) 1987, SI 1987/1423

**15.  Document disclosure of which would be injurious to public interest: saving (Ord 24, r 15)**

The foregoing provisions of this Order shall be without prejudice to any rule of law which authorises or requires the withholding of any document on the ground that the disclosure of it would be injurious to the public interest.

## ORDER 26

### INTERROGATORIES

**1.  Discovery by interrogatories (Ord 27, r 1)**

(1) A party to any cause or matter may in accordance with the following provisions of this Order serve on any other party interrogatories relating to any matter in question between the applicant and that other party in the cause or matter which are necessary either—

(a)    for disposing fairly of the cause or matter, or
(b)    for saving costs.

(2) Without prejudice to the provisions of paragraph (1), a party may apply to the Court for an order giving him leave to serve on any other party interrogatories relating to any matter in question between the applicant and that other party in the cause or matter.

(3) A proposed interrogatory which does not relate to such a matter as is mentioned in paragraph (1) may not be administered notwithstanding that it would be admissible in oral cross-examination of a witness.

(4) In this Order,

'interrogatories without order' means interrogatories served under paragraph (1);
'ordered interrogatories' means interrogatories served under paragraph (2) or interrogatories which are required to be answered pursuant to an order made on an application under rule 3(2) and, where such an order is made, the interrogatories shall not, unless the Court orders otherwise, be treated as interrogatories without order for the purposes of rule 3(1).

(3) Unless the context otherwise requires, the provisions of this Order apply to both interrogatories without order and ordered interrogatories.

**2.  Form and nature of interrogatories (Ord 26, r 2)**

(1) Where interrogatories are served, a note at the end of the interrogatories shall specify—

(a)    a period of time (not being less than 28 days from the date of service) within which the interrogatories are to be answered;
(b)    where the party to be interrogated is a body corporate or unincorporate which is empowered by law to sue or be sued whether in its own name or in the name of an officer or other person, the officer or member on whom the interrogatories are to be served; and
(c)    where the interrogatories are to be served on two or more parties or are required to be answered by an agent or servant of a party, which of the interrogatories each party or, as the case may be, an agent or servant is required to answer, and which agent or servant.

(2) Subject to rule 5(1), a party on whom interrogatories are served shall, unless the Court orders otherwise on an application under rule 3(2), be required to give within the period specified under rule 2(1)(a) answers which shall (unless the Court directs otherwise) be on affidavit.

## 3. Interrogatories without order (Ord 26, r 3)

(1) Interrogatories without order may be served on a party not more than twice.

(2) A party on whom interrogatories without order are served may, within 14 days of the service of the interrogatories, apply to the Court for the interrogatories to be varied or withdrawn and, on any such application, the Court may make such order as it thinks fit (including an order that the party who served the interrogatories shall not serve further interrogatories without order).

(3) Interrogatories without order shall not be served on the Crown.

## 4. Ordered interrogatories (Ord 26, r 4)

(1) Where an application is made for leave to serve interrogatories, a copy of the proposed interrogatories shall be served with the summons or the notice under Order 25, rule 7, by which the application is made.

(2) In deciding whether to give leave to serve interrogatories, the Court shall take into account any offer made by the party to be interrogated to give particulars, make admissions or produce documents relating to any matter in question and whether or not interrogatories without order have been administered.

## 5. Objections and insufficient answers (Ord 26, r 5)

(1) Without prejudice to rule 3(2), where a person objects to answering any interrogatory on the ground of privilege he may take the objection in his answer.

(2) Where any person on whom ordered interrogatories have been served answers any of them insufficiently, the Court may make an order requiring him to make a further answer, either by affidavit or on oral examination as the Court may direct.

(3) Where any person on whom interrogatories without order have been served answers any of them insufficiently, the party serving the interrogatories may ask for further and better particulars of the answer given and any such request shall not be treated as service of further interrogatories for the purposes of rule 3(1).

## 6. Failure to comply with order (Ord 26, r 6)

(1) If a party fails to answer interrogatories or to comply with an order made under rule 5(2) or a request made under rule 5(3), the Court may make such order as it thinks just including, in particular, an order that the action be dismissed or, as the case may be, an order that the defence be struck out and judgment be entered accordingly.

(2) Without prejudice to paragraph (1), where a party fails to answer ordered interrogatories or to comply with an order made under rule 5(2), he shall be liable to committal.

(3) Service on a party's solicitor of an order to answer interrogatories made against the party shall be sufficient service to found an application for committal of the party disobeying the order, but the party may show in answer in the application that he had no notice or knowledge of the order.

(4) A solicitor on whom an order to answer interrogatories made against his client is served and who fails without reasonable excuse to give notice thereof to his client shall be liable to committal.

## 7.  Use of answers to interrogatories at trial (Ord 26, r 7)

A party may put in evidence at the trial of a cause or matter, or of any issue therein, some only of the answers to interrogatories, or part only of such an answer, without putting in evidence the other answers or, as the case may be, the whole of that answer, but the Court may look at the whole of the answers and if of opinion that any other answer or other part of an answer is so connected with an answer or part thereof used in evidence that the one ought not to be so used without the other, the Court may direct that that other answer or party shall be put in evidence.

## 8.  Revocation and variation of orders (Ord 26, r 8)

Any order made under this Order (including an order made on appeal) may, on sufficient cause being shown, be revoked or varied by a subsequent order or direction of the Court made or given at or before the trial of the cause or matter in connection with which the original order was made.

**ORDER 38**

EVIDENCE

*I  General rules*

## 1.  General rule: witnesses to be examined orally (Ord 38, r 1)

Subject to the provisions of these rules and of the Civil Evidence Act 1968 and the Civil Evidence Act 1972, and any other enactment relating to evidence, any fact required to be proved at the trial of any action begun by writ by the evidence of witnesses shall be proved by the examination of the witnesses orally and in open Court.

**Note:** Amended by Rules of the Supreme Court (Amendment) 1969, SI 1969/1105; Rules of the Supreme Court (Amendment No 4) 1979, SI 1979/1542

## 2.  Evidence by affidavit (Ord 38, r 2)

(1), (2) . . .

(3) In any cause or matter begun by originating summons, originating motion or petition, and on any application made by summons or motion, evidence may be given by affidavit unless in the case of any such cause, matter or application any provision of these rules otherwise provides or the Court otherwise directs, but the Court may, on the application of any party, order the attendance for cross-examination of the person making any such affidavit, and where, after such an order has been made, the person in question does not attend, his affidavit shall not be used as evidence without the leave of the Court.

## 3.  Evidence of particular facts (Ord 38, r 3)

(1) Without prejudice to rule 2, the Court may, at or before the trial of any action, order that evidence of any particular fact shall be given at the trial in such manner as may be specified by the order.

(2) The power conferred by paragraph (1) extends in particular to ordering that evidence of any particular fact may be given at the trial—

(a)  by statement on oath of information or belief, or

(b)  by the production of documents or entries in books, or

(c)  by copies of documents or entries in books, or

(d)  in the case of a fact which is or was a matter of common knowledge either generally or in a particular district, by the production of a specified newspaper which contains a statement of that fact.

## 4.  Limitation of expert evidence (Ord 38, r 4)

The Court may, at or before the trial of any action, order that the number of medical or other expert witnesses who may be called at the trial shall be limited as specified by the order.

## 12.  Evidence at trial may be used in subsequent proceedings (Ord 38, r 12)

Any evidence taken at the trial of any cause or matter may be used in any subsequent proceedings in that cause or matter.

## 13.  Order to produce document at proceeding other than trial (Ord 38, r 13)

(1) At any stage in a cause or matter the Court may order any person to attend any proceeding in the cause or matter and produce any document, to be specified or described in the order, the production of which appears to the Court to be necessary for the purpose of that proceeding.

(2) No person shall be compelled by an order under paragraph (1) to produce any document at a proceeding in a cause or matter which he could not be compelled to produce at the trial of that cause or matter.

*II  Writs of subpoena*

## 14.  Form and issue of writ of subpoena (Ord 38, r 14)

(1) A writ of subpoena must be in Form No. 28, 29, or 30 in Appendix A, whichever is appropriate.

(2) Issue of a writ of subpoena takes place upon its being sealed by an officer of the office out of which it is issued.

(3) Where a writ of subpoena is to be issued in a cause or matter which is not proceeding in a District Registry, the appropriate office for the issue of the writ is the Central Office or, if the cause or matter has been set down for trial outside the Royal Courts of Justice, either the Central Office or the registry for the district comprising the city or town at which the cause or matter has been set down for trial.

(4) Where a writ of subpoena is to be issued in a cause or matter which is proceeding in a District Registry, the appropriate office for the issue of the writ is—

(a)  that registry, or

(b)  if the cause or matter has been set down for trial at a city or town not comprised in the district of that registry, either that registry or the registry for the district comprising that city or town, or

(c)  if the cause or matter has been set down for trial at the Royal Courts of Justice, either the Central Office or the Registry in which the cause or matter is proceeding.

(5) Before a writ of subpoena is issued a praecipe for the issue of the writ must be filed in the office out of which the writ is to issue; and the praecipe must contain the name and address of

the party issuing the writ, if he is acting in person, or the name or firm and business address of that party's solicitor and also (if the solicitor is the agent of another) the name or firm and business address of his principal.

**Note:** Amended by Rules of the Supreme Court (Amendment) 1969, SI 1969/1105; Rules of the Supreme Court (Amendment No 5) 1971, SI 1971/1955

### 15. More than one name may be included in one writ of subpoena (Ord 38, r 15)

The names of two or more persons may be included in one writ of subpoena ad testificandum.

### 16. Amendment of writ of subpoena (Ord 38, r 16)

Where there is a mistake in any person's name or address in a writ of subpoena, then, if the writ has not been served, the party by whom the writ was issued may have the writ re-sealed in correct form by filing a second praecipe under rule 14(5) indorsed with the words 'Amended and re-sealed'.

### 17. Service of writ of subpoena (Ord 38, r 17)

A writ of subpoena must be served personally and, subject to rule 19, the service shall not be valid unless effected within 12 weeks after the date of issue of the writ and not less than four days or such other period as the Court may fix, before the day on which attendance before the Court is required.

**Note:** Amended by Rules of the Supreme Court (Amendment) 1969, SI 1969/1105; Rules of the Supreme Court (Amendment No 2) 1980, SI 1980/1010

### 18. Duration of writ of subpoena (Ord 38, r 18)

Subject to rule 19, a writ of subpoena continues to have effect until the conclusion of the trial at which the attendance of the witness is required.

**Note:** Amended by Rules of the Supreme Court (Amendment) 1969, SI 1969/1105

### 19. Writ of subpoena in aid of inferior court or tribunal (Ord 38, r 19)

(1) The office of the Supreme Court out of which a writ of subpoena ad testificandum or a writ of subpoena duces tecum in aid of an inferior court or tribunal may be issued is the Crown Office, and no order of the court for the issue of such a writ is necessary.

(2) A writ of subpoena in aid of an inferior court or tribunal continues to have effect until the disposal of the proceedings before that court or tribunal at which the attendance of the witness is required.

(3) A writ of subpoena issued in aid of an inferior court or tribunal is duly served on the person to whom it is directed not less than 4 days, or such other period as the court may fix, before the day on which the attendance of that person before the court or tribunal is required by the writ that person shall not be liable to any penalty or process for failing to obey the writ.

(4) An application to set aside a writ of subpoena issued in aid of an inferior court or tribunal may be heard by a Master of the Queen's Bench Division.

...

*IV  Expert evidence*

## 35.  Interpretation (Ord 38, r 35)

In this Part of this Order a reference to a summons for directions includes a reference to any summons or application to which, under any of these Rules, Order 25, rules 2 to 7, apply and expressions used in this Part of this Order which are used in the Civil Evidence Act 1972 have the same meanings in this Part of this Order as in that Act.

## 36.  Restrictions on adducing expert evidence (Ord 38, r 36)

(1) Except with the leave of the Court or where all parties agree, no expert evidence may be adduced at the trial or hearing of any cause or matter unless the party seeking to adduce the evidence—

  (a)  has applied to the Court to determine whether a direction should be given under rule 37 or 41 (whichever is appropriate) and has complied with any direction given on the application, or

  (b)  has complied with automatic directions taking effect under Order 25, rule 8(1)(b).

(2) Nothing in paragraph (1) shall apply to evidence which is permitted to be given by affidavit or shall affect the enforcement under any other provision of these Rules (except Order 45, rule 5) of a direction given under this part of this Order.

**Note:** Amended by Rules of the Supreme Court (Amendment No 2) 1980, SI 1980/1010; Rules of the Supreme Court (Amendment) 1987, SI 1987/1423

## 37.  Direction that expert report be disclosed (Ord 38, r 37)

(1) Subject to paragraph (2), where in any cause or matter an application is made under rule 36(1) in respect of oral expert evidence, then, unless the Court considers that there are special reasons for not doing so, it shall direct that the substance of the evidence be disclosed in the form of a written report or reports to such other parties and within such period as the Court may specify.

(2) ...

**Note:** Amended by Rules of the Supreme Court (Amendment No 4) 1989, SI 1989/2427

## 38.  Meeting of experts (Ord 38, r 38)

In any cause or matter the Court may, if it thinks fit, direct that there be a meeting 'without prejudice' of such experts within such periods before or after the disclosure of their reports as the Court may specify, for the purpose of identifying those parts of their evidence which are in issue. Where such a meeting takes place the experts may prepare a joint statement indicating those parts of their evidence on which they are, and those on which they are not, in agreement.

**Note:** Amended by Rules of the Supreme Court (Amendment) 1987, SI 1987/1423

## 39.  Disclosure of part of expert evidence (Ord 38, r 39)

Where the Court considers that any circumstances rendering it undesirable to give a direction under rule 37 relate to part only of the evidence sought to be adduced, the Court may, if it thinks fit, direct disclosure of the remainder.

**Note:** Amended by Rules of the Supreme Court (Amendment) 1987, SI 1987/1423

# Appendix 2

## TABLE OF PRESCRIBED PLEADINGS AND FORMS OF EVIDENCE IN FAMILY PROCEEDINGS

The manner of commencement and forms of supporting evidence in particular proceedings are prescribed in family cases. Generally they are prescribed by rules (Family Proceedings Rules 1991, SI 1991/1257: Family Proceedings Courts (Children Act 1989) Rules 1991, SI 1991/1395; Rules of the Supreme Court 1965; County Court Rules 1981). Sometimes they are judge-made (see for example *H v M* [1992] 1 FLR 229). This table is intended as a convenient guide to the pleadings and forms of evidence prescribed for particular matters. Included are not only the originating process, but also interlocutory applications where it is important to understand the distinction between pleadings and evidence (for example interrogatories and the replies thereto). Wherever affidavit evidence is prescribed or ordered, the deponents should, on the application of the other party, generally be made available for cross-examination (County Court Rules 1981, ord 20, rr 5–7; Rules of the Supreme Court 1965, Ord 38, r 2). Where they are unavailable, their evidence will be admissible subject to the provisions of the Civil Evidence Act 1968, which permits, in prescribed circumstances, the admission of hearsay in civil proceedings. Hearsay is admissible in all cases concerning the 'upbringing, maintenance or welfare of a child' (Children (Admissibility of Hearsay Evidence) Order 1993, SI 1993/631). The effect of the Civil Evidence Act 1995 will be the abolition of the rule against the admission of hearsay evidence in civil proceedings. This will result in the admission of hearsay evidence in family proceedings not covered by the Children (Admissibility of Hearsay Evidence) Order 1993, such as ancillary relief and divorce proceedings.

Where proceedings are to be commenced by originating summons in the High Court, the invariable rule is that they are to be commenced by originating application if brought in the county court.

**Glossary to Table**

| | |
|---|---|
| ARPS 1996 | Ancillary Relief Pilot Scheme – Draft Rule 25 July 1996 |
| CA 1989 | Children Act 1989 |
| CAA 1985 | Child Abduction Act 1985 |
| CCR 1981 | County Court Rules 1981 |
| CSA 1991 | Child Support Art 1991 |
| DVMPA 1976 | Domestic Violence and Matrimonial Proceedings Act 1976 |
| FLA 1986 | Family Law Act 1986 |
| FPC(CA)R 1991 | Family Proceedings Court (Children Act 1989) Rules 1991 |
| FPC(CS)R 1993 | Family Proceedings Court (Child Support) Rules 1993 |
| FPR 1991 | Family Proceedings Rules 1991 |
| RSC 1965 | Rules of the Supreme Court 1965 |
| MCA 1973 | Matrimonial Causes Act 1973 |
| MFPA 1984 | Matrimonial and Family Proceedings Act 1984, ss 12–27 |
| MHA 1983 | Matrimonial Homes Act 1983 |

| Business | Pleading | Rule | Evidence | Rule |
|---|---|---|---|---|
| divorce | petition | FPR, r 2.2 | oral | FPR, r 2.28 |
| nullity | petition | FPR, r 2.2 | oral | FPR, r 2.28 |
| judicial separation | petition | FPR, r 2.2 | oral | FPR, r 2.28 |
| presumption of death and dissolution of marriage MCA 1973, s 19 | petition | FPR, r 2.2 | oral | FPR, r 2.28 |
| declaration of marital status FLA 1986, s 55 | petition | FPR, r 3.12 | affidavit | FPR, r 3.16 |
| declaration of parentage FLA 1986, s 56(1)(a) | petition | FPR, r 3.13 | affidavit | FPR, r 3.16 |
| declaration of parentage CSA 1991, s 27 | written application (no prescribed form) | FPC(CS)R, r 4(1) applying FPC (CA)R, rr 2–16 | written statement attested/ affirmed | FPC(CA)R, rr 9 and 12 |
| declaration of legitimacy/ legitimation FLA 1986, s 56 (10)(b) and (2) | petition | FPR, r 3.14 | affidavit | FPR, r 3.16 |
| declaration of overseas adoption FLA 1986, s 57 | petition | FPR, r 3.15 | affidavit | FPR, r 3.16 |
| applications under MCA 1973, s 10(2) | notice: Form M12 | FPR, r 2.45(1) and (3) | affidavit | FPR, r 2.45(2) |
| ancillary relief MCA 1973, ss 23 and 24 | notice: Form M11 (or M13 if prayed for in Petition or Answer) | FPR, r 2.53 | affidavit | FPR, r 2.58(2) |
| ancillary relief (pilot scheme) | Form A | Draft Rule ARPS, Part 1 | Form E sworn | Draft Rule ARPS, Part 2 |
| reasonable maintenance MCA 1973, s 27 | Form M19 | FPR, r 3.1 | affidavit | FPR, r 3.1(2) |
| alteration of maintenance agreements MCA 1973, s 35 | Form M21 | FPR, r 3.2 | affidavit | FPR, r 3.2(2) |

| Business | Pleading | Rule | Evidence | Rule |
|---|---|---|---|---|
| alteration of maintenance agreements after death of party MCA 1973, s 36 | Form M22 | FPR, r 3.3 | affidavit | FPR, r 3.3(2) |
| variation of financial relief orders MCA 1973, s 31 | originating summons/ application | FPR, r 3.3 | affidavit | FPR, r 3.3(2) |
| order restraining attempt to defeat ancillary relief claim MCA 1973, s 37 | M11 | FPR, r 2.68 | affidavit | FPR, r 2.68(2) |
| financial relief after overseas divorce MFPA 1984, Part III, ss 12–27 | | | | |
| leave to apply for financial relief after overseas divorce MFPA 1984, s 16 | ex parte originating summons Form M25 | FPR, r 3.17(1) | affidavit | FPR, r 3.17(1) and (2) |
| application for order for financial relief/avoidance of transactions – MFPA 1984, Part III | originating summons | | affidavit | FPR, r 3.18(1) |
| application preventing transaction MFPA 1984, s 24 | originating summons Form M27 | FPR, r 3.19(1) | affidavit | FPR, r 3.19(1) |
| proceedings under CA 1989 | prescribed forms | FPR, r 4.4 and Appendix 1 Forms C1–C54 | written statements oral evidence | FPR, rr 4.17–4.21 |
| wardship | originating summons | FPR, r 5.1 | affidavit | FPR, r 5.1(1) |
| CAA 1985 | originating summons | FPR, r 6.7 | affidavit | FPR, r 6.2 |
| Married Women's Property Act 1882 | originating summons Form M23 | FPR, r 3.6 | affidavit | FPR, r 3.6(1) |
| MHA 1983, ss 1 and 9 | originating summons Form M23 | FPR, r 3.8 | affidavit | FPR, r 3.8 |

| Business | Pleading | Rule | Evidence | Rule |
|---|---|---|---|---|
| DVMPA 1976 | originating summons Form No 10 | RSC, Appendix A originating application Form CCR, N16 | affidavit | FPR, r 3.9 |
| discovery by interrogatories (in defended causes RSC Ord 26 applies as modified by FPR, r 2.21) | interrogatories | | affidavit | RSC Ord 26, r 1 |
| in county court: CCR Ord 14, r 11 (applied to family cases by FPR, r 1.3) | | | | |
| request for further information in ancillary relief applications, FPR, r 2.63 | letter/ questionnaire | | reply: written statement and copy documents | |
| production appointment FPR, r 2.62(7) | summons | | documents | |
| Application under Bankers' Books Evidence Act 1879 | summons | | copies of bank records | |

# Appendix 3

## PROCEDURAL CHECKLIST FOR INSTRUCTING EXPERTS[1]

In order to assist the practitioner to instruct an expert smoothly, the following checklist has been devised. It will not, of course, cover all cases and it is not, in any event, complete on its own; reference should be made back to the authorities themselves.

(1) Consider the questions of experts as early as possible in the proceedings, and always keep in mind any funding implications, whether your client is on legal aid or paying privately.

(2) Identify the issues which the expert is to address.

(3) Consider whether a joint instruction of one expert between two or more parties might suffice, and pursue this line if feasible.

(4) Identify the expert to be instructed (whether jointly or by your client alone), checking, in principle only (no documents at this stage), that he:

    (a)   has the correct expertise
    (b)   is willing to act
    (c)   is available to report in time
    (d)   is available to appear as required (get his availability dates if the dates for court hearings are not yet fixed).

Preferably obtain a letter from him setting all this out.

(5) Make sure your client understands the duties with regard to the disclosure of any report you obtain, even if adverse.

(6) If so instructed, file the application for leave in accordance with the rules; this should be done as early as possible in the proceedings.

(7) File and supply to the other parties at least 10 days before the leave hearing an explanation of the area of expertise of the expert and the reasons why the court should grant leave; it may be helpful also to draft a proposed letter of instruction and list of documents to be sent to the expert at this early stage.

(8) Consider in detail what directions the court should be granting on the leave application and canvass the views of the other parties in advance (reference to the specimen directions in *Re C (Expert Evidence: Disclosure: Practice)* [1995] 1 FLR 204 should help); if sufficient is agreed, prepare a first draft of a proposed order and have copies available for the court and other parties to work with.

---

1    This checklist was prepared by Jill Black QC and first appeared in *The Family Court Practice* (Family Law, 1999): commentary on Family Proceedings Rules 1991, SI 1991/1247, r 4.18.

(9) Ensure attendance at the leave hearing by a legal representative who is fully informed about the case.

(10) If leave is granted, abide by any specific directions that may have been given. They are likely to be fairly detailed and all further steps listed below will be subject to them.

(11) Sort out and copy the documents that the expert needs to see, being careful that your selection is relevant and sufficient. Even if a court bundle is not yet in existence, tether the documents and number the 'bundle' right through so that the expert can refer to passages conveniently in his report. If your numbering system can be agreed with the other parties and translated in due course into the numbering in the court bundle, so much the better.

(12) Send a letter of instruction (including a list of documents supplied to the expert) to the expert, together with copies of the documents. Draw the expert's attention in the letter to any particular directions that affect him and, in any event:

- (a) set out precisely the issues which you want him to address
- (b) summarise the context in which his opinion is sought
- (c) invite him to seek any further information/documentation he needs from you
- (d) make sure he appreciates he will be required to meet with other experts before the hearing to establish areas of agreement/disagreement and to embody these in a statement
- (e) be clear about deadlines for the meeting with other experts, reporting to the court etc
- (f) depending on how experienced the expert is as a witness, consider forwarding to him (or offering to forward) a selection of the authorities setting out guidance as to how an expert should approach his task in a children's case.

The draft letter of joint instruction of an expert, which is annexed to the Children Act Advisory Committee Annual Report 1994/95 and is set out as Best Practice Note of January 1996 in Part IV of *The Family Court Practice 1999*, may prove a helpful starting point. However, account needs to be taken of the reservations expressed by Wall J about it in *Re CB and JB (Care Proceedings: Guidelines)* [1998] 2 FLR 211.

(13) Send a copy of your letter of instruction and list to other parties.

(14) Include the letter and list in the court bundle.

(15) On receipt of the other side's letter of instruction and list, send them to your expert. Also send, from time to time, any new papers that may be relevant to the expert's view, including the other side's expert's report and, in most cases, the guardian ad litem's report. Update your expert scrupulously on other relevant developments as well.

(16) Serve and file your expert's report on receipt and ensure that you receive a copy of the other parties' reports as scheduled.

(17) Ensure that, where there is more than one expert on a particular issue and their views are different, they meet before the hearing to attempt to reach agreement or to limit the issues between them, thereafter identifying areas of agreement and dispute and encapsulating them in a further statement(s) for the court. Depending on the form of the statement(s), it may be necessary to arrange for a separate schedule to be drawn up isolating what is agreed and what is not. This can be the responsibility of the guardian ad litem or local authority or of one of the other parties. Ensure that the schedule etc is served on all parties and filed with the court.

(18) If your expert should change his advice, communicate this to the other parties and have him record it in a form that is appropriate for the court.

(19) Consider with the other parties how best to arrange the timing of the oral evidence of the experts at the hearing – do they wish to sit in on each other's evidence, can evidence of a similar sort be grouped together on a particular day etc? Calculate carefully the time set aside for the experts' evidence so that arrangements can be made for them to attend without being kept

waiting and so that they do not run the risk of having to return on another unscheduled occasion to conclude. Inform your expert of when he is to attend and make sure that the other parties are also aware.

(20) Where an expert's view appears to be uncontentious, check with the other parties that he will not be required to attend to give oral evidence (ensuring that there is a clear understanding as to whether or not the expert's report will still form part of the bundle for the court's attention or not) and notify him as soon as possible.

(21) If all the experts are of one view which points to only one tenable conclusion for the proceedings, draw this to the attention of the court at the pre-trial directions hearing so that the substantive hearing can be planned accordingly.

(22) At all times, keep in mind any legal aid implications that the experts' opinions may have.

(23) If difficulties of any kind are encountered, seek further directions.

# Index

References are to paragraph numbers and Appendices.